D0746491

Readings in **CANADIAN FOREIGN POLICY**

Readings in **CANADIAN FOREIGN POLICY**

Classic Debates & New Ideas

Third Edition | Edited by **Duane Bratt & Christopher J. Kukucha**

OXFORD
UNIVERSITY PRESS

OXFORD

UNIVERSITY PRESS

Oxford University Press is a department of the University of Oxford.
It furthers the University's objective of excellence in research, scholarship,
and education by publishing worldwide. Oxford is a registered trade mark of
Oxford University Press in the UK and in certain other countries.

Published in Canada by
Oxford University Press
8 Sampson Mews, Suite 204,
Don Mills, Ontario M3C 0H5 Canada

www.oupcanada.com

Copyright © Oxford University Press Canada 2015

The moral rights of the authors have been asserted

Database right Oxford University Press (maker)

First Edition published in 2007
Second Edition published in 2011

All rights reserved. No part of this publication may be reproduced, stored in
a retrieval system, or transmitted, in any form or by any means, without the
prior permission in writing of Oxford University Press, or as expressly permitted
by law, by licence, or under terms agreed with the appropriate reprographics
rights organization. Enquiries concerning reproduction outside the scope of the
above should be sent to the Permissions Department at the address above
or through the following url: www.oupcanada.com/permission/permission_request.php

Every effort has been made to determine and contact copyright holders.
In the case of any omissions, the publisher will be pleased to make
suitable acknowledgement in future editions.

Library and Archives Canada Cataloguing in Publication

Readings in Canadian foreign policy : classic debates & new ideas
/ edited by Duane Bratt & Christopher J. Kukucha. — Third edition.

Includes bibliographical references.
ISBN 978–0–19–900831–5 (pbk.)

1. Canada—Foreign relations—Textbooks. I. Bratt, Duane, 1967–,
author, editor II. Kukucha, Christopher John, editor III. Title: Canadian foreign policy.

FC242.R43 2015   327.71   C2014-907915-X

Cover image: ©iStockPhoto.com/grajte

Oxford University Press is committed to our environment.
Wherever possible, our books are printed on paper which comes from responsible sources.

Printed and bound in the United States of America

1 2 3 4 — 18 17 16 15

Contents

Preface

The first two editions of *Readings in Canadian Foreign Policy: Classic Debates and New Ideas* were a pleasant surprise. The book's formula of combining classic articles with newer, more issue-specific ones appealed to students, instructors, and researchers alike. When Oxford University Press approached us about writing a third edition, we had specific ideas about how to improve upon the first two collections. The result is a larger text with a number of new original articles from both established and younger scholars.

Part 1, our theoretical section, has the fewest changes. The original articles by John Holmes, David Dewitt and John Kirton, and Stephen Clarkson all remain in the collection. Each of these classic articulations of the three mainstream perspectives (middle power, principal power, and satellite) is complemented by updated contributions from Tom Keating, John Kirton, and Brian Bow and Patrick Lennox. Additional theoretical perspectives are provided by Nicole Wegner (feminist/constructivism) and Sean McMahon (neo-Gramscian). Three historical chapters were also added at the beginning of this section: John Kirton identifies the 10 most influential books in Canadian foreign policy; Claire Turenne Sjolander and Heather A. Smith respond to Kirton; and Adam Chapnick offers an important historical review of the period from 1945 to 1968.

Parts 2 and 3 continue to examine the external and domestic determinants of Canadian foreign policy. Previous selections by Paul Gecelovsky (prime minister) and Patrice Dutil (DFAIT/DFATD) remain, but have been updated to include information from the years of the Harper government. New to this edition are chapters from Christopher Kirkey and Michael Hawes (polarity), Geoffrey Hale (US), Charles Burton (China), Paul Heinbecker (G8/G20), Gerald J. Schmitz (Parliament), Anita Singh (diasporas), and David Carment and Joe Landry (civil society).

Parts 4, 5, and 6—the issue-specific sections—have been completely revamped. The security section begins with a historical analysis of Canadian defence policy by Kim Nossal. This is followed by chapters by Stéphane Roussel and Jean-Christophe Boucher (Quebec security culture), Doug Ross (US/NORAD/NATO), and Rob Huebert (the Arctic). In the trade and economic issues section, there are updated chapters by Elizabeth Smythe (investment) and Stephen McBride (the 2008–09 financial crisis) and new chapters by Michael Hart (trade) and Duane Bratt (energy policy). In the final section of the volume, which focuses on social considerations, there are chapters by Heather Smith (environment), Stephen Brown (foreign aid), and David Black (Africa).

We have also kept, and updated, the pedagogical features that were introduced in the first and second editions: section introductions, bibliographies, list of key terms, and a list of important dates in Canadian foreign policy.

Acknowledgements

As noted in the first edition, we are fortunate to participate in a community of scholars that is diverse and collegial. Despite obvious differences, there is an ongoing commitment to dialogue and quality of research. We hope this continues in the future.

As with the first two editions of this book, we enjoyed working with the folks at Oxford University Press. Besides the staff at OUP, we are also indebted to the anonymous reviewers who provided excellent advice on how to improve the first and second editions.

Finally, both of us are fortunate to be surrounded by people who provide the required support and inspiration for a project such as this.

Chris Kukucha

Thanks again to Duane for another positive collaborative experience. We've shared a lot together over a number of years. You are an important and valued person in my life. I also appreciate the ongoing love and support of my family.

Duane Bratt

Once again, my collaboration with Chris could not have gone more smoothly. It is always nice to work with someone who is not just a colleague but also a friend. I also want to recognize the patience of my wife Teresa and my children Chris and Dorothy as I went through another book project.

Permissions

The editors gratefully acknowledge the use of the following material:

Black, David. "The Harper Government, Africa Policy, and the Relative Decline of Humane Internationalism," in Heather A. Smith and Claire Turenne Sjolander, eds., *Canada in the World: Internationalism in Canadian Foreign Policy*. Toronto: Oxford University Press, 2012: 217–37. Reprinted by permission of the publisher.

Chapnick, Adam. "Canadian Foreign Policy, 1945–1968" from "Victims of Their Own Success? Canadians and their Foreign Policy at the Onset of the Cold War". First published in *Zeitschrift für Kanada-Studien* 30/1 (2010), 9–23.

Clarkson, Stephen . "The Choice to Be Made". "Conclusion," in Clarkson ed., *An Independent Foreign Policy for Canada?* Toronto: McClelland and Stewart, 1968: 253–71. Reproduced by permission of the author.

Dewitt, David B. and John Kirton. "Three Theoretical Perspectives", *Canada as a Principal Power: A Study in Foreign Policy and International Relations* (Toronto: John Wiley and Sons, 1983), 13–20. Reproduced by permission of the authors.

Hart, Michael . "Breaking Free: A Post-Mercantilist Trade and Productivity Agenda for Canada," *Commentary #357*. C.D. Howe Institute: Toronto, August 2012.

Heinbecker, Paul. "Canada's World Can Get a Lot Bigger: The Group of 20, Global Governance and Security," The School of Public Policy, University of Calgary, Research Papers 4/5 (May 2011). Reprinted with permission from The School of Public Policy at the University of Calgary.

Holmes, John. "Most Safely in the Middle", *International Journal* 39/2 (Spring 1984), 366–88. Reprinted by permission of SAGE.

Huebert, Rob. "Canadian Arctic Sovereignty and Security in a Transforming Circumpolar World," *Foreign Policy for Canada's Tomorrow #4*. Canadian International Council: Toronto, 2009.

Hurrell, Andrew. 2007. *On Global Order* (Oxford University Press), p. 9

Kirton, John J. "The 10 Most Important Books in Canadian Foreign Policy". *International Journal* 64/2 (Spring 2009) pp. 553–64. Reprinted by permission of Sage.

Nossal, Kim Richard. "Defending the 'Realm': Canadian Strategic Culture Revisited", *International Journal* 59:3. Summer 2004: 503–520. Reprinted by permission of Sage.

Roussel, Stéphane and Jean-Christophe Boucher. "The Myth of the Pacific Society: Quebec's Contemporary Strategic Culture," *American Review of Canadian Studies* 38/2 (August 2008), 165–87. Reprinted by permission of Taylor & Francis.

Sjolander, Claire Turenne and Heather A. Smith. "The practice, purpose, and perils of list-making: A response to John Kirton's '10 most important books on Canadian foreign policy'". *International Journal* 65/3 (Summer 2010), 751–62. Reprinted by permission of Sage.

Smith, Heather. "Choosing Not to See: Canada, Climate Change, and the Arctic," *International Journal* 65/4 (Autumn 2010), 931–42. Reprinted by permission of Sage.

Contributors

David Black is professor in political science and director of the Centre for Foreign Policy Studies at Dalhousie University.

Jean-Christophe Boucher is assistant professor of political science at MacEwan University.

Brian Bow is associate professor of political science at Dalhousie University.

Duane Bratt is professor of political science in the Department of Policy Studies at Mount Royal University.

Stephen Brown is professor at the School of Political Studies at the University of Ottawa.

Charles Burton is associate professor in the Department of Political Science at Brock University.

David Carment is a professor of international affairs at the Norman Paterson School of International Affairs, Carleton University, and Fellow of the Canadian Defence and Foreign Affairs Institute (CDFAI).

Adam Chapnick is associate professor of defence studies at the Royal Military College of Canada and deputy director of education at the Canadian Forces College of Canada.

Stephen Clarkson is professor emeritus in the Department of Political Science at the University of Toronto.

David B. Dewitt is the vice-president of programs at the Centre for International Governance Innovation (CIGI).

Patrice Dutil is professor in the Department of Politics and Public Administration, and a member of the Yeates School of Graduate Studies, at Ryerson University.

Paul Gecelovsky has held academic appointments at the University of Lethbridge, the University of Western Ontario, and the University of Windsor.

Geoffrey Hale is professor in the Department of Political Science at the University of Lethbridge.

Michael Hart holds the Simon Reisman Chair in Trade Policy and is Professor of International Affairs at the Norman Paterson School of International Affairs at Carleton University.

Michael Hawes is CEO of Fulbright Canada and professor, Department of Political Studies, at Queen's University (on leave).

Paul Heinbecker is a retired Canadian career diplomat and distinguished fellow at the Centre for International Governance Innovation (CIGI).

John Holmes (1910–88) served in the Department of External Affairs in the late 1940s and the 1950s and was later the head of the Canadian Institute of International Affairs.

Rob Huebert is professor of political science and associate director of the Centre for Military and Strategic Studies at the University of Calgary.

Tom Keating is professor in the Department of Political Science at the University of Alberta.

Christopher Kirkey is professor of political science and director of the Center for the Study of Canada at State University of New York (SUNY) College at Plattsburgh.

John Kirton is professor of political science and director of the G8 Research Group at the University of Toronto.

Christopher J. Kukucha is a professor in the Department of Political Science at the University of Lethbridge.

Joseph Landry is a Ph.D. student at the Norman Paterson School of International Affairs, Carleton University.

Patrick Lennox is a fellow with the Centre for Foreign Policy Studies, Dalhousie University.

Stephen McBride is professor in the Department of Political Science at McMaster University.

Sean McMahon is an assistant professor in the Department of Political Science at the American University in Cairo.

Kim Richard Nossal is professor in the Department of Political Studies at Queen's University.

Stéphane Roussel is professor and Canada Research Chair in Canadian Foreign and Defence Policy at l'École nationale d'Administration publique (ENAP).

Douglas A. Ross is professor of political science at Simon Fraser University.

Gerald Schmitz is an independent scholar and former principal analyst for international affairs, Parliamentary Information and Research Service, Library of Parliament, Ottawa.

Anita Singh is a research fellow in the Centre for Foreign Policy Studies at Dalhousie University.

Claire Turenne Sjolander is professor in the School of Political Studies, and vice-dean, Graduate Studies, Faculty of Social Sciences, at the University of Ottawa.

Heather Smith is professor of international studies at the University of Northern British Columbia.

Elizabeth Smythe is professor of political science and program coordinator, Political Economy, at Concordia University College of Alberta.

Nicole Wegner is a Ph.D. candidate in the Department of Political Science at McMaster University.

Readings in **CANADIAN FOREIGN POLICY**

Studying Canadian Foreign Policy: Varying Approaches

PART I

What Is Canadian Foreign Policy?

Historically, Canada has attempted to define its foreign policy in both explicit and implicit terms. *Canada in the World*, the 1995 government white paper on foreign policy, for example, stated that "domestic policy is foreign policy. Foreign policy is domestic policy."[1] Lester Pearson, on the other hand, famously suggested that "foreign policy is domestic policy, but with your hat on." Ottawa's 2003 *Dialogue on Foreign Policy* also articulated three main "pillars": ensuring global security and the security of Canadians, promoting the prosperity of Canadians and global prosperity, and projecting Canada's values and culture.[2] These three pillars were reinforced in the 2005 International Policy Statement, released by Paul Martin's Liberal government, which stated that its foreign policy would rest on "three core priorities—prosperity, security, and responsibility."[3] The Conservative government of Stephen Harper (2006–present), however, has suggested a significant break with past practices. Speaking to the General Assembly of the United Nations in October 2013, John Baird, Canada's Minister of Foreign Affairs, made it clear that "Canada's government doesn't seek to have our values or our principled foreign policy validated by elites who would rather 'go along to get along.'"[4] In doing so, Baird was overtly suggesting that, unlike previous governments, Canada now pursued a "principled" foreign policy. Unfortunately, this government has yet to clearly define what these values are.

This volume examines the relevance of these statements in the context of security, trade, and social issues. This text also argues that most studies of Canadian foreign policy tend to focus on one aspect of a state's external relations, such as international developments, the domestic policy process, or the role of individuals. In the Canadian case, therefore, a more holistic framework should be adopted in evaluating foreign policy. As Kim Nossal has made clear, "foreign policy is forged in the nexus of three political environments—international, domestic, and governmental. It is within these three spheres that the sources, or the determinants, of a state's foreign policy are to be found."[5]

As the following discussion also suggests, however, Canadian foreign policy must be conceptualized beyond the new policies and priorities of specific governments. Specifically, is it possible to identify broader, entrenched practices, illuminated by various theoretical perspectives that can be consistently identified in Canada's foreign relations? If so, serious questions are raised about Baird's argument of a dramatic shift in Canadian foreign policy. Baird, however, would simply dismiss this observation, and likely this book, as an "elite" exercise by those simply trying to "go along to get along."

Therefore, in order to fully evaluate Canada's foreign relations over an extended period of time, it is essential to consider issues of system, process, and change. In terms of systemic issues, there is the obvious understanding that international developments have an impact on Canada's global relations and that these external variables can take many forms. For most Western developed states, including Canada, foreign policy is guided by certain ideational assumptions regarding the international system, namely realist and neo-liberal institutionalist perspectives. These perspectives accept the reality of a state-centric, competitive, anarchic international system in both political and economic relationships. Cooperation is still possible at the international level, however, in the form of regimes and other institutions, which allows for an evaluation of both absolute and relative gains. It is important to note that this does not restrict Canada's ability to pursue issues related to its own self-interest. Realist and most liberal international relations (IR) theory is based on the understanding that sovereignty and anarchy are realities, and Canada has demonstrated repeatedly that these options will be embraced in the formulation of Canadian foreign policy. Neo-idealism also accepts liberal efforts to engage civil society and promote greater democratization.

Non-state actors are also influenced by many of the same realist and neo-liberal systemic considerations, especially corporate and sectoral interests. At the same time, however, many also have very different "structural" assumptions that are instead guided by gender, class, or ethnicity. These "critical" approaches challenge the basic, core organizing principles of the modern state system and represent alternative international structural interpretations. It is important to understand that these considerations can also shape the foreign policy of states, namely in the form of non-traditional factors not usually accounted for in realist or neo-liberal frameworks.

In addition, Canadian foreign policy is influenced by "process" issues, which can include domestic institutional factors such as constitutional and judicial realities; the role of the prime minister, provincial premiers, cabinets, and executives at both levels of government; federal and provincial legislatures; bureaucratic interests; and intergovernmental relations linked to international affairs. Process factors, however, must also examine non-institutional inputs. Sectoral actors, for example, consist of industry associations, specific corporations, individual executives, advisory groups, and consultative links with federal government departments or officials. In addition, societal interests—which are typically treated as secondary considerations in studies of Canadian foreign policy—incorporate organized labour, environmental groups, First Nations, civil society, and a wide range of other non-governmental actors. Finally, ideational issues focus on how "dominant ideas" are transferred, or entrenched, at both levels of analysis, contributing to exploitative relationships related—but not limited—to ideology, class, gender, ethnicity, and culture.

To fully understand process-related issues, causal relationships must also be explored, especially in terms of state autonomy. Specifically, the international and domestic activities of institutional, sectoral, societal, and ideational actors should be evaluated. In addition, these observations must account for the transnational activity *between* states that contributes to policy convergence. International pressures related to treaties, financial markets, and global capital can also lead to limitations of domestic autonomy, although this will vary greatly from sector to sector.[6] Also missing, however, is the acknowledgement that domestic actors can have a direct impact on the international system. The institutional policies of central and non-central governments, for example, are often transferred between levels of analysis as states consult, negotiate, and implement agreements.

Finally, any discussion of foreign policy must incorporate a review of "change" that moves beyond traditional discussions of state autonomy. Although Baird is correct in pointing out significant differences in Canada's foreign relations under the Conservatives, using the criteria adopted for this volume, the change is not holistic. Specifically, "change" must identify developments that represent a pattern of relations that are significantly different from previous relationships. This could include shifts in power-based capabilities, re-interpretations of regime-based norms and standards, and/or membership in international institutions. To be fair, there is evidence that Harper's foreign policy represents a shift from those of previous governments. Examples include disengagement from the United Nations and Commonwealth and much higher support, especially in rhetorical pronouncements, for Israel. What is not different, however, is the primary systemic and process variables that drive Canadian foreign policy. Canada's foreign relations continue to be guided by the assumption that states pursue self-interest, be it values or other priorities, in an anarchical international system. A complex array of domestic pressures will also influence Canada's approach to managing this anarchy.

Therefore, in order to fully evaluate "change" and foreign policy outcomes, it is essential to engage critical theoretical interpretations of foreign policy. In fact, tangible benefits can be gained by including these issues in rational, realist, or neo-liberal approaches. In terms of trade policy, for example, issues of class are relevant to the role of organized labour and civil society's backlash to neo-liberalism within the state, while also being relevant to the obvious economic disparities between the developed and developing world. Gender-based NGOs and social movements also place pressure on states at both the international and domestic levels, although liberal feminists would take a much different view of the neo-liberal patriarchy than would those with a socialist or more critical perspective. Ethnic and cultural issues present further challenges in terms of neo-liberalism's insensitivity to non-Western-oriented economic considerations and issues of collective rights. All of these social issues are relevant to questions involving state autonomy and the level-of-analysis problem, in terms of structure, process, and change.

The chapters in this volume will evaluate numerous Conservative foreign policy initiatives. Many will support Baird's claim of change. Others will highlight the political motives for these shifts in policy and question the lack of emphasis on normative considerations, despite claims of a new "principled" approach to Canada's foreign relations.

How Is Canadian Foreign Policy Studied?

Traditional frameworks

Chapters 4–6 in Part 1 outline the traditional frameworks for analyzing Canadian foreign policy. Maureen Appel Molot, in a seminal article, points out that the vast majority of the thinking about Canadian foreign policy has been preoccupied with Canada's place in the world—its role, status, position, influence, and power.[7] Three different images have prevailed: Canada as a middle power, a principal power, or a satellite power. The dominant image is of Canada as a middle power. Historically, middle powers were perceived as situated below the great powers of the United States, Russia, the United Kingdom, France, China, Germany, and Japan. The middle power perspective assumes that Canada has an important role to play both in multilateral and bilateral regimes and in institutions because of its wealth, geographic location, and human capacity. Initially, Canada's functional role in strong multilateral regimes was viewed as a way of constraining the *realpolitik* of great power rivalry by providing an alternative rules-based mechanism for ensuring world order.

Several authors have adopted this approach when examining the evolution of Canadian foreign policy. The most prominent observer of Canada as a middle power was John Holmes.[8] His classic discussion of being "safely in the middle," in Chapter 4, touches on a number of traditional themes. Tom Keating, a contemporary expert who has re-evaluated this perspective, focuses more on the principle of multilateralism and reflects the increasing tendency of some scholars to question the utility of categorizing states as middle powers due to the ambiguity of this standing in the contemporary international system. Specifically, Keating has argued that Canadian policy-makers have repeatedly relied on both economic and security regimes to fulfill a wide range of foreign policy objectives. Ottawa has, at times, pursued unilateral and selected bilateral arrangements, but over time "these alternatives are deviations from the norm, are short-lived, and are frequently combined with complimentary multilateral activities."[9] Keating's update to the middle power in this volume examines the potential "twilight of multilateralism in Canadian foreign policy." In doing so, he reinforces Baird's assertion of change, at least in terms of the Conservative commitment to multilateralism. Interestingly, however, Keating points to the possibility of "significant change" in the twenty-first century, which Canada will be poorly situated to influence due to its inability to engage a multilateral process that will likely oversee a redesign of international order. Kim Nossal and Andrew Cooper have also addressed Canada's traditional role as a middle power.[10]

An alternative image is that of Canada as a principal power. Canada has many capabilities—abundant natural resources, high levels of technology, well-educated people, a high standard of living, and membership in exclusive groups like the G7/8 and G20—that rank it far ahead of other middle powers. Principal power theorists argue that Canada is able to pursue its own policies in the international system with relatively little interference. The first to acknowledge this position was James Eayrs, who wrote in 1975 that the rising importance of oil-producing states, the increasing significance of natural resources in the global political economy, and the declining economic status of the United States all increased Canadian power.[11] Norman Hillmer and Garth Stevenson also adopted this approach in 1977 when they suggested that Canada was not a "modest power."[12] It was David Dewitt and John Kirton, as noted in Chapter 5, who argued most strongly in favour of Canada being labelled a "principal power" because of the decline in status of the United States. Although they were writing almost a decade after Eayrs, they also cited a decrease in American hegemony that portrayed Canada as an "ascending power" whose "star was on the rise."[13] In his update, Kirton reflects on the theoretical legacy of his work with Dewitt and provides additional evidence of the principal power thesis by highlighting Canada's abundant natural resources (water, oil, potash, and uranium); declarations by other major powers that Canada is one of them; trade agreements; its military deployment to Afghanistan; and its role in the G8 and G20. Although the popularity of the principal power approach has declined in recent years, it still serves as a core foundation for studying Canadian foreign policy.

Another alternative image—and the opposite of the principal power approach—is that Canada is a peripheral-dependent/satellite country. In this conception, Canada moved seamlessly from existing as a British colonial dependency to being pulled into the orbit of the American empire. The origins of the satellite model date back to the 1920s, when Archibald MacMechan complained that Canada was becoming nothing more than a "Vassal State" of the United States.[14] A.R.M. Lower also echoed this sentiment in the 1940s when he described Canada as a "subordinate state" or "satellite" to its American neighbour.[15] The satellite approach gained increasing momentum during the 1960s when several observers argued that Canada was adopting policy decisions that were deferential to the United States, especially in terms of military and security issues. Although George Grant touched on many of these themes in *Lament for a Nation*,[16] the most prominent voice of the satellite movement in terms of Canadian foreign policy came from Stephen Clarkson. For Clarkson the problem was largely one of leadership: senior officials were not willing to distance themselves from American influence.[17] The answer, as described in Chapter 6, was to aggressively protect Canadian sovereignty by promoting greater government intervention in the economy through the establishment of mechanisms such as the Foreign Investment Review Agency (FIRA) and the National Energy Program (NEP). More recent contributors sympathetic to this argument include Stephen McBride, John Helliwell, and Alex Michalos.[18] Stephen Clarkson has recently re-entered the debate by suggesting that institutions such as the North American Free Trade Agreement (NAFTA) and the World Trade Organization (WTO) have imposed a "supraconstitution" that constrains "authority that was once the exclusive preserve of domestically elected legislatures."[19] Clarkson presents a brief retro-spective of *An Independent Foreign Policy* as an addendum to Chapter 6. Brian Bow and Patrick Lennox, in honour of the fortieth anniversary of *An Independent Foreign Policy*, brought together a new generation of Canadian scholars to reconsider Clarkson's thesis.[20] Based on the conclusions of this book, Bow and Lennox provide an update to Chapter 6.

As previously mentioned, Maureen Appel Molot argued that the traditional approaches to the study of Canadian foreign policy—especially the middle, principal, and satellite models discussed in the three chapters preceding Chapter 7—are no longer adequate for a number of reasons. Not only do the traditional methods fail to evaluate the complexity of Canadian foreign policy in terms of a holistic analysis of system, process, and outcome, but they also suffer from the following weaknesses:

a)   They are atheoretical, with only implicit ties to IR theory.

b)   The approaches fail to focus on domestic politics and/or international/domestic linkages (the level-of-analysis problem).

c)   Problems and opportunities related to Canadian foreign policy are largely scrutin-ized through the lens of state autonomy. Other more critical approaches are required.

d)   There is no real discussion of economic issues (trade and finance).

In addition, non-institutional actors, both sectoral and societal, are usually ignored. For these and other reasons, David Black and Heather Smith have called for the application of non-traditional models in the study of Canadian foreign policy. In particular, they argue, models are needed that explore "the interaction between state, society, and global levels of analysis."[21]

Non-traditional models

Gender-based analysis is one of the main non-traditional models. This perspective explores, in the words of Deborah Stienstra, "how gender relations are shaped and how they, in turn, shape Canadian foreign policy."[22] Stienstra's article, which was written in the mid-1990s, was particularly critical of the fact that, despite an increase in the application of gender-based analysis in the study of international relations, such analysis had not been extended to exam-ining Canadian foreign policy. This was a groundbreaking study that added to the voice of a group of scholars led by Sandra Whitworth, Heather Smith, Edna Keeble, and Claire Turenne Sjolander that critiqued Canada's international role from a feminist perspective.[23] Specifically, it is argued that "women and gender issues have been excluded from the study of Canadian foreign policy" because the "feminine is devalued in the way that people think."[24]

In Chapter 7, Nicole Wegner adopts a discourse-based gendered analysis to evaluate Canada's military operation in Afghanistan. Wegner begins by examining the masculinized military training of Canadian soldiers and the inconsistency of these soldierly tasks with the duties traditional Canadian peacekeepers were often asked to perform. The discourse around Afghanistan was different, however, and was portrayed in terms of Canada fighting to eliminate terrorism, as opposed to peacekeeping. In many cases, the government of Canada also emphasized the gendered oppression exercised by the Taliban, and the Canadian military's "heroic" efforts to end these discriminatory practices. The masculine image of soldiers as fighters was not eliminated from the discourse, but it was downplayed, creating instead a "strange hybrid of soldier and helper." In doing so it both opened and limited potential military initiatives and shaped a public understanding of the Canadian military not always consistent with reality.

A second critical perspective is neo-Gramscian structural analysis and "dominant-class" theory, which is reviewed by Sean McMahon in Chapter 8. Antonio Gramsci (1891–1937) was an Italian socialist, activist, and political theorist. His *Prison Notebooks*, not published in English until the 1970s, was filled with critical commentary about socialism, capitalism, communism, and fascism. Robert Cox and Stephen Gill have applied many of Gramsci's ideas to the study of world politics.[25] Of particular importance is the now neo-Gramscian notion of hegemony whereby the institution and maintenance of a world order serves the interests of the dominant social class in a wide range of states. Gramscian hegemony, then, is not based on coercive force, but on consent gained through intellectual and moral leadership. McMahon uses the Gramscian approach to assess Canada's extensive role in the North Atlantic Treaty Organization's recent military intervention in Libya. McMahon questions what he suggests was Canada's disproportionate involvement compared to other NATO members. Ultimately, he concludes that the global and local interests of a hegemonic financial bloc drove Canadian involvement. Globally, the NATO mission provided an opportunity to displace an ongoing surplus of international capital. Locally, Canada's military role reaffirmed the neo-liberal hegemony of Canadian society.

Plan of the Book

This book is structured with three primary goals in mind. The first goal is to illustrate that the setting of Canadian foreign policy exists at the intersection of the international, state, and societal levels of analysis. The second goal is a thorough examination of the stated purposes of Canadian foreign policy, namely physical security, economic prosperity, and the promotion of Canadian values. The third goal aims to draw attention to some of the weaknesses in the Canadian foreign policy literature and to offer a critical, or more holistic, approach to studying Canada's global relations.

Part 1 develops the various mainstream and critical approaches to the study of Canadian foreign policy identified in this introduction. Before delving into the theoretical debates discussed above, Part 1 provides some context through three historical chapters. Chapter 1, written by John Kirton, assesses the scholarly attention to Canadian foreign policy by identifying the most influential books on the subject. Many of the authors that Kirton recognizes are contained in this volume. Chapter 2 is a reprinted rebuttal to Kirton's list by Claire Turenne Sjolander and Heather Smith, first published in *International Journal*.

Chapter 3, written by Adam Chapnick, describes the major events of Canada's foreign relations from the end of World War II to 1968. Since international relations scholars use history as a laboratory to test theories, it is important that students have a basic understanding of how Canada's role in the world has evolved since World War II.

Part 2 examines the constraints and opportunities facing Canada in the international environment through an examination of the shifting polarity of the international system, bilateral relations with the United States and China, and Canada's role in the G20. Part 3 shifts to an analysis of the major domestic actors that shape, make, and implement Canadian foreign policy: the prime minister, parliament, bureaucracy, diasporas, and civil society. Part 4, the first of three issue-specific sections, examines Canada's pursuit of international peace and security through a historical analysis of Canadian defence policy, the erosion of Canada's military capabilities, its Arctic security strategy, and the question of a pacifist culture in Quebec. Part 5 examines Canada's pursuit of economic prosperity through international trade, Canada's response to the global financial crisis, and the importance of foreign investment and energy to the Canadian economy. Part 6 begins with Heather Smith's critique of Canada's international approach to climate change. Selections that analyze Canada's foreign policy in relation to foreign aid and African development complete the section.

Notes

1. Canada, *Canada in the World: Government Statement* (Ottawa: Canada Communications Group, 1995), 4.

2. Department of Foreign Affairs and International Trade, *A Dialogue on Foreign Policy: Report to Canadians* (Ottawa: Communications Services Division, 2003).

3. Canada, *Canada's International Policy Statement: A Role of Pride and Influence in the World—Diplomacy* (Ottawa: Government of Canada, 2005), 5.

4. Ian MacDonald, "John Baird Brings the Politics of Conviction to the United Nations," *The Gazette*, 2 October 2013, A1-19.

5. Kim Richard Nossal, *The Politics of Canadian Foreign Policy*, 3rd ed. (Scarborough, ON: Prentice-Hall, 1997), 7.

6. George Hoberg, Keith G. Banting, and Richard Simeon, "The Scope for Domestic Choice: Policy Autonomy in a Globalizing World," pp. 252–99 in Hoberg, ed., *Capacity for Choice: Canada in a New North America* (Toronto: University of Toronto Press, 2002).

7. Maureen Appel Molot, "Where Do We, Should We, Or Can We Sit? A Review of Canadian Foreign Policy Literature," *International Journal of Canadian Studies* 1, 2 (Spring–Fall 1990), 77–96.

8. John W. Holmes, *Canada: A Middle-Aged Power* (Toronto: McClelland and Stewart, 1976); John W. Holmes, *The Shaping of Peace: Canada and the Search for World Order, 1943–1957* (Toronto: University of Toronto Press, 1979).

9. Tom Keating, *Canada and World Order: The Multilateralist Tradition in Canadian Foreign Policy*, 2nd ed. (Don Mills, ON: Oxford University Press, 2002), 23.

10. Kim Nossal, *The Politics of Canadian Foreign Policy*; Andrew F. Cooper, *Canadian Foreign Policy: Old Habits and New Directions* (Scarborough, ON: Prentice-Hall, 1997); Andrew F. Cooper, Richard A. Higgott, and Kim Richard Nossal, *Relocating Middle Powers: Australia and Canada in a Changing World Order* (Vancouver: UBC Press, 1993).

11. James Eayrs, "Defining a New Place for Canada in the Hierarchy of World Power," *International Perspectives* (May–June 1975): 15–24.

12. Norman Hillmer and Garth Stevenson, eds., *A Foremost Nation: Canadian Foreign Policy in a Changing World* (Toronto: McClelland and Stewart, 1977).

13. David B. Dewitt and John Kirton, *Canada as a Principal Power: A Study in Foreign Policy and International Relations* (Toronto: John Wiley and Sons, 1983), 38.

14. Archibald MacMechan, as cited in Nossal, *The Politics of Canadian Foreign Policy*, 61.

15. A.R.M. Lower, as quoted in Phillip Resnick, "Canadian Defence Policy and the American Empire," in Ian Lumsden, ed., *Close the 49th Parallel Etc: The Americanization of Canada* (Toronto: University of Toronto Press, 1970), 99.

16. George Grant, *Lament for a Nation: The Defeat of Canadian Nationalism* (Toronto: McClelland and Stewart, 1965).

17. Stephen Clarkson, ed., *An Independent Foreign Policy for Canada?* (Toronto: McClelland and Stewart, 1968).

18. Stephen McBride, *Paradigm Shift: Globalization and the Canadian State* (Halifax: Fernwood, 2001); John Helliwell, *Globalization and Well-Being* (Vancouver: UBC Press, 2002); Alex C. Michalos, *Good Taxes: The Case for Taxing Foreign Currency Exchange and Other Financial Transactions* (Toronto: Dundurn, 1997); Alex C. Michalos, "Combining Social, Economic and Environmental Indicators to Measure Sustainable Human Well-Being," *Social Indicators Research* 40 (1997): 221–58.

19. Stephen Clarkson, *Does North America Exist? Governing the Continent after NAFTA and 9/11* (Toronto: University of Toronto Press, 2008), and Stephen Clarkson, *Uncle Sam and Us: Globalization, Neoconservatism, and the Canadian State* (Toronto: University of Toronto Press, 2002).

20. Brian Bow and Patrick Lennox, eds., *An Independent Foreign Policy for Canada? Challenges and Choices for the Future* (Toronto: University of Toronto Press, 2008).

21. David R. Black and Heather A. Smith, "Notable Exceptions? New and Arrested Directions in Canadian Foreign Policy Literature," *Canadian Journal of Political Science* 26, 4 (December 1993): 745–75.

22. Deborah Stienstra, "Can the Silence be Broken? Gender and Canadian Foreign Policy," *International Journal* 50, 1 (Winter 1994–5): 126–27.

23. For other examples of gender analysis in Canadian foreign policy see Claire Turenne Sjolander, Heather A. Smith, and Deborah Stienstra, eds., *Feminist Perspectives on Canadian Foreign Policy* (Don Mills, ON: Oxford University Press, 2003); Edna Keeble and Heather A. Smith, *(Re)Defining Traditions: Gender and Canadian Foreign Policy* (Halifax: Fernwood, 1999).

24. Keeble and Smith, *(Re)Defining Traditions*, 20.

25. Robert W. Cox, "Gramsci, Hegemony and International Relations: An Essay in Method," *Millennium, Journal of International Studies* 12, 2 (Summer 1983): 162–75; Stephen Gill, *American Hegemony and the Trilateral Commission* (Cambridge: Cambridge University Press, 1990); Stephen Gill, ed., *Gramsci, Historical Materialism, and International Relations* (Cambridge: Cambridge University Press, 1993).

1

The 10 Most Important Books on Canadian Foreign Policy

John J. Kirton

Key Terms

Gender   Middle Power
Generation   Region
International Relations Theory   Satellite

In many ways the scholarly study of Canadian foreign policy has become a rich, robust, and rapidly growing field. It is now well over a century old, if one dates its inauguration from the publication of Goldwin Smith's *Canada and the Canadian Question* in 1891, a book that understood that Canada's relationship with the United States was properly part of, or even at the centre of, the field.[1] From 1945, when many of today's scholars start their scrutiny, to 1995, the detailed bibliographies compiled under the auspices of the Canadian Institute of International Affairs recorded works of all kinds as relevant to the subject. Since then, the explosion of material has been too vast for this careful bibliographic compilation to be published in print, especially as the Internet has arrived to help others take on the task in electronic form.

Since 1970, courses on Canadian foreign policy have become staples of universities' undergraduate curricula across Canada, accompanied by selective forays into the United States and beyond. These courses have been mounted and delivered in the first instance by the doctoral students produced by John Holmes, with some help from James Eayrs, at the University of Toronto over many years. More recently, the 6500-member International Studies

Association has created a separate Canadian Studies section that has been nourishing, expanding, and honouring its senior scholars since its inception. There are now over a dozen articles reviewing the state of the Canadian foreign policy field![2] There are also several that reflect on its connection with, and theoretical inheritance from, international relations as a whole.[3] All signs thus suggest that the study of Canada's foreign policy has gone prime time on a global scale.

But amidst this proliferating scale, scope, and self-reflection, there remains an unanswered question: Is Canadian foreign policy really a self-contained scholarly field with an intellectually coherent, progressive research tradition, defined by seminal books of creative inspiration and continuing relevance at its core? There are good reasons to doubt that it is, especially in contrast with the larger field of international relations in which it properly resides. Here foundational works such as those by Thucydides, Hans Morgenthau, Robert Keohane and Joseph Nye, John Ruggie, Kenneth Waltz, and Alexander Wendt are used, disputed, or at least recognized and referred to by all. In contrast, the study of Canadian foreign policy has long been an endeavour involving those from many disciplines, starting with history and law. It has also been one to which practitioners from government, the media, research institutes, and the business community contribute a great deal. And it has always had its "second solitude," an important French-language literature centred in Quebec, which has long enriched the few who have been able or willing to read it on the other side of Canada's great linguistic divide.

To determine whether there is a coherent field of Canadian foreign policy based on broadly recognized, intellectually generative foundational works, this study identifies and justifies the impact of the top 10 most important books on Canadian foreign policy of all time. Part 2 focuses on books rather than journal articles as the probable source of the foundational centrepieces, given the small number of journals, especially peer-refereed ones, focused on the subject over many years. It further aims at works of enduring importance, reducing the "recency bias" that would otherwise propel today's biggest hits, most prolific scholars, curricular fashions, and policy favourites to the top of the list. It thus sets aside the standard mechanical metrics of citation indices and Google hits to probe the content of the "top 10" and explore how they shaped thinking, research, and teaching for many years in the past—and probably will for many years to come. This is thus the list of Canadian foreign policy's finest wines that have aged well enough to be continuously copied, adapted, and selectively consumed directly by the dedicated purists in the profession today.

Given the diverse and fast-moving shape of the field, it is unlikely that all scholars currently teaching and researching in it will agree with every book on the list. Those raised as realists, liberal institutionalists, world systems political economists, or constructivists in the diverse field that Canadian foreign policy has become, and those from different generations, geographic regions, genders, and language groups, will have their own special selections.[4] But virtually all should recognize the works on this top-10 list, accept most as clear choices or credible candidates, and be able to mount a considered case to explain why the personal favourite that has been omitted is better than one or more of the ones that have made it on. In addition to representing the personal picks of someone who has taught and researched Canadian foreign policy for more than 30 years, this list should thus serve as the beginning of a debate about what the field is, based on what its best books are. Others are welcome to suggest and justify their own "blasts from the past" in the years ahead.

The Key Scholars in Canadian Foreign Policy Today

If a book is to be important, its innovative ideas should stand at or near the centre of the field today. It is thus useful to begin by identifying somewhat systematically the top 10 scholars of Canadian foreign policy, what books appear most often on the syllabi of the undergraduate courses on the subject across Canada, and from where both groups draw their central intellectual inspiration.

The best available published evidence about the top 10 scholars of Canadian foreign policy comes from the TRIP survey of international relations faculty in 10 countries, published in February 2009. Although it specifically asked respondents to "[l]ist four IR scholars whose work has had the greatest influence on Canada's foreign policy in the past 20 years," the answers provide a reasonable indication of scholarly importance, especially if influence on government policy and the public's thinking are taken as a responsibility of the scholars' role. See Table 1.1 for the results.

These results show a strong representation of political scientists whose teaching and research has concentrated on Canadian foreign policy over two or three decades, and who have authored most of the textbooks available today. It also shows some reasonable balance by theoretical tradition, **generation**, **gender**, and **region**, especially in its inclusion of two scholars who live and work outside Canada. The most notable imbalance is the slender representation of francophone Quebecers, only one of whom appears on the list.

Amidst this diversity a strong historical footprint appears: the intellectual legacy of John Holmes and James Eayrs looms large in the work of first-ranked Kim Richard Nossal, third-ranked Denis Stairs, and sixth-ranked John Kirton. Several others, such as fourth-ranked Andrew F. Cooper, have been substantially influenced by their work.

To identify which scholars' books are actually used in undergraduate classes on Canadian foreign policy across Canada, a survey was conducted of all relevant syllabi available on the web. The results, also reported in Table 1.1, show the importance of *Readings in Canadian Foreign Policy*, edited by

Table 1.1 Most Important Scholars in Canadian Foreign Policy

Scholar	Most influential Rank (share %)	Most used Rank (share)	Combined Rank (share)
Both lists			
Kim Richard Nossal	1 (46)	3 (4)	1 (4)
John Kirton	6 (12)	2 (5)	2 (8)
Tom Keating	7 (11)	5 (3)	3 (12)
Andrew F. Cooper	4 (20)	9 (1)	4 (13)
Stéphane Roussel	9 (6)	8 (2)	5 (17)
Most influential only			
Janice Stein	2 (35)		
Denis Stairs	3 (29)		
Jack Granatstein	5 (13)		
Jennifer Welsh	7 (11)		
Claire Turenne Sjolander	9 (6)		
Joseph Nye	9 (6)		
Thomas Homer-Dixon	9 (6)		
Most used only			
Duane Bratt		1 (6)	
Christopher Kukucha		1 (6)	
Fen Osler Hampson		3 (4)	
Brian Tomlin		5 (3)	
Norman Hillmer		5 (3)	

Notes: "Most influential" is the response to the question, "List four IR scholars whose work has had the greatest influence on Canada's foreign policy in the past 20 years," in answer to the survey whose results were reported by Richard Jordan and his colleagues.[5] "Most used" refers to those authors whose books appeared as core works most often on the syllabi of undergraduate courses on Canadian foreign policy taught in Canada in 2008–9. The author is grateful to Zaria Shaw for conducting this survey of 25 courses and the compilation of its results from the 42 books being used.

Source: TRIP Survey of International Relations Faculty of 10 Countries, retrieved from http://irtheoryandpractice.wm.edu/projects/trip/Final_Trip_Report_2009.pdf.

Duane Bratt and Christopher Kukucha in 2007, and the volumes of the *Canada Among Nations* series, appearing with a different but overlapping set of editors every year.[6] Yet it also shows the importance of monographs produced as textbooks by Kim Nossal, John Kirton, and Tom Keating, and of five co-authored works from Brian Tomlin and Fen Osler Hampson.[7] While no research work is sufficiently central to rank highly on the list, the selections in the Bratt–Kukucha reader provide a strong indication of the most important scholars and books from the past for the field today. Here there is a strong reliance on works by Stephen Clarkson, John Kirton, and Cranford Pratt, with two contributions each, and by John Holmes, Tom Keating, Maureen Appel Molot, Claire Turenne Sjolander, and Mark Neufeld, whose writings fill out the opening section of the book. Among the small set of five scholars who are listed as both "most influential" and "most used," Kim Nossal also appears in the Bratt–Kukucha reader.

To enrich these systematic surveys with direct reputational data, several of the leading scholars in the field, currently active in both Canada and the United States, were asked over the past two years to identify their choice of the two most important books. In their answers, there was only one work written by a journalist, *While Canada Slept*, by Andrew Cohen. There were two from long-time career practitioners: *The Washington Diaries* by Allan Gotlieb, and *Decision at Midnight* by Michael Hart and William Dymond. There were also several historians, led by Jack Granatstein, Norman Hillmer, and C.P. Stacey. There were none from lawyers or economists. The field for political scientists has become a largely self-contained, autonomous, scholarly one.

There was a high degree of consistency, both in the scholars and in their books selected. Nossal led the list, followed by Holmes, Eayrs, and Kirton; then Stairs and Cooper; and finally Clarkson, Charles Doran, Michael Tucker, and Michael Hawes. These results are quite consistent with those who were judged as producers of, or whose work lies behind, the most influential and most-used books today. With this foundation, it is time for judgment to be exercised in selecting the top 10 books, listed in chronological order below.

The Top 10 Most Important Books in Canadian Foreign Policy

1. R.A. MacKay and E.B. Rogers, *Canada Looks Abroad*
2. James Eayrs, *The Art of the Possible: Government and Foreign Policy in Canada*
3. Stephen Clarkson, ed., *An Independent Foreign Policy for Canada?*
4. John Holmes, *The Better Part of Valour: Essays on Canadian Diplomacy*
5. Bruce Thordarson, *Trudeau and Foreign Policy: A Study in Decision-Making*
6. Denis Stairs, *The Diplomacy of Constraint: Canada, the Korean War, and the United States*
7. Peyton Lyon and Brian Tomlin, *Canada as an International Actor*
8. Charles Doran, *Forgotten Partnership: U.S.–Canada Relations Today*
9. Andrew F. Cooper, Richard Higgott, and Kim Richard Nossal, *Relocating Middle Powers: Australia and Canada in a Changing World Order*
10. Kim Richard Nossal, Stéphane Roussel, and Stéphane Paquin, *Politique internationale et défense au Canada et au Québec*

Note: It was agreed at the outset that this list would exclude works produced either alone or with co-authors or co-editors by John Kirton (the author of this article) or by David Haglund and Joseph Jockel (co-editors of the *International Journal*).

1. R.A. MacKay and E.B. Rogers, *Canada Looks Abroad* (London: Oxford University Press, 1938)

Published in 1938, this was the launch volume of the *Canada in World Affairs* series produced by the Canadian Institute of International Affairs. Successive volumes in the series provided a detailed description of the subject through to J.L. Granatstein and Robert Bothwell's *Pirouette: Pierre Trudeau and Canadian Foreign Policy* in 1990.[8] But more importantly, MacKay and Rogers's outline of the policy options for practising, and the underlying logic for analyzing, Canadian foreign policy created the classic trilogy that has defined the field ever since.[9] Its option of the "league" outlined the liberalist–internationalist approach of Canada as a **middle power** that has dominated the study, if not the conduct, of Canadian foreign policy to this day. Its option of "North America" (Canada) as a small, isolated state close to the US alone offered what became the **satellite** approach. And its option of "empire" presented Canada as a country consequential for the global balance of power, and thus a foremost nation or principal power, as the later complex neo-realist approach would claim.

2. James Eayrs, *The Art of the Possible: Government and Foreign Policy in Canada* (Toronto: University of Toronto Press, 1961)

In the two decades following the Second World War, the fusion of policy-makers and scholars created a consensus on the concept of Canada as a middle power. But it produced no autonomous scholarly logic to show how this, or any alternative, might be correct. The first career-long scholar in the field, recognizable as a social scientist by the standards of today, was James Eayrs, whose influence has been profound. Eayrs wrote largely as a historian in his multi-volume series, *In Defence of Canada*. He also wrote more as a critical journalist in such works as *Northern Approaches, Diplomacy and Its Discontents*, and *Fate and Will in Foreign Policy*.[10]

But it was his masterful *The Art of the Possible: Government and Foreign Policy in Canada* that stands out as perhaps the single most influential work in the field to this day. Published in 1961, it set the field's continuing focus and framework on the making of Canadian foreign policy. It systematically identified and explored the external, societal, governmental, and individual determinants of Canadian foreign policy, introducing to the field the levels of analysis that Waltz had pioneered in the study of international relations as a whole.[11] Nossal, Kirton, and Thordarson are intellectually direct descendants of Eayrs, while Denis Stairs and Douglas Ross are enriched as well by *In Defence of Canada*.

3. Stephen Clarkson, ed., *An Independent Foreign Policy for Canada?* (Toronto: McClelland and Stewart, 1968)

Soon after Eayrs established the field as a social science, there erupted a plethora of normatively inspired, policy-oriented books arguing that Canada was or should be a multilateralist middle power, or that it was and should not be a dependent satellite of the United States. From this deluge, the single work with the most enduring impact is George Grant's 1965 *Lament for a Nation*.[12] But the one book from the energetic 1960s that re-established and enriched Canadian foreign policy as a social scientific field, as well as having a significant policy influence, was Stephen Clarkson's 1968 collection, *An Independent Foreign Policy for Canada?* In addition to the remarkable insights in its individual chapters, its concluding analytical synthesis defined a logically coherent framework for capturing the content of Canadian foreign policy. Its outline of an independent foreign policy offered several key concepts for what was later codified as the complex neo-realist perspective. It did so long before James Eayrs wrote his 1975 article, which is widely viewed as the inspiration for this approach.[13]

4. John Holmes, *The Better Part of Valour: Essays on Canadian Diplomacy* (Toronto: McClelland and Stewart, 1970)

It was at the end of this period of great intellectual innovation that John Holmes, the epitome of the diplomat-turned-scholar, arrived on the scholarly scene in full force. Along with Eayrs, he is the most influential author in the field to this day. His two-volume work, *The Shaping of Peace: Canada and the Search for World Order,* written at the peak of his career, is the *In Defence of Canada* for those who think Canadian foreign policy is in essence not about defence and war but about diplomacy and peace, based on international institutions, with the United Nations at the core.[14] Indeed, with Eayrs the realist, Clarkson the critical political economist, and Holmes the liberal internationalist, the three wise men had all taken their place on the playing field. Holmes, however, was ultimately not a historian, as Eayrs had been intellectually at the start. Rather, he was a policy commentator and essayist of consummate skill, as displayed in *Life with Uncle* and *A Middle-Aged Power.* His best collection was his first, *The Better Part of Valour,* published in 1970. In its wonderfully readable way, it offered the core insights of the liberal internationalist perspective that those with "tidy minds" could later arrange into a theory that could co-exist and compete with the theories and interpretations that Eayrs and Clarkson would create.

5. Bruce Thordarson, *Trudeau and Foreign Policy: A Study in Decision-Making* (Toronto: Oxford University Press, 1972)

It was not only at or near the political economy department of the University of Toronto that the scholarly field of Canadian foreign policy was formed. Thanks to Peyton Lyon, Brian Tomlin, and Lester Pearson (when he left political life), Carleton University's Norman Paterson School of International Affairs was active at an early stage.

Carleton's first work of enduring scholarly consequence, in keeping with the generational revolution of the time, came from one of its students, Bruce Thordarson, in 1972: *Trudeau and Foreign Policy: A Study in Decision-Making.* It offered three case studies of key decisions at the outset of the Trudeauvian era—an advance from Eayrs's seminal study of the single Suez crisis in 1956. It examined external, societal, and governmental determinants across the levels of analysis more systematically than Eayrs had in 1961. Far more convincingly than the biographical vignettes that adorned *In Defence of Canada,* it concluded that it was not international fate but individual will that mattered.[15] And it connected causes directly to effects, showing how Trudeau's personal belief system drove changes in Canadian foreign policy itself.

6. Denis Stairs, *The Diplomacy of Constraint: Canada, the Korean War, and the United States* (Toronto: University of Toronto Press, 1974)

It was, however, Denis Stairs who really brought the Eayrsian and Holmesian inheritances together in *The Diplomacy of Constraint: Canada, the Korean War, and the United States* in 1974. This was the quintessential case study, an approach pioneered by John Holmes and expanded by his graduate students in their seminar at the University of Toronto for many years. Stairs's book was a multidimensional marvel, relying both on documents, when available, and on specialized oral interviews. And it invented the concept—the "diplomacy of constraint"—at the core of the liberal internationalist theory of Canadian foreign policy, as the foundation on which the entire edifice could deductively be built.

7. Peyton Lyon and Brian Tomlin, *Canada as an International Actor* (Toronto: Macmillan, 1979)

Carleton reappeared at the end of the 1970s in the form of Peyton Lyon and Brian Tomlin's *Canada as an International Actor* in 1979. The book certified Lyon's status as a true scholar, as distinct from the recently retired foreign service officer with policy convictions that he had been when he wrote *The Policy Question* in 1963. The book introduced Brian Tomlin, who pioneered the use of quantitative methods in the field, even if he was to move to more mainstream methods with great skill in his later work. The 1979 book was a productive fusion of quantitative and qualitative methods that showed, whatever the predispositions of the senior author, that Canada was more than a mere middle power with only modest relative capability in a changing world.

8. Charles Doran, *Forgotten Partnership: U.S.–Canada Relations Today* (Baltimore: Johns Hopkins University Press, 1984)

Canadian foreign policy has long been a subject of more than merely local interest. Non-Canadians have made important book-length contributions, notably William T.R. Fox, Annette Baker Fox, Melvin Conant, John Sloan Dickey, Jon McLin, Roger Frank Swanson, and Joseph Nye, Jr., in his co-authored work with Robert Keohane, *Power and Interdependence,* in 1977. But the standout contribution is Charles Doran's *Forgotten Partnership: U.S.–Canada Relations Today,* published in 1984.[16] It offered an integrated argument that articulated the core concepts and relationships for the model of special partnership that extended the liberal internationalist theory to Canadian foreign policy toward, and with, the United States. Along with only William Fox, who wrote *The Super-Powers: The United States, Britain, and the Soviet Union* in 1944 and *A Continent Apart: The United States and Canada in World Politics* in 1985, Doran was a leading scholar of international relations whose insights in his *The Politics of Assimilation: Hegemony and Its Aftermath* enriched his study of Canadian foreign policy in his several subsequent books devoted to this subject alone.

9. Andrew Fenton Cooper, Richard Higgott, and Kim Richard Nossal, *Relocating Middle Powers: Australia and Canada in a Changing World Order* (Vancouver: UBC Press, 1993)

The end of the Cold War, the Soviet empire, and the Soviet Union forced students of Canadian foreign policy to consider whether their inherited ideas remained relevant for the new age. Many concluded they did. Tom Keating updated the liberal internationalist middle power argument in *Canada and World Order* in 1993 and 2002, and Stephen Clarkson the peripheral dependent satellite one, after his *Canada and the Reagan Challenge* in 1982, in *Uncle Sam and Us: Globalization, Neoconservativism, and the Canadian State* in 2002 and *Does North America Exist? Governing the Continent after NAFTA and 9/11* in 2008. But Andrew F. Cooper and Kim Richard Nossal innovatively came together with an Australian colleague, Richard Higgott, to ask the question in a comparative context, in a way that was embedded in new concepts of international relations. The resulting *Relocating Middle Powers: Australia and Canada in a Changing World Order* inspired a subsequent cascade of conceptual innovation by Cooper and Nossal to enrich the field for the new age.[17]

10. Kim Richard Nossal, Stéphane Roussel, and Stéphane Paquin, *Politique internationale et défense au Canada et au Québec* (Montreal: Les Presses de l'Université de Montréal, 2007)

The final work on the top 10 list is *Politique internationale et défense au Canada et au Québec,* by Kim Richard Nossal, Stéphane Roussel, and Stéphane Paquin. It is the only book to survive the strong bias against recent volumes that cannot yet prove that they will stand the test of time. This book is the most recent version of Nossal's English-language *The Politics of Canadian Foreign Policy,* a work that modernized the Eayrsian focus on the making of Canadian foreign policy and has served as a core textbook since its first publication in 1985. The current version infuses the distinctiveness of Quebec and represents the first major fusion of anglophone and francophone scholarship in the field. It thus shows that there is, at long last, a single field of Canadian foreign policy, reflective of the rich diversity that the subject itself contains.

Questions for Review

1. Who are the most influential scholars in Canadian foreign policy?
2. What measures does Kirton use to identify the top 10 scholars of Canadian foreign policy?
3. Are there important conclusions reached regarding theoretical tradition, gender, region, and generation?
4. How important is **international relations theory** in the study of Canadian foreign policy?
5. Is this textbook important in evaluating the 10 most important books on Canadian foreign policy?

Suggested Readings

Black, David R., and Heather A. Smith. 1993. "Notable Exceptions? New and Arrested Directions in Canadian Foreign Policy Literature." *Canadian Journal of Political Science* 26, 4 (December): 745–74.

Hawes, Michael K. 1984. *Principal Power, Middle Power, or Satellite? Competing Perspectives in the Study of Canadian Foreign Policy*. Toronto: York Research Programme in Strategic Studies.

Keating, Tom. 2013. *Canada and World Order: The Multilateralist Tradition in Canadian Foreign Policy*. 3rd ed. Don Mills, ON: Oxford University Press.

Nossal, Kim Richard. 1997. *The Politics of Canadian Foreign Policy*. 3rd ed. Scarborough: Prentice-Hall.

Smith, Heather A., and Claire Turenne Sjolander, eds. 2013. *Canada in the World: Internationalism in Canadian Foreign Policy*. Don Mills, ON: Oxford University Press.

Notes

1. Goldwin Smith, *Canada and the Canadian Question* (Toronto: Hunter, Rose, 1891).
2. These started with Michael Hawes, *Principal Power, Middle Power, or Satellite?* (Toronto: York Research Programme in Strategic Studies, 1984); Maureen Appel Molot, "Where do we, should we, or can we sit? A review of Canada's foreign policy literature," *International Journal of Canadian Studies* 1, 2 (Spring–Fall 1990), 77–96; Denis Stairs, "Will and circumstance and the postwar study of Canadian foreign policy," *International Journal* 50 (Winter 1994–5), 9–39; and Daizo Sakuraba, "The contending approaches to Canadian foreign policy and Canada–US relations: A reinterpretation of literature," *Proceedings of the Sixth Tsukuba Annual Seminar on Canadian Studies*, 1995, 50–70.
3. Axel Dorscht and Gregg Legare, "Foreign policy debate and realism," *International Perspectives*, November–December 1986, 7–10; Axel Dorscht, Tom Keating, Gregg Legare, and Jean-François Rioux, "Canada's international role and 'realism,'" *International Perspectives* (September–October 1986), 6–9: Axel Dorscht, Ernie Keenes, Gregg Legare, and Jean-François Rioux, "Canada's foreign policy," *International Perspectives* (May–June 1986), 4–6; John Kirton, "Realism and reality in Canadian foreign policy," *International Perspectives*, January–February 1987, 3–8; David Haglund and Tudor Onea, "Sympathy for the devil: Myths of neoclassical realism in Canadian foreign policy," *Canadian Foreign Policy* 14 (Spring 2008), 53–67.
4. Paul Gecelovsky and Christopher Kukucha, "Canadian foreign policy: A progressive or stagnating field of study?" *Canadian Foreign Policy* 14 (Spring 2008), 109–19.
5. Richard Jordan, Daniel Maliniak, Amy Oakes, Susan Peterson, and Michael J. Tierney, "One discipline or many? TRIP survey of international relations faculty in 10 countries," Institute for the Theory and Practice of International Relations, College of William and Mary, Williamsburg, VA: February 2009.

6. Duane Bratt and Christopher J. Kukucha, eds., *Readings in Canadian Foreign Policy: Classic Debates and New Ideas* (Don Mills, ON: Oxford University Press, 2007).

7. Notably Brian Tomlin, Norman Hillmer, and Fen Osler Hampson, *Canada's International Policies: Agendas, Alternatives, and Politics* (Don Mills, ON: Oxford University Press, 2008).

8. J.L. Granatstein and Robert Bothwell, *Pirouette: Pierre Trudeau and Canadian Foreign Policy* (Toronto: University of Toronto Press, 1990).

9. Douglas Ross, *In the Interests of Peace: Canada and Vietnam, 1954–1973* (Toronto: University of Toronto Press, 1984).

10. James Eayrs, *Fate and Will in Foreign Policy* (Toronto: Canadian Broadcasting Corporation, 1967).

11. Kenneth Waltz, *Man, the State, and War: A Theoretical Analysis* (New York: Columbia University Press, 1959).

12. George Grant, *Lament for a Nation: The Defeat of Canadian Nationalism* (Toronto: McClelland and Stewart, 1965).

13. James Eayrs, "Defining a new place for Canada in the hierarchy of world power," *International Perspectives*, May–June 1975, 15–24.

14. John Holmes, *The Shaping of Peace: Canada and the Search for World Order, 1943–1957*, 2 vols. (Toronto: University of Toronto Press, 1979, 1982).

15. James Eayrs, *In Defence of Canada: Peacemaking and Deterrence* (Toronto: University of Toronto Press, 1972).

16. By way of disclosure, although I, along with David Haglund and Joseph Jockel, received my doctorate at the Johns Hopkins University School of Advanced International Studies, I had graduated with a Ph.D. supervised by Roger Frank Swanson before Doran arrived to lead the Center of Canadian Studies there.

17. Andrew F. Cooper, *Canadian Foreign Policy: Old Habits and New Directions* (Scarborough, ON: Prentice-Hall Allyn and Bacon Canada, 1997).

2 The Practice, Purpose, and Perils of List-making: A Response to John Kirton's "10 Most Important Books on Canadian Foreign Policy"

Claire Turenne Sjolander and Heather A. Smith

Key Term

Intellectual Legacy

In the Spring 2009 issue of *International Journal*, John Kirton published his list of the "10 most important books on Canadian foreign policy." He framed his "top 10" list as a response to what he believes to be the one remaining unanswered question about the field: "Is Canadian foreign policy really a self-contained field with an intellectually coherent, progressive research tradition, defined by seminal books of creative inspiration and continuing relevance at its core?"[1] Although Kirton suggests that there are "good reasons to doubt that it is" (554), the exercise of producing such a list convinces him that "there is, at long last, a single field of Canadian foreign policy, reflective of the rich diversity that the subject itself contains" (564). In putting forward his list, Kirton invites others to offer their own suggestions and amendments, presenting it as "the beginning of a debate about what the field is, based on what its best books are" (556), rather than as the *definitive* statement of the best books in the field. Despite this, Kirton does go on to argue that "virtually all" scholars should accept most of his selections as "clear choices or credible candidates," and where readers' personal favourites have been omitted, these

scholars should be able to "mount a considered case to explain why the personal favourite that has been omitted is better than one or more" of Kirton's own personal favourites (555).

In responding to Kirton's article, we are taking up the invitation to interrogate what constitutes the academic field of Canadian foreign policy. In doing so, it is neither our intent nor our desire to produce an alternative list of books in response to Kirton's top 10. Rather, we want to raise questions about the entire enterprise of list production, whether those lists are of the most important books, of the most used books, or of the most influential scholars.[2] The act of defining a field "based on what its best books are" is an exercise that is inherently political, and not only for the reason that Kirton identifies—that "it is unlikely that all scholars currently teaching and researching in [Canadian foreign policy] will agree with every book on the list" (555). While we may (and will) query the selection of books that Kirton has included on his list, it is not the choice of individual books that causes us the greatest consternation. Rather, our concern is with the fact of producing such a list in the first instance, particularly when the objective of the effort is to demonstrate the supposed self-contained and coherent research tradition existing in *the* field. In this inherently political exercise, Kirton is tracing the boundaries of the field as *he* sees it, and in so doing, defining its most important theoretical questions and traditions, thereby effectively marginalizing or dismissing other questions and traditions as less significant, perhaps irrelevant, and certainly not consistent with the "coherent research tradition" that he believes now defines the field. As such, the practice, purpose, and perils of the list-making enterprise merit serious discussion, which we propose to undertake by looking both at Kirton's list, and at the implicit messages behind the list-making.

The Practice of List-making

Kirton begins his article by situating his own list-making effort within the context of other "lists." In particular, he looks at the 2009 TRIP survey of the top international relations/Canadian foreign policy scholars in order to establish a list of the most influential scholars of Canadian foreign policy. He supplements this "most influential" list with a list of the 10 most used books appearing on the 25 undergraduate Canadian foreign policy 2008–9 syllabi available to him on the Web, which he deems the "most used" textbook list. He then presents us with his list of the 10 most important books on Canadian foreign policy. His criteria for the selection of the 10 most important books, aside from being personal favourites, seem to include "innovative ideas [that] stand at or near the centre of the field today" (556). He wants to look at works of "enduring importance, reducing the 'recency bias' that would otherwise propel today's biggest hits, most prolific scholars, curricular fashions, and policy favourites to the top of the list" (555).

Interestingly, Kirton's criteria for the top-10 books list do not seem to apply to the most used

textbooks list. As we have noted, his textbooks list draws from 2008–9 undergraduate course outlines (the institutional affiliation for these course outlines remains a mystery) and seems to justify some sort of academic standing for the authors thus identified. While some of the textbooks on that list are first rate, one has to wonder what such a list would look like if Kirton drew from course outlines dating from 2005 or 2000 or 1990? If the list of most-used textbooks was created from course outlines dating from 2005, prior to the publication of Kirton's own text, *Canadian Foreign Policy in a Changing World*, and the Duane Bratt and Christopher J. Kukucha-edited volume, *Readings in Canadian Foreign Policy: Classic Debates and New Ideas*, what would the list of most-used textbooks look like? Would Kim Nossal's multiple edition volume be ranked first? Would Kirton not appear at all on the list where he currently ranks second over Nossal? And how do we square the fact that Kirton rejects the use of journal articles in favour of a top-10 list of books on the grounds that there is but a small number of journals and peer-reviewed articles, when he uses the Bratt and Kukucha reader to legitimize his list of most-used and most influential scholars—a reader that draws several of its chapters from journal articles?[3]

The production of the list of influential scholars identified by the TRIP survey is at least transparent, even if it is completely appropriate to ask what such a list is really measuring. Kirton's list of the most-used textbooks, on the other hand, lacks such methodological transparency and is subject to the recency bias he seeks to avoid in his top-10 books list. The volumes and course outlines upon which he builds his textbooks list are obviously subject to change depending upon the publication of new textbooks and the seriousness of the marketing efforts of textbook publishers. The practice of list-making, however, makes static that which is dynamic. In the absence of clear methodological justification, the building of both the most-used and most-important books lists appears to be at least as much the result of cherry-picking personal favourites as it is about the imposition of transparent or objective criteria. How a list is created matters.

The Purpose of List-making

Whatever the practice of producing these lists, the purpose of reporting on the "most influential" or "most used" lists is obscure, since their relationship to the "top 10 books" list is never fully explained. The presentation of these lists does, however, allow Kirton to make affirmations about the **intellectual legacy** and influences shaping the thinking of some of those figuring on these other two "top 10" lists. It is important to note that Kirton presumes to trace the intellectual heritage influencing but a very few of the scholars appearing on one or the other (or both) lists. He describes Kim Nossal, Denis Stairs, and John Kirton as the intellectual descendants of John Holmes and James Eayrs, while Andrew Cooper is positioned as having been "substantially influenced" (557) by their work. Kirton thus "establishes" the intellectual trajectory of four of the 17 scholars figuring on these two lists, although he suggests that the Holmes and Eayrs influence is seen in the work of "several [unnamed] others." Given the uncertain relationship between the "most used books" or the "most influential scholars" lists and Kirton's ultimate list of the 10 most important books, it seems reasonable to assume that the lists are presented so as to frame Kirton's assessment of the importance of one selected set of intellectual influences in Canadian foreign policy. This assessment, as well as the results of his conversations over two years with "leading scholars in the field" (558), added to his own professional experience, provides the basis for Kirton's identification of his 10 most important books.[4]

What does the top-10 books list teach us about the field of Canadian foreign policy as perceived by John Kirton? First, as Kirton himself notes, his field is remarkably anglophone. André Donneur, for decades one of the most prolific and dedicated Québécois scholars of Canadian foreign policy, does not rate a mention by Kirton anywhere in his article, nor do other Québécois analysts such as Louis Balthazar, Paul Painchaud, Albert Legault, Louis Bélanger, Gordon Mace, or Nelson Michaud, among many others. While Kirton bemoans the fact that the other lists he examines suffer from the "notable imbalance" of a "slender representation of francophone Québécois" (557), his own list reproduces the same imbalance, including only one book with francophone Québécois co-authors, in partnership with Kim Nossal, in the translation and substantial adaptation of Nossal's "classic" English-language textbook, *The Politics of Canadian Foreign Policy.* This seems somewhat ironic, given Kirton's acknowledgement that there is "an important French language literature centred in Québec" (555)—one he acknowledges, but subsequently ignores.

This deafness to francophone voices is hardly surprising. Claire Turenne Sjolander's 2008 review of the content of Canadian foreign policy course syllabi revealed a complete absence of French-language material from courses taught in English. Stéphane Roussel's examination of the frequency with which English-speaking authors in Canadian foreign policy cite their French-speaking colleagues concluded that "French-speaking researchers *are . . . cited four times less than what one can expect*" based on the volume of their contributions to the field, regardless of the language (French or English) in which their work is published.[5] There are consequences to this deafness: Turenne Sjolander's analysis, for example, noted that courses taught in French were far more preoccupied by the role of the provinces in foreign policy formulation than were their English counterparts.[6] More significantly, Roussel's study pointed to the fact that national unity and its potential foreign policy consequences are virtually ignored by Canada's English-speaking scholars when compared to their French-speaking colleagues, suggesting that an issue of considerable importance to the academic foreign policy discussion in Québec is virtually absent from conversations in the rest of the Canadian foreign policy scholarly community.[7] In displaying this deafness to francophone voices, Kirton's academic field of Canadian foreign policy is being constructed in a particular way—in this case, in a way that is deaf to an issue of substantial theoretical and empirical importance.

The second observation to be made about Kirton's top-10 books list is that his field is also solidly male. While Kirton is satisfied that the combined list of the most influential scholars and the most used books reflects "some reasonable balance by theoretical tradition, generation, gender, and region" (557), his own list of the top 10 books does not include a *single* woman.[8] Arguably, one could suggest that the presence of female scholars in Canadian foreign policy (as in many other academic disciplines) has only recently begun to increase, making it almost certain that Kirton's stated bias in favour of "works of enduring importance" (or as he labels them, "Canadian foreign policy's finest wines" [555]) would draw books from a very slender pool of female authors. Yet, as is the case for Kirton's linguistic deafness, his gender blindness is not without its consequences either. As Jérémie Cornut, Heather Smith, and Stéphane Roussel demonstrated in recent work, in areas attracting substantial attention in the study of Canadian foreign policy, such as Canada–US relations or defence policy, scholarship by women has been underrepresented (as a proportion of women researchers in the field), whereas in other areas, attracting less attention and thus generating less scholarship, such as gender, First Nations, international law, aid and humanitarian assistance, or the environment, female scholars have been

overrepresented as a percentage of their total numbers.[9] What is considered "central" or "core" to the field thus has substantial consequences for who is (and whose books are) included on the list of the 10 most important books in *the* field.

It is, of course, not only women and francophones who are absent; Kirton's list is also uniformly white. This racial dimension potentially distorts his field as well; influential works such as Sherene Razack's 2004 *Dark Threats and White Knights: The Somalia Affair, Peacekeeping, and the New Imperialism*, for example, reveal the centrality of intersectional analysis as a tool to deconstruct recent Canadian peacekeeping missions.

If the potential consequences for our understanding of *the* field of who is excluded from the list thus start to become clear, what of those who figure *on* the list? MacKay and Rogers; Eayrs; Clarkson; Holmes; Thordarson; Stairs; Lyon and Tomlin; Doran; Cooper, Higgott and Nossal; and Nossal, Roussel, and Paquin. Kirton provides his readers with a brief justification for each of the chosen texts, and it is not our purpose here to review the arguments he marshals in favour of each of his choices. Rather, we are interested in what these books have in common—if indeed they have anything in common. What do these books taken together tell us about the state of the field in Kirton's vision of Canadian foreign policy?

To answer the question, we don't need to look further than Maureen Appel Molot's often-cited review of the state of the field in Canadian foreign policy. In her review, Molot concludes that there have been two primary focuses to Canadian foreign policy literature, at least until the late 1980s (the period during which the article was written). The first preoccupation of the literature, she argues, has been around "Canada's place in the world, a preoccupation with status, position, influence, and power." This concern with place is most closely identified with John Holmes and his elaboration of a liberal internationalist perspective to Canadian foreign policy. The second major theme she identifies is policy formulation—literature that "investigates the way in which Canadian foreign policy is made and the role of institutions—governmental and non-governmental—in the process."[10] This theme is the intellectual legacy of James Eayrs, with his focus on decision-making and the determinants of foreign policy. On Kirton's list, MacKay and Rogers, Clarkson, Holmes, Stairs, Lyon and Tomlin, Doran, and Cooper et al. are clearly concerned with place, while Eayrs, Thordarson, Stairs, Doran, and Nossal et al. are interested in the processes and determinants of foreign policy formulation. Molot's review, however, does not celebrate this state of affairs, but rather points to a field that "is rather narrow in the range of issues it has examined."[11] The field's obsession with the two major themes captured by Kirton's list has produced a literature that is "highly descriptive . . . [having] left many important questions about Canadian foreign policy and Canada's place in the world unasked and, therefore, undebated."[12] Following upon this argument, Black and Smith pointed both to areas in Canadian foreign policy that have shown some theoretical sophistication (moving beyond the "largely descriptive" moniker attributed to the field by Molot), as well as to areas where the field can usefully move, drawing from the broader debates and theoretical innovations found in the literatures of international relations and comparative politics.[13] In other words, at least 20 years ago, criticisms about the narrowness of a field of Canadian foreign policy defined as focusing on only two broad themes were already being clearly articulated. Kirton's belief that his top-10 books list must include only the finest (well-aged) wines succeeds in reproducing and thereby enshrining the narrowness of the field critiqued by Molot, painting it in a static light, impervious to the intellectual and theoretical debates that have characterized international relations, among other disciplines. If these 10 books

represent the finest wines of the field, it seems to stand to reason that Canadian foreign policy includes only two vintages: "place" (the Holmes vintage) and "policy formulation" (the Eayrs vintage).[14]

The irony, of course, is that the existence of other vintages among the wines of Canadian foreign policy has been recognized for some time. In the introduction to his third edition, Kim Nossal tells us that his approach to the study of Canadian foreign policy cannot ask the questions that motivate a myriad of other possible perspectives on the field, be they perspectives informed by international political economy, post-modernism, or gender. "In short," Nossal argues, "these are not approaches that one can merely 'add' to a traditional approach and 'stir'—at least, not if one wishes to do them justice. Rather, these are approaches that require a (re)construction of the project *de novo*."[15] Kirton's top-10 books list, however, dismisses these approaches entirely, all the while claiming that there now exists "a single field of Canadian foreign policy" reflecting the rich diversity of the subject matter. He makes one passing reference to "world systems political economists, or constructivists" (555) in his discussion of the diversity of the field, but doesn't even see fit to include reference to the wealth of critical literature in his third footnote, which *lists* literature reviews reflecting on theoretical connections to the broader international relations literature. Rather, the footnote contains a selection of articles on realism. If we take seriously Christine Sylvester's observation that "who and what is in and who and what is out: it's all in the footnotes," then it is clear that the dismissal is not just about books, but also about perspectives.[16]

On one level, it could be argued that these more critical perspectives are newer, and that the books that speak from these perspectives are too recent to be included on Kirton's list of finest wines. His own requirement that books have proven that they can withstand the test of time is waived in the inclusion of the final book on his list, however.

From Kirton's perspective, the rich diversity of which he is so pleased appears to have been assured from the moment Nossal decided to collaborate with Roussel and Paquin in the adaptation of his textbook for the 2007 French-language edition, for this guaranteed that the new version of the book would be "infuse[d with] the distinctiveness of Québec" and would "represent the first major fusion of anglophone and francophone scholarship in the field" (564). The diversity, then, appears to come from Kirton's ability to include two francophone co-authors and one French-language text (subsequently translated into English) on his list—all the while preserving the intellectual lineage represented by the Holmes and Eayrs vintages. This "fusion" does not address any concern with the way in which the discipline is defined, for it does not upset the centrality of the two dominant vintages. Where diversity is reduced to two vintages, however, it is legitimate to ask whether any real diversity exists. As Molot contended in 1990, there is much that is left unasked and undebated in the representation of the field of Canadian foreign policy through the books that have been included on Kirton's list.

The Perils of List-making

While Kirton's attempt to identify the most important works of the field is not without interest, inasmuch as it spurs us to think about the way in which we define our field of study, the exercise of list-making is one that needs to be problematized. In the introduction to their 2010 book, *Canadian Foreign Policy in Critical Perspective*, Marshall Beier and Lana Wylie frame the issue eloquently. Examining disciplinary endeavours, Beier and Wylie make the point that mainstream scholarship has made a virtue of theoretical parsimony, allowing it to claim coherence in a world that critical scholarship would argue to be far messier than the mainstream would

accept. The need to simplify, however, "necessarily leaves out many voices, ideas, interests, and perspectives." In constructing a list of important books that consolidates the claim that the intellectual heritage of the field is to be found in only two vintages, Kirton has presented a list of books that share broad assumptions about the world and the key challenges within it. In representing the field through this list, however, the messiness of the world about which the field is supposed to speak is made silent. As Beier and Wylie go on to point out, "it is important to recognize that power . . . works through this very formula for coherence because it subtly draws authority for each successive voice, and for all in sum, from an aesthetic of consensus that itself functions by placing at least a thread of continuity beyond critical examination."[17] If each book on Kirton's list represents an extension of the Holmes or Eayrs vintages, then who is to question that these two vintages do not represent the sum of approaches or perspectives to the study of Canadian foreign policy? If the 10 most important books, spanning the decades from 1938 to 2007, owe their importance to their connection with their twin intellectual forebears, than how is it possible to question that these two vintages are not the most significant ones to the study of the field, even today? In producing his list, Kirton has provided us with a "comfort text"—a narrative of the field that reinforces mainstream assumptions of what and who constitute Canadian foreign policy and, by extension, who doesn't.[18] The production of the list of the 10 most important books reproduces a narrow understanding of our field, which sends signals about its nature to scholars and students. Kirton's list reinforces the anglophone, mainstream, white, male dominance of the field without even a nod to alternative work.

It is not necessary to subscribe to a particular perspective to acknowledge that it exists. There are surveys and assessments of the field that attempt to represent its full breadth.[19] Such inclusiveness is important because, regardless of our own perspectives as individual scholars, we must understand that our work is potentially part of a disciplining project. Who and what we include matters. If Canadian foreign policy is as Kirton describes it, we leave out indigenous voices, women's voices, and the voices of those who do not write or speak in English, among many others. The signal is sent that the inclusion of alternative voices is not part of the project of Canadian foreign policy and, by extension, not part of an academic project that tells the world who and what Canada is.

Lists such as those constructed by Kirton also have implications for our peers and our students. Imagine that you are a young francophone or feminist scholar with a newly minted Ph.D. Do you see a place in the field for yourself? Anecdotal evidence suggests that young scholars working in critical traditions with an interest in things Canadian do not fashion themselves as Canadian foreign policy scholars, but rather, as feminist scholars or critical security scholars, precisely because they see little or no space for their work at the core of the field. Lists such as those created by Kirton have personal and career implications for those who could and should be part of our community.

Finally, who and what do our increasingly diverse students see when they read the Kirton list? Do they see themselves and their experiences? What does the Kirton list tell our students about dissent and debate? How do we encourage critical thinking when all we offer in our classes are Kirton's two vintages? Surely our role as teachers is to encourage broadly based critical thinking that not only allows, but also promotes, exposure to the breadth of the field, from mainstream discussions of multilateralism to critical assessments of war trauma.[20] Teaching should not be about the promotion of only one set of ideas, and if it is, it does a disservice to our students, as well as to ourselves.

Conclusion

As Kirton notes, the study of Canadian foreign policy has come to be dominated largely by political scientists (558), and indeed, political scientists not only figure disproportionately as authors on his list of the 10 most important books but are also disproportionate in their numbers in our own reference to alternative works and perspectives. In a conversation among political scientists, therefore, it would seem more than appropriate to insist that we be self-conscious about the political choices we make, the political messages we send, and the political consequences of the things we advocate. List-making is not neutral, and the act of producing a list normalizes a certain construction of *the* field. If we truly wish to ensure that *our* field of study becomes and remains as progressive and as rich as Kirton wishes it to be, then it is not by elaborating an artificially coherent list of anything or anyone that we do so. Rather, we must ensure that *our* field is open, dynamic, and welcoming of a myriad of perspectives—that it reflects the messiness of the world in which we live. If we fail to do so, we reproduce patterns of power in the construction of an arbitrary consensus that excludes many voices and many colleagues, and *our* field will be much the poorer for it.

Questions for Review

1. What is the purpose in trying to measure who are the most influential scholars in Canadian foreign policy?

2. Why is it important to acknowledge issues of region, language, gender, race, and theoretical interpretation when evaluating Kirton's list?

3. Does list-making potentially contribute to intellectual marginalization?

4. Why do the authors not construct their own list of the top books on Canadian foreign policy?

Suggested Readings

Beier, J. Marshall, and Lana Wylie, eds. 2010. *Canadian Foreign Policy in Critical Perspective*. Don Mills, ON: Oxford University Press.

Black, David R., and Heather A. Smith. 1993. "Notable exceptions? New and arrested directions in Canadian foreign policy literature." *Canadian Journal of Political Science* 26, 4 (December): 745–74.

Cox, Robert W. 1986. "Social forces, states and world orders: Beyond international relations theory," pp. 204–54 in

Robert O. Keohane, ed. *Neorealism and its Critics*. New York: Columbia University Press.

Molot, Maureen Appel. 1990. "Where do we, should we, or can we sit? A review of the Canadian foreign policy literature." *International Journal of Canadian Studies* 1, 2 (Spring–Fall): 77–96.

Neufeld, Mark. 2004. "Pitfalls of emancipation and discourses of security: Reflections on Canada's 'security with a human face.'" *International Relations* 18, 1: 109–23.

Notes

1. John Kirton, "The 10 most important books on Canadian foreign policy," *International Journal* 64, 2 (Spring 2009): 553–64. Henceforth, materials cited or quoted from the Kirton article will be indicated by page number(s) in parentheses in the text.

2. We refer here to the lists cited or composed by Kirton in his article.

3. In personal communication, Bratt and Kukucha expressly denied any attempt to choose articles for their reader so as to construct or represent wholly "*the* field" of Canadian foreign policy, making Kirton's reliance on the text as one of his legitimation techniques particularly ironic.

4. The identity of Kirton's "leading scholars" is unknown, but it certainly does not include all the scholars named by the TRIP survey, The College of William and Mary, Williamsburg, VA, February 2009.

5. Stéphane Roussel, "About solitudes, divorce, and neglect: The linguistic division in the study of Canadian foreign policy," in J. Marshall Beier and Lana Wylie, eds., *Canadian Foreign Policy in Critical Perspective* (Don Mills, ON: Oxford University Press: 2010), 159. Italics in original.

6. Claire Turenne Sjolander, "Two solitudes? Canadian foreign policy/Politique étrangère du Canada," *Canadian Foreign Policy* 14, 1 (2008): 106.

7. Roussel, "About solitudes," 165.

8. The "reasonable" gender representation is assured by the "most influential" list, which includes three female scholars. Kirton's "most used books" list does not include a single woman (suggesting only that female scholars of Canadian foreign policy had not published a recent

textbook picked up by the authors of the 2008–9 web-available course syllabi).

9. Jérémie Cornut, Heather A. Smith, and Stéphane Roussel, "On the margins? Women and gender in the study of Canadian foreign policy," paper presented at the annual meeting of the Canadian Political Science Association, Montreal, 11–12 June 2010. This is particularly evident in the area of gender and foreign policy, where 93.4 per cent of the scholars publishing in the area are women.

10. Maureen Appel Molot, "Where do we, should we, or can we sit? A review of Canadian foreign policy literature," in Duane Bratt and Christopher J. Kukucha, eds., *Readings in Canadian Foreign Policy: Classic Debates and New Ideas* (Don Mills, ON: Oxford University Press, 2007), 62.

11. Ibid., 68–69.

12. Ibid., 63.

13. David R. Black and Heather A. Smith, "Notable exceptions? New and arrested directions in Canadian foreign policy literature," *Canadian Journal of Political Science* 26, 4 (December 1993).

14. Place is clearly important to Kirton as well. Interestingly, one or more of the authors of each of the 10 books listed has a clear relationship to one of the three universities best known by John Kirton: Johns Hopkins University, Carleton University, and, most especially, the University of Toronto.

15. Kim Richard Nossal, *The Politics of Canadian Foreign Policy* (Toronto: Prentice-Hall Canada, 1997), xv.

16. Christine Sylvester, "Anatomy of a footnote," *Security Dialogue* 38, 4 (2007): 547.

17. J. Marshall Beier and Lana Wylie, "Introduction: What's so critical about Canadian foreign policy?" in J. Marshall Beier and Lana Wylie, eds., *Canadian Foreign Policy in Critical Perspective* (Oxford: Oxford University Press, 2010), xv.

18. Marysia Zalewski, "Distracted reflections on the production, narration, and refusal of feminist knowledge in international relations," in Brooke A. Ackerly, Maria Stern, and Jacqui True, eds., *Feminist Methodologies for International Relations* (Cambridge: Cambridge University Press, 2006), 47.

19. In addition to Black, Smith, and Molot, mentioned earlier, see for example, Kim Richard Nossal, "Home-grown IR: The Canadianization of international relations," *Journal of Canadian Studies* 35, 1 (2000): 95–114; or Heather A. Smith, "The disciplining nature of Canadian foreign policy," pp. 3–14 in Beier and Wylie, *Canadian Foreign Policy in Critical Perspective*.

20. Alison Howell, "The art of governing trauma: Treating PTSD in the Canadian military as a foreign policy practice," pp. 113–25 in Beier and Wylie, *Canadian Foreign Policy in Critical Perspective*.

3 Canadian Foreign Policy, 1945–1968

Adam Chapnick

Key Terms

Functional Principle

The Golden Age of Canadian Foreign Policy

The Gray Lecture

The question of whether foreign policy has been, or indeed should be, determined by interests or values has dominated recent analyses of Canada's role in the world.[1] It is an intriguing issue, characterized aptly, albeit provocatively, by the former Canadian ambassador to the United States, Allan Gotlieb, as a clash between realists and romantics.[2] It has no definitive answer. Typically, foreign policy practitioners in Ottawa have preferred caution to bold international initiatives, but there have been sufficient exceptions to justify entire books meant to promote and demonstrate the contrary.[3] Moreover, both approaches have some basis in Canada's post-Second World War history. The first decade favours Gotlieb's realists, while the second is more consistent with the vision of his romantics.

The typical starting point for Gotlieb's realists is Canada's so-called **golden age**, the period generally understood to have begun shortly after the end of the Second World War during which international circumstances, the domestic political environment, and popular attitudes at home were all compatible with the pursuit of a Canadian foreign policy that served a widely accepted definition of the national interest to an unprecedented extent.[4] By the mid-1950s, in spite of the acclaim brought to Canada when its former secretary of state for

external affairs, Lester B. Pearson, accepted the Nobel Peace Prize, that age was coming to an end. The opportunities to exert a consistently disproportionate role in world affairs were more limited, just as Ottawa became saddled with unrealistic, popular expectations to demonstrate Pearsonian-like leadership abroad.[5]

Unable, or unwilling, to admit Canada's relative decline publicly, from the late 1950s through the 1960s, successive Conservative and Liberal governments took their country's self-proclaimed middle power role too seriously, or so the realists maintain.[6] To them, the period from 1957 to 1968 was a time when rhetoric flourished, and increasing numbers of Canadians believed that they had no national interests other than world peace. Such romanticism was nurtured by the political leadership, with one prime minister even announcing with pride, "so far as Canada is concerned, support of the United Nations is the cornerstone of its foreign policy."[7]

To the romantics, even if "the post-golden age may not deserve the laudatory epithets" of the previous period, it nonetheless "entrenched the essential continuity of Canadian internationalism . . . . [T]he accumulated Canadian distinction and prestige were too good to be either ignored or resisted."[8]

Ottawa's commitment to selfless, value-laden participation on the world stage in the 1960s—and its success in promoting its worldly agenda—was hardly different from the approach and effectiveness of Canada's political and diplomatic elite 20 years earlier.

Regardless of which interpretation seems more plausible, by 1968, pride in the previous decade's accomplishments seemed to disappear, replaced by condemnation of an era alleged to have been characterized by excessive national self-confidence and blindness to global realities. Almost immediately upon taking office, Prime Minister Pierre Elliott Trudeau called for a foreign policy review. The resultant white paper, *Foreign Policy for Canadians*, rejected his immediate predecessors' approach to international engagement. As historian Robert Bothwell has explained, Trudeau's government contended that Canadian foreign policy "had become the handmaiden of a misguided devotion to international institutions. Along the way, Canada's national interest had been lost, or at least submerged, and Canada had earned itself the reputation of an international busybody."[9] Academic differences over whether Trudeau was right persist to this day.

While making no claims to comprehensiveness, nor to any greater insight than those of the historians and political scientists who have attempted this exercise before, the rest of this chapter seeks to summarize Canada's foreign policy experience between 1945 and 1968. It does so by dividing the nearly quarter century into three phases: the early postwar (1945–53), which favours Gotlieb's realists; the time of transition (1954–57), which provides evidence suitable to either interpretation; and the age of romanticism (1957–68), which speaks for itself. While coming to no specific conclusions, it is more sympathetic to the realist point of view, if only because, as Lester Pearson once said, "The true realist is the man who sees things both as they are and as they can be."[10]

Canadian Foreign Policy in the Early Postwar Period, 1945–1953

The Second World War stimulated a dynamic transformation of the international power structure that had significant implications for Canada's external status and standing. The changes began with the fall of France in 1940. To that point, while the Canadian government had been committed to the global conflict alongside the British and French militaries, the national contribution had been relatively insignificant and unimpressive. Prime Minister William Lyon Mackenzie King brought his country into the war united, if also unprepared, and initially his primary concern was keeping obligations to a minimum.[11] When France fell, however, Canada became Great Britain's most significant wartime ally. Ottawa's engagement with the conflict and its influence upon it—in both economic and military terms—necessarily increased.

France's decline was followed by a series of fundamental changes that overtook Europe and Asia during the Second World War. Leading states like Great Britain saw their economies depressed and their fiscal infrastructure devastated. Other former and future powers, like China, Japan, and Germany, were left in political disarray. As a result, for a short period in the late 1940s, those states whose geography had shielded them from the destruction of the conflict, like Canada, emerged disproportionately strong and capable of exerting unusual influence on international developments.

Also strengthened by the outcome of the war was Ottawa's most significant economic and military ally, the United States. Moreover, in the 1940s Washington was open to cooperating with like-minded nations to consolidate an international anti-communist network.[12] Canada was among the United States' most valuable partners both in the

Cold War and in the development of a new global economic order, and the State Department, along with its executive leaders, was therefore more apt to include Ottawa in high-level discussions than it had been in the past or would be in the future.

The end of the Second World War also coincided with the creation of a new system of global governance. Between 1943 and 1947, at a time when much of the developed world was shifting its focus to reconstruction, Canada was able to play a significant role in the founding of a series of critical multilateral organizations, including (chronologically) the International Monetary Fund (IMF), the International Bank for Reconstruction and Development, the United Nations, the General Agreement on Tariffs and Trade (GATT), and what is known today as the North Atlantic Treaty Organization (NATO).[13] Certainly, the Canadian negotiators were taken seriously because of their abilities, but one cannot deny the opportunities that were created by the difficulties experienced by Canada's allies and associates.

Finally, from the more narrow perspective of global security, although a majority of North Americans felt relatively safe prior to the Second World War, with the launch of the first atomic weapons on Hiroshima and Nagasaki in August 1945, the international community encountered a danger that left no person entirely secure. At a time when only the United States had mastered atomic technology, those in the possession of the materials necessary to build the bombs became disproportionately important. Canada, the only allied power with an active uranium producing and refining industry, again found itself in a position of influence.[14]

In summary, changes at the global level that began with the fall of France in 1940 and extended into the early postwar period provided an opening for states like Canada to exert unusual authority on the world stage. There was room for countries who were unaccustomed to playing a major role to

act boldly if they so chose. Nonetheless, not every state that would soon be called a middle power embraced the opportunity.[15] In this context, one must consider issues and events at the national level that facilitated Ottawa's specific effort.

The first, and perhaps the most significant, was the state of the Canadian economy. Although there were initial challenges in the immediate postwar period, after 1946, real GDP in Canada rose every year during the next decade (and indeed into the early 1970s). Consumption increased, as did business investment. Oil and gas reserves were discovered in Alberta, and national projects like the Trans-Canada Highway created jobs and stimulated an already vibrant domestic market. Growth rates into the early 1950s were also impressive, allowing for new government spending and enterprise.[16] Canada's economic strength lent it international credibility, while the stability that strength provided gave Ottawa freedom to concern itself with matters beyond the country's borders.

The federal government's control over its often disgruntled provinces was also unusually strong. In 1941, Mackenzie King used his wartime powers to impose a series of tax rental agreements that provided the federal government with overwhelming control over the national economy. In exchange for their cooperation, the provinces received unconditional transfer payments. Tax rentals were not replaced by tax sharing until 1957 and by tax collection agreements in 1962.[17] Until then, intergovernmental relations rarely ventured into the realm of foreign policy, leaving Ottawa with one less factor to consider as it developed and implemented its global strategy.

Not only did the federal government and the provinces demonstrate a degree of unity in their outlook on external relations (if only because the provinces were otherwise occupied and constrained), so did Canada's political parties. The period that followed the conscription crisis of 1944 was one of refreshing parliamentary cooperation on the world stage. The Liberal prime minister, Mackenzie King, invited the Conservatives' House leader, Gordon Graydon, and the Co-operative Commonwealth Federation's leader, M.J. Coldwell, to join the Canadian delegation to the United Nations' founding conference in San Francisco. Representation during subsequent meetings of the UN General Assembly through the early years of the Cold War was also multipartisan.[18] This civilized environment enabled the federal government to consistently advance a clear vision of Canada's role in the world. In January 1947, Secretary of State for External Affairs Louis St Laurent pledged that "in its external relations the government in office should strive to speak and to act on behalf of the whole of Canada and in such manner as to have the support of all the Canadian people regardless of party affiliation at home." What has since become known as the **Gray Lecture** remained the standard statement of the nation's foreign policy principles for at least a decade.[19]

Canada spoke with one voice in world affairs, and its government had a coherent grand strategy.[20] As St Laurent explained, ever since the battles of the Second World War had ended, his country had become an active player in the conflict against communism on the side of political liberty, the rule of law, and the values of humanity. No longer could Canadians remain isolated in North America; in the postwar world, they had both a duty and a responsibility to promote their international interests, as well as those of their allies. Ottawa was a secondary power, and could not be expected to contribute to the same extent as some of its global peers. But it would do what it could, and would likely exert its most significant influence through multilateral organizations and institutions.

The government advanced this vision effectively because its relationships with the media and the public service were exceptionally strong. For a brief period in Canada's national history, all three groups largely agreed on the importance of active participation on the world stage and of cooperating to spread their message to the widest possible audience. As historian Patrick Brennan has explained, for the journalists, "getting the story straight necessitated the closest of contacts with the establishment that formulated and implemented foreign policy." Moreover, he has noted, "admiration for the brainpower and dedication [within the Department of External Affairs] . . . was eclipsed only by the degree of respect and affection the press, and especially the top-ranked men, had for [Lester] Pearson."[21]

The Department of External Affairs and its related public service agencies were populated by a selfless group of internationalists whose talents and acclaim were appreciated beyond Canada's borders. Louis Rasminsky was a leading voice in the creation of the International Monetary Fund and the World Bank. Hume Wrong was treated with the utmost respect as Ottawa's long-time ambassador in Washington. Norman Robertson was on America's short list to become the United Nations' first secretary-general, and John Read was one of the original nominees to the International Court of Justice in 1946. At a time when foreign ministries were playing a significant role across the Western world, Canadian diplomats were well prepared to make a difference.[22]

Finally, members of the public were supportive of global engagement without demanding direct input into the process. They expressed pride in their country's achievements during and after the Second World War while permitting their external representatives the freedom to operate without overt concern for the domestic political ramifications of their initiatives.[23] The mandarins acted accordingly, balancing pragmatism with idealism while never losing track of Canada's national interests. Once politics re-entered the equation in the mid-1950s, the national foreign policy process deteriorated.

Until then, as John Holmes has argued (and as St Laurent had predicted), Ottawa's most significant contributions to world affairs arose primarily out of its participation in international institutions.[24] Canada's **functional principle**—the philosophical basis of Canadian international engagement from the middle of the Second World War onward—meant that the country could make its most significant difference in the world when engaged in issues for which it had pre-existing expertise as well as an interest in active participation.[25] A corollary to this principle was that strategic effect would come more easily in areas that concerned the great powers the least. It therefore made sense to show initiative in the development of the International Court of Justice, in global reconstruction efforts (through the United Nations Relief and Rehabilitation Administration), and even on such mundane issues such as the composition of the UN secretariat.[26] As a non-great power, it was in Ottawa's interest to function within an international system of rules and regulations. As a nation whose economic prosperity was unusually dependent on foreign trade, it made sense for Canada to establish constructive working relationships with members of the developing world. And blessed with an able diplomatic corps, the Canadian government understood that its global initiatives stood their greatest chance of implementation within multilateral institutions developed primarily by Canada's leading wartime allies.

The fast-growing Department of External Affairs was similarly active in the evolution of the British Commonwealth. In 1950, Canada helped establish the Colombo Plan, the first formal development assistance program for Africa. During the Korean War (1950–53), the Canadian military made a notable, albeit not exceptional, contribution as part of a British Commonwealth division.[27] Finally, an effective relationship with India facilitated Lester Pearson's diplomatic success during the Suez Crisis. In every case, Ottawa recognized the importance of counterweights. There was never any doubt that the United States was Canada's most important ally—at Washington's request, Ottawa did not recognize Communist China after Mao's victory over the nationalists in 1949; it supported hot pursuit into Chinese territory during the Korean War; and it negotiated a series of bilateral and binational defence agreements, including 1957's North American Air Defense Command—but the benefits of diversification were rarely forgotten either.[28]

Nor did the Canadian government neglect its broader international responsibilities and obligations. Support for the military during the Cold War reached its peak during the Korean conflict.[29] The Department of External Affairs expanded dramatically throughout the first postwar decade. Ottawa's commitment to international development, although limited, increased in importance as decolonization progressed. Canada contributed on time and disproportionately to the UN's operating and supplementary budgets throughout the 1940s and 1950s. The quality of Canadian personnel was similarly impressive.

Finally, it was rare for the political leadership to promise more than it could deliver. As St Laurent explained, Canada always kept "in mind the limitations upon the influence of any secondary power." The senior members of his Department of External Affairs were aware that "no society of nations can prosper if it does not have the support of those who hold the major share of the world's military and economic power." There was "little point" in a country of Canada's stature "recommending international action, if those who must carry the major burden of whatever action is taken are not in sympathy."[30]

The Foreign Policy Transition, 1954–1957

Between 1954 and 1957, Canadian foreign policy underwent an ironic transition. Ottawa was recognized publicly for its global achievements. The romantic assessment of its ability to make a difference on the world stage, held by an increasing number of national analysts and commentators, appeared to be justified. And yet, from a strategic perspective, the government's efforts to effect global change caused it to depart from the recipe for influence that had served it so well over the previous decade.

In 1954, Canada accepted a seat on an exclusive subcommittee of the United Nations' disarmament commission. The position placed it on relatively equal footing with four of the five great powers. (Only China was excluded.) The following year, the federal government co-sponsored a resolution praising the establishment of the International Atomic Energy Agency.[31] These actions might well have represented global leadership, but they also constituted a significant change in foreign policy. Back in 1946, when the Soviet Union introduced an unhelpful resolution on disarmament, the Canadian delegation to the UN had declined to respond publicly. Its reasoning was made clear in a subsequent publication. Ottawa did not "consider it appropriate that a population which had never had armed forces which might constitute a threat to the peace of the world should take the lead" on nuclear issues. Such issues, noted the Department of External Affairs' 1946 report on the UN, were best left to the United States.[32] Less than 10 years later, the national attitude was different. The political leadership no longer deferred automatically to Canada's great power allies.

There were grounds for this more optimistic approach to policy-making. The death of Joseph Stalin in 1953 created an improved international context in which an increasingly moderate and conciliatory Soviet Union seemed open to compromise and de-escalation of the Cold War. In 1955, Paul Martin (Sr), the federal cabinet minister who led the Canadian delegation to the UN while Secretary of State for External Affairs Lester Pearson was away in Moscow, lobbied successfully for an agreement among the great powers to admit 16 new members to the UN General Assembly. His efforts ended a long-standing impasse between the United States and the Soviet Union.[33] In the new global environment, it seemed as if Canada could and would make a difference. At the same time, however, Martin's actions broadened traditional understandings of the Canadian national interest. Certainly, the new United Nations better reflected the contemporary geopolitical environment, but it also empowered the international community to counter the inclinations of Canada's greatest ally, the United States.[34]

Martin's successful initiative inspired Canadian analysts to expect more from their country. Not much later, the 1956 Suez Crisis amplified the public pressure on the government in Ottawa to be noticed abroad. In January 1957, as the United Nations Emergency Force became operational, a writer for the magazine *Saturday Night* proclaimed "a kind of break-through to new levels of responsibility for Canada in the world." To Maxwell Cohen, Lester Pearson's Nobel Prize-worthy intervention and assistance in establishing the first modern international peacekeeping force—the United Nations Emergency Force—marked "a turning point in the Canadian world role inside and outside the United Nations."[35]

Indeed it did, but not for the reasons that Cohen suggested. As historian Trevor Lloyd has documented, rather than launching it, the Suez Crisis *concluded* an exceptional period in the practice of Canadian external relations.[36] Whether the 1954–57 period should be considered the end of the realists' golden age or the prelude to a decade of romanticism is therefore unclear. It is more certain that what followed was a period of adjustment and romantic thinking, enabled, if not encouraged, by a changing set of global and domestic circumstances.

Romanticism and Canadian Foreign Policy, 1957–1968

Although many in Canada failed to realize it, the world in 1957 was a different place than it had been when Germany and Japan surrendered in 1945.[37] The international power structure, which seemed so fluid at the end of the war, had solidified. The Cold War had entrenched the United States and Soviet Union as superpowers within a bipolar system. Beneath them, the nations of Europe, whose economies had been so ravaged by the total war of the early 1940s, had recovered and begun to unite, and the relative strength and influence of countries like Canada consequently diminished. Although recent research notes that Canada's strong *British* ties remained evident into the 1960s, there is no doubt that Canadians were less *European* in 1957.[38] Moreover, the symbolic and historical links to the Commonwealth began to eclipse the real ones.

The old British Empire was no more and, just as the return of Europe had affected Canada's position in world affairs, so too did the "rise of the rest." In the words of historian Paul Kennedy, the admission of 40 former colonies to the United Nations in the 1960s meant that "the old UN system . . . with its majority of votes in the North, would never be the same again."[39] It did not take long for Canada's influence in the General Assembly, where the non-aligned movement came to dominate, to weaken.

Certainly, as a so-called middle power, Ottawa still served as a reliable, non-colonial Western ally in the Cold War. But its opinions were often less important than those of states such as India, whose influence over the non-aligned community caused the superpowers to take notice. At the Geneva Conference of 1954—meant to finalize the resolution of the Korean War and deal with a pending crisis in Indochina—Canada was not consulted before its allies, at India's insistence, appointed it to serve on

international commissions on supervision and control (ICSCs) in Vietnam, Laos, and Cambodia. Caught in the awkward position of having been volunteered for an assignment for which it was not prepared, Ottawa concluded that it had no choice but to accept, regardless of whether serving on the ICSCs advanced Canada's own national interests.[40]

The Geneva experience was indicative of an evolution in the US approach to international relations which affected Canada significantly. More aggressive and less consultative, Washington under Dwight Eisenhower, John F. Kennedy, and Lyndon Johnson struggled to understand Ottawa and its concerns.[41] Moreover, as the size of the US economy and defence industry expanded, so did the discrepancy in power between the United States and its associates. The incentive to take Canadian opinions seriously decreased in conjunction with Canada's declining ability to play a significant role in US foreign policy initiatives.

The global governance system upon which Canada depended so strongly also faced challenges in the late 1950s and early 1960s. A trend towards greater regionalism in Europe limited the impact of the GATT negotiations until an agreement to lower tariffs was finally reached in 1967.[42] In 1958, the new French president, Charles de Gaulle, came to see NATO differently than its ruling elite. The conflict led to France's withdrawal from the organization's integrated military command. The great powers chose to work outside of the United Nations to deal with the escalating situation in Vietnam. The United Nations failed to deter Washington's disastrous Bay of Pigs invasion in 1961, and the Security Council's actions to quell an ongoing crisis in the Congo were less effective than supporters of the organization might have anticipated, or hoped.[43]

Nuclear proliferation also contributed to the changing nature of the international power dynamic. Whereas the postwar period began with a single nuclear-armed state, by 1964 the Soviet

Union, Great Britain, France, and China had all joined the nuclear club. In the United States in particular, Eisenhower's New Look—an approach to continental and European defence that relied heavily on the nuclear deterrent—alienated Canadian moderates.[44] Ottawa could still lobby actively for disarmament, but Canadians now had to present their case to multiple actors, none of whom had sufficient incentive to listen.[45]

Finally, as the postwar period evolved, the impact of the foreign ministries across the western world decreased. Improvements in information technology provided global leaders with more immediate access to both each other and the general public. Announcements and speeches that used to be the purview of foreign ministers became responsibilities of heads of government, and personal, summit-level diplomacy gained a new prominence. In Canada, the replacement of the long-governing Liberals with John Diefenbaker's inexperienced group of Progressive Conservatives increased the challenges facing an intermediate-sized power.[46] The new Canadian government lacked competent ministers with foreign policy experience. The sudden death of Diefenbaker's first appointee as secretary of state for external affairs, Sidney Smith, meant that after having a single representative in the portfolio for close to a decade, in 1959 Canadians welcomed their fourth foreign minister in just over three years.

The domestic situation was also tenuous. Consumption spending declined significantly in 1957 and 1958, and exports stagnated. By 1961, unemployment was more than double what it had been four years earlier.[47] The economy began to recover in 1962, but by then Canadians had grown even more tightly attached to their social programs, and increasingly determined to expand the size and scope of the welfare state regardless of the impact on federal allocations for foreign affairs and defence. The provinces—whose constitutional responsibilities included social policy—gradually reasserted their power in negotiations with their federal partners, and spending that might once have been dedicated to international security was redirected towards priorities at home.[48]

Parliamentary debate during the Suez Crisis—the Conservatives accused the Liberals of abandoning Great Britain during its gravest time of need—effectively ended the anti-communist Cold War consensus that had largely determined the direction of Canadian foreign policy since 1945. In 1957, Prime Minister Diefenbaker chose not to attend a bipartisan dinner celebrating Liberal rival Lester Pearson's Nobel Prize. His Progressive Conservatives further undermined any plans to strategize about Canadian interests from a long-term perspective by using potentially damaging anti-American rhetoric in their efforts to sway voters to their side.[49] "It's me against the Americans, fighting for the little guy,"[50] argued Prime Minister Diefenbaker during his failed campaign for re-election in 1963. Pearson's more centrist Liberals, equally afraid of losing public support, reduced their emphasis on international relations altogether, insulating them from specific criticisms but also leaving them unable to effectively redefine a unifying vision of Canadian foreign policy for the future.[51]

The great triad of the early postwar period—the media, the civil service, and the federal government—also crumbled. By the mid-1950s, a new generation of reporters had embraced a more combative approach to political journalism.[52] The Conservative government looked upon its public servants as what Diefenbaker called *Pearsonalities*, and the bond between the executive and the mandarins was never the same.[53] Beginning with the establishment of the Royal Commission on Government Organization in 1960 (the Glassco Commission), the Department of External Affairs encountered public criticism for its organizational and administrative attitudes and "general distrust of outsiders"[54] which affected departmental morale and, in time, capabilities.[55]

The mandarinate was not all to blame. Neither Conservative Howard Green (1959–63) nor Liberal Paul Martin Sr (1963–68) were as effective in advancing Canadian interests as their predecessor as secretary of state for external affairs, Lester Pearson, had been. Green was hard-working and dedicated, but his strong will deprived Ottawa of some of the flexibility it needed to play an effective global role. His advocacy of disarmament won him accolades from certain elements of the Canadian population—particularly those who believed that "the celebration of idealist optimism could win over the fixation on 'effectiveness'"[56]—but his romantic determination to collaborate with like-minded countries at the UN regardless of the views of Ottawa's great power allies ensured that the world body's resolutions had limited impact.[57]

Green was, according to defence analyst Joseph Jockel, the "decisive voice" in reneging on Ottawa's commitment to participate in NORAD's "Operation Skyhawk" in 1959, leaving Washington frustrated and dismayed. The following year, the secretary of state for external affairs' opposition to nuclear weapons created irresolvable tension with Minister of National Defence Douglas Harkness. The dispute, and Diefenbaker's unwillingness to settle it, left the Conservative cabinet deadlocked on the pressing issue of Canada's NORAD (and NATO) obligations for over two years.[58] Harkness's resignation failed to clarify the Conservative government's security policy, and contributed to the Liberals' return to power in 1963.

The new prime minister, Lester Pearson, placed the much more experienced Paul Martin in charge of foreign affairs. Nevertheless, the naked ambition of the former and future candidate for the Liberal Party leadership hardly benefited Canada's global credibility. Martin was successful at times—he was instrumental in organizing a UN peacekeeping

expedition to Cyprus, for example—but he often aimed too high, as romantics often do, and as a result drew attention to his country's limitations as much as he did to its strengths. As Robert Bothwell has rightly pointed out, "Some thought [Martin] had difficulty distinguishing small points from larger issues. Some were uneasy at his ability to reinterpret the record in his own favour. Many of them would have agreed with the American official Bill Bundy, who when asked to summarize his impression of Martin said that he was 'pas sérieux', someone not to be taken seriously."[59] Martin's miscalculation of the power of, first, Blair Seaborn and then Chester Ronning to mediate between the United States and the People's Army of Vietnam in the mid-1960s underlined his overconfidence in his own, and Canada's, power to effect change in US policy. By the later 1960s, he was struggling to maintain the full confidence of Pearson's cabinet and less able to advance dramatic initiatives.

In spite of the challenges, Canada's record during the 1957–68 period was not without its achievements, and these successes help explain why romantics see a continuity of Canadian foreign policy accomplishments throughout the period that followed the golden age. Ottawa continued to be an active supporter of the United Nations, and its participation in new peacekeeping missions in Lebanon, the Congo, Yemen, West New Guinea, and Cyprus enhanced its reputation as a leading player in global peace support operations.[60]

Canada also remained active within the British Commonwealth, with Prime Minister Diefenbaker drawing positive attention to his country when he criticized South Africa over its policy of apartheid at the Meeting of Commonwealth Prime Ministers in 1961. At the time, no other white Commonwealth leader was willing to demonstrate the same courage. Diefenbaker's relations with Britain were less successful—his foolish call to divert 15 per cent of Canadian trade to Great Britain in 1957 and his vocal opposition to London's efforts to join the European Common Market in 1960 alienated British political leaders—but his outspoken advocacy of human rights and his commitment to official development assistance through the Colombo Plan drew accolades from some of Canada's smaller partners and allies.

Under Lester Pearson, Canada and the United States resolved an awkward dispute over power generation on the Columbia River System. Subsequently, confronted with provincial demands that none of his predecessors had been forced to contemplate, Pearson faced down the foreign policy challenges that accompanied the Quiet Revolution in Quebec through a combination of ad hoc policies and clever diplomatic negotiation. His efforts enhanced Canada's relationship with a number of developing francophone countries in Africa, even if they were less well received in Charles de Gaulle's France. Finally, in 1965, Ottawa and Washington completed the Auto Pact, a major victory for Canadians that came about in spite of massive American disappointment in the Canadian prime minister's outspoken criticism of US policy in Vietnam just months earlier.

Perhaps most important to a general understanding of Canadian foreign policy in the post-1957 period—and therefore worthy of somewhat more detailed analysis here—is the publication of a seemingly innocuous diplomatic report on the state of the Canadian–American relationship, *Canada and the United States: Principles for Partnership*, in June 1965. The work appeared during a time of significant cultural upheaval in North America and beyond. The 1960s witnessed the coming of age of the baby boomers: the sons and daughters of the veterans of the Second World War. This exceptionally large demographic cohort had the numerical power to be a force in global politics at a young age and a natural inclination to challenge authority. Access to a growing number of publicly funded universities gave them a platform to air their concerns. And with the US war in Vietnam growing in

intensity, and American investment in Canada increasing concurrently, they had an ideal target. In the words of two Canadian historians, by the mid-1960s in Canada, "anti-Americanism had become the national sport."[61]

The impact on discussions of foreign policy was immediate. A book published by CBC journalist James M. Minifie in 1960, *Peacemaker or Powder-Monkey: Canada's Role in a Revolutionary World*, which blamed Canada's close relations with the United States for depriving Ottawa of the international influence that it had exercised so effectively during the Suez Crisis, spawned a virtual industry in Canada dedicated to ending Ottawa's perceived deference to American geopolitical initiatives. Minifie and his followers advocated neutrality as a recipe for independence and counselled (romantically) a return to global leadership that should have come naturally to a well-regarded non-colonial power.[62] By 1965, then, Canadian–American relations had been deteriorating for a number of years, and a binational study of how to improve them was a laudable political undertaking.

The authors of what became known as the Merchant-Heeney Report were good choices on paper, but ill-suited to the mood of the time. A former US ambassador to Canada, Livingston Merchant, and a former Canadian ambassador to the United States, Arnold Heeney, were part of an older, conservative generation of foreign policy practitioners. Their argument that, in the case of bilateral disputes, both countries would be better served if resolutions were negotiated "in private, through diplomatic channels,"[63] ignited a storm of protests and divided Canadians along generational lines. Heeney's colleagues, mandarins who had served during the golden age, understood and supported the report's pragmatism. New Canadian nationalists, including a future foreign minister—Lloyd Axworthy—were furious. One of them, a philosophy professor at the University of Toronto, condemned "the bankruptcy of this approach to world affairs." Others argued only somewhat less emotionally for a new approach to Canadian foreign policy that was less dependent on the aims and interests of the United States.[64]

The debate had not been resolved by 1968, when Pierre Trudeau came to power, but the new prime minister's electoral victory—along with Egypt's abrupt dismissal of the United Nations Emergency Force in 1967—was a symbolic turning point nonetheless. Old ideas that had defined Canada's place in the world for over two decades seemed initially to have little place in Trudeau's Ottawa. It was time for a new foreign policy, one that placed Canada first, regardless of allies' criticisms or concerns.[65]

* * *

At least initially, Trudeau combined the realism and romanticism of his predecessors. He sought to redefine Canadian national interests, but he did so in a way that appealed to the public's sense of moral righteousness and de-emphasized the significance of the United States to Ottawa's international conduct.[66] As a result, there was no clear winner in the realists versus romantics debate, only a new opportunity to revisit the question of what did, and should, motivate Canada's behaviour on the world stage.

Just over 40 years later, not much has changed.

Questions for Review

1. Why is the period 1945–68 often referred to as the golden age in Canadian foreign policy?
2. What international factors allowed Canada to contribute greatly to international affairs in the 1945–68 period?
3. What domestic factors allowed Canada to contribute greatly to international affairs in the 1945–68 period?
4. How does Chapnick distinguish between three phases: 1945–53 realism; 1954–57 transition; and 1957–68 romanticism?

Suggested Readings

Chapnick, Adam. 2005. *The Middle Power Project: Canada and the Founding of the United Nations*. Vancouver: UBC Press.
Cohen, Andrew. 2003. *While Canada Slept: How We Lost Our Place in the World*. Toronto: McClelland and Stewart.

Gotlieb, Allan. 2005. "Romanticism and Realism in Canada's Foreign Policy." *Policy Options* (February): 16–27.
Hilliker, John, and Donald Barry. 1995. *Canada's Department of External Affairs*. Vol. 2: *Coming of Age, 1946–1968*. Montreal and Kingston: McGill-Queen's University Press.

Notes

1. See, for example, Michael Hart, *From Pride to Influence: Towards a New Canadian Foreign Policy* (Vancouver: UBC Press, 2008), 320–35; Michael Byers, *Intent for a Nation* (Toronto: Douglas & McIntyre, 2007), 6–16, 215–41; Steven Kendall Holloway, *Canadian Foreign Policy: Defining the National Interest* (Peterborough, ON: Broadview Press, 2006), 5–18; Roy Rempel, *Dreamland: How Canada's Pretend Foreign Policy Has Undermined Sovereignty* (Montreal and Kingston: McGill-Queen's University Press, 2006) 1–7, 151–75; Jennifer Welsh, "Are interests really value free?,"

Literary Review of Canada 14, 9 (November 2006): 1–5; and Denis Stairs, "Myths, morals, and reality in Canadian foreign policy," *International Journal* 58, 2 (Spring 2003): 239–56.

2. Allan Gotlieb, "Romanticism and realism in Canada's foreign policy," *Policy Options*, February 2005, 16–27.

3. See, for example, the contrast between Adam Chapnick, "Peace, order, and good government: The 'conservative' tradition in Canadian foreign policy," *International Journal* 60, 3 (Summer 2005): 635–50; and Costas Melakopides, *Pragmatic Idealism: Canadian Foreign*

Policy, 1945–1995 (Montreal and Kingston: McGill-Queen's University Press, 1998).

4. For a more complete assessment of the golden age, see Adam Chapnick, "The golden age: A Canadian foreign policy paradox," *International Journal* 64, 1 (Winter 2008–9): 205–21.

5. Peyton V. Lyon, "The evolution of Canadian diplomacy since 1945," pp. 13–33 in *De Mackenzie King à Pierre Trudeau: quarante ans de diplomatie canadienne*, ed. Paul Painchaud (Quebec: Presses de l'université Laval, 1989), specifically p. 21; and Trevor Lloyd, *Canada in World Affairs 1957–1959* (Toronto: Oxford University Press, 1968), 8.

6. On middle powers, see Adam Chapnick, "The Middle Power," *Canadian Foreign Policy* 7, 2 (Winter 1999): 73–82; and Chapnick, "The Canadian Middle Power Myth," *International Journal* 55, 2 (Spring 2000): 188–206.

7. John Diefenbaker, quoted in Canada, Department of External Affairs, *Report of the Department of External Affairs 1957* (Ottawa: Queen's Printer, 1958), 2.

8. Melakopides, *Pragmatic Idealism*, 52.

9. Robert Bothwell, *Alliance and Illusion: Canada and the World, 1945–1984* (Vancouver: UBC Press, 2007), 278.

10. L.B. Pearson, *Democracy in World Politics* (Toronto: S.J. Reginald Sanders and Co., 1955), 121.

11. C.P. Stacey, *Canada and the Age of Conflict*, vol. 2, *1921–1948: The Mackenzie King Era* (Toronto: University of Toronto Press, 1981), 272–74, 281. On King and national unity before the war, see J.L. Granatstein and Robert Bothwell, "'A self-evident national duty': Canadian foreign policy, 1935–1939," *Journal of Imperial and Commonwealth History* 3, 2 (January 1975): 212–33. On Canada's unpreparedness, see Adrian W. Preston, "Canada and the higher direction of the Second World War, 1939–1945," pp. 98–102 in B.D. Hunt and R.G. Haycock, eds., *Canada's Defence: Perspectives on Policy in the Twentieth Century* (Toronto: Copp Clark, 1993).

12. Allan P. Dobson and Steve Marsh, *US Foreign Policy since 1945*, 2nd ed. (London and New York: Routledge, [2001] 2006), 29.

13. Tom Keating, *Canada and World Order: The Multilateralist Tradition in Canadian Foreign Policy*, 2nd ed. (Toronto: Oxford University Press, [1993] 2002); Adam Chapnick, *The Middle Power Project: Canada and the Founding of the United Nations* (Vancouver: UBC Press, 2005); Kathleen Britt Rasmussen, "Canada and the reconstruction of the international economy, 1941–1947," Ph.D. dissertation (University of Toronto, 2001).

14. Robert Bothwell and William Kilbourn, *C.D. Howe: A Biography* (Toronto: McClelland and Stewart, 1979), 168–69, 213.

15. On the differences, for example, between Canada and Australia at the end of the war, see Chapnick, *The Middle Power Project*, 143–44.

16. Kenneth Norrie, Douglas Owram, and J.C. Herbert Emery, *A History of the Canadian Economy*, 3rd ed. (Scarborough: Thomson Nelson, 2002), 374–79.

17. Ibid., 347, 396.

18. John English, "'A Fine Romance': Canada and the United Nations, 1943–1957," in *Canada and the Early Cold War, 1943–1957*, ed. Greg Donaghy (Ottawa: Department of Foreign Affairs and International Trade, 1998), 77.

19. St Laurent, quoted in Chapnick, "The Gray Lecture and Canadian citizenship in history," *American Review of Canadian Studies* 37, 4 (Winter 2007): 448. See also, Hector Mackenzie, "Shades of Gray? 'The Foundations of Canadian Policy in World Affairs' in Context," *American Review of Canadian Studies* 37, 4 (Winter 2007): 459–73.

20. David Pratt, *The Ross Ellis Memorial Lectures in Military and Strategic Studies: Is there a Grand Strategy in Canadian Foreign Policy?* (Calgary: Canadian Defence and Foreign Affairs Institute, 2008).

21. Patrick H. Brennan, *Reporting the Nation's Business: Press–Government Relations during the Liberal Years, 1935–1957* (Toronto: University of Toronto Press, 1994), 142, 143. Pearson left the foreign service to become Louis St Laurent's secretary of state for external affairs in 1948. On Pearson's abilities, see John W. Holmes, "The Unquiet Diplomat—Lester B. Pearson," *International Journal* 62, 2 (Spring 2007): 300, 302.

22. For more detail, see J.L. Granatstein, *The Ottawa Men: The Civil Service Mandarins, 1935–1957* (Toronto: University of Toronto Press, [1982] 1998).

23. Robert Bothwell and John English, "The View from Inside Out: Canadian Diplomats and Their Public," *International Journal* 39, 1 (Winter 1983–84): 65. See also Chapnick, *The Middle Power Project*, 149; John W. Holmes, *The Shaping of Peace: Canada and the Search for World Order, 1943–1957*, vol. 2 (Toronto: University of Toronto Press, 1982), 332–33; and Arthur Andrew, *The Rise and Fall of a Middle Power: Canadian Diplomacy from King to Mulroney* (Toronto: J. Lorimer, 1993), 32. Polls from the period confirm Canada's support for internationalism as well as evidence of their relative ignorance of world affairs. On internationalism, see Canadian Institute of Public Opinion, 10 January 1945, cited in *Public Opinion Quarterly* (Spring 1945): 106–7; on the lack of sophisticated understanding, see Gallup Poll #186, May 1944, in which 50 per cent of respondents declared themselves either not familiar with or undecided on whether the United Nations had been making progress. Cited at www.library.carleton.ca/ssdata/surveys/doc/gllp-49-may186-cbk. Retrieved 1 August 2008.

24. Holmes, *The Shaping of Peace*, 2 vols. (Toronto: University of Toronto Press, 1979, 1982).

25. On Canada's functional principle, see Chapnick, *The Middle Power Project*, 23–24; and Chapnick, "Principle for Profit: The Functional Principle and the Development of Canadian Foreign Policy, 1943–1947," *Journal of Canadian Studies* 37, 2 (Summer 2002): 68–85.

26. Canada, Department of External Affairs, *Report of the First Part of the First Session of the General Assembly of the United Nations* (Ottawa: King's Printer, 1946), specifically 28.

27. In historian Robert Bothwell's words, "The Canadian contribution to the war was large enough to be noticed, though not enough to weigh decisively in the balance when important American interests were at stake." See his *Alliance and Illusion*, 89.

28. On the related ideas of "the diplomacy of constraint" and "defence against help," see Denis Stairs, "The diplomacy of constraint," pp. 214–26 in Norman Hillmer, ed., *Partners Nevertheless: Canadian–American Relations in the Twentieth Century* (Toronto: Copp Clark, 1989), and Donald Barry and Duane Bratt, "Defense against help," *American Review of Canadian Studies* 38, 1 (Spring 2008): 63–89.

29. Canada had largely demilitarized after the Second World War but rebuilt its armed forces aggressively in response to the UN's call to engage in Korea. The Canadian military remained relatively strong through the 1950s and into the 1960s.

30. Louis St Laurent, *The Foundations of Canadian Policy in World Affairs* (Toronto: University of Toronto Press, 1947), 33.

31. Canada, DEA, *Report of the Department of External Affairs 1955* (Ottawa: Queen's Printer, 1956), 8. On Canada's significant role in the IAEA, see Duane Bratt, *The Politics of CANDU Exports* (Toronto: University of Toronto Press, 2006).

32. Canada, DEA, *The United Nations 1946: Report of the Second Part of the First Session of the General Assembly of the United Nations* (Ottawa: King's Printer, 1947), 37.

33. On Martin's experience, see Greg Donaghy and Don Barry, "Our Man from Windsor: Paul Martin and the New Members Question, 1955," pp. 3–20 in *Paul Martin and Canadian Diplomacy*, ed. Ryan Touhey (Waterloo: Centre on Foreign Policy and Federalism, 2001).

34. Tom Keating, *Canada and World Order: The Multilateral Tradition in Canadian Foreign Policy*, 2nd ed. (Don Mills: Oxford University Press, [1993] 2002), 103; and John Holmes, *The Shaping of Peace*, vol. 2, 346. For more idealistic assessments, see Canada, DEA, *Canada and the United Nations 1954–55* (Ottawa: Queen's Printer, 1956), 30; and John Hilliker and Donald Barry, *Canada's Department of External Affairs*, vol. 2, *Coming of Age, 1946–1968* (Montreal and Kingston: McGill-Queen's University Press, 1995), 122.

35. Maxwell Cohen, "A new responsibility in foreign policy," *Saturday Night*, 19 January 1957, 28. On UNEF, see Michael K. Carroll, *Pearson's Peacekeepers: Canada and the United Nations Emergency Force, 1956–67* (Vancouver: UBC Press, 2009).

36. Lloyd, *Canada in World Affairs 1957–1959*. Lloyd's analysis of the end of the so-called golden age remains as valuable as anything that has been written since. For more contemporary analyses, see Andrew Cohen, *While Canada Slept: How We Lost Our Place in the World* (Toronto: McClelland and Stewart, 2003), and Robert Greenhill, "The decline of Canada's influence in the world—what is to be done about it?" *Policy Options*, February 2005, 34–39.

37. On the romantic impulse, see Cohen, *While Canada Slept*. For the most fervent defence of the romantic interpretation of this period, see Melakopides, *Pragmatic Idealism*. Prime ministerial speeches from the late 1950s and early 1960s express similar sentiment. See Arthur E. Blanchette, ed., *Canadian Foreign Policy 1955–1965: Selected Speeches and Documents* (Toronto: McClelland and Stewart, 1977).

38. On the British connection, see Phillip Buckner, ed., *Canada and the Age of Empire* (Vancouver: UBC Press, 2004).

39. Paul Kennedy, *The Parliament of Man: The Past, Present, and Future of the United Nations* (New York: Random House, 2006), 121.

40. Holmes, *The Shaping of Peace*, vol. 2, 203; Bothwell, *Alliance and Illusion*, 197.

41. John Herd Thompson and Stephen J. Randall, *Canada and the United States: Ambivalent Allies*, 4th ed. (Athens and London: University of Georgia Press, [1994] 2008), 199.

42. On Canadian trade policy during the period, see Michael Hart, *A Trading Nation: Canadian Trade Policy from Colonialism to Globalization* (Vancouver: UBC Press, 2002), 204–68.

43. On the Congo, see Kevin A. Spooner, *Canada, the Congo Crisis, and UN Peacekeeping, 1960–64* (Vancouver: UBC Press, 2009).

44. Thompson and Randall, *Canada and the United States*, 197–98.

45. The lobbying itself, taking place at the same time as Canada was accepting nuclear weapons as part of its NATO obligations, was a prime example of the country's romanticism. See, for example, "Statement by General E.L.M. Burns, representative of Canada on the First Committee of the United Nations, 30 October 1961," cited in Blanchette, *Canadian Foreign Policy 1955–1965*, 57–62.

46. On the problems with new governments, see George C. Perlin, *The Tory Syndrome: Leadership Politics in the*

Progressive Conservative Party (Montreal and Kingston: McGill-Queen's University Press, 1980).

47. Norrie et al., *A History of the Canadian Economy*, 381.

48. The exception to this argument is spending on foreign aid, which increased dramatically. Given how little of the federal budget was allocated to aid in the first place, however, these numbers are relatively unimportant. On the challenges with the provinces, and the romantic face placed upon them, see, for example, "Statement issued by the Secretary of State for External Affairs, Mr. Paul Martin, 23 April 1965," cited in Blanchette, *Canadian Foreign Policy 1955–1965*, 409–10.

49. Norman Hillmer and J.L. Granatstein, *For Better or For Worse: Canada and the United States into the Twenty-First Century* (Toronto: Thomson Nelson, 2007), 194; Hilliker and Barry, *Canada's Department of External Affairs*, 135.

50. Quoted in Hillmer and Granatstein, *For Better or for Worse*, 208. Beginning in 1961, the newly formed New Democratic Party was no better.

51. See, for example, Bothwell, *Alliance and Illusion*, 260–63.

52. Brennan, *Reporting the Nation's Business*, xi.

53. Hilliker and Barry, *Canada's Department of External Affairs*, 134–43; H. Basil Robinson, *Diefenbaker's World: A Populist in Foreign Affairs* (Toronto: University of Toronto Press, 1989), 6–9; and Adam Chapnick, *Canada's Voice: The Public Life of John Wendell Holmes* (Vancouver: UBC Press, 2009), 94–102.

54. Gilles Lalande, *The Department of External Affairs and Biculturalism*, vol. 3 of *Studies of the Royal Commission on Bilingualism and Biculturalism* (Ottawa: Queen's Printer, 1969), 14.

55. Hilliker and Barry, *Canada's Department of External Affairs*, 198–208.

56. Melakopides, *Pragmatic Idealism*, 58.

57. Canada, Department of External Affairs, *Report of the Department of External Affairs 1960* (Ottawa: Queen's Printer, 1961), v, 11, 14. See also Peyton Lyon, *Canada in World Affairs 1961–1963* (Toronto: Oxford University Press, 1968), 280. For more on Green specifically, see his speeches in Blanchette, *Canadian Foreign Policy 1955–1965*.

58. Joseph T. Jockel, *Canada in NORAD 1957–2007: A History* (Montreal and Kingston: McGill-Queen's University Press, 2007), 52–66.

59. Bothwell, *Alliance and Illusion*, 217.

60. Martin, "Peacekeeping: Some prospects and perspectives," cited in Blanchette, *Canadian Foreign Policy 1955–1965*, 46–52.

61. Hillmer and Granatstein, *For Better or For Worse*, 230.

62. James M. Minifie, *Peacemaker or Powder-Monkey: Canada's Role in a Revolutionary World* (Toronto: McClelland and Stewart, 1960).

63. Quoted in Chapnick, *Canada's Voice*, 168.

64. Charles Hanly, "The Ethics of Independence," in *An Independent Foreign Policy for Canada?*, ed. Stephen Clarkson (Toronto: McClelland and Stewart, 1968), 27. See the rest of the Clarkson collection for an indicative sample of the new nationalist views of the time. For a retrospective analysis, see Brian Bowe and Patrick Lennox, eds., *An Independent Foreign Policy for Canada? Challenges and Choices for the Future* (Toronto: University of Toronto Press, 2008), and in particular, the editors' introductory chapter. For a sampling of popular views, see Editorial, *Toronto Daily Star*, 13 July 1965, 6; Bruce Hutchison, "The prickly neighbours," *Winnipeg Free Press*, 22 July 1965; and James Eayrs, *Diplomacy and Its Discontents* (Toronto: University of Toronto Press, 1971), 49–58.

65. For an excellent summary, see John Holmes, *Canada: A Middle-Aged Power* (Toronto: McClelland and Stewart, 1976), 8–19.

66. Most striking was the result of his foreign policy review, *Foreign Policy for Canadians*, which included six books detailing Canada's foreign policy priorities, none of which focused on the United States.

4 Most Safely in the Middle

John W. Holmes

Medio tutissimus ibis.

—Ovid

Key Terms

Foreign Policy
Functional Middlepowermanship

Helpful Fixer
Middle Power

It seemed like sound advice for Canada when we were launched after the Second World War into the giddy world of international diplomacy: "You will go most safely in the middle." There was enough of Mackenzie King in it to carry the cabinet and enough forward motion for an impatient body of foreign service officers and a public that seemed more anxious than Mr King to accept rather than avoid commitments. He probably sensed all along, however, a Canadian disinclination to pay much for status or to maintain the requisite armed forces for an aspiring major power. Mr King did not much like the classification "middle" power. As far as status was concerned, he regarded it as somewhat demeaning to be ranked with, say, Mexico, but he had little zeal for the entangling responsibilities such as, for example, membership in a United Nations commission to seek the peaceful reunification of Korea. In any case, the idea that Canada was a middle power did gain wide acceptance. What we had considered ourselves before is hard to say, our preference for smallness when contributions were in order conflicting with the sense of bigness that came from being the second largest country in the world. The ambiguity has persisted.

What has become of the middle power and its role in the past 25 years? At the end of the fifties we seemed to have got it neatly defined. The term **middle power** had been conceived in the first place as a way of explaining to the world that Canadians were of greater consequence than the Panamanians but could not take on the obligations of the Americans, or even the French. It was useful in encouraging a wallflower people to get responsibly involved in keeping the peace and unleashing the world economy while at the same time warning them that they should not expect to wield the influence of a "great" power. Canada's early forays into international diplomacy encouraged confidence that we were needed and, if we did not set our sights too high, that we could impinge. Mackenzie King's conviction that we should keep our noses out of distant problems because we had no distant interests was turned upside down. That became our qualification for intermediary therapy in the United Nations and elsewhere. So "middle" power took on an unexpected meaning. Altogether it fitted very well a country that was recognizing that it could best work through combinations and through international institutions; there were three major associations (the United Nations, the Commonwealth, and the North Atlantic Treaty Organization) and many minor ones that fitted our needs aptly. The variety, furthermore, made us more confident of the freedom of movement we had come to cherish in a long history of groping for our own place in the sun.

The high point had come in 1955 and 1956 when our accomplished leaders, Paul Martin Sr and Lester Pearson, with wide if not universal international acclaim, led the lesser powers in the General Assembly in revolt against great power arrogance over the issues of new members and the Suez. The replacement, shortly afterwards, of this skilled team by the inexperienced Conservatives slowed us down but did not substantially alter the concept. The satisfactions, however, diminished, and as new issues—the rise of the Third World, nuclear escalation, continental economics, provincial claims in **foreign policy**—began to press us harder, one could see that "middlepowermanship," while still a valid concept, did not tell us much about how to handle 90 per cent of the agenda that crowds the day of a foreign service officer.

It was really only after the so-called golden decade of the middle power had passed that we began to grow self-conscious about it. Having been as guilty as any in analyzing and defining this mystic role, I became worried by the mid-sixties over the glorification and formalization of a kind of diplomacy that was really just commonsensical and not as unique as we were hinting. At a conference in Banff in 1965 I asked: "Is there a future for middlepowermanship?" The irony would, I thought, be grasped by a generation who knew Stephen Potter. The term *brinkmanship* had been coined by James Reston to deflate John Foster Dulles, but it was then incorporated into the language as if Dulles had said it himself. I should have listened to Charles Lamb: "Clap an extinguisher on your irony, if you are unhappily blessed with a vein

of it." The mood in the land was earnest. A new breed of scholars was now adding greatly to our sophistication in terms of foreign policy but seeking somewhat too arduously to define the indefinable. The word *middlepowermanship* began to buzz. Editors and politicians needed something to cling to, and in a time of increasing uncertainty the illusion gained ground that the multifarious range of international involvements could be subsumed in a succinctly definable "foreign policy."

There was already an anxiety to cling to what seemed fleeting glories. More regrettable was the consuming interest in what one might, if one still dared, call *rolemanship*. For scholars it was less seductive than for politicians. There was nothing wrong in the efforts, scientific or intuitive, to draw a bead on Canada in world politics and economics, provided the abstractions were restrained and not pressed too far. Middlepowermanship got boring, however, and by the end of the sixties a new prime minister proclaimed a revolt. He questioned whether the national interest had been adequately served in all the strenuous *helpful fixing*—another term that was drafted ironically but interpreted solemnly—that went with middlepowermanship. Pierre Trudeau's grasp of foreign policy and diplomacy was dubious, but he was posing a question being widely asked by an "attentive public" disenchanted with formulae too oft repeated. The "role of a middle power" was under critical review. The idea had become increasingly associated with "peacekeeping," and attitudes to that proud Canadian function were soured by the expulsion of the United Nations Emergency Force (UNEF) from Egypt in 1967 and the embarrassment and frustrations of trying, as a member of three international supervisory commissions, to control the peace in Indochina at war.

It was certainly time for a review, but it is unfortunate that the role of the middle power had become confused with "do-goodism," constantly misconstrued in a debate over "nationalism" and "internationalism." The idea gained ground that somehow the national interest of Canada, particularly its economic interests *vis-à-vis* the United States, had been sacrificed because Lester Pearson was off at the United Nations for a few days a year. A much greater number of public servants and cabinet ministers, among them the redoubtable C.D. Howe, had been guarding our trade and commerce than those few engaged in the high-profile acts in New York or Geneva. Canada had been drawn into accepting responsibilities for world order because it was wanted. Canadians had not gone looking for distinguished service, although in general they welcomed the challenge. If there was any soliciting of such assignments it was tentative. The determination to play as effective a role as was possible for a middle power was based on a very hard-headed calculation of national interest at the end of a war in which too many Canadians had been killed, following a Depression in which too many Canadians had starved. It was a firm rejection of the prewar assumption that Canada could escape disaster by dancing on the periphery. It was taken for granted that there was no national interest greater than the preservation of a world in which Canadians could survive and prosper. Collective defence and collective law as the best means of serving and protecting Canada itself were better understood by those who had passed through the thirties and forties than by later generations who, nurtured on the new "victimization" school of Canadian history, took a more claustrophobic view of the national interest.

It was of course always arguable ad hoc that some national interest had been ill-defended, but it was intellectually slipshod to see this in either/or terms. The same simple thinking was evident in the simultaneous debate over the efficacy of "quiet diplomacy," associated persistently with feckless middlepowermanship. That quiet diplomacy had quite often failed to move other powers, especially the United States, was easy to prove, but it did not follow that loud shouting would have moved a mountain either. It was still not widely recognized that there are no sure ways and means for a middle power to get its way at all, that abstractions are to be handled with care, and that a more discriminating look at specifics is a better way to further the national interest and avoid despair.

The attack on classical middlepowerism came from two directions. There were those on the right who thought all Canada's energies should be directed to selling apples and reactors. The more articulate critics on the left did want Canada to play a grand peace-inducing role in the world but thought that we were hindered by our alignment. They saw "uncommitment" as a means to a worthy end. Then, almost inevitably, "independence" came to be seen as an end in itself. In particular that meant independence of the United States, partly, it was thought, because we could not be regarded as objective actors in world diplomacy if we were allied to one of the superpowers, and partly because the close economic tie was believed to be intimidating us from foreign policies that would serve specifically Canadian ends and help to keep the world in balance. The independentist school of thought strayed from the Canadian tradition of regarding independence functionally. We had pursued self-government but not independence from Britain for the simple reason that our national interests seemed better served that way. We needed Britain as counterweight and the prestigious Foreign Office to conduct Canadian diplomacy on the cheap. *Independence* was a Yankee word that even Mackenzie King rejected. In practice we acted independently when we wanted to and joined a team when that was more useful. The new nationalism was based on a persistent misreading of the postwar period, popularized regrettably by a great Canadian historian, Donald Creighton. The assumption that the Canadian government had embraced "continentalism" with enthusiasm when they had broken with the shackles of the British is an anti-American version of our history based ironically on the tenets and mythologies of certain American scholars. It is essentially anti-Canadian also because it assumes Canadian incompetence. Since our historians have been able to delve into postwar Canadian as well as American files, the record has been very considerably revised, but "Canada as victim" lingers on in textbooks to which students are still subjected. It suffuses also much masochistic comment on our foreign policy, which does not accord us even middle power status.

In all this clamour the pursuit of the national interest got derailed, and the role of this middle power confused. That Mr Trudeau has worked his way eventually to his predecessor's concept of the basic national interest would seem to have been proved latterly by his dedication to reconciliation between North and South and the restoration of the dialogue between East and West. He was, nevertheless, responsible initially for setting Canadians off on a few false scents and for leaving the impression that there occurred in the early seventies a profound change in Canadian foreign policy. The Pearson–Martin years of the sixties were written off as more of the same old middle-powermanship, although with less spectacular results. The extent to which change has been attributable in fact more to the turning earth than to policy planning in Ottawa has been ignored. Already during the Diefenbaker regime it was clear that the configuration of power in which this middle state had flourished was becoming unhinged.

The world has changed and we along with it. The intensification of economic competition in the world at large, the price of oil, nuclear escalation, the banking crises, the relative decline of both the United States and Canada in the world economy, and the rigidifying of East–West as well as North–South relations have profoundly affected the states of North America. They have altered our predicaments and challenged the rules and habits by which we have played. If we seek the causes for patterns of change in Canada–US relations, for example, I suggest that we are more likely to find them in these alterations than in the philosophical stance and the *Weltanschauung* of Mr Trudeau. Because Pierre Trudeau is one of the few statesmen around with a sophisticated philosophy and a reasonably consistent prospect of the world, Canadians, and other peoples as well, tend to see him as causal rather than influential. That is even more true of his critics than his admirers. When I say that he is reasonably consistent, I am aware of perceived contradictions in his attitudes to nuclear weapons or economic protectionism, but his philosophy does embrace paradox. He must be a politician as well as a philosopher, and he is constrained by the will of cabinet colleagues and the Liberal caucus. His *Weltanschauung* of 1983 is not that of 1968, and he is probably more willing than most prime ministers (male or especially female) to admit that he has changed his mind—although not much. That his views, his beliefs, and his prejudices have considerably influenced Canadian foreign policy is undeniable. He has certainly changed the style.

My main point, however, is that Canadian policies in recent years have been determined more by what has happened in Washington or Houston, Brussels, or Tegucigalpa, than by what has been decided or sought in Ottawa. I suggest, although without total conviction, that Canadian policies would not have been very different if there had been another Liberal leader or a longer Conservative government during these years. The range of Canadian foreign policies is considerably more restricted by basic geopolitical, economic, and cultural factors than critics and opposition spokesmen assume, and the room for radical change is circumscribed. I am not hereby proclaiming, as do our archaic Marxists, that Canada is a bound victim of American imperialism. We have considerably more room for manoeuvre than most middle powers, but even superpowers have a limited range of choice in these intervulnerable times.

The reason for the undue attention to Trudeauism is probably to be found in the prime minister's stance on foreign policy when he came to office. Foreign policy was not his major preoccupation, and at least until recently it has not been. His views on the subject were highly academic, reflecting those widely held by many other professors at that time. His exposure to the contradictions of actual policy-making was limited. In fact he revealed a certain lack of understanding of what foreign policy, diplomacy, and the foreign service were all about. He was impatient of the diplomats because they had to obtrude certain inescapable facts of international life on his visions. He mistakenly thought embassies abroad were engaged simply in reporting on the world scene and could be replaced by more subscriptions to *Le Monde* or the *New York Times*. Among his many misjudgments was his insistence that Canadian policy had been too reactive. In his innocence he failed to see that, however energetic and imaginative Canada could be in the world, it could not hope to shape in advance the circumstances to which it would have to respond.

For these reasons Mr Trudeau wanted a brand new foreign policy for Canadians. We and our allies were led to expect radical change. Attracting most attention were his questioning of Canada's commitment to NATO and its failure to establish relations with the Beijing government. He set in motion a review that culminated in the white paper, *Foreign Policy for Canadians*—in fact a collection of many-hued brochures on various aspects of foreign policy in which loyal civil servants sought to distil what they thought the prime minister would want, tempered by the advice given during the review by "the people" (mostly politicians and professors). It was time for a thorough review of postwar policies in a changing world, and the effort was worthwhile. The white

paper suffered, as it was bound to suffer, from the fact that no government can discuss its relations with other countries in complete candour, as one might in a post-graduate thesis. Beneath the inevitable circumlocutions were pockets of sound advice. It was a learning experience for the PM and all concerned; but the booklets are primarily of interest now as indicators of the philosophical base from which Mr Trudeau set out to learn about foreign policy.

To his credit he did listen and learn to a greater extent than his critics have allowed. Within a year he had accepted the argument that NATO was a good thing and that Canada should withdraw not all but only half its forces from the European theatre. He soon found out that events in faraway Africa would require him to play the mediatory role expected of Canada in the Commonwealth, whether he sought to save the world or leave it to others to patch up. He proved to be a good diplomat and decided that the Commonwealth was also a good thing.

He learned too that his favourite project of recognizing the People's Republic of China was more complex than just standing up to the Department of External Affairs and the Yankees; it would involve extended and fancy diplomatic negotiation by his best professionals before a satisfactory formula could be reached. The professionals were not opposed to recognizing Beijing, but they did not want their prime minister to fall on his face. They had to make sure at an uncertain time that Canadian recognition would not be rejected by the Chinese. The satisfactory result was attributable not only to his policy and the eventual acceptance by Beijing of a clever formula covering the Taiwan problem, but also to the coincidence of a shift of Chinese policy toward more normal international relations. Washington was less upset because of the new China policy being conceived by Henry Kissinger. Mr Trudeau deserves credit for making a commitment about China before an election and sticking to it, but recognizing Beijing was not a new policy.

Canadian governments since 1949 had stated that intention but had always been stalled by some temporary obstacle. There was more in the way of a new will and new circumstances than new policy.

It is not surprising, however, that the impression was left that we were being ushered into a revolutionary change in direction. When the world proved intractable and perversely went its own course, policy did not look all that new. So there was a tendency, not so much by Mr Trudeau as by his devotees, to offer a somewhat rearranged version of what had gone on before in order to simulate contrast. Previous leaders, as mentioned earlier, were portrayed as having been too intent on international high jinks to protect the store. Those in Washington and elsewhere who had actually faced the formidable C.D. Howe in his defence of Canada's industrial program or Lester Pearson's polite but really quite resonant diplomacy were puzzled, but no matter. The conviction of a new national stubbornness was an essential element of Trudeaumania—even if it was not really a part of Trudeau's own philosophy.

A man by profound conviction anti-nationalist, concerned with broader issues than trans-border bargaining, was made to seem like a red-hot nationalist when nationalism was in the wind. Canada's so-called "economic nationalism" of the seventies, whether wise or unwise, was in fact attributable not to the PM's philosophy but to the threat of American "economic nationalism" as perceived in the import surcharge and the domestic international sales corporations (DISC) legislation of 1971. It was a reactive policy. The misinterpretation has persisted, particularly in the United States, and it is little wonder that American business circles, rallied by the *Wall Street Journal,* have of late ascribed the disease they call Canadian economic nationalism to the anti-American vagaries of this exotic Canadian leader. In this confusion they are, of course, stoked by their admirers in Calgary now that anti-nationalism has become trendy. Mr

Trudeau is a nationalist in the sense that he wants to strengthen the Canadian fabric. He wants Canada to be influential abroad as a model of internal internationalism, of peaceful living together. He has said many times that a failure of Canadians to maintain our kind of federation would be viewed with dismay throughout the world because most countries now have to consolidate more than one language and tribe. He emphatically rejects the kind of nationalism that is simple anti-Americanism. He is more inclined to take Canada's independence for granted than to make a false goal of it—and that is healthy. As Harald von Riekhoff has pointed out, "Trudeau's reasoning is . . . most firmly linked to the global society paradigm and has less of the traditional state-centric orientation."[1] The middle power is seen as the model power.

There was detectable a new will, or a new stubbornness, in certain aspects of foreign policy. Or was it renewed will? In 1945 it had been largely an alteration of will rather than a whole new philosophy of foreign policy that led Canada into its new era of world diplomacy. A new impulse was perhaps required. Lester Pearson had reluctantly agreed in the early sixties to accept nuclear weapons because we had promised our allies to do so. His stated intention was, however, to negotiate decently with NATO to get out of that role. That process was delayed, and Mr Trudeau pressed it to a conclusion. Lester Pearson had hoped to transfer at least some of the forces in Europe to Canada, which, he had always insisted, was part of the NATO front. Mr Trudeau showed a stronger will to defy criticism and act, but he scaled down his original intentions regarding NATO very considerably and emphatically accepted the importance of the treaty as an element of detente, and of Canadian participation in it. Mr Pearson had always wanted to recognize Beijing but never had adequate support in cabinet or the country to act boldly. Mr Trudeau made his pledge before the election and had to go through with it.

A clearer example of this new will of the seventies, frequently cited, was the Arctic Waters Pollution Prevention Act of 1970 in which the government, responding to a chauvinistic hullabaloo over the northern voyage of the American tanker *Manhattan*, proclaimed unilaterally a 100-mile zone which the coastal state would police and defied the International Court of Justice to intervene. It was said that this bold act differed from the previous habit of Canadian governments to go for a compromise. There is some truth in this. The act may have been attributable in part to the easier confidence of a man who had been less exposed to the corrosive game of international compromise, but it was also in the spirit of traditional **functional middlepowermanship**. It was in fact a compromise with the domestic demand for the claiming of Arctic sovereignty *tout court*. It claimed precisely what was needed for practical purposes without grandiloquence. It asserted the right of a lesser power not only to challenge but also to push along international law when the great powers were intransigent—reminiscent somewhat of Paul Martin's defiance over new members of the United Nations in 1955. It was certainly successful, for the Americans and others were soon proclaiming an analogous principle in the 200-mile economic zone favoured at the United Nations Conference on the Law of the Sea. It launched the Trudeau administration on its most effective and laudable international enterprise, a leading and highly constructive role in the most important contribution to world order since San Francisco. It was the culmination of efforts, which had actually begun during the Diefenbaker regime in 1958–60, to adapt the historic maritime laws to a new age. It was "helpful fixing" of the highest order, a worthy contribution to international structure in which, furthermore, the Canadian national interest has been somewhat more than decently advanced.

The rejection of the grand enterprise by the Reagan administration was a disastrous blow, but instead of submission in Ottawa there has been firm resistance accompanied by quiet diplomacy. In the classical tradition of Canada's United Nations activities there have been persistent efforts, not by hortatory rhetoric but by unobtrusive collaboration with other middle powers, to seek out the compromises that might enable the Reaganites to return to the fold. The **helpful fixers**—our old associates the Scandinavians, the Australians, etc.—have been labelled, even by the Americans, as "the good Samaritans."[2] Plus, *peut-être, c'est la même chose*. It has not yet achieved the desired goal, but the strategy is long range. The constructive leadership and brilliant diplomacy of the Canadians in the whole evolution of the United Nations Law of the Sea has enabled survivors like me to insist that their fixing is as helpful as it was in the golden decade; it is just that now it is performed in exhausting nocturnal negotiations beyond the television cameras. They serve alike the national and the international interest, mindful of the wise admonition of an eighteenth-century essayist, William Shenstone: "Laws are generally found to be nets of such a texture as the little creep through, the great break through, and the middle-sized are alone entangled in."

So where does all this leave the role of a middle power in the eighties? Those who think foreign policy is simple proclaim confusion and inconsistency, and, of course, decline. Those who realize the complexities might more charitably detect a learning experience not only for the prime minister but for all the citizenry. We have been aided by an expanding crop of political scientists and historians, cutting through the mythologies and, of course, occasionally creating new ones. In accordance with the times, the debate became excessively ideological in the late sixties and early seventies. The ideologies were usually imported and hard to fit to the real facts of a middle power that had been pretty successfully defying a great capitalist power for a couple of centuries, and which had also been an imperialist power of sorts in its own right. The political scientists and historians are by no means untinged by ideology, but the more clinical approaches are bearing fruit, as we rise for snatches of air above the fog of clichés. There has been, unhappily, a new fog of unintelligibility that keeps the masses unconverted, but one must in this case believe in the trickle-down theory.

There is abroad in the land a new pragmatism, often mistakenly identified as conservatism because it rejects the simplicities of the left as well as those of the far right, and is too often obscured from editors and speechifiers by their dedication to partisan combat. The persistent effort to identify the major parties with certain foreign policies is perverse. The extent to which foreign policy is determined more by the changing scene than by changing ministers is shown in the fact that in 1984 the Conservatives are seeking election on the grounds that the Liberals have messed up Canada's relations with the United States. That is one of the grounds on which the Liberals ousted the Conservatives in 1963. Is it perhaps also of some significance that the leaders of all three political parties say that they are cleaving to the middle ground in the Ovidian tradition even though they are tempted to please variant audiences with immoderate pitches.

It may be counted as progress that the role of a middle power is now seen in a more discriminating way. History has provided the scholars with many more case studies than they had when our world was new. There is a groping for different terms. James Eayrs sees Canada as a "foremost power," and John Kirton and David Dewitt call it a "principal power." Those terms are in themselves interesting because they challenge the more popular assumption that Canada has sunk in the international pecking order. Our power is, of course, infinitely broader and stronger than it was in the golden decade, but there is more competition. The concept of power is regarded more searchingly. The nuclear

power of the super-players is increasingly seen as inapplicable, deluding them into assumptions about the extent to which they can manage the world. Distinctions are being made between military, economic, and diplomatic influence. Canada's claim to be an effective middle power in security questions was made in the forties on the strength of its major contribution to the allied forces during the war. After we had demobilized, however, we were ourselves reluctant to sustain the military strength required to maintain that kind of clout in the United Nations or NATO. The stark contradictions became apparent with the call to support the United Nations cause in Korea in the summer of 1950. When we had to match our high-flown rhetoric about the United Nations and collective security with deeds, the Canadian public realized that the barracks were bare. Our medium-rare reputation in the United Nations now depended on the skills of our diplomacy rather than the might of our arms. We were propelled for a short time into high-level company because we had been one of the three atom powers of 1945, but we soon realized that when you are not a major contributor to the problem you can't make very convincing offers to deal with it. In any case the influence we had in arms control circles rested less on our own nuclear capacity than on the diplomatic prowess and reputation of two generals turned ambassadors, McNaughton and Burns.

It was in any case Canada's economic capacity that first gave it recognition as an important actor and which has proved much more enduring. The military capacity we could offer was for peacekeeping rather than peace-enforcing, and it was important not for its quantity but for its quality, especially technological. Our particular kinds of middling power have had to be assessed in terms of their applicability. We have our wheat and our diplomacy and certain skilled and bilingual soldiers to offer, but military power in the abstract has really mattered little to our role as a middle power. It can be argued, in the abstract of course, that our influence in NATO would be increased from fair to middling if our military contribution was increased, but when one gets down to concrete decisions it is harder to see that there would be much difference. It is true, of course, that if we had no armed forces and were non-aligned, we would almost certainly get shorter shrift from all our allies. Whether that immaculate position would give us greater moral strength in world affairs is the subject of persistent debate, with the skeptics still dominant in Ottawa.

From the beginning Canada's approach to the role of a middle power was functional. We had demanded our due place in allied decisions on *matériel*, where we counted, during the war and made our first pitch for appropriate representation in postwar bodies over the United Nations Relief and Rehabilitation Administration on the grounds that we would be a major supplier. The issue was distorted by our ill-advised campaign to get a special place on the Security Council, not as a great power but as a middle power deserving attention for military merit. God knows what would have happened had the cabinet grasped the financial and manpower implications of maintaining that heady status. After the Korean enterprise, when the Security Council tacitly abandoned its pretensions to maintain a workable system of universal collective security and devoted itself to "helpful fixing," the irrelevance of military force to a special status in its deliberations or to sustain across-the-board middle power became obvious. It had nothing to do with the strength of Canada's voice in the International Monetary Fund, the General Agreement on Tariffs and Trade (GATT), or the International Wheat Agreement where we mattered a good deal more.

Judging our power by its applicability ad hoc should save us from delusions. It might enlighten (without entirely discouraging) those who see foreign policy largely as a simple matter of taking resonant stances on wickedness in a naughty world.

We have too much debate about stances and too little about method. It is the cynics rather than the do-gooders who profit from that situation. Economic sanctions, whether against the Soviet Union or South Africa, are considered as moral gestures, but they ought to be carefully calculated as means to some definable end. Otherwise we risk the kind of reverse suffered over the pretentious sanctions against the USSR over Afghanistan. A successful foreign policy requires concentrated attention. Denouncing villains is sloppy diplomacy. In most issues the problem is not identifying the villain but coping with the predicament. Some of the time we are all more or less guilty.

When Prime Minister Trudeau initiated his peace campaign in the autumn of 1983 he was wise to furnish himself with specific proposals worked out by the professionals with long direct experience of the realities of arms control negotiations. The early successes of Canada as a middle power were attributable to our skill in producing sound ideas for the general rather than just the Canadian interest. That is the way to be listened to. In various international institutions our representatives, whether they are our scientists in the World Meteorological Organization or the United Nations Environment Programme or our engineers or our diplomats, are still being constructive without getting headlines. That is how the international infrastructure is laid. The Canadians agree or disagree with the Americans and balance the national and international interest ad hoc. What they do is sensational only in the long haul and largely ignored by the media for regrettable but understandable reasons; so the perpetual disparagers hold sway. The more dogged nationalists repeat their irrelevant slogans about Canadian foreign policy being an echo of Washington's, revealing thereby their essential anti-Canadianism and their ignorance of the substance of a modern foreign policy. The anti-nationalists on the right display, as they did in imperial days, their lack of confidence in the intelligence and capacity of their own people, by advocating simple docility to a greater power. But in real foreign policy there is such a long agenda, so many ways of succeeding or failing, and these generalizations are almost always wide of the mark. Pleading the rights of a middle power as such is one of the generalizations that will rarely get us far. Applying pressures surgically has got us a good deal. The public has to think functionally, and in this it is now getting some good leadership from a new crop of scholar analysts—at least when it can get the gist of what they are saying.

How useful is it then to talk still of the role of a middle power? The hierarchies, such as they were, are breaking down and the categorization of states shifts. Countries are what they are for all kinds of historical, geographical, and other reasons. Each is unique, and all bilateral relationships are special. Cuba or Israel often act like great powers, and South Africa is treated as one by its enemies. Aside from the somewhat anachronistic categorization of five great powers in the Security Council, there is no fixed classification of states in the United Nations. Countries pay their dues in accordance with individual assessments based largely on economic factors. Membership in the so-called Western European and Others group assures Canada of a reasonable chance for election to the Security Council or other bodies. We still have the advantage of not being tied too tightly to any bloc in multilateral diplomacy, an attribute traditionally associated with our kind of middlepowerism. Loyalty to collective NATO agreements and perceptions of basic common interests properly limit our freedom of action somewhat. So does a sense of respect for the feelings of Commonwealth or francophone associates and the large neighbour. Our greater need for an open world economy restricts our instinct for protection. There is, however, much more flexibility in our situation than is usually assumed. No country has an "independent foreign policy."

In the beginning Canada had regarded blocs as obstacles to sound decision-making, and we have always rejected the idea of a conformist NATO or Commonwealth voting bloc, as distinct from a consultative group. As the number of members of United Nations bodies has increased we have come to realize the importance of blocs in overcoming the anarchy of multilateral negotiation. They work best, however, if the membership shifts in accordance with the subject, as has been the case pre-eminently in the United Nations Conference on the Law of the Sea. As one of the coastal states, we often opposed our major allies while paying due respect to their concern for certain strategies on which we too depend. On other issues we worked with other partners. We accept the validity of the Group of 7 as a voting and bargaining instrument while protesting against the kind of across-the-board voting on political issues that is a major cause of stalemate in the General Assembly. On the Law of the Sea we are a major power because of our fish and nickel and enormous seacoast, and we can confidently act as such. In nuclear matters our endeavours are better conceived as lateral rather than frontal, except in the matter of the proliferation of uranium or reactors. Although we could hardly expect to settle, for example, the Soviet–Chinese border dispute, in other conflicts there is quite often something we can do in good company if we retain a due sense of proportion.

Ours is not a divine mission to *mediate*, and the less that far-too-specific verb is used the better. It is the mission of all countries, and in particular all statesmen and diplomats, with the probable exception of Albanians, to be intermediaries or to seek out compromises in the interests of peace. Our hand is strengthened by acknowledged success, but it is weakened if planting the maple leaf becomes the priority. Whether or not the role of a middle power is now an exhausted concept (or just a boring one), the fact is that the world still needs a good deal of the kind of therapy we thought of as "middlepowermanship."

Our idea of the role of great powers is just as much in need of review. It is doubtful whether the great, and especially the super-, powers ever had as much sway in the managing of the globe as is implied in current theory. In the early postwar years the United States had the economic and military wherewithal and the residual authority that went with it to act almost as a surrogate United Nations while some kind of world order was being established. This was done with widespread if not universal, and certainly not formal, assent from the world community. It did not "run" the United Nations, however. It could influence the voting and often, though not always, block by rough or smooth means what it did not like. It was never able to "control" the votes of a majority because to get support it had to make concessions. It is well not to exaggerate the erstwhile power of the United States now that we are concerned with diluting it. The world must cope with an American administration that wants to revive the past. Aside from Mr Reagan and friends, there seems to be wide agreement that the United States cannot count any more on the kind of authority it once had. By the same token the United States cannot be counted upon for that kind of management or for the residual resources. It was never the ideal arrangement, but what is now to be feared is that there will be no management at all.

The obvious alternative to unilateralism is multilateralism, but the latter is, as the painful lessons of over 40 years make clear, extraordinarily difficult to achieve. Hence the fears that beset us all as a familiar framework of power crumbles. In inveighing against the abuses of power, great, middle, or small, we tend to forget the responsibility that goes with each gradation of power. The transition from superpower dominance to a healthier distribution is not going to be accomplished simply by

demanding that the supers surrender. What, if anything, the Russians are doing about it in their bloc heaven only knows. The Americans, on our side, tend too simply to see this as letting their allies supply more funds and troops while they go on making the decisions as demanded by their system of government. The rest of us want first of all to share in the decision-making but have to struggle with the paradoxes between something like cantonal democracy and the veto. Middle powers and the lesser greats have to show leadership in accepting wider responsibilities even when that means risking American displeasure. That kind of foreign policy requires positive thinking. There is everything to be said for persuading the superpowers and their proxies to withdraw from Central America, the Middle East, and all of Africa, but that is only a beginning. Something still must be done about the endemic problems of El Salvador, Lebanon, Afghanistan, Grenada, and Chad. We have been arguing that these problems may be ascribed to domestic causes rather than to foreign conspiracies, and that means they will not be solved simply by American or Soviet or Cuban withdrawal. They threaten the security of Canadians or New Zealanders as much as they do that of Texans or Ukrainians.

If there is still a point in Canadians seeing ourselves as a middle power in the eighties, it may be to discipline ourselves. When we found a mission as intermediary mediums we began to get some grip on our Canadian capabilities. When a definition that was analytical and descriptive came to be seen as prescriptive we got a little frenetic. However we still need guidelines to cling to and knowing one's strength remains a sound principle. If we are now more discriminating and calculating in our estimates of our own as well as others' powers, so much the better. Skepticism about spreading our good offices too wide may have induced a sense of proportion about the number of rescue missions, crusades, or moral interventions a country of 25 million can conduct at one time. We have to contend with the persistent feeling of other countries that we are smug, self-righteous, and officious. Our moral majority may want the government to pass judgment on every misbehaviour in the world, and no doubt they will feel better if we do so, but it is the surest way to undermine the beneficent role of a middle power. It is furthermore a kind of cop-out by some well-intentioned people whose attention might better be directed to the baffling contradictions we face over policies that hit closer to home. If one were to judge from questions in the House of Commons, one might conclude that Canadian foreign policy was largely a matter of deciding what to do about El Salvador and South Africa.

The middle power that is a major power in the world economy is caught in dilemmas not unlike those of a major military power, and they require hard thinking. It is not only a question of deliberately using power. There is also the inescapable question of withholding it. Canada cannot help, for example, being a food power of decisive proportions and a producer of a wide array of mineral resources. It is not difficult to reject as immoral the idea of using food as a weapon to gain political ends, but if food is so scarce that it has to be rationed, on what bases do we make it available and to whom? That is the kind of issue we face in a rudimentary way with our none-too-plentiful energy supplies in the International Energy Agency. How much greater our problems will be if, with our broad territory and small population, we have to feed the new billions of Asians and Latin Americans. The experience of economic sanctions over Rhodesia and Afghanistan has led us to the too simple conclusion that they don't work and that's that. But the concept of sanctions is inseparable from the trading and aiding that are recognized as high priorities of Canadian foreign policy. We will grapple with these issues more safely in the middle of international institutions. The United Nations system remains of central importance because we of all

countries need international disciplines, but where our vote really matters now is not in the Assembly or Security Council but in GATT or the International Monetary Fund or the World Bank, which are at least as important parts of the United Nations as is the General Assembly. Those are the places where, for example, we register our differences with the United States over Nicaragua or Grenada in votes on loans that count. Our positions on the increase of financing for the Fund or the International Development Association are not decisive but they can be marginally so.

The distinguished British scholar, Denis Brogan, told Canadians 30 years ago, "The very fact that Canada is now one of the treasure houses of the world makes the naive isolationship of the inter-war years . . . impossible. A uranium producing country cannot be neutral."[3] That means not privilege but responsibility for a middle power. One thing that has changed is that the role of a middle power costs more, not just financially but politically. Helpful fixing in the postwar period impinged much less on the priorities of the electorate. When the big international issues now are resources and coastal waters, defence spending, Asian imports, and non-tariff barriers—the things on which our future depends—the ridings will be less quiescent. Our idea of foreign policy has been stretched, and it is no longer true to say that it is not a major issue in elections. Public awareness of the long-range view for a middle power is more essential than ever.

It was in the setting of the wide international community that Canada first saw itself as a "middle" power. Like all other countries Canada was adapting itself to the shift of power from Europe to the United States. There was never a question, as legend has it, of a conscious decision to transfer allegiance from the British to the American protector. Canadian governments worked hard to restore the triangular balance in which we had felt comfortable, to bring Europe and America together in alliance, and to create the international institutions in which we could be ourselves. It was a giant step out of the colonial mentality. Although American power was more nearly omnipotent then than it is now, we had not become so much obsessed by it. Increasingly one feels that Canadians see their foreign policy only in the context of American foreign policy. The fact that it would be seen in better perspective if we compared it with those of other countries our size, with our European allies, with Australia, or with Mexico, is ignored in the single-minded concentration on what Reagan or Shultz, Mrs Kirkpatrick or Dan Rather, are up to. It is not a matter of being pro- or anti-American; the obsession is common to both.

If the Americans have come to dominate our foreign policy, it is not, as nationalists have thought, by arm-twisting and threatening sanctions. We have let the American media capture us for their debate. The danger is not that we support their policies; we associate ourselves just as often with the critics. It is rather that our minds are on what the United States is or should be doing, not how we, with our very different kind of role to play in the world, should be acting. It is irresponsible. Statements by politicians and others often imply that our foreign policy consists simply of approving or disapproving of American actions. When we criticize the Russians for shooting down airliners or take action against them over Afghanistan, this is persistently described as supporting or not supporting the Americans, as if we were helping them out in their private struggle with the Russians and not pursuing our own quarrel with aggressors in the broad company of the United Nations and NATO. By treating NATO as a United States-dominated organization, we and the Europeans have only helped to make it so and dimmed in the process the moral strength of the alliance. Surely the lesson of Canadian experience of middlepowermanship is that we can be a stronger world citizen and a stronger ally if we act in accordance with our own wisdom. The colonial tradition dies hard. It was reported (incorrectly, I hope) that one of our major political parties had been unable to reach a position over Grenada because it did not know whether to follow Mr Reagan or Mrs Thatcher. That is a kind of "middle" policy that I thought we had long since abandoned. As Norman Snider wrote recently in *The Globe and Mail*, "Canadians would be better advised to suppress all those neo-colonial urges to jump up and salute at the most powerful English-speaking nation around and continue to do their own thinking."[4]

It is unfortunate that the excesses of the nationalists of a few years ago helped to discredit the kind of healthy, self-respecting nationalism that Canada needs to combat the cringing anti-nationalism, the idolatry of foreign gods, from which we suffer at present. Surely there is a middle way here that is more sensible and safer and in our own best tradition. Is it so demeaning in a churning world to maintain our peculiar reputation for good sense, moderation, a will to see all sides of a question, and an instinct for compromise? Must we call that mediocrity?

Questions for Review

1. What motivated Canada to conceive of the concept of middle power?
2. What other countries are also middle powers?
3. What are the dimensions of middlepowermanship?
4. Is Canada a middle power today?

Suggested Readings

Chapnick, Adam. **2009.** *Canada's Voice: The Public Life of John Wendell Holmes*. Vancouver: UBC Press.

Holmes, John W. 1976. *Canada: A Middle-Aged Power*. Toronto: McClelland and Stewart.

Holmes, John W. 1970. *The Better Part of Valour: Essays on Canadian Diplomacy*. Toronto: McClelland and Stewart.

Lennox, Patrick. 2010. "John W. Holmes and Canadian international relations theory." *International Journal* 65, 2 (Spring): 381–90.

Notes

1. "The Impact of Prime Minister Trudeau on Foreign Policy," *International Journal* 33, 2 (Spring 1978): 268.
2. Leigh S. Ratiner, "The Law of the Sea: A Crossroads for American Foreign Policy," *Foreign Affairs* 60 (Summer 1982): 1015.
3. "An Outsider Looking In," Canada's Tomorrow Conference, Quebec City, 13–14 November 1953.
4. "Rethinking our Allegiance," *The Globe and Mail*, 3 December 1983, L9.

UPDATE

The Twilight of Multilateralism in Canadian Foreign Policy?
Tom Keating

Key Terms

International Order

Intervention

Multilateralism

Responsibility to Protect

United Nations

Values

Introduction

Canadian foreign policy has undergone a transition since the end of the Cold War in ways that have had a significant effect on the country's commitment to and involvement in multilateral diplomacy and international institutions. The transition is a reflection both of shifts in the global political economy and in successive Canadian governments' approach to both the substance of foreign policy and to the instruments employed in pursuit of this policy. The global political economy has passed through two significant phases since the end of the Cold War. The first was an extended period of Western hegemony reinforced by American unipolarity and a considerable degree of hubris around Western values, democratic principles, and liberal economic practices. The second phase has been marked by a slight but not insignificant shift in global power away from a unipolar system, resulting from the growth of emerging powers and a diminution in Western hubris in the face of American withdrawal and the limited efficacy of Western-led interventions and neo-liberal practices. The result for Canadian foreign policy has been manifest in its engagement with multilateral diplomacy and international institutions—from an attempt to redesign these along the lines of explicitly Western norms to one marked by greater selectivity mixed with significant degrees of withdrawal, accompanied at times by hostility towards various forms of **multilateralism**. These developments raise serious questions about the government's interest and ability to participate constructively in a multilateral process for what may prove to be a significant redesign of international order for the twenty-first century.

The Multilateral Era

The association between Canadian foreign policy and multilateralism has been long-standing. Canada emerged as an independent state on the world stage from the platform of the League of Nations and pursued greater autonomy from the United Kingdom and the United States through its commitment to and participation in multilateral institutions in the post-World War II environment. Throughout the postwar period, Canadian policy officials were often among those states seeking to push these institutions into more active roles. This was done in a manner that would not offend the major powers, so that they would remain involved, if not always actively engaged or strongly committed to the work of the institutions. For Canadian policy-makers, multilateral institutions provided both a platform for a more active role in global affairs and one from which they might have some influence. Multilateral institutions were also useful for deflecting the necessary but potentially stifling effects of a close bilateral relationship with its principal economic and security ally the US. Throughout the last half of the twentieth century, multilateralism proved to be a valuable instrument for pursuing a variety of foreign policy objectives that served core Canadian security and economic interests. In short, it was not for others, but for Canada's own interests, that multilateralism was used so extensively. The value that multilateralism provided as an instrument of foreign policy, however, meant that it was valued in principle. In turn, protecting and promoting the principle and the practice of multilateralism became, at times, as important as the substantive policy objectives that multilateralism facilitated. For this reason throughout the history of the **United Nations** (UN), the Commonwealth, the North Atlantic Treaty Organization (NATO), the General Agreement on Tariffs and Trade (GATT) and other multilateral ventures, Canadian diplomacy was often directed at making the process work in the face of the indifference or opposition of other powers large and small.

The widespread acceptance and use of multilateralism in contemporary global politics has seemingly encouraged the view that this is a normal and permanent feature of interstate relations. In the early days of the post-World War II order, however, there was nothing certain or secure in this move to a more institutionalized multilateral order. Canadian foreign policy officials spent much of their time keeping the multilateral process afloat, because its standing was so very tenuous. The growth of international institutions and multilateral processes in number, scope, and range of responsibilities attests to the success of this idea. Yet as is often noted, these institutions have not been able to keep up with the many responsibilities that member governments have placed on their agendas. The UN is most frequently cited for its many failings, but the World Trade Organization (WTO), the International Monetary Fund (IMF), the multilateral framework to address climate change, and many others are open to criticism as well. Such criticisms are easy to level and not without foundation, but they ignore at least two critical issues. One is that these institutions have been asked to take on responsibilities far beyond what anyone expected them to do. For example, the very idea that the UN would or should be engaged in dismantling a country's weapons system was unheard of until the end of the Cold War when the topic was first breached. A mere 20 years later, the institution is roundly condemned for not doing so more quickly or thoroughly. The second caveat is to recognize that these institutions are very much at the mercy of their member governments, both in terms of what they are asked or expected to do and in terms of the capabilities that are provided to them for conducting such activities.

Transitioning Multilateralism

Robert Cox (1989) has noted that the "commitment to the process of building a more orderly world system is quite different from seeking to impose an ideologically preconceived vision of the ideal world order" (p. 827). Since the end of the Cold War, Canadian governments have leaned strongly in the direction of the latter. Drawing initially from the view that Western liberal **values** prevailed in the Cold War, and operating under the security blanket of American unipolarity, Canada along with other Western governments began pressing international and regional institutions to advance liberal values. In the economic realm this began in the 1980s and progressed through the widespread application of the Washington consensus in bilateral and multilateral agreements and conditional aid programs designed to foster economic and political reforms in recipient states. In addition, Canada and other governments encouraged more active **interventions** in states experiencing domestic conflict or where civilian populations were at risk. These interventions in the former Yugoslavia, Somalia, and Haiti also sought to promote liberal democratic values and to punish regimes that fail to respect such values. Both the Mulroney and Chrétien governments actively pursued these interventions and were active in multilateral forums promoting reforms that would entrench human rights and democratic norms in existing institutions. The Canadian government also played a leading role in the establishment of the International Criminal Court (ICC) and in the International Commission on Intervention and State Sovereignty that developed the principle of **Responsibility to Protect** (R2P).

One can read into these practices an attempt to use multilateral diplomacy and international institutions to design an **international order** based more firmly on substantive principles reflecting human rights, democracy, and liberal economic practices. This would, in turn, compromise the sovereignty of states and create a more permissive environment for intervention in circumstances where such values had been violated. From the perspective of the Canadian government's approach to multilateralism, this marked a significant change in perspective. Previously, Canadian officials tended to accept the pluralism that litters the international system and sought to accommodate these differences within the multilateral framework provided by international institutions. In the last decade of the twentieth century, Canadian diplomacy was influenced by a desire to remake the institutions and through them the member states such that pluralism would be replaced by a common society of liberal democratic states. As Andrew Hurrell (2007) has noted, the enterprise was suspect from the start, in large measure because it could not be divorced from the power and interests of the Western governments in pursuing this reform.

> The transformationist rhetoric about "post-Westphalia" substantially overstates the degree to which we have in fact moved beyond a state- and sovereignty-based order—in terms of politics, law, and morality. . . . [T]he precarious and insecure political foundations of both liberal solidarism and other alternative modes of governance mean that the aspirations of this normatively ambitious international society remain deeply contaminated by the preferences and interests of powerful states; that where solidarist cooperation is weak or breaks down, the older imperatives of pluralist international society continue to flourish; that even when genuinely consensual, the promotion of solidarist values both depends on, and reinforces, the power and privileges of the dominant state or groups of states. We are therefore not dealing with a vanished or vanishing Westphalian world, as much transformationist writing suggests, but rather with a world in which solidarist and cosmopolitan conceptions of governance coexist, often rather unhappily, with many aspects of the old pluralist order (p. 9).

A telling illustration of this comes from the ICC, which again was designed to embody values surrounding human rights and civilian immunity from violent conflict, and represents a considerable advancement on the system of impunity that surrounded state practice. In this case, a significant degree of support was achieved and many states signed on, including most African governments, reflecting at least some measure of support for the principles involved. In practice, however, the ICC has been most effective and persistent in pursuing African leaders and warlords. That they might bear some guilt is in most cases unquestionable, and while the failure of other governments to come on board might explain their lack of accountability, the differential treatment suggests that the ICC might be motivated or influenced by factors other than justice. The prevalence of African statespersons and warlords in the dockets or on the indictments of the ICC make it look like a very targeted, if not even racist institution. Looks might betray, but the image is not unimportant. Whatever the validity of the particular cases, the overall effect has not been positive. In response, African governments have raised the possibility of a mass withdrawal. Some might say good riddance, but if one were concerned about advancing human rights, norms, and practices, one might also conclude that an opportunity had been missed to engage these states in a more fulsome and constructive conversation around such practices. Such a conversation might seek to empower rather than punish and might start from a principle of inclusiveness rather than righteousness.

The Libyan intervention of 2011 also presents an example of both how far the system has come and how fragile the consensus remains. Just as the Americans turned away from Rwanda because of the casualties they suffered in Somalia, so too have Russia and China turned away from Syria in part because of the belief that they were misled in Libya. There are, of course, other factors at play in Syria that would have made a consensus on a common cause more problematic, but the Libyan experience made these governments leery of yielding any ground to a UN Security Council resolution authorizing any form of intervention. Yet it was clear at the time of the UN resolution authorizing the intervention in Libya that all members of the Security Council were in agreement with the principle of protecting civilians and the responsibility of the international community to do something to carry out this principle. In the end, however, the Libyan case illustrates the fragile nature of the existing international order that has been significantly liberalized over the last 20 years.

Transitioning Canadian Foreign Policy

Much has been made of Canadian Prime Minister Stephen Harper's apparent disregard for the UN. The media highlighted his decision to visit the Tim Hortons headquarters instead of addressing the annual session of the UN General Assembly in 2009. Three years later, he was a few blocks away from UN headquarters in New York City receiving an award. Less than two miles away, the UN General Assembly was meeting in its annual session. A short cab ride would have taken the prime minister across town so that he could address the Assembly. Instead he limited his speaking engagement to the members of the Appeal of Conscience Foundation, taking the time to lament the UN's tendency to give credibility to dictators. In September 2013, the prime minister made it to the UN building while the Assembly was in session, but limited his appearance to those involved in the much touted maternal health initiative—and once again avoided the flotsam of the international community that had gathered in the General Assembly. It seems to be the case that Harper is not comfortable in the Assembly given that it welcomes the likes of the president of Iran.

There is indeed much not to like about many of the countries that are members of the UN. The worst have engaged in brutal acts of repression against their own citizens, others target political, religious, and ethnic minorities for explicit forms of discrimination, some engage in torture, while others engage in an excessive amount of corruption and state intervention in economic affairs. These acts are very different from the ideas, values, and practices that animate the Canadian polity and economy. This is, however, nothing new. The world has never been a pristine place, and the states that have populated the planet for the past 400 years have never shared a common set of values, let alone conducted their relations with others or their domestic populations on the basis of these values. Indeed, Canada's own history is sprinkled with some of the practices we now condemn in others.

Times have changed, however, and many groups and some governments, including the Canadian government, are now aspiring for a global consensus around some of these values. As discussed above, this is not purely a reflection of the current government. While Prime

Minister Harper may be loath to admit any semblance of inspiration from previous governments, this more values-based agenda for Canadian foreign policy harkens back to the last days of the Mulroney government and came to be enshrined in the foreign policy of the Liberal governments that followed in the 1990s and early 2000s. Moreover, there was an explicit effort to redefine multilateral institutions such that they should reflect and support such values. There was also widespread acceptance of the view that intervention to "convert" recalcitrant societies would also be permitted. While the partisan-inspired Harper government has sought to distance itself from these initiatives, as some were initiated by a Liberal government, its practices have been more similar than the partisan rhetoric might suggest. If anything, the dogmatism of "Canadian" values seems more firmly entrenched. It has, however, been complemented with a more trenchant critique of multilateral diplomacy and international institutions that harbour those not in accord with these values.

John Baird (2012) has stated that Canadian foreign policy will be guided by an agenda promoting "freedom, dignity and security," an agenda guided by the principle that "doing what is morally right is in our national interest." This dignity agenda rings similar to what some referred to as the Obama doctrine, which intended to move "beyond a hollow, sloganeering 'democracy promotion' agenda in favor of 'dignity promotion,' to fix the conditions of misery that breed anti-Americanism and prevent liberty, justice, and prosperity from taking root" (Ackerman 2008). The government has also been very clear in indicating that it has little interest in pursuing multilateral diplomacy. It has repeatedly invoked the mantra that it will not "go along to get along" in adopting the view that participating in a multilateral diplomatic process (or, it would seem, in an institutional setting) with states not in agreement with our values will not only compromise such values but give succour to those who do not abide by them. Trotting out the over-used appeasement reference from the very different and thus totally irrelevant context of the 1930s, Baird's (2011) address to the UN General Assembly argued that "Canada does not just 'go along' in order to 'get along.' We will 'go along' only if we 'go' in a direction that advances Canada's values: freedom, democracy, human rights and the rule of law . . . . The Second World War taught us all the tragic price of 'going along' just to 'get along.' It was accommodation and appeasement that allowed fascism to gather strength. As Winston Churchill said, 'An appeaser is one who feeds a crocodile, hoping it will eat him last.' We respect state sovereignty, but Canada will not 'go along' or look the other way when a minority is denied its human rights or fundamental freedoms.'"

This suggests a very different view of multilateralism on the part of Canadian policy-makers, something akin to what Antonio Franceschet (2013) refers to as "conditional multilateralism." As Ferry de Kerckove (2013) describes it, "The present government clearly seems to prefer intergovernmental groupings where sovereignty is unfettered and major players' consensus is the rule." Harper's approach to foreign policy seeks to make a clear and significant distinction between friends—those who think and act like us—and others, and has little time for the latter unless there are tangible economic benefits to be pursued. "Henceforth, he vowed, Canadian foreign policy would take three approaches: to make common cause with democratic allies—'our true friends'—to deal 'openly and fairly' with other nations, though 'we will not deceive ourselves about those relationships,' and finally 'to recognize clear and unequivocal threats' to global security and to speak out against them" (Ibbitson 2012a). John Kirton (2012) has also noted the preference that Harper's foreign policy displays towards liberal democratic regimes. The concentration enables the government to stick to its values agenda and castigate those who have not reformed.

The statements reinforce the central role that values are to play in Canadian foreign policy. The practice is not always as clear. It is difficult to say whose morals are to be applied: the prime minister's or those held by other Canadians—for example, environmentalists or social justice advocates. Another matter is how rigidly they are to be adhered to: in all relations with all states, or with a select few? What is absolutely clear is that one would not be able to travel very far on this planet without encountering some who hold different values, not just as matters of expediency but also as matters of conviction. What guidance would a dignity agenda provide for how we interact with them—or would we ignore them, as seems at times to be the case in the government's attention to working with narrowly defined like-minded states? We will need to share the planet with them, breathe the same air, and share the same oceans, whether we like their politics or not. As indicated earlier, there is little evidence that the international community has evolved to the point where such a common moral framework, even if it were to be defined in a manner that truly represented the morals of Canadians, could guide a foreign policy that would consistently meet our interests.

Not surprisingly, there is much room for inconsistency in the application of a values-based foreign policy to be overly committed to a dignity agenda. There is also too much pluralism in the global community to seek such a substantive consensus around values. Any effort to limit one's relations to only those like-minded states means a narrower foreign policy. Perhaps in the end this is what policy-makers have in mind: a Canada less involved in the affairs of the world and more narrowly focused on only those issues that matter most to Canadians. While such an isolationist approach might be defensible, it would seem to be less reflective of one of the most internationalized states in the global community. With nearly 25 per cent of the Canadian population foreign-born, defending a policy that would operate in such restricted circles is more difficult.

What is also very clear from the government's behaviour is that its commitment to not going along tends to waver when economic interests are at stake, as revealed in its efforts to expand its trade relationship with China. Therein lies one of the problems with trying to pursue in a dogmatic fashion a values-based foreign policy. Such a policy is often incompatible with other interests such as trade (China) or investment (Canadian mining practices in any number of countries). When presented in the missionary mode, as has been done by Canadian officials since the early 1990s, expectations that are difficult to achieve and risks that are difficult to avoid are both raised, as experiences and outcomes in Afghanistan and Libya clearly demonstrate. The obvious point here is that moral righteousness is a fine idea but a very difficult one for any government to pursue with any consistency. The necessary qualifications and exceptions render the very idea of a values-based foreign policy problematic. It tends to become self-selective since the moral hubris is usually focused on weak states that carry little political and especially economic interest for Canada. It also leads to grandstanding at international meetings that lends little credence, given the afore-mentioned selectivity, to the credibility of the policy and the efficacy of Canadian diplomacy, however meagre the efforts on that front might be.

It would be wrong to conclude that the declining engagement with diplomacy and multilateral institutions persists through all aspects of Canadian foreign policy: the government *has* taken a more active role around some international economic institutions and remains actively engaged in the G20. It has been supportive of institutional reform at the World Bank and IMF, acknowledging the increased economic power of emerging markets by yielding its voting shares and position to Brazil, which has displaced Canada among the top 10 members of the IMF. It has also sought to strengthen the accountability surrounding the G20 and remains supportive of using multilateral connections around such initiatives as improving maternal health and protecting potential child brides. At the same time, however, the government does not hesitate to call into question the credentials of selected G8 and G20 members such as Russia. It has also devoted more time and effort to a series of bilateral trade agreements with relatively minor trading partners while ignoring the staggering multilateral framework. The latter could be as much a result of the WTO's failings as of Canada's declining interest and capabilities, though the contrasts with the 1970s and 1980s are apparent. Its approach to both the Americas and the Asia-Pacific regions has tended to focus on selected bilateral partners rather than turning to regional organizations such as the Organization of American States (OAS) or the Association of Southeast Asian Nations (ASEAN). This might also account for its late arrival at the more limited multilateral Trans-Pacific Partnership. Stephen Brown and Michael Olender (2013) have also demon-strated the significant decline in Canadian involvement in multilateral development activ-ities. Overall, the dominant pattern has been a discernible shift away from multilateral diplomacy and active institutional engagement.

One alleged outcome of Canada's new foreign policy was the failure to win a seat on the UN Security Council in 2011. As Denis Stairs (2011) has discussed, there were likely other reasons for this as well. In the context of the place of multilateralism in Canadian foreign policy, what is most telling about the Security Council election was the general level of disinterest displayed by the Conservative government, both prior to and following the election. The Harper government showed little concern about the Security Council vote until the very last minute, with a rather perfunctory campaign. The government was also relatively quick in making clear that it had no plans to contest a seat on the Council in the near future. All of this could be attributed to an attitude of "if you know you are going to lose, pretend to be not interested." Instead it seems to reflect a genuine lack of interest, as further illustrated by Harper's failure to address the UN General Assembly even when he was in the building or a mere few blocks away. The snub is both obvious and sincere; there are few kind words for the organization in any of the speeches by the prime minister or his foreign minister. Again, many will argue that there are all kinds of good reasons for such an attitude, but it is a departure from past practice. Even in the midst of the Zionism-as-racism fiasco of the mid-1970s and Yasser Arafat's address to the Assembly, or the Reagan government's assault on the organization in the 1980s, Harper's predecessors defended the inherent value of the organization for Canadian foreign policy. Former Prime Minister Brian Mulroney did so again in his reaction to the Harper government's approach. In a meeting with *The Globe and Mail*'s editorial board, he referred to the UN as "a vital instrument" of the Canadian commitment to multilateralism and went on to say that "We don't have the strength to impose our will or get our way at all times . . . We need the instruments of international harmony" (Ibbitson 2012b).

Whither the Multilateralist Tradition?

Antonio Franceschet (2013) has made a distinction between conditional multilateralism and principled multilateralism. Briefly put, *conditional multilateralism* refers to relations or institutions based on select membership criteria that is based on shared values, such as the proposed Assembly of Democracies. *Principled multilateralism* refers to a more universal approach to multilateralism—to multilateralism as a principle, a value in and of itself, for bringing disparate states together in a process that encourages dialogue and compromise. This is where the idea of multilateralism as an inclusive process through which states can reach accommodations and consensus remains a significant virtue, one that will not be sustained by default, but one that must be maintained—preferably in good working order. It has become evident under the Conservative government of Stephen Harper that any interest in multilateralism demonstrates a strong preference for the former as compared to the latter. The government seems to have little time and attention for dealing with governments that do not share our values and practices or with institutions that grant these governments any credibility. The disdain that Canada's current leaders frequently exhibit towards multilateral institutions seems to reflect their discomfort in dealing with governments with which they do not agree, and while one satisfying solution may be to closet Canada in a community of liberal democratic states, the rest of the world will be moving ahead regardless and the emerging international order will be designed by this larger community. A gated community in a larger, more diverse, and complicated world may seem like a safe haven, but it might also increasingly feel like an isolated and insecure exile with little prospect for security or prosperity.

The prospects for the future of multilateralism might not be very dim, as emerging powers have sought greater access to any number of regional and multilateral institutions. These emerging powers also seem inclined to commit resources, albeit in selected areas, even in circumstances where they have little opportunity for input in the design of the operations or the institutions. As these governments seem to be stepping up their game, the prospects for Canada playing a successful and effective role in such a framework appear limited for reasons in addition to the shifts in policy discussed here. Aside from the predilections of the current political leadership, other conditions may have encouraged the development of such a policy. To the extent that a succession of Canadian governments has sought to infuse institutions with Canadian values, the inherent difficulties of such an enterprise might be cause for resentment. Related to this, however, have been the limited capabilities with which these governments have attempted to advance such reforms. The government no longer sees the need to make the contributions to international society that we once did, especially in the realms of diplomacy and development assistance. Advocating for major political and economic reform in other states while progressively reducing the diplomatic, development, and military capabilities to support such efforts has been a recipe for failure. At the same time, Canadian foreign policy has become ever more strongly tied to a narrow view of its national interest, a concern raised by Cranford Pratt nearly 30 years ago. A shift to a more instrumentalist approach to international institutions has accompanied this view. Canada does not consider these institutions and the practice of multilateralism as important as it once did.

The changing landscape of global power means that international order will be redesigned. It is not yet clear how or what the precise outcome will be. It is clear that Western efforts to redesign international order along more liberal lines have likely come to an end. That is not to say that Western values will have no place in the emerging international order or that any new order will be inherently illiberal. It is to say, however, that efforts by Western powers, including Canada, must start from the recognition that international society remains pluralistic and that efforts to impart Western values onto such a society will require at the very least a greater degree of inclusiveness and responsiveness to the different viewpoints at play in this society. It will also mean considerably less hubris than that which informed Western efforts to stamp liberal values across international society for the past two decades, a hubris that remains all too apparent in Canadian foreign policy. We have not reached the stage of a new "cold" or "hot" war, but we are nowhere near the degree of consensus that is often assumed in Western efforts to dictate how other states must act. We are also woefully inept at having either the capacity or the commitment to undertake such transformation, regardless of the ethical justification for doing so. Conditions in such places as Afghanistan, Haiti, and Libya attest to this. Where there have been some signs of success, such as perhaps Bosnia and Kosovo, Stairs (2011) reminds us that these interventions should not mislead us, for Canada "is not a very muscular power and in any case it should not confuse its own good luck with a special aptitude for efficacious social engineering abroad, or for resolving some of the far more challenging problems that are confronted by others" (p. 12).

The shifts in power in the international society have created a host of new powers, some of which seem interested in playing a more active role in multilateral frameworks and have as great a capacity to do so as the Canadian government seems willing or able to deploy. Canada's relative position in this global hierarchy of power will also continue to decline. The Conference Board of Canada (2006) has forecast that by 2020, "Canada will account for less than 2 per cent of the world's gross domestic product (GDP), only 1 per cent of the world's military expenditure and just 0.5 per cent of the world's population" (p. 2). Much of this is, of course, beyond any government's control, and it will be a very difficult trend to slow down, let alone reverse in any significant way. "A genuine reason for the Canadian relative decline in capability is that middle powers with huge capacity for growth—and experiencing rapid growth—are ascending from the bottom of the central system. As they ascend, they take power share away from the rich, middle powers like Canada that are not growing as fast. Three states in particular are in a position to challenge the standing of Canada. They are China, India, and Brazil, perhaps in the order of their size of impact" (Doran 2005, pp. 695–96). These states are poised to make a more significant contribution to the design of international order in the future. That they will make this contribution differently than did Canada and its postwar allies goes without saying. "The result is a world with a dramatically altered power structure in which Canada can hardly expect to be noticed in the way it was in the early post-World War II decades. The issues are different. The demands are different. The distribution of power is different" (Stairs 2011, p. 7). The real issue is how different it will be and how Canadian interests will be served in this new international order. The other issue is: What, if anything, can the Canadian government contribute to its content?

The withdrawal of diplomatic activity, indeed even interest, in all but the most select areas suggests a government with little interest in the machinery of international relations. The constant preaching about values and the repeated statements by policy officials of their refusal to stand down reflect a commitment to select principles that holds no room for compromise (unless it seems there is a trade relationship worth pursuing). Canadian foreign policy increasingly takes the form of a weekly church service where the principal activities are a sermon and a collection plate, followed by a small gathering to which only the converted are welcome. Multilateral diplomacy—indeed diplomacy in any form—requires meeting with adversaries, negotiation, and compromise. It is not a matter of indoctrination or conversion, although all participants involved might so desire. The same is true of the UN. It is representative of the world we live in, not the exclusive club one might prefer to join, and as with any sort of association, there will be parties with whom one does not get along, indeed with whom one might be in conflict. If such conflicts are to be resolved, the opportunity must be seized: "Be they deeply frustrating at times, international organizations do offer a window to the world, and Canada cannot be as great a country as it deserves if it does not use that window" (de Kerckove 2013).

Conclusion

In summary, we find that a combination of three factors have brought on a significant change in Canadian support for and contribution to multilateralism. The first has been the growing prominence and continued significance of a values-based foreign policy. The second has been a growing disenchantment with multilateral institutions and with working alongside states that do not share our values. A third has been a precipitous decline in Canada's diplomatic resources, including our development funds. Loss of interest in the multilateral process, complemented by a declining commitment of resources for conducting foreign policy, alongside the pursuit of a values agenda that does not resonate widely, has left the Canadian government on the sidelines of many pressing issues. The government seems not only comfortable, but also somewhat proud of standing alone. The rest of the world, however, is moving ahead, and emerging powers are taking a much greater interest in multilateralism. This may be good news for the process of global governance, though its content, to be determined by others, may not serve Canadian interests as well as the post-World War II institutions have. There may be little we can do about this, but unlike the 1940s, when the multilateral framework was being created and the Canadian government was very much present at the creation, today as the framework is being redesigned for the twenty-first century, the Canadian government has apparently left the building.

Questions for Review

1. How is Tom Keating's overview of multilateralism different from John Holmes's reflections on the middle power approach?
2. How did Canada's approach to multilateralism shift during the governments of Brian Mulroney and Jean Chrétien? Why did it not matter that these were Conservative and Liberal governments?
3. Do values shape Stephen Harper's Conservative government's approach to multilateral institutions? Is this similar or different compared to previous eras? Does this lead to an inconsistent approach to multilateral institutions in Canada's foreign relations?
4. What are the possible implications of Canada's current multilateral foreign policy in the wake of a shifting international order?

Suggested Readings

Bull, Hedley. 1977. *The Anarchical Society: A Study of Order in World Politics*. London: Macmillan.

Chapnick, Adam. 2000. "The Canadian Middle Power Myth." *International Journal* 55, 2 (Spring): 188–206.

Cooper, Andrew F., Richard A. Higgott, and Kim Richard Nossal. 1994. *Relocating Middle Powers: Australia and Canada in a Changing World Order*. Vancouver: UBC Press.

Keating, Tom. 2010. "Whither the Middle Power Identity? Transformations in the Canadian Foreign and Security Milieus," in Nik Hynek and David Bosold, eds. *Canada's Foreign and Security Policy: Soft and Hard Strategies of a Middle Power*. Don Mills, ON: Oxford University Press.

Nossal, Kim Richard. 2000. "Home-Grown IR: The Canadianization of International Relations." *Journal of Canadian Studies* 35, 1 (Spring): 95–114.

References

Ackerman, Spencer. 2008. "The Obama doctrine." *The American Prospect*, 19 March. Available at http://prospect.org/article/obama-doctrine.

Baird, John. 2011. "Address to the United Nations General Assembly." New York, 26 September. Available at www.international.gc.ca/media/aff/speeches-discours/2011/2011-030.aspx?lang=eng.

———. 2012. "Address to the Montreal Council on Foreign Relations." Montreal, 14 September. Available at www.international.gc.ca/media/aff/speeches-discours/2012/09/14a.aspx.

Brown, Stephen, and Michael Olender. 2013. "Canada's fraying commitment to multilateral development cooperation," pp. 158–87 in Hany Besada and Shannon Kindornay, eds.

Multilateral Development Cooperation in a Changing Global Order. London: Palgrave.

Conference Board of Canada. 2006. "Facing the risks: Global security trends and Canada." *Executive Action* (February).

Cox, Robert. 1989. "Middlepowermanship, Japan, and future world order." *International Journal* 44, 4 (Autumn): 823–62.

de Kerckove, Ferry, 2013. "Conservative multilateralism is possible." *Ottawa Citizen*, 1 August. Available at http://www2.canada.com/ottawacitizen/news/archives/story.html?id=ef6439b5-6a9e-46e7-8c7e-be6be44b1eb8.

Doran, Charles F. 2005. "Explaining ascendancy and decline: The power cycle perspective." *International Journal* 60, 3 (Summer): 685–701.

Franceschet, Antonio. 2013. "Must international coercion be multilateral? Three response types." Paper delivered to the Prairie Provinces Political Science Association Annual Meeting, Banff, AB, (September).

Hurrell, Andrew. 2007. *On Global Order.* Oxford: Oxford University Press.

Ibbitson, John, 2012a. "Canada gives cold shoulder to the UN," *The Globe and Mail*, 1 October. Available at www.theglobeandmail.com/news/politics/canada-gives-cold-shoulder-to-the-un/article4581231/.

———. 2012b. "Mulroney's advice to Harper: Don't give up on the United Nations; 'We need the instruments of international harmony,' former prime minister tells current PM." *The Globe and Mail*, 4 October. Available at www.theglobeandmail.com/news/politics/mulroneys-advice-to-harper-dont-give-up-on-the-united-nations/article4588688/.

Kirton, John. 2012. "Vulnerable America, capable Canada: Convergent leadership for an interconnected world." *Canadian Foreign Policy Journal* 18, 1: 133–44. Available at http://dx.doi.org/10.1080/11926422.2012.674381.

Stairs, Denis. 2011. "Being rejected in the United Nations: The causes and implications of Canada's failure to win a seat in the UN Security Council." CDFAI Policy Update Paper, Calgary (March).

5 Three Theoretical Perspectives

David B. Dewitt and John J. Kirton

Key Terms

Complex Neo-Realist Perspective   Principal Power

Despite their differences over themes, interpretations, and values, scholars of Canadian foreign policy share an implicit interest in a single set of fundamental questions about Canada's behaviour in international affairs. These questions have been developed through public debate concerning Canada's role abroad.

The first debate centred on whether Canada should use its new formal freedom from the United Kingdom, attained in the 1931 Statute of Westminster, to sustain the League of Nations, enhance Canada's position as a North American nation, or support Britain in maintaining a broader global balance of power.[1] Although support for this last alternative was reflected in Prime Minister W.L. Mackenzie King's September 1939 decision to enter the Second World War and in Canada's substantial contribution to the Allied cause, the end of the war saw a new debate between those preferring a retreat to quasi-isolationism and those urging active international participation commensurate with Canada's new material strength.[2] The victory of the latter group gave Canada two decades under prime ministers Louis St Laurent, John Diefenbaker, and Lester Pearson during which the precepts of liberal internationalism evolved. The 1968 election of Prime Minister Pierre Trudeau's Liberal government began a new debate about whether Canada was reverting to the isolationist and continental instincts of the interwar era, modifying its internationalist traditions to reflect new circumstances, or defining a new approach to Canadian behaviour abroad.[3]

Out of this debate has emerged the need for a more explicit, rigorous, and comprehensive analytical framework for the study of Canadian foreign policy. By drawing upon the literature of Canadian foreign policy, general foreign policy analysis, and international relations, it is possible to identify the most fundamental questions about Canada's international behaviour.[4]

Based on the thesis that a country's external activities and international presence are related to its size and capabilities—population, resources, and specialized skills and knowledge—a central challenge for students of international affairs and foreign policy has been to determine the relationship between these attributes and international behaviour. In the Canadian context, a postwar issue has been whether Canada's attributes are sufficient to propel it from its former status as a minor actor through small- and middle-power ranking to a more prominent place in the community of nation-states. In the shadow first of the United Kingdom and more recently of the United States, Canada has been perceived as a regional power without a region, and recognized as a middle-range partner in the Western coalition. One set of questions relating to this issue concerns Canada's historic position, or *rank*, in the hierarchy of the international system; the next questions provide the explanatory focus for Canada's *activity, association*, and *approach to world order*, examining the relative significance of *external, societal*, and governmental determinants.

The Central Questions of Foreign Policy Analysis

International Presence

Rank

Virtually all students of foreign policy begin their explorations with a perception of a state's historical experience. Formulated into models that may try to account for the past, these evolutionary myths are partly the inherited results of exposure to particular historical traditions, partly ideological or philosophic orientations conditioning one's interpretations of evidence, and partly crude summations of easily measurable attributes. Yet in most cases, they are grounded in an underlying conception of whether the state's capacity to pursue its national interests—most basically, self-help in a competitive international system—is being diminished, maintained, or expanded over time.[5]

What is Canada's place in the international system relative to that of other states? The concern with defining Canada's position was heightened by its leading international stature at the end of the Second World War, when a newly emerging world order was being shaped out of the ruins of global conflict. Canada's ability to influence these efforts was seen as being linked directly to its ascribed status. In the study of international relations, this focus on a state's rank has been sustained by mounting evidence of the salience of national capabilities in determining foreign policy behaviour.[6]

The question of rank includes the state's relative capability, as measured by a standard set of objective attributes such as population size and distribution, indigenous fuel supplies, and size of standing armed forces. It is also concerned with the position that it ascribes to itself and that it asserts internationally, and with the acknowledged status ascribed to it by other international actors.[7] It includes the consistency of these elements across varying international systemic configurations, geographic regions, substantive issue areas, and critical power resources.[8] And it is based on the state's maintenance of minimum levels of performance in meeting the basic requisites of statehood—notably security, sovereignty, and legitimacy.[9]

International Behaviour

Activity

The importance of a state's international ranking—both ascribed and achieved—is based upon the hypothesized relationship between rank and externally oriented behaviour.[10] The primary aspect of a state's behaviour is the activity it directs toward other actors in the international realm. Concern here centres on the *degree* of a state's activity, or the simple volume of interaction it has with its "targets" abroad; the *variety* of this activity, or the similarity across time, issues, and targets in the volume and intensity of action; and the *diffusion* of this activity among targets abroad.[11]

Association

Association is the intersection of one state's external activities with those of another, and includes the question of *initiative*—the extent to which the state maintains its membership in an existing group, participates in forming a new or altered group, or acts without direct reference to any group. It embraces a country's *commitment*—the time, resources, and effort expended to produce similarity between the country's own position and the group position.

And it contains the element of *focus*, or the extent to which the central target of the country's activity lies within or outside existing or emerging groups.[12] Characterized by degrees of conflict and cooperation, association can be measured by the extent to which a country's activity is similar in time, content, and target to that of other states.

Approach to World Order

Also relevant is a state's attempt to foster a global order in which relationships are organized into regimes and institutions that promote a particular distribution of political power and economic resources.[13] The first aspect is the *degree* to which the state considers that order should be registered in a comprehensive, well developed, interrelated, and autonomous network of international organization and law. A subsequent aspect is that of *scope*, that is, the extent to which a state seeks to ensure that international order, at all levels of institutionalization, has the full, active participation of all members of the state system, and embraces a broad range of subjects. A third aspect is *transformation*, the extent to which a state supports moderate specific alternatives or more permanent alterations in the structure of existing and emerging regimes and organizations.

Determinants of International Behaviour

External Determinants

To explain a country's particular pattern of activity, association, and quest for order, most scholars focus on the stimuli that a country receives from states and organizations abroad, whether or not these are directed at it. Their initial interest centres on the *relative salience* of this external environment—the extent of variation in a state's foreign policy behaviour caused by these states and organizations as compared to the variations explained by forces at home.[14] A further concern is the *scope* of relevant external determinants—the number and range of states and international organizations with a direct impact on a state's foreign policy behaviour. A third issue deals with a state's *sensitivity* to external stimuli—the immediacy, directness, and specificity with which external events and conditions affect the decisions of leaders and the behaviour they authorize.[15] Finally, interest centres on *actor relevance*—the identity of those particular major powers, groupings of middle and smaller powers, and leading international organizations that have the most salient, wide-ranging, and immediate impact on a state's foreign policy behaviour.

Societal Determinants

A similar set of questions arises in regard to domestic influences on a state's international behaviour.[16] The *relative salience* of domestic organizations is of fundamental concern, as is the issue of the *scope* of societal actors—the extent of differentiated, specialized, and autonomous non-governmental institutions that have a direct impact on foreign policy behaviour.[17] Further aspects are the *sensitivity* of the government to these organizations and the *relevance* of particular actors, notably Parliament, political parties, interest groups, labour, media, business communities, and provincial governments. Also of importance is the country's profile of population, resources, and technology, and the impact of these critical factors on the structure and activity of societal actors.

Governmental Determinants

The final set of questions addresses the influence of the executive branch of a state's central government on foreign policy-making and ensuing behaviour.[18] The central questions remain the relative overall *salience* of governmental factors, the *scope* of institutional differentiation and autonomy, the state's *sensitivity* to its foreign policy process, and the *relevance* of specific governmental actors.[19] Attention is directed at the relevance of the prime minister and his or her closest associates, the government's foreign office, and especially the domestically oriented departments and agencies responsible for critical changes in the state's pattern of growth in population, resources, and technology.[20] The complexity of the modern state requires that attention be given to the central foreign policy's coordinative structures and processes in attempts to define autonomously and implement overarching conceptions of the national interest.[21]

Table 5.1 provides a schematic overview of the seven basic foreign policy questions and the predictions of each of the three theoretical perspectives.

Table 5.1 Theoretical Perspectives on Canadian Foreign Policy: Predictions Based on Ideal Types

Foreign Policy Questions	Liberal Internationalism	Peripheral Dependence	Complex Neo-realism
1. Rank	middle power	small, penetrated power	principal power
2. Activity			
Degree	active participation	low interaction	global involvement
Variety	responsible participation	undifferentiated interactive	interest-based involvement
Diffusion	multiple participation	imperial-focused interaction	autonomous bilateral involvement
3. Association			
Initiative	combination	adherence	unilateralism
Commitment	consensus	acquiescence	divergence
Focus	constraint	support	diversification
4. Approach to World Order			
Degree	moderate institutionalization	existing institutionalization	revised institutionalization
Scope	multilateralization	hegemony and marginal universalism	concert
Transformation	reformation	marginal redistribution	modification
5. External Determinants			
Relative Salience	moderate	high	low
Scope	moderate	low	high
Sensitivity	moderate	low	high
Actor Relevance			
United Kingdom	moderate	high	low
United States	moderate	high	low
USSR	moderate	low	high
China	moderate	low	high
Large European States and Japan	moderate	low	high
Non-European Middle Powers	high	low	moderate
Small European States	high	low	moderate
Other Small States	high	low	moderate
NATO	moderate	low	high
United Nations	high	low	moderate

continued

Table 5.1 *continued*

Foreign Policy Questions	Liberal Internationalism	Peripheral Dependence	Complex Neo-realism
6. Societal Determinants			
Relative Salience	moderate	low	high
Scope			
Institutional Differentiation	moderate	low	high
Institutional Autonomy	moderate	low	high
Sensitivity	moderate	low	high
Actor Relevance			
Parliament	high	low	moderate
Parties	high	low	moderate
Associational Interest Groups	moderate	low	high
Labour	moderate	low	high
Media	low	moderate	high
Business Community	low	moderate	High
Provincial Governments	low	high	moderate
Critical Capabilities	resources and technology	resources	population, resources, and technology
7. Governmental Determinants			
Relative Salience	moderate	low	high
Scope			
Institutional Differentiation	moderate	low	high
Institutional Autonomy	moderate	low	high
Sensitivity	moderate	low	high
Actor Relevance			
Prime Ministerial Group	moderate	low	high
Department of External Affairs	high	low	moderate
Foreign Service Departments	low	moderate	high
Other Domestic Departments	low	moderate	high
Agencies and Crown Corporations	low	moderate	high
Central Foreign Policy			
Coordinative Structures	moderate	low	high

The Complex Neo-Realist Perspective

Preoccupied with the powerful challenge that peripheral dependence presents to liberal internationalism, students of Canadian foreign policy have devoted relatively little attention to the possible relevance of a third interpretive perspective, one derived from the realist theory that has dominated the study of international relations as a whole. As expressed in the major work of its most popular proponent, Hans Morgenthau, classic realism highlights the ceaseless interplay among great powers preoccupied with maximizing their military security by manipulating the balance of power to secure a fragile stability within an international system characterized by anarchy.[22] It portrays this central theme of the history of international relations as a cyclical pattern in which the short-term stability produced by a balance of power is followed by a breakdown of this equilibrium, leading to war and the creation of a new transitory balance. It focuses almost exclusively on the small set of great powers involved in arranging the balance, the military security interests that motivate their activity, the conflictual quest for advantage relieved only by temporary military alliances, and the structure of the resulting balance of power as the only form of order that a context of anarchy allows.

Given the fundamental fact of anarchy, states are portrayed as giving predominant weight to external determinants, as each is preoccupied with monitoring and adjusting to shifts in the balance abroad. Neither societal nor governmental processes are given significance as determinants, since they are forced by the requirements of the security dilemma to be aggregated in advance, within the impermeable shell of the sovereign state, as "factors of national power" and "quality of leadership," respectively.

This standard realist portrait has had little appeal to students of Canadian foreign policy, for several reasons. Generally, it seemed intuitively irrelevant to the dilemmas of a newer country, beset internally by regional and ethnic cleavages and foreign penetration, preoccupied by a full array of nation-building imperatives, and confronted externally with the necessities of managing interdependencies in collaboration with like-minded but vastly more powerful neighbours. More precisely, preoccupation with security dilemmas, military interests, and the instruments of force appeared secondary to practitioner and scholar alike. For both, armed conflict had been an intermittent, somewhat discretionary concern, always conducted in association with larger external powers, and aimed centrally at sustaining the systems of deterrence within which the primary tasks of foreign policy were pursued.

Realist precepts seemed to be further contradicted by the fundamental features of Canada's historic emergence as a nation. Until well after the First World War, Canada's external *vision* had been affected by a profound and practical attachment to a stable and benign British imperial system.[23] During the interwar period, in a deliberate effort to distinguish themselves from the United Kingdom and the central European system, Canadian leaders eagerly embraced a North American identity defined by the very absence of power politics and by the invention of a uniquely cooperative and peaceful form of international relations.[24] After the Second World War, the very tenacity with which American leaders adopted realism as a justification for their policy of global containment engendered skepticism on the part of Canadian leaders, armed with the legacy of distinctive visions and experienced in detaching themselves from the doctrines and accompanying demands of their imperial leaders abroad.

To the attitudes of heritage was added an accident of history. It was the fate of the modern phase in the study of Canadian foreign policy to emerge at a time when the dominant actor in the international system, the United States, was itself moving beyond the immediate demands of the security dilemma, and when the precepts of realism were beginning to lose their intellectual appeal.[25] At the outset of the 1960s, the emergence of an apparent bipolar stability, confirmed by the outcome of the Berlin and Cuban crises, provided American scholars and their Canadian counterparts with the vision of a system in which security was assured in the short term, rendered permanent by the new nuclear balance, and superseded by the tasks of enhancing abroad a range of values formerly perceived as subordinate.[26] In such a mood, there was little incentive to continue debates about Canada's precise role in North American defence and nuclear deterrence or general concerns about its place in a North Atlantic alliance.[27] Realism seemed to have little to offer the student of Canadian foreign policy.

As America's global dominance faced new challenges in the late 1960s, so too did the precepts of standard realism. The emerging dynamics of global politics provided an empirical foundation for a renewed interest in a realist theory considerably more complex, as were the dilemmas it addressed.[28]

The "complex neo-realist" perspective begins by accepting the fundamental premise of standard realism: the primacy of politics. It sees separate states pursuing distinctive interests in an international milieu in which no natural harmony of interests exists. Its new contribution is the emphasis it places on the prevalence of international order—tentatively defined by the convergence of the interests of principal actors leading to an emerging stable global system, but still grounded in the values of an internationally predominant power.[29] Most importantly, it highlights the complex constellation of interests and values that states and non-state actors in such an ascendant, system-defining position are able to pursue.[30]

Complex neo-realism thus focuses on the role of hegemonic powers in ensuring, defining, and extending international order in a system in which universal values remain secondary, in which a common security calculus and interest in balance provide no substitute, and in which leadership is required to transform convergent interests into stable order.[31] It sees the history of international relations characterized by the rise to positions of international primacy of a succession of hegemonic powers, with periods of balance among roughly equal powers as relatively rare, temporary, and particular to periods in which one state has lost its hegemony before another has emerged.[32] And in the critical transition from balance to hegemony, it highlights the way in which order may be defined by a concert of **principal powers**.

Collectively substituting for states exercising individual hegemony, such principal powers are not merely the familiar great powers of realist theory.[33] Rather, they are principal states in three senses. First, they are the states in the international hierarchy that stand at the top of the international status ranking, collectively possessing decisive capability and differentiated from lower-ranking powers by both objective and subjective criteria. Second, they act as principals in their international activities and associations, rather than as agents for other states or groupings, or as mediators between principals. And third, they have a principal role in establishing, specifying, and enforcing international order.

At the heart of a state's position as a principal power is its possession of surplus capability: a margin of strength in a broad array of sectors well beyond that required to meet the basic requisites of statehood and the minimal performance expected of modern states.[34] Surplus capability relieves principal powers of the tyranny of responding to short-term security dilemmas and provides them with the luxury of basing their international behaviour on the outcomes of political debates within their societies and on the definitions provided by their state apparatus. Surplus capability thus provides such states the discretion to act autonomously, on the basis of internal choices, on a global stage. Such choices derive not from an exclusive or predominant concern with security but from a multiplicity of values in which priority is given to those political interests that integrate, assign weights to, and provide coherence to specific concerns of military, economic, social, and cultural spheres.[35] This configuration of internal values is embedded in a historically evolved and distinctive array of specialized capabilities, which channels the external activity of a principal power and renders it competitive with those of its counterpart.[36] Surplus and specialized capability together enable principal powers to define the characteristics of international order in a way that disproportionately reflects their distinctive values and to extend that order, and hence their values, into member states throughout the international system.[37]

Traditionally, scholars of Canadian foreign policy have not conceived of their country as having the capabilities or performing the functions of a principal power. Yet, led by key individuals within the state apparatus, they have begun in the past two decades to develop from themes that move in that direction.[38] The first such theme, developed from 1960 to 1968, was a thrust toward globalism, especially significant because of the intent to employ aid as an instrument to advance specifically Canadian interests worldwide, on a bilateral basis. Canada extended its formal diplomatic presence to all regions and major capitals in the world, dealt with quite distinctive cultural groupings, and supplemented conventional diplomacy by the deliberate use of such new techniques as cultural relations and development assistance.[39]

The most dramatic manifestation was the programmatic and geographic expansion of Canada's development assistance. Constituting the major division between the distributive thrust of liberal internationalism and the globalist thrust of complex neo-realism, this transition was initiated in the 1960s when significant Canadian aid began to be deployed in specific francophone countries for the domestic political purpose of meeting the challenges to Canadian foreign policy from Quebec and France.

A second major theme, which emerged from 1968 to 1971, advocated an interest-based initiation of external behaviour. Rejecting the reactiveness that they thought characterized Canadian foreign policy in the Pearsonian approach, dissatisfied

domestic critics and officials of the new Trudeau government sought to ensure that the Canadian government would be capable of discerning future trends at home and abroad, identifying their impact on Canadian interests, and formulating policies in advance, enabling Canada to withstand the impact of forces from abroad and thereby to maximize its self-determined interests. This emphasis presumed both a direct focus on national interests as the basis for policy calculation, and the initiation of policies and programs having little direct dependence on the international situation at the time.[40] In its initial form, this theme of internationally projected values offered the image of a "new" Canada whose policies—concerned with such values as bilingualism, ethnic relations, federalism, techniques of parliamentary government, income redistribution, and environmental protection—provided an example for other states to emulate and a foundation for Canadian behaviour abroad. After 1973 it was enriched by an emphasis on a third major theme: the way in which unique Canadian assets—deriving from its small, diverse, skilled population, its extensive resource base, and its developed technology—gave Canada a more active role in defining a new international order based on these values.[41]

The emergence of these major themes of principal-power capability and behaviour is logically based on a series of premises and precepts that address the seven central questions of foreign policy analysis from the perspective of complex neo-realism. In application to Canada's post-Second World War foreign policy experience, this begins with a view, similar to the other perspectives, of an international system characterized by the disappearance, over the years 1945 to 1957, of the United Kingdom's hegemonic legacy and its replacement by an American hegemony. However, in contrast to liberal internationalism and peripheral dependence, complex neo-realism sees the key factor as the erosion of the hegemonic position of the United States from

1968 onward.[42] Canada's international experience is seen as one of secular, sustained development, reflected most profoundly in its steadily increasing ability to define, advance, secure, and legitimize distinctive national interests and values in a competitive process with adversaries and associates.[43]

In response to the question of international rank, the **complex neo-realist perspective** portrays Canada, particularly since 1968, as an ascending principal power in an increasingly diffuse, non-hegemonic international system.[44] Placed in the context of the most prevalent global configuration—a top tier of eight powers, with an average of seven involved in the central, European-based system, and nine on a global basis if the central and peripheral systems are combined—Canada is argued to be part of the classically defined "top tier" group.[45]

In addition to a location in this configuration, principal powers have three specific characteristics. The first is a rank roughly comparable to other states in the top range, unexcelled by states outside it, and closer to those within than to outside states immediately below.[46] The second is a set of organizations and instruments sufficient to help deter significant direct assaults on its homeland and to provide a strategic presence abroad. The third consists of special rights in determining and preserving international order in political, military, and economic spheres, together with distinctive values and sufficiently strong influence to attract the attention of other principals and to help define the orientation of some lesser states.

With these criteria, the complex neo-realist argument asserts that Canada's objective capability—grounded in the relative size, breadth, and diversity of its natural resources, advanced technology, and skilled population and in other standard calculations of national power—places it predominantly within the top tier of the system.[47] Canada's designated rank is reinforced by its involvement in groupings composed of members drawn exclusively or predominantly from this top tier.[48] While acknowledging Canada's lack of independent nuclear and conventional military deterrence, complex neo-realism recognizes that Canada's military capability at home and abroad directly contributes to strategic stability in several critical regions. Moreover, it assigns Canada a prominent position within the top tier in defining and managing global regimes in major-issue areas and leadership within a distinctive grouping or network of lesser states on such questions.[49]

The degree, variety, and diffusion of Canada's external activities provide the initial indication of aspects of its international behaviour that characterizes it as an emerging principal power. The degree of Canadian activity is expressed by the maintenance of permanent political involvement in virtually all regions, sectors, and forums of world politics. Such global involvement is registered in the consistently high volume of interactions in which Canada engages with a large number of actors abroad. Grounded in a need to continuously manage a state's immediate, direct, durable interests, global involvement arises when several relatively stringent conditions are met: the existence of societal actors sufficiently powerful to influence behaviour and critical security interests or commitments; the presence of a full range of concerns and values that give the international behaviour additional significance; the recognition that behaviour is based at least partly on state-specific interests, vulnerabilities, and values, rather than universal doctrines; and the desire of partner countries to maintain the involvement.

From these conditions, the variety of activity is defined as one of interest-based involvement predicated on the distinctively national interests and values previously identified as the touchstone of Canadian participation. Canadian policy and behaviour are likely to exhibit some inconsistency over time and across issues as officials also seek to make their contributions in the context of past efforts while maintaining congruence with the accumulated expectations and interests of others. Such activity may appear as a large number of highly complex patterns quite distinct from one another, irregular and seemingly unpredictable as a variety of interests and decision strategies compete.

As a further consequence of Canada's global behaviour, the diffusion of activity is seen as a tendency toward autonomous bilateral involvement. Reflecting the need to develop and maintain direct ties worldwide, distinctive effort is made on specific state-to-state relations while relatively less involvement occurs with international organizations having universal membership. In this mode, new and multiple membership, concern with balance across affiliations, and stress on fluidity assume lesser prominence. Priority is given to employing the state's resources in servicing the particular interest of each specific bilateral relationship. In practice, this suggests a fuller and more equal association with a larger number of non-universal organizations and, more importantly, the development of direct bilateral relations with groups and actors beyond the Anglo-American sphere. More specifically, in this thrust bilateral diplomatic representation on a resident basis is given and received with most actors, posts acquire a "multiprogram" character, regular visits by heads of government increase, and joint organizations are formed with regional bodies and individual countries.

From the complex neo-realist perspective, this tendency toward global, interest-based, bilateral activity is supplemented by associative behaviour characterized by a set of competitive orientations: a predisposition toward unilateral initiatives, a divergence in policy commitment, and a diversification of focus away from any associated imperial state. Emphasizing unilateral initiatives, Canada's diplomatic behaviour does not necessarily concentrate on inducing other states to act, does not

require their active cooperation, passive support, or subsequent imitation for success, and is therefore not heavily dependent on calculations of their likely behaviour for its initiation. In short, this diplomatic behaviour is not a heavily context-dependent attempt to preserve or engender cooperative arrangements, but rather a self-motivated effort to operate within the confines of the existing system to national advantage. A desire to act primarily with equivalent states on the one hand, and to maintain relatively exclusive spheres of influence on the other, reinforces this emphasis on selective involvement of other actors as dictated by each issue.

The second competitive tendency, divergence, is reflected in actions in which relatively little effort is made to ensure consistency with the actions of other states and in which dissimilar actions often result. Positions may be taken at variance with those of members in existing groups, and sometimes this exercise of leadership will initiate a new grouping. Little emphasis is given to offsetting the weight of a given bloc or eroding bloc cleavages. As a result, Canada often adopts positions on major issues discrepant with those of traditionally associated states.

The third and most significant competitive tendency is that of diversification, manifested in active efforts to concentrate behaviour on actors other than an associated imperial power or its groups, with the aim of obtaining alternative sources of resources such as information, markets, investment, and general political support. In particular, it involves a deliberate attempt to forge relations and assume compatible positions with other states that are roughly equivalent in status or even more powerful and thus capable of serving as a substitute for, or rival to, the traditional imperial power. Diversification rests on the following beliefs: that in the absence of such action, existing behavioural domination by the prevailing imperial power would continue; that this is not in Canada's interest; that Canada has the power to force a more acceptable balance by itself; and that this effort can be sustained even in the face of active opposition from the imperial power.

In overseas relations, the rivalry induced by diversification is constrained somewhat by the fundamental responsibility of all major powers to preserve a general balance of power and reduce the likelihood of war. However, these tasks are performed by individual as well as collective actions, rest on negotiated settlements among equals more than on compromises forwarded or facilitated by other parties, and provide only an overarching framework in which major power interests are pursued in a competitive fashion. Within this framework, diversification engenders the establishment of cooperative relationships with other major or emerging powers as an alternative to its affiliation with an associated imperial power. At that point the process may extend into an intensive and increasingly competitive relationship in which Canada becomes involved in the internal political processes of its new partner, incompatible interests become apparent, and diplomatic conflict results. Alternatively, the continuation and reinforcement of a close, cooperative relationship may result in an effort at counterweight, in which the new partner is deliberately invoked as an ally directly against the preferences of the previous imperial power.

Canada's pursuit of diversification within North America breeds an emphasis on arm's-length diplomacy. Bilateral relations with the United States resemble those between any two sovereign states with unified governments: formally equal while differing in objective, formulating national positions in advance, guarding information, and seeking to outmanoeuvre adversaries, link issues, and dominate policy implementation. Within Canada itself, the corresponding value of an autonomous society prompts a reliance on strategies that prohibit outright further American penetration and actively reduce the existing American presence.

In an emerging principal power, in the complex neo-realist view, the defence of national interests and the promotion of distinctive values engender a strong incentive to follow and promote a detailed conception of world order compatible with its purposes. The first manifestation of this incentive is an active effort to revise the existing patterns of international institutionalization. Believing that such frameworks preserve old values and inhibit emergent powers from securing equality with their established counterparts, these states reduce their verbal and material support for the standard set of international institutions, seek to forge alternative organizations or informal groupings, and forge alliances with new states that have attained success within the existing order. Moreover, efforts to promote a well-developed, highly autonomous, and fully consistent structure of international law are reduced, on the grounds that such constructions introduce rigidities that impede the process of revision.

A second component of a complex neo-realist approach to world order is the promotion of principal-power concerts through the creation of groupings in which effective participation is restricted to states within the top tier, and more particularly to states with a rank equal to or greater than one's own. Premised on the recognition of Canada's principal-power rank and claims, this tendency is directed at strengthening the distinction between groups made up exclusively of principal powers and mixed groups of principal and lesser powers. In addition, it increasingly transfers important questions from the latter to the former in the interests of a more rapid and realistic revision and more effective management of the international order.

Modification of the existing international order in keeping with its distinctive interests and values is the third criterion of a principal power's approach to world order. Accepting the basic legitimacy of those structures that allowed it to ascend to principal-power status, Canada devotes few resources to conducting direct, comprehensive assaults on the formal framework of existing institutions. Yet, in an attempt to reinforce its new position, it seeks to forge alliances with those who have successfully manipulated the existing system and who are likely candidates for major-power status in the near future. And in an effort to register the particular contribution it can make to the management of the global system and to secure the support of emerging powers who sustain its position, it forwards distinctive conceptions of what a new international order should be.

Implicit in complex neo-realist writing is the assumption that these action tendencies and doctrines are sustained by an external environment rather more open and less concentrated than in the classical formulation. This configuration, when combined with Canada's principal-power status, reduces to a low level the overall salience of the external environment, disperses its influence across a wide number of states, and endows a multitude of states with a noticeable, if minor, impact on Canadian behaviour. Thus complex neo-realism assigns the "imperial" actors—the United Kingdom and the United States—a significantly reduced role in providing a stimulus, framework, and referent for Canadian behaviour. At the same time it allows the major European powers, and Japan, the Soviet Union, and China, a relatively high impact, not only by providing a broader affiliation to balance Canada's relations with the United States but also in serving as comparable, autonomous actors in their own right.

The significant weight attached to the positions and initiatives of these major states reduces to a moderate level the significance of the smaller European and overseas middle powers as associates of Canada in international diplomacy and as a factor when Canada undertakes autonomous action. Within this sphere, attention shifts from states with a historical relationship with Canada to those with similar socio-cultural attributes or convergent population, resource, and technology characteristics and to those emerging into the major-power realm. Finally, the United Nations, as the institutional codification of an increasingly obsolete pattern of international relations, declines to a moderate position as an influence on Canadian behaviour, while the North Atlantic Treaty Organization (NATO), a more restricted body with a direct role in security and in defining systems, experiences an offsetting increase.[50] Moreover, a much greater influence is enjoyed by such new, restricted-membership, task-specific bodies as la Francophonie, the Namibia Contact Group within the Security Council, the Organisation for Economic Co-operation and Development, the International Energy Agency, the London Suppliers Group on nuclear materials, and the Western Economic Summits held since 1975.

A complex neo-realist orientation perceives the domestic environment as being marked by the emergence of highly salient, ongoing disputes over foreign policy issues, grounded in the interest of autonomous major organizations throughout the national society. The high importance of domestic organizations rests in the first instance on the likelihood that the country's possession of a surplus margin of capability allows for and prompts an effective debate within society about the purposes for which that power should be employed. Furthermore, the existence of routine global involvements by societal organizations increases the number of actors whose primary interests are affected by foreign affairs, who possess direct, specialized international expertise, and who thus have legitimate, divergent perspectives about the best course to pursue. Moreover, the stress on national interest and initiative emphasizes the desirability of considering domestic sources and taking the time for domestic actors to mobilize, organize, and debate. Together these factors produce a domestic process that, in conformity with a pluralist conception of politics, contains a highly developed set of differentiated institutions, each autonomously defining and pursuing specific interests among societal competitors and organizations in the external and governmental realm. Thus, Canada's international behaviour becomes highly sensitive to such societal factors.

The depth and durability of these societal interests give the overtly political and directly accessible institutions—Parliament and the party system—only a moderate role in influencing government behaviour. In contrast, associational interest groups, labour, the media, and the business community all enjoy a high degree of influence, in keeping with the precepts of interest-group theory. Finally, provincial governments possess a moderate degree of influence. The result is a highly dispersed and evenly balanced process, in which all types of institutions and especially those organizations whose strength is based on population, resource, or technological capabilities, have substantial impact.

Within the executive branch of the federal government, complex neo-realism predicts the existence of a decision-making process resembling bureaucratic politics, but one in which strong central coordinative mechanisms operate to produce overall order. The decision-making process of government is viewed as highly salient in foreign policy behaviour, resulting from the vigorous debate taking place among a well-developed constellation of organizational subunits capable of registering their missions with considerable specificity. Within this constellation, a relatively moderate influence is assigned to the Department of External Affairs and its career foreign service officer corps; a high degree of influence, in contrast, is assigned to other foreign service departments and domestic departments. Exercising dominant influence are those within the prime ministerial group and in the central foreign policy coordinative structures closest to it, given their role in defining overarching values and the overall national interest. Indeed, great emphasis is placed on the emergence of a large, highly specialized, and tightly controlled set of such coordinative structures as a means for integrating and transcending the multitude of powerful competing missions within the government and competing interests within domestic society. Therefore, Canadian foreign policy behaviour is argued to be, in the context of complex neo-realism, highly sensitive to key governmental actors but durable, interrelated, and comprehensive nonetheless.

These three theoretical perspectives on Canadian foreign policy provide our entry into the study of Canada's postwar international behaviour. Determinations about the usefulness, accuracy, and validity of each one must be made in the context of the empirical record, not on an *a priori* basis.

Questions for Review

1. How is state power measured?
2. How is international behaviour measured?
3. What determines a country's international behaviour?
4. Is Canada a principal power today?

Suggested Readings

Dewitt, David J., and John J. Kirton. 1983. *Canada as a Principal Power: A Study in Foreign Policy and International Relations.* Toronto: John Wiley and Sons.

Eayrs, James. 1975. "Defining a New Place for Canada in the Hierarchy of World Power." *International Perspectives* (May/June): 15–24.

Hawes, Michael K. 1984. *Principal Power, Middle Power, or Satellite?* Toronto: York Research Programme in Strategic Studies.

Kirton, John J. 2007. *Canadian Foreign Policy in a Changing World.* Toronto: Thomson Nelson.

Notes

1. R.A. MacKay and E.B. Rogers, *Canada Looks Abroad* (London: Oxford University Press, 1938). See also Robert Bothwell and Norman Hillmer, eds., *The In-Between Time: Canadian External Policy in the 1930s* (Toronto: Copp Clark, 1975). The most authoritative history of this period is contained in C.P. Stacey, *Canada and the Age of Conflict, vol. 1, 1867–1921* (Toronto: Macmillan, 1977), and *vol. 2, 1921–1948* (Toronto: University of Toronto Press, 1981).

2. John W. Holmes, *The Shaping of Peace: Canada and the Search for World Order, 1943–1957*, 2 vols. (Toronto: University of Toronto Press, 1979, 1982). On the move toward the war and its legacy, see James Eayrs, *In Defence of Canada*, 4 vols. (Toronto: University of Toronto Press, 1964, 1965, 1972, 1980).

3. See Dale Thomson and Roger Swanson, *Canadian Foreign Policy: Options and Perspectives* (Toronto: McGraw-Hill Ryerson, 1971); Peter Dobell, *Canada's Search For New Roles: Foreign Policy in the Trudeau Era* (London and New York: Oxford University Press, 1972); Peyton V. Lyon, "A Review of the Review," *Journal of Canadian Studies* 5 (May 1970): 34–47; Lyon, "The Trudeau Doctrine," *International Journal* 26, 1 (Winter 1970–71): 19–43; James Hyndman, "National Interest and the New Look," *International Journal* 26 (Winter 1970–71): 5–8; and Kal Holsti, *Proceedings of the Standing Committee on External Affairs and National Defence*, Statement no. 7, 19 July 1971.

4. The most influential framework provided by students of general foreign policy analysis is presented in James N. Rosenau, "Pre-theories and Theories of Foreign Policy," pp. 27–92 in R.B. Farrell, ed., *Approaches to Comparative and International Politics* (Evanston, IL: Northwestern University Press, 1966). For a view of the development and application of this framework, see Patrick McGowan and Howard Shapiro, *The Comparative Study of Foreign Policy: A Survey of Scientific Findings* (Beverly Hills, CA: Sage Publications, 1973); and James N. Rosenau, ed., *Comparing Foreign Policies: Theories, Findings and Methods* (Toronto: John Wiley and Sons, 1974).

5. The prevalence of such myths and models in the social sciences is noted, by specific example, in Larry Ward et al., "World Modelling: Some Critical Foundations," *Behavioral Sciences* 23 (May 1978): 135–47. The major traditions in Canadian historical writing are discussed in Carl Berger, ed., *Approaches to Canadian History* (Toronto: University of Toronto Press, 1967); and Berger, *The Writing of Canadian History: Aspects of English-Canadian Historical Writing: 1900 to 1970* (Toronto: Oxford University Press, 1976). A brief portrait of the implicit models in the writing on Canadian foreign policy

is offered in John W. Holmes, "After 25 years," *International Journal* 26, 1 (Winter 1970–71): 1–4.

6. Kal Holsti, *International Politics: A Framework for Analysis*, 3rd ed. (Englewood Cliffs, NJ: Prentice-Hall, 1977), 390; Maurice East and Charles Hermann, "Do Nation-Types Account for Foreign Policy Behaviour?' pp. 269–303 in Rosenau, ed., *Comparing Foreign Policies*.

7. The best treatment of the classic formulations of relative capability, position, and status is provided in Martin Wight, *Power Politics* (Harmondsworth, England: Penguin, 1979). For modern extensions and applications, see Klaus Knorr, "Notes on the Analysis of National Capabilities," in James N. Rosenau et al., eds., *The Analysis of International Relations* (New York: Free Press, 1972); Knorr, *The Power of Nations: The Political Economy of International Relations* (New York: Basic Books, 1975); and Ray Cline, *World Power Trends and US Foreign Policy for the 1980s* (Boulder, CO: Westview Press, 1980). Recent applications to individual states include Ezra Vogel, *Japan as Number One: Lessons for America* (Cambridge, MA: Harvard University Press, 1979); and Wolfram Hanrieder, "Germany as Number Two? The Foreign and Economic Policy of the Federal Republic," *International Studies Quarterly* 26 (March 1982): 57–86. Yet to appear is a piece in this tradition arguing the case for "Canada as Number Seven."

8. See K.N. Waltz, *Theory of International Politics* (Reading, MA: Addison–Wesley, 1979); Charles Pentland, "The Regionalization of World Politics: Concepts and Evidence," *International Journal* 30, 4 (Autumn 1975): 599–630; William Zimmerman, "Issue Area and Foreign Policy Process: A Research Note in Search of a General Theory," *American Political Science Review* 67 (December 1973): 1204–12; William C. Porter, "Issue Area and Foreign Policy Analysis," *International Organization* 34 (Summer 1980): 405–28; A.F.K. Organski, *World Politics*, 2nd ed. (New York: Knopf, 1968); and W.W. Rostow, *The World Economy* (Austin: University of Texas Press, 1978).

9. Following the treatment in Joseph Frankel, *International Relations in a Changing World* (Toronto: Oxford University Press, 1979), 8–27, *security* is defined as the possession of defined, externally recognized boundaries unlikely to be changed in the short term by outside force. *Sovereignty* is defined as the capacity of the central government to enforce its jurisdiction and preserve the identity of its major societal institutions, and *legitimacy* as its ability to attract regularly high degrees of voluntary compliance from its citizenry.

10. The three basic categories of externally oriented behaviour are formed by viewing state behaviour at progressively higher levels of analysis: activity (acting state), association

(state in interaction with other states), and order (system of interacting states). Each of these categories is divided in turn by the three stages of behaviour offered in events data analysis: emission, transmission, and reception or impact. See J. David Singer, "The Level of Analysis Problem in International Relations," pp. 77–92 in Klaus Knorr and Sidney Verba, ed., *The International System: Theoretical Essays* (Princeton, NJ: Princeton University Press, 1961); and Charles Hermann, "What Is a Foreign Policy Event?" pp. 295–321 in Wolfram Hanrieder, ed., *Comparative Foreign Policy: Theoretical Essays* (New York: David McKay, 1971).

11.   *Diffusion* is defined more specifically as the number of, balance among, and intensity of relations with the targets of Canadian action abroad. Analytically, the impact of Canadian behaviour on a target transforms Canadian "activity" into "relations." It thus leads to the next level of analysis—association—in which attention is directed at the internal character of a pattern of relations (or a "relationship").

12.   Analytically, because the overall focus of Canadian behaviour is directed at the distribution of power in the international system and can affect that distribution, it gives rise to the subsequent concern with order, or the structure of the international system that a given distribution of power yields.

13.   The basic concept of world order is discussed in Hedley Bull, *The Anarchical Society: A Study of Order in World Politics* (New York: Columbia University Press, 1979). See also Robert Tucker, *The Inequality of Nations* (New York: Basic Books, 1977). For a current debate on regimes, see *International Organization* 36 (Spring 1982), entire issue.

14.   The importance of systemic attributes, such as the actions of individual states on a state's international activity, is argued in James Harf et al., "Systemic and External Attributes in Foreign Policy Analysis," pp. 235–50 in Rosenau, ed., *Comparing Foreign Policies.* Evidence that the relative status and salience of external actors has a particular impact on Canadian foreign policy behaviour is contained in Don Munton, "Lesser Powers and the Influence of Relational Attributes: The Case of Canadian Foreign Policy Behaviour," *Études internationales* 10 (September 1979): 471–502. *Salience* includes the concept of vulnerability, which refers to "the relative availability and costliness of the alternatives that the actors face." It is defined as "an actor's liability to suffer costs imposed by external events even after policies have been altered" and is measured by "the costliness of making effective adjustments to a changed environment over a period of time." Robert O. Keohane and Joseph S. Nye, Jr. *Power and Interdependence: World Politics in Transition* (Boston: Little, Brown, 1977), 13.

15.   Compare the concept of sensitivity as degree and speed of costly impacts from, and responsiveness to, outside events, including social, political, and economic contagion effects, "before policies are altered to try to change the situation." Keohane and Nye, *Power and Interdependence*, 12–13.

16.   For an introduction to the literature on domestic sources of foreign policy, see Henry Kissinger, "Domestic Structure and Foreign Policy," *Daedalus* 95 (Spring 1966): 503–29; James N. Rosenau, ed., *Domestic Sources of Foreign Policy* (New York: Free Press, 1967); McGowan and Shapiro, *Comparative Study*, 107–32; and Peter J. Katzenstein, ed., "Between Power and Plenty: Foreign Economic Policies of Advanced Industrialized States," *International Organization* 31 (Autumn 1977).

17.   For societal determinants, a further breakdown of scope includes the concepts of institutional differentiation and autonomy derived from Samuel Huntington, *Political Order in Changing Societies* (New Haven, CT: Yale University Press, 1968), and the discussion of penetrated political societies in Rosenau, "Pre-theories and Theories." On the dual nature of the influence relationship between domestic and governmental actors in the Canadian case, see Denis Stairs, "Publics and Policy Makers: The Domestic Environment of the Foreign Policy Community," *International Journal* 26, 1 (Winter 1970–71): 221–48; and Stairs, "Public Opinion and External Affairs: Reflections on the Domestication of Canadian Foreign Policy," *International Journal* 33, 1 (Winter 1977–78): 128–49.

18.   See Richard Snyder, H.W. Bruck, and B.M. Sapin, eds., *Foreign Policy Decision Making* (New York: Free Press, 1962); Graham Allison, *Essence of Decision: Explaining the Cuban Missile Crisis* (Boston: Little, Brown, 1971); McGowan and Shapiro, *Comparative Study*, 65–106; and, most usefully, Stephen D. Krasner, *Defending the National Interest: Raw Material Investments and US Foreign Policy* (Princeton, NJ: Princeton University Press, 1978); Alfred Stepan, *The State and Society: Peru in Comparative Perspective* (Princeton, NJ: Princeton University Press, 1978); and Eric A. Nordlinger, *On the Autonomy of the Democratic State* (Cambridge, MA: Harvard University Press, 1981).

19.   "A principal task of research is to determine the extent to which any particular state (a) is procedurally neutral and allows an autonomous and competitive process of interest aggregation to present binding demands on the state, (b) is a class instrument in which the full range of its coercive, administrative and legal powers is used to dominate some class fractions and protect others, or (c) achieves some degree of autonomy from civil society and thus contributes its own weight to civil society." Stepan, *State and Society*, xii–xiii.

20.   These three groups emerge from most empirical analyses of a state's foreign policy apparatus; for example, I.M.

Destler, *President, Bureaucrats and Foreign Policy: The Policy of Organizational Reform* (Princeton, NJ: Princeton University Press, 1972).

21. These coordinative structures and processes are staffed by what Stepan terms the "strategic elite" and depend for their efficacy on the "ideological and organizational unity of that elite," Stepan, *State and Society*, xiii.

22. Hans Morgenthau's classic work is *Politics among Nations: The Struggle for Power and Peace* (New York: Knopf, 1948). Other classic works in the realist tradition, broadly conceived, are E.H. Carr, *The Twenty Years' Crisis, 1919–1939: An Introduction to the Study of International Relations* (New York: St Martin's Press, 1939); Raymond Aron, *Peace and War: A Theory of International Relations* (New York: Praeger, 1967); and Bull, *Anarchical Society*.

23. Carl Berger, *The Sense of Power: Studies in the Idea of Canadian Imperialism, 1867–1914* (Toronto: University of Toronto Press, 1970).

24. Don Page, "Canada as the Exponent of North American Idealism," *The American Review of Canadian Studies* 3 (Autumn 1973): 30–46.

25. John H. Herz, "Rise and Demise of the Territorial State," *World Politics* 9 (July 1957): 473ff; and Herz, *International Politics in the Atomic Age* (New York: Columbia University Press, 1959). See also the criticisms summarized in Stanley Hoffman, *The State of War: Essays on the Theory and Practice of International Relations* (New York: Praeger, 1965).

26. This broadening of the concepts of security and national interest and the introduction of a more prominent role for values and moral considerations were led by Arnold Wolfers, *Discord and Collaboration* (Baltimore: Johns Hopkins University Press, 1962).

27. For example, R.J. Sutherland, "Canada's Long-Term Strategic Situation," *International Journal* 17 (Summer 1962): 199–233; James Eayrs, "Sharing a Continent: the Hard Issues," pp. 55–94 in J.S. Dickey, ed., *The United States and Canada* (Englewood Cliffs, NJ: Prentice-Hall, 1967); Klaus Knorr, "Canada and Western Defence," *International Journal* 18 (Winter 1962–63): 1–16; and Melvin Conant, *The Long Polar Watch: Canada and the Defence of North America* (New York: Harper and Row, 1962). From an earlier period, see the great classics, J.B. Brebner, *North Atlantic Triangle: The Interplay of Canada, the United States and Great Britain* (Toronto: Ryerson, 1945); "A Changing North Atlantic Triangle," *International Journal* 3 (Autumn 1948): 309–19; and Harold Innis, *Great Britain, the United Nations and Canada* (Nottingham: University of Nottingham Press, 1948).

28. For the best summaries, see Keohane and Nye, *Power and Interdependence*; and Stanley Hoffman, *Primacy or World Order: American Foreign Policy since the Cold War* (New York: McGraw-Hill, 1978).

29. Wight, *Power Politics*, 30–40; and Jeffrey Hart, "Dominance in International Politics," *International Organization* 30 (Spring 1976).

30. Hans Morgenthau, *The Purpose of American Politics* (New York: Knopf, 1960); Arnold Wolfers, "Statesmanship and Moral Choice," *World Politics* 1 (January 1949): 175–95; and Wolfers, *Discord and Collaboration*. While this broader conception of interests and values follows many of the recent extensions of realist thinking, it does *not* embrace the globally derived, universally common, or inherent "cosmopolitan values," argued in John H. Herz, "Political Realism Revisited," *International Studies Quarterly* 25 (June 1981): 182–97, and suggested in Stanley Hoffman, *Duties Beyond Borders: On the Limits and Possibilities of Ethical International Politics* (Syracuse, NY: Syracuse University Press, 1981). Essentially, our argument asserts that balance-of-power dynamics do not usually prevent a state from acquiring a position of hegemony, that such states have "milieu" goals, and that such goals are partially determined by a historically engendered conception of national values.

31. The major works that provide the basis in the general literature for our complex neo-realist model are George Liska, *Imperial America: The International Politics of Primacy* (Baltimore: Johns Hopkins University Press, 1967); Raymond Aron, *The Imperial Republic* (Englewood Cliffs, NJ: Prentice-Hall, 1974); and David Calleo, *The Imperious Economy* (Cambridge, MA: Harvard University Press, 1982). Equally important is a stream of literature focusing on the dynamics within and between states, which give rise to processes of hegemony. See, in particular, Nazli Choucri and Robert C. North, *Nations in Conflict: National Growth and International Violence* (San Francisco: W.H. Freeman, 1975).

32. See A.F.K. Organski, *World Politics*, 364–67; and Wight, *Power Politics*, 30–40.

33. On great powers, see Wight, *Power Politics*, 41–53.

34. The concept of surplus capability is drawn from Charles Kindleberger, "Dominance and Leadership in the International Economy," *International Studies Quarterly* 25 (June 1981): 245. In our formulation, it is not only an absolute criterion based on internal capability but also a criterion relative to domestic demands, external security threats, and ultimately the demands for creating international order that are bred by different external distributions of power.

35. Collectively, a particular configuration of interests and values is termed "the national interest." The traditional, security-focused concept of national interest has met with considerable skepticism from scholars of international politics, for reasons well summarized in James N. Rosenau, "National Interest," pp. 34–40 in David L. Sills, ed., *International Encyclopedia of the Social Sciences*, vol. 2

(New York: Crowell, Collier, and Macmillan, 1968). Our concept derives from subsequent efforts to defend and refine the concept, such as Joseph Frankel, "National Interest: A Vindication," *International Journal* 24 (Autumn 1969): 717–25; Donald Nuechterlein, *National Interests and Presidential Leadership: The Setting of Priorities* (Boulder, CO: Westview Press, 1978); and, especially, Krasner, *Defending the National Interest*. In our conception, the national interest is a set of premises, perceptions, and policy-relevant priorities that is durable (extending for a minimum of, say, five years), comprehensive (in embracing interests from several issue areas or sectors of society), interrelated (in specifying the relationships among interests), internally prioritized (in providing a particular scale of order or weighting to components), and general (in relating directly overarching values that structure the scale of priorities). In process terms, "the national interest" is seen in broad foreign policy declarations, doctrines, or the calculus underlying seminal decisions when these endure beyond the electoral cycle, actively involve a number and range of government departments, require extensive interdepartmental interaction, engender interdepartmental conflict or major efforts at harmonization, and stimulate more than formal authorization, monitoring, or servicing activities from the chief executive group or central coordinative structures. Thus "the national interest" embraces both "interests," which are specific to societal sectors and government departments and affected by decision in a direct and immediate way, and "values," which are general to society and the state and produced by the chief executive group and central coordinative structures. Because society lacks unified control and central coordinative structures, interests are primarily the preserve of society, while values reside primarily in the state.

36. The concept of specialized capabilities is drawn from Choucri and North, *Nations in Conflict*, 14–43.

37. In short, they present the possibility of leadership, as conceived in Kindleberger, "Dominance and Leadership."

38. In addition to the works cited in the introduction, our presentation of complex neo-realism draws on the following literature in the Canadian foreign policy field: Hyndman, "National Interest and the New Look"; Ivan Head, "The Foreign Policy of the New Canada," *Foreign Affairs* 50 (January 1972): 237–52; "Dossier Canada," *Politique Internationale* 12 (Summer 1981): 181–302; A.E. Gotlieb, "The Western Economic Summits," Notes for Remarks to the Canadian Institute for International Affairs, 9 April 1981, Winnipeg; and Charles Doran, "Politics of Dependency Reversal: Canada," Paper prepared for the International Studies Association Annual Meeting, 21–24 March 1979, Toronto.

39. Note the co-existence of the two themes in the prescriptions of Escott Reid in "Canadian Foreign Policy, 1967–1977," *International Journal* 22, 2 (Spring 1967): 171–81. Distinctive cultural groups included, most notably, the francophone countries and the People's Republic of China.

40. See Stephen Clarkson, ed., *An Independent Foreign Policy for Canada?* (Toronto: McClelland and Stewart, 1968), 253–69; and Hyndman, "National Interest and the New Look."

41. See Head, "Foreign Policy of the New Canada"; and James Eayrs, "Defining a New Place for Canada in the Hierarchy of World Power," *International Perspectives,* May/June 1975: 15–24.

42. More particularly, we see the United States acquiring hegemony from 1945 to 1960 and exercising stable, virtually unchallenged "high" hegemony from about 1960 through 1967.

43. Robert Bothwell, Ian Drummond, and John English, *Canada since 1945: Power, Politics and Provincialism* (Toronto: University of Toronto Press, 1981).

44. "Canada is a large power; to call us a 'middle power' is inaccurate . . . . As an immigrant country, with a barely developed national resource base to our economy, and a rapidly adapting capability in technology and processing, we are to some extent only now beginning to reach our true potential." A.E. Gotlieb, "Canada–US Relations: The Rules of the Game," Christian A. Herter Lecture Series, The Johns Hopkins School of Advanced International Studies, 1 April 1982, Washington DC, 4, 10. The term *principal power* is used by Marc Lalonde, "Le Canada et l'indépendance énergétique du monde libre," *Politique Internationale* 12 (Summer 1981): 206.

45. A.F.K. Organski and Jacek Kugler, *The War Ledger* (Chicago: University of Chicago Press, 1980), 43.

46. For an illustration of this calculation, see Gotlieb, "Western Economic Summits."

47. For an example of a national capabilities presentation, see Peyton V. Lyon and Brian W. Tomlin, *Canada as an International Actor* (Toronto: Macmillan, 1979), 56–76.

48. Such groupings include the Western Economic Summit, the Namibia Contact Group, and, less clearly, the four-power Caribbean Consultative Group, the 1970 uranium cartel group, the initial London Suppliers Group on nuclear materials, the executive directors of the International Monetary Fund, and, historically, the United Nations Atomic Energy Commission.

49. These groupings include states in the Commonwealth and Francophonie, particularly those from the Caribbean and Africa and, less clearly, small and middle powers from the North Atlantic region. One very stringent measure of such states is the group that Canada has represented at one time as an executive director on the International Monetary Fund: Norway, Iceland, Ireland, Jamaica, Guyana, Barbados, and the Bahamas. From this

perspective, the standard observation of Canada—as a "regional power without a region" because of the dominating presence of the United States—overlooks the three major poles of Canada's regional sphere: as a transcontinental and trans-Atlantic power, beginning with Confederation in 1867 and culminating in the admission of Newfoundland into the Dominion in 1949; as a northern power, symbolized by the Arctic Waters Pollution Prevention Act of 1970 and conceptualized in Franklyn

Griffiths, *A Northern Foreign Policy* (Toronto: Canadian Institute of International Affairs, 1979); and as a Caribbean power, based on this historic Canada–West Indies trade and currently registered in Canada's leading role in development assistance in the region.

50. More precisely, within the United Nations, greater emphasis is given to the Security Council and to the new generation of organizations and special conference groupings created in the 1970s to deal with new "global" issues.

Canada as a Principal Power 2010

John J. Kirton
Revised May 6, 2010

UPDATE

Key Terms

Complex Neo-Realist Perspective

Principal Power

Introduction: Canada as a Principal Power 1983

In *Canada as a Principal Power: A Study in Foreign Policy and International Relations*, published in 1983, David Dewitt and I argued that Canada was emerging as a **principal power** in a more diffuse international system, as identified by a new **complex neo-realist perspective** on Canadian foreign policy. At the time, the work seemed significant on several counts.

First, the suggestion that Canada could be a principal power broadened the scholarly and policy debate beyond the traditional duelling dichotomy of Canada as a middle power or satellite (Granatstein 1969). Inspired by James Eayrs's (1975) brilliant but breezy insight, it recaptured and modernized the intellectual richness of the initial trichotomy of policy patterns and options that had been present at the creation of the systematic study of Canadian foreign policy in R.A. MacKay and E.B. Rogers, *Canada Looks Abroad,* in 1938 (Hawes 1984, Bratt and Kukucha 2007, Kirton 2009).

Second, *Canada as a Principal Power* was arguably the first fully theoretical work on Canadian foreign policy in that it offered three competing, logically interrelated sets of specified concepts covering all the major dimensions of the behaviour and determinants of Canadian foreign policy and capable of empirical application and disconfirmation. While others had offered core concepts, notably Denis Stairs's (1974) *The Diplomacy of Constraint,* or systemically explored the determinants of key decisions, as in Bruce Thordarson's (1972) *Trudeau and Foreign Policy*, only in 1983 did a comprehensive theoretical, empirically testable edifice arrive.

Third, that theoretical edifice was explicitly grounded in the larger theories of international relations and foreign policy, rather than treating Canadian foreign policy as a subject of merely local conceptualization and concern. While earlier international relations concepts such as "middle power" and dependency theory had enriched the study of Canadian foreign policy, *Canada as a Principal Power* explicitly drew on the major modern international relations theories from within the realist, liberal institutionalist, and political economy/world systems traditions and was designed to be used for a study of Canadian and comparative foreign policy.

Fourth, as subsequent scholars correctly recognized, this theory was a systemic one (Tomlin et al. 2008). It argued that Canada was emerging as a principal power in, and because of, a more diffuse international system. Its systemically grounded theory flowed from the two most influential international relations works of the time. First, Kenneth Waltz's (1979) *Theory of International Politics,* with its stark emphasis on the structural significance of relative capability among major powers, and second, Robert Keohane and Joseph Nye, Jr.'s (1977) *Power and Interdependence,* with its new emphasis on sensitivity and vulnerability in an era when systemic interdependence as a parallel component of the structure of the international system was taking hold. The work sought to pull the study of Canadian foreign policy beyond an idiographic concern with individuals, histories, and biographies to become part of, benefit from, and contribute to the large community of international relations scholars. It also began to move the study of Canadian foreign policy from the supply-side driver of relative capabilities as the key cause of a country's international behaviour to the demand-side driver of vulnerabilities, with a richer conception of both the supply and demand sides than those traditionally at work.

Canada as a Principal Power received considerable critical acclaim upon publication. But it did not immediately inspire a host of other scholars or doctoral students to develop or apply its theoretical innovations in major works (Molot 1990). In part this was due to bad timing. James Eayrs's initial insight in 1975 that Canada was now a "foremost nation," and the full-blown "principal power" claim to which this gave rise, seemed sensible in the energy-short, détente-bathed mid-1970s. However, it proved to be incorrect and implausible in the mid-1980s as Canada suffered from a severe recession, as Ronald Reagan seemed to restore the United States' hegemonic primacy, and as the superpower Soviet Union expanded into Afghanistan. These events seemed to make the diffusing international system of the 1970s disappear into a new world of tight, Cold War bipolarity, as the closed, insensitive, and invulnerable billiard ball-like polities of conventional realism returned.

Moreover, the primary Canadian audience, somewhat correctly, saw that the book closely charted, and was theoretically inspired by, the doctrines and doings of the governments of Prime Minister Pierre Elliott Trudeau that had started in 1968 but that had disappeared, amidst the disgrace of a bandwagoning public, in 1984. Nor were they designed to be normative, and thus useful to the ongoing policy and political practice in which too many scholars of the subject are involved. It thus easily fell out of favour, especially when some scholars of Canadian foreign policy in the cash-strapped 1990s turned their talents to producing short policy-oriented papers on the problems of the moment.

More importantly, the book's complex concepts were not easy to comprehend and digest. Additionally, *Canada as a Principal Power* did not fully develop the conceptual insights that logically flowed from its theoretical foundations. It took another quarter of a century for one of the co-authors to do that, in *Canadian Foreign Policy in a Changing World,* published in

2007. With that elaboration and its application to 25 years of evidence after the theory was first offered, it is now possible to assess how theoretically valuable and empirically prescient and accurate *Canada as a Principal Power* has been. While that assessment must ultimately come from the co-authors' colleagues, the basic case for the defence is offered below.

Theory 2010

The fully elaborated argument, flowing from the 1983 foundations, rests on five central elements, some of which were implicit or obscured in the original work.

The first is the central argument that Canada is not in and of itself a principal power. Rather, it is a principal power only in a changing world defined by the severe, sustained, and probably irreversible decline of the United States as a system-dominant power; by the diffusion of its "released" relative capability to a diffuse set of rising powers rather than a single challenger; by the emergence of a new, expanded top tier of principal powers; and by the location of Canada in that top tier rather than the one below. This elaboration makes clear that this is a systemically grounded theory, and imposes four specific systemic conditions—decline, diffusion, top tier expansion, and Canadian inclusion—that must exist if the argument of Canada's emergence and establishment as a principal power is to prove true.

The second element was to specify an anchor of invariants for starting to explain and predict how Canada, or any other country in this system, would behave once these systemic conditions and the societal and governmental determinants within the country changed. With sovereign, exclusive, territorial states in a structurally anarchic system as a starting point, it argued that Canada, like all countries, has six essential national interests—survival, sovereignty, security, territory, legitimacy, and relative capability—from which its foreign policy flows. This theory was able to give pride of place to the recurrent national unity challenge as a survival threat to Canadian foreign policy, allowed people to measure how well Canada was doing in defending its national interests compared to all the other polities in the present or past, and helped us conclude from the evidence that Canada could be the most successful country in the world since the Westphalian system first arose way back in 1648. Such success as a state allowed Canada as a nation increasingly to seek and secure its distinctive national values, a concept first theorized and then empirically identified as anti-militarism, environmentalism, multiculturalism, openness, globalism, and international institutionalism. The theory entered into and drew from the new debate about whether Canadian foreign policy does or should derive from interests or from values, and from which ones in each case.

The third element, coming at the systemic, societal, and state levels, was the concept of neo-vulnerability (Kirton 1993). Joseph Nye's initial concept of vulnerability, probably inspired by the OPEC oil shock of 1973, was based on a deliberate state action aimed at and designed to hurt a target state. The concept of neo-vulnerability extended Nye's insight to include and emphasize how non-state, indeed non-human, activities and processes that were unintended and untargeted could spread anywhere to afflict even the most powerful polity, whose unilateral, protectionist, or isolationist policy changes could not remove or reliably reduce the vulnerability to national interests and distinctive national values (as well as mere preferences) that thus arose. These new security threats were conceptualized and identified in 1993 as terrorist, ecological, and drug- and health-related (Kirton 1993). Immediately after the chapter specifying them went to press, terrorists associated with Al Qaeda hit the twin towers in New York City and killed nearly 3,000 Americans on 11 September 2001. By September 2005, the United States had "lost a city" to Hurricane Katrina, in a physical realization of what had only been the constructed imagination of nuclear war gamers in the city-trading deterrence age. By the classic calculus of the "body count," the world's most capable principal power, the United States, had become the most vulnerable one, while the least capable principal power, Canada, remained, despite the Air India tragedy, the least vulnerable one.

The fourth theoretical element was the explicit articulation of the parsimonious but powerful principal power paradox. It stated that, as states gain in relative capability, they become less policy-takers and more policy-makers within the international system, with the result that external determinants have less salience in shaping their foreign policy and societal and governmental determinants have higher salience in doing so. This logic united the cause-and-effect components of the seven basic questions of foreign policy analysis on which the three theoretical perspectives of liberal internationalism, peripheral dependence, and complex neo-realism were based. Given the argument that Canada was emerging as principal power, this pointed to a future in which individual determinants within the governmental ones—even ultimately the beliefs and skill of an individual prime minister—could actually matter in the making of Canadian foreign policy and its results for Canada and the world. This element restored democratic policy accountability and human agency to a systemically rarefied world in which the leader of Canada was previously only a rationally confined calculator of systemic determinants, or socialized out of the Canadian political system if, as with John Diefenbaker in 1962, he or she failed that stark systemic test. The principal power paradox also predicted a future in which a Canada doing so well in defending its national interests could focus in its foreign policy on forwarding Canada's distinctive national values as the foundation for a new world order. Pierre Trudeau successfully started this tradition in the late 1960s, and under Prime Minister Paul Martin, Canada asserted its vision of itself within the international community in the 2005 *International Policy Statement—A Role of Pride and Influence in the World*.

The fifth element was to advance beyond the trend of Canada emerging, declining, or staying the same, to specify a threshold or a level at which Canada would actually arrive as a principal power in a changing and much changed world. Specifying thresholds, like making point predictions, is a difficult task, and securing further clarity here is a task that remains. But the theory contained so many components that could be used to trace and test the dynamics, and thus the ability of Canada to secure its desired approach to world order, that by 2007, in *Canadian Foreign Policy in a Changing World*, I concluded that Canada had now emerged as a principal power in a much changed world. Those focused parochially on Canada's new prime minister, Stephen Harper, had their doubts. But those focused on a changing world saw a broader picture. With the United States afflicted by possible political and military defeats in Iraq and Afghanistan as well as by a global financial crisis, and with China, India, and Brazil gaining economic and political influence, in part through the new G20 summit, the specified systemic conditions for this bold assertion appear to be materializing.

Evidence 2010

Canada as a Principal Power was constructed on the premise that the facts do matter, despite whether commentators in downtown Toronto like what their prime minister in Ottawa is doing. The ultimate test of the work is whether it accurately predicted an actual or potential future for Canadian foreign policy, or predicted the major alternatives if the systemic conditions unfolded in an empirically different but theoretically well-defined way. Amidst the many empirical applications to be made before a definitive conclusion can be reached on this point, a few fundamental facts stand out to suggest that this empirical test might have been met.

The first concerns objective capability and the long list of critical components of power or performance on which Canada stands number one in the world. These include uranium production, potash, fresh water, coastlines, temperate forests, and livable and multicultural cities. Canada is first in the production of hydroelectricity and third in natural gas, prompting Prime Minister Stephen Harper to assert Canada's intentions of being a "clean energy superpower." Canada's position in the specified top tier of seven to nine powers is bolstered by its second place rank in territory and in having, thanks to Alberta's tar sands, at least the world's second largest oil reserves. Canada's objective capabilities in terms of resources, population, and technology suggest a principal power ranking.

The second fact concerns the asserted position and acknowledged status. Prime Minister Kim Campbell's 1993 statement that Canada is a major power, and Prime Minister Harper's declaration abroad that Canada is an emerging energy superpower, make the 1983 claim that Canada was emerging as a principal power look modest. In 2006 in London, British Prime Minister Tony Blair presented Canada as a major superpower in the energy field.

To Canadians themselves in Calgary in 2007, Blair predicted that Canada will become one of the most powerful countries in the world. Among current leading commentators outside of Canada, in 2008 Fareed Zakaria concluded that "Canada is becoming a major power." He described Canada as a benign neighbour of the United States, with better broadband, health care and automotive manufacturing, a troop contributor to the American-led, UN-endorsed mission in Afghanistan, and a core part of the global British Empire in its illustrious past (Zakaria 2008: 29).

The third fact concerns activity and association. Canada now has six full bilateral free trade agreements and is negotiating one with Europe—the largest market in the world—in a Trudeauvian diversification dream finally come true. Moreover, since 1990, Canada has become a highly war-prone country, going to war ever more expansively and always winning, or at least not yet losing. Canada's longest engagement in Afghanistan remains to be won.

The fourth fact concerns the approach to world order. Canada has not only advanced highly authentic and ambitious conceptions, but achieved them as well. Under the agency of Prime Minister Paul Martin, Canada advocated for and secured the Responsibility to Protect principle, the antithesis of Article 2(7) of the UN Charter and anchor of the Westphalian system, now collectively affirmed by the leaders of virtually every country in the world. As Canada's finance minister in 1999, Paul Martin invented the Group of Twenty (G20), a group of systemically significant states that leapt to leaders' level summit meetings in 2008 in response to the American-turned-global financial crisis and the financial vulnerability it entailed. The G20 is now the central forum for global economic governance, working alongside the more established Group of Eight (G8). In 2010, Canada will chair the G8 major market democracies' summit, and co-chair the newly institutionalized G20 summit meeting. Its place at the centre of global governance is well entrenched.

Conclusion

Any serious theory lives on in the mind of its creator, its predictions constantly challenged by new observables and frequently beleaguered by self-doubt. In that spirit, it is important to note two possible threats, beyond the globally existential issues of nuclear and climate vulnerability, which could dislodge Canada from its now established principal power perch. The first, from faraway Afghanistan, is the first war that Canada could, having fought for so long, actually lose, with consequences for the country that can only be predicted by going beyond Canada to the comparative foreign policy realm.

The second threat touches on national unity, the core component of the first national interest of survival. It is the haunting reminder from René Lévesque's important article "For an Independent Quebec," in *Foreign Affairs* in 1976, that federal government policy constituted "demographic genocide" for Canada's francophone population. Canada prides itself on a multiculturalism founded by francophones and that includes the First Nations population as part of the essence of this distinctive national value. How Canadian foreign policy can solve that compounding problem is a challenge of the first order.

The theory put forth in *Canada as a Principal Power* is still relevant today in explaining Canadian foreign policy. In 2010, Canada has emerged as a principal power, particularly in the energy field. As Canada continues to shift from being a policy-taker to a policy-maker in the international system, Canadian politicians will play an increasingly influential role in international affairs, promoting distinctive Canadian national values and interests in the world.

Questions for Review

1.   How is state power measured?
2.   How is international behaviour measured?
3.   What determines a country's international behaviour?
4.   Is Canada a principal power today?

Suggested Readings

Dewitt, David J., and John J. Kirton. 1983. *Canada as a Principal Power: A Study in Foreign Policy and International Relations*. Toronto: John Wiley and Sons.

Eayrs, James. 1975. "Defining a New Place for Canada in the Hierarchy of World Power." *International Perspectives* (May/June): 15–24.

Hawes, Michael K. 1984. *Principal Power, Middle Power, or Satellite?* Toronto: York Research Programme in Strategic Studies.

Kirton, John J. 2007. *Canadian Foreign Policy in a Changing World*. Toronto: Thomson Nelson.

References

Bratt, Duane, and Christopher J. Kukucha, eds. 2007. *Readings in Canadian Foreign Policy: Classic Debates and New Ideas*. Don Mills, ON: Oxford University Press.

Eayrs, James. 1975. "Defining a New Place for Canada in the Hierarchy of World Power." *International Perspectives* (May/June): 15–24.

Granatstein, J.L. 1969. *Canadian Foreign Policy Since 1945: Middle Power or Satellite?* Toronto: Copp Clark.

Hawes, Michael K. 1984. *Principal Power, Middle Power, or Satellite?* Toronto: York Research Programme in Strategic Studies.

Keohane, Robert O., and Joseph S. Nye, Jr. 1977. *Power and Interdependence: World Politics in Transition*. Boston: Little, Brown.

Kirton, John J. 1993. "The Seven-Power Summit as a New Security Institution," pp. 335–57 in David Dewitt, David Haglund, and John Kirton, eds. *Building a New Global Order: Emerging Trends in International Security*. Don Mills, ON: Oxford University Press.

———. 2007. *Canadian Foreign Policy in a Changing World*. Toronto: Thomson Nelson.

———. 2009. "The Ten Most Important Books on Canadian Foreign Policy." *International Journal* 64 (Spring): 553–64. (Also reprinted in Duane Bratt and Christopher J. Kukucha, eds. *Readings in Canadian Foreign Policy: Classic Debates and New Ideas*. 2nd ed. Don Mills, ON: Oxford University Press, 2011.)

MacKay, R.A., and E.B. Rogers. 1938. *Canada Looks Abroad*. London: Oxford University Press.

Molot, Maureen Appel. 1990. "Where Do We, Should We, Or Can We Sit? A Review of Canadian Foreign Policy Literature," *International Journal of Canadian Studies* 1, 2 (Spring–Fall): 77–96.

Stairs, Denis. 1974. *The Diplomacy of Constraint: Canada, the Korean War, and the United States*. Toronto: University of Toronto Press.

Thordarson, Bruce. 1972. *Trudeau and Foreign Policy: A Study in Decision-Making*. Toronto: Oxford University Press.

Tomlin, Brian W., Norman Hillmer, and Fen Osler Hampson. 2008. *Canada's International Policies: Agendas, Alternatives, and Politics*. Don Mills, ON: Oxford University Press.

Waltz, Kenneth N. 1979. *Theory of International Politics*. Reading, MA: Addison-Wesley.

Zakaria, Fareed. 2008. *The Post-American World*. New York: W.W. Norton & Co.

6 The Choice to Be Made

Stephen Clarkson

Key Terms

Independent Foreign Policy
Nationalists

Quiet Diplomacy

In most cases, disagreements over Canadian foreign policy appear to revolve round matters of fact. *Continentalists* believe that our membership in NATO increases our political influence, while *nationalists* reject the link between the Atlantic alliance and Canada's international effectiveness. Yet only part of the dispute is really concerned with "hard facts." The major points at issue are questions of evaluation and interpretation. We can establish as facts what amounts of money and manpower we devote to our NATO commitments, but this does not *prove* continentalists right in their contention that our contribution of guns and troops increases Canada's power in West Europe or Washington. Nor does it *prove* **nationalists**' contrary thesis that the influence we may have is not worth the cost that would better be devoted to peacekeeping through an international police force. In both cases the authors are really invoking the support of conflicting assumptions to which they make the tacit appeal that political influence through collective action is desirable in continentalists' view (insignificant in nationalists'), that the communist threat is serious (or unreal), that the Atlantic area is more (or less) important to Canada than the under-developed world, and so on . . . .

Two Alternatives

Once we recognize this, we can see that the key to the often confusing debate on what Canadian foreign policy should be can be found in the underlying clash between two opposing foreign policy theories. Each theory contains a complete, if implicit, explanation of the world situation and of Canada's role in it, including a view of the American relationship and a statement of objectives for Canadian diplomacy. Let's follow current fashion and call the contending theories *quiet* and *independent*. By the *quiet* foreign policy approach I mean the official policy as expressed in statements, the government's practice as seen over the last five years, and the image projected by our diplomats in their execution of this policy. Although [what] is referred to throughout this book as an **independent foreign policy** has not been systematically articulated as a coherent doctrine, I shall present briefly what appear to me to be the major positions of each theory in order to crystallize their differences and so make possible a choice between these opposing approaches to Canada's foreign policy.

The International Situation

Quiet Approach

As in the late 1940s and 1950s, the world is still polarized along ideological lines between the forces of Communism and the West. Despite the splits in the Marxist–Leninist bloc, the defence of the free world is still the major priority. Revolution is a continuing threat to world stability, especially in the under-developed continents of Asia, Africa, and Latin America. This makes it all the more important to contain Communism in Vietnam and Cuba lest the whole Third World fall to the Reds like a row of dominoes. The United States is the only power able to pursue a containment policy on a world-wide basis. Its allies must support this effort.

Independent Approach

The stabilization of Soviet and European communism has reduced the former Communist military threat to the West, turning the Cold War into a cold peace. The major world problem is no longer the East–West ideological confrontation but the North–South economic division of the world into rich and poor. Revolution is less a Red menace than an aspect of achieving the urgently needed socio-economic transformations in the under-developed world; in any case it is no direct threat to our society. Naive American impulses to save the world from Communism are misguided, out of date, and a menace to world peace. The breakdown of the monolithic unity of both the Communist and Western blocs gives middle powers like Canada greater margins for independent manoeuvre.

Canada's National Interests

Quiet Approach

As a Western, democratic, and industrial country, Canada's national interests are essentially similar to those of our continental neighbour and friend, the United States, which is still the arsenal and defender of the free world. Worrying about national unity is of far less importance than pulling our weight in the Atlantic alliance. Collective security is the only defence against new Hitlers or Stalins; we must not forget the lessons of 1939 and 1948.

Independent Approach

A less ideologically but more socially concerned view of the world shows that Canada's national

interests coincide more with general progress than with the maintenance of the United States superpower status. Our external economic and political interest in trade with Communist countries diverges from American restrictions against "trading with the enemy." Canada's internal political divisions and our national identity crisis create another urgent national task for our policy: reinforce Canada's sense of bicultural personality.

Independence

Quiet Approach

Foreign policy independence is an illusion in the present-day world unless it is defined as head-in-the-sand isolation. We might just as well try to cut Canada off from North America and float out into the Atlantic. Independence must also mean a narrow and harmful anti-Americanism.

Independent Approach

Far from being illusory, independence—being able to control one's own socio-economic environment—is an essential condition for the healthy development of the nation-state. Independence means neither isolation nor anti-Americanism, unless making up our own minds on the merits of individual foreign policies is considered un-American.

Interdependence

Quiet Approach

Relations of interdependence are the situations within which middle powers must normally operate. Alliances and supranational organizations provide Canada with the best way to exercise influence and be useful in day-to-day international affairs. Ties of interdependence also guarantee weaker powers [protection] against arbitrary action by the strong, both by binding the superpowers to listen and by giving the small a forum within which to unite their forces.

Independent Approach

Obligations freely undertaken in cooperation with other countries are perfectly legitimate if they improve both the national and the world situation, for example, IMF or GATT. Interdependence can create new opportunities that can be exploited to further the national interest commercially and increase our influence diplomatically. Fulfilling our many international commitments is the staple of our diplomatic activity and the means of building our influence. But we must be ready to use this credit when initiatives are needed. Too much interdependence can become glorified dependence.

International Objectives

Quiet Approach

In the light of this analysis of the international situation and our national interests, we should strive to defend the status quo, nurturing our influence in Washington and helping maintain the solidarity of the Western alliance as the expression of our commitment to internationalism and the defence of democracy. Our order of priorities should be the American relationship first, then the Atlantic Alliance, finally the developing countries. All our actions should keep in mind the central importance of collective actions as the appropriate activity of a middle power.

Independent Approach

Given the more relaxed international environment and our internal need for a more distinctive foreign activity, Canadian objectives should outgrow our anti-communism to embrace the aims of international equality and socio-economic modernization. This may entail more economic sacrifice and more tolerance of revolutionary change, but an enlightened nationalism requires re-evaluating our aims in terms of the most pressing needs of the whole world and will refuse to hide behind any alliance apron strings. Accordingly the "third world" should now come first in our priorities as the affairs of the Atlantic community can more easily take care of themselves. Our American relationship should not prejudice these international priorities.

Overall Foreign Policy Strategy

Quiet Approach

Our general strategy should be affiliation, or close alignment and cooperation, with our superpower neighbour to achieve maximum diplomatic power by our influence on the Western bloc leader. We can only enjoy this influence by accepting the American foreign policy framework and restraining our urge to criticize the Americans. This then gives us access to the inner corridors of US power.

Independent Approach

Canada is too unimportant in Washington's worldview for us to have significant direct influence on American foreign policy. Our strategy should be to act directly in a given situation after making an independent evaluation of the problem. Except for continental matters of direct Canadian–American concern, influence on Washington would normally be a secondary objective. Even then, our power to affect Washington's policy will depend on our international effectiveness, not our allegedly "special" relationship.

Tactics to Implement the Strategy

Quiet Approach

Quiet diplomacy describes the foreign policy method most appropriate to implement an affiliation strategy. It puts special emphasis on confidential, friendly contacts with our allies, primarily the Americans, so that any differences that may arise are ironed out before they can reach crisis proportions and come out in the open. American views should be anticipated and taken into consideration as part of our own policy-making. Publicity is to be avoided, as are public declarations of criticism by our leader. Rather, our role should be to seek common ground between those in disagreement.

Independent Approach

Communications between our diplomats and those of other countries are by definition quiet. Carrying on our routine diplomatic business will therefore be unobtrusive. But there is no reason to make quietness a cardinal feature of our foreign policy, for this is to renounce in advance one of the most effective of a small power's bargaining tools: the use of exposure and public pressure to strengthen our position against a big power. If we have something to say and want to be heard, we must speak up. In dealing with the State Department, which has dozens of importunate allies to cope with, not to mention its enemies, the demure may earn some gratitude from harried American diplomats. It does not follow that the "smooth" diplomat will get more response than his "raucous" rival.

Foreign Policy Style

Quiet Approach

Our international style for quiet diplomacy should be that of the discreet professionals who operate outside the glare of the TV lights and the prying eye of the press in close harmony with the diplomats of our allies, unobtrusively husbanding our stock of goodwill and influence. This would maintain our credit as a responsible friend in Washington, preserve our special access to inside information and so maximize our ability to affect American policy-making when we do disagree privately with it.

Independent Approach

A hush-puppy style may be proper for our diplomats but is not the manner that our political leaders should adopt if they want to reinforce the Canadian identity. Without having to bang their shoes on the United Nations podium they could adopt a more assertive stance that makes clear Canada's existence as a bicultural nation with a unique set of policies. It is unrealistic not to be concerned with the "public relations" aspect of our foreign policy, since the way we present ourselves in the world—our international image—has a direct bearing on our international effectiveness. To this extent, it is true that the posture of independence is a vital part of the policy.

The American Relationship

Quiet Approach

As it is this relationship that gives Canada special influence through our geographical, political, and psychological proximity, nurturing the American relationship should have highest priority. We should not question the ultimate goals of the United States that has, after all, world-wide responsibilities for the defence of the free world. In addition we must realize that Canada cannot survive economically without the goodwill of the Americans upon whom we depend for our high standard of living. It would be "counterproductive" to try to influence American policies by publicly opposing them. This would only reinforce the extremist elements advocating the policies we opposed.

Independent Approach

Our relations with the United States are "special" because of the disparity of our power and the degree to which we depend on American trade and capital inflows. We should for this reason devote careful attention to our relations, especially if we are planning international moves of which they do not approve. The huge military and political power of the US should make us particularly critical of American policies however well-intentioned the Average American may be. Our well-being is not a product of bounteous concessions made by the US but of economic development considered to be to both countries' advantage. Our relationship should be governed by this awareness of mutual benefit. There is no evidence that independent actions strengthen extremism in the US. If we really wish to influence American public opinion, we have to make it clear what policy we advocate. There is no better way than actually pursuing it.

Retaliation

Quiet Approach

We are so dependent on the American economy that we cannot afford to do anything that might annoy them, such as taking some foreign policy initiative that displeases Congress or the administration. The price of independence would be a 25 per cent drop in our standard of living. . . . We are, after all, the little pig that must be eternally vigilant lest the big pig roll over. . . . We cannot increase this risk by provoking it to roll deliberately. In such areas as the Defence Production Sharing Agreements we gain enormously from being able to bid on American defence contracts. The share of the US market we have won pays for our own purchases of American war material at prices cheaper than we could produce it ourselves. We cannot afford the luxury of independence, whatever our conscience might say, since independent actions might jeopardize these arrangements.

Independent Approach

The possibility of retaliation is present in all international relationships. It is true that we are more vulnerable to American than the US is to Canadian retaliation, but we must not forget that retaliation is a reaction of last resort showing that all milder negotiation has failed. By being willing to use the whole armoury of diplomatic weapons—bilateral and multilateral, informal and public—we could reduce the dangers of retaliation conjured up by the all-or-nothing approach of quiet diplomacy. We must realize that as the little power, we have important advantages. We can concentrate our whole attention on defending our interests in the continental relationship, which, from the American point of view, is but one of dozens of issues of greater importance. We have important hostages in Canada, the very subsidiaries that are the instruments of US political and economic pressure. We can also use the threat of mobilizing public opinion to strengthen our hand against possible intimidation and economic blackmail. Our goodwill and our favourable image in the United States as a long-standing friend is a further asset we should not ignore.

Internal Impact of Foreign Policy

Quiet Approach

The internal implications of our diplomacy are negligible and should remain so. Foreign policy should be practised to achieve specific external goals and not to boost the national ego. If Canadians have an identity problem, they should cure it themselves, not resort to artificial stimulation. Similarly, we should not let our concern for internal problems of biculturalism distort our foreign policy. External affairs and internal politics should be kept in their proper places. Quebec should not drag foreign policy into its federal arguments with Ottawa.

Independent Approach

It is impossible to dissociate external from internal policies if only because external relations are carried out by all branches of government—finance, commerce, defence, and citizenship are involved and even the provinces, quite apart from external affairs. Foreign policy must in any case be seen as only one aspect of the government's total network of policies. We cannot afford *not* to exploit the nation-building potential of our foreign policies, since the way others perceive us—dynamic and bicultural, or ineffectual and divided—can strengthen, or undermine, our own national identity. Similarly, if we accept French-Canadian desires for cultural equality and Quebec's demands for greater self-control, our foreign policy should reflect and reinforce Canada's new binational politics.

The "quiet" approach to our foreign policy is not an extremist absurdity, however unlike most nations' foreign policy doctrines it may appear. It is the rationale of Canadian diplomacy. The over-riding concern for kid-glove relations with our American neighbours was articulated in 1965 by the Merchant-Heeney Report with all the hallmarks of official policy. The feeling of economic dependence is not an opposition charge but a situation acknowledged by the prime minister himself.[1] The surprisingly unsophisticated cold warrior analysis complete with the domino theory of Asian communism is heard time after time from our diplomats, both senior officers and newly inducted recruits. In our discussions with these foreign service officers during our ULSR [University League for Social Reform] seminars, we found them cut off from the Canadian public whose views they take to be adequately expressed by *Globe and Mail* editorials or questions posed in the House of Commons. More disconcerting is the professionals' scorn for the amateur that colours their attitude toward the value of the public's opinion. Quiet diplomacy is enshrined as the conventional wisdom of our federal political establishment.

Independence Yes, Quiet Diplomacy No

However accepted this doctrine may be, I would submit that it is no longer suitable for Canadian foreign policy in the late sixties. It is inappropriate, first of all, for the reasons stated in the "independent" replies to the "quiet" positions summarized above: its view of the world is 10 years out of date; its understanding of Canada's international needs and capabilities is hopelessly circumscribed.

"Quiet" foreign policy is also unacceptable in a mass democracy. If, to be effective, our quiet foreign policy must be carried on in complete secrecy so that even its successes should not be known lest they compromise further success . . . how are the voters ever to know whether the policy is justified? Are they simply to accept the protestations of diligence and sincerity by the minister of external affairs or the prime minister and the assurances of our diplomats, all claiming to plead impartially in their own cause? Until all the files are open . . . we cannot know for sure. But even then, how would proof be certain? To be sure that the quiet approach had been the more effective, it would be necessary to show what results the independent approach would have produced in exactly the same circumstances—an obviously impossible condition. We cannot wait 50 years for the files to be open, even if they did promise final proof. Quiet diplomacy has been practised long enough for the onus to be on its defenders to demonstrate their case. The record does not lend them very strong support. Such a diplomatic success as Pearson's constructive role in the 1956 Suez crisis is an example of independent initiative, well-conceived at an appropriate time . . . .

When the defenders of quiet diplomacy expound on our influence in Washington, their argument raises more doubts. To start with, they are hard put to provide empirical evidence of Canada's power to make Washington act in the way we want. They go on to insist that this putative special influence in Washington is the basis for Canada's power in other countries who take us seriously, because they assume we have a unique path to American waiting chambers. But they then warn that we should not actually try to use this influence for this would undermine this special position and so our international status. Strange logic, a sophisticated rationalization for inaction. Influence is like credit: it has to be used to exist. The quiet diplomatists manage to underrate Canada's real power to act by exaggerating our potential influence.

The alternative to quiet diplomacy is not "raising a row"; it is developing an independent foreign policy. Independence means above all striving for maximum effectiveness. Those times when Canada has been most clearly effective it has acted directly, achieving negotiations in Korea or the exclusion of South Africa from the Commonwealth. This means neither that it acted alone nor against a big power. Kicking Uncle Sam in the shins or twisting the lion's tail has no necessary part in any of Canada's more independent actions. Canadians are not even aware that our enlightened aid program toward Tanzania was pushed forward despite Dar-es-Salaam's rupture of relations with Britain. Such acts are satisfactory because they are effective. They are effective because the Canadian initiative itself contributed directly to achieve the particular goal. They achieved this goal because in these situations the Canadian government acted flexibly; not out of deference or automatic loyalty to another power. To act flexibly means to make up one's own mind—to be independent.

To make independence the standard for our foreign policy is not to opt out of the many undramatic areas of collective diplomacy in which Canada makes a continuing major contribution at a supranational level. Nor does independence imply anti-Americanism, however much the bogey of "making a row" is raised. Deciding policies on their own merits may well lead to disagreement with American policy. Still there is no reason to inflate such policy disagreements to disastrous proportions unless the defendants of quiet diplomacy really believe the Americans to be the most vindictive politicians on earth . . . . [W]we have followed a line directly counter to American policy on a problem of the highest sensitivity, Cuba, and still not suffered retaliation. The point is that if we diverge, it is not for the sake of a quarrel but to practise what we feel to be the correct policy, after due consideration of the Americans' reasons. It is hard to believe that a more assertive Canadian foreign policy would be countered in Washington by a concerted anti-Canadian policy. The more truculent General de Gaulle has become, the gentler has been the Americans' treatment of France. With so much direct investment in Canada, it is unlikely that the Americans, in Baldwin's phrase, would want to get rid of a blemish on the finger by amputating the arm.

Independence also requires realism in our conception of the American relationship. Our interactions with the US are so intense and multitudinous at all levels of political, economic, cultural, and personal contact that we should make a fundamental distinction between our foreign policies on one hand and our American policies on the other. While pursuing what we consider to be the best policy abroad, it is in our interest to place the strongest emphasis on the maintenance of good neighbourly relations with the US. In all matters of mutual concern, whether financial investment, tariff policy, resource development, or cultural interchange, the policies of both countries toward each other must continue to be formulated in close consultation. We clearly have an essential unity of self-interests with the Americans in our continental partnership. But partnership requires equality, and equality implies independence . . . .

An independent foreign policy is an ethically just policy. Continentalists attack the critics of quiet diplomacy for being "ostentatiously on the side of virtue, regardless of practical consequences." One can heartily agree that a "tub-thumping moralistic approach" is distasteful and that a disregard for practical consequences is irresponsible. Yet an argument for independence is not *moralistic* for raising *moral* problems.

Nationalists argue that an independent approach is necessarily more ethical for it requires an autonomous calculation for every policy of the probable consequences both for Canada and for those our policy will affect. It is the defenders of quiet diplomacy who are open to the charge of moralism if they cling dogmatically to a moral judgment of American policy made 20 years ago.

An independent foreign policy also presupposes responsibility. As only a free man is considered responsible for his actions, only a nation which makes its own decisions can be considered in charge of its destiny and can expect its citizenry to believe in its integrity. And like the youth who can only develop maturely if they liberate themselves from parental controls, the nation-state can only achieve full expression if it is master in its own house, able to act in the community of nations as a fully responsible entity.

The Problem of Reform

If independence is more desirable as an overall guideline for our foreign policy, why is quietness still the guiding light of Canadian diplomacy? Not from American pressure. Nor for lack of international scope, particularly in the under-developed world. The conclusion must be that the problem is here at home. Yet we can hardly blame public opinion. The opinion polls, for all their inaccuracies, indicate that the general public's views have been consistently more nationalist on foreign policy issues like Vietnam, the Dominican Republic, and China than the government.[2] All the major parties have, at the very least, strong wings in favour of a more independent diplomacy. Predominant editorial opinion, church statements, students groups, and academic protests complete the general picture of a public opinion that increasingly rejects quietness.

It would be superficial to conclude with facile exhortations to the leadership to change its policy.

The conditions are so favourable for an independent foreign policy that the persistence of a quiet approach indicates more fundamental problems are involved. If we are to make some proposals for reform, we must assess the underlying reasons for this anomalous state of affairs. These are threefold and interconnected: a decision-making structure that isolates the government from public participation and control; an elitist ideology for the civil service that legitimizes this insulation; and a leadership that perpetuates this situation.

The foreign policy-making process is almost completely sealed off from the normal give and take between public and government. Even members of Parliament have no significant access to this "closed circuit." In a recent article surveying the problems of the Department of External Affairs, the undersecretary of state for external affairs, Marcel Cadieux, deals quite extensively with his relationship with the minister. Yet, with the exception of consulting university specialists, he makes no mention of the contribution that members of the public, parliamentarians included, can make to the formation of the nation's foreign policy. "Without public understanding," he concedes, "we can hardly hope to develop Canada's role in world affairs."[3] He doesn't seem to feel that the public has any greater part to play than to stand and wait, deferentially yet comprehendingly, in the spectators' boxes.

It is institutional security from criticism that makes quiet diplomacy the natural ideology of the diplomatic caste. It gives a theoretical justification for the handling of all business by routine bureaucratic channels. If foreign policy is the private domain of the administrator, he or she need not take seriously clamour, interest group opinion, or, God forbid, parliamentary interference. Public discussion of foreign policy problems is fine and even desirable, our diplomats will hasten to profess, so long as it does not disturb their professional activity.

The crucial link in this combination of institutional isolation and bureaucratic elitism is its endorsement by the leadership. Paradoxically the Liberal leaders bring an unprecedented background of experience to their handling of foreign affairs. Yet Mr Pearson, the Nobel Prize winner, has turned the "unobtrusive oil can" tactics, which led to his own international successes in the mid-fifties, into a dogma which frustrates the continuation of this early record. Mr Martin, for all his concern for his public image, is unable to convey to the nation a convincing and unambiguous understanding of what Canada can achieve internationally and has not been able to transmit the growing public concern for foreign policy questions into revised governmental policies. Nor has he shown any sign of opening the major issues of foreign policy, such as the decision to renew the NORAD agreement, to public debate in parliament. Institutions, ideology, and leadership: we have here a troika of conditions that require basic reforms and changes. Yet remedies cannot be solely of relevance to our foreign policy. We face a general problem of Canadian democracy—the responsiveness of governmental policy and the civil service to public scrutiny and control. Reforms needed in this area of public policy are needed in other branches as well:

> All bureaucracy is conservative, but the conservatism of diplomatic bureaucracy is in a class by itself. The ethos of diplomacy is an ethos of suspicion—suspicion tempered by skepticism, snow tempered by ice. The foreign service officer is a nay-sayer in statecraft, the abominable no-man of diplomacy. His mission in life is to preserve the status quo from those who propose to alter it.[4]

. . . [T]he problem of foreign policy change is the problem of subjecting bureaucratic inertia to some reasonable form of public control.

Let the Public in

The first step is to open the process of policy-forming so that the expression of expert, informed, and articulate opinions can have a major impact on foreign policy-making. Yet in this age of McLuhan, our channels for public participation in politics are still using a Walter Bagehot technology. Gallup polls give irregular insights into public views on simplified issues, but their findings are ignored unless politically exploitable. A partial solution is to put the measuring of attitudes on a regular and scientific basis, possibly by a research institute that would, by continuous sampling, make "what public opinion wants" no longer a subject for guesswork. More important, structural change such as the activation of the parliamentary committee on foreign affairs. . .could institutionalize the public scrutiny of foreign policy in a way compatible with the parliamentary system. To be meaningful, the committee would need a full-time research staff and would have to be able to require testimony from expert and interested groups as well as diplomats. While such a watchdog committee could not actually make policy, the defence committee hearings on tri-service unification have proved that basic public issues can be brought out into the open for thorough airing. The hearings would also provide our diplomats with a link to articulate opinion; they would start to see themselves as public servants rather than tight-lipped agents.

Another by-product would be important, if intangible. Coverage of the committee hearings by mass media would help give the public a sense of being involved in this hitherto exclusive area of policy. Other ways should be initiated to increase the public's interest in foreign policy.

If our foreign activity is to have the strength of public participation, the public must be sufficiently informed. Never have ordinary people been so exposed by instant communications to international events, so bombarded with journalistic commentary and academic debate. Never have they had such a high level of education to absorb this information. But the data on Canadian foreign policy with which the public could come to policy conclusions is not made available. The change that is needed here is less quantitative than qualitative. To make public opinion aware of Canada's foreign policy problems, mass media and newspaper reports must relate their analysis of foreign affairs to Canadian external activity.

Civil Masters or Civil Servants?

To change from a quiet to a more independent approach to our foreign policy will require a transformation of the values of the practitioners, the diplomats in the Department of External Affairs. So long as the personnel of external affairs maintain a secretive, distrustful attitude toward the public, an independent foreign policy is doubly stymied. An informed, alert public opinion cannot be developed if extensive, relevant information is not made regularly and easily available. As long as external affairs maintains its Mandarin mystique explicitly tied to quiet diplomacy and anti-communism, the civil servants would be likely to block the implementation of an alternative foreign policy, even if the government should desire it.

To change our diplomats from civil masters to civil servants will require a change in their ideology. A partial measure is to modify the environment they enter when they are recruited into the service so that the values they absorb conform to the desire of the public and the views of the leadership. In France, for example, recruits to all branches of the upper civil service receive three full years of practical and theoretical training at the National Administration School where they absorb the dynamic, nationalist values of the French state and so start their career as activist, not conservative, civil servants. The excellence and dynamism of the French civil service is one of the principal reasons for the impact of de Gaulle's foreign policy in Europe. Rather than have our new diplomats absorb willy-nilly the smug, conservative attitudes of the established bureaucracy, an introductory training program—needed in any case to improve technical and linguistic competence—could give them an awareness of the role that the political leadership wants Canada to play and a consciousness of the challenge of achieving these goals in a democratic framework.

To prevent the diplomats from becoming cut off from public and informed opinion they need continual "professional retraining" just as any doctor or engineer. Sabbatical leaves for research and senior staff officer courses are needed if our international crisis managers are to keep up intellectually with the rate of change of the crises they are entrusted to manage.

Leadership from the Top

No change in our diplomats' value system and no structural reform will be very productive without a third innovation: dynamic leadership. The muddling through of the quiet approach will continue until Canada's leaders realize that determination and a clear articulation of political objectives are needed to turn potentiality into reality. Canada is wealthy, strong, and developed. It does not need the mountain-moving voluntarism of Mao Tse-Tung. It simply needs a leadership that can make it clear to the public—if not in a little *Red Book* at least in a *White Paper*—what role Canada can play and how its objectives are to be achieved. This would give a sense of direction to the unusual talents in our diplomatic service and harness the force of public opinion behind this effort.

Partnership with Quebec

It is finally necessary to remove the uncertainty overshadowing the future of confederation. Although Quebec nationalism has made a major contribution to the development of a more independent Canadian activity, particularly in starting an aid program to the French-speaking African states, the open diplomatic warfare between Ottawa and Quebec that broke out in conjunction with de Gaulle's visit to Quebec is rapidly becoming self-destructive.

It is time to come to some firm decision whether or not Quebec can satisfy its international aspirations as a special province in the federation acting both through Ottawa and autonomously in its areas of provincial jurisdiction. This is essentially an issue for Quebecers to decide, though their compatriots can reasonably urge that the debate be fair and full before any irrevocable step is taken. It is for the French-Canadian intellectuals to spell out the costs and benefits of special status in the federation versus complete separation. Their English-speaking colleagues can point out, however, why they would like Quebec to stay in the effort to develop a new foreign policy. Not only does Quebec's wealth add strength to Canada's foreign power but, more importantly, Quebec's culture and technology makes it possible for the total Canadian international effort in the under-developed world to have a unique impact. But the only finally convincing argument is the demonstration that Ottawa can mount a foreign policy that would be more independent and more effective than the foreign role that Quebec could play by itself, as a single state. Quiet diplomacy has failed to provide this proof.

It is our belief that an independent foreign policy could give this proof to French and English Canadians alike by, first, rejecting its lingering anti-communism and downgrading the Cold War alliances while, second, redirecting its resources and redefining its priorities to a determined support for the political, economic, and social needs of the developing countries—both through its multilateral diplomacy in international organizations and by directly making Canada a "great power in foreign aid."[5]

The Public Should Choose

We need more open diplomats, we need more public participation in policy-making. But most of all we need to choose: between the quiet, continental foreign policy we have followed in the main over the past decade and an independent foreign policy.

Notes

1. Interview published in *Maclean's*, July 1967, 52.
2. Unpublished paper presented to the ULSR by Roman March, Carleton University.
3. Marcel Cadieux, "La Tache du Sous-Secrétaire d'État aux Affaires extérieures," *International Journal* 22, 3 (Summer 1967): 527.
4. James Eayrs, *Fate and Will in Foreign Policy* (Toronto: Canadian Broadcasting Corporation, 1967), 50.
5. A phrase coined by Escott Reid in a speech to the Kiwanis Club, Toronto, 27 September 1967, when he argued that Canadian aid should be expanded from $300 million to $1 billion in five years.

The Choices That Were Made and Those That Remain

Re-reading "The Choice to be Made"—the conclusion to the book, *An Independent Foreign Policy for Canada?*, that I edited four decades ago after organizing a year-long process of discussions between many Canadian diplomats and a cross-disciplinary group of younger academic colleagues—gave me a strange feeling. *Plus ça change*. And much has changed in Canada's international, continental, and domestic context. *Plus c'est la même chose*. And much also remains the same in our seemingly eternal debate about Canada's role in the world.

The Context: *Plus Ça Change*

Let's pass in review how things were back then, what's happened since, and how they are now in the three scales that condition the country's foreign policy: the global, the continental, and the domestic.

Global Balance of Forces

Forty years later, the global balance of forces then is almost unrecognizable compared to today. Then, in the late 1960s, the Cold War standoff between East and West seemed frozen forever.

Although some non-aligned countries in the developing world kept their distance from both camps, Canada, which was on the flight path for long-range bombers and intercontinental missiles between the Soviet Union and the United States, had no choice but to support the Pentagon's strategy, however mad—and the Mutually Assured Destruction on which the United States' second-strike nuclear-retaliation doctrine was based was, literally, mad. Even when outrage at the United States' imperialist efforts to force its will on Vietnam had Canadians demonstrating by the thousands outside American consulates, Ottawa dissented from Washington's policy at its peril, since the fear of US economic retaliation was the ever-present subtext of Canada's international disagreements with Uncle Sam.

Since then, with the collapse of the Soviet Union, the United States passed from being the hegemonic entity of the West—its capitalist partners had supported Washington's construction of a liberal global order after the Second World War—to being the hegemonic entity of the world: in 1995, the launch of the World Trade Organization (WTO) created a global economic order using a made-in-the-US rule book to which almost every country willingly subscribed.

Having been invited, on Pierre Trudeau's watch, to join the Economic Summit, the exclusive club of the seven most powerful states, Canada had been an actively contributing participant as the new trade regime was negotiated. Although its relative power in the global hierarchy declined with the rise of China, India, and Brazil, Ottawa occasionally managed to take the lead in brokering multilateral agreements such as the International Criminal Court and the treaty banning anti-personnel landmines, even in the face of Washington's opposition.

Now, following 9/11, when the United States subordinated its economically hegemonic role to its militarily imperialist persona, which unilaterally and arbitrarily tried to spread American values in the Middle East by force, poles of resistance have sprung up. The future economic colossus, China, is even threatening America's sense of energy security by buying a share in Alberta's oil resources.

Based as it was on evident misinformation and miscalculation, Washington's rogue behaviour in Iraq generated such dismay among the Canadian public that the country's political elite was obliged to back away from its default position of supporting the United States. And, even though Paul Martin vowed to repair the relations with the George W. Bush administration that he felt had been imprudently broken by his predecessor, Jean Chrétien, he was impelled by the public's distaste for Rumsfeld militarism to decline support to the US National Missile Defense program.

Canada's Position on the Continent

Much has changed in Canada's political economy position in North America. In the late 1960s, Canada was striving to find ways to reduce the bleeding caused by its US-owned economy by constructing a more nationally focused market that would be less vulnerable to damaging American actions.

Since then, a decade's experimentation with a more nationally focused industrial strategy flamed out in the early 1980s with the ambitious but disastrously timed National Energy Program. John Turner's self-immolation in the 1984 federal election handed power to Brian Mulroney who, having sworn to give Washington the benefit of the doubt, proceeded to join with then-President Ronald Reagan to sign a declaration of economic disarmament called the Canada–United States Free Trade Agreement (CUFTA). CUFTA locked Ottawa into a set of rules designed to subordinate the country's resources and manufactured production to the needs of the American economy.

Once Washington had established precedents to foreclose Canadian economic autonomy, it expanded the continental scope of what Ronald Reagan called the economic constitution of North America by including Mexico in this integrative régime. With the North American Free Trade Agreement (NAFTA) extending the WTO's massive and intrusive rules, Canada found itself saddled with an external constitution that sounded the death knell of an independent Canadian capitalism capable of competing with the United States. Canada's wealth remains dependent on pumping oil (for which the US thirst is insatiable), developing other economic niches (which are complementary but not competitive with US industries), hewing wood (which the US resists buying beyond the point that threatens rival US forestry interests), and, probably, drawing water (that is, diverting water southwards, an issue that is already on the agenda in the Great Lakes and southwestern states).

Now, following close to two decades of border-lowering economic integration, Canada has been hit with Washington's latest strategic doctrine, a "war on terror" focused on a border-raising, national security priority. Whereas Canadian leaders were able to dissent over the American position on Iraq, they have no freedom to diverge over its border policies because, in the Bush administration's view, security trumps trade. If Ottawa does not satisfy Washington that the Canada–US boundary is secure against terrorists—meaning that its immigration policies, its anti-terrorism secret policing, and its passport control processes meet with the approval of the Department of Homeland Security—the economic arteries that now flow from North to South will be blocked.

Canada's Domestic Scene

By 1968, the federal and provincial governments had put in place the health care system that was to become, with the Canadian flag, a defining element of Canada's national identity.

Since then, the relatively generous system of social-policy support for the unemployed, the poor, single parents, and the aged, which had been nurtured during the Trudeau years, came under attack by neoconservative budget slashing. The public's passion for health care, however, convinced politicians to restore those financial cuts. Meanwhile, Trudeau's immensely popular Charter of Rights and Freedoms gave millions of non-British and non-French immigrants a sense of security that theirs was not a second-class citizenship.

Now, differences between Canadian and American values grow ever greater. In sharp contrast to the fundamentalist conservatism espoused in the White House, the US Supreme Court, and the Congress, the Canadian government has followed the Canadian Supreme Court's lead by legalizing same-sex marriage and decriminalizing the possession of marijuana. These attitudinal differences underpin the continuing debate within Canada over its own foreign policy.

The Debate: *Plus C'est La Même Chose*

Canadian attitudes have changed little; Canadians remain anxiously obsessed with how to get along with their one and only neighbour in the face of its sometimes laudable but often destructive behaviour. As they look overseas, they remain worried about their standing in the rest of the world and how best to contribute to resolving its most urgent issues.

Interested academics, along with a limited number of journalists and civic-minded citizens, study how to understand these problems. The analytical and normative positions resulting from this consideration continue to fall into two distinct schools of thought, generating a debate that seems as irreconcilable as it is eternal.

Because its global, continental, and domestic context has changed, so too have the goalposts for the debate about Canada's foreign policy choices moved. Because the Cold War's demise has relieved Ottawa of the imperative to support the United States on the major issues, the foreign policy field it faces is considerably broader. But because the WTO and NAFTA have tied one hand behind the government's back and because there are very few economic sectors that remain under Canadian ownership and control, the field is also much shorter. Nevertheless, there are still two main schools of thought, two teams, as it were, which rally their supporters to propound opposing positions.

Continentalists

A century ago Canadian imperialists expounded the view that the Dominion of Canada's prime goal should be to retain its connection with the British Empire in order to guarantee its military security, its economic well-being, and its cultural identity. They reflected the interests of exporters who shipped their produce to Great Britain, importers who shipped consumer goods back across the Atlantic, the banking community that financed this commerce, and the intellectuals whose careers depended on nourishing their links with Oxford and Cambridge in the "mother country."

At that time, nationalists who wanted autonomy from the Empire looked to the United States as a progressive haven, relations with which could help burnish the Dominion's prospects as a self-sufficient and fast-growing, but more autonomous, society.

Four decades ago, the pattern had shifted: pro-British imperialists had become pro-American continentalists. Those wanting to extend relations with the United States were the dominant resource and manufacturing corporations for which continental integration promised economic salvation. Continentalists, as "The Choice to be Made" explained, admonished Canadians to support US foreign policy whether it was right or wrong. As the hearth of freedom in the Cold War, Washington should not be criticized. Furthermore, Canada's influence in the world depended on proving its influence in Washington's corridors of power. Being on the inside—pulling our own weight, being seen as sound—was the precondition for being effective in international forums. Even when we disagreed with Washington, we were advised not to speak our mind lest we risk being punished. Continental integration should be accelerated, they argued, since the interdependence of the two economies provided Canada with some insurance against Washington's arbitrary action; if it tried to punish Canada, the United States would really be harming its own interests.

Since then, the same logic pushed Ottawa to negotiate CUFTA and NAFTA and abandon the previous strategy of developing a self-standing economy.

Now, in the aftermath of 9/11, Canadian continentalists have made the same arguments. Ottawa should support US military policy in Iraq and the National Missile Defense, not because these are sensible policies but because Canada might be punished for not toeing the American line. Canada's global influence depends on being seen as insiders in Washington where our advice is heeded. Criticizing American policy, they argue, will only alienate our American interlocutors and be self-defeating.

Nationalists

The economic nationalist position has long been ambivalent. While admired by some for its great social, technological, and intellectual achievements, the United States was also seen as a threat to Canadian security. Interdependence really meant a dependence that shut down the possibility for creative action abroad. Rather than practising "quiet diplomacy," nationalists felt that Ottawa should develop a public diplomacy that spoke its mind. This could be valuable itself in buttressing Canadians' sense of their bilingual and multicultural identity.

Since then, nationalists have been mainly on the losing side of the debate. While they could take some comfort from Pierre Trudeau's occasional forays on the world scene and from Brian Mulroney's defiance of both Margaret Thatcher and Ronald Reagan over apartheid in South Africa, they had to mourn their two defeats over free trade and resign themselves to the country's economic-policy castration and consequently to its ever-closer and dependent integration in the American system.

Lloyd Axworthy's surprisingly successful ventures in low-cost niche diplomacy—the International Criminal Court and the landmine treaty—proved the nationalist view that public diplomacy could produce effective foreign policy. But the Department of Foreign Affairs and International Trade had been too drained of funds, personnel, and morale from years of neoconservative budget-cutting for Axworthy's muscular "damn-the-torpedoes" approach to continue under other leadership.

Now, the nationalists enjoy a clear, if temporary, advantage. The American application of unilateral, pre-emptive war in Iraq has proven such a patent disaster that "ready-aye-ready" solidarity with George Bush has almost no traction outside the boardrooms of the Canadian Council of Chief Executives (CCCE). Even the CCCE has been consternated by Washington's blatant disregard of its NAFTA commitments in defying dispute panel rulings that remanded US countervailing and anti-dumping duties levied against Canadian softwood lumber exports. Other examples of Washington's unprincipled protectionism—most glaringly, its prolonged ban on imports of Canadian beef—make continentalist arguments a hard sell. Nevertheless, Canada remains locked into its external constitution, just as its negotiators intended. Advocates of greater autonomy have few power levers at their command.

In the final analysis, the Canadian foreign policy debate between continentalists and nationalists remains just as unresolvable as that between the ideological right and left in domestic politics. The two schools are rooted in different value systems and support opposing corporate and citizen interests. Deploying actual evidence has little effect. Turning to the reforms advocated four decades ago, it is clear that much of what I recommended then has actually been implemented. White papers have been written on foreign policy issues, Parliament's Standing Committee on Foreign Affairs and International Trade has held hearings across the country on the major issues facing Canada and produced substantial reports, and public opinion polls are constantly commissioned in order to take the electorate's pulse.

The mandarinate—the diplomatic elite which kept its foreign policy cards close to its vest—has vanished, and its place of dominance over Canadian foreign policy has been assumed by trade policy analysts inspired by an equally exclusive and arrogant ideology. It was the reverse takeover of the old Department of External Affairs in 1982, when the trade commissioners were moved to Sussex Drive from the Department of Industry, Trade, and Commerce, which led to Canadian foreign policy being hijacked by a mania for free trade agreements. Similar to the old Ottawa mandarinate in their anti-democratic elitism, but inspired by a messianic and economics-based faith in neoconservative market deregulation, they drove out considerations of Canada's national interests as a global power in order to hitch the country to America's destiny.

Now that the future of the United States seems decidedly less rosy; now that India, Brazil, and even Mexico are moving up the power hierarchy behind China; now that many Canadians have taken the future into their own hands by operating across national borders in non-government organizations that are directly coping with pandemics and rebuilding failed states, the continentalist–nationalist debate has taken on a renewed relevance. If the United States has become a rogue imperial power whose policies exacerbate rather than remedy global warming, expand rather than contain nuclear proliferation, provoke rather than stifle terrorism, and speed rather than slow the spread of HIV/AIDS, there is a powerful argument to "go around" the United States, as former Defense Secretary Robert McNamara recently urged the international community.

Many foreign policy choices have been made over the past four decades, but many still remain to be made day by day and year by year. Given the ineradicably deep gaps separating the normative positions of continentalists and nationalists, what choices Ottawa should make will continue to be debated. Forty years from now, it would be surprising if the debate had been definitively resolved. With luck, students and scholars in the middle of the twenty-first century will conclude that the choices made in this period contributed to averting the social, economic, and environmental disasters that were facing both Canadians and the world during this century's first decade.

Questions for Review

1. What is Clarkson's distinction between the quiet approach and the independent approach? Why is it important to make internal and international distinctions when applying these approaches?
2. How has Stephen Clarkson's perspective changed in his update? Does Canada remain a satellite today?
3. Does Clarkson still identify continentalists and nationalists in Canada's contemporary foreign policy? If so, why does this remain an important distinction?

Suggested Readings

Bow, Brian, and Patrick Lennox, eds. 2008. *An Independent Foreign Policy for Canada? Challenges and Choices for the Future.* Toronto: University of Toronto Press.

Clarkson, Stephen, ed. 1968. *An Independent Foreign Policy For Canada?* Toronto: McClelland and Stewart.

Clarkson, Stephen. 2002. *Uncle Sam and Us: Globalization, Neoconservatism, and the Canadian State.* Toronto: University of Toronto Press.

Clarkson, Stephen. 2011. *Dependent America? How Canada and Mexico Construct U.S. Power.* Toronto: University of Toronto Press.

The "Independence" Debates, Then and Now: False Choices and Real Challenges

Brian Bow and Patrick Lennox

UPDATE

Key Terms

Quiet Diplomacy   Special Relationship

The advent of the Obama era in American diplomacy seemed to bring with it much hope for a more ambitious and proactive Canadian foreign policy. Unshackled from George W. Bush's "with us or against us" mindset, and inspired by Barack Obama's promise to rebuild America's reputation abroad through multilateral engagement, Canada might have been expected to try to reinvigorate a stagnant foreign policy that had gotten bogged down in—and devolved almost exclusively into—the bloody counter-insurgency in southern Afghanistan. But the Harper government instead turned its focus inward, and Canadian voters seemed not merely acceptant, but generally approving.

Through much of this decade, most Canadians were confident their country was on steady ground but worried that the United States under the Bush administration was headed for trouble (particularly, but not only, in Iraq). So there were frequent calls for Canada to break away from the United States and pursue a more "independent" foreign policy. These calls fell silent in late 2008 and early 2009, however, with the election of a popular new president and the onset of the ongoing global recession. International political challenges were multiplying, but Ottawa was caught up in the petty intrigues that go with minority government, and the Canadian public wanted its leaders to focus on getting the country's financial house in order. To the extent that Canada has actually had a foreign policy over the last couple of years, it has mainly centred on efforts to try to limit casualties until the clock runs out on our commitment to Kandahar; to negotiate bilateral trade or investment agreements wherever that seemed relatively easy; and generally to follow America's diplomatic lead on global finance, climate change, the Honduras coup, and reconstruction in Haiti.

The debate over whether Canada can and should pursue an "independent" foreign policy, in other words, has faded into the background for now; but it is only a matter of time before it erupts again. It is a natural, possibly inescapable, side effect of Canada's unique position in the world, which is always simmering on the edge of Canada's political consciousness, and flares up from time to time into a full-blown existential crisis. Because Canada is profoundly dependent on the United States for its prosperity, its security, and its capacity to have a significant impact on the wider world, Canadians recognize a need to stick close to the Americans, to try to influence them, and to avoid provoking them. However, because of that very same dependency, because there are subtle differences between Canadian and American political cultures, and because Canada doesn't face the same global strategic challenges that the US does, Canadians also have an impulse—particularly in times when the two countries seem to be going in markedly different directions—to try to increase self-reliance, to find new international partners, and to make a show of pursuing different priorities.

In the 1960s, the war in Vietnam raised doubts about Canada's traditional commitment to work closely with the US and prompted Canadian nationalists to demand a more "independent" foreign policy. But proponents of the traditional approach pushed back, arguing that striking an independent posture would bring few tangible gains and might come at a high price, in terms of lost influence and lost economic advantages. Stephen Clarkson summarized this wide-ranging debate in terms of a dichotomy between the proponents of **quiet diplomacy** and the advocates of "independence." His characterization of the debate gives us a good sense of the battle lines in 1968, and we can see strikingly similar divides in the more recent debates about how Canada ought to relate to the Bush administration, particularly in the controversy over whether or not Canada should support the US-led invasion of Iraq.

But, as we argued in our 40-years-later revisiting of the "independence" debate, Clarkson's stark dichotomy oversimplified and distorted the original debate, and pulled our attention away from other, more crucial challenges for Canadian foreign policy.

In Clarkson's summary, the proponents of quiet diplomacy are portrayed as inflexible, timid, and generally out of step with the major historical developments of the day. They are so caught up in the Cold War rivalry that they cannot see the emergence of a new global order in which Canada might play new roles and have new partners. The advocates of independence, on the other hand, are wonderfully clever and brave, having apparently figured out not only how to resolve all of the inherent dilemmas haunting Canadian foreign policy-makers, but how to do so in a way that would satisfy Canadians' moral convictions, and even reconcile the clashing priorities of Canada's various regions and ethnic groups. Setting aside the question of whether the "independentists" of the late 1960s really had all the answers, it's important to be clear that their "quiet diplomacy" rivals weren't nearly as hidebound and morally bankrupt as Clarkson made them out to be. Most of those arguing for maintaining Canada's traditional partnership with the US didn't like the Vietnam War any more than their critics did, but judged that Canada could have more of an impact on what happened in southeast Asia—or virtually anywhere else in the world—by sitting down at the table with the Americans and trying to nudge them in the right direction, rather than by trying to act alone. Canadian leaders could be critical of the US from time to time, as Pearson was in his Temple University speech, but only where there was a real impasse, and only within the context of a generally close and collaborative relationship.

When we fast-forward almost 40 years to the war in Iraq, we find the Chrétien government facing a similar choice. But Chrétien, unlike Pearson, chose to go with the flow of public opinion, mounting the soapbox and loudly proclaiming Canada's independent stance. Chrétien's decision was of course very popular with voters and did much to burnish his otherwise dubious foreign policy legacy, but it was not without costs. The break over Iraq raised questions in the US about whether Canada was really a reliable ally and a close friend to the US, which made American policy-makers less receptive to subsequent Canadian appeals for consideration on lumber quotas, beef restrictions, and border controls. There was no clear-cut and direct retaliation, just as Clarkson's independentists would have expected, but there was still a price to be paid, just as the proponents of quiet diplomacy worried there might be. Moreover, since Chrétien felt compelled to offset the break over Iraq by increasing Canada's commitment to Afghanistan, we could also see at least some of the casualties suffered there in recent years as another part of the indirect costs of our foreign policy independence. Critics of the quiet diplomacy approach might argue that it has been discredited by Canada's experience in Afghanistan, since our close collaboration with the US, and all of the sacrifices made in the dusty hills of Kandahar province, do not seem to have done much to secure Canadian influence in Washington. The evidence on that score is mixed, however, and the earning of "diplomatic capital" in Afghanistan was clearly undercut by lingering recriminations over Iraq.

Clarkson was right in arguing that the divide between proponents of quiet diplomacy and advocates of independence was not so much a philosophical one, but rather one based on different hunches about the answers to *factual* questions: Does the US reward Canada for taking a collaborative approach to foreign policy? Does it punish Canada for challenging the US on foreign policy issues? Does Canada have the capacity to act alone? Are there other potential international partners for Canada, and could Canada reconcile these new partnerships with its economic interdependence with the US? When and where does "doing well" by working closely with the US conflict with our impulse to "do good" by acting on Canadian values?

Unfortunately, recent iterations of the independence debate are still driven mostly by hunches and loaded anecdotes, because we have not made much progress over the last 40 years in finding solid answers to these pivotal questions, building from well-developed theories, and anchored in systematic empirical research. We seem to think we already know, intuitively, everything there is to know about Canada–US relations, so study of the relationship has been set aside in favour of other, more "exotic" places and problems, and a once-lively field of research is becoming an academic backwater. Given what is at stake for Canada, a clear and pressing need exists for greater efforts to understand the nature of the bilateral relationship, the inner workings of American government and society, and the way that the two countries relate to the wider world. And that understanding can only come through substantial investment of resources, and a more intensive and sustained engagement between academics, policy-makers, and the general public.

But there are some things that we do know. Canada can make up its own mind about whether or not to stand beside the United States, but it can never really stand shoulder to shoulder with the global colossus that lives next door. There is a certain sense of partnership and mutual obligation which sustains the old idea of a **special relationship** between the two countries, but there is also Canada's profound dependency on the US for both its security and its prosperity. There is a clear hierarchy in the bilateral relationship, and all of our philosophical debates over the best approach to managing our relations with the US must be predicated on a clear-eyed recognition of the underlying material reality that fundamentally limits and directs our choices.

We should be clear here that there *are* choices to make, and they are important ones. Over the last 40 years, successive Canadian governments (and the people who vote for them) have chosen to allow the country's capacity to exercise an effective foreign policy to rust out. Our military, our development aid programs, and our foreign service are all under-funded, politically neglected, and at least a little bit demoralized. It should be obvious that choosing not to make these investments now will come at some cost to Canada further down the road, whether one considers oneself a proponent of quiet diplomacy or an advo-cate of independence. Without the means to fight, to aid and support, or to innovate and lead, Canada can neither win a seat at the table with the US nor act alone. Thus while the independence debate will always be with us, the crucial debate for today is probably the much more fundamental one over whether this country is serious about having a foreign policy at all.

Questions for Review

1. Why do Brian Bow and Patrick Lennox suggest Clarkson's dichotomy might create "false choices"? What are the challenges for Canada identified by the authors?

2. Is Canada a satellite today?

Suggested Readings

Bow, Brian, and Patrick Lennox, eds. 2008. *An Independent Foreign Policy for Canada? Challenges and Choices for the Future*. Toronto: University of Toronto Press.

Clarkson, Stephen, ed. 1968. *An Independent Foreign Policy For Canada?* Toronto: McClelland and Stewart.

Clarkson, Stephen. 2002. *Uncle Sam and Us: Globalization, Neoconservatism, and the Canadian State*. Toronto: University of Toronto Press.

Clarkson, Stephen. 2011. *Dependent America? How Canada and Mexico Construct U.S. Power*. Toronto: University of Toronto Press.

7 (De)constructing Foreign Policy Narratives: Canada in Afghanistan

Nicole Wegner

Key Terms

Critical Discourse Analysis
Discourse
Hyper-Masculinization
Militarism

National Identity
Peace Enforcement Operation
Peacekeeping
Sovereignty

Discourse Analysis as a Method for Foreign Policy Studies

Many approaches to the study of foreign policy begin with theory and a methodological plan. Discourse analysis, broadly understood, begins with a research topic (Fairclough et al. 2011). Driven by curiosity about what the Canadian military was doing in Afghanistan, we explore in this chapter how the analysis of narratives in foreign policy **discourse** can be used in the understanding of Canada's military mission in Afghanistan from 2001–2011. The stories told about Canada's foreign policy have important implications, as they not only function to explain what the country's foreign policy role was, but also serve as a mechanism for (re)defining its **national identity** in the international arena.

Discourse analysis is a tool for understanding International Relations (IR) that is growing in importance. George (1994) explains that these tools of analysis help to explain how "textual and social processes are intrinsically connected and [can be used] to describe . . . the implications of this connection for the way we think and act in the contemporary world" (p. 191). Scholars in various disciplines have utilized and defined discourse analytical methods in different ways. **Critical discourse analysis** is a tool for examining social practices and political orders that are generally accepted as natural. The (re)telling of these practices, orders, or what are commonly perceived as truths serves to (re)construct them as so-called common sense. Embedded in all forms of language, cultural and ideological assumptions presented within these discourses often occur below the level of conscious awareness (Fairclough 2001).

Therefore, discourses do not exist out in the world; rather they are "*structures* that are actualized in their regular use by people in discursively ordered relationships" (Shapiro 1989, p. 11).

The term *discourse* lies in an analytical category that describes a multitude of meaning-making resources (Fairclough et al. 2011). Discourses operate as systems of signification: "things do not mean (the material world does not convey meaning); rather, people construct the meaning of things, using sign systems (predominantly, but not exclusively linguistic)" (Milliken 1999, p. 229).

In other words, the commonly assumed "truths" that are taken for granted as the foundation for foreign policy are actually discursively constructed "regimes of truth" (Foucault 1980) that contain powerful political and cultural meanings (Gusterson 1999; Mustapha 2008). These regimes come into existence through various political practices, related as much to the "constitution of various subjectivities as to the intentional action of pre-determined subjects" (Campbell 1998, p. 17). Simply put, the assumptions present in foreign policy are both consciously and subconsciously (re)created through the stories and narratives told about these events.

Discourse Analysis and Identity (Re)construction

If, then, foreign policy is (re)constructed through multiple social practices and orders, it can be useful to break these discursively constituted orders into three broad categories: *Representations* of the world, social *relations* among people, and people's social and personal *identities* (Fairclough et al. 2011, p. 370).

Foreign policy does not just make sense of the world; it gives us a place within it. It determines "us," both in the sense of the discursive boundary (in other words, delineations between "us" and "them") and also in the imagined caricature or myth of who "we" are or what "we" are like. Interestingly, this does not describe an individual's personal self, even if many foreign policy myths are affective in their ability to evoke personal identification with their messages.

Exploring narratives is important, as narratives are "the primary way by which human experience is made meaningful" (Polkinghorne 1988, p.1). They "enable and limit representation—and representation shapes our world and what is possible within . . . [narratives which] are profoundly political" (Wibben 2011, p. 43). While the specific political implications of national self-imagining are beyond the scope of this chapter, it is important to

emphasize that policy options or exclusions are produced and reproduced through these narratives. How Canada's international identity is defined will influence how and what policy decisions appear sensible and possible and what do not. The narratives present in foreign policy discourse therefore (re)construct: (1) the nature of the international arena, and (2) Canada's imagined identity.

Defining the International

Campbell (1998) explained that the boundaries of a state's identity are secured by the representation of danger integral to foreign policy. Simply put, state boundaries are justified by the threat of what is beyond the borders—that is, danger. The protection of national security interests is a narrative present in Canada's foreign policy stories: the Canadian military is necessary to defend **sovereignty** (at home and abroad) because sovereignty must be (according to this narrative) defended militarily. Campbell explained that "the paradigm of sovereignty operates on the basis of a simple dichotomy: sovereignty versus anarchy" (1998, p. 65). If sovereignty is something that requires continuous defence by the military, then, in this narrative, the assumed alternative is that Canada *would not defend* sovereignty, a state of affairs which would result in anarchy and would not allow for the maintenance of international order. In the Hobbesian, traditionalist understanding of international politics, anarchy is equated with chaos, danger, and violence.

"The state of nature is shock therapy. It helps subjects to get their priorities straight by teaching them what life would be like without sovereignty. It domesticates by eliciting the vicarious fear of violent death in those who have not had to confront it directly" (Butler 1990, p. 133). Post-9/11, the stories of Canada as a sovereignty-preserving nation contribute to the (re)construction of how the *international* is imagined. They also serve to silence critics of Canadian foreign policy who may question any actions that the Canadian Forces undertake in protecting sovereignty through the emphasis on imminent danger of chaos and death (as imagined through narratives of terrorism). The focus on terrorism as a threat to security abroad and at home emphasizes the need for **militarism** in Canadian foreign policy to secure and protect national sovereignty, specifically in the post-9/11 environment.

If international politics are understood as "externalization and totalization of dangers and the mobilization of populations to control these dangers" (Campbell 1998, p. 62), then militarism in foreign policy is performed "in the name of a social totality that is never really present, that always contains traces of the outside within and that is never more than an effect of the practices by which total dangers are inscribed" (Campbell 1998, p. 62). International threat—a danger that is always closely lurking on artificial state boundaries—therefore becomes a justification for ascribing particular roles to the Canadian Forces (such as the need to fight terrorism).

Canada's International Identity

It should be noted that the homogenous identity traits ascribed to Canada in foreign policy narratives gloss over the complexity of the units within the state. The association or disassociation with particular national imaginings is most interesting, then, because for citizens it has nothing to do with what they individually do or how they act: most citizens have no direct contact with military policies in Afghanistan. However, they like to imagine complicity in how these foreign policy decisions are made. As discourse can also act to constitute the citizenry as a political community (Fairclough et al. 2011, p. 370), the narratives used in this discourse help to construct a social identity for Canada and Canadians.

The articulation of the narratives that explain Canada's role in the foreign politics and policies also creates imagery in which the national identity and identification is (re)constructed. These narratives are not exclusive, but dominate the discourse in describing not only *what* the Canadian Forces were doing, but also redefine what it is Canadians represent in the imagined international sphere. These are not mutually exclusive constructs, as they reinforce possible or impossible logics for foreign policy action and self-identification. For analytical purposes within the discourse on Afghanistan, these explanations and identity constructions can be distilled into three narratives that defined Canada's military role within Afghanistan: Canada Fighting Terrorism, Canada the Humanitarian, and Canada the Loyal Ally. Although multiple narratives and sub-narratives are present in the discourse on Canada's military mission from 2001 to 2011, an analysis of the discourse suggests these three narratives are most prominent. As noted by Turenne Sjolander, the objectives underlying Canada's military mission in Afghanistan were "at best—rhetorically ambiguous" (Turenne Sjolander 2009, p. 78). There were tensions and confusion over which role Canada was performing or should have been performing, although these roles were not necessarily mutually exclusive. Using Munton's (2003) terms to differentiate these actions as active internationalism (otherwise called peacemaking in a defensive war) and liberal internationalism (humanitarianism, developmental assistance, and traditional peacekeeping), Turenne Sjolander (2009) explained that, although the two roles in practice are not in opposition, the images of Canadian international roles that they evoke are different and play a different role in the Canadian imagination. As other works have discussed the narrative of Canada the Humanitarian (Bell 2010; Turenne Sjolander and Trevenen, 2011), this chapter focuses on the narrative that articulated Canada's role (and therefore perceived identification) as a nation that fights terrorism. This narrative is not necessarily distinct from the other narratives, as they often overlap; however, it is the deconstruction of this narrative that shows how discourse analysis can be a useful tool for the study of Canadian foreign policy.

Canada: A Peacekeeper Image

Mythologies surrounding present-day military operations involve powerful narratives that sustain and create legitimacy for the wars they narrate. Stories are usually told from a particular perspective, and that narration (re)produces and shapes opinions and realities. Since many individuals have never and may never experience international conflict or war situations, first-hand accounts are told to the public through other media. Government public relations campaigns inform the public, but modern conflict is also reported through mass media—online, print, radio, and television. Analysis of this discourse is important in understanding how a public audience digests the narrative and how this informs and (re)produces the way that groups of people (re)constitute national identity. International engagement is performative in the sense that nationhood and national identity are created when "we" are separated from "them."

Canada's international identity has long been characterized (or perhaps more appropriately, caricaturized) by Canadian military involvement in traditional **peacekeeping**. The imagery of the blue-helmeted soldier who participates in positive and heroic service work overseas creates a sentiment of pride and identity amongst Canadian citizens and politicians across the spectrum (Dorn 2005). National memory promotes a core myth of Canada as a "selfless middle-power, acting with a kind of moral purity not normally exhibited by contemporary states" (Whitworth 2006, p. 85). However, the nature of international peacekeeping has long since been the traditional role of a ceasefire monitor. Post-World War II peacekeeping was mostly

non-combative, using soldiers as monitors for an already-established peace under the supervision of a UN-mandated mission. Over the latter decade of the twentieth century, however, peacekeeping developed into multi-faceted, complex operations that often occurred in areas where there was no established peace. The term *peacekeeping* has been distorted, resulting in a lack of clarity about what these missions actually encompass; "[p]eacekeepers, including Canadians, recently have been serving where there is no complete peace to keep. In other words, war can be seen as a form of peacekeeping" (Jockel 1994, pp. 5–6).

From 2001 onward, an interesting (re)defining of the Canadian Forces identity took place through narratives of the role of soldiers presented in the discourse and through questioning what sorts of policies were being implemented in Afghanistan. The discourse promoted three major narratives that define both the soldier and the purpose of the mission. First, the Canadian Forces are, and should be, increasingly capable in military proficiency and are serving their role as terrorist-fighters, front-line combatants who protect Canadians at home from potential security risks abroad. Second, the Canadian Forces might not be peacekeeping, but they retain the moral goodness and objectives of the country's former peacekeeper role through a commitment to a multilateral, neo-liberal, and Afghan-condoned intervention that serves the Afghan people. Third, the Canadian Forces are upholding the nation's responsibility to its NATO allies by contributing forces to a morally important and security-dependent mission.

These narratives are most aptly summed up in the 2008 Report by the Independent Panel on Canada's Future Role in Afghanistan:

> Canada's commitment in Afghanistan matters because it concerns global and Canadian security, Canada's international reputation,

and the well-being of some of the world's most impoverished and vulnerable people. Our commitment is important because it has already involved the sacrifice of Canadian lives. (Independent Panel 2008).

An analysis of the (re)defining of roles that Canadian Forces soldiers play in foreign policy studies provides a unique perspective on how Canada's actions as a nation can be understood. As national self-identifications are represented (or understood as being represented) by the actions of the Canadian Forces, it is this connection that allows an exploration of how Canada's identity (or imagining of its identity) is (re)constructed through discourse. A discussion of Canada's perceived role as a nation fighting terrorism follows.

Subtitle: Canada Fighting Terrorism

The Canadian government's military commitments to Afghanistan had clear rationalizations linked to the 9/11 terror attacks and Canadian obligations to NATO alliance commitments (Bratt 2011, pp. 316–17). Military action in Afghanistan was justified by a need to deter terrorism:

> We need to address threats to our security before they reach our shores. Canada therefore has a responsibility to ensure that the extremists who would harm us and our allies can no longer find refuge in Afghanistan (Parliament of Canada 2006).

Military historians and security studies academics alike had criticized the lack of funding to the Canadian Forces that occurred in the 1980s and 1990s, a period when peacekeeping was heavily promoted and romanticized as a role better suited for the Canadian Forces. Accelerating a change in the Canadian security environment following 9/11, the Harper government articulated narratives encouraging the reimagining of the Canadian Forces—not as a peacekeeping mediator but as a more militarized and combat-capable institution:

> [O]ur government is close to finalizing a long-term plan to thoroughly reverse the so-called "rusting out"of the Canadian forces . . . . [W]e need to build a first-class modern military and keep it that way. Ladies and gentlemen, I believe Canada should be a leader in the world, not a follower. And in today's dangerous world, Canada must have a credible military to be a credible leader. You understand that countries that cannot or will not make real contributions to global security are not regarded as serious players. They may be liked by everybody; they may be pleasantly acknowledged by everybody. But when the hard decisions get made, they will be ignored by everybody (Government of Canada 2008).

The identification of Canadian Forces soldiers as increasingly militaristic, combat-capable individuals constructs an image of Canada that extends beyond the helpful-fixer, middle-power role that was hailed in the latter half of the twentieth century. Images of soldiers fighting terrorists with advanced military equipment in faraway deserts not only redefine the military, but also redefine Canada in an international context. The underlying message in the above quotation is that Canada's international reputation is linked to its military ability. The ability of the military to be "first class" infers the necessity of the Canadian Forces soldier to be masculinized, "tough," and combat-ready.

Feminist and critical security studies scholars have raised concerns about the **hyper-masculinization** that occurs in military training. (Whitworth 2006). The projection of the soldier as tough, rational, strong, or warrior-like is commonly criticized in feminist scholarship, which has been wary of the binary-divisive definition (and therefore oversimplification) of what it means to be a soldier. For feminists, this is often related to the privileging of masculinized qualities and the exclusion of feminized or other attributes. However, this has not always accurately captured the identity confusion that has occurred within the Canadian Forces (CF). The identification of the CF with a history of peacekeeping has meant in the past that Canadian soldiers struggled with what Whitworth (2006) called the crisis of masculinity—unlike their American counterparts. As militaries require a particular ideology of manliness in order to function properly, soldiers are trained in ways that promote masculinized values: encouragement of violence and aggression, and individual conformity to military discipline, as well as an emphasis on homophobia and heterosexism (Whitworth 2006, p. 16). Whitworth identified a problematic contradiction: many of the messages that soldiers receive about appropriate soldierly behaviour are fundamentally at odds with their expected duties in peacekeeping operations. Whitworth examined incidents such as the murder of a Somali teenager, and hazing practices that involved homoerotic and racist embarrassment tactics—which explain how the socially reproduced image of peacekeepers has often been at odds with the environment within which soldiers operate.

However, since the government of Canada has been clear that the nation's involvement in Afghanistan was *not* a peacekeeping mission, it can be suggested that this shift in policy role offers some reprieve from Whitworth's concerns of soldierly purpose. Rather than a traditional peacekeeping mission, Canada's involvement has been identified as a "**peace enforcement operation**" as provided for under Chapter VII of the United Nations Charter: a "collective use of force, under international law, to address a threat to international peace and security posed by continuing

disorder in Afghanistan" (Government of Canada 2008). The country's role has been to "counter the terrorist threat" by ensuring that Afghanistan does not again "revert to the status of sanctuary and head office for global terrorism" (Independent Panel 2008). In this formulation, what Canada was doing was fighting terrorism abroad to provide security at home. This rationalization was most prominent in the discourse from 2001 to 2007. Most often, this explanation of the country's role in Afghanistan was tied to retaliatory efforts against terrorist attacks in North America:

> Following the horrific terrorist attacks of September 11, 2001, the United Nations Security Council (UNSC) authorized the mission of the International Security Assistance Force (ISAF) in Afghanistan to assist the Afghanistan Interim Authority in providing security in and around Kabul (Government of Canada 2007).

The focus on fighting terrorism and providing security was not made in isolation. Frequent reference was made to Canada's 3D policy (Defence, Diplomacy, Development), with a heavy emphasis on placing security as the first and most important *D* to be accomplished. Prime Minister Harper explained that "the stark reality is that there can be no progress in Afghanistan without security—the security provided by the sacrifice and determination of our men and women in uniform" (CBC News 2007). Parliamentary reports released in both 2007 and 2008 noted that it was the government and the media's excessive emphasis on this aspect of the Canadian mission (i.e., fighting Taliban terrorists) that caused a lack of public support for CF activity in Afghanistan.

Discussion of on-the-ground activities of CF members has usually been in reference to their military successes against insurgents: "Canadian troops have been clearing Taliban out of the Panjwayi and

Zhari districts, claiming success in finding and killing key Taliban leaders" (Parliament of Canada 2007). While the media had been cautious about portraying insurgent Afghan fighters in a negative way, both military representatives and government reports defined the Taliban as antagonistic:

> The Taliban are not just attacking the ISAF forces. They have attacked mosques where moderate imams preach against them. They have attacked hospitals and other social services funded by the international community. They have murdered teachers who provide instruction to girls. . . . Taliban and al Qaeda insurgencies, fuelled by drug traffickers, corrupt officials, and common criminals . . . are the primary, direct military threat to the security of Afghanistan (Parliament of Canada 2007, pp. 28, 31).

In contrast to the pejorative imagery of the Taliban, the Canadian Forces have been portrayed as heroic, militarized, and efficient warriors. In 2006 the Canadian Forces launched a media campaign to address the shortage of active members. Tested in Atlantic Canada, the CAD$3-million campaign was created to increase recruitment numbers—a goal of 6,500 new personnel was set for 2007 (Ramage 2006). Unlike the Canadian Forces recruitment campaign of the 1990s—"There's No Life Like It"—which depicted video-game-like sequences and techno music, the new ads were filled with dark, trancelike music and short, hazy video clips of soldiers doing search and rescue domestically and internationally (CanWest MediaWorks 2008). Canadian television journalist Graham Richardson noted, "It [was] certainly an aggressive push for more soldiers, a move that the Forces desperately need to make" (Smith 2006).

The video campaign was aired on television and through Internet advertising banners. There were three 60-second ads containing different imagery but bearing the same floating slogans: "Fight Fear;" "Fight Distress;" "Fight Chaos;" "Fight with the Canadian Forces." The campaigns included one ad that specifically showed images of CF members in Afghanistan, breaking down doors and rescuing civilians.

The images present an interesting dichotomy: an exciting, thrill-filled job that involves an element of danger (though not *too* much danger) but that also means helping, rescuing and saving Canadians. Those images depicted perfectly the struggle and conflicting narratives about how the role of Canadian Forces should be understood. They fight—but the advertisements did not show them killing, firing weapons, or performing other overtly militarized activities. They help—but not in an overly feminized or emotional way. The forces were depicted as a strange hybrid of soldier and helper, but this distorts the ways that the public is able to understand the caricatures presented. The overlapping of narratives (Canada as a terrorist-fighting nation and Canada as a humanitarian, peacemaking nation) were used at times to justify what the government has called "the expenditure of Canadian blood and treasure abroad" (Parliament of Canada 2007, p. 12).

The images presented contribute to the understanding of what foreign policy options are possible and acceptable. In these images, the Canadian soldier does not kill or fire weapons. This contributes to frustration and confusion about the deaths of Canadian soldiers in Afghanistan. The war story constructed in these commercials omits the possibility of death. This is a unique way that discourse functions to create not only expectations, but facilitates the ways a nation understands foreign policy.

It also limits the agency and ability of those being rescued. As the Canadian military mission ended in 2011 and the start of the new training mission began, it did so in a discursive context where groups of individuals previously understood to be in need of rescue and aid were given greater political control over their country.

Conclusion

Discourse analysis as a tool in studying foreign policy offers a unique way to understand power relationships that shape how and what policy options might be pursued. The stories told about Canada's foreign policy have important implications, as they not only function to explain what the country's foreign policy role was but also serve as a mechanism for (re)defining its national identity in the international arena. How Canada's national identity is understood either opens or omits possibilities for action and practice. It is the identification of "who" Canada represents (a nation fighting terrorism, a helpful fixer, or a loyal ally) that influences the types of policies pursued and the ways that the citizenry will understand them.

Questions for Review

1. What is meant by "deconstruction" of foreign policy narratives?
2. How can looking at the messages within discourse help to better understand decision-making in foreign policy circles?
3. If discourse analysis is a methodology, what sorts of tools and activities are used when putting this methodology into practice?
4. If discourse analysis allows analysts to see biases (and omissions) in the telling of foreign policy, how can we account for our own biases when we deconstruct and analyze narratives?
5. What perspectives are omitted in the dominant narratives told about Canada's military role in Afghanistan?
6. Since the removal of Canadian military operations in Afghanistan (2011), what national image or identity markers has Canada been associated with?

Suggested Readings

Campbell, David. 1998. *Writing Security: United States Foreign Policy and the Politics of Identity.* Minneapolis: University of Minnesota Press.

Razack, Sherene. 2004. *Dark Threats and White Knights: The Somalia Affair, Peacekeeping, and the New Imperialism.* Toronto: University of Toronto Press.

Richler, Noah. 2012. *What We Talk About When We Talk About War.* Fredericton: Goose Lane.

Stein, Janice Gross, and Eugene Lang. 2007. *The Unexpected War: Canada in Kandahar.* Toronto: Penguin Canada.

Turenne Sjolander, Claire. 2009. "A funny thing happened on the road to Kandahar: The competing faces of Canadian internationalism?" *Canadian Foreign Policy* 15, 2: 78–98.

Whitworth, Sandra. 2006. *Men, Militarism, and un Peacekeeping: A Gendered Analysis.* New Delhi: Viva.

Wibben, Annick T.R. 2011. *Feminist Security Studies: A Narrative Approach.* New York: Routledge.

References

Bell, Colleen. 2010. "Fighting the war and winning the peace: Three critiques of the war in Afghanistan," pp. 58–71 in Marshall J. Beier and Lana Wylie, eds. *Canadian Foreign Policy in Critical Perspective.* Don Mills, ON: Oxford University Press.

Bratt, Duane. 2011. "Afghanistan: Why did we go? Why did we stay? Will we leave?," pp. 316–28 in Duane Bratt and Christopher J. Kukucha, eds. *Readings in Canadian Foreign Policy: Classic Debates and New Ideas.* 2nd ed. Don Mills, ON: Oxford University Press.

Butler, Judith. 1990. *Gender Trouble: Feminism and the Subversion of Identity.* New York: Routledge.

Campbell, David. 1998. *Writing Security: United States Foreign Policy and the Politics of Identity.* Minneapolis: University of Minnesota Press.

CanWest MediaWorks Publications. 2008. "Canadian Forces launch dark, edgy ad campaign." 16 April. Available at http://www.canada.com/story.html?id=5dddfa9c-e047-46a3-940b-d1fba2f7a687.

CBC News. 2007. "Canada leads by example on world stage, says PM." 25 September. Available at www.cbc.ca/news/ world/ story/2007/09/25/harper-foreignpolicy.html.

Dorn, A. Walter. 2005. "Canadian peacekeeping: Proud tradition, strong future?" *Canadian Foreign Policy Journal* 12, 2: 7–32.

Fairclough, Norman. 2001. *Language and Power*. 2nd ed. London: Longman.

Fairclough, Norman, Jane Mulderrig, and Ruth Wodak. 2011. "Critical discourse analysis," pp. 357–78 in Teun van Dijk, ed. *Discourse Studies: A Multidisciplinary Introduction*. 2nd ed. London: Sage.

Foucault, Michel. 1980. *Power/Knowledge*. Brighton, UK: Harvester.

George, Jim. 1994. *Discourses of Global Politics: A Critical (Re)Introduction to International Relations*. Boulder, CO: Lynne Rienner.

Government of Canada. 2007. *Canada's Mission in Afghanistan: Measuring Progress*. Report to Parliament (February).

———. 2008. "PM unveils revised motion on the future of Canada's mission in Afghanistan." 21 February. Available at http://www.pm.gc.ca/eng/news/2008/02/21/pm-unveils-revised-motion-future-canadas-mission-afghanistan-0.

Gusterson, Hugh. 1999. "Missing the end of the Cold War in international security," pp. 319–42 in Jutta Weldes, Mark Laffey, Hugh Gusterson, and Raymond Duvall, eds. *Cultures of Insecurity: States, Communities, and the Production of Danger*. Minneapolis: University of Minnesota Press.

Independent Panel on Canada's Future Role in Afghanistan. 2008. *Final Report*. Ottawa: The Panel (January).

Jockel, Joseph T. 1994. *Canada and International Peacekeeping*. Washington, DC: Center for Strategic and International Studies.

Milliken, Jennifer. 1999. "The study of discourse in international relations: A critique of research and methods." *European Journal of International Relations* 5, 2 (June): 225–54.

Munton, Don. 2003. "Whither internationalism?" *International Journal* 58, 1 (Winter): 155–80.

Mustapha, Jennifer. 2008. "Threat construction in post-9/11 US foreign policy discourses: Implications for (critical) security in Southeast Asia." Presented at the Canadian Political Science Association Conference, Vancouver, 4 June.

Parliament of Canada. 2006. Standing Committee on National Defence. Statement by the Hon. Gordon O'Connor. 30 May. Available at http://www.parl.gc.ca/HousePublications/Publication.aspx?DocId=2230358&Language=E&Mode=2&Parl=39&Ses=1.

———. 2007. *Canadian Forces in Afghanistan: Report of the Standing Committee on National Defence*. House of Commons (39th Parliament, 1st session, June). Available at http://www.parl.gc.ca/content/hoc/Committee/391/NDDN/Reports/RP3034719/nddnrp01/nddnrp01-e.pdf.

Polkinghorne, Donald E. 1988. *Narrative Knowing and the Human Sciences*. Albany: State University of New York Press.

Ramage, Norma. 2006. "Advertising is war." *Marketing Magazine*, 2 October. Available at http://www.marketing-mag.ca/brands/advertising-is-war-19941.

Shapiro, Michael. 1989. "Textualizing global politics," pp. 11–22 in James Der Derian and Michael Shapiro, eds. *International/Intertextual Relations*. Lexington, MA: Lexington Books.

Smith, Roger. 2006. "Canadian Forces ads zoom in on combat mission." CTV News, 13 September.

Turenne Sjolander, Claire. 2009. "A funny thing happened on the road to Kandahar: The competing faces of Canadian internationalism?" *Canadian Foreign Policy* 15, 2: 78–98.

Turenne Sjolander, Claire, and Kathryn Trevenen. 2011. "Constructing Canadian foreign policy: Myths of good international citizens, protectors, and the war in Afghanistan," pp. 44–57 in Duane Bratt and Christopher J. Kukucha, eds. *Readings in Canadian Foreign Policy: Classic Debates and New Ideas*. 2nd ed. Don Mills, ON: Oxford University Press.

Whitworth, Sandra. 2006. *Men, Militarism, and UN Peacekeeping: A Gendered Analysis*. New Delhi: Viva.

Wibben, Annick T.R. 2011. *Feminist Security Studies: A Narrative Approach*. New York: Routledge.

8 Hegemony in the Local Order and Accumulation in the Global: Canada and Libya

Sean McMahon

Key Terms

Crisis of Overaccumulation
Entrepreneurial Canadian
Responsibility to Protect

Transnational Historic Bloc
Value

Introduction

The Annales School historian Fernand Braudel "pointed out [that] history comprises a relatively fast-moving events-time (*histoire événementielle*), and a much slower-moving time of structural change (*longue durée*)."[1] The events-time history of the Libyan conflict is as follows: protests began on 15 February 2011. Unlike protests in Egypt and Tunisia, "[f]rom the beginning, 'the movement' in Libya took the form of an armed revolt firing on the army."[2] The struggle "followed the logic of a civil war from a very early stage" due in large measure to the almost immediate involvement of the American Central Intelligence Agency (CIA).[3] On 22 February, the Arab League suspended Libya, and the United Nations (UN) Security Council issued a press statement that called on the government of de facto President Muammer al-Qadhdhafi "to meet its responsibilities to protect its people."[4]

Four days later, the Security Council adopted Resolution 1970, which imposed an arms embargo on Libya and travel bans on select Libyans, and, for only the second time, referred a situation to the International Criminal Court for prosecution. As the violence persisted into early March, a chorus of calls for the imposition of a no-fly zone above Libya went up from regional organizations including the Gulf Cooperation Council (GCC), Organization of the Islamic Conference, and the Arab League. Around this same time, the National Transitional Council (NTC) was coalescing and being recognized as the legitimate representative of the Libyan people. On 17 March al-Qadhdhafi, as was his rhetorical style, called those involved in the movement against his regime "cockroaches," and the Security Council adopted Resolution 1973.[5] The signal importance of this resolution is that it "marked the first time the Council had authorized the use of force for human protection [in accordance with the **responsibility to protect** doctrine] against the wishes of a functioning state."[6] On 19 March, Operation Odyssey Dawn was initiated with American, British, and French air strikes being launched against Libyan assets.

The American-initiated operation was transferred to the North Atlantic Treaty Organization (NATO) on 31 March and was renamed Operation

Unified Protector. On 4 April, the US withdrew from direct combat operations, and 10 days later, US President Barack Obama, French President Nicolas Sarkozy, and British Prime Minister David Cameron published a common letter that clearly articulated their political objective in Libya: al-Qadhdhafi had to go.[7] In mid-August Tripoli fell, and two months later, al-Qadhdhafi was captured—and killed on 20 October. Three days after that, Libya's "liberation was declared"; Operation Unified Protector ended on 31 October. Finally (and interestingly, given the clear instrumentalization of the **value** of protection to realize NATO's political objective), on 7 December, Brazil, Russia, India, China, and South Africa (the BRICS) submitted a letter to the UN General Assembly and Security Council calling "for a thorough examination of the conformity of the actions taken by the coalition with the provisions of Resolutions 1970 and 1973."[8]

The Canadian state and its repressive apparatuses mobilized for war against Libya as soon as Resolutions 1970 and 1973 were adopted. Canada abided by and then exceeded the requirements of Resolution 1970 to impose additional sanctions, including a ban on financial transactions with the government of Libya.[9] Three days after the adoption of Resolution 1973, Prime Minister Harper candidly endorsed the imperial removal of a de facto head of state under the cover of protecting civilians: "[h]e [al-Qadhdhafi] simply will not last very long . . . . I think that is the basis on which we're moving forward. If I am being frank here, that is probably more understood than spoken aloud. But I just said it aloud."[10] This major foreign policy decision was unanimously supported in the House of Commons. When asked about the decision the next day, the Leader of the Official Opposition, Michael Ignatieff, said he would "be calling for a motion in the House of Commons to formally approve the mission." His foreign affairs critic, Bob Rae, said: "[w]e don't see [the bombing of Libya] as a partisan issue between

Liberals and Conservatives," and "I don't see Libya as a game-changer." And the leader of the New Democratic Party, Jack Layton, said it was appropriate for Canada to be part of the mission.[11] Through Operation Mobile, Canada contributed two frigates, seven CF-18 planes, as well as refuelling and reconnaissance aircraft to the Libya campaign. Canadian Forces flew a disproportionate amount of the bombing sorties, almost 1,000 by the end of the war.[12] And a Canadian was operational commander of NATO's Operation Unified Protector. When all was said and done, the apparatuses' deployment against Libya cost the Canadian state CAD$103 million.[13]

Throughout the operation, the Canadian state was given cover by its ideological apparatuses. The media and its so-called experts labelled al-Qadhdhafi an "odious thug" who could thrillingly be "blown to smithereens,"[14] and a "monster" comparable to Saddam Hussein.[15] Canadians were also reassured that their state had started the war with the best of intentions and "had responded the way it should."[16] Academics, too, performed their political function. They spuriously claimed that Libya was on the cusp of a genocide comparable to that of Rwanda;[17] reminded Canadians of al-Qadhdhafi's "deadly degradation of his people;"[18] claimed al-Qadhdhafi's actions were "intolerable" and that Canada had to take a stand;[19] and when the war dragged into its fifth month, again made sensationalist and paradoxical claims of a "blood bath" and that the war made for a more humane world.[20]

As with all matters that are represented as widely agreed upon and obvious, this policy demands interrogation. Why was Canada involved in the Libya operation? It is facile to answer because Canada is a member of NATO. Other NATO members, most notably Germany, did not support UN Resolution 1973. Furthermore, other members of NATO, including usually staunchly supportive Poland, refused to participate in Operation Unified Protector. In fact, only 14 of the alliance's 28 members contributed war materiel. So why was Canada disproportionately involved in the operation?

Canadian involvement in the war on Libya can only be properly understood by locating the policy in the politics of structural time. My argument is that the Canadian state supported the Libya campaign and participated as it did in the service of global and local interests of the **transnational historic bloc** led by finance capital. Globally, the war facilitated accumulation on the part of this bloc by temporally displacing the ongoing crisis of surplus capital. Locally, the war on Libya supported this bloc's political project in Canada by reaffirming a neo-liberal nationalist ideology. The war was against value, including people, in Libya and resistant subordinate social forces in Canada's politico-economic order; Operations Mobile and Unified Protector were material attacks in Libya and techniques of social domination in Canada.

I execute this argument in four stages. First, I explain my analytical apparatus. More specifically, I adumbrate the specific ideas and insights I deploy from the historical materialist tradition. Second, I demonstrate that the prevailing readings of the war on Libya, including Canada's participation in it, are, at best, analytically deficient and, at worst, ahistorical and bereft of critical reflection. It must be noted that commentaries on Canadian policy vis-à-vis Libya are almost non-existent, so much of this review is cast in the broader terms of the global political-economic order. Third, I explain how the war on Libya temporally displaced the problem of surplus capital and served an ideological function in Canada. Fourth, I conclude with some thoughts regarding local social implications of the Canadian involvement in the war.

Historical Materialism

Historical materialism is a neglected and marginalized approach to foreign policy analysis. In contrast to the field's heavy reliance on the concept of national interest and ontology of like states, historical materialism is premised on the labour theory of value and assigns ontological primacy to production.[21] For the present purpose, human labour is the source of all value under capitalism,[22] and value is determined by the socially necessary labour–time taken up in a commodity's production.[23] Rather than a number in the market of exchange, value is a social relation, and money is the social expression of value.[24] In essence, social structures, practices, ideas, and identities are all products of how societies are organized to produce value in the form of commodities.[25]

There are myriad implications of historical materialism's ontology. Most germane to this discussion is the framework's rejection of the very assumption of *foreign* policy. According to Lenin, "[t]o separate 'foreign politics' from politics in general, or, still worse, to contrast foreign politics to home politics is fundamentally wrong."[26] In keeping with this idea, historical materialism posits a tripartite conceptualization of politics in which the structure of production "below" the state produces power institutionalized in certain forms of states which, in turn, create certain world orders. A "historic bloc is the term applied to the particular configuration of social classes and ideology" that structures production.[27] A transnational historic bloc is a configuration of social forces across different states that share material interests and ideological perspectives.[28] While the transnational historic bloc has common interests, the realization of those interests differs across political economies because of the specific national histories of the structures of accumulation, including resistances to the bloc's project. The current order's transnational historic bloc is led by finance capital and its ideology is neo-liberalism.

In dialectical fashion, world orders also (re)structure relations of production at the local level using the state as a "transmission belt."[29] Specific organizations of production and configurations of social forces—say, Canada's or Egypt's—are all part of the same unity of the global political economy; they are differently connected to different spheres of state in the world order. There is no equality in these relations. The world order, while it affects all states, is a manifestation of social relations in the societies of the powerful states (determined, of course, by how the production process was structured in the specific instance). In the current historical moment, the world order is increasingly non-hegemonic because social relations within the powerful countries are, to varying degrees, increasingly non-hegemonic.

Now, for historical materialism, the manner in which capitalism structures the production process is rife with internal contradictions. One such contradiction is that capitalism succeeds so well in accumulating capital (understood "as value 'in motion' undergoing a continuous expansion through the production of surplus value") that capital overaccumulates.[30] This is capitalism's surplus capital problem: capital is produced in such abundance that processes that will facilitate more accumulation are exhausted. Capital is like any other commodity in the sense that when its supply rises while demand remains elastic, its value falls. When this condition becomes acute because the accumulated quantities of surplus capital can no longer be turned to profitable uses, crises ensue.[31]

While crises borne of surplus capital are never resolved, mechanisms have been devised to defer—temporally displace—them. One such mechanism is long-term investments. The construction of road systems, airports, and dams consume surplus capital for a time, thereby enabling the remaining capital to retain its value. Militarism, with its construction of bases and development and stockpiling of destructive technologies, performs the same function.[32] When they do occur, these "crises

entail the devaluation, depreciation and destruction of capital."[33] This is by no means a universal process, however. Crises destroy the value of *some* capital so the remaining capital can accumulate more value. War is the most spectacular means of temporarily addressing crises of surplus capital. War literally destroys value in the forms of human labour and fixed capital while concomitantly creating new profitable uses for the remaining surplus capital (destroyed infrastructure must be rebuilt).[34] If, as Harvey so eloquently says, "[d]evaluation is the underside of overaccumulation,"[35] then politics, locally and globally, are about imposing the costs of devaluation on some social forces while realizing opportunities to (over)accumulate for others.

Some final thoughts about what this necessarily limited sampling of the historical materialist tradition means for the study of Canadian policy in the global order specifically: in the contemporary moment, the production of value "below" the Canadian form of state, as in the global order, is structured according to the interests of the transnational historic bloc led by finance capital.[36] The Canadian state-as-intermediary is implicated locally and globally in distributing the costs and opportunities of **crises of (over)accumulation** according to the interests of this social force. These distributions and their attendant (re)ordering of social relations, understood as policy, are not exclusively material. The historical materialist tradition also has an ideological dimension.[37] Policy, materially and ideologically, entails contradictions, including repatriating to the local practices and values performed in the global structure. Ultimately, what is imagined on both sides of the border (cognitive and international) is dialectically related: state policy "out there" comes "home," and policy "at home" produces policy "out there."

Having explained that my analysis is based on Canada's existence in the organization of the global political economy's production of value, with its attendant contradictions and crises, and *not*, say, its middle ranking in the global hierarchy or role and capabilities as a principal power, I now review analyses of the war on Libya and Canada's role in it.

Why Did Canada Bomb Libya?

Canada's "acts of war" against Libya, as Prime Minister Harper called them, were executed almost without debate or critical reflection.[38] According to Engler, Canada bombed Libya to: 1) justify purchase of the F-35 fighter plane, 2) serve the interests of Canadian corporations such as Suncor and SNC-Lavalin, 3) substantiate the Conservatives' "principled" foreign policy, and 4) provide the West with a modicum of control over a region in flux.[39] Putting aside the empty rhetorical nature of the third reason and the fact that the interests of the imperial powers were never seriously challenged by the changes in Egypt and Tunisia (to which I will return), Engler's first two points are reasonable, particularly when you consider that most of the bombing sorties were conducted by the NATO members that are also partners in the F-35 development program. These points do not go far enough, however. Talking about profit as Engler does—political in the form of servicing the interests of the Conservatives' military-industrial complex constituency, or economic—stays in the domain of the market. It does not penetrate to the level of production. Cast in these essential terms, the fighter plane and accessing the Libyan political economy are about addressing the surplus capital problem. The militarism of the plane consumes surplus capital, and reconstruction and expansion of the means of oil exploitation provide investment opportunities for the remaining capital to further accumulate.

In her commentary "Blame R2P [Responsibility to Protect]: The intellectuals go to war," Wente seems to claim that Canadian policy is determined by liberal intellectuals.[40] Wente's tirade is ahistorical; Matthews makes the point that Canada abandoned the responsibility-to-protect doctrine almost immediately after shepherding it to UN adoption in 2005.[41] The commentary is only notable for broaching the prevailing connection made with the war on Libya—namely that it was the realization of the responsibility-to-protect doctrine. According to Dunne and Gifkins, "the early response to Libya in 2011 has shown that the United Nations Security Council is able to give effect to the '**responsibility to protect**' norm."[42] Zifcak sees much the same thing.[43] Cronogue argues that coercive humanitarian intervention remains legitimate even after its performance in Libya and entanglement in a web of strategic and pragmatic concerns.[44] For Bellamy and Williams, the war on Libya demonstrated that the Security Council will not be inhibited in its actions by respect for state sovereignty, having "broken through the final constraint on humanitarian intervention—the nominal consent of the host state."[45] Most interestingly, Pommier, too, sees the responsibility to protect as the basis of the intervention in Libya, but wonders aloud if the doctrine paradoxically died through its realization in Libya—if the doctrine is collateral damage of the Libyan operation it authorized.[46]

Readings making this connection cannot be taken seriously. First, as Falk notes, the limited nature of the UN mandate to protect civilians "was disregarded almost from the outset."[47] He goes on to remark that "[i]t is extremely disturbing that a restricted UN mandate was ignored and that the Security Council did not reconsider the original mandate or censure NATO for unilaterally expanding the scope and nature of its military role."[48] And in speculation reminiscent of Pommier's reflections, Falk asserts that "[b]y ignoring the UN 's limits, NATO may have destroyed the prospect for future legitimate uses of the principle of responsibility to protect."[49] The obvious instrumentalization and immediate exceeding of this doctrine to realize the imperial removal of a head of state belies these readings, but this is not the end of the matter.

While Falk raises the issue of "the selectivity of Libya's application of the [responsibility to protect] norm,"[50] it is impossible to accept the claim that the American empire that invaded and occupied Iraq (with the assistance of its British ally, to the cost of 2 million lives) and wantonly kills Afghanis, Pakistanis, and Yemenis with its drones asymmetrically valued Libyan lives. Moreover—and this is where Canadian policy in particular is exposed as nakedly disingenuous—all of these supposed champions of civilian protection continue to support Israel in its commission of war crimes and crimes against humanity against the civilian population of Gaza.[51] Further still, it is impossible to ignore the imperial epistemology so obviously embedded in the reality that the constraint of state sovereignty will only be broken through in the post-colonial world. This same epistemology, for example, precludes the very thought of intervening to stop the American drone program, which by any reasonable standard constitutes war crimes. The responsibility to protect doctrine is little more than a mechanism that "gives the hegemonic power ideological legitimization for intervening in weaker countries against noncompliant regimes."[52] To think otherwise requires suspension of all disbelief.

Getting past this apologia for power, more critical analyses of the war highlight interests in oil, counter-revolutionary vigilance, precluding the establishment of a gold dinar currency, destroying Libya—effectively Lebanonizing it—and establishing a location for the Africa Command (AFRICOM) base in Africa. The oil interest is the most obvious—so obvious, in fact, that Poland's prime minister alluded to it when explaining his country's non-participation in Operation Unified Protector. Prime Minister David Tusk refused to allow Poland to join the bombing campaign, saying "that is one of the reasons for our restraint . . . . If we want to defend people against dictators, reprisals, torture and

prison, that principle must be universal and not invoked only when it is convenient, profitable or safe."[53] This interest is not a compelling explanation for the war for the simple reason that capital associated with the imperial states already had access to Libyan oil. Echoing Engler, Ismi argues that the "Western attack on Libya [was] motivated mainly by the Egyptian and Tunisian revolutions taking those countries out of Washington's control."[54] Wallerstein similarly argues that the war on Libya was a deliberate distraction from Saudi Arabia, as the region's primary comprador state, crushing what he calls the "second Arab revolt."[55] On the face of it, this reading, too, seems plausible. Its problem, though, is that the political protests and changes that occurred in states such as Egypt and Tunisia were not revolutionary and did not remove them from the American imperial order.[56] Saudi Arabia's policies were certainly heavy-handed —pushing for war on Libya, effectively invading Bahrain—but its response to these events does not confirm the events as revolutionary. Instead, the reformist nature of the events confirm NATO's war on Libya and Saudi policy as intensely reactionary.

Three critical analyses of the war remain. They come progressively closer to the essential reason for the NATO attack. The first speculates that the attack was, literally, a currency war. Russia Television reports that the war was "about the gold dinar—a single African currency made from gold . . . . [African and Arab states would] sell oil and other resources around the world only for gold dinars. It is an idea that would shift the economic balance of the world; a country's wealth would depend on how much gold they [sic] have, not how many [American] dollars they [sic] trade."[57] Cockburn, citing Brown, communicates much the same idea.[58] This explanation—that the war was about ensuring that the dollar remained the world's reserve currency—is plausible for the same reasons that it is a plausible explanation for the US invasion and occupation of Iraq in 2003.[59] Second, according to Amin, the war was part of a larger imperial project to destroy Arab societies in the Middle East.[60] Said offered the same suggestion as the US rushed to attack Iraq: "[p]erhaps even the idea is to turn Iraq into civil war Lebanon."[61] Both proffer much the same motivations for this policy, namely that the destruction of first Iraq and then Libya served the imperial and regional interests of the US, Israel, and the Gulf States. Third—and this is a point made by a number of authors—the war was waged to allow for the establishment of AFRICOM's headquarters in Africa (currently it is based in Germany).[62] Libya had to be attacked and al-Qadhdhafi removed to make way for an imperial installation all African states have hitherto unanimously rejected.

Given's Canada's location in the global political economy, these critical analyses can shed some light on Canadian policy on the war on Libya. Interests represented by the Canadian state do not want the US dollar replaced as the global reserve currency, for example. As piercing as they are, however, these analyses do not get to the essence of the matter. Currency is a matter in the domain of market circulation. Proper understanding of the war on Libya requires descending to the level of production. By the same token, the imperialism that necessitates the destruction of Arab societies and locating of military bases is not imperialism for its own sake but rather imperialism for the sake of accumulation. The destruction of Libyan society and the relocation of AFRICOM are not imperial ends in themselves, but rather the means to temporally displace the surplus capital problem.

I now turn to an elaboration of this analysis.

Accumulation Globally and Hegemony Locally

The war on Libya was one iteration of the displacement of the ongoing global crisis of surplus capital—the crisis had already been displaced to Iceland, Greece, Italy, and Spain—and a means through which the governing historic bloc realized its political project in Canada. This section has two parts. First, I adumbrate the mechanics of the war's temporal displacement of the surplus capital problem and show how the surplus capital problem was bound up with the politics of the war. Second, I explain how Canadian participation in this expression of the global crisis served the interests of the transnational historic bloc locally, in Canada.

The devaluation of capital is clear in the war's momentary violence as well as its future militarism. The destruction of Libyan society noted by Amin was, essentially, the destruction of value in Libyan society. NATO destroyed all manner of fixed capital investments, including roads and airports. It also destroyed value in the form of people, particularly valuable people in fact. Until the war, the use and distribution of oil rents in Libya had meant that Libyans had one of the highest per capita incomes in Africa. The rents produced Libyans who enjoyed high literacy rates and high life expectancy at birth.[63] In terms of human development, Libya was the second-highest ranked African society, and one of only two to achieve a rank of "high" in the United Nations Development Programme index.[64] The NATO attack destroyed the second-most valuable African country and the second-most valuable Africans.

These high-value targets were destroyed with equally high-value munitions. According to Barry, "[i]t appears that NATO air attacks exclusively used precision weapons and that no dumb bombs were dropped."[65] This is supported by the fact that the European allies exhausted their supplies of precision-guided munitions and had to access US stockpiles.[66] Putting aside the nonsensical claim that precision weapons somehow save lives, the ever increasing use of technologically advanced weapons means the destruction of ever larger stores of surplus capital. Obviously, more capital is destroyed in the explosion of a cruise missile than in that of an artillery piece. Crucial to note in this regard is that, given the distribution of tax burdens in the imperial states, value destroyed in state procured armaments means the disproportionate destruction of value from labour, while leaving finance capital largely intact for future accumulation. Technology is a consumptive mechanism, and the more advanced the technology of state violence, the better it addresses the problem of surplus capital.

Recall that (over)accumulation and devaluation are dialectically related. Even before the war ended, the violent devaluation of Libyan capital was seen as opening new opportunities for (over)accumulation. The opportunity presented by the tendering of reconstruction contracts for Libya's destroyed infrastructure was characterized as a "bonanza."[67] The *Independent* expressed this part of the process most pointedly with an article entitled "Dash for profit in post-war Libya carve-up."[68] Of course, the investments would not have had to be rebuilt for multibillion dollar profits if they had not been destroyed in the first place. While Brun and Hersh are right that "military destruction is neither environmentally friendly nor energy saving," it does (re)affirm remaining value.[69] The kind of death and destruction performed in Libya and lamented by many authors is in the logic of the finance capital class-led transnational historic bloc.

The manner in which the war temporally displaced the surplus capital problem was not limited to value destruction and accumulation through reconstruction. The war was also used to further increase militarism. This is obvious in the case of the AFRICOM base. In appearance and superficial function the base is a tool of imperial control of Africa. In terms of the essence of value, the base consumes considerable surplus capital: USD\$1.4 billion in 2010 alone.[70] Less talked about (but with the potential to consume even more surplus capital, and not just in Canada) is increased military spending across NATO members. As was the case with reconstruction, the

war on Libya was deployed to argue for more future militarism before it was even finished. In June 2011, US Secretary of Defense Robert Gates "warned of 'a dim if not dismal future' [for NATO] unless more member nations scaled up their participation in the alliance's activities," including military spending.[71] NATO's Secretary-General delivered much the same message, saying that "[a]t the current rate of cuts [to defense spending], it is hard to see how Europe could maintain enough military capabilities to sustain similar operations in the future."[72] The chorus of increased militarism was sung not only by politicians. The Centre for European Reform claimed "the new division of labour between Europe and the US [epitomized by Operation Unified Protector] can only work if European governments continue to invest in their militaries."[73] And according to the Atlantic Council, the "best outcome for the alliance would be if Libya serves as a wake-up call in European capitals to protect core defense capabilities even as they manage fiscal austerity."[74]

Leaving aside the glaring contradiction of using a war purportedly waged to make the world more humane to argue for increased militarism, what is interesting about all of these calls is they were framed by economic crisis. Rasmussen observed that "NATO's sea and air mission in Libya is the first major military engagement undertaken since the global financial crisis," and that "[t]he economic challenges that European nations face are immense, but that must not prevent them from seeing the wider strategic picture" lest they turn the economic crisis into a security crisis.[75] The Atlantic Council asserted that Operation Unified Protector was "even more remarkable given the Alliance mustered the political will and resources to pull this off during an existential financial and economic crisis for Europe."[76] This concern and surprise are misplaced. War-making on the part of imperial states is not dependent on available resources in a moment of crisis, such that austerity measures will reduce war-making. Instead, crises are dialectically related to surpluses of capital, such that the larger the surplus, the more catastrophic the crisis, and the more the need for its displacement through, among other mechanisms, war. War and militarism are not political policies that run contradictory to capitalist crisis. They are temporary remedies for crisis. Because they selectively consume surplus capital and create opportunities to invest portions of the remaining capital, imperial wars like that waged against Libya and militarism are more, *not* less, needed in moments of crisis.

The politics of the war are explained by the asymmetrical distribution of the costs of capital devaluation and opportunities for accumulation realized through the destruction of Libya. The Security Council vote on Resolution 1973 was 10 in favour, none opposed, with 5 abstentions. The abstentions, cast by Brazil, China, Germany, India, and Russia, have been explained through reference to the responsibility-to-protect doctrine.[77] For all of the aforementioned problems with the doctrine, these interpretations are wrong-headed. Cast in terms of value and the problem of surplus capital, however, the vote makes perfect sense. The major capitalist states on the Council that supported the resolution—the US, UK, France, Portugal—are in the process of furthering neo-liberal restructuring, ostensibly in response to crisis, and have seen domestic hegemonies increasingly called into question as a result. They needed a military means of temporarily addressing the economic crisis and its ideological consequences. Those state/society complexes not suffering under the weight of so much overaccumulated capital, and its political implications, abstained. Privately owned value in Brazil, China, Germany, India, and Russia did not need other capital destroyed by surplus capital in the form of bombs to protect the value of the remaining capital and provide it more opportunities to accumulate while reinforcing domestic power

relations. This division between those states in most desperate need of having the financial crisis temporarily addressed (their support of the war and securing outlets for surplus capital) and those not needing it (not supporting the war and not securing outlets for surplus capital) was starkly drawn by an official with the Libyan rebel oil firm AGOCO when he "said the company [might] have difficulties working with China, Russia, and Brazil which opposed tough sanctions on Gaddafi." To modify the adage somewhat: to the victor go opportunities to temporarily alleviate crises of surplus capital.

So, why Libya specifically? Libya was made the space in which the surplus capital crisis was temporarily addressed for two interrelated reasons: 1) the nature of value in the Libyan political economy, and 2) the political economy's relative isolation in and autonomy from the global politico-economic order. In 2011, the value invested in Libya was almost exclusively Libyan. Libya was home to little capital of the transnational historic bloc because sanctions imposed in the 1980s had only started to be lifted in 2003. This meant that when war was being debated by the UN, no significant value represented by the belligerent states would be violently destroyed. Libya could be targeted precisely because the space was not home to considerable amounts of transnational capital. Furthermore, the value of the society was not already an existing imperial possession. Value was destroyed in Libya under the guise of the responsibility to protect (but not in Palestine or Bahrain)—not because Libyans as people are asymmetrically valued, but because the other spaces are already imperial possessions. What Cronogue called Libya's "nation-specific condition" was that it was a space still available for imperial division.[78] The instrumentalization of the doctrine in those other spaces would have come at the expense of another imperial power. Libya offered an opportunity to further divide spoils among the imperial states; it did not require a *re*division.

The Libya-was-a-war-of-overaccumulated-capital reading also holds for the (non)participation of NATO members in Operation Unified Protector. Societies experiencing an acute crisis of surplus capital, neo-liberal restructuring, and challenges to local ideological hegemony participated militarily in the war on Libya; for example, Greece, Italy, and Spain. Conversely, societies relatively unaffected by crisis and material and ideological reordering—say, the Czech Republic, Germany, and Poland—did not participate. With the exception of Portugal, while not all NATO military participants in the war on Libya experienced severe capitalist crisis, all those members experiencing severe crisis were military participants.

Now, of course, by serving the material interests of the transnational historic bloc, the war on Libya served the material interests of nominally Canadian social forces party to the bloc. Recall in this regard Engler's mention of Suncor and SNC-Lavalin. The fact, though, that Canada had not suffered the acute effects of crisis means Canadian involvement in the war on Libya was more about the policy's ideological function than accumulation. Canada bombed Libya to provide the governing historic bloc with a legitimizing narrative in "support of an increasingly fragile domestic hegemony."[79] In this sense, Canada participated for the same ideological reasons as the more materially affected member states of NATO.

Nationalist ideologies are produced. Operations Mobile and Unified Protector reproduced a particular imagining of the Canadian nation, of what it means to be Canadian. In November 2011, Canada's Senate, through its celebration of the Libya campaign, ideologically reproduced Canadians as free, responsible, and superior. To start, the ceremony honoured Lieutenant-General Charles Bouchard and members of the state's repressive apparatuses. Then, as part of the ceremony, the Governor General declared that: "[t]ogether, you embody our commitment to international law, to the rights and freedoms we cherish in a democratic society, and to the personal values of duty, honour, and service." The Prime Minister explained that: "we believe that in a world where people look for hope and cry out for freedom, those who talk the talk of human rights must from time to time be prepared to likewise walk the walk;" and "soldier for soldier, sailor for sailor, airman for airman, the Canadian armed forces are the best in the world."[80]

This theatre reproduced a specific nationalist ideology. First, honouring the operational commander and members of the state's repressive apparatuses was the governing historic bloc's way of identifying ideal members of the Canadian political community.[81] Canadians were given the model to which they should aspire. Second, Canadians were reminded that, *inter alia*, ideal Canadians are committed to rights and freedoms. Given how the governing historic bloc has recast Canadianness over the past 30 years, the rights and freedoms to which ideal Canadians are committed are those exclusively of the market, and they "reflect the interests of private property owners, businesses, multinational corporations, and financial capital."[82] Model Canadians cherish the freedom to, say, move about the country applying their entrepreneurial skills—read: equalizing low wages across regions. Third, the values of ideal Canadians are personal. Located again in the *longue durée* political process of redefining Canadianness, these values are individual in nature. They are not social. This individualization is part and parcel of the discourse of individual responsibility.[83] The Libya mission afforded the historic bloc another opportunity to remind Canadians that ideal Canadians take ownership of their condition; they pay for their health care; they pay to educate their children; they adjust to the vicissitudes of the market. Model Canadians do not think in terms of social rights and entitlements, and others are not obliged to them.[84] Ultimately, model Canadians do not make claims of others. They realize their values themselves; they did so globally through Operation Mobile and they do so locally by having minimal expectations of other members of Canadian society and the state. The performance of this nationalist ideology distinguishes model Canadians from all other people, and model Canadians are the best people in the world.

In effect, Operation Mobile reaffirmed the neo-liberal subject of Canada, what Brodie has called the **entrepreneurial Canadian**.[85] Concomitantly, the campaign again defined this Canadian's relationship with the state. The state is his/her military protector. It is not an economic protector. As such, the state demands some of the highest levels of military spending since World War II while members of social forces not party to the governing historic bloc increasingly incur the costs of their social reproduction and are made increasingly insecure in the face of other state policies such as support for the Trans-Pacific Partnership. Most Canadians are no healthier or better educated for the war on Libya, but they have proven they are not "denuded, postmodern pacificists."[86]

The transnational historic bloc has long been realizing its neo-liberal project in the Canadian political economy. The ongoing production of the nationalist ideology of the entrepreneurial Canadian is integral to this project. The disembedding of capital from social and political constraints, for example, is facilitated by the entrepreneurial Canadian.[87] (S)he encourages privatization and the free movement of capital and commodities, accepts unemployment-inducing monetarism, and demands a minimalist state. In essence, the entrepreneurial Canadian realizes policies that enable finance capital to accumulate more capital and power in the Canadian politico-economic order. This accumulation of capital and power and realization of the neo-liberal project does not proceed

without contestation, however. Opposition to the Multilateral Agreement on Investment is ready evidence that this contestation grows. In this war between social forces, the governing historic bloc is increasingly eager for victories that will enable it to ideologically allay resistances. The otherwise unremarkable events in Libya were seized upon because they afforded just such a deployment: by reaffirming the neo-liberal Canadian, the war provided further ideological cover for the reproduction of neo-liberal social relations of production in a space where they are under increasing strain. Locally, the Libya campaign extended the historic bloc's dominance by reinforcing among subordinate social forces a nationalist ideology that materially benefits and empowers dominant social forces, particularly finance capital.

Globally, the war on Libya was a displacement of capitalism's crisis of surplus capital. It selectively consumed and opened new processes for the accumulation of value in a manner that served the interests of the transnational historic bloc. The Canadian state participated militarily because Operation Mobile served the ideological function, for the governing historic bloc, of reaffirming the entrepreneurial Canadian and, by extension, re-legitimizing the bloc's project in the Canadian political economy.

Conclusion

The Canadian state participated in the war on Libya because Operations Mobile and Unified Protector served the material and ideological interests of the transnational historic bloc in the global political economy and Canadian structure of accumulation.

My analysis has two notable implications for Canadians, particularly members of subordinate social forces. First, Canada will increasingly repatriate to the local political economy those policies the state performs in the global order. Already, the long occupation of Afghanistan has produced an increasingly deleterious militarism in Canadian society. As bothersome as this new normal is, even more worrying is the fact that imperial war abroad to consume surplus capital means the negation of democracy at "home." The more Canadians commit wars such as that against Libya, and the more they imagine themselves as entrepreneurial citizens, the more they will privilege private property and individual responsibility over a sense of sociality and its attendant conceptualizations, including rights and expectations. Second, undoubtedly Canadians will soon be urged on to another war, again under the cover of humanitarianism. Capitalist crisis makes war more likely, not less. The ongoing crisis of overaccumulated capital is increasingly acute, which means, in turn, that the transnational historic bloc will again seek temporary relief through the consumption and destruction of value. The war on Libya was another in a long line of iterations of the displaced global crisis of surplus capital, but it will not be the last.

Questions for Review

1. Identify and explain three central elements of the historical materialist approach.
2. What do you make of the prevailing explanations for the war on Libya? Do you find the responsibility-to-protect argument convincing?
3. How did the war on Libya address the global crisis of surplus capital?
4. Describe the Canadian identity ideologically reaffirmed through Operation Mobile. How would you imagine "Canadianness" differently?

Suggested Readings

Bellamy, Alex J., and Paul D. Williams. 2011. "The new politics of protection? Côte d'Ivoire, Libya and the responsibility to protect." *International Affairs* 87, 4: 825–50.

Brun, Ellen, and Jacques Hersh. 2012. "Faux internationalism and really existing imperialism." *Monthly Review* 63, 11 (April): 36–48.

Cox, Robert W. 1987. *Production, Power and World Order: Social Forces in the Making of History.* New York: Columbia University Press.

Cox, Robert W., with Timothy J. Sinclair. 1996. *Approaches to* *World Order.* Cambridge: Cambridge University Press.

Harvey, David. 2006. *The Limits to Capital.* London: Verso.

Ismi, Asad. 2011. "The empire strikes back: Libya attacked by the U.S. and NATO." *Canadian Centre for Policy Alternatives Monitor* (May): 20–21. Available at www.policyalternatives.ca/publications/monitor/middle-east-revolution-part-iii.

Neufeld, Mark. 2004. "Pitfalls of emancipation and discourses of security: Reflections on Canada's 'security with a human face.'" *International Relations* 18, 1 (March): 109–23.

Notes

1. Robert W. Cox, "Middlepowermanship, Japan, and future world order," in Robert W. Cox, with Timothy J. Sinclair, *Approaches to World Order* (Cambridge: Cambridge University Press, 1966), p. 251.
2. Samir Amin, "Libya is neither Tunisia nor Egypt," *MRZine*, 24 May 2011. Available at http://mrzine.monthlyreview.org/2011/amin240511.html.
3. International Crisis Group, *Popular Protest in North Africa and the Middle East (V): Making Sense of Libya*, No. 107, 6 June 2011, p. 1. See Mark Mazzettie and Eric Schmitt, "C.I.A. agents in Libya aid airstrikes and meet rebels," *New York Times*, 30 March 2011. Available (by subscription) at www.nytimes.com/2011/03/31/world/africa/31intel.html?_r=4&adxnnl=1&seid=auto&smid=tw-nytimesglobal&adxnnlx=1382102128-s8pWtLNkGaRQI09ojZspcA.
4. United Nations Security Council, Department of Public Information, "Security Council press statement on Libya," SC/10180—AFR/2120, 22 February 2011. Available at www.un.org/News/Press/docs/2011/sc10180.doc.htm.
5. BBC News Middle East, "Libya protests: Defiant Gaddafi refuses to quit," 22 February 2011. Available at www.bbc.co.uk/news/world-middle-east-12544624.
6. Alex J. Bellamy and Paul D. Williams, "The new politics

of protection? Côte d'Ivoire, Libya and the responsibility to protect," *International Affairs* 87 (2011): 825.

7. Bruno Pommier, "The use of force to protect civilians and humanitarian action: The case of Libya and beyond," *International Review of the Red Cross* 93 (December 2011): 1067.

8. Ibid., p. 1079.

9. CBC News, "Canada imposes additional sanctions against Libya," 27 February 2011. Available at www.cbc.ca/news/politics/canada-imposes-additional-libyan-sanctions-1.1017281.

10. CTV News, "Canada will fight to protect Libyan civilians: Harper," 19 March 2011. Available at www.ctvnews.ca/canada-will-fight-to-protect-libyan-civilians-harper-1.620889.

11. Mark Iype, "Harper gains advantage with Libya participation: Experts," 20 March 2011. Available at Canada.com, www.canada.com/news/Harper+gains+advantage+with+Libya+participation+experts/4474092/story.html.

12. Tom Blackwell, "Canada contributed a disproportionate amount to Libya air strikes: sources," *National Post*, 25 August 2011. Available at http://news.nationalpost.com/2011/08/25/canada-contributed-a-disproportionate-amount-to-libya-air-strikes-sources/.

13. James Cudmore, "Libyan mission racked up $11M in hotel bills," CBC News, 20 September 2012. Available at www.cbc.ca/news/politics/libyan-mission-racked-up-11m-in-hotel-bills-1.1198074.

14. Margaret Wente, "Why are we at war in Libya?" *The Globe and Mail*, 22 March 2011. Available at www.theglobeandmail.com/commentary/why-are-we-at-war-in-libya/article623626/.

15. Global News, "Looking at Libya," 26 June 2011. Available at www.cigionline.org/articles/2011/06/looking-libya.

16. Jeffrey Simpson, "Canada went into Libya with lofty ideals and little knowledge," *The Globe and Mail*, 15 June 2011. Available at www.theglobeandmail.com/commentary/canada-went-into-libya-with-lofty-ideals-and-little-knowledge/article625312/; *Global News*, "Looking at Libya."

17. Elizabeth Dickinson, "Does the world belong in Libya's war?" *Foreign Policy*, 18 March 2011; with response "Yes. Now let's hope it's not too late," Romeo Dallaire with Jeffrey Bernstein, Available at www.foreignpolicy.com/articles/2011/03/18/does_the_world_belong_in_libyas_war?page=0,1.

18. Aurel Braun, "Human Rights Council burnished Libya's image," *Toronto Star*, 27 February 2011. Available at www.thestar.com/opinion/editorialopinion/2011/02/27/human_rights_council_burnished_libyas_image.html.

19. Anthony Seaboyer, "Libya and Canadian military action: Queen's University expert," 2 March 2011. Available at http://m.queensu.ca/media/newsreleases/libya-and-can-adian-military-action-queens-university-expert.

20. Fen Hampson, "Libya's bigger lesson? There are no lessons," *iPolitics*, 29 August 2011. Available at www.ipolitics.ca/2011/08/29/fen-hampson-libyas-bigger-lesson-there-are-no-lessons/. Lloyd Axworthy, "In Libya, we move toward a more humane world," *The Globe and Mail*, 23 August 2011. Available at www.theglobeandmail.com/commentary/in-libya-we-move-toward-a-more-humane-world/article626440/.

21. Timothy J. Sinclair, "Beyond international relations theory: Robert W. Cox and approaches to world order," in Robert W. Cox, with Timothy J. Sinclair, *Approaches to World Order* (Cambridge: Cambridge University Press, 1966), p. 8.

22. David Harvey, *The Limits to Capital*, new and updated ed. (London: Verso, 2006), p. xxiii.

23. Karl Marx, *Capital: Volume One*, trans. Ben Fowkes (New York: Vintage, 1977), p. 129.

24. Harvey, *The Limits to Capital*, p. 12.

25. Sinclair, p. 9.

26. V.I. Lenin, *Lenin on Imperialism: The Eve of the Proletarian Social Revolution* (Peking: Foreign Language Publishing House, 1960), p. 18.

27. Robert W. Cox, *Production, Power, and World Order: Social Forces in the Making of History* (New York: Columbia University Press, 1987), p. 409.

28. Ibid., p. 7.

29. Robert W. Cox, "Towards a post-hegemonic conceptualization of world order: reflections on the relevancy of Ibn Khaldun," in Robert W. Cox, with Timothy J. Sinclair, *Approaches to World Order* (Cambridge: Cambridge University Press, 1966), p. 154.

30. Harvey, *The Limits to Capital*, p. 83.

31. Ibid., p. xxiii.

32. Rosa Luxemburg, "The Accumulation of Capital—An Anti-Critique," in Rosa Luxemburg and Nikolai Bukharin, *Imperialism and the Accumulation of Capital*, ed. Kenneth J. Tarbuck (London: Penguin, 1972), p. 60.

33. Harvey, *The Limits to Capital*, p. 97.

34. Ibid., p. 329.

35. Ibid., p. 195.

36. William Coleman and Tony Porter, "'Playin' along': Canada and global finance," pp. 241–64 in Wallace Clement and Leah F. Vosko, eds., *Changing Canada: Political Economy as Transformation*, (Montreal and Kingston: McGill-Queen's University Press, 2003).

37. Mark Neufeld, "Pitfalls of emancipation and discourses of security: Reflections on Canada's 'security with a human face,'" *International Relations* 18, 1 (March 2004): 120.

38. CBC News, "Harper: Libya air mission poses risks," 19 March 2011. Available at www.cbc.ca/news/world/harper-libya-air-mission-poses-risks-1.977098.

39. Yves Engler, "Why Canada attacked Libya," 29 March 2011. Available at http://yvesengler.com/2011/03/29/why-canada-attacked-libya/.

40. Margaret Wente, "Blame R2P: The intellectuals go to war," *The Globe and Mail*, 26 March 2011. Available at www.theglobeandmail.com/commentary/blame-r2p-the-intellectuals-go-to-war/article623734/.

41. Kyle Matthews, "Canada's abandonment of the responsibility to protect," *Centre for International Policy Studies*, 20 September 2012. Available at http://cips.uottawa.ca/canadas-abandonment-of-the-responsibility-to-protect/.

42. Tim Dunne and Jess Gifkins, "Libya and the state of intervention," *Australian Journal of International Affairs* 65 (November 2011): 515–29.

43. Spencer Zifcak, "The responsibility to protect after Libya and Syria," *Melbourne Journal of International Law*, 13 (June 2012): 59–93.

44. Graham Cronogue, "Responsibility to protect: Syria[,] the law, politics and future of humanitarian intervention post-Libya." *International Humanitarian Legal Studies*, 3 (2012): 124–59.

45. Bellamy and Williams, p. 847.

46. Pommier, p. 1079.

47. Richard Falk, "Libya after Qaddafi," *The Nation*, 14 November 2011, p. 6.

48. Ibid., p. 6.

49. Ibid.

50. Ibid.

51. Sean F. McMahon, "Challenging Canada's myths about its role in Palestine," *Electronic Intifada*, 18 May 2010. Available at http://electronicintifada.net/content/challenging-canadas-myths-about-its-role-palestine/8828.

52. Elle Brun and Jacques Hersh, "Faux internationalism and really existing imperialism," *Monthly Review*, April 2012, p. 37.

53. "Polish PM chides Europe over Libya 'hypocrisy,'" *Reuters*, 9 April 2011. Available at www.reuters.com/article/2011/04/09/poland-eu-libya-idAFLDE73806T20110409.

54. Asad Ismi, "The Empire strikes back: Libya attacked by the U.S. and NATO," *Centre for Canadian Policy Alternatives Monitor*, May 2011. Available at www.policyalternatives.ca/publications/monitor/middle-east-revolution-part-iii.

55. Immanuel Wallerstein, "The great Libyan distraction," *iwallerstein.com*, 1 April 2011. Available at www.iwallerstein.com/great-libyan-distraction/.

56. Sean F. McMahon, "Egypt's social forces, the state, and the Middle East order," pp. 151–72 in D. Tschirgi, W. Kazziha, and S.F. McMahon, eds., *Egypt's Tahrir Revolution* (Boulder, CO: Lynne Rienner, 2013).

57. Russia Television, "Gaddafi gold-for-oil dollar-doom plans behind Libya 'mission'?" *YouTube*. Available at www.youtube.com/watch?v=GuqZfaj34nc.

58. Alexander Cockburn, "What's really going on in Libya?" *Counterpunch*, 15–17 April 2011. Available at www.counterpunch.org/2011/04/15/what-s-really-going-on-in-libya/.

59. William R. Clark, *Petrodollar Warfare: Oil, Iraq and the Future of the Dollar* (Gabriola, BC: New Society Publishers, 2005).

60. Samir Amin, "An imperialist springtime? Libya, Syria, and beyond," *MRZine*, 28 April 2012. Available at http://mrzine.monthlyreview.org/2012/amin280412.html.

61. Edward Said, "The Arab condition," *Al-Ahram Weekly*, 22–28 May 2003. Available at http://weekly.ahram.org.eg/2003/639/op2.htm.

62. Brun and Hersh, p. 46; Ismi, "The Empire strikes back: Libya attacked by the U.S. and NATO"; and Amin, "An Imperialist springtime? Libya, Syria, and beyond."

63. International Crisis Group, p. 1.

64. United Nations Development Programme, *Human Development Report 2011—Sustainability and Equity: A Better Future for All* (New York: United Nations Development Programme, 2011).

65. Ben Barry, "Libya's lessons," *Survival* 53 (October–November 2011): 8.

66. Ian Brzezinski, "Lesson from Libya: NATO alliance remains relevant," *National Defense*, November 2011: 18.

67. Sebastian Tong, "Analysis: Investors eye promise, pitfalls in post-Gaddafi Libya," *Reuters*, 22 August 2011. Available at www.reuters.com/article/2011/08/22/us-libya-investment-idUSTRE77L4NG20110822.

68. Jerome Taylor, Kevin Rawlinson, Laurie Martin, and Charlotte Allen, "Dash for profit in post-war Libya carve-up," *The Independent*, 24 August 2011. Available at www.independent.co.uk/news/business/news/dash-for-profit-in-postwar-libya-carveup-2342798.html.

69. Brun and Hersh, p. 37.

70. African Human Security Working Group, Frequently Asked Questions. Available at http://africahumansecurity.weebly.com/faqs.html.

71. Thom Shanker, "Defense secretary warns NATO of 'dim' future," *New York Times*, 10 June 2011. Available at www.nytimes.com/2011/06/11/world/europe/11gates.html?_r=0.

72. Anders Fogh Rasmussen, "NATO after Libya," *Foreign Affairs* 90 (July/August 2011): full text.

73. Tomas Valasek, *What Libya says about the future of the transatlantic alliance* (London: Centre for European Reform, 2011), p. 5.

74. Damon M. Wilson, "Learning from Libya: The right lessons for NATO," *Issue Brief—Atlantic Council*, September 2011 (Washington, DC: Atlantic Council of the United States, 2011), p. 3.

75. Rasmussen, "NATO after Libya."

76. Wilson, p. 1.

77. See Bellamy and Williams, p. 844, and Pommier, p. 1068.
78. Cronogue, p. 126.
79. Neufeld, p. 120.
80. "Harper hails Libya mission as 'great military success,'" *The Globe and Mail*, 24 November 2011. Available at www.theglobeandmail.com/news/politics/harper-hails-libya-mission-as-great-military-success/article4106634/.
81. Janine Brodie, "On being Canadian," eds., *Reinventing Canada: Politics of the 21st Century* (Toronto: Prentice-Hall, 2003), p. 20.
82. David Harvey, *A Brief History of Neoliberalism* (Oxford: Oxford University Press, 2007), p. 7.
83. Janine Brodie and Linda Trimble, "Reinventing Canada: An overview," in Janine Brodie and Linda Trimble, eds., *Reinventing Canada: Politics of the 21st Century* (Toronto: Prentice-Hall, 2003), p. 7.
84. Ibid., p. 7.
85. Brodie, pp. 18–30.
86. Wilson, p. 2.
87. Harvey, p. 11.

Selected Bibliography

Comprehensive Texts

Byers, Michael. 2007. *Intent for a Nation.* Vancouver: Douglas and McIntyre.
Cohen, Andrew. 2003. *While Canada Slept: How We Lost Our Place in the World.* Toronto: McClelland and Stewart.
Cooper, Andrew F. 1997. *Canadian Foreign Policy: Old Habits and New Directions.* Scarborough, ON: Prentice-Hall.
Eayrs, James. 1963. *The Art of the Possible: Government and Foreign Policy in Canada.* Toronto: University of Toronto Press.
English, John, and Norman Hillmer, eds. 1992. *Making a Difference? Canada's Foreign Policy in a Changing World Order.* Toronto: Lester.
Granatstein, J.L., ed. 1986. *Canadian Foreign Policy: Historical Readings.* Toronto: Copp Clark Pitman.
Hart, Michael. 2008. *From Pride to Influence: Towards a New Canadian Foreign Policy.* Vancouver: UBC Press.
Holloway, Steven Kendall. 2006. *Canadian Foreign Policy: Defining the National Interest.* Peterborough, ON: Broadview Press.
James, Patrick, Nelson Michaud, and Marc J. O'Reilly, eds. 2006. *Handbook of Canadian Foreign Policy.* Lanham, MD: Lexington Books.
Keating, Tom. 2013. *Canada and World Order: The Multilateralist Tradition in Canadian Foreign Policy*, 3rd ed. Don Mills, ON: Oxford University Press.
Kirton, John. 2007. *Canadian Foreign Policy in a Changing World.* Scarborough, ON: Nelson Education.
MacKay, R.A., and E.B. Rogers. 1938. *Canada Looks Abroad.* London: Oxford University Press.
Michaud, Nelson, and Kim Richard Nossal, eds. 2001. *Diplomatic Departures: The Conservative Era in Canadian Foreign Policy, 1984–93.* Vancouver: UBC Press.
Munton, Don, and John Kirton, eds. 1992. *Canadian Foreign Policy: Selected Cases.* Toronto: Prentice-Hall.
Nossal, Kim Richard. 1997. *The Politics of Canadian Foreign Policy*, 3rd ed. Scarborough, ON: Prentice-Hall.
Nossal, Kim Richard, Stéphane Roussel, et Stéphane Paquin. 2007. *Politique international et défense au Canada et au Québec.* Montréal: Les Presses de l'Université de Montréal.
———. 2011. *International Policy and Politics in Canada.* Toronto: Pearson Canada.
Smith, Heather A., and Claire Turenne Sjolander, eds. 2013. *Canada in the World: Internationalism in Canadian Foreign Policy.* Don Mills, ON: Oxford University Press.
Tomlin, Brian W., Norman Hillmer, and Fen Osler Hampson. 2008. *Canada's International Policies: Agendas, Alternatives, and Politics.* Don Mills, ON: Oxford University Press.
Tucker, Michael. 1980. *Canadian Foreign Policy: Contemporary Issues and Themes.* Toronto: McGraw-Hill Ryerson.
Tucker, Michael J., Raymond B. Blake, and P.E. Bryden, eds. 2000. *Canada and the New World Order.* Toronto: Irwin.

Welsh, Jennifer. 2004. *At Home in the World: Canada's Global Vision for the 21st Century*. Toronto: HarperCollins.
Canada Among Nations, an annual edited volume, is organized around a timely theme. It is a product of the
Norman Paterson School of International Affairs (NPSIA) at Carleton University and is currently published
by the Centre for International Governance Innovation (CIGI) in partnership with NPSIA.

Academic Journals

Articles on Canadian foreign policy can be found in many peer-reviewed academic journals
around the world. That being said, however, there are two journals that specialize in the
study of Canadian foreign policy. The Canadian International Council, founded in 1928 as
the Canadian Institute for International Affairs, is Canada's oldest association for the discussion of international events and Canada's place in the world. The CIC publishes the
International Journal. *International Journal* has been published quarterly since 1946 and
has been the starting point of many of the most important debates in Canadian foreign
policy. *Canadian Foreign Policy Journal*, which was started in 1995, is published by the
Norman Paterson School of International Affairs at Carleton University. This journal
includes articles from practitioners, academics, and media representatives, as well as
roundtable discussions, documents, and book reviews.

Literature Reviews and Perspectives on Canadian Foreign Policy

Black, David R., and Heather A. Smith. 1993. "Notable Exceptions? New and Arrested Directions in Canadian
Foreign Policy Literature," *Canadian Journal of Political Science* 26, 4 (December): 745–75.
Blanchette, Arthur E. 1977. *Canadian Foreign Policy 1955–1965: Selected Speeches and Documents*. Ottawa:
Carleton Library.
———. 1980. *Canadian Foreign Policy 1966–1976: Selected Speeches and Documents*. Ottawa: Carleton Library.
———, ed. 1994. *Canadian Foreign Policy 1977–1992: Selected Speeches and Documents*. Ottawa: Carleton
University Press.
Granatstein, J.L. 1969. *Canadian Foreign Policy Since 1945: Middle Power or Satellite*. Toronto: Copp Clark.
Hawes, Michael K. 1984. *Principal Power, Middle Power, or Satellite? Competing Perspectives in the Study of
Canadian Foreign Policy*. Toronto: York Research Programme in Strategic Studies.
Molot, Maureen Appel. 1990. "Where Do We, Should We, Or Can We Sit? A Review of Canadian Foreign Policy
Literature," *International Journal of Canadian Studies* 1, 2 (Spring–Fall): 77–96.
Nossal, Kim Richard. 2000. "Home-Grown IR: The Canadianization of International Relations," *Journal of
Canadian Studies* 35, 1 (Spring): 95–114.
Stairs, Denis. 1994. "Will and Circumstance and the Postwar Study of Canadian Foreign Policy," *International
Journal* 50, 1 (Winter): 9–39.

Middle Power Perspectives

Andrew, Arthur. 1993. *The Rise and Fall of a Middle Power*. Toronto: Lorimer.
Axworthy, Lloyd. 2003. *Navigating a New World: Canada's Future*. Toronto: Vintage.
Chapnick, Adam. 2000. "The Canadian Middle Power Myth," *International Journal* 55, 2 (Spring): 188–206.
———. 2009. *Canada's Voice: The Public Life of John Wendell Holmes*. Vancouver: UBC Press.
Cooper, Andrew F. 1997. *Niche Diplomacy: Middle Powers after the Cold War*. Toronto: Macmillan.

Cooper, Andrew F., Richard A. Higgott, and Kim Richard Nossal. 1994. *Relocating Middle Powers: Australia and Canada in a Changing World Order*. Vancouver: UBC Press.

Dewitt, David B. 2000. "Directions in Canada's International Security Policy: From Marginal Actor at the Centre to Central Actor at the Margins," *International Journal* 55, 2 (Spring): 167–87.

Holmes, John W. 1970. *The Better Part of Valour: Essays on Canadian Diplomacy*. Ottawa: Carleton Library; Toronto: McClelland and Stewart.

———. 1976. *Canada: A Middle-Aged Power*. Ottawa: Carleton Library; Toronto: McClelland and Stewart.

Hynek, Nik, and David Bosold, eds. 2010. *Canada's Foreign & Security Policy: Soft and Hard Strategies of a Middle Power*. Don Mills, ON: Oxford University Press.

Pratt, Cranford, ed. 1990. *Middle Power Internationalism: The North–South Dimension*. Montreal and Kingston: McGill-Queen's University Press.

Principal Power Perspectives

Dewitt, David B., and John J. Kirton. 1983. *Canada as a Principal Power: A Study in Foreign Policy and International Relations*. Toronto: John Wiley and Sons.

Eayrs, James. 1975. "Defining a New Place for Canada in the Hierarchy of World Power," *International Perspectives* (May–June): 15–24.

Hillmer, Norman, and Garth Stevenson, eds. 1977. *A Foremost Nation: Canadian Foreign Policy in a Changing World*. Toronto: McClelland and Stewart.

Hampson, Fen Osler, and Maureen Appel Molot. 1996. "Being Heard and the Role of Leadership," pp. 3–20 in Fen Osler Hampson and Maureen Appel Molot, eds., *Canada Among Nations 1996: Big Enough To Be Heard?* Ottawa: Carleton University Press.

———. 1998. "The New Can Do Foreign Policy," pp. 23–55 in Fen Osler Hampson and Maureen Appel Molot, eds., *Canada Among Nations 1998: Leadership and Dialogue?* Don Mills, ON: Oxford University Press.

Hampson, Fen Osler, Michael Hart, and Martin Rudner. 2000. "A Big League Player or Minor League Player?," pp. 1–25 in Fen Hampson, Michael Hart, and Martin Rudner, eds., *Canada Among Nations 1999: A Big League Player?* Don Mills, ON: Oxford University Press.

Kirton, John. 1999. "Canada as a Principal Financial Power: G7 and IMF Diplomacy in the Crisis of 1997–99," *International Journal* 54, 4 (Autumn): 603–24.

———. 2002. "Canada as a Principal Summit Power: G/8 Concert Diplomacy from Halifax 1995 to Kananaskis 2002," pp. 209–32 in Norman Hillmer and Maureen Appel Molot, eds., *Canada Among Nations 2002: A Fading Power*. Don Mills, ON: Oxford University Press.

Lyon, Peyton, and Brian Tomlin. 1979. *Canada as an International Actor*. Toronto: Macmillan of Canada.

Satellite Power Perspectives

Bashevkin, Sylvia. 1991. *True Patriot Love: The Politics of Canadian Nationalism*. Toronto: Oxford University Press.

Bow, Brian, and Patrick Lennox, eds. 2008. *An Independent Foreign Policy for Canada? Challenges and Choices for the Future*. Toronto: University of Toronto Press.

Clarkson, Stephen, ed. 1968. *An Independent Foreign Policy for Canada?* Toronto: McClelland and Stewart.

———. 1985. *Canada and the Reagan Challenge: Crisis and Adjustment, 1981–85*. Toronto: Lorimer.

———. 2002. *Uncle Sam and Us: Globalization, Neoconservatism, and the Canadian State*. Toronto: University of Toronto Press.

Clarkson, Stephen, and Matto Mildenberger. 2012. *Dependent America? How Canada and Mexico Construct US Power*. Toronto: University of Toronto Press.

Doran, Charles. 1996. "Will Canada Unravel?" *Foreign Affairs* 75 (September/October): 97–109.

Grant, George. 1965. *Lament for a Nation: The Defeat of Canadian Nationalism*. Toronto: McClelland and Stewart.

Hampson, Fen Osler, and Maureen Appel Molot. 2000. "Does the 49th Parallel Matter Anymore?," pp. 1–27 in Fen Osler Hampson and Maureen Appel Molot, eds., *Canada Among Nations 2000: Vanishing Borders*. Don Mills, ON: Oxford University Press.

Macleod, Alex, Stéphane Roussel, and Andri van Mens. 2000. "Hobson's Choice: Does Canada Have any Options in its Defence and Security Relations with the United States?," *International Journal* 55, 3 (Summer): 341–54.

Molot, Maureen Appel, and Norman Hillmer. 2002. "The Diplomacy of Decline," pp. 1–33 in Norman Hillmer and Maureen Appel Molot, eds., *Canada Among Nations 2002: A Fading Power*. Don Mills, ON: Oxford University Press.

Critical Approaches

Beier, J. Marshall, and Lana Wylie, eds. 2010. *Canadian Foreign Policy in Critical Perspective*. Don Mills, ON: Oxford University Press.

Howard, Peter, and Reina Neufeldt. 2000. "Canada's Constructivist Foreign Policy," *Canadian Foreign Policy* 8, 1 (Fall): 11–38.

Keeble, Edna, and Heather A. Smith. 1999. *(Re)Defining Traditions: Gender and Canadian Foreign Policy*. Halifax: Fernwood Publishing.

Neufeld, Mark. 1995. "Hegemony and Foreign Policy Analysis: The Case of Canada as a Middle Power," *Studies in Political Economy* 48: 7–29.

Roussel, Stéphane, and Charles-Philippe David. 1998. "Middle Power Blues," *American Review of Canadian Studies* 28 (Spring/Summer): 131–56.

Turenne Sjolander, Claire, and David R. Black. 1996. "Multilateralism Re-constituted and the Discourse of Canadian Foreign Policy," *Studies in Political Economy* 49 (Spring): 7–36.

Turenne Sjolander, Claire, Heather A. Smith, and Deborah Stienstra, eds. 2003. *Feminist Perspectives on Canadian Foreign Policy*. Don Mills, ON: Oxford University Press.

Stienstra, Deborah. 1994. "Can the Silence be Broken? Gender and Canadian Foreign Policy," *International Journal* 50, 1 (Winter): 103–27.

External Factors and Canadian Foreign Policy

Canadian foreign policy is greatly affected by two different aspects of the international environment: 1) the international system in which Canada must operate (geography, anarchy, polarity, etc.); and 2) Canada's place in that international system. The first aspect of the international environment comprises sets of variables that are givens, "in the sense that every foreign policy maker must confront them without being able to challenge them easily or rapidly."[1] The first of these aspects is explored by Christopher Kirkey and Michael Hawes in Chapter 9. They examine the impact on Canadian foreign policy when the international system changed from the stable bipolarity of the Cold War era to a new era marked by American unipolarity. This systemic change has meant that Ottawa now has much greater freedom of movement in pursuing its foreign policy. The second aspect of the international environment was discussed in the articles on middle power, principal power, and satellite power in Part I.

The rest of Part II focuses on the different external actors, individual states, and international organizations that Canada confronts in the international system. Canada's relationship with these external actors provides it with a number of constraints and opportunities in conducting its foreign policy.

This history of Canadian foreign policy since the end of the Second World War has been defined by the tension between bilateralism[2] and multilateralism. From pre-Confederation until 1945, Canada's foreign policy was a balancing act between two different bilateral relationships: the United Kingdom and the United States. Since 1945, it has been a balancing act between a bilateral relationship with the United States and a multilateral impulse through international organizations. At times, Canada has sought to distance itself from the United States, as with the Third Option initiative of the early 1970s, but at other times Canada has sought greater collaboration with the Americans, such as the decision to pursue a comprehensive trade agreement in the 1990s. Part II highlights both bilateralism and multilateralism, with chapters on Canada's bilateral relationship with the United States and China, as well as a chapter on Canada and the G20.

Canada's geography, security, economy, and culture are all inexorably intertwined with the United States. Over $2 billion in trade and half a million people cross the border each day. There also exists a vast collection of ties between family, friends, interest groups, sports leagues, and businesses on both sides of the border. These connections have been formalized in a number of different institutions including the International Joint Commission (IJC), Permanent Joint Board on Defence, NORAD, and the North American Free Trade Agreement (NAFTA). Further complicating matters is the power imbalance that exists between Canada and the United States. The US is the world's only superpower, with great wealth and military might, and Canada is a medium-sized country with roughly 10 per cent of its neighbour's population and economic size. Given the massive multi-disciplinary but asymmetrical relationship that exists between Canada and the United States, it is safe to say that no international connection is more fraught with dangers for the Canadian government.[3] When prime ministers become too close to American presidents—as Louis St Laurent did with Dwight Eisenhower, or Brian Mulroney did with Ronald Reagan—they are criticized for abandoning Canadian autonomy. However, when their relationships become too distant—such as between John Diefenbaker and John Kennedy, or Pierre Trudeau and Richard Nixon, or Jean Chrétien and George W. Bush—they are criticized for abandoning Canadian security and economic interests.[4]

Geoffrey Hale, in Chapter 10, summarizes the Canadian–American relationship across three broad sets of policy domains: trade-commercial, psychological-cultural, and institutional-procedural. Hale does not examine bilateral defence relations, but these are covered in other places in the book, especially by Sean McMahon (Chapter 8) and Douglas Ross (Chapter 20).

Just as the United Kingdom was an alternative major trading partner to the United States in the early part of the twentieth century, China has emerged as that alternative in the twenty-first century. While Duane Bratt discusses Canada–China relations exclusively in the energy sector (see Chapter 25), Charles Burton looks at the whole bilateral relationship in Chapter 11. Burton shows that Ottawa has tried to balance economic considerations with the promotion of human rights in its dealings with Beijing and that the Harper government has moved from one end of the spectrum to the other during its successive mandates.

International organizations comprise a second set of external factors. Canada is a great supporter of international organizations and belongs to most universal organizations (United Nations, World Bank, World Trade Organization, International Monetary Fund, International Criminal Court), regional organizations (North Atlantic Treaty Organization, Organization of American States, North American Free Trade Agreement), and historic/linguistic organizations (Commonwealth and Francophonie). Tom Keating has argued that Canada's interest in multilateral institutions has been due to both external sources (Canada's middle power position, trade dependency, and as a counterweight to the US) and domestic sources (activist Canadian politicians and officials, public opinion, and civil society).[5] Canada's role in the newest of these international organizations—the G20—is discussed in the last chapter in Part II.

In 2010, Canada hosted both the G8 in Huntsville, Ontario, and the G20 in Toronto, Ontario. Canada has jealously guarded its inclusion in the G8, but over the years, the G8 seemed an anachronism due to the rise of the BRIC countries (Brazil, Russia, India, and China). It was significant, then, that when the global financial crisis hit in 2008, it was the G20, not the G8, UN, or IMF, that became the key international forum. Ironically, former Prime Minister Paul Martin was a key catalyst for the formation of a G20.[6] Given the changing roles, responsibilities, and membership of these ad hoc (but important) international clubs, Canada's role in the G8 and G20 needs to be assessed. Paul Heinbecker, a former Canadian ambassador to the United Nations, provides such a discussion in Chapter 12, arguing that the G20 can complement, but not replace, existing international organizations, especially the United Nations. He also suggests that if the G20 endures, as seems likely, the trend of the prime minister's being the personification of the government of Canada on the international stage will continue.

Notes

1. Kim Richard Nossal, *The Politics of Canadian Foreign Policy*, 3rd ed. (Scarborough, ON: Prentice-Hall, 1997), 8.
2. This has also been called continentalism or regionalism.
3. See Robert O. Keohane and Joseph S. Nye, Jr., *Power and Interdependence: World Politics in Transition* (Boston: Little, Brown, 1977).
4. For a historical account see Lawrence Martin, *The Presidents and the Prime Ministers: Washington and Ottawa Face to Face: the Myth of Bilateral Bliss, 1867–1982* (Toronto: Doubleday, 1982).
5. Tom Keating, *Canada and World Order: The Multilateralist Tradition in Canadian Foreign Policy*, 2nd ed. (Don Mills, ON: Oxford University Press, 2002), 1–16.
6. Paul Martin, "A Global Answer to Global Problems," *Foreign Affairs* 84, 3 (May/June 2005), 2–6.

9 Canada in an Age of Unipolarity: Structural Change and Canadian Foreign Policy[1]

Christopher Kirkey and Michael Hawes

Key Terms

Alliance
Anarchic

Distribution of Capabilities
Great Power

Introduction

When one looks for an explanation as to why the government of Canada pursues a particular foreign policy strategy, as opposed to another equally compelling strategy (or what might appear to be an equally compelling strategy), a striking pattern quickly emerges. Most academics whose careers revolve around understanding Canadian foreign policy, along with many of their colleagues in the world of policy studies, argue that the key factors (indeed, the defining or determining factors) behind the planning and implementation of Canada's foreign policy are domestic. Interestingly, while the relative weighting of the various domestic determinants changes from time to time and from government to government, a striking consistency exists with respect to their continuing importance and indeed their dominance as an explanatory variable. There is no doubt that state-level explanations, especially those focusing on the respective foreign policy priorities and decisions of successive Canadian governments and their leaders, are directly relevant to and, as such, highly persuasive in explaining the specifics of Canada's engagement with the international community. They help us to understand pivotal political

decisions, key shifts in policy directions over time, and the approaches of governments with distinctly different understandings of what constitutes the Canadian national interest.

What is equally striking from our perspective is that very little attention is paid to subnational, transnational, regional, and system level variables. The latter is, perhaps, the most startling, given that we are still living in the wake of one of the most transformative moments in contemporary history—namely, a profound and undeniable shift from a highly structured and clearly bipolar international order to a much more complex and clearly unipolar world order. There has been very little serious scholarly examination of the extent to which these profound structural changes have affected Canada's foreign policy. Most serious accounts of Canadian foreign policy, defence policy, and, to a modestly lesser extent, development policy, direct us to national (and often mono-causal) explanations. More specifically, they direct our attention to internal or domestic factors that are specific to Canada to explain Ottawa's foreign policy priorities, actions, and activities. To the extent that external factors are considered, the focus has typically been on other actors; more specifically, on states, on international or regional organizations and, again to a lesser extent, on nongovernmental organizations (NGOs). These analyses tend to focus on the extraordinary impact the United States has had on Canada when it comes to foreign policy, though even here the impact is often seen in terms of Canada's dependence on the large US consumer market as opposed to US foreign policy priorities and the need for greater coherence in North America. To a lesser extent (and certainly less so in recent years), there has been something of a focus on the importance of **alliances** like the North Atlantic Treaty Organization (NATO), international organizations like the United Nations, and even on NGOs. It is worth noting, however, that Canada's traditional interest in peacekeeping, in multilateral management, and in collective security have been replaced by a heightened interest in Canada's overall prosperity and in the pursuit of new opportunities.

The broader international political and economic system, namely the context in which all of this behaviour takes place, is viewed by analysts and by the government (assuming that they consider it at all) as a simple outcome. This chapter argues that this view of foreign policy is incomplete, lacks nuance, and misses important (sometimes determining) realities. Foreign policy is not made in a vacuum, nor should it reflect some independent and impenetrable domestic environment. Rather, foreign policy decisions and priorities must be understood within the prevailing realities of the international system.

This essay sets out, in broad terms, to identify and assess the central characteristics of the unipolar international political system and to specifically examine what unipolarity means for Canadian foreign policy. Recent changes in the structure of the international system, we would argue, have provided successive Canadian governments with significantly increased freedom to consider and ultimately pursue high profile foreign policy initiatives. While not in and of itself determinative as an explanation for Canada's external behaviour—domestic variables, as noted above, are integral to any sophisticated and nuanced explanation of Canada's foreign policies and priorities—the structure of the international system has an important and consequential impact on Ottawa's engagement with the international community. In *Realism and International Politics*, Kenneth Waltz succinctly reminds us, in what is now a classic contribution to the theory of international politics, that "structures [have the tendency to] shape and shove; they do not determine the actions of states."[2] The **anarchic** structure of the international political system and the prevailing **distribution of capabilities** within it must be regarded as the *independent* variable, and the formulation and execution of foreign policy by states such as Canada as the *dependent* variable. This essay focuses on how a profound structural change—transitioning from the post-World War II bipolar Cold War system (1945–1991), which featured two great powers (the United States and the Soviet Union), to a system that today is widely considered to be unipolar and post-Cold War—might affect a nation's foreign policy. The United States is now widely recognized as the sole **great power**, alone possessing the political will, military might, and economic clout to play that key leadership role. This situation, we would argue, has created considerable unfettered latitude in foreign policy for nations like Canada.

In short, this chapter argues that this fundamental shift in the structure of the international system is of considerable import to Canadian foreign policy for two compelling reasons: first, the operational characteristics that define a unipolar environment, which are strikingly different than previous multipolar or bipolar moments, create a unique series of incentives and constraints that impact directly on foreign policy behaviour; and second, the current unipolar international system is likely to persist for some time, and consequently the success of Canadian foreign policy must recognize and be grounded in this reality.[3]

The Structure of the International Political System and Polarity

The most salient feature of the international system, dating back well before the 1648 Treaty of Westphalia and the emergence of the modern nation-state system, is its fundamentally anarchic character. To the extent that systemic structures exist at all, they depend on a consensus and on the willingness of states to support and legitimize them. The world, in short, lacks an overarching central authority or a "common interstate government."[4] It is a highly decentralized, loosely coordinated social realm populated by many types of actors—including states, international organizations like the United Nations, regional political bodies like the European Union, alliances and other collective defence arrangements like the North Atlantic Treaty Organization, and scores of diverse non-governmental organizations—in which states stand out as the preeminent actors. States are the highest political authority in the system, though they do, on occasion, concede or pool sufficient sovereignty to meet or achieve some specific common purposes. Within this anarchic international system, material resources or capabilities are distributed in a recognizably uneven fashion, with some states having a greater level of military, economic, social, and political assets than others.[5] Individual states that possess significant combined capabilities relative to other states are regarded as great powers. Kenneth Waltz, in his *Theory of International Politics*, reminds us that

"the economic, military and other capabilities of nations cannot be sectored and separately weighed. States are not placed in the top rank because they excel in one way or another. Their rank depends on how they score on all of the following items: size of population and territory, resource endowment, economic capability, military strength, political stability and competence."[6]

The distribution of capabilities in the international political system has changed over time, resulting in three particular configurations: multipolarity, with three or more great powers (1648–1945); bipolarity, featuring two great powers (1945–1991); and unipolarity, with the United States as the sole great power. The latter, in our view, represents the current state of the system and has since 1991.[7] Each of these configurations has proven to have important implications for the foreign policy of individual states. While not "determining" per se how a state behaves externally, the number of great powers present at any given time serves to create discernible constraints and opportunities for states. States, in response, formulate and conduct foreign policy in accordance with "differently structured international-political systems."[8]

A. Multipolarity

Multipolarity, the most commonplace distribution of capabilities witnessed in the international political system, is identified by:

- the existence of at least three great powers;
- the fact that the existence of a number of great powers can result in multiple threats from multiple sources. These threats can quickly shift—reflecting the flexibility embedded in a multipolar system—and be reconfigured from one grouping to another;[9]
- unclear and uncertain sources of threat. As Waltz so aptly observes, "who is a danger to whom and who can be expected to deal with

threats and problems are matters of uncertainty";[10]

- efforts to balance threats (through deterrence or defence), given the number of great powers, are decidedly more complicated (requiring some sense of who, when, where, and how to respond), and an increase in the probability of misperception and miscalculation (in the resolve, capabilities, and political actions of others) by great powers;[11]
- each great power, in addition to relying on internal capabilities to balance threats, seeking, in the first instance, to secure their survival through external efforts; namely, among other things, to actively participate in alliances. Great powers in a multipolar system are "militarily dependent on one another because none can defend itself alone";[12]
- membership of the great powers in, and the specific purposes of, a given alliance, which can be subject to rapid and significant shifts in coalitions and policy.[13] As explained by Glenn Snyder and Paul Diesing, a multipolar system allows for great variance in the alignment of great powers: "Structure provides incentives to align but does not affect who aligns with whom. Each major state is potentially an ally or adversary of any other one. Actual alignments are determined, not by system structure, but by the particular conflicts and common interests of states and by a process of competitive bargaining."[14]
- the inherent danger, as Robert Jervis reminds us, of formal obligations vested in alliance membership for great powers. Such membership dramatically circumscribes the flexibility and freedom for independent foreign policy decision-making;[15] and,
- the possibility of international crises and war, which are more likely to escalate and difficult to extinguish.[16]

B. Bipolarity

Bipolarity is a condition marked by several related characteristics, including, but not limited to, the following:

- the presence of only two preponderant powers in the international political systems, in this case, the United States of America and the Soviet Union;
- competition between the great powers (militarily, territorially, economically, ideologically), which will be truly global in scope and decidedly zero-sum in nature. This competition will encourage calculated and strategic foreign policy initiatives and responses. The intensity of the competition is prone to episodically facilitate "unnecessary conflicts along the peripheries"[17] resulting from "exceedingly competitive or aggressive policies that may trigger crises and war";[18]
- clarity of threat for the great powers. Each great power must realize that the other great power poses, by a measure that exceeds any other, the single greatest threat to its survival. The need to balance power against only one rival weakens the possibilities of miscalculation, "misperception, confusion and unpredictable interaction" in the formulation and exercise of foreign policy.[19] This is what Waltz called "the clarity of dangers" and "the uncertainty about who has to face them";[20]
- each great power, in the absence of other potential great powers and the presence of subordinate allies, recognizing and subscribing to the need to first and foremost independently (read: internally) provide defensive and deterrent capabilities to balance power. In short, each great power is reliant on itself for its continued survival;
- alliances (like NATO and the Warsaw Pact Treaty Organization) that, while established

and operationalized, "merely formalize a built-in polarity."[21] Given the significant differences in material resources among states, these were helpful but added "relatively little" and, as such, were not "indispensable" to the great powers.[22] As Jervis put it, "under bipolarity superpowers do not need allies because they have sufficient resources";[23]

- the structural reality that provides the necessary condition for the great powers to effectively, as Robert Gilpin put it, "control and regulate interactions within and between their respective spheres [East and West] of influence."[24] As such, allies in a bipolar configuration have very little opportunity—that is, they enjoy little bargaining leverage—to have an impact on the foreign policy decisions of the great powers except on issues of tremendous need and in the absence of attractive alternative options;[25]

- the defection of allies, under conditions of bipolarity, which will have no salient impact on the overall health of the prevailing balance of power. "Third parties," Waltz reminds us, "are not able to tilt the balance of power by withdrawing from one alliance and by joining the other";[26] and,

- a distribution of capabilities that is vulnerable to two potential critical developments: the inability or failure of one of the two great powers to maintain the balance; and the emergence of a new great power.[27]

C. Unipolarity

There is a significant and increasingly more sophisticated body of scholarship by international relations scholars on the emergence, impact, and durability of the unipolar system. Unipolarity, as a condition, and the current unipolar system, as a fact, are chiefly characterized by:

- the presence of a "gross imbalance of power in the world," featuring only one great power, in this case the United States;

- the absence of a current and/or imminent hostile state-level or national threats to the survival of the great power;

- increased influence of the great power, far fewer restraints on its external behaviour (a condition of "minimal constraint," according to Martha Finnemore), and the likelihood, given the absence of a counterweight with equal capabilities, of its increasing the scope and range of its involvement throughout the international political system—what Jervis calls "excessive expansion";[28]

- the built-in, internal dynamics embedded in a unipolar structure, which by definition imply and facilitate a relaxed, permissive environment for all states—an environment that contains the necessary framework (especially regarding the diminution of constraints and the increase in meaningful opportunities for external behaviour) for states with sufficient capabilities.

- the great power's eschewing the norms, rules, and conditions central to international institutions and multilateral arrangements and instead favouring what Stephen Walt calls "ad hoc coalitions of the willing," assembled "less for [the] capabilities they produce than for the appearance of legitimacy they convey."[29]

- balancing against potential national security threats that is undertaken even more so through independent development and deployment of internal capabilities.[30]

- the prompting of other states—either independently or through vehicles such as alliances—to attempt to balance against the great power;[31] and,

- likely impermanence, given the fluid distribution of capabilities over time in the international political system (principally driven by the uneven growth of states). In the words of Christopher Layne, unipolarity is a temporary "geopolitical interlude."[32]

What are the principal effects of a unipolar international political system on the purpose, role(s) and scope of alliances, specifically those alliances that were in place (meaning operational) prior to the advent of the unipolar moment and that were then and are now currently led by the sole great power?[33] One might predict that with the removal of external threat(s), the need for and logic of such alliances is eliminated. After all, alliances created in the international political arena to balance against threats (to address the constant sense of insecurity felt by states in an anarchic environment), which are in turn, as Stephen Walt points out, a direct function of a state's aggregate power, its geographic proximity, its offensive capability, and the perceived aggressiveness of its intentions, are surely rendered unnecessary.[34]

Indeed, while there is a literature that argues that the relevance of alliances is highly contestable in the context of the current international order, the remaining alliances, in the absence of a situation where balancing is provided by the existence of a small number of great powers, are subject to the following realities. First, they are prone to expand in scope (reflecting an increase in the number of participants and in the territorial reach) as the dominant power works to extend and consolidate its hegemonic position in the international system. Second, they are directed to serve political ends (at least in the first instance) as they are defined and determined by the great power. Lastly, with the exception of cost savings and reasons of political symbolism, alliances are even more dispensable in the unipolar than in a bipolar structure—a key result being that states allied with the sole great power will see a decrease in bargaining power, and "leverage opportunities" will

dramatically decline.[35] The transformation of the United States-dominated North Atlantic Treaty Organization (NATO) speaks directly to these points. Since 1991, NATO's membership, purpose, and geographic footprint (consider recent engagements/missions in Afghanistan, Somalia, and Libya) has grown considerably while actively serving political initiatives principally shaped and defined in Washington.[36]

Polarity: The Implications for Canadian Foreign Policy

What does this mean, both theoretically and practically, for Canadian foreign policy? What impact has the structural presence of a single great power in the international political system since 1991 had on Canada's external behaviour? We begin by first examining the powerful systemic forces that affected Canadian foreign policy and that were brought on by the system that immediately preceded the current unipolarity—the bipolar world dominated by the ideological conflict between United States and the Soviet Union.

Apart from the recognition that the international system was bipolar, the overriding consideration for Canada was the identity of one of the two poles—namely, the United States. As a committed ally of the United States in an ideologically hostile environment, Canada's range of external action was clearly circumscribed and constrained. Its bargaining power and influence (both with the United States and on the management and direction of salient issues in and with the international system) was, for the most part, muted. Canada depended on the United States for its continued existence in the nuclear age, and was overwhelmingly a "consumer of security."[37] Restraints on independent foreign policy initiatives that either challenged the core direction of American security and economic policies or possibly threatened to contribute to a crisis between the great powers were real and tangible.

Indeed, the structural conditions of the bipolar system encouraged Canada, in the first instance, to pursue a coherent post-World War II foreign policy strategy for nearly 50 years, focusing on one singular element: policies and actions designed to contribute to the maintenance of political, economic, and social order in the international political system. This objective was, arguably, most visibly manifested in Canada's thoroughgoing engagement in international institutions and the creation of, and commitment to, peacekeeping operations around the globe.[38] Conversely, selective opportunities for Canada to meaningfully engage in international affairs were available, provided the issue was not part of the fundamental matrix of the Soviet–American relationship.

Canada, it must be noted, would have had considerably less influence and fewer opportunities—and the constraints would have been even tighter—had one of the two great powers not been the United States. In short, Canada's long-standing (albeit positive) relationship with the United States (described by Arnold Wolfers as the "extreme of amity") directly served to prevent Canada from being subjected to the full range of structural effects lesser states might normally experience in a bipolar arrangement.[39] The high point in Canada's leverage with the United States came in the late 1940s and persisted through to the early 1960s. During this time, the principal means available for the Soviet Union to launch a devastating atomic attack against the United States was through the use of long range bomber aircraft, an attack that would require the use of Canadian airspace, in that the bombers and/or missiles would overfly Canadian territory en route to the United States.[40] The need for access by the United States to

Canadian airspace and territory to counter this threat (there were no attractive military and/or geographic alternatives available to Washington) benefited Canada. Canada's ability to demonstrate that it was effectively contributing, albeit selectively and on a small military/economic/human scale to the defence of the West, was important.

How times have changed. What has the collapse of the Soviet Union, and the advent of the unipolar structure of the international political system (led by our principal ally, the United States) meant for Canadian foreign policy? Foreign policy decision-makers, political and bureaucratic, in Ottawa should openly recognize the implications for Canada of the recent emergence of unipolarity. Of critical importance to Canada is the fact that the sole remaining great power is not the Soviet Union but instead a well-established and largely predictable partner and friend: the United States. Indeed, a unipolar system dominated by the former Soviet Union—one that continued to be viewed as a genuine threat—would have promoted very different policies and actions by Canada since 1991. Second, the dynamics of the current system have further eroded Canada's ability to influence the United States (which was not meaningful in the bipolar context) except on issues of tremendous need to the former and in the absence of attractive alternatives. Unipolarity has also meant an end to the Cold War, during which time Canada felt obligated to (but no longer has to) disproportionately focus its external behaviour on identifying and implementing mechanisms to maintain international order.

In a unipolar system, Canada has considerably more opportunity and far less constraints on its foreign policy behaviour. Simply put, in a non-zero-sum unipolar environment, the structural reality of the system is more permissive in character, disposing and encouraging states with considerable material capabilities, such as Canada, to more actively engage, indeed even champion leadership roles on issues it defines as important to itself and the international community, whether they are security-oriented in nature or revolve around normative notions of distributive justice. Prime examples of Canadian external behaviour since 1991 that can at least in part be attributed to the permissive and flexible characteristics of the current unipolar distribution of capabilities in the system include championing both the Mine Ban Treaty and the International Criminal Court; rejecting participation in both the US-led coalition war against Iraq and Washington's plans for ballistic missile defence; and participating in military activities (including combat) in Afghanistan, Kosovo, Somalia, and Libya. This even in the face of seemingly divergent foreign policy pursuits of Liberal governments led by Jean Chrétien and Paul Martin (principally characterized as following a human security agenda reliant on "soft power") and Conservative minority and majority governments under Stephen Harper (with a dominant emphasis on defence and security supported by hard military capabilities).

In this environment, Canada is also less likely to defer or blindly conform to the policies, interests, and rules advanced by the United States government. Active participation in international institutions will, under the condition of unipolarity, prove to be more acute for Canada. The structural logic of such a system suggests that Canada will continue to participate in previously established and potential new international institutions and rules-based multilateral social arrangements for two key reasons: first, to help offset the external behaviour of the great power by attempting to modify or constrain the use of unilateral US power; and second, to provide forums through which Canada can enhance its foreign policy autonomy and international standing.

Conclusion: Recognizing Structural Effects

This essay has demonstrated that a comprehensive and nuanced understanding of Canadian foreign policy must include a careful examination of the structural dynamics at work in the international system. That anarchic system, currently marked by a condition of unipolarity, is central to explaining Ottawa's external behaviour. The emergence of a unipolar world in 1991, coupled with a clear sense of who the remaining great power was, has generated its own set of incentives and constraints (embedded in the unipolar structure of our world) for Canadian foreign policy. Unipolarity has most especially provided the necessary precondition that has "allowed" Canada—now far less circumscribed in its capacity to independently engage in significant foreign policy pursuits—to commit itself to a wide range of (at times seemingly divergent) foreign policy initiatives. Structure in and of itself, Waltz correctly reminds us, "does not by any means explain everything."[41] It does, however, provide the necessary foundational prism from which to analyze the conduct of Canadian foreign policy.

Questions for Review

1. Why do most accounts that seek to explain Canadian foreign policy behaviour principally, if not overwhelmingly, rely on domestic factors?

2. Why is the structure of the international political system integral to understanding the foreign policy of states?

3. What are the most salient characteristics of multipolarity, bipolarity, and unipolarity?

4. What does the current unipolar distribution of capabilities mean for the planning and implementation of Canadian foreign policy?

Suggested Readings

Gilpin, Robert. 1981. *War and Change in World Politics.* Cambridge: Cambridge University Press.

Hawes, Michael, and Christopher Kirkey. 2012. "Canada in a unipolar world (?): New directions in Canadian foreign policy." *Canadian Foreign Policy Journal* 18, 1 (special issue – March), 2–8.

Ikenberry, G. John, Michael Mastanduno, and William C. Wohlforth. 2009. "Unipolarity, State Behavior, and Systemic Consequences." *World Politics* 61, 1 (January), 1–27.

Jervis, Robert. 1997. *System Effects: Complexity in Political and Social Life.* Princeton, NJ: Princeton University Press.

Waltz, Kenneth N. 1979. *Theory of International Politics.* Reading, MA: Addison-Wesley.

Waltz, Kenneth N. 2008. *Realism and International Politics.* New York: Routledge.

Wolfers, Arnold. 1962. *Discord and Collaboration: Essays on International Politics.* Baltimore: Johns Hopkins University Press.

Notes

1. This chapter draws, in part, from arguments advanced in Christopher Kirkey and Nicholas Ostroy, "Why is Canada in Afghanistan? Explaining Canada's military commitment," *American Review of Canadian Studies* 40, 2 (June, 200–13, 2010); and Michael Hawes and Christopher Kirkey, "Canada in a unipolar world (?): New directions in Canadian foreign policy," *Canadian Foreign Policy Journal* 18, 1 (March 2012), 2–8.

2. Kenneth N. Waltz, *Realism and International Politics* (New York: Routledge, 2008), p. 211. The seminal work of Kenneth Waltz places direct emphasis on the significance of the structure of the international political system as an independent variable in influencing foreign policy behaviour. See in particular Kenneth N. Waltz, *Man, the State and War: A Theoretical Analysis* (New York: Columbia University Press, 1959); Waltz, *Theory of International Politics* (Reading, MA: Addison-Wesley, 1979); and Waltz, *Realism and International Politics*. David Haglund, in a recent contribution, reminds us "that extreme caution is in order when one sets out to 'prove' how these structural forces exert their impact." David Haglund, "Orders and borders: Unipolarity and the issue of homeland security," *Canadian Foreign Policy Journal*, 18, 1 (March 2012), p. 15.

3. We reject the argument advanced by Christopher Layne that "The Unipolar Era has ended and the Unipolar Exit has begun." A relative and comparative qualitative and quantitative measurement of capabilities in 2014 fully suggests that the current system is unipolar, with the United States as the sole great power. For Layne's argument, see Christopher Layne, "This time it's real: The end of unipolarity and the *Pax Americana*," *International Studies*

Quarterly 56, 1 (March 2012), 203–13. For a recent compelling statement affirming the operation and durability of the position of the United States in the current unipolar system, see Josef Joffe, *The Myth of America's Decline: Politics, Economics and a Half Century of False Prophecies* (New York: W.W. Norton, 2014).

4. Joseph M. Grieco, *Cooperation among Nations: Europe, America, and Non-Tariff Barriers to Trade* (Ithaca, NY: Cornell University Press, 1990).

5. As described by Arthur Stein: "There are asymmetries in international politics. Some nations are more powerful than others." Arthur Stein, *Why Nations Cooperate: Circumstance and Choice in International Relations* (Ithaca, NY: Cornell University Press, 1990), p. 23.

6. Kenneth N. Waltz, *Theory of International Politics*, p. 131.

7. For the fullest statement on the effects of changes to the distribution of capabilities (i.e., power) in the international political system and the process of systemic change in international politics, see Robert Gilpin, *War and Change in World Politics* (Cambridge: Cambridge University Press, 1981).

8. Waltz, *Theory of International Politics*, p. 72.

9. John Lewis Gaddis, "The long peace: Elements of stability in the postwar international system," in Sean M. Lynn-Jones and Steven E. Miller, eds., *The Cold War and After: Prospects for Peace* (Cambridge: MIT Press, 1993), p. 11.

10. Waltz, *Realism and International Politics*, p. 61. For similar reasoning from Waltz, see *Theory of International Politics*, p. 165.

11. On the difficulties of great power coordination in a multipolar world, see John J. Mearsheimer, "Back to the future:

Instability in Europe after the Cold War," in Lynn-Jones and Miller, eds., *The Cold War and After: Prospects for Peace*, p. 152. On miscalculation, see Gilpin, *War and Change in World Politics*, p. 89.

12. Robert Jervis, *System Effects: Complexity in Political and Social Life* (Princeton, NJ: Princeton University Press, 1997), p. 112.

13. "In multipolar systems," Waltz writes, "there are too many powers to permit any of them to draw clear and fixed lines between allies and adversaries and too few to keep the effects of defection low. With three or more powers flexibility of alliances keeps relations of friendship and enmity fluid and makes everyone's estimate of the present and future relation of forces uncertain." *Theory of International Politics*, p. 168.

14. Glenn H. Snyder and Paul Diesing, *Conflict Among Nations: Bargaining, Decision Making, and System Structure in International Crises* (Princeton, NJ: Princeton University Press, 1977), p. 474.

15. As Jervis puts it: "Great powers may have to fight not because they have direct conflicts of interest but because the alternative is to endanger their security by losing a necessary partner to defeat or defection." Robert Jervis, *System Effects: Complexity in Political and Social Life*, p. 112.

16. See Mearsheimer, "Back to the future: Instability in Europe after the Cold War," p. 150. For the fullest analysis of the structure of international crises, see Snyder and Diesing, *Conflict among Nations: Bargaining, Decision Making, and System Structure in International Crises*.

17. Robert Jervis, "Unipolarity: A structural perspective," *World Politics* 61, 1 (January 2009), p. 197.

18. Stephen Van Evera, "Primed for peace: Europe after the Cold War," in Lynn-Jones and Miller, eds., *The Cold War and After: Prospects for Peace*, p. 223. As a scholar and government practitioner, Henry Kissinger was not attracted by the workings of bipolarity: "A bipolar world loses the perspective for nuance; a gain for one side appears as an absolute loss for the other. Every issue seems to involve a question of survival. The smaller countries are torn between a desire for protection and a wish to escape big-power dominance. Each of the superpowers is beset by the desire to maintain its preeminence among its allies, to increase its influence among the uncommitted, and to enhance its security vis-à-vis its opponent. The fact that some of these objectives may well prove incompatible adds to the strain on the international system." Henry A. Kissinger, *American Foreign Policy: Three Essays* (New York: W.W. Norton, 1969), p. 56.

19. John Lewis Gaddis, "International relations theory and the end of the Cold War," in Lynn-Jones and Miller, eds., *The Cold War and After: Prospects for Peace*, p. 355.

20. Waltz, *Theory of International Politics*, p. 172.

21. George Liska, *Nations in Alliance: The Limits of Interdependence* (Baltimore: Johns Hopkins University Press, 1962).

22. Ibid., p. 171.

23. Jervis, *System Effects: Complexity in Political and Social Life*, p. 112.

24. Gilpin, *War and Change in World Politics*, p. 29.

25. According to Jervis, because the distribution of power cannot be much changed by their actions, the great powers' "allies lose their ability to influence their larger partners." Jervis, *System Effects: Complexity in Political and Social Life*, p. 115. In Waltz's examination of the post-World War II period (written in 1979), he notes that "although concessions to allies are sometimes made, neither the United States nor the Soviet Union alters its strategy or changes its military dispositions simply to accommodate associated states." Waltz, *Theory of International Politics*, p. 170.

26. Waltz, *Theory of International Politics*, p. 169.

27. Gilpin, *War and Change in World Politics*, pp. 90–91.

28. Jervis, "Unipolarity: A Structural Perspective," p. 197. According to Stephen Walt, "the United States can now contemplate actions it would have quickly rejected when the Soviet Union was intact." Stephen M. Walt, "Alliances in a unipolar world," *World Politics*, 61, 1 (January 2009), p. 94. Jervis comments that "what is most striking about American behavior since 9/11 is the extent to which it has sought not to maintain the international system but to change it. One might think that the unipole would be conservative, seeking to bolster the status quo that serves it so well. But this has not been the case." Jervis, "Unipolarity: A structural perspective," p. 204. For further examination on the scope and range of great power behaviour in a unipolar world, see Waltz, *Realism and International Politics*, pp. 197–229, 246–50; Jack Snyder, Robert Y. Shapiro, and Yaeli Bloch-Elkon, "Free hand abroad, divide and rule at home," *World Politics* 61, 1 (January 2009), 155–87; and Martha Finnemore, "Legitimacy, hypocrisy, and the social structure of unipolarity: Why being a unipole isn't all it's cracked up to be," *World Politics* 61, 1 (January 2009), 58–85.

29. Stephen M. Walt, "Alliances in a unipolar world," p. 117.

30. For a brief discussion on the relationship between unipolarity and war—local, regional, and systemic—see Seyom Brown, *The Causes and Prevention of War* (New York: St. Martin's Press, 1994), p. 72.

31. Regarding the considerable obstacles to effective balancing behaviour under a condition of unipolarity, see Stephen M. Walt, "Alliances in a unipolar world," pp. 96–97.

32. Christopher Layne, "The unipolar illusion: Why new great powers will arise," in Lynn-Jones and Miller, eds., *The Cold War and After: Prospects for Peace*, p. 246. For the argument that several other past periods in the

international political system can also be considered unipolar, see Layne's full article, pp. 256–71. On the temporary nature of our current situation, Waltz observed that "the American aspiration to freeze historical development by working to keep the world unipolar is doomed." Waltz, *Realism and International Politics*, p. 220.

33.   For the fullest statement on alliance formation under unipolarity, see Walt, "Alliances in a unipolar world."

34.   See Stephen M. Walt, *The Origins of Alliances* (Ithaca, NY: Cornell University Press, 1987). Other important contributions to examine the formation, purposes, functioning and maintenance of alliances include Mancur Olson, *The Logic of Collective Action* (Cambridge, MA: Harvard University Press, 1971); Liska, *Nations in Alliance: The Limits of Interdependence*; Evan Luard, *The Balance of Power: The System of International Relations, 1648-1815* (New York: St. Martin's Press, 1992); Samuel P. Huntington, *The Clash of Civilizations and the Remaking of World Order* (New York: Simon & Schuster, 1996); and Waltz, *Theory of International Politics*.

35.   Walt, "Alliances in a unipolar world," p. 220. Indeed, a careful study of Canada's marked activism with NATO in the unipolar period—especially Canada's willingness to engage in combat missions—finds that Ottawa's participation is chiefly driven by its "desire to please the United States." Kenneth M. Holland, "How unipolarity impacts Canada's engagement with the North Atlantic Treaty Organization," *Canadian Foreign Policy Journal* 18, 1 (March 2012), p. 52.

36.   Philip Stephens, "NATO's long drift towards irrelevance," *Financial Times*, 24 September 2010, p. 9; and Philip Stephens, "Politicians should pay up for NATO—or shut it down," *Financial Times* (8 March 2013), p. 13.

37.   Waltz, *Theory of International Politics*, p. 70.

38.   Tom Keating, *Canada and World Order: The Multilateralist Tradition in Canadian Foreign Policy* (Toronto: McClelland and Stewart, 1993).

39.   Arnold Wolfers, *Discord and Collaboration: Essays on International Politics* (Baltimore: Johns Hopkins University Press, 1962), p. 26.

40.   Joseph T. Jockel, *No Boundaries Upstairs: Canada, the United States, and the Origins of North American Air Defence, 1945-1958* (Vancouver: UBC Press, 1987).

41.   Waltz, *Theory of International Politics*, p. 174.

10 Canada–US Relations: Proximity and Distance in Perspective

Geoffrey Hale

Key Terms

Asymmetries in Canada–US Relationship
Buy American
Continuum of Policy Relationships
Intermesticity

Performance Legitimacy
Transgovernmental Relations
Value Chains

Canada's relations with the United States are among the most important priorities of its foreign and international policy relations. Canadians and their governments generally desire to take advantage of the opportunities of living next to the world's foremost economic, diplomatic and military power. At the same time, continuing differences in size and power between the two countries—and the progressive shift in global economic activity away from advanced industrial countries—increase the challenges of framing domestic and foreign priorities and policies that serve Canadians' diverse interests and enable Canadian governments to preserve policy discretion amid pervasive interdependence.

Many aspects of Canada–US relations are best understood through the concepts of interdependence, **intermesticity** (the blurring of traditional distinctions between domestic and international policies, and asymmetries), structural differences in size, power, and national perspectives (and relative awareness) of the relationship, and its place within each country's broader national priorities.

This chapter frames the major enduring features of Canada's policy relations with the United States, along with significant developments that have begun to reshape bilateral relations in the twenty-first century. It summarizes the principal objectives and trade-offs across three broad sets of policy domains: trade-commercial, "psychological-cultural," and "institutional-procedural"[1] for managing bilateral policy relations, along with the major forces shaping their evolution in recent years. Traditional diplomatic and defence/security relations are addressed in other chapters in this edition.

Enduring Features of the Canada–US Relationship

The enduring reality of Canada–US relations is characterized by several major **asymmetries**. The United States is Canada's principal foreign policy preoccupation and largest trade and investment partner. From a US foreign policy perspective, Canada is a useful but largely peripheral ally capable of complementing US policy initiatives but little more. Economic relations with Canada have long been subsets of US domestic politics and policies. Paradoxically, bilateral foreign and security relations have traditionally been most important from an American perspective, while economic relations generally have loomed largest to the Canadian outlook in recent years.[2] Major US policy and economic shifts, ranging from intensified fears of terrorism after the attacks of 9/11, to periodic spasms of trade protectionism, the meltdown of the US housing market in 2007–8, or shifts in US energy and environment policies, often trigger disproportionate effects and corresponding political responses in Canada. The most persistent challenge facing Canadian political leaders and diplomats is to secure the attention and responsiveness of their American counterparts to bilateral issues amid the constant clangour of international and domestic politics.[3] Indeed, for many Americans, relations with Mexico have become substantially more important to US interests—for good or ill—than relations with Canada.

At the same time, the US maintains broader and deeper administrative or **transgovernmental relations** with Canada across dozens of executive departments and agencies than with any other country, reflecting relatively similar administrative cultures,

overlapping interests, and extensive day-to-day dealings on defence, public security, finance, the environment, and a wide range of other regulatory issues. These relationships are vital to managing the two countries' interdependence that results from North American economic integration—particularly given the very limited willingness of either government to pursue closer *political* integration or to create the bi- or trinational institutions necessary to facilitate it. These realities, along with extensive cross-border engagement of business and other societal interests, has contributed to a considerable decentralization of policy relations in both countries, sometimes described as a "shift from 'government' to 'governance.'"[4] The result is a **continuum of policy relationships** (see Figure 10.1) ranging from conflicting to "independent" policy development in each country, to "parallelism" (characterized by the pursuit of similar policy objectives but often using differing combinations of policy instruments and settings reflecting differences in domestic political traditions and trade-offs), through cooperation, collaboration and, in some cases, actual policy harmonization.

Table 10.1 North America in context—2012

	United States		Canada		Ratio
Population (million)	318.8		34.8		9.2 : 1
GDP (million USD)	15,940		1,819		8.8 : 1
GDP per capita (USD)	49,965		52,219		
GDP per capita (USD, PPP*)	49,922		43,734		
Trade as % of GDP	31.1		62.1		
Services trade as % of GDP	6.8		10.6		
Inward foreign direct investment (FDI) from Canada, US ($CAD billion, % of Canada's FDI)	289.4	40.7% (% of total)	326.5	51.5% (% of total)	
Trade with Canada, US (goods %)	16.1		60.0		
Share of goods exports to Canada, US	18.9		73.2		

*purchasing power parity

Sources: World Economic Forum; World Bank; national statistical agencies; Department of Foreign Affairs, Trade and Development Canada (2013); United States Census Bureau; author's calculations.

Conflict -------- Independence ------- Harmonization

|-Parallelism-|-Coordination-|-Collaboration-|

Figure 10.1 The Binational or Regional Policy Continuum

Source: Gattinger and Hale, *Borders and Bridges: Canada's Policy Relations in North America* (2010), 13.

However, the past decade has also seen both major policy shifts and institutional developments. Rising Canadian energy exports to the US after 2000 have increased the relative significance of cross-border environmental issues, involving both cooperation and significant tensions among cross-border environmental groups. The rapid growth of intra-North American trade in the 1990s has given way to a broader diversification of trade and investment beyond North America, particularly with developing Asia-Pacific region economies,[5] reflecting the faster growth of developing economies, fluctuating terms of trade and exchange rates since 2000, and infrastructure constraints.

As a result, a growing component of bilateral relations involves meetings of national leaders and cabinet-level and senior officials through numerous specialized institutions for policy cooperation. These dealings range from regional meetings of national leaders and G20 meetings of finance ministers, through specialized organizations such as the Financial Stability Forum, the World Trade Organization, World Intellectual Property Organization (WIPO), World Customs Organization (WCO), International Organization of Securities Commissions (IOSCO), the Arctic Council, regional trade negotiations for a Trans-Pacific Partnership, and many more. These trends point towards the integration of decentralized North American governance processes within related international policy systems, reflecting Stephen Clarkson's observation that there is no single recipe for managing the US relationship, because there is no single power centre in the American system of government."[6] The decentralization of Canada–US policy processes may also be seen in the emergence of specialized and subnational cross-border networks for facilitating policy cooperation, including the activities of individual provincial governments.

The Psychological-Cultural Relationship

Public opinion in both Canada and the United States is one of the most significant constraining or enabling variables for Canadian governments in their management of cross-border relations. The pervasiveness of American political, economic, and cultural influences in Canadian life provokes a wide range of popular emotions, ranging from attraction and selective emulation to resentment and various forms of defensive nationalism.[7] A 2008 federal study notes broad similarities in cultural attitudes in cross-border regions: Atlantic Canada and New England; Ontario and the US Midwest; Canada's Prairies and the US Plains states; and British Columbia and the US Pacific Coast states. However, sharp cultural differences between most Canadian provinces and the American South became much more visible during the presidency of George W. Bush (2001–9).[8]

Contrary to expectations raised during the free trade debates of the 1980s, closer economic integration has not resulted in greater cultural similarities between the two countries, mitigating Canadians' traditional fears of American power.[9] However, closer economic cooperation remains heavily contingent on **performance legitimacy** reflected in tangible economic or social benefits for Canadians, while Canadian political leaders frequently seek to tailor parallel policies with "made-in-Canada" rhetoric aimed at preserving responsiveness to varied domestic interests.[10] As a result, periodic US policies towards Canada that ignore or threaten Canadian interests, whether deliberately or (more often) inadvertently, can prompt intense public resentment in Canada, potentially disrupting the broader relationship. Major examples include post-9/11 US border security arrangements, protracted disputes over softwood lumber, and other trade irritants such as US **Buy American** policies.[11]

Canadian political leaders generally recognize the value of maintaining cooperative relations with the White House, but are often cautious of being seen to be *too* close, even when individual presidents, often liberal Democrats, are relatively popular in Canada. Historically, Canadian public opinion has been less receptive to close relations with presidential administrations seen to be more assertive in the use of American power. Conversely, Canadians often overestimate the capacity of American presidents to address cross-border irritants within the relatively decentralized US domestic political system, and are correspondingly disappointed with the glacial pace of political and regulatory responses to Canadian concerns, most of which are peripheral to the priorities of American leaders.

These realities contribute to a major paradox of Canadian efforts to influence American policies towards Canada. Americans generally have positive attitudes towards Canada and Canadians, based on the general perception that Canadians are "nice neighbors" who are "much like us."[12] However, this goodwill is balanced by very limited awareness of the practical details of the relationship. As a result, many aspects of bilateral relations are subject to the cross-cutting pressures of American interest group politics, requiring persistent efforts by Canadian diplomats to explain how particular cross-border policies emerging from the bureaucracy or Congress may help or harm not only Canadian interests but also *American* interests engaged in cross-border trade or cultural exchanges.[13]

Bilateral relations can also be complicated by the tendency of US politicians and commentators to use Canadian actions or comparisons with Canada to score political points in domestic political debates. Of course, Canadian politicians frequently do exactly the same thing in making positive or adverse comparisons with a wide variety of American policies and political outlooks, depending on their partisan or ideological agendas. As a result, both Canadian and US governments often deal with bilateral issues at a technical level—under the political radar—particularly when their policy goals coincide or are complementary. Canadian governments in particular may dress up parallel policies in the language of "made-in-Canada" policies, emphasizing areas of national distinctiveness. But when policy goals diverge on significant bilateral issues, each country's diplomats must be careful to avoid the appearance of meddling in the other country's domestic politics, while at the same time quietly engaging in advocacy for their respective interests.

Complicating bilateral relations is the reality that significant domestic interests in each country may oppose policy choices taken by their respective governments on major bilateral issues. For example, Canadian environmental interest groups have been more likely to side with counterparts in the United States than with their development-oriented governments regarding conflicts related to forest industry practices or large-scale energy or pipeline expansion. Similarly, US environmental interest groups have invested heavily in supporting Canadian environmental interest groups opposed to Canadian domestic pipeline projects in recent years.[14]

The Trade-Commercial Relationship

Canada's economic relations with the United States have been the most important dimension of the bilateral relationship since the 1980s, although the nature of this relationship has changed significantly during that period. The US remains Canada's largest export market: 73.2 per cent of goods exports in 2012, and Canada's largest source of and destination for foreign investment.[15] (See Table 10.1.) Canada remains the US's largest export market (18.9 per cent in 2012) and trading partner. It is the largest source of US energy imports—particularly oil (27.8 per cent of imports in 2012, 11 per cent of market share), and natural gas (94 per cent of imports, 8 per cent of market share)—even if rising American production levels have reduced import dependence in recent years.[16]

The two economies have become deeply integrated in many ways. Several major industries including automotive, steel, aerospace, information technology, and railways function as North American rather than national industries, while many others are characterized by extensive cross-border interdependence. Some major Canadian banks now have more branches in the US than in Canada, prompting complex manoeuvres to limit the effects of US financial sector regulations on operations of Canadian banks outside the United States.[17] Although trade irritants (including persistent "Buy American" policies) remain, US trade remedy actions that were a major impetus to negotiating the Canada–US Free Trade Agreement (CUFTA) in 1986–88 have virtually ceased since 2004.[18]

Canada–US trade relations have gone through three major eras since the late 1980s. The negotiation of CUFTA and the North American Free Trade Agreement (NAFTA) were part of a multi-track strategy of trade liberalization that involved both closer integration of regional markets and the broadening of multilateral trade agreements through the General Agreement on Tariffs and Trade to include service industries, foreign investment, food safety, and other regulations traditionally treated as primarily domestic policies. Canada's trade with the US grew rapidly during the 1990s, partly in response to freer trade and the integration of cross-border supply chains.

The pace of integration slowed after 2001, reflecting tighter border security in the aftermath of the 9/11 terrorist attacks, rising Canadian exchange rates resulting from the post-2000 commodities boom, and growing US interest in negotiating preferential trade agreements outside North America, paralleling broader global negotiations—a process known as "competitive liberalization."[19] Although manufacturing exports peaked in mid-decade, energy and other commodity exports (except forest products) grew rapidly (see Table 10.2).

Table 10.2 Canada's shifting export patterns: 1999–2012

(Per cent of Canadian merchandise exports)	1999	2003	2008	2012	Change 1999–2012
Automotive products	27.0	22.4	12.6	14.8	−12.2
Machinery and equipment	19.3	17.4	15.4	14.5	−4.8
Industrial goods and materials	14.6	15.3	22.4	22.9	+8.3
Forestry products	13.1	11.3	7.3	6.6	−6.5
Energy products	7.9	14.8	24.2	22.7	+13.8
Agricultural and fishing products	7.1	7.5	8.9	10.4	+3.3
Other consumer goods	7.4	8.1	6.4	6.0	−1.4

Source: Statistics Canada (2013), CANSIM Table 228-0059; author's calculations.

The 2008–9 financial crisis and recession led to a 31 per cent drop in Canadian goods exports to the US—24.4 per cent overall, although trade volumes have recovered slightly in subsequent years.[20] The slow US recovery from the financial crisis, growing American environmental opposition to Canadian energy exports, and disproportionate levels of economic growth in major emerging markets have led the Harper government to pursue a series of trade negotiations outside North America, including US-led negotiations for a Trans-Pacific Partnership (TPP) after 2011.[21]

Bilateral trade relations are affected by three broad sets of issues, mediated through each country's domestic political system: structural changes in the North American and global economies; parallel or cooperative national policies intended to facilitate trade; and periodic irritants—usually resulting from unilateral actions by one country—that require careful management to avoid becoming structural irritants in the relationship.

Structural Economic Changes

Structural economic changes since 2000 have affected Canada and the US in different ways. The rise of China and other Asia-Pacific economies contributed to rising global prices for many Canadian commodities, stimulating major investment flows, especially in Western Canada, and contributing to rising exchange rates, particularly against the US dollar. Although non-resource-related manufacturers have faced more difficult adjustments, these trends have contributed to rising living standards for a broad cross-section of Canadians—in sharp contrast to income stagnation and polarization in the United States.[22] However, the inherently cyclical character of commodity markets and prices demands a commitment to economic and market diversification to mitigate national or regional vulnerability to such cycles.

The broad shift in manufacturing activities and employment from advanced industrial to developing economies has affected the United States as much as Canada, although exchange rate shifts have contributed to some "reshoring" in recent years. However, changing patterns of comparative advantage have greatly increased the importance of tradable services, particularly those related to innovation and intellectual property, to the US economy. As a result, a major goal of US trade policies is to expand intellectual property protections, whether through international negotiations or persistent pressure on trading partners, leading Canada to revise its copyright laws in recent years, if not as much as desired by Washington.[23]

US trade policies under the Bush administration (2001–9) were generally outward looking—if partly hamstrung by intensified border security measures after 9/11. However, reckless domestic fiscal and credit policies, combined with rising energy prices and a breakdown of immigration policies, contributed to a combination of record trade deficits, a real estate bubble, and relative income stagnation for most American households. These trends increased public suspicion of closer North American integration, effectively undercutting closer cooperation with Canada and Mexico under the Bush administration.[24] The slow-motion collapse of the housing market after 2006 triggered a financial crisis in 2007–8 that affected much of the industrial world and increased protectionist pressures in the US Congress. Whether in response to the Bush administration's border security policies or to threats of protectionism during the Obama administration, Canadian responses to an inward-looking America were frequently reactive and defensive: attempting to maintain open borders and unrestricted trade, but making selective concessions as necessary to achieve these objectives. The Bush administration's efforts to promote closer trilateral cooperation on trade and security issues gave way to a two-track approach, sometimes called "dual bilateralism," after 2009, as the Obama administration attempted to negotiate parallel border security, trade facilitation, and regulatory cooperation agreements with Mexico and Canada.

A Market-Driven Relationship

Trends towards North American and global economic integration have also contributed to another major structural change: greater specialization and decentralization of economic activity. The primarily market-driven (or "bottom up") character of Canada–US economic relations is driven largely by the decisions of many thousands of businesses, and millions of consumers and investors. As such, it reflects the interaction of geographic dispersion, multiple industry sectors, diverse financial structures and regulatory systems. The transgovernmental dimension of bilateral relations is discussed further below.

Apart from a handful of industry sectors—mainly transportation, telecommunications, and cultural sector businesses—Canadian governments have reduced barriers to both inward and outward foreign investment since the 1980s. Both have grown rapidly relative to the size of Canada's economy, as noted in Table 10.3. Canadian firms have greatly expanded their activities in the United States and beyond North America, while levels of foreign direct investment (FDI) have grown significantly in Canada. However, since 1997, FDI by Canadian-based companies in foreign countries has generally exceeded levels of FDI by foreign-based firms in Canada.

These trends have contributed to the growing integration of many firms in complex value chains

and supply chains, so that Canadians, Americans, and increasingly Mexicans "make things together" rather than just "selling things to one another."[25] However, traditional trade in commodities and finished goods remains significant to bilateral economic relations. Supply chains are business networks used to source raw materials and intermediate goods for processing, production, and then distribution through their final point of sale. More recently, trade analysts emphasize the emergence of **value chains**, also called "trade in tasks"—processes by which "bits of value [are] added in many different locations."[26] Product specialization in value chains may involve a variety of companies, often located in different countries, which specialize in producing intermediate inputs (components *and* related services such as design and marketing), which are then processed or assembled elsewhere into finished industrial and consumer products.[27] Trade-in-tasks further expands Canadian-based firms' participation in export markets by "supplying firms in the U.S. and other advanced economies that are selling to emerging markets."[28] These factors tend to increase pressures on governments from businesses in deeply integrated sectors to coordinate or parallel domestic regulations across national borders to reduce transaction costs and facilitate cross-border trade, thereby intensifying existing patterns of transgovernmental relations.

Regulatory Cooperation and Transgovernmental Relations

The effects of continuing North American integration can be seen in extensive sector-level policy cooperation. A 2004 federal report indicated that at least 14 federal departments and many more federal and provincial agencies maintain extensive cross-border relations with their American counterparts.[29] The nature of transgovernmental relations from sector to sector depends on four major factors:

Table 10.3 Foreign direct investment stocks as percentage of GDP

	Outbound	Inbound	Ratio
1990	14.5	19.4	0.752
2000	32.8	29.3	1.117
2011	38.6	34.3	1.127

Source: UNCTAD; author's calculations.

- the degree to which responsibilities for policy development are centralized or decentralized within each country;
- the number and diversity of domestic interest groups in each country implicated by and engaged with proposed policy shifts;
- the extent to which relations among cross-border economic and social interests are sufficiently integrated to contribute to policy harmonization, rather than the accommodation of diverse domestic interests and institutions through policy parallelism;
- the relative emphasis on distributive issues of domestic politics, as opposed to international economic competitiveness.[30]

Figure 10.2 provides a comparative outline of sectoral patterns of policy integration within North America. In the electricity sector, although provincially owned Crown corporations remain the dominant suppliers of electricity in most provinces, utilities in both countries have negotiated common reliability standards under the North American Electric Reliability Corporation (NERC). Canadian and US energy regulators meet regularly to exchange information on regulatory processes and cross-border projects between the two countries.[31]

Deep integration of the North American auto industry has contributed to the harmonization of environmental, safety and fuel economy standards between the US, Canada, and increasingly Mexico. Washington, Ottawa, and Ontario worked together closely in 2009 to bail out bankrupt General Motors and Chrysler, with Canadian involvement based on preservation of its existing share of bilateral production.[32]

Canadian corporations (and governments) have raised capital in US financial markets for many years, resulting in the "cross-listing" of many large firms on Canadian and US stock exchanges, and extensive cross-border investments by financial

sector firms in both countries—leading to selective adaptation of American corporate governance rules by provincial regulators in Canada. US and Canadian food inspectors and regulators have worked closely for many years to promote parallel approaches to food safety, given extensive cross-border trade in agricultural and food products. However, differences in each country's regulatory processes create persistent barriers to closer regulatory harmonization.

Pressure from closer policy and regulatory coordination comes most frequently from business organizations whose members have operations on both sides of the border. Increased security measures at the border increase transaction costs for exporters and shippers, reducing the efficiency of North American supply chains, particularly for smaller shipments going back and forth across the border. The Beyond the Border process initiated in 2011 is the latest in a series of cooperative efforts to streamline trade and travel across the border through mutual recognition of border inspections, information sharing on travellers, closer law enforcement cooperation, increased preclearance of cross-border truck shipments to reduce border wait times, and closer cooperation on border infrastructure.[33] Several government agencies are also working together to coordinate the development of sectoral regulations in each country to remove or reduce technical differences that increase cross-border transaction costs and that don't have corresponding public benefits.

Border management issues often involve complex local political sensitivities that require careful management of state and local as well as national interests. US passport requirements introduced after 9/11 triggered strong negative reactions from border communities, eventually resulting in provisions for state *and* provincial governments to issue "enhanced" driver licences which met American security requirements.[34] Building new border

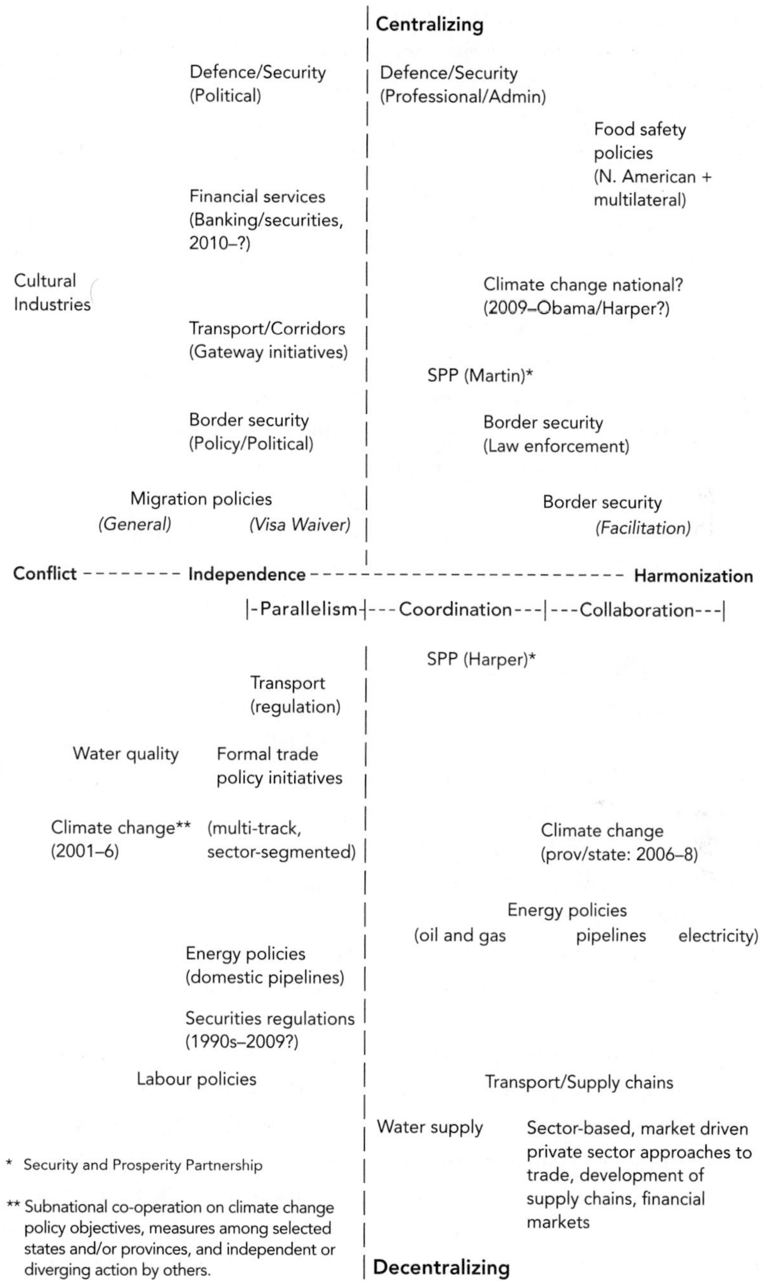

Centralizing

Defence/Security
(Political)

Defence/Security
(Professional/Admin)

Food safety
policies
(N. American +
multilateral)

Financial services
(Banking/securities,
2010–?)

Cultural
Industries

Climate change national?
(2009–Obama/Harper?)

Transport/Corridors
(Gateway initiatives)

SPP (Martin)*

Border security
(Policy/Political)

Border security
(Law enforcement)

Migration policies

(General)   (Visa Waiver)

Border security

(Facilitation)

Conflict -------- Independence --------------------------- Harmonization

|-Parallelism-|---Coordination---|---Collaboration---|

SPP (Harper)*

Transport
(regulation)

Water quality   Formal trade
policy initiatives

Climate change**   (multi-track,
(2001–6)   sector-segmented)

Climate change
(prov/state: 2006–8)

Energy policies
(oil and gas   pipelines   electricity)

Energy policies
(domestic pipelines)

Securities regulations
(1990s–2009?)

Labour policies

Transport/Supply chains

Water supply   Sector-based, market driven
privately sector approaches to
trade, development of
supply chains, financial
markets

* Security and Prosperity Partnership

** Subnational co-operation on climate change
policy objectives, measures among selected
states and/or provinces, and independent or
diverging action by others.

Decentralizing

Figure 10.2 Mapping Economic, Institutional, and Policy Integration

Adapted from Gattinger and Hale, eds., *Borders and Bridges: Canada's Policy Relations in North America* (2010), 372.

infrastructure, including roads and bridges, can involve years of navigation through different regulatory systems and competing local interests, often triggering political controversy. The owners of the Ambassador Bridge, which spans the Detroit River between Detroit, Michigan, and Windsor, Ontario, and which carries 28 per cent of cross-border trade, spent more than USD $30 million on an unsuccessful 2012 state referendum to block construction of a new bridge.[35] In 2013, Ottawa and Michigan formalized an agreement for Canadian taxpayers to fund the construction of a new Detroit–Windsor bridge, with the cost to be repaid from toll revenues (although US government funding arrangements were not confirmed at time of writing.)[36] Similar improvements on Ontario's Niagara frontier have long been delayed by political and regulatory conflicts in and with New York State.[37]

Managing Trade Disputes

Canada's relative dependence on US markets has long made security of access a central Canadian priority, regardless of other policy priorities. Conversely, lesser US dependence on trade with Canada and dominance of the US legislative branch over the executive branch typically make reciprocity a key principle of US trade politics and policy processes—often resulting in unilateral actions by American domestic interests to leverage their domestic influence to enforce their policy preferences.[38] US concerns over Canadian trade practices have focused largely on intellectual property issues, including limited resources against counterfeit products, and on Canada's protectionist supply management practices in agriculture.[39]

Trade disputes arising from protectionist US actions are most difficult to resolve either when regionally significant US interests can mobilize protectionist coalitions in Congress, or when diverging provincial policies limit Ottawa's capacity to develop a consistent negotiating position.

Canadian governments can take several approaches to such disputes: politicization (usually for domestic consumption); litigation through US domestic, NAFTA, or WTO processes; or negotiation (shaped by the economic, legal, and political circumstances of each case).[40]

Entrenched US domestic interests can often frustrate attempts at trade liberalization. For example, American sugar interests spent USD$49 million on political contributions and lobbying in 2008–12 to preserve domestic price supports and trade barriers aimed at Brazilian and Mexican imports, as much or more than Canadian imports, frustrating countervailing efforts by food and candy manufacturers.[41] Litigation against major trading powers, whether the US or EU, is a long, time-consuming process that usually requires building large enough coalitions of aggrieved trading partners to make WTO-authorized sanctions economically and politically effective.

Both US and Canadian domestic politics—especially differences among provincial regulatory and negotiating positions—contributed to the persistence of disputes over Canadian softwood lumber exports between 1982 and 2006. The Harper government negotiated the most recent managed trade agreement on softwood lumber to avert a constitutional challenge to NAFTA in American courts and enable negotiations on a wide range of other issues crowded out by the softwood dispute.[42] Subsequent disputes have been managed through the arm's-length London Court of International Arbitration.

Long-running disputes over Canadian cattle imports—most recently over US country-of-origin-labelling legislation—reflect internal US disputes among domestic and export-oriented ranchers, meat processors, and retailers mediated through Congress. Although some Canadian observers have suggested pursuing harmonized food safety standards through negotiations,[43] the nature of American domestic debates means that any such approach will probably require shifts in White House priorities and the Congressional balance of power.

Similarly, the efforts of environmental interest groups since 2008 to block the Keystone XL pipeline have become a focal point in American partisan and ideological debates over energy and environmental policies. Although the Harper government has offered periodically to negotiate joint environmental standards to create a "level playing field" for energy development in both countries, the polarized and gridlocked status of US domestic politics have precluded any such arrangements, while encouraging Canadian governments to pursue other infrastructure and market opportunities for Canadian energy exports. These trends are likely to be reinforced by growing American energy self-sufficiency, driven by the rapid growth of US shale oil and gas production.[44]

Although many business interests in both countries view continuing progress towards North American integration as central to the international competitiveness of American as well as Canadian business interests, political and market uncertainties require Canadian governments to pursue a two- (or multi-) track approach paralleling US initiatives. On one hand, Canadian government officials are attempting to coordinate domestic regulatory processes with American counterparts, while negotiating broader regulatory cooperation agreements with US, Mexican, and Asia-Pacific nations through the Trans-Pacific Partnership.[45] On the other, they are attempting to diversify trade and investment by negotiating other, "modern" trade and economic agreements with the European Union (and other countries), and by promoting wider trade diversification strategies that recognize the progressive shift of economic activity and power towards major developing economies. The latter have accounted for almost 80 per cent of global growth in recent years.[46]

The Institutional-Procedural Dimension

A persistent challenge of Canadian diplomacy towards the United States is to secure the attention of senior American policy-makers on terms conducive to the pursuit of mutual interests. As noted above, these processes are often complicated by the realities of intermesticity—the blurring of traditional distinctions between domestic and international policies in both countries. This section addresses three separate elements of cross-border diplomacy: relations between national leaders and their senior advisors, Canadian diplomats' engagement of Congress, and the continuing engagement of provincial premiers in bilateral relations.

Positive relations between national leaders do not guarantee outcomes favourable to Canada in bilateral policy relations. However, the presence or absence of good relations can contribute to or detract from bureaucratic incentives to facilitate the management of particular files, ranging from comprehensive cooperation on border management issues to rules governing Canadian charter flights carrying NHL hockey teams. The prime minister and president might discuss bilateral issues at international leaders' meetings of the G8, Council of the Americas, the APEC Economic Leaders' Meeting, and other organizations, or on occasional visits between Washington and Ottawa.

The diplomatic style of prime ministers ranges from "centralized activism" to "decentralized incrementalism,"[47] depending on circumstances. Given the breadth of bilateral relations and the range of political actors capable of supporting or obstructing major policy changes—especially in the US—prime ministers need to focus on a handful of major priorities in dealing with American presidents, while being sensitive presidents' priorities on broader international issues. Paul Martin centralized control over major policy issues in the Privy Council Office during his time in office. Stephen Harper initially decentralized policy management to line departments on all but a handful of major issues, while rigidly centralizing government communications, including supervision of the public relations activities of Canadian diplomats.[48]

Both the Beyond the Border process for cooperation on border security and trade facilitation issues and the Regulatory Cooperation Council process initiated in 2011 employed extensive central agency coordination intended to engage high-level officials in the US executive branch. The Canadian embassy in Washington plays an active role in building relationships with US policy- and lawmakers, as well as with important policy communities in Washington, DC, and through its network of consulates across the country.

Canadian diplomats also closely monitor activities of the US Congress that have the potential to affect bilateral relations. As Congress plays a leading role in most areas of US domestic policy, its actions can often affect Canadian interests, whether intentionally or (more often) inadvertently. The fragmentation of the US legislative (and appropriations) processes requires careful observation and strategic analysis of policy initiatives, risks, and opportunities, and the building of relationships with members of Congress and their staff to help craft strategies to influence legislative developments. Two key strategies used by Canadian diplomats involve cooperation with various American domestic interest groups with overlapping legislative and policy interests on specific issues, and the identification of specific constituency interests that might influence positions taken by particular senators or members of the House of Representatives.[49]

However, Canadian diplomats must be careful not to be seen to "meddle" in US domestic politics, particularly by taking sides on major issues of partisan controversy. This requires considerable delicacy, particularly on issues such as acid rain (during the Reagan administration), and proposed US passport requirements under the George W. Bush administration, when Canadian government positions were at odds with the policy preferences of the White House or of major executive departments. When Republican leaders sought to champion building of the Keystone XL pipeline during the 2012 presidential primaries, Ottawa instructed Canadian diplomats to suspend their lobbying activities on the issue until after the election.[50]

Differences between the Canadian and American federal division of powers have long given provincial governments a significant stake in engaging cross-border relations central to their provincial interests. Provincial premiers regularly attend meetings of regional governors' associations in the United States, along with regular cross-border gatherings such as those of the Conference of New England Governors and Eastern Canadian Premiers. The Pacific NorthWest Economic Region (PNWER) brings together provincial and state legislators, officials, and business and community leaders from 10 jurisdictions to address a wide range of cross-border issues—often leading to joint representations to governments in Ottawa and Washington. Individual states and provinces also maintain relations of varying depth and intensity, although these are often interrupted by different electoral cycles and turnover of key decision-makers.[51]

Provincial governments play a leading role on regionally sensitive cross-border issues such as improving environmental standards on the Great Lakes or negotiations for the pending renewal of the Columbia River Treaty. However, successful cross-border cooperation generally requires shared policy goals and the willingness of both a state governor and provincial premier to invest the time, effort, and political capital to pursue those goals over an electoral cycle. Examples include Ohio's Bob Taft on Great Lakes water issues in the 2000s, and BC's Gordon Campbell and California's Arnold Schwarzenegger on the Western Climate Initiative.

Although Quebec and Alberta both maintain representative offices in Washington, DC, several other provinces keep a number of government relations consultants, including former senior Canadian and American diplomats, on retainer to monitor major developments and to provide policy advice on US government initiatives that affect their interests.[52]

Conclusion

Canada's persistent interdependence with the United States and the reality of North American economic integration ensure heightened Canadian sensitivities to changes in American economic conditions and policy priorities. On one hand, Canadian policy-makers seek to maintain a capacity for choice in their domestic and international policies, within the constraints imposed by the realities of interdependence. On the other, they must take American priorities and political conditions into account when attempting to influence American policies towards Canada.

The diversity of policy issues and economic and social interests in each country that are implicated by the multidimensional character of Canada–US relations ensures, as Dyment has suggested, that there are a series of "enduring situation(s) to be managed" rather than a "problem to be solved."[53] Whether in various aspects of its bilateral relations or in its attempts to diversify its trade and investment relations outside North America in response to changing patterns of global economic activity, Canada remains a relatively small, necessarily open actor balancing its relations with a variety of large, self-absorbed economic powers, especially the United States.

Canada's location in North America requires continued care and attention to bilateral relations. However, absent the kinds of formal policy coordination that are severely constrained by each country's political institutions and policy trade-offs, the evolving nature of the global economy also requires Canada to engage the US and other economic powers in a broader range of international policy venues. These realities are likely to increase rather than decrease the complex, intermestic, alternately cooperative and contested character of bilateral relations for the foreseeable future.

Questions for Review

1. What major areas of continuity and change in Canada–US relations are discussed in the chapter?

2. The chapter discusses four separate dimensions of the Canada–US relationship. Summarize how each one affects the nature of the relationship in each country, whether from the standpoints of governments or of particular economic and societal interests.

3. In what major ways has the trade-commercial dimension of the Canada–US relationship changed since the 1990s? What major factors help to explain these changes?

4. What underlying factors lead different observers to perceive the relationship as "corporate-dominated" and "decentralized" or "bottom-up" in character? How do these different outlooks help to explain different perspectives of relationships between state and society?

5. In what major ways do differences between US and Canadian federal divisions of powers affect relations between each country's central governments? Between and among central and subnational governments?

Suggested Readings

Anderson, Greg, and Christopher Sands, eds. 2011. *Forgotten Partnership Redux: Canada–U.S. Relations in the 21st Century*. Amherst, NY: Cambria Press.

Canada. Standing Committee on Foreign Affairs. 2002. *Partners in North America: Advancing Canada's Relations with the United States and Mexico*. Third Report. Ottawa: House of Commons (December).

Clarkson, Stephen. 2008. *Does North America Exist? Governing the Continent after NAFTA and 9/11*. Toronto: University of Toronto Press.

Dyment, David. 2010. *Doing the Continental: A New Canadian–American Relationship*. Toronto: Dundurn Press.

Gattinger, Monica, and Geoffrey Hale, eds. 2010. *Borders and Bridges: Canada's Policy Relations in North America*. Don Mills, ON: Oxford University Press.

Hale, Geoffrey. 2012. *So Near Yet So Far: The Public and Hidden Worlds of Canada–U.S. Relations*. Vancouver: UBC Press.

Sands, Christopher. 2009. *Toward a New Frontier: Improving the U.S.-Canadian Border*. Washington, DC: Brookings Institution (July).

Van Assche, Ari. 2012. *Global Value Chains and Canada's Trade Policy: Business as Usual or Paradigm Shift?* IRPP Study #32. Montreal: Institute for Research on Public Policy (June).

Notes

1. Charles Doran, *Forgotten Partnership: U.S.–Canada Relations Today* (Baltimore: Johns Hopkins University Press, 1984); Geoffrey Hale, *So Near Yet So Far: The Public and Hidden Worlds of Canada–U.S. Relations* (Vancouver: UBC Press, 2012).

2. Doran, *Forgotten Partnership*; Hale, *So Near Yet So Far*; Carl Ek and Ian F. Fergusson, *Canada–U.S. Relations*, CRS Report # 96-397 (Washington, DC: Congressional Research Service, Library of Congress, 5 April 2012).

3. Allan Gotlieb, *"I'll be with you in a minute, Mr. Ambassador"* (Toronto: University of Toronto Press, 1991); Denis Stevens, "Remarks to the Annual Meeting of the Association for Canadian Studies in the United States," Tampa, FL, 20 November 2013.

4. Monica Gattinger and Geoffrey Hale, "Borders and Bridges," pp. 3–8 in Monica Gattinger and Geoffrey Hale, eds., *Borders and Bridges: Canada's Policy Relations in North America* (Don Mills, ON: Oxford University Press, 2010).

5. Andrew Card and Thomas Daschle, *U.S. Trade and Investment Policy*, Independent Task Force Report # 67 (New York: Council on Foreign Relations, September 2011); Geoffrey Hale, "In Pursuit of Leverage: The Evolution of Canadian Trade and Investment Policies in an Increasingly Multipolar World," *Canadian Foreign Policy Journal* 18,1 (March 2012), 106–19.

6. Canada, Standing Committee on Foreign Affairs, *Partners in North America: Advancing Canada's Relations with the United States and Mexico*, Third Report (Ottawa: House of Commons, December 2002), 218; see also Stephen Clarkson, *Does North America Exist? Governing the Continent after nafta and 9/11* (Toronto: University of Toronto Press, 2008).

7. Hale, *So Near Yet So Far*, 77–84; Mark Milke, "Limits on Deliberative Democracy: A Study of Canadian Political Culture and How Attitudes Toward the United States Shape Canadian Political Debates," Ph.D. dissertation, University of Calgary, 2008; David Dyment, *Doing the Continental: A New Canadian-American Relationship* (Toronto: Dundurn, 2010).

8. Canada, Policy Research Institute, *The Emergence of Cross-Border Regions Between Canada and the United States: Reaping the Promise and Public Value of Cross-Border Regional Relationships—Final Report* (Ottawa: Industry Canada, November 2008).

9. Michael Adams, *Fire and Ice: the United States, Canada, and the Myth of Converging Values* (Toronto: Penguin, 2003).

10. Matthew Mendelsohn, Robert Wolfe, and Andrew Parkin, "Globalization, Trade Policy and the Permissive Consensus in Canada," *Canadian Public Policy* 28, 3 (2002): 351–71; George Hoberg, ed., *Capacity for Choice: Canada in a New North America* (Toronto: University of Toronto Press, 2003).

11. Hale, *So Near Yet So Far*, 276–301.

12. Ibid., 84–90.

13. Gotlieb, *"I'll be with you in a minute, Mr. Ambassador"*; Cameron D. Anderson and Laura B. Stephenson, *Moving Closer or Drifting Apart? Assessing the State of Public Opinion on the U.S.-Canadian Relationship* (London, ON: Canada–U.S. Institute, University of Western Ontario, April 2010); Hale, *So Near Yet So Far*.

14. Vivian Krause, "U.S. cash vs. oil sands," *Financial Post*, 15 October 2010, FP11; Vivian Krause, "The war on Canadian oil," *Financial Post*, 3 December 2013, FP11.

15. Canada, Department of Foreign Affairs, Trade and Development, *Trade Investment and Economic Statistics* (Ottawa: Office of the Chief Economist, October 2013).

16. U.S. Energy Information Administration, "U.S. Imports by Country of Origin: Petroleum and Other Liquids"

(Washington, DC: 27 November 2013); U.S. Energy Import Administration, "Natural Gas Monthly" (Washington, DC: April 2013).

17. Bill Curry, "Canada raising alarm over Volcker rule," *The Globe and Mail*, 14 February 2012, B3; Barbara Shecter, "Canada dodges Volcker's full impact," *Financial Post*, 11 December 2013, FP1.

18. Hale, *So Near Yet So Far*, p. 68.

19. Geoffrey Hale and Stephen Blank, "North American Economic Integration and Comparative Responses to Globalization—Overview," pp. 21–40 in *Borders and Bridges: Canada's Policy Relations in North America*; Jeffrey J. Schott, ed., *Free Trade Agreements: U.S. Strategies and Priorities* (Washington, DC: Institute for International Economics, 2004).

20. Canada, Department of Foreign Affairs and International Trade, *Canada's State of Trade: 2011—Trade and Investment Update*. Ottawa: DFAIT, 2011.

21. Tiff Macklem, "Global Growth and the Prospects for Canada's Exports," Speech to the Economic Club of Canada (Toronto, 1 October 2013), available at http://www.bankofcanada.ca/2013/10/global-growth-and-prospects-canada-exports/; Mike De Souza, "Tories aim to diversify natural resource exports," *Ottawa Citizen*, 9 December 2013, A4.

22. Philip Cross, *Dutch Disease, Canadian Cure: How Manufacturers Adapted to the Higher Dollar* (Ottawa: Macdonald-Laurier Institute, January 2013); Craig Alexander and Frances Fong, "Income and Income Inequality: A tale of two countries" (Toronto: TD Economics, 11 December 2012).

23. Ian F. Fergusson, William H. Cooper, Remy Jurenas, and Brock R. Williams, *The Trans-Pacific Partnership Negotiations: Issues for Congress*, CRS Report # 42694 (Washington, DC: Congressional Research Service, Library of Congress, 17 June 2013).

24. Greg Anderson and Christopher Sands, *Negotiating North America: The Security and Prosperity Partnership* (Washington, DC: Hudson Institute, September 2007); Jerome R. Corsi, *The Late, Great USA: The Coming Merger with Mexico and Canada* (Los Angeles: World Ahead Media, 2007).

25. Stephen Blank, "North American Integration: Looking Ahead," mimeo (July 2005).

26. Gene M. Grossman and Esteban Rossi-Hansberg (2008), "Trading Tasks: A Simple Theory of Offshoring," *American Economic Review* 98,5: 1978–97.

27. Bill Dymond and Michael Hart, *Navigating New Trade Routes: The Rise of Value Chains and the Challenges for Canadian Trade Policy*, Commentary # 259 (Toronto: C.D. Howe Institute, March 2008); Ari Van Assche, *Global Value Chains and Canada's Trade Policy: Business*

as Usual or Paradigm Shift?, IRPP Study # 32 (Montreal: Institute for Research on Public Policy, June 2012), 3–26.

28. Macklem, "Global Growth and the Prospects for Canada's Exports," 9.

29. Dieudonné Mouafo, Nadia Ponce Morales, and Jeff Heynen, *A Compendium of Canada–U.S. Relations* (Ottawa: Canada School of Public Service, 2004).

30. David A. Lake, "Open economy politics: a critical review," *Review of International Organizations* 4,3 (September 2009): 219–44; Geoffrey Hale and Monica Gattinger, "Variable Geometry and Traffic Circles: Navigating Canada's Policy Relations in North America," pp. 371–75 in *Borders and Bridges: Canada's Policy Relations in North America*.

31. Monica Gattinger (2010), "Canada–United States Energy Relations: From domestic to North American energy policies," pp. 214–18 in Glen Toner, Leslie A. Pal, and Michael J. Prince, eds., *Policy: From Ideas to Implementation* (Montreal and Kingston: McGill-Queen's University Press, 2010).

32. Christopher Waddell, "The Auto Industry Bailout: Industrial Policy or Job-Saving Social Policy?," pp. 150–67 in G. Bruce Doern and Christopher Stoney, eds., *How Ottawa Spends: 2010–2011* (Montreal and Kingston: McGill-Queen's University Press, 2010).

33. United States, White House, and Canada, Privy Council Office, *Beyond the Border Implementation Report* (Washington and Ottawa, December 2012).

34. Geoffrey Hale, "People, Politics and Passports: Contesting Security, Trade and Travel on the US–Canadian Border," *Geopolitics* 16, 1 (2011): 27–69.

35. Paul Egan, "With $31 million, Manuel (Matty) Moroun spends more than anyone ever on a state ballot proposal," *Detroit Free Press*, 27 October 2012.

36. Roy Norton, "The New International Trade Crossing," *Dome Magazine*, 16 August 2013.

37. Christopher Sands, "Towards a New Frontier: Improving the U.S.–Canadian Border," (Washington, DC: Brookings Institution, July 2009); Robert J. McCarthy and Tom Precious, "Cuomo, Canadian ambassador tout Peace Bridge deal," *Buffalo News*, 27 June 2013.

38. Judith Goldstein, "International Forces and Domestic Politics: Trade Policy and Institution Building in the United States," pp. 211–35 in Ira Katznelson and Martin Shefter, eds., *Shaped by War and Trade: International Influences on American Political Development* (Princeton, NJ: Princeton University Press, 2002); I.M. Destler, *American Trade Politics*, 4th ed. (Washington, DC: Institute for International Economics, 2005).

39. Fergusson et al., *The Trans-Pacific Partnership Negotiations*, 14, 26–29.

40. Hale, *So Near Yet So Far*, 276–301.

41. Peter Wallsten and Tom Hamburger, "Lawmakers find protecting sugar easy to swallow," *Washington Post*, 8 December 2013, A1.

42. Daowei Zhang, *The Softwood Lumber War* (Washington, DC: Resources for the Future, 2007); Hale, *So Near Yet So Far*, 285–94.

43. Alexander Moens and Amos Vivancos Leon, *Mandatory Country of Origin Labeling: The Case for a Harmonized Canada–US Beef and Pork Regulatory Regime, Fraser Forum* (Vancouver: Fraser Institute, July/August 2012).

44. Geoffrey Hale (2010), "Canada–US Relations in the Obama Era: Warming or Greening," pp. 24–43 in Doern and Stoney, eds., *How Ottawa Spends, 2010–2011*; De Souza, "Tories aim to diversify natural resource exports."

45. Fergusson et al., *The Trans-Pacific Partnership Negotiations.*

46. Macklem, "Global Growth and the Prospect for Canada's Exports," 9–13.

47. Hale, *So Near Yet So Far*, 110.

48. Confidential interviews, Foreign Affairs and International Trade Canada (2005–11).

49. Allan Gotlieb, *The Washington Diaries, 1981–1989* (Toronto: McClelland and Stewart, 2006); Colin Robertson, "CDA_USA 2.0: Intermesticity, Hidden Wiring, and Public Diplomacy," pp. 268–85 in Jean Daudelin and Daniel Schwanen, eds., *Canada Among Nations 2007: What Room for Manoeuvre?* (Montreal and Kingston: McGill-Queen's University Press, 2008); Hale, *So Near Yet So Far*, 147–74.

50. Interview, Foreign Affairs and International Trade Canada (2012).

51. Hale, *So Near Yet So Far*, 198–223.

52. Ibid., 220–21.

53. Dyment, *Doing the Continental*, 32.

11 The Dynamic of Relations between Canada and China

Charles Burton

Key Terms

Foreign Direct Investment

Human Rights

Defining the direction and priorities for Canada's engagement of China is arguably the most complex and contentious foreign policy issue faced by Canada's political leadership. China is a very significant rising power that challenges Canada's national interests in international relations across economic, political, and strategic security aspects.

The Politics of Canada–China Relations

How Canada should best respond to the challenge of the rise of China is a controversial and high profile domestic political issue that receives considerable attention in the Canadian media. Moreover, China inspires a great deal of passion among diverse elements of the Canadian population. Canadian political parties struggle to strike the right balance between economic concerns and **human rights** in the formulation of their statements on China policy.

An unusual political consensus has formed between the right wing and left wing of the Canadian political spectrum on how to further Canada's interests in China. Both sides strongly condemn the Chinese state's human rights violations and China's political and economic activities in the Third World. Canadian political leftists and rightists are allied in

urging that the government of Canada adopt strong measures to counter the threat to Canada's economic and political security of Chinese state investment in Canada, and of Chinese state-sponsored economic and political espionage activities directed at Canada.

Political discourse on these aspects of Canada–China relations tends to assume a highly polarized and polemical nature. Charged denunciations of alleged Chinese government duplicity in its domestic human rights violations, **foreign direct investment** policies, and foreign espionage activities by supporters of the Canadian right wing and left wing political perspectives typically elicit a strongly dismissive response from those who identify with and speak for Canada's business and "centrist" political interests. The centrists hold that harshly worded criticism of Chinese government domestic and foreign policy are informed by irrational ideological biases and not based in verifiable facts. This centrist view enjoys support of moderate elements within the Conservative Party and has been consistently affirmed by the policy statements of the Liberal Party of Canada since the late 1960s (Office of the Hon. Ujjal Dosanjh 2009). This centrist policy perspective asserts that the government of the People's Republic of China should be treated with due respect because that government represents a friendly nation with which Canada should establish a strong "strategic

partnership" to achieve high levels of mutually beneficial trade and investment. Indeed, the proponents
of this perspective on the Canada–China relationship strongly caution that Canada's future economic
prosperity is critically dependent on getting our relations with the government of China "right."
Furthermore, as a matter of high national priority,
the government of Canada should be vigorous in
developing an action plan for greatly enhanced
engagement of China. Failing to do so will have significant negative consequences for Canada's economic future (Bouw 2009; Burney 2009; Evans 2013;
Jiang 2009; Jiang 2012).

Outside of government, organizations funded
by monied interests who are active in the China
trade (such as the Canada China Business Council,
the Canadian International Council, and the Asia
Pacific Foundation), as well as large Canadian corporations (such as the Power Corporation of
Canada, Bombardier, and SNC-Lavalin), exert substantial pressure on governments to put more priority on engendering friendly relations with the
Chinese communist regime to mutual economic
benefit. On the other hand, public advocacy organizations such as Amnesty International, Chinese–
Canadian expatriate pro-democracy groups, the
Falun Gong, and Tibetan and Uyghur diaspora
organizations in Canada urge that the government
of Canada engage the government of China more
vigorously on human rights concerns. They also
demand more active pursuit by the RCMP and
Foreign Affairs, Trade and Development Canada
(DFATD) of allegations that Chinese diplomats and
Chinese cyber-hackers illegally harass expatriate
Chinese citizens in Canada (Burton 2009c).

Moreover, tensions exist within the government of Canada between agencies and departments
whose mandate is to further Canada's trade and
economic interests abroad—particularly between
DFATD and those agencies and departments whose
mandate it is to ensure Canada's national security,
such as the Royal Canadian Mounted Police (RCMP),

the Canadian Security Intelligence Service (CSIS),
and the Communications Security Establishment
Canada (CSEC).

Canada's China policy is also a prominent issue
in mainstream partisan political posturing.
Governments are criticized by political opposition
parties for sacrificing Canada's commitment to social
justice and human rights and Canada's national
security to curry favour with China's communist
regime and thereby promote trade and investment
between Canada and China. But governments are
also denounced for raising Canada's concerns over
human rights and allegations of Chinese state espionage in Canada, thereby putatively inhibiting the
expansion of Canada's economic interests in China,
which are considered critically important to Canada's
sustained future prosperity. Canada's China policy
is thereby highly politicized and tends to be the subject of simplistic partisan rhetoric at the level of
popular political debate.

But beyond the use of China policy as a device
to score partisan political advantage, once in power,
Canadian political leaders of all political stripes get
pulled in many directions over how to engage China
in a way that serves Canada's economic interests without sacrificing the liberal democratic values that legitimate the political authority of governments in
Canada's parliamentary system. Because of the
unusually high public profile of Canada's China policy
and the very significant prominence the matter
assumes in political lobbying, the Prime Minister's
Office has taken close and detailed interest in relations
with China at a very senior level in recent Liberal and
Conservative governments (Burton 2011).

Canada's National Interest in Relations with the People's Republic of China (PRC)

Despite the domestic political contention over how
Canada should define its national priorities in this

complicated dynamic of relations with China, in the larger frame, strong cross-partisan consensus exists on the aspect that Canada should engage in relations with the PRC. Over the years, Canada has adopted a highly consistent approach to relations with China; this approach is highly resonant with the Canadian foreign policy doctrine articulated in the Department of Foreign Affairs 1995 foreign policy statement *Canada in the World*. This document sees Canada's foreign policy as based on "three pillars of diplomacy": 1) the promotion of prosperity and employment; 2) the protection of Canada's national security, within a stable global framework; and 3) the projection of Canadian values and culture abroad (Government of Canada, DFAIT 1995).

As to the first pillar, Canada wants fair and reciprocal trading agreements with China— Canada welcomes Chinese investment. But in his 2012 press conference announcing the Canadian government's approval of the China National Offshore Oil Corporation's (CNOOC) $15 billion acquisition of the Canadian energy firm Nexen, Prime Minister Harper made it clear that Canada will not allow the Chinese state to gain dominant control of Canadian economic resources through full acquisition of Canadian resource companies by Chinese state firms. Canada *does* very much encourage Chinese state firms to invest in Canadian enterprises as minority shareholders (Burton 2012b, 2012c).

Regarding the second pillar, Canada continues to investigate Chinese state espionage, including cyber-espionage, directed at Canadian economic, political, and military targets. Canada collaborates with like-minded nations in multilateral forums to encourage the Chinese regime to follow the norms of responsible global citizenship.

Finally, with regard to the third pillar on projection of Canadian values and culture abroad, as the 1995 statement puts it: "Canada is not an island: if the rights of people abroad are not protected, Canadians will ultimately feel the effects at home.

They understand that our economic and security interests are served by the widest possible respect for the environment, human rights, participatory government, free markets and the rule of law. Where these are observed, there is a greater prospect of stability and prosperity. . . . Their observance, therefore, is both an end in itself and a means to achieving other priority objectives." This 1995 statement has stood the test of time and still informs Canada's engagement with China today.

The popular perception that the rise of China is concomitant with the US's economic decline and the gradual winding down of the US's role as the pre-eminent global superpower adds to the sense of urgency for Canada's government to come up with politically viable ways to greatly enhance engagement with China as a rising power. The United States might also reduce its imports of Canadian oil due to US economic decline and to expansion of domestic production of shale oil and natural gas resulting from the increasing development of hydraulic fracturing (fracking) extraction technology. Moreover, US buyers at present can negotiate purchase of Canadian energy products at prices lower than global commodity prices because the US is virtually a monopoly buyer of Canadian oil. Therefore, the only way to stave off a decline in sales of Canadian oil and natural gas and to get the proper value for oil exports to the US is for Canada to diversify its energy export markets—primarily by dramatically expanding sales to China. According to the proponents of this view, it is therefore imperative that Canada build infrastructure for the export of Canadian gas and oil sands oil via the laying of a Northern Gateway pipeline from Alberta to the coast of northern BC for transshipment onward to Asia, primarily to China. Ideally, the massive investment necessary to make this happen, including construction of port facilities in Northern BC and other related infrastructure, would involve large inputs of capital from Chinese sources. However, environmentalists and indigenous Aboriginal bands through whose territory the pipeline would pass are mounting court challenges to this pipeline project, challenges that could significantly delay or even kill it (Blanchfield 2012; Jiang 2010; Kheiriddin 2013).

Barriers to Engagement between Canada and China

The nature of the relationship between Canada and China is fraught with complications due to incompatibilities between Canada's liberal democratic system and China's one-party authoritarian regime.

The Origins and Character of the Current Chinese Regime

The current Chinese regime is the People's Republic of China. The PRC was established in 1949 after the victory of the Communist Party's army over the Chinese Nationalist Party (KMT) forces in the Civil War in China, which followed the defeat of the Japanese in the Second World War.

The People's Republic of China is a one-party state whose political legitimacy is based on achieving Communism through Marxist revolution as being the ultimate purpose of the regime (18th CPC National Congress 2012). China's current political system is categorized as a Leninist system. It remains patterned on the political norms of the Soviet Union under the totalitarian dictatorship of Joseph Stalin. All organized political opposition to the rule of the Communist Party of China is strictly prohibited.

All forms of media in China—radio, TV, newspapers, magazines, books, and the Internet—are strictly controlled by the Central Propaganda Department of the Communist Party of China's Central Committee.

The Chinese judiciary is not independent. Chinese courts at all levels are subordinate to corresponding political and legal affairs commissions, which answer to their corresponding Communist Party committee. All judges and lawyers in China

ultimately are answerable to the authority of the Politics and Law Commission of the Central Committee of the Communist Party of China.

In the 1950s, all Chinese commercial enterprises of any size were nationalized and became functions of Chinese government ministries in a socialist, comprehensively planned, and integrated state economic system (Lawrance 1998).

The intention of the post-1949 Chinese regime was that the socialist planned economy would lead to a just and equitable distribution of the nation's wealth and that the planning would lead to more rational economic development and higher growth rates than a market-regulated economy. Furthermore, the promise of the Marxist ideology promulgated by the Chinese Communist Party was that China would inevitably develop towards the achievement of Communist utopia, even as early as 1966.

But instead, throughout the 1960s and 1970s, the utopian proletarian revolutionary policies of the Chinese Communist Party led to disappointing economic results. China's socialist planned economy stifled individual initiative and was inefficient in allocation of production, leading to chronic problems of shortages of critical economic inputs. The expansion of the economy fell short of high rates of population growth over those years. This was in sharp contrast to the very high growth rates of market economies in Japan, Taiwan, Hong Kong, and South Korea over the same period.

Furthermore, most Chinese people found China's "socialist" culture dispiriting. Food, clothing, and most consumer goods were subject to strict rationing. Religious observance and much of classical Chinese high culture and popular culture were banned as "remnants of feudalism." Modern fashion, foreign pop music and movies were banned as "decadent bourgeois trash." For most Chinese people, life in Mao's "revolutionary" China was impoverished both materially and spiritually.

Despite the comprehensive police and security apparatus designed to suppress all forms of political dissent, pervasive popular dissatisfaction with the Communist Party's political program intensified through the 1970s. By 1976, public demonstrations against the party's failing political program of revolution and socialism began to break out in Beijing and elsewhere in the country. Many felt that the party's harsh rule was under threat of being overthrown by popular demand. The death of the regime's founding supreme leader, Chairman Mao Zedong, in September 1976 eventually led to political factional struggle. The Maoist "leftists" were removed from power. Just over two years after Mao's death and under the new supreme leader, Deng Xiaoping, the Communist Party of China implemented a program of "opening and reform," and demand for political change abated. China's Marxist ideology was gradually phased out, and a market economy system meant to stimulate economic growth and improve the living standards of China's citizens gradually phased in. High rates of sustained economic growth far exceeding expectations rapidly followed. China's historic, dramatic, and comprehensive rise to power has been the consequence.

But the Chinese state did not reprivatize the national state enterprises. These continue to be functions of the Chinese state under the overall coordination of the Chinese Communist Party's leadership. And there is still no independent rule of law in China. Politically, China remains a one-party Leninist regime. There is no social space for true civil society outside of the authority of the party-state, which has no democratic political institutions. The political authority of the unelected Standing Committee of the Political Bureau of the Central Committee of the Chinese Communist Party is paramount and unchallengeable.

Implications of Regime Incompatibility for Canada's Engagement of China

The fundamental incompatibilities between the Chinese and Canadian political systems present a significant challenge to Canada's realization of its foreign policy agenda in relations with China. These incompatibilities have an impact on all three pillars of Canada's foreign policy doctrine: promotion of Canada's prosperity, protection of Canada's national security, and the projection of Canadian values abroad.

China is able to exercise a high degree of coordination between its economic engagement and its political engagement with foreign powers. Of course the members of the Communist Party of China committees that direct Chinese state enterprises hope to maximize profit in their foreign investments. They have some advantage in this regard because Chinese state enterprises, as functions of the Chinese state, are able to comprehensively draw on all Chinese state resources to enhance their business competitiveness abroad. This includes Chinese state espionage agencies, which can provide state enterprises with covertly obtained economic data and purloined intellectual property, technologies, and proprietary production processes that give Chinese state enterprises a business advantage over their foreign competitors. These state benefits are of course not readily available to the smaller, non-state commercial enterprise Canadian counterparts of Chinese businesses (McGregor 2012).

At the same time, the Communist Party of China's control and direction of Chinese state enterprise gives the Chinese state the economic leverage to strengthen and further China's national political goals and strategic engagement with foreign nations. For example, nations that resist Chinese government pressure to refuse to meet with His Holiness the Dalai Lama are consistently threatened by Chinese diplomats with the spectre of economic retaliation by Chinese state firms. They are warned that these firms prefer to engage in business with nations that are deemed "friendly" to China (Duggal 2012). These threats have not been realized in the case of Canada. But they have gone beyond rhetoric and had significant economic impact on other nations' trade and investment projects in China (Ghosh 2013). Similarly, the Chinese government expressed its discontent with the government of Norway over the Nobel Peace Prize being awarded to imprisoned Chinese political dissident Liu Xiaobo in 2010, and retaliated with economic sanctions that banned Chinese state firms from pursuing contracts with Norwegian firms (Fuchs and Klann 2010; Wong and Morillo 2010).

There are concerns that the Chinese state firms engaged in trade and investment in Canada, in addition to being motivated by profit, might also be employed by the government of China to realize other state goals in Canada. For example, the government of Canada has disallowed Chinese telecommunications enterprise Huawei from competing for contracts to supply software and equipment to Canadian government communications networks for fear that Huawei would be compelled by the Chinese military to insert software routines into its equipment that would allow Chinese security agencies to have access to Canadian secret government communications (Weston 2012). This government decision is comparable to similar decisions by the governments of other Western nations, including Australia and the United States (Lu Yueyang 2012; US House of Representatives 2012). Huawei insists that it is not a Chinese state enterprise but acknowledges that it does have a branch of the Chinese Communist Party at the top of its management structure. The firm also receives research grants from the government of China and is able to offer foreign purchasers of its software and equipment favourable financing terms through Chinese state banks. Huawei has made highly competitive bids to install wireless telephone technology on behalf of major Canadian firms, including Wind, Bell, and Telus (Burton 2012d). There is concern that the founder of Huawei has a background in the Chinese People's Liberation Army (PLA), and therefore Huawei might be a front for Chinese security agencies (Reuters 2013). Some

allege that Huawei's software supporting its hardware sold abroad includes routines that would facilitate Chinese cyber-espionage or even allow the shutdown of critical Canadian infrastructure in time of war. But there is no hard evidence supporting these serious allegations.

In 2012, the bid by CNOOC to acquire a Canadian oil firm, Nexen, was the subject of considerable controversy and debate. CNOOC went to considerable lengths to satisfy the terms of the Investment Canada Act (Government of Canada, Industry Canada 2002). The key for CNOOC to gain approval for the acquisition was to demonstrate that the Nexen acquisition would be a net benefit to Canada. To this end, CNOOC promised to locate their head office for overseas operations in Calgary and to maintain Nexen's corporate responsibility programs. CNOOC also offered a significant financial incentive for Nexen shareholders. Their $15 billion offer was some 60 per cent over the value of Nexen shares (CNOOC Canada Inc. press release 2012).

Nevertheless, this acquisition inspired a very high profile public debate over a period of months. Opposition came from both the right and left wing of Canada's political spectrum (Barlow 2012; Ibbitson 2012). Questions were raised about CNOOC's environmental record in Burma, about the proclivity of Chinese state firms to flout foreign laws with regard to bribery, tax evasion, and labour standards, and about the use of imported Chinese labour in the operation of Chinese state firms abroad. There were further concerns about whether the Chinese state would take advantage of CNOOC's presence in Canada to engage in economic espionage, and about the transfer of Canadian technologies to other Chinese state firms without payment of licensing fees. As well, there was speculation that if the Chinese state got its foot in the door through this $15 billion investment, other Chinese state firms would invest much larger sums in the acquisition of other Canadian companies (Jordan 2012). It was felt that if the Chinese state obtained a significant degree of control over critical Canadian economic assets, this control would give a foreign power undue political and economic leverage over decisions of the government of Canada, including Canada's ability to respond to Chinese human rights abuses domestically and the Chinese government's support for the regimes of undemocratic political dictators in the third world (Burton 2012a).

But there was also very strong lobbying by some Canadian business interests for the government of Canada to approve this deal and in general to welcome further extensive Chinese state investment in Canada. These business interests indicated that there was no basis for thinking that CNOOC had any intentions with regard to Nexen except to gain a foothold into the highly profitable export potential of Canada's oil sands (Trudeau 2012; Woo 2013).

Canadian policy on this matter was clarified by an extraordinary press conference by the prime minister in December 2012 at which he said that, while the government of Canada would approve CNOOC's acquisition of Nexen, the approval represented "not the beginning of a trend but rather the end of a trend. When we say Canada is open for business, we do not mean that Canada is for sale to foreign governments. To be blunt, Canadians have not spent years reducing the ownership of sectors of the economy by our own governments, only to see them bought and controlled by foreign governments instead" (Payton 2012; Burton 2012b, 2012c).

Of course, due to the integrated nature of the Chinese political/economic/social regime, it stands to reason that Canadian companies that have been able to successfully participate in Chinese communist business networks would also support all aspects of the Chinese regime in its engagement with Canada including, consciously or unawares, providing "fronts" for facilitating Chinese state espionage. As the director of CSIS, Richard Fadden, has indicated: "Certain state-owned enterprises and private firms

with close ties to their home governments have pursued opaque agendas or received clandestine intelligence support for their pursuits here. When foreign companies with ties to foreign intelligence agencies or hostile governments seek to acquire control over strategic sectors of the Canadian economy, it can represent a threat to Canadian security interests" (Campion-Smith 2012).

Similar issues of systemic incompatibility and distrust on the part of Canadians toward Chinese assurances of goodwill and fair play in trade dealings have also bedevilled the expansion of Canada's investment in China (Akin 2012). Expansion of Canada's trade relations with China is far from commensurate with the high growth rates in China's economic development, particularly since the mid-1990s. Canadian businesses are too often reluctant to invest in China because of concerns over lack of protections for contractual relations with potential Chinese business partners. There are many accounts of Chinese partners transferring intellectual property and proprietary manufacturing processes to other Chinese concerns without the permission of the Canadian firm and without paying licensing fees for the Canadian intellectual property. Seeking recourse through the Chinese courts can be problematic due to the lack of independence of Chinese justice and pervasive issues of corruption and bribery in the Chinese judicial system. The Chinese business culture is rife with gift-giving practices and under-the-table exchanges of favours that allow public officials to supplement their very low civil service salaries. Rent-seeking behaviour by Chinese managers of state enterprises and local government offices who are responsible for taxation and imposition of fees, for issuing of permits, and for environmental and labour regulations is a constant fact of life for any commercial enterprise operating in China, including Canadian business. By law, Canadian companies are not permitted to engage in bribery in their operations abroad. As a consequence, Canadian firms in China can be subject to arbitrary changes in regulations and to the imposition of taxes and fees that force them to abandon their China operations (Burton 2009c). Pressure can also be strong to agree to transfer Canadian technologies to the Chinese state as a condition of continuing to operate in the Chinese market (Lubman 2013).

With a view to addressing this, Canada began to negotiate with China a Foreign Investment Promotion and Protection Agreement (FIPA) in 1994 (Government of Canada, DFAIT 2012b). The agreement was signed in September 2012 and ratified by Parliament two years later. The intent of the agreement was to ensure that investors in each other's country would receive the same treatment as domestic firms and that contract disputes would be subject to arbitration by a neutral third party offshore. Court challenges have been mounted by Aboriginal groups, supported by the Green Party, both of which are concerned that implementation of this agreement would lead to un-environmentally friendly mining operations by Chinese state firms in the Canadian North (Bertrand 2013; Hong 2012). The agreement is similarly opposed by the New Democratic Party and by right wing elements within the Conservative Party who fear that it will give Chinese state firms significant advantage in their investments in Canada, but will not lead to a level playing field for Canadian firms wishing to invest in China (Radia 2013).

In a similar vein, the Canada–China Economic Complementarities Study was completed in August 2012 (Government of Canada, DFAIT 2012a). This study could form the basis for negotiation of a much touted free trade agreement between Canada and China (Ivison 2012). The Complementarities Study has been effectively shelved and no movement toward free trade negotiations is apparent (Simpson 2013). This likewise reflects Canadian skepticism about the motivation of the Chinese government in proposing free trade between Canada and China as a means to redress the current trade disparities between the two nations and to dramatically intensify economic engagement between Canada and China.

Human Rights as a Constraint in the Development of Canada–China Relations

China's population comprises close to a quarter of all humanity, and about 40 times Canada's population. Despite relatively low per capita GDP, China is a leading global economic power because of its huge size. So China has an enormous power advantage over Canada in both bilateral and multilateral engagement. But Canada puts great importance on relations with the People's Republic of China, as expressed by the fact that China was the first place John Baird travelled to shortly after being named minister of foreign affairs (Clark 2011).

Certainly Canada–China relations were a low priority for the Harper Conservatives over their years as a minority government. For the first five years, prior to the achievement of a majority government in 2011, the government of Stephen Harper was largely consumed by domestic issues and with maintaining and consolidating its fragile hold on power. So foreign relations in general were not a primary focus of the early period of this government. Moreover, there was a distinct lack of foreign policy expertise at the senior levels of the Conservative leadership when the Conservative Party first came to power. Mr. Harper himself made clear that he had not been much engaged in foreign policy prior to becoming prime minister (Heinbecker 2010). The Harper government's first three ministers of foreign affairs—Peter MacKay, Maxime Bernier, and Lawrence Cannon—kept the portfolio at a relatively low profile in Canada and abroad. Only with the appointment of John Baird in May 2011 did a strong figure who enjoyed the marked confidence of the prime minister step into the position of minister of foreign affairs. By that time, the Conservatives had a majority in Parliament and, more confident of their position domestically, were able to focus on furthering Canada's interests internationally.

Moreover, the Conservatives sought to establish a China policy distinct from the approaches to China of the Liberal past. Some of it might have had to do simply with political branding—carving out a fresh and distinctive Conservative political approach to relations with China. But certainly for deeply felt reasons of ideology the Conservatives have been more comfortable dealing with democratic regimes. India is a democracy, so de-emphasizing relations with the Communist government in Beijing and putting more focus on developing closer ties with the democratic government in New Delhi might have been viewed as a possible direction for the new government's aspiration to make its mark by new and innovative Canadian foreign policy. But while China had been grouped with Brazil, Russia, India, and South Africa in the Martin government's foreign policy statement, the bottom line was that China's economy is larger and far more critical to ensuring Canada's future economic prosperity than Brazil, Russia, India, and South Africa put together (Alessi 2012). Canada had to deal with China. India simply could not displace China in Canada's foreign relations priorities.

China is a permanent member of the United Nations Security Council. On a number of occasions the government of Canada has urged Security Council condemnation of the behaviour of UN member-states, behaviours deemed by Canada as inconsistent with UN norms, where China has opposed condemnation or sought to water down UN resolutions. These often involve states with which China has close trade arrangements, including Sudan, Iran, Zimbabwe, and North Korea. In general, Canada encourages China to become fully compliant with international political and economic regimes (Burton 2009a, 2009b). But statements by officials of the Chinese government suggest that China does not feel bound by international regimes that were established without the consent of the PRC because they predate its involvement in larger matters of global governments and transnational relations (Potter 2003).

Nevertheless, the government of the People's Republic of China did sign the UN's International Covenant on Civil and Political Rights (ICCPR) in 1998. And indeed China has ratified most of the major UN human rights covenants (University of Minnesota Human Rights Library n.d.). From 1998 to 2005, Canada engaged in a government-to-government bilateral human rights dialogue coordinated by the International Organizations Department of the Ministry of Foreign Affairs of the People's Republic of China. The government of China suggested this form of confidential government-to-government bilateral engagement on human rights issues in exchange for Canada's ceasing to support a resolution against China in the UN Human Rights Commission annual meetings. Under Foreign Affairs Minister Lloyd Axworthy there was an expectation that if the government of China understood the Canadian perspective on the benefits of framing domestic and international policy in way that was mindful of human rights norms, China would better appreciate the importance of a free civil society to good governance and stable democratic development and therefore move to make the appropriate political reforms in China's political institutions to strengthen the rule of law through an independent judiciary. Along these lines, CIDA approached the Chinese authorities proposing to offer training for Chinese foreign ministry officials on how to report to the UN on compliance with the ICCPR after China ratified. Canada also initiated a major CIDA program to train Chinese judges at about this time (Burton 2006; Kamm 2012).

But Canada ceased the bilateral human-rights-dialogue mode of engagement with the government of China in 2006 when it became apparent that it was having no impact on Chinese state behaviour with regard to international human rights. Canada's "quiet diplomacy" approach to continuous allegations of China's state-sanctioned flouting of international human rights norms had the effect of tacitly sanctioning Chinese state behaviours that violate the language, cultural, and religious rights of Uyghurs, Tibetans, and other minority ethnic groups, as well as pervasive violations of universal human entitlements to freedom of expression, freedom of association, and fundamental political rights of citizenship.

China inserted a statement in the National Constitution of the People's Republic of China promising to "uphold human rights" in 2004 (Second Session of the Tenth National People's Congress 2004). But Chinese officials have argued that cultural, historical, and developmental factors have prevailed against implementation of universal human rights norms for the time being until conditions allow (Burton 2009c; Xinhua News Agency 2012b). More recently, the government of China (under the new leadership of Communist Party Chairman Xi Jinping) has adopted a harder line, banning discourse on "universal values," "civil society," "civil rights," "judicial independence," and so on, in the Chinese media and in universities and think tanks (Carlson 2013).

Nevertheless, at all bilateral meetings, Prime Minister Harper and senior ministers continue to engage the Chinese leadership on China's human rights record and to stress this point in post-summit press briefings (Clark 2011). But Chinese media reports on visits by senior Canadian officials or visits by senior Chinese officials to Canada typically do not mention that human rights issues were discussed (Xinhua News Agency 2011). It appears that any significant movement on human rights issues by the Chinese authorities will be indicative of fundamental transformation of the nature of China's authoritarian communist party regime. But it is difficult to assess the effectiveness of Canada's program to promote the Canadian "values agenda" in China.

Conclusion: Pending Issues in Canada–China Relations

On the face of it, the prospects for intensification of Canada's bilateral engagement with China should be very strong. In recent years, the Chinese state has suffered significant losses of property and investment after violent, non-democratic regime change in some Third World dictatorships (Xinhua News Agency 2012a). Therefore, Chinese state enterprises increasingly favour investment in stable democracies with comprehensive rule of law. Canada clearly fits the bill. And Canada's oil and natural gas and other mineral resources, including potash, are very much in demand by the Chinese regime to sustain China's continuing economic growth.

Canada also requires enormous investment to fully exploit the oil sands resources, and for infrastructure to develop port facilities in Northern BC and pipelines and other transportation links to facilitate diversifying our trade to China and other Asian destinations. China also represents a rapidly expanding market not only for Canadian commodities, but also services, including banking and insurance, in which Canada is a world leader. Getting into the Chinese market would do much to promote Canada's future prosperity. Moreover, Chinese is the third most spoken language in Canada after English and French. Canadians of Chinese origin comprise more than 4 per cent of Canada's population, so this should give Canada a natural advantage in interaction with China (Government of Canada, Statistics Canada n.d.).

So Canada and China are very evidently a good fit for each other for comprehensive development of mutually beneficial relations. But as discussed above, incompatibility issues between the political economic systems of Canada and China continue to pose a significant challenge to broadening and deepening relations between our two countries in a meaningful way.

Most of Canada's recent bilateral agreements with China have been rather low level. For example, China extended Approved Destinations Status to Canada in 2009, which means that Chinese passport holders now have the right to leave China for the purpose of tourism in Canada (Government of Canada, Office of the Prime Minister 2009). But more than 120 countries achieved this status ahead of Canada (Arita, Edmonds, La Croix, and Mak 2009).

In 2013, Canada and China reached an agreement on sharing the proceeds of transnational crime (Government of Canada, DFATD 2013b). Negotiations on this began in 1999. This agreement allows Canada to compensate the Chinese police with assets seized in Canada for the costs of police investigations in China that break drug rings and organized transnational financial fraud schemes.

Potentially even more important, FIPA negotiations were completed in 2013, almost 20 years after they started (Government of Canada, DFATD 2012). The bottom line appears to be that Chinese investments already enjoy protection in Canada because Canada has a fair and impartial judicial system that does not discriminate against foreign investors, so there is no incentive for the Chinese regime to offer protection of Canadian investment in China. The 2013 FIPA is arguably problematic because through it, China gained certain concessions from Canada without really providing effective assurance for Canadian investors seeking to exploit the Chinese market.

Apart from economics, the growing problem of corrupt Chinese officials seeking refuge in Canada and Chinese organized criminal gang elements fleeing to Canada has not been satisfactorily addressed by the logical solution of a Canada–China

extradition treaty (Huang 2009). Aside from the problem that China imposes the death penalty for a broad range of crimes, including white-collar crimes, Canadian courts are reluctant to send people back to China to face charges because Canadian judicial authorities feel anyone accused of a crime in China cannot obtain fair and impartial justice and due process of law there. Chinese people alleged to have committed serious crimes in China, even murder, have not been made accountable for what they've done once they touch base in Canada. Indeed, many are suspected of working for the overseas operations of Chinese triad gangs after fleeing to Canada. And Canada has not been able to repatriate Chinese nationals alleged to have committed serious crimes in Canada who have fled to China before arrest by the Canadian police (Burton 2009c).

Many issues of this nature could be addressed if mutual trust and compatible institutions allowed productive cooperation between Canada and China. But both trust and compatible institutional mechanisms for bilateral collaboration are severely lacking, and the understandable lack of rapport between Prime Minister Harper and his Chinese counterparts is a soft factor that reflects this regrettable reality.

From Beijing's perspective, Canada is just one of dozens of middle powers with whom China seeks markets for its exports and investment in sectors critical to China's economic needs, but with whom China has little interest in meaningful political relations (Burton 2009c). Genuine strategic partnerships are sought by China with other permanent members of the UN Security Council or with surrounding nations, particularly Japan and South Korea, and possibly India in future years, but Canada simply does not matter that much to China. We offer little that cannot be obtained by China elsewhere. Canada needs China more than China needs Canada.

Relations between Canada and China could be intensified if China made the transition to a democratic system akin to that of the political democratization that took place in Taiwan, South Korea, or Japan (all of whom share with China a Confucian political legacy) in the latter part of the last century. Thanks to the spread of alternative political discourse in China—at odds with the Chinese state media—that has been facilitated by the enthusiastic adoption of social media by the hundreds of millions of users of smart phones, tablets, and networked computers in China in recent years (Schiavenza 2013); at odds with China's official political norms, Chinese young people more and more identify themselves as citizens with inherent entitlement to human rights. But despite this, objectively speaking, the current regime shows no sign of imminent collapse. China has no charismatic political opposition leaders like Lech Walesa or Vaclav Havel, who oversaw the transition from Leninist systems in Poland and Czechoslovakia respectively and who might inspire a twenty-first-century "Beijng spring." That is not to say that Canada should no longer continue to support progressive agents of political and legal change through government-funded development programming in "good governance, democratic development and human rights" (Government of Canada, DFATD 2013a).

A balanced policy of combining the "hard" aspects of economic and security factors with the "softer" aspect of promoting Canadian values in China is in Canada's national political interest, not only because liberal democracies promote stable economic regimes but also because political systemic reform in China would go a long way to breaking down the systemic incompatibilities that so inhibit the natural intensification of bilateral engagement between Canada and China in all spheres of international relations.

Questions for Review

1. What is the relationship between promotion of trade and promotion of Canadian values in Canada–China relations?
2. Should the Canadian government concern itself with the human rights of Chinese citizens in China?
3. Should Chinese state-owned enterprises be permitted to make major investments in Canada?
4. Is Canada's pursuit of a "strategic partnership" with China in Canada's long-term interest?

Suggested Readings

Burton, Charles. 2009. *A Reassessment of Canada's Interests in China and Options for Renewal of Canada's China Policy.* Toronto: Canadian International Council (CIC). Available at http://dspace.cigilibrary.org/jspui/handle/123456789/23874.

Evans, Paul. 2013. "Dancing with the dragon: as China surges to new heights, can Canada keep step?" *Literary Review of Canada* 21, 3 (April). Available at http://reviewcanada.ca/essays/2013/04/01/dancing-with-the-dragon/.

Jiang, Wenran. 2009. "Seeking a strategic vision for Canada–China relations." *International Journal* 64, 4 (Autumn): 891–909.

Paltiel, Jeremy. 2010. *Canada in China's Grand Strategy.* China Papers No. 6. Toronto: Canadian International Council (CIC). Available at http://cic.verto.ca/wp-content/uploads/2011/05/Canada-in-Chinas-Grand-Strategy-Jeremy-Paltiel1.pdf.

Potter, Pitman B., and Thomas Adams, eds. 2011. *Issues in Canada–China Relations.* Toronto: Canadian International Council (CIC). Available at http://opencanada.org/features/reports/issues-in-canada-china-relations/.

Poy, Vivienne, and Huhua Cao, eds. 2011. *The China Challenge: Sino-Canadian Relations in the 21st Century.* Ottawa: University of Ottawa Press. Available at www.ruor.uottawa.ca/en/bitstream/handle/10393/23096/China_Challenge.pdf?sequence=1.

References

18th CPC National Congress. 2012. *Constitution of Communist Party of China*. Available at http://news.xinhuanet.com/english/special/18cpcnc/2012-11/18/c_131982575.htm.

Akin, David. 2012. "Majority says spike Chinese takeover of Canada's Nexen." *Toronto Sun*, 23 August. Available at www.torontosun.com/2012/08/23/majority-says-spike-chinese-takeover-of-canadas-nexen?utm_source=facebook&utm_medium=recommend-button&utm_campaign=Majority says spike Chinese takeover of Canada's Nexen.

Alessi, Christopher. 2012. "Does the BRICS group matter?" Interview with Martin Wolf of the *Financial Times*. Council on Foreign Relations. 30 March. Available at www.cfr.org/emerging-markets/does-brics-group-matter/p27802.

Arita, S., C. Edmonds, S. La Croix, and J. Mak. 2009. *The Impact of Approved Destination Status on Chinese Travel Abroad: An Economic Analysis*. Available (with account) at http://proxy.library.brocku.ca/login?url=http://search.ebscohost.com/login.aspx?direct=true&db=ecn&AN=1083249&site=eds-live&scope=site.

Barlow, Maude. 2012. "Challenging the Harper government's handling of CNOOC takeover of Nexen." Council of Canadians. 10 December. Available at www.canadians.org/node/3468.

Bertrand, Julie. 2013. "Hupacasath gets ready for final round in Canada China FIPPA [sic] fight." *Alberni Valley Times*, 27 May. Available at www.avtimes.net/news/local/hupacasath-gets-ready-for-final-round-in-canada-china-fippa-fight-1.232217.

Blanchfield, Mike. 2012. "China to push 'win–win' energy pact with Canada on Harper visit, envoy says." *Global News*, 23 January. Available at http://globalnews.ca/news/202763/china-to-push-win-win-energy-pact-with-canada-on-harper-visit-envoy-says/.

Bouw, Brenda. 2009. "Canada should accept different values than China, focus on economic ties." *Canadian Press*, 16 October. Available at http://news.ca.msn.com/money/article.aspx?cp-documentid=22304079.

Burney, Derek. 2009. "Canada must outgrow its juvenile relationship with China." *The Globe and Mail*, 9 April. Available at http://v1.theglobeandmail.com/servlet/story/RTGAM.20090409.wcoessay0411/business.

Burton, Charles. 2006. "Assessment of the Canada–China bilateral human rights dialogue." Department of Foreign Affairs and International Trade. Available at http://charlesburton.webplus.net/page38.html.

——. 2009a. "For a more sophisticated engagement with China." *The Globe and Mail*, 27 November. Available at www.theglobeandmail.com/commentary/for-a-more-sophisticated-engagement-with-china/article4395546/.

——. 2009b. "Sino-Canadian relations on slow boat to nowhere." *Toronto Star*, 6 March. Available at www.thestar.com/opinion/2009/03/06/sinocanadian_relations_on_slow_boat_to_nowhere.html.

——. 2009c. *A Reassessment of Canada's Interests in China and Options for Renewal of Canada's China Policy*. Toronto: Canadian International Council (CIC). Available at http://dspace.cigilibrary.org/jspui/handle/123456789/23874.

——. 2011. "The Canadian policy context of Canada's China policy since 1970." In Vivienne Poy and Huhua Cao, eds. *The China Challenge : Sino-Canadian Relations in the 21st Century* (p. 32). Ottawa: University of Ottawa Press. Available at www.ruor.uottawa.ca/en/bitstream/handle/10393/23096/China_Challenge.pdf?sequence=1.

——. 2012a. "CNOOC's bid for Nexen is a key move on China's global chess board: If this deal goes through, China will assume a major voice in government consultations on Canada's energy policy." *Toronto Star*, 22 August. Available at www.thestar.com/opinion/editorialopinion/2012/08/22/cnoocs_bid_for_nexen_is_a_key_move_on_chinas_global_chess_board.html.

——. 2012b. "Stephen Harper's decision on CNOOC finally gets the China connection right: In Canada's relations with the People's Republic of China, it is better to be respected than loved." *Toronto Star*, 10 December. Available at www.thestar.com/opinion/editorialopinion/2012/12/10/stephen_harpers_decision_on_cnooc_finally_gets_the_china_connection_right.html.

——. 2012c. "Stephen Harper's new trade rules safeguard Canada's interests." *The Globe and Mail*, 8 December. Available at www.theglobeandmail.com/commentary/stephen-harpers-new-trade-rules-safeguard-canadas-interests/article6136355/.

——. 2012d. "Weighing Huawei in Canada." *Embassy*, 17 October. Available at www.embassynews.ca/opinion/2012/10/16/weighing-huawei-in-canada/42632.

Campion-Smith, Bruce. 2012. "Spy agency warns of espionage risk with foreign takeovers: Cyber-attacks, home-grown terrorism and corporate espionage are among threats facing Canada, CSIS director warns in his annual report." *Toronto Star*, 21 September. Available at www.thestar.com/news/canada/2012/09/21/spy_agency_warns_of_espionage_risk_with_foreign_takeovers.html.

Carlson, B. 2013. "The 7 things you can't talk about in China: China's top propaganda officials have issued new restrictions banning seven topics deemed to be 'dangerous Western influences.'" *Toronto Star*, 30 June. Available at www.thestar.com/news/world/2013/06/30/the_7_things_you_cant_talk_about_in_china.html.

Clark, Campbell. 2011. "Effusive John Baird wraps up China visit with praise for 'strategic partner.'" *The Globe and Mail*, 20 July. Available at www.theglobeandmail.com/news/politics/ottawa-notebook/effusive-john-baird-wraps-up-china-visit-with-praise-for-strategic-partner/article616103/.

CNOOC Canada Inc. 2012. "CNOOC Limited enters into definitive agreement to acquire Nexen Inc." Press release (23 July). Available at www.cnoocltd.com/encnoocltd/newszx/news/2012/2062.shtml.

Duggal, S. 2012. "Meeting with famed Tibetan a balancing act for PM." *Embassy*, 5 February. Available at www.embassynews.ca/news/2012/05/02/meeting-with-famed-tibetan-a-balancing-act-for-pm/41544.

Evans, Paul. 2013. "Dancing with the dragon: As China surges to new heights, can Canada keep step?" *Literary Review of Canada*, 21, 3 (April). Available at http://reviewcanada.ca/essays/2013/04/01/dancing-with-the-dragon/.

Fuchs, Andreas, and Nils-Hendrik Klann. 2010. "How credible are China's threats of economic retaliation in the context of bilateral disputes?" *VOX*, 10 November. Available at www.voxeu.org/article/dalai-lama-effect-and-china-s-potential-trade-response-nobel-peace-prize.

Ghosh, Palash. 2013. "David Cameron and China: Could the Dalai Lama cost Britain billions in trade and investments?" *International Business Times*, 7 May. Available at www.ibtimes.com/david-cameron-china-could-dalai-lama-cost-britain-billions-trade-investments-1241657.

Government of Canada, Department of Foreign Affairs and International Trade (DFAIT). 1995. *Canada in the World: Canadian Foreign Policy Review*.

Government of Canada, DFAIT. 2012a. "Canada–China Economic Complementarities Study." 15 August. Available at www.international.gc.ca/trade-agreements-accords-commerciaux/agr-acc/china-chine/index.aspx?lang=eng.

Government of Canada, DFAIT. 2012b. "Background on the Canada–China Foreign Investment Promotion and Protection Agreement (FIPA) negotiations." Available at www.international.gc.ca/trade-agreements-accords-commerciaux/agr-acc/fipa-apie/china-chine.aspx?lang=eng.

Government of Canada, Department of Foreign Affairs, Trade and Development (DFATD). 2012. "Agreement between the Government of Canada and the government of the People's Republic of China for the promotion and reciprocal protection of investments." Available at www.international.gc.ca/trade-agreements-accords-commerciaux/agr-acc/fipa-apie/china-text-chine.aspx.

Government of Canada, DFATD. 2013a. "Policy for CIDA on Human Rights, Democratization and Good Governance." Available at www.cida.gc.ca/acdi-cida/acdi-cida.nsf/eng/REN-218124821-P93.

Government of Canada, DFATD. 2013b. "Stepping up the fight against transnational organized crime." Available at www.international.gc.ca/media/aff/news-communiques/2013/07/04b.aspx.

Government of Canada, Industry Canada. 2002. *Investment Canada Act*. Available at www.ic.gc.ca/eic/site/ica-lic.nsf/eng/home.

Government of Canada, Office of the Prime Minister. 2009. "China grants Canada approved destination status." Available at http://pm.gc.ca/eng/media.asp?id=3004.

Government of Canada, Statistics Canada. N.d. "The Chinese community in Canada: A growing community." Available at www.statcan.gc.ca/pub/89-621-x/89-621-x2006001-eng.htm.

Heinbecker, Paul. 2010. *Getting Back in the Game: A Foreign Policy Playbook for Canada*. Toronto: Key Porter.

Hong, Beth. 2012. "Canada–China FIPPA agreement may be unconstitutional, treaty law expert says." *Vancouver Observer*, 17 October. Available at www.vancouverobserver.com/politics/canada-china-fippa-agreement-unconstitutional-treaty-law-expert-says.

Huang, Y. 2009. 前中国驻加大使梅平：中国半数经济犯藏在加拿大 ("Former Chinese Ambassador to Canada Mei Ping: Half of China's Economic Criminals are Hiding in Canada"). *Chinese Global Times*, 25 June. Available at http://blog.ifeng.com/article/2853086.html.

Ibbitson, John. 2012. "Harper can't ignore opposition to Nexen sale by his political base." *The Globe and Mail*, 1 August. Available at www.theglobeandmail.com/news/politics/harper-cant-ignore-opposition-to-nexen-sale-by-his-political-base/article4453670/.

Ivison, John. 2012. "Ottawa eyeing full-blown free trade agreement with China." *National Post*, 11 September. Available at http://news.nationalpost.com/2012/09/11/ottawa-eyeing-full-blown-free-trade-agreement-with-china/.

Jiang, Wenran. 2009. "Seeking a strategic vision for Canada–China relations." *International Journal* 64, 4 (Autumn): 891–909.

———. 2010. *The Dragon Returns: Canada in China's Quest for Energy Security*. *China Papers* No. 19. Toronto: Canadian International Council (CIC). Available at www.opencanada.org/wp-content/uploads/2011/05/The-Dragon-Returns_-Canada-in-China%E2%80%99s-Quest-for-Energy-Security-Wenran-Jiang1.pdf.

———. 2012. "China in Canada, part 3: We need a plan." *Financial Post*, 19 January. Available at http://opinion.financialpost.com/2012/01/19/china-in-canada-part-3-we-need-a-plan/.

Jordan, Pav. 2012. "Nexen bid part of China's plan to become resources powerhouse." *The Globe and Mail*, 23 July. Available at www.theglobeandmail.com/report-on-business/international-business/asian-pacific-business/nexen-bid-part-of-chinas-plan-to-become-resources-powerhouse/article4436971/.

Kamm, John. 2012. "Afterword: What future for human rights dialogues?," pp. 332–41 in Timothy B. Weston and Lionel

M. Jensen, eds. *China in and beyond the Headlines.* Lanham, MD: Rowman and Littlefield.

Kheiriddin, Tasha. 2013. "Crude awakening: What if Obama rejects Keystone?" *iPolitics*, 29 July. Available at www.ipolitics.ca/2013/07/29/385799/.

Lawrance, Alan. 1998. *China under Communism.* London and New York: Routledge.

Lu Yueyang, Maggie. 2012. "Australia bars Huawei from broadband project." *The New York Times*, 26 March. Available at www.nytimes.com/2012/03/27/technology/australia-bars-huawei-from-broadband-project.html.

Lubman, Stanley. 2013. "Outside the law: Lessons from a Chinese hostage-taking." *Wall Street Journal*, 9 July. Available at http://blogs.wsj.com/chinarealtime/2013/07/09/outside-the-law-lessons-from-a-chinese-hostage-taking/.

McGregor, Richard. 2012. *The Party: The Secret World of China's Communist Rulers.* New York: Harper Perennial.

Office of the Hon. Ujjal Dosanjh. 2009. Commentary: "A Stronger Canada–China Relationship." Available at http://newpartnership.wordpress.com/what-theyre-saying/.

Paltiel, Jeremy. 2010. Canada in China's Grand Strategy. China Papers No. 6. Toronto: Canadian International Council (CIC). Available at http://cic.verto.ca/wp-content/uploads/2011/05/Canada-in-Chinas-Grand-Strategy-Jeremy-Paltiel1.pdf.

Payton, Laura. 2012. "Government OK's foreign bids for Nexen, Progress Energy." CBC News: Business, December 7. Available at www.cbc.ca/news/business/story/2012/12/07/cnooc-nexen-takeover.html.

Potter, Pitman B. 2003. "Globalization and economic regulation in China: Selective adaptation of globalized norms and practices." Washington University *Global Studies Law Review* 2, 1 (January): 119–50.

Potter, Pitman B., and Thomas Adams, eds. 2011. *Issues in Canada–China Relations.* Toronto: Canadian International Council (CIC). Available at http://opencanada.org/features/reports/issues-in-canada-china-relations/.

Poy, Vivienne, and Huhua Cao, eds. 2011. *The China Challenge: Sino-Canadian Relations in the 21st Century.* Ottawa: University of Ottawa Press. Available at www.ruor.uottawa.ca/en/bitstream/handle/10393/23096/China_Challenge.pdf?sequence=1.

Radia, Andy. 2013. "New Democrats make last-ditch effort to stop FIPPA trade deal with China." *Yahoo! News Canada*, 18 April. Available at http://ca.news.yahoo.com/blogs/canada-politics/democrats-one-last-ditched-effort-stop-fipa-trade-153206421.html.

Reuters. 2013. "Former CIA boss says aware of evidence Huawei spying for China." *The Globe and Mail*, 19 July. Available at www.reuters.com/article/2013/07/19/us-huawei-security-idUSBRE96I06I20130719.

Schiavenza, Matt. 2013. "WeChat—not Weibo—is the Chinese social network to watch." *The Atlantic*, 30 July. Available at www.theatlantic.com/china/archive/2013/07/wechat-not-weibo-is-the-chinese-social-network-to-watch/278212/.

Second Session of the Tenth National People's Congress. 2004. *The Constitution of the People's Republic of China.* Available at www.npc.gov.cn/englishnpc/Constitution/node_2825.htm.

Simpson, Jeffrey. 2013. "We have pandas, but no trade deal with China." *The Globe and Mail*, 3 July. Available at www.theglobeandmail.com/commentary/we-have-pandas-but-no-trade-deal-with-china/article12936621/.

Trudeau, Justin. 2012. "Why the CNOOC–Nexen deal is good for Canada." 19 November. Available at http://o.canada.com/news/national/justin-trudeau-why-the-cnooc-nexen-deal-is-good-for-canada.

U.S. House of Representatives, 112th Congress. 2012. "Investigative report on the U.S. national security issues posed by Chinese telecommunications companies Huawei and ZTE. 8 October. Available at http://intelligence.house.gov/committee-report/investigative-report-us-national-security-issues-posed-chinese-telecommunications.

University of Minnesota Human Rights Library. N.d. "Ratification of International Human Rights Treaties—China." Available at www1.umn.edu/humanrts/research/ratification-china.html.

Weston, Greg. 2012. "Chinese firm's Canadian contracts raise security fears." CBC News: Politics, 15 May. Available at www.cbc.ca/news/politics/story/2012/05/15/pol-weston-huawei-china-telecom-security-canada.html.

Wong, Gillian, and Isolda Morillo. 2010. "China steps up retaliation against Norway for Nobel." *The Globe and Mail*, 12 October. Available at www.theglobeandmail.com/news/world/china-steps-up-retaliation-against-norway-for-nobel/article4328793/.

Woo, Yuen Pau. 2013. "State-owned enterprise investment in Canada: The next chapter." Asia Pacific Foundation of Canada, 12 June. Available at www.asiapacific.ca/editorials/presidents-view/39355.

Xinhua News Agency. 2011. "Canada links future with China." *China Daily*, 15 August. Available at www.chinadaily.com.cn/imqq/china/2011-08/15/content_13111737.htm.

———. 2012a. "China asks Libya to compensate for companies' losses." *China Daily*, 7 March. Available at http://usa.chinadaily.com.cn/china/2012-03/07/content_14780113.htm.

———. 2012b. "China highlights human rights in law revision." *China Daily*, 8 March. Available at www.chinadaily.com.cn/china/2012-03/08/content_14786362.htm.

12 Canada's World Can Get a Lot Bigger: The Group of 20, Global Governance, and Security

Paul Heinbecker

Key Terms

G8

G20

Global Governance

Sovereign Debt Crisis

The International Context

Globalization continues to change our world before our eyes and, notwithstanding the constant repetition of bad news by today's 24-hour news cycle, largely for the better. Since 1950, gross world product has increased more than eightfold and average per capita income has more than tripled. Since 1990, almost 500 million people have climbed out of poverty.[1] Average life expectancy has increased by almost 50 per cent. The global literacy rate has increased from 56 per cent in 1950 to 82 per cent in 2004.[2] Despite the predations of terrorism and the failing of fragile states, the world remains largely at peace. According to a report of the independent UN High-Level Panel on Threats, Challenges and Change in 2005, there were fewer interstate wars between countries large or small in the second half of the twentieth century than in the first half, despite a nearly fourfold increase in the number of states.[3] And the number of intra-state wars declined dramatically since 1992, before increasing slightly since 2003.[4]

Most countries, including most major countries, increasingly put economic prosperity at the heart of their foreign policy. The US is a major exception, although there are signs that hard economic times and vast deficits are forcing reconsideration there too. Further, the sheer destructiveness of contemporary military technology, even "conventional" technology, makes war between major states increasingly irrational and improbable, except by inadvertence or miscalculation. Most states have too much at stake economically and socially to risk a roll of the military dice.

People in almost every region are healthier, richer, better educated, more secure and better connected electronically—as well as more numerous—than ever before. More than two billion people have access to the Internet, and more than five billion have access to cell phones, which together are becoming a tool of democratization or, at least, public information and protest.[5] People are more and more linked to each other and have progressively greater access to information, as the revolution in Cairo's Tahrir Square showed. As a consequence, governing this world presents challenges more complex than ever before. States remain predominant in global decision-making, but technology is making it possible for more and more people to be involved in the world beyond their borders and for more and more individuals and groups to affect the environment in which states conduct their foreign (and national) policy. The same phenomenon affects the operations of multilateral organizations.

Although the US will long remain the pre-eminent state, Asian political and economic power is growing perceptibly and the centre of economic gravity is shifting eastward and southward. China, though far behind the US by most economic, social, and military measures, is making rapid progress,[6] as are other emerging economies, with the result that in the decades ahead, no country will determine unilaterally the course of world events. At the same time, competition between states is at least as much economic as military in character, with the size of a state's Gross Domestic Product (GDP) and its attractiveness to others in terms of quality of life increasingly a currency of power and influence. We are entering into a time either of enhanced cooperative governance if we are wise or zero-sum international competition if we are foolish. The G20 could be decisive in determining which it is to be.

The global institutions through which the world governs itself have been struggling for over a generation to respond to the world's rapidly changing expectations and demands. The UN, the International Monetary Fund (IMF) and the World Bank have for some considerable time faced challenges of effectiveness, efficiency, and legitimacy as they have considered whether and how to acknowledge the emergence of new powers and to accommodate growing popular engagement. The **G8** has faced similar problems. The **G20**, potentially the most important innovation in **global governance** since 1976, when the G7 was formed, or even since the creation of the UN and Bretton Woods institutions in the 1940s, is important both for what it is—a body whose membership is a frank acknowledgment of the power shifts underway in the world—and for what it can potentially do to help world leaders cooperate to deliver effective global leadership and governance, if those leaders have the wit and will to use it effectively and creatively.

This chapter attempts to answer three key sets of questions:

- How well is the G20 doing, and what does the future likely hold for it? Will it complement or conflict with the G8, the UN and other global institutions with security avocations? Is the G20 still necessary?
- What are the consequences of the G20 for international politics and security likely to be?
- How will all of this affect Canada, particularly Canadian foreign policy, and what should Canada do about it?

The Short, Largely Successful, but so far Mostly Economic, History of the G20

The G20's Origins

The origins of the Group of 20[7] are traceable to the successive financial crises at last century's end—the Mexican peso crisis, the Asian financial contagion, and the Russian default—when it became clear that existing institutions were inadequate to meet the challenges they faced. Then-finance minister Paul Martin and his US treasury secretary counterpart, Lawrence Summers, among others, recognized that the G7[8] of leading industrial countries was unable to respond effectively to financial crises because the governments seated around the table were not able to carry out or enforce the decisions they made. Crucial players, capable of resisting G7 decisions or ignoring them altogether, were absent. To remedy the problem, Martin called into being the G20 finance ministers group, which thereafter met as an entity. In Martin's words in 2001, "[n]obody's going to follow a G7 dictate. They [the emerging powers and the faltering economies] have got to be at the table and be part of the solution."[9] Further, even though the G20 represented the lion's share of global GDP, large parts of the world were not represented and the hope was that countries like South Africa, and others, would take a leadership role in their regions, promoting best practices and sound policies.

As the heat of that financial moment cooled so, too, did the ardour of finance ministers for their G20—possibly a harbinger of things to come for prime ministers as the "Western Financial Crisis" subsides. The G20 finance ministers, as an institution, nevertheless endured and engaged in meaningful debate in a frank, informal manner, seeking consensus, building habits of cooperation, and creating personal relationships that were ready to be called on when the time came to do so. When Martin subsequently became prime minister in 2003, he perceived before many other leaders did the rapidity with which power realities in the world were changing. To respond to the times, he called for upgrading the G20 to the level of leaders, and he also commissioned Canadian think tanks, notably the Centre for International Governance Innovation (CIGI) in Waterloo and the Centre for Global Studies at the University of Victoria, in cooperation with Brookings, Princeton, Oxford, and others, to research the modalities of such an upgrade. In 2005 he wrote that "an effective new [leaders'] group, focused on practical issues of global importance, is something that the world very much needs."[10]

It was an innovative idea whose time had not quite come, however, meeting inertia and even resistance in several G8 capitals, and above all in Washington where president George W. Bush was simply not interested in participating in one more multilateral summit group where US power and freedom to manoeuvre would be constrained by combinations of others less powerful. Further, most G8 members were comfortable in their small, familiar, like-minded group, where they could talk

relatively freely with one another. Further, the prestige and thus domestic partisan political advantage that such exclusivity appeared to confer were also factors; better to be seen in the intimate company of the instantly recognizable (by the public) powerful Western leaders than that of the less *médiatique arrivistes*—to be a big fish in a smaller pond. They preferred to enlarge their group informally, inviting other leaders, and heads of international organizations, to join the proceedings only on issues for which their presence could not be avoided. Various formulations were used; for example, G8 + others and G8 + G5, all of which had the G8 as the core.

At the same time, the emerging powers, especially China and Brazil, but also India and Mexico, did not relish the idea of being "outreach" countries. As their global significance grew rapidly, their impatience with attending G8 sessions only on the sufferance of their "betters" grew apace. They formed their own counter-group, the G5, a divisive development that was likely to complicate global problem-solving rather than facilitate it. When subsequently the G20 leaders came into being, the five agreed among themselves that they would not acquiesce in an organic link between the G8 and G20 processes.[11] The G20 was to be new, one of the few international bodies in which the major existing powers and the major emerging powers were to meet on the basis of formal equality, unlike the UN Security Council with its permanent and non-permanent members, or the major international financial institutions, where voting power is weighted. Nor were caucuses of the eight and five to become the norm within the G20, although the G8 has continued to meet separately.

As the financial system rapidly melted down in the fall of 2008 and as G8 leaders, especially those in Washington, peered into the economic abyss, all reticence about including the emerging powers in their midst evaporated. The G5, for its part, welcomed the idea of being part of something that was not an appendage of the G8. All eagerly grasped the ready-made idea of the G20, and President Bush, apparently at the urging of President Sarkozy of France, convened the group in Washington to try to chart a course away from the precipice. Thus was born the leaders' G20, a made-in-Canada idea and foreign policy success, albeit not because of any enthusiasm for it in Conservative-governed Ottawa after Martin left office. The G8 was, at least initially, Prime Minister Stephen Harper's preferred grouping.

The G20 Record So Far

The G20 as an entity has been effective and has the potential to be more so, although progress on its economic agenda has slowed as it addresses domestically sensitive problems. It has met five times since its inception in 2008 and has succeeded in pulling the world back from the abyss of another Great Depression, undertaking some of the financial re-engineering needed to prevent a recurrence. The G7 finance ministers and the G20 leaders saved—not too strong a word—the international financial system from collapse.

On 10 October 2008, facing the very real risk that markets would just not open on the following Monday and that there would be a run on British banks, with demonstration effects elsewhere, finance ministers agreed they would do whatever it took to prevent the banks from defaulting, unfreeze credit and money markets, re-establish lending, assure confidence in national deposit and guarantee programs, and restart secondary markets for mortgages and other securitized assets. Fortunately, it largely worked.

At the Washington G20 meeting a few weeks later, heads of governments signalled that they recognized that the world had a problem and pledged to work cooperatively to address it. All leaders agreed to take steps to unfreeze credit, "fix" their banks (Canada was exempted), launch financial reforms, avoid protectionism, and stimulate their economies. At the next meeting in London in the spring, leaders undertook to pump large sums—a trillion dollars, using creative accounting—into the international economy through the IMF and other international financial institutions (IFIs), to the benefit largely of the large emerging economies. Leaders effectively reversed the descent into economic depression, launching reform of the international financial regulatory system, modernizing international financial institutions and undertaking to recognize in structural terms the growing power and influence of the emerging market countries. They created the Financial Stability Board (FSB),[12] a potentially major international institutional innovation, intended to provide better international oversight of the financial system and develop capital and liquidity standards for systemically important financial institutions.

In Pittsburgh in the fall, as the danger of a depression receded, the leaders proclaimed the G20 as the "primary institution for [their] economic cooperation"[13] and charted the transition from crisis to recovery with the Framework for Strong, Sustainable and Balanced Growth (FSSBG), commissioning work on what had to be done to achieve a new "balanced" growth model in the future.

In Toronto the following June, Canada's game plan was for the G20 to concentrate on meeting past commitments on the core agenda, and to hand off progress to Seoul. Ottawa focused the summit agenda on four critical areas:

- Supporting the recovery and laying the foundations for the FSSBG.
- Following through on required reforms to the regulation and management of financial sectors.
- Strengthening international financial institutions, particularly the World Bank and the IMF, through reforms to their governance and strengthening of their resources.
- Resisting protectionism and seeking enhanced liberalization of trade and investment.[14]

Leaders found themselves having to respond to the suddenly urgent **sovereign debt crisis** in Europe triggered by Greece. Prime Minister Harper, who had earlier written to other leaders about deficits, proposed precise targets for winding them down. With his counterparts from Britain, Germany, and France, he favoured sending the markets a signal of fiscal consolidation—that is, that leaders understood that they needed to rein in unsustainable deficits and public debt in advanced economies, although they also recognized that such consolidation had to be balanced against the continuing implementation of fiscal stimulus in some countries and a rebalancing in global demand, with a particular emphasis on emerging economies to offset the slower growth in the developed world.

US President Barack Obama, for his part, worried that the recovery was not yet self-sustaining and emphasized, therefore, leaving the door open to increased stimulus spending, the large government deficits notwithstanding. Ultimately, G20 leaders under Harper's chairmanship effectively decided to do both, agreeing that they would complete their planned fiscal stimulus programs, but also setting targets of a 50 per cent deficit reduction by 2013 and a stabilized or improving debt-to-GDP ratio by 2016, thereby sending a clear signal to markets that they recognized that budget deficits could not go on forever. The British had already moved to cut spending in order to get their fiscal books in order and others promised to do so. Others, especially the newly emerging economies, argued that they didn't have a deficit and debt problem and that they needed to continue to spend on development; in any case, the countries that had caused the crisis should get their own houses in order first. The emerging economies were effectively excused from the deal, as were the Japanese whose fiscal problems were put in the "too difficult" category. To block a British, French, and German push for an international bank tax that would have unfairly burdened Canadian banks, which had not been part of the problem, the Harper government actively sought allies and made common cause with some of the emerging economies, notably China and India.

In Toronto, leaders also made progress on the goal of financial sector reform. In particular, leaders agreed on the need to recalibrate upwards requirements regarding the amount and quality of capital held by banks. Leaders agreed on the importance of creating a strong regulatory framework, including the need to create a more effective system for oversight and intervention. The G20 was also able to deliver on a number of earlier commitments, including ensuring $350 billion in general capital increases for multilateral development banks, which would allow them to nearly double their lending. The group also endorsed recent reforms at the World Bank and called for an acceleration of efforts to advance additional quota and governance reforms at the IMF. On both quotas and "voice," leaders recognized that the situation at the IMF, with its northern and western, especially European, over-representation, remained inequitable, seriously undermining the legitimacy of the organization and support for it in the rest of the world. Leaders also renewed their commitment to avoid protectionism and to conclude the Doha Development Round of trade negotiations.[15] Overall, the G20 took forward its "core" agenda, dealt with the sovereign debt crisis, and put in train work for Seoul and beyond.

Following Toronto, Bank of Canada Governor Mark Carney commented that successful implementation of the G20 financial reform agenda, when combined with the peer review process of the FSB and external reviews by the IMF, should increase actual and perceived systemic stability. At the same time, he warned that while the right promises had been made, implementation was less encouraging.[16] It was evident already then that the G20 was becoming a victim of its own success, having achieved enough progress to lessen the urgency of going further, and thereby taking at least some of the drive out of the financial reform effort.

In the lead-up to Seoul, the G20 struggled to come to grips with currency valuation and credit-easing policies and their significance for current account and trade imbalances. The US and others, including Canada, took one side and China and Germany took another, with the US blaming China for currency manipulation to maintain its export-led growth, China criticizing the US for unilaterally creating excessive credit through "quantitative easing," and some other countries openly or covertly agreeing with one or the other or both. It is a sign of how tendentious discussions among the group had become on monetary policy that the veteran and very sober German politician and Finance Minister Wolfgang Schäuble characterized US policy as "clueless"—not the usual vocabulary used in these august circles—for, in his judgment, pumping too much financial liquidity into the market which would destabilize some countries' financial systems and risk provoking international defensive responses. South African and Brazilian finance ministers echoed Schäuble's concerns.[17]

Policy Responses to the Imbalances Were Creating Strange, or at Least New, Bedfellows

In Seoul, the cracks in solidarity evident in Toronto on the causes of trade and current account imbalances and on currency values became fissures. The group effectively split several ways on this issue, but did manage to establish a 2011 target for agreeing on "indicative guidelines" by which to assess imbalances and to consider what, if anything, to do about them. G20 countries were able to agree on the need for new financial rules to render the international financial system more resilient, reduce the "moral hazard" of major financial institutions relying on governments to bail them out, limit the buildup of systemic risk,

and support stable economic growth.[18] The G20 adopted new capital and liquidity requirements for banks that will, however, only be implemented starting on January 1, 2013, and only fully phased in by January 1, 2019, ostensibly out of concerns for constricting lending and thereby aborting the recovery, but likely also because of the effective lobbying by Wall Street in Washington. Priority attention was also given to the regulation of commodity derivatives markets, which have been blamed for commodity price volatility and the food crisis of 2008.

The Seoul summit will likely be remembered for registering the importance of the emerging economies in the G20, both by virtue of its non-G8 locus and by the shift in the content of the agenda. Thanks mainly to Korean leadership, "development" in the sense of economic growth, rather than the traditional donor-recipient paradigm, was added to the G20 agenda. Seoul also put the issue of cross-border capital flows on the G20 macro-prudential regulatory agenda, advocating the creation of "financial safety nets" to safeguard smaller states from volatile financial flows and obviate the need for the self-insurance of large reserves, which contribute to the imbalances problem. G20 leaders also endorsed IMF reforms that will give developing countries greater influence in the institution. China will become the third largest IMF shareholder, bypassing Germany, as part of an overall six per cent transfer of voting power to dynamic and underrepresented economies.

The Future of the G20 and its Place in Global Governance

The G20: A Work in Progress

Because of the currency and liquidity disputes, the general public perception of the results of Seoul was negative, even if progress was made on a number of key issues (IMF reform, financial regulation, development, etc.). In the spring of 2011, finance ministers and central bankers made progress in reconciling the divergent views of the US, which has the world's largest trade deficit, with those of China and Germany, who have the two largest surpluses, on establishing indicators of the causes of the imbalances, and in financial reform challenges that remain, especially as regards reserve currencies and capital market volatility as well as cross-border financial institutions being too big to fail and the need to give the new FSB the authority and capacity to do its job effectively. They also agreed that G20 countries' accounting for more than five per cent of G20 GDP will be reviewed, reflecting the greater potential for spillover effects from larger economies.

The Washington summit communiqué foresaw "addressing other critical challenges" such as fossil fuel subsidies, energy security and climate change, food security, rule of law, and the fight against terrorism, poverty, and disease.[19] There was also a need for the international community to address water scarcity, reform of the UN Security Council, and arms control. The G20 has, nevertheless, stuck close to its self-prescribed economic and financial mandate.

For everyone's sake, G20 leaders do have to get the economics and financial issues right, as well as the related reforms to the governing rules and regulations. Undoubtedly, the group will be judged primarily on its success in re-engineering the financial system to preclude, as much as possible, recourse to risky financial practices that can bring the entire world to the brink of economic disaster. But over time, and likely not very much time, G20 leaders will probably complement their financial and economic agenda with deliberations on other issues that require their attention. Experience derived from the G8 has been that when leaders come together, the temptation is irresistible to take advantage of each other's presence to discuss the pressing issues of the day, whatever they are and whatever

the agenda of the meeting they are attending may be. Nor do most want to delve too deeply into the technical details of international finance, preferring to leave that task to finance ministers and national bank governors.

The next G20 summit will be held in France, and its host, Sarkozy, speaking before an annual gathering of French ambassadors in July 2010, signalled his preference for an expansive agenda:

> . . . now that relative calm has returned, there is a temptation to limit the G-20's ambitions to implementing its decisions, supplementing them in 2011 by expanding regulation where it remains insufficient, verifying the implementation of tax exchange information agreements, adopting strong measures to fight corruption, strengthening the mandate of the Financial Stability Board and, more broadly, re-examining the prudential framework of banking institutions to avoid a repetition of the recent crisis. Completing the work that is under way is important—the G-20's credibility depends on it. But is it enough?[20]

He then answered his own question, asserting that "sticking with this agenda would condemn the G-20 to failure and the world to new crises." It would also condemn the world to cope with its major governance problems using organizations and institutions that were created in other times, partly at least to address other issues.

In January 2011, Sarkozy refined his priorities for the next summit in Cannes, identifying three overall priorities that France would invite G20 leaders to address, namely:

1. Continuing reform of the international monetary system to ensure that the decisions taken at the last five G20 summits are put into practice, particularly as regards financial regulation,

greater stability of the international monetary system, volatility in currency values, volatile capital flows that destabilize developing economies, as well as indicators to measure global economic imbalances.

2. The need to control the volatility of commodity prices, including oil and agricultural products, notably wheat (commodities of particular interest to Canada, especially to Western Canada), possibly through a code of conduct on food aid and emergency stocks.

3. Reform of global governance.

On the last, Sarkozy's ambitions stretch from creating a G20 secretariat; to promoting innovative financing for development such as some version of "the Tobin tax" on international financial transfers; giving the International Labour Organization (ILO) more weight in global governance; setting up a minimum standard of universal social protection; fulfilling financial commitments on climate change; and infrastructure projects in Africa. UN reform, particularly UN Security Council reform, which had earlier been an explicit part of the French governance reform package, was put on the back burner.

The G20 and the G8: Redundant or Complementary?[21]

The Canadian government has been one of the principal defenders of the ongoing utility of the G8, with Harper arguing that the G8 and G20 have distinct but complementary roles to play. He apparently sees the G20 as focusing on finance and economics and the G8 on democracy, development assistance (it was at Huntsville that Harper promoted the multibillion dollar initiative on maternal and children's health[22]) and peace and security.[23]

Not everyone is convinced by the logic of these divisions, especially as regards economics and development, as China, India, Brazil and South Africa are deeply involved economically in the Third World. Non-G8 members of the G20 are sceptical of the need for the continuing existence of the G8, even wary of it. G8 members seem generally disposed to continue the G8's existence although some, including particularly Obama, have expressed doubts. Sarkozy, the host of the next G8 in 2011, seems noncommittal, remarking to the gathering of French ambassadors last summer that while France would prepare the next G8 summit with the requisite care, ". . . some have said [the G8] is condemned. Others believe it has a rosy future if it refocuses on security issues and its partnership with Africa. The future will decide."[24]

Ultimately the G20 seems destined to supplant the G8. The time demands of summit diplomacy—exceeding a dozen gatherings per year and more for some leaders—as well as the wear and tear on leaders of travel across time zones and the impatience of those leaders with redundancies of forums and issues, militate in favour of dispensing with the G8. For example, at Huntsville and Toronto, both the G8 and the G20 addressed themselves to Haiti's problems, with the G8 discussing Haiti's security needs and the G20 focusing on economic challenges. Had there been the will to do so, some moderately agile drafting would have made it possible to address these issues in one session. Unless the G20 falls into deadlock, the odds are that the G8 will go the way of the Group of Major Emitting Countries, which has near identical membership to the G20, and which has not met since the L'Aquila, Italy, summit in 2009.

The G20 and the United Nations

One of the most important governance questions facing the international community is what the relationship is to be between the G20 and the UN. Both are creatures of the wills of their member states, and are in some respects complementary instruments for promoting global governance and international cooperation, and, in other respects, potentially competitive. The G20 has the ability to assist the UN in coming to grips with intractable global problems, notably climate change, by importing greater consensus into UN deliberations. It can also impart a reform trajectory to the UN that is difficult to generate otherwise. The UN, for its part, can extend the G20's effectiveness, "ratifying" G20 decisions and thus lending greater legitimacy to them. Getting the relationship between the G20 and the UN right holds the prospect of considerable benefits all around.

The Enduring Value of the UN[25]

The UN Charter provides the rule book for the conduct of international relations which all states, including G20 states, usually see it as in their interest to respect—and have respected. If the UN didn't exist, to quote the old cliché, the world would have to invent it, if the world could marshal the political will to do so in the absence of a stimulus as powerful as the Second World War.

An underappreciated reality is that the UN is a kind of motherboard of global governance, performing its own core functions but also enabling other entities, for example, the United Nations International Children's Fund (UNICEF), to work better as well. Were there no UN with its universal membership, the restrictive G20 would be much more controversial and its decisions much more contested—and resented. The North Atlantic Treaty Organization (NATO), for its part, needs the UN to certify the legitimacy of its operations in, for example, Afghanistan and Libya, and to complement NATO's military efforts there with civilian development programs. The UN also makes it possible for initiatives such as the Millennium Development Goals (MDGs) to be subcontracted out efficiently. The reverse is also true. The products

of other entities, potentially including the G20, are imported into the UN for consideration by its larger membership and, where possible, endorsement, as the Ottawa Treaty on anti-personnel landmines; the Responsibility to Protect; and the Global Fund to Fight AIDS, Tuberculosis and Malaria have been. From peacekeeping, peace enforcement and peace-building to international criminal justice systems, sustainable development, refugee protection, humanitarian coordination and food relief, democracy and electoral support, human rights conventions, health protection, landmine removal and managerial accountability and oversight, the organization has been innovating and equipping itself to acquit its increasingly demanding responsibilities. As a consequence, the UN has a broader presence in the world than any other organization except the United States, and much substantive expertise in dealing with contemporary challenges, such as instability, fragile states, and natural disasters.

The results of the UN's efforts are impressive—and vital. In 2009, the UN High Commissioner for Refugees (UNHCR) protected 36 million people, including refugees, the stateless, the internally displaced, returnees and asylum-seekers.[26] In 2009, the World Food Programme (WFP), operating in 75 countries, fed almost 102 million people.[27] The World Health Organization (WHO), which, in its earlier years, led the successful program to eradicate smallpox, is now close to eliminating poliomyelitis. As a consequence of the work of the WHO and its private partners, including Rotary International, polio infections have fallen by 99 per cent since 1988, and some five million people have been spared paralysis. With the assistance of the WHO and UNICEF, the immunization of children for the six major vaccine-preventable diseases—pertussis, childhood tuberculosis, tetanus, polio, measles and diphtheria—has risen dramatically. For example, about 20 per cent of the world's children had been inoculated in 1980 for measles, but this had risen to an estimated 82 per cent by 2009.[28] At least 90 per cent will be immunized by 2015, the target date of the MDG. Global coverage of infants for hepatitis B in 1990 was one per cent, but in 2009 it was 70 per cent.[29] Meanwhile, the WHO has also been coordinating the world's response to SARS, the avian flu and the H1N1 virus. This work has been belittled in some unenlightened quarters as mere international social work. It is social work, but it delivers very real human and national security benefits, which the G20 is unequipped to deliver.

At the same time, the UN suffers from problems that have accumulated since 1945. Disagreements, often grounded in genuine differences of interests, persist between the rich northern countries and the G77, between the permanent five members of the Security Council and the rest, between climate changers and climate victims, between Israelis and Arabs (and Muslims more generally), between Indians and Pakistanis, and between North Korea and South Korea and the US, and so on. These various disputes and failures hinder the UN's effectiveness and, as a consequence, diminish its efficacy.

Similarities and Differences, Complementarities and Dissonances[30]

The UN is an organization with a written charter endorsed by 192 countries, an extensive body of international law and rules created under its auspices by its members, a General Assembly of member states, a Security Council, an international court, a Secretary-General and a professional secretariat of 63,450.[31] Just under 100,000 soldiers and police serve under the UN flag in 15 current operations.[32] The UN disposes of a combined annual budget of about $10 billion in contributions from its member countries to support its operations. This is a modest cost compared to the budgets of most governments; the Canadian federal budget totals approximately $260 billion.

The UN's legitimacy is derived essentially from the adherence of its 192 member states to the UN Charter and from the work the world body performs on behalf of its members around the world. A web of several hundred treaties negotiated under UN auspices gives expression to the wishes of its members and helps to regulate the behaviour of governments towards each other and towards their own people. The UN meets at the level of Permanent Representatives and other diplomats and is in near-constant session, addressing an open-ended agenda that extends from peace and war to economic and social development. Leaders from around the world participate in large numbers in the annual General Debate in the General Assembly each September and in occasional, quite exceptional, Security Council sessions. For example, in September 2009, Obama convened the Security Council at heads-of-state and government level to promote progress on nuclear arms control and disarmament.

The G20, by contrast, is more virtual than concrete, has no international legal personality, is not an organization at all, and is scarcely an institution. It has no charter, no brick and mortar assets, no standing secretariat thus far (continuity is theoretically assured by a troika of immediately previous, current, and next host countries) and no research capacity beyond that which its member states and international organizations supply. The G20's work is supported professionally by the World Bank, IMF, the Organisation for Economic Co-operation and Development (OECD), ILO, WTO, and UN.

The G20 also works with the new FSB to address vulnerabilities, to develop and implement strong regulatory, supervisory, and other policies in the interest of financial stability, and to monitor and report on progress in strengthening financial regulation. The G20 has set up a large number of working and expert groups, each co-chaired by a G8 member and an emerging economy country, covering a range of mainly economic issues in considerable detail.

Fundamentally, though, the G20's effectiveness depends on the exceptional international standing of its members, who number some of the most powerful countries on earth, on the strength of the consensus they can fashion on given issues and on their willingness to act in concert to give expression to that consensus.

The G20's legitimacy derives from its success in redressing the crucial economic and financial crises of 2008–9. It also derives from the fact that its membership accounts for 90 per cent of global GDP, 80 per cent of world trade, and 67 per cent of the planet's total population. The G20 has no budget, but its members have shown they are capable of committing truly vast resources under its auspices if circumstances warrant. These characteristics do not confer the legitimacy inherent in universality, but nor are they trivial. When the G20 reaches agreement, a large part of whatever problem it is addressing is on the way to resolution.

The G20's effectiveness is immeasurably enhanced by virtue of the fact that it meets at the level of heads of government. At the same time, while G20 members can bind themselves individually and collectively, if they can reach agreement among themselves, they cannot bind others. They need to work through more universal bodies, including, ultimately, the UN, to get their decisions endorsed by non-G20 member countries.

Although the UN works best when consensus reigns among the major powers, the latter are often at loggerheads in the organization. It is not always clear whether it is the intractability of the problems the UN handles that causes divisions, or the UN's divisions that make the problems intractable. In any case, the countries of the "North" and the countries of the overlapping Non-Aligned Movement and G77 are often at ideological odds with each other and working to cross-purposes. Unlike the G8, the G20 members have the built-in advantage of spanning the infamous North–South divide, its members

having places in the UN's disparate political groups and in all five geographic regions, as well. The G20 could make a major contribution to improving the effectiveness of the UN if it could iron out some of the differences that divide its members and import that agreement into UN deliberations.

To the extent, therefore, that G20 membership induces a sense of common purpose among the 20 and diminishes its members' identification with geographic or other groups, cooperation under UN auspices would be made easier and more productive. As has been the case in the IMF, consensus by the G20 on a particular need could be a powerful stimulus to action and reform at the UN. Conversely, the very existence of the G20 and its evident capacity to act outside of UN parameters if non-G20 UN members are dilatory or obstructive, create an incentive for the UN to act and cooperate. Those in the UN who cling to ideological positions could find the organization they are obstructing bypassed altogether.

Not surprisingly, much of the UN's membership is apprehensive of the G20. They recognize that the G20 came into existence when and how it did because a myriad of political and structural problems prevented existing institutions, principally the G8 and the IMF, but also the UN proper, from addressing the global financial crisis effectively. They realize that similar impediments are obstructing progress on other global issues more directly under the UN's purview, and they are well aware that the G20 is capable of sidestepping the UN when disagreements prevent effective action.

At the same time, they are troubled by the G20's structural shortcomings. Despite the presence at the G20 table of some developing countries, no place is reserved for the poorest, least developed countries, and no one is carrying their proxies. Also problematic, the capable smaller countries of the UN such as Norway, Switzerland, Chile, Singapore, and New Zealand, are absent from G20 tables as well, effectively depriving G20 deliberations of these countries' generally constructive and frequently innovative diplomacy. The Norwegian Foreign Minister, Jonas Gahr Støre, who presides over one of the most widely respected and effective small country diplomacies in the world, said bluntly in the lead-up to the Toronto and Muskoka summits last year that "the spirit of the Congress of Vienna, where great powers assembled to effectively govern the world, has no place in the contemporary international community. The G-20 is sorely lacking in legitimacy and must change." While acknowledging that "there is value in having an effective, smaller forum of nations, equipped to act quickly when necessary," he warned that "if the G-20 cooperation should effectively result in decisions being imposed on the great majority of other countries, it will quickly find itself stymied."[33]

It is in the interest of the countries of the G20 to work out an effective relationship with the G172 (i.e., the UN members not also members of the G20) because the more the 172 are excluded, the less they will have confidence in the ultimate fairness and efficacy of the multilateral system, and the less interest they will have in responding to G20 wishes. Global problems require global solutions and, as Bruce Jones of Brookings has pointed out, "however much influence the G20 have, the problems they confront are the kind where the weakest link can break the chain."[34] Unless smaller states see their views reflected in decision-making processes, or at least judge that their interests have been duly and fairly taken into account, they are unlikely to "buy into" the solution of whatever is at issue. This kind of unresponsiveness can have repercussions in, for example, the G172's attitudes towards illegal migration, transnational crime and the drug trade, international terrorism and piracy, evasion by unscrupulous industries of climate change regulations, the prevention of the spread of pandemics of infectious disease, and collaboration on financial regulation, notably regarding tax havens and banking reforms, and so on.

The G20 needs to take outreach seriously, in ways consistent with efficacy and inclusion as well. There are several steps the G20 can take, none of which will be fully satisfactory to those who are absent, but all of which are likely to be better than nothing. Most fundamentally, the chair of the G20 in a given year will need to consult others beyond his/her G20 counterparts on the G20 agenda and seek substantive rather than pro forma input through, for example, the African Union (AU), ASEAN, the Shanghai Cooperation Organization, the Gulf Cooperation Council, the Organization of American States, and so forth.

A further idea is to adopt at least an informal constituency approach, so that G20 leaders at the table, or some of them, carry de facto proxies of those not present. Canada and the UK could, for example, "represent" the Commonwealth. Canada and France could do the same for the Francophonie, while Mexico and Brazil could carry briefs for Latin America, and so on. This would imply effective consultation with members of the constituency before G20 meetings and timely debriefings and cooperation afterwards. A variation on this idea is that G20 finance ministers should form a council to take strategic decisions on the international monetary system, effectively replacing the IMF monetary and financial committee, with each G20 country representing a constituency of smaller countries, mirroring the IMF's system of constituencies.[35] At the same time, the more effectively the G20 worked with the UN, the less need there would be for outreach and for G20 members to try to represent constituencies, informal or otherwise. In order to ensure a voice for the G172 at the G20 table, especially for the poorest, the UN Secretary-General could attend the G20 as a matter of right, as could the heads of the IMF and the head of the World Bank when economic issues were on the agenda. While the Secretary-General works for the G20 as well as the G172, it is in the latter capacity that he/she can give voice to the absent. As is the case with the EU, the AU and any other transcendent political unions could attend as a matter of convention. Further, the UN (and the Bretton Woods organizations) could be encouraged to contribute their perspectives and ideas at G20 preparatory ministerial meetings and working groups.

There are numerous global issues on which the G20 and the UN can help each other, but two stand out: Security Council reform and climate change.

The G20 and Reform of the Security Council

UN Security Council is the world's top security table. It is empowered under Chapters VI and VII of the UN Charter to authorize the use of force, and is the only international body that has that legal right. Signatories of the North Atlantic Treaty pay due deference to the UN Charter and undertake under its Article I "to refrain in their international relations from the threat or use of force in any manner inconsistent with the purposes of the United Nations." Under Article V of the Treaty, they pledge to come to each other's defence "in exercise of the right of individual or collective self-defence recognized by Article 51 of the Charter of the United Nations." The Security Council is also equipped by Chapter VII of the UN Charter with the power to "legislate" for all member countries, for example its post-9/11 decision to deny terrorists access to the world's financial system, a power that the self-appointed G8 and G20 do not (and should not) have.

The Council's writ covers peace and security, fairly broadly defined. Major international political and security issues continue to be brought to the UN for deliberation and decision where possible and for surveillance and management where solutions are not possible. For example, the US successfully sought Security Council authorization in 2001 to use military force in Afghanistan in response to 9/11 and

again in 2011 in Libya, but was denied authorization by the Council in 2003 to use military force to topple Saddam Hussein's regime in Baghdad. The Israeli–Lebanese war of 2006 was brought to the Council for a diplomatic conclusion. Further, the international sanctions in response to the alleged Iranian nuclear weapons program are currently coordinated in the Council. There are literally dozens of less high-profile issues on the Council's docket.

There is no prospect that the G20 will ever supplant the Council. The five permanent members of the Security Council are unlikely in the extreme to acquiesce in any sort of formal encroachment by the G20 onto Council turf and in doing so to undermine their own privileged positions there. The Council is too valuable to them. There is, though, a strong argument for the G20 members to invest greater effort in making the Council work better. G20 leaders could, for example, debate certain issues among themselves and import whatever consensus they can reach into the Council via their Permanent Representatives, as the G8 did to end the Kosovo war in 1999. G20 members could also participate more actively in Council-sanctioned, UN-led military missions. Participation by G20 countries, including Canada, would upgrade the UN's capacity to act effectively. G20 leaders could also inject high-level political energy periodically into issues of surpassing importance, as Obama did in 2009 in chairing a Security Council session devoted to arms control and disarmament.

One issue on which the G20 could make a major contribution is reform of the UN Security Council, specifically the number and composition of permanent seats. For a generation, member states of the UN have endeavoured vainly to revamp Council membership. Several emerging market countries—who are members of the G20—see themselves as entitled to permanent Security Council seats by virtue of their significant and growing standing in international relations. Further, neither Africa nor Latin America has a permanent seat on the Council, whereas Europe has two permanent seats, three counting Russia. For the aspirant countries, a Council that does not reflect contemporary power realities is unrepresentative and illegitimate. Worse, it is ineffective, and their solution is to enlarge the Council to include themselves as permanent members.

Others do not equate enlargement with reform and regard the whole idea of permanency with distrust. Some opponents of an increase of permanent seats cite the cases of Darfur, Rwanda, Srebrenica, and others to argue that the Council has a performance deficit more than a representational deficit. They contend that more members do not necessarily increase the Council's effectiveness, and that permanency is, in any case, incompatible with accountability. Further, opponents of adding permanent seats favour democratic, electoral practices over autarchic, anachronistic privilege.

It happens that there is a potentially useful overlap between the G20 and the Security Council in the next period. Ten G20 members (six G8 members) will be on the Council in 2011, as will five of the leading six aspirants for permanent Council membership. While the overlap might lessen the perceived need for the G20 to address political issues, it also presents an opportunity that might not come soon again to solve this chronic problem. Whether the G20 wishes to seize it remains to be seen.

The G20 and Climate Change[36]

The leaders' G20 was created to deal with the last economic crisis. The next economic crisis might well be driven by an inadequate global response to climate change. Preventing climate change, the mother of all tragedies of the commons, was never going to be easy. There are only a few examples in modern history of humanity coming together in its own enlightened self-interest to change its collective course on a major governance issue: World War III

has been avoided (so far), the widespread proliferation of nuclear weapons has (largely) been averted and the ozone layer has been (mostly) preserved.

For climate change, as for most overarching global issues, the crucial negotiations have usually taken place in the back rooms of large gatherings, among groups of 20 or so of the most engaged countries. In the Copenhagen conference in November 2009, even that process was bypassed as five countries—the US, China, Brazil, India, and South Africa, some of the worst polluters—cut a deal among themselves that they then offered to others on a take-it-or-leave-it basis. The Copenhagen solution, however, was inadequate substantively and unfair procedurally. While it had some merit—more than 70 countries, including 35 developing countries, signed on to the deal and pledged to take "nationally appropriate actions"—it lacked targets and timetables and it back-end-loaded its promises of financial assistance to poorer countries harmed by a problem the richer countries created. Further, G20 members from the EU and Japan, South Korea, Saudi Arabia, Mexico, Australia, Turkey, Indonesia, and Russia were sidelined from the backroom negotiations, as was Canada, itself a significant generator of greenhouse gases (GHG) and the leading foreign supplier of oil, gas, electricity, and uranium to the worst GHG emitter, the US. Nor were the innocent victims represented.

More progress was made at Cancun, Mexico, in November 2010 and a more constructive, even hopeful tone was established for subsequent negotiations. United Nations Framework Convention on Climate Change (UNFCCC) Executive Secretary Christiana Figueres called it "a new beginning . . . not what is ultimately required but [an] essential foundation on which to build greater, collective ambition."[37] Nevertheless, in the absence of any prospect of progress in the US Congress on climate change, much had to be kicked down the road to Durban in the fall of 2011 and likely beyond the next US presidential and congressional elections in 2012.

World Bank President Robert Zoellick encapsulated the challenge when he called for "reaching real results on the ground while at the same time working on overall international regimes and arrangements, and not letting the perfect be the enemy of the good."[38] A notable accomplishment at Cancun in this respect was agreement to create a program—Reducing Emissions from Deforestation and Forest Degradation (REDD)—that uses market and financial incentives to reduce GHG emissions from deforestation and forest degradation. Elsewhere, coalitions of the willing have been turning to "bottom-up" actions on a national and regional basis, although that course risks making the world a crazy quilt of incompatible regulations and trade protectionism masquerading as climate sensitivity.

It would make sense for climate change, starting perhaps with its economic and development dimensions, to be put on the G20 agenda, given the fundamental disagreements that continue to bedevil progress, particularly over who bears the major responsibility for creating the problem and on whom it is incumbent to act first and do most to fix it. But the greater the extent to which the G20 can narrow differences between themselves on principles and import some consensus into the necessarily larger UN negotiating framework, the more likely it is for progress on climate change to be made.

The UN remains a necessary but not sufficient response to globalization, as is the G20. The inescapable conclusion is that there is room and need for both the UN and the G20, and for cooperation between them. Effective global governance depends considerably on the success of both the nascent G20 and of the sexagenarian UN. The UN embodies universality and the G20 efficacy. Together, they can produce synergies, with the G20 strengthening the UN by reducing the gaps among the major powers on contentious issues, making decision-making in the world body easier and more effective, with the UN returning the favour by extending the G20's effectiveness vis-à-vis the G172, a group that the G20 cannot command but whose cooperation it does need. The UN, for its part, needs to be sensibly responsive and strategically savvy, resisting the blandishments of its ideological "spoilers." And the G20 needs to take the initiative to develop an effective modus operandi with non-members of the group to resolve legitimate issues of inclusion and exclusion, and to find a way to give voice in its deliberations to the less powerful poorer countries and to the small but very competent richer ones.

The G20: Stock-Taking and the Future

On the eve of the Seoul summit, former prime minister Martin, the godfather of the G20, said that it was "critical that it complete the cycle from global crisis-responder to global steering committee, for that is what is required if globalization is to work."[39] That transition has not yet happened. The G20 has done comparatively well in pursuing financial re-engineering but has done less well in addressing the highly political tasks of resolving the current account, trade, and budget imbalances conundrum, whose causes lie deep in the economic philosophies and internal practices of the world's largest economic players. Nor has the G20 made much progress on issues of a more indirect economic character, and still less on security issues. More fundamentally, the G20 has yet to develop a consensus on the nature of what ties them together—that is, global interdependencies.

The G20 has shown that it can generate policy consensus and coordination when its members manifest the requisite political will to drive reform on major global challenges. It is the best solution so far to the legitimacy/efficiency trade-off, combining inclusiveness and representativeness, albeit far from universality with capacity and effectiveness.[40] But it is not a panacea.

While consensus is easier to generate in smaller bodies than the UN General Assembly or large international conferences, it is not yet clear how much easier in practice it is to do so in the G20. National interests are not a factor of the setting in which they are addressed, and ways of thinking and acting established over generations are not modified easily. Further, for the heretofore hegemonic US, G20 partnership needs to mean not just hearing others before deciding and acting, but rather developing shared assessments and engaging cooperatively—rusty skills in Beltway-bound Washington.

For some others, notably China and India, if the G20 is to prosper, their conceptions of their interests need expanding to include more fully the well-being and effectiveness of the institution, which has to be more than the sum of disparate interests if it is to work. Further, it is not clear that they and Brazil, among others, see the G20 as a more cordial venue in which to pursue their interests than the UN whose legitimacy, solidarity, and universality they value. Further, some are wary of the risk inherent in small group negotiations of being "jammed" into making deals, as China apparently felt was the case in the backroom bargaining at the climate change negotiations in Copenhagen. For the G20 to prosper and achieve its potential, all 20 governments will have to reconcile self-interest with the common interest, and privilege cooperation over autarchy, multilateralism (or at least plurilateralism) over unilateralism, the effective over the merely efficient, and the legal over the expedient. All of this is easier said than done, especially in the absence of the unifying power of major common threats.

There are practical problems, too. First, the G20 agendas are too technical for many leaders to handle, even supported by the informal sherpa process. It is unrealistic to expect a group of leaders, most of whom are not themselves technically expert and all of whom are lacking the luxury of time, to resolve complex multidimensional problems in brief, informal meetings. Such technical issues should be the province of G20 finance ministers and central bankers who, in contrast, meet several times a year

and are backed up by dedicated ministries and staffs. A professional secretariat (or "non-secretariat"), building on formal G20 ministerial processes, might help leaders cope better.

Second, G20 members' disparate cultures, values, governance, and economic philosophies, domestic political structures and imperatives, and unequal levels of economic and social development make finding common ground difficult. Internal communications and logistical challenges among the G20 make that task more difficult.

English is not quite a *lingua franca* for the G8, but it is even less so for the G20. About half of the latter's participants have to rely on translation, making cacophony a risk (even the UN uses only five official languages) and diminishing the spontaneity of exchanges. The more translation is necessary in the course of discussions, the more the conversation is stilted and the more formalized and less spontaneous the process becomes. Further, the more technical the issues—notably as regards the intricacies of international finance—the less some leaders are comfortable discussing them extemporaneously and the more they have recourse to talking points setting out their positions, further formalizing the proceedings and shifting the emphasis from the search for compromise to the defence of interests, thereby rendering the leaders' experience as something akin to a political root canal. If the G20 is to progress, it will need to leave economic and technical details to finance ministers and bank governors, and deal instead with the politics of international relations where only they have the authority to cut the deals needed to advance global governance.

Logistically, the G20 suffers from disadvantages of size, at least compared to the G8, and operates less intimately. Meeting rooms are bigger than at G8 sessions and thus less conducive to generating familiarity among the participants. To obtain the maximum benefits from the meetings of the G20, the number of people at the table needs to be tightly restricted. The leaders need proximity and intimacy to really understand each other's perspectives—especially their disparate political interests and limitations—and to engage each other. Distance across large tables destroys spontaneity and favours formality and disengagement. As a consequence, only 20 government leaders should have dedicated seats at the G20 table. One or two additional rotating seats, as in the UN Security Council, could be allocated to non-government leaders to use when invited by the host chair to speak. Or perhaps there could be inner and outer circles, with national leaders seated at the inner ring and institutional leaders at the outer.

If the experience of the G8 is any guide—and it is in the interests of the G20 as an institution that it should be—frequent contact will lead to better understanding of the political constraints within which others must operate. As participants come to know each other better and to the extent that the common ground between them expands, misunderstandings, miscalculations, and unrealistic expectations are likely to diminish and more practicable and cooperative ideas to emerge. An effective G20, in which its members meet frequently and work cooperatively, can instill a greater sense of community among countries accustomed to seeing each other in competitive terms.

Evidence so far is that the G8, though broadly like-minded, is unlikely to constitute a formal caucus within the G20, although the EU will informally do so. While the migration of economic and political power to Asia is generating a growing Asian voice in the G20, the competitive nature of the various bilateral relationships within the region makes the emergence of an Asian caucus unlikely. Nor, for similar reasons, are the countries of the other regions likely to band together. The existence in one institution of 20 of the world's most significant and capable states with disparate interests does increase the probability of temporary, issue-based alliances

forming within the group as problems and opportunities come to the fore and then retreat. Former British prime minister Lord Henry Palmerston's insight that nations have no permanent friends, just permanent interests, seems likely to come back into vogue in the G20.

A further likely development is cross-regional cooperation among the G20 countries that are not great powers but that nonetheless have compelling strategic interests in a stable and prosperous world and the capacity to intervene—for example, the effort by Turkey and Brazil to mediate the international dispute over the alleged Iranian nuclear weapons program. Whether within the G20 or outside of it, there is ample scope for new partnerships to develop in the realms of security, development, global governance and international institutional innovation. There is also room, indeed a need, for cooperation between G20 members and capable G172 members.

Several lessons can reasonably confidently be drawn from the G20 experience thus far. First, in order to address major crises effectively, it is imperative to bring all the key stakeholders into the discussion. Second, the broadening of the circle of participants sets in train a process of power-sharing and pluralistic decision-making whose full import is probably not even now adequately assimilated around the world, not even by its members. Third, the interest of the participants in the forum thus created wanes as the crisis triggering its creation retreats. The pace of progress has slowed perceptibly as meeting has succeeded meeting and the recession has eased. The instinct to cooperate in a crisis yields to national interests and nationalist habits as the crisis recedes and the lifeboat reaches less turbulent waters.

The fourth lesson, perhaps the most important at this stage, is that expectations need to be kept realistic. The demands on the G20 for immediate, concrete results have been enormous and to some extent understandable considering the financial stakes. But the demands are also unsatisfiable; the issues are difficult and progress is going to be neither easy nor fast. G20 leaders would be wise not to issue promises in order to create the impression that they are doing something and should not establish markers for the sake of appearing accountable.

While it is right for the public and the media to expect results, it is a mistake to judge the efficacy of the group on the basis of the contents of one communiqué or another at one summit or another. The issues the G20 are wrestling with are complex. A true appreciation of the progress that the G20 is making or not making in resolving them requires a longer view. Understanding the problems, reaching agreements on them, fulfilling them, assessing the results and recalibrating approaches take time. Further, the very process of 20 of the most powerful leaders in the world meeting regularly and probing each other's arguments and reassessing their own is important in itself. It is through such interaction and cooperation that leaders grow intellectually and that they progress from the gritty imperatives of domestic politics to the higher plains of global statesmanship. In any case, it is better that leaders be talking than fighting; to paraphrase former British prime minister Sir Winston Churchill: jaw-jaw is better than war-war.

G20 members should not shrink from making the difficulty of achieving reforms clear to the media and the public. Allowing themselves to be pressured into presenting a happy, unified message of cooperation just to get through a media-intensive event risks either misrepresenting the views of some or settling for the lowest common denominator in their negotiations; either outcome undermines the credibility of the process and increases the pressure for more artificial results. As Alan Beattie of the *Financial Times* has argued, G20 communications need to reflect the increasing detail of the debate and its lengthening time horizon.[41]

The larger story of the G20, including its much criticized performance at Seoul, is not that the G20

is failing to resolve intractable issues but that the issues are intractable and the G20 is trying to solve them. In any case, there is no other forum where prospects for agreement are any better. Just leaving the problems to the market to sort would have punishing consequences all round.

The G20 and Canada

The Importance of Summitry and Personal Diplomacy[42]

As few doubt the axiom that it is better to be a policy-maker than a policy-taker, the most coveted seats in the world are at the G20 table. It is at these summits where the world's leading countries address themselves to the world's most important and urgent economic issues. Having a place at that table positions leaders to do good by contributing to the improvement of global governance, protecting their people's interests, and advancing their own political standing. It also gives leaders opportunities to develop, at relatively low transaction cost, personal relationships with each other that can be invaluable down the road.

Like most other countries, Canada needs opportunities and vehicles to advance its foreign policy interests. The G20 provides both. It is enormously in Canada's interest to be present in G20 summits and in a position to influence the discussions and conclusions to advance its ideas. While no one attending G20 gatherings forgets for a moment which countries around the table are the most powerful and which leaders are in the strongest political positions, the second-tier leaders have the opportunity nevertheless to advance their ideas to the group. In such intimate gatherings, the quality of the ideas a leader can offer can offset disadvantages in size.

For Canada, as for most other major countries, the prime minister's leadership is essential to advance Canadian interests internationally. Personal diplomacy by leaders is important because it is one of the surest ways of getting important issues addressed by their counterparts. Given that in every capital, but especially in the major capitals of G20 countries, there is tremendous competition for the leaders' time and attention, and, like everyone else, those leaders have only 24 hours in their days, some things, even important things, will never come to their attention. For Canada to get an issue to the top of another leader's agenda, especially if the issue matters more to Canada than it does to the country in question, it is important that there be a personal relationship between the leaders, and that the leaders' programmers realize that their principals value it and want to preserve it. Such relationships facilitate the scheduling of bilateral meetings and the maintenance of telephone contact between meetings. They force both stocktaking by the respective bureaucracies and decision-making by the leaders. The G20 is an excellent vehicle for developing personal relationships.

Personal relations are vital,[43] and the onus inevitably is on the smaller partner to take the initiative to get issues important to them addressed. In his memoirs, former prime minister Brian Mulroney observed how hard he worked to make sure Canada was noticed, and "that membership [in the G8] was personified so that others could see that Canada and its leadership were making a contribution." His close personal relationships with former US presidents Ronald Reagan and George H. W. Bush were indispensable to his broad international influence and in solving bilateral issues. His influence in Washington reinforced his effectiveness abroad and, conversely, his influence in the world enhanced his effectiveness in Washington. Summitry made it possible for him to develop relationships with European leaders including French president François Mitterrand, British prime minister Margaret Thatcher, German chancellor Helmut Kohl and Russian president Boris Yeltsin, among others, and to sustain this extraordinary network. What was true for Mulroney is true for all Canadian prime ministers, including Harper.

Summitry is challenging for any leader. The number of multilateral summits has multiplied over the years and the issues addressed at these gatherings have become more encompassing, more numerous and, substantively and politically, more important. Summits of various kinds happen on average more than once a month (for the Canadian prime minister and include the G20, the G8, the UN General Debate, the Commonwealth, the Francophonie, the EU, NATO, Asia Pacific Economic Cooperation (APEC), the Summit of the Americas, the Caribbean and North American Free Trade Agreement-related events, as well as sectoral conferences like Climate Change in Copenhagen, and the Commission on Information and Accountability for Women's and Children's Health in Geneva, among others). The physical wear and tear is significant, the travel is time-consuming, the stakes are frequently high, much of the media tends to score the event in terms of winners and losers and the outcomes are only partly programmable (for example, the Birmingham G8 summit in 1998 had to respond to the Pakistan and Indian nuclear tests that took place shortly beforehand, and the Toronto G20 summit had to respond to the sovereign debt crisis).

Participation in international summits, meetings, and conferences constitutes important, even necessary, growth opportunities for newly elected/appointed leaders. Summits expose them to the political needs, expertise, personalities and, in some cases, unsparing judgments of the only peers they have (German chancellor Helmut Schmidt and others were so critical of Canadian economic policies at the G8 summit in Bonn in 1978 that when prime minister Pierre Trudeau came home, he abruptly changed them[44]). Summits require leaders to expand their intellectual horizons and to check their instincts and theories against reality (Reagan was an exception, sticking close to the talking points on his 4 × 6 cards, and apparently immune to criticism, including from Trudeau, for doing so).

Hosting summits is a great deal more demanding than simply attending them, as the host takes charge of herding the guests, developing an agenda cooperatively with other governments, conducting the proceedings and endeavouring to deliver outcomes that serve his own political and policy needs and that are reasonably acceptable to fellow leaders, while hoping for as many favourable judgments as possible from his own media and population. Used strategically, these summit meetings also afford prime ministers opportunities to conduct bilateral business with other participants, obviating the need for additional travel.

Largely as a consequence of the frequency, significance, and breadth of the agendas of summits, prime ministers are increasingly becoming the personification of Canadian diplomacy, although an integrating world ensures that there is plenty to keep foreign ministers busy. It is a very demanding responsibility and, whatever the talents of a prime minister, to function optimally he or she needs to draw on the research strengths and vast experience of a professional public service. The public visibility of a prime minister at a summit is the proverbial tip of the iceberg of the massive preparatory effort.

Partly because of the G20, international diplomacy has become increasingly economic in character. The financial crisis of 2008 and its enormous scope and complexity have demanded specialized expertise, very considerably increasing the international role of Finance and Bank of Canada officials who have been extraordinarily effective in supporting Harper and Flaherty in G20 summit discussions of complex and crucial finance and banking issues. On the non-financial aspects of summits, DFAIT and CIDA provide the essential support, including the very influential role of the prime minister's personal representative, or sherpa, in summit parlance.

What Should Canada Do?[45]

It is evident in an age of multiple centres of power that summitry is only going to become more important.

We need therefore first to register in our collective consciousness just how significant summitry is for Canada and to recognize that the G20 is central to that reality. It is at summits that the world's most important governance issues are deliberated and decided upon, affecting Canadian sovereignty, security, and prosperity. No other organization or institution, at least potentially, offers more advantages and opportunities to us to advance crucial interests than the G20 does. The creation of a G2 or a G5 would force us to rely on others to protect our vital interests, a dubious proposition at best. We should, therefore, treat the effectiveness of the G20 as a Canadian national interest and work at making it happen.

Second, we should cement Canadian membership in the G20 by making ourselves as useful and indispensable to the institution as possible. We are there as a right, with an economy that ranks us in the top 10 or 11 in the world now and which seems likely to rank us well into the top 20 even if the emerging countries grow as rapidly as expected. But our reputation has lost some of its lustre in recent years and we need to ensure that our enviable and legitimate strengths are not deprecated and our standing not further downgraded.

Third, we need to regard G20 membership as the near equivalent of a permanent seat for Canada on the UN Security Council; this is all the more true now that we have little prospect of sitting again on the Council for several years. We should endeavour, therefore, to shape G20 agendas to promote our own interests. We should engage actively on financial reform and institutional innovation and promote the discussion of non-financial issues in the G20, notably the economic development of the world's poorer countries, UN reform, climate change, and energy security.

Fourth, at the same time, we should work to rebuild our diminished standing at the UN, which remains the pre-eminent body for global governance. The UN Charter provides the rule book for the conduct of international relations and also enables

IMF/EB	G20	G8	G5	UNSC
Argentina	Argentina			
Australia	Australia			
Belgium				
Brazil	Brazil		Brazil	Brazil
				Bosnia
Canada	Canada	Canada		
China	China		China	China
				Colombia
Denmark				
Egypt				
	European Union	European Union		
France	France	France		France
				Gabon
Germany	Germany	Germany		Germany
India	India		India	India
	Indonesia			
Iran				
Italy	Italy	Italy		
Japan	Japan	Japan		
				Lebanon
Lesotho				
Mexico	Mexico		Mexico	
Netherlands				
				Nigeria
				Portugal
Russia	Russia	Russia		Russia
Saudi Arabia	Saudi Arabia			
	South Africa		South Africa	South Africa
	South Korea			
	Spain *Defacto member			
Switzerland				
Thailand				
Togo				
	Turkey			
United Kingdom	United Kingdom	United Kingdom		United Kingdom
United States	United States	United States		United States

Figure 12.1 Memberships of International Organizations and Institutions, 2011

other entities, including the G20 and other organizations, to work better as well. A strong reputation at the UN as a constructive power would reinforce our effectiveness in the G20. The reverse is also true.

Fifth, we should work to promote a reciprocal beneficial relationship between the nascent G20 and the United Nations. The G20 can make the UN more effective by importing consensuses among the major powers, where that is achievable, into UN deliberations. The UN can make the G20 more effective by extending the latter's reach and facilitating cooperation with the G172 who are not at the G20 table but whose cooperation is needed, for example, on curtailing international crime or terrorism. Both institutions are needed, but neither is sufficient on its own and cooperation between the two is likely to yield synergies. We could promote coherence between the two by holding the G20 summits in New York at the same time as the UN General Debate each fall, as most leaders attend. That would save wear and tear on leaders by deleting one major trip and save a vast amount of money, taking advantage of the extensive security for leaders already afforded by the UN each fall.

Sixth, we should devise strategies for developing and managing effective bilateral and multilateral relationships with each G20 country, especially the emerging economies of the G20, notably China, India, Brazil, Korea, Turkey, and Indonesia. Effective relationships with these countries would virtually guarantee an effective foreign policy and win us respect in Washington to boot. The G20 summits provide a ready-made and very cost-effective instrument for developing more effective personal relationships with the leaders of arguably the 20 most important countries in the world.

Seventh, we should create issue-specific alliances in the G20, beyond the more familiar relationships among the old G8. The like-minded groupings of the Cold War have disintegrated as the EU united, old enemies became partners, other powers emerged and the nature of international security challenges changed. Further, there is an emerging need for cooperation and new partnerships among countries that are not themselves great powers by traditional definition but that nonetheless have both compelling strategic interests in a stable and prosperous world and the diplomatic capacity and political disposition to make a significant difference.

Eighth, as the poorest states are not represented at the G20, and nor are some of the most effective smaller countries, notably Norway, the Netherlands, Chile, and Singapore, we should work towards finding a solution to the efficiency (fewer countries around the table) and inclusivity (all countries around the table) conundrum. Canada could make itself the champion of the importance of the G20's taking into account—genuinely and effectively—the views of the 172 countries that are not members of the G20. It is a role that our diplomatic traditions and residual competencies position us to play superbly.

Ninth, we should reinvest in diplomacy as the Americans, for example, are doing to prepare for a world where international diplomacy will be every country's first line of national security.

Tenth, we should develop a network of Canadian think tanks and universities to reinforce the expertise available inside the public service, researching these issues and conducting track II diplomacy to develop informal international consensuses on issues that governments might not be able to achieve directly.

Questions for Review

1. What was the impetus for the creation of the G20?

2. Should the G8 survive after the creation of the G20?

3. In what ways can the G20 support the work of the United Nations?

4. How has the G20 changed the making of Canadian foreign policy?

Suggested Readings

Harper, Stephen. 2010. "From Canada to Korea: Advancing Global Leadership through the G-8 and G-20." Presented at the G20 Seoul Summit, the G-20 Research Group, Munk Centre for International Studies, University of Toronto (November).

Heinbecker, Paul. 2010. *Getting Back in the Game: A Foreign Policy Playbook for Canada.* Toronto: Key Porter.

Jones, Bruce. 2010. *Making Multilateralism Work: How the G-20 Can Help the United Nations.* Washington, DC: Brookings Institution for The Stanley Foundation (April).

Martin, Paul. 2005. "A Global Answer to Global Problems." *Foreign Affairs* 84, 3 (May/June): 2–6.

Saran, Shyam. 2010. *Global Governance and Emerging Economies—An Indian Perspective.* Presented to ICRIER/Konrad Adenauer Foundation Seminar.

Smith, Gordon S., and Peter Heap. 2010. "Canada, the G8 and the G20: A Canadian Approach to Shaping Global Governance in a Shifting International Environment." University of Calgary School of Public Policy, *SPP Research Papers* 3, 8 (November).

Notes

1. Sources: Compiled by Earth Policy Institute, with 1950–1979 from Worldwatch Institute, *Signposts 2001,* CD-ROM (Washington, DC: 2001) (Worldwatch update of Angus Maddison, *Monitoring the World Economy 1820–1992* [Paris: OECD, 1995]); 1980–2005 from International Monetary Fund, *World Economic Outlook Database,* at www.imf.org/external/pubs/ft/ weo/2006/02/data/index.htm, updated September 2006; United Nations, *World Population Prospects: The 2004 Revision* (New York: 2005); United States Department of Commerce, Bureau of Economic Analysis, "Implicit Price Deflators for Gross Domestic Product," Table 1.1.9, revised 30 August 2006, at www.bea.gov; UNESCO Institute for Statistics, Data on Illiteracy, for Population Age Fifteen and Older: www.uis.unesco.org; Economic and Social Council E/CN.9/2010/3, 28 January 2010.

2. See the UNESCO Literacy Report 2008 at www.uis.unesco.org/template/pdf/Literacy/LiteracyReport2008.pdf.

3. See A/59/565, "A More Secure World: Our Shared Responsibility," Report of the High-Level Panel on Threats, Challenges and Change, 2 December 2004, p. 12.

4. Human Security Report Project, Human Security Report 2009/2010: *The Causes of Peace and the Shrinking Costs of War,* pre-publication (Vancouver: HSRP, 2010), forthcoming in print from Oxford University Press Brief, Figure 10.1.

5. Eric Schmidt and Jared Cohen, "The Digital Disruption: Connectivity and the Diffusion of Power," *Foreign Affairs* (November/December 2010).

6. But according to Branko Milanovic in *The Haves and the Have-Nots,* as quoted by Doug Sanders in *The Globe and Mail,* 22 January 2011: "Even as the Chinese worker has gone from $525 per year to $5,000 in two decades, the average American worker has gone from about $25,000 to $38,000." The income gap has widened in favour of the American.

7. For an interesting and detailed assessment of North–South relations see Shyam Saran, *Global Governance and Emerging Economies: An Indian Perspective* (paper presented to the ICRIER/Konrad Adenauer Foundation Seminar, 2010). Saran was a former Indian foreign secretary and national security adviser to Prime Minister Manmohan Singh.

8. The US, Germany, the UK, France, Italy, Japan, and Canada.

9. Interview with Paul Martin, Canada's Minister of Finance and Chair of the G20, conducted by Candida Tamar Paltiel, G8 Research Group, 18 November 2001, Ottawa.

10. Paul Martin, "A Global Answer to Global Problems," *Foreign Affairs* 84, 3 (May/June 2005): 2–6.

11. See Saran, *Global Governance and Emerging Economies.*

12. "The Global Plan for Recovery and Reform," official communiqué issued by G20 leaders for the G20 London Summit, 2 April 2009.

13. Pittsburgh G20 leaders' summit communiqué, 29 September 2009.

14. Len Edwards, Canadian "sherpa," speech to the Annual General Meeting of the Korea–Canada Society, Ottawa, 3 November 2010.

15. Prime Minister Stephen Harper, "From Canada to Korea: Advancing Global Leadership through the G8 and G20," presented at the G20 Seoul Summit 2010: *Shared Growth Beyond Crisis,* the G20 Research Group, Munk School of Global Affairs, University of Toronto (November 2010).

16. Bank of Canada Governor Mark Carney's speech, 10

September 2010.

17. "China, Germany, and South Africa criticize US stimulus," BBC Business News, 5 November 2010.

18. Prime Minister Lee Myung-bak, President, Republic of Korea, at the G20 Seoul Summit 2010: *Shared Growth Beyond Crisis*, the G20 Research Group, Munk School of Global Affairs, University of Toronto (November 2010).

19. Declaration of the Summit on Financial Markets and the World Economy, G20 Special Leaders' Summit on the Financial Situation, Washington, DC, 14–15 November 2008.

20. President Nicolas Sarkozy, adapted from an address to the 18th Ambassador's Conference, 25 August 2010, Elysée Palace, Paris.

21. For a fuller treatment of the relationship between the G8 and the G20, see Gordon S. Smith and Peter Heap, "Canada, the G8 and the G20: A Canadian Approach to Shaping Global Governance in a Shifting International Environment," University of Calgary School of Public Policy, *SPP Research Papers* 3, 8 (November 2010).

22. The Canadian initiative succeeded in attracting quite substantial funding—pledges equaled $7.3 billion—but also drew the ire of some of our partners, notably the Americans, for our determination to exclude funding for abortion, a policy posture that had earlier been adopted by the Bush administration, but explicitly rejected by the Obama administration. US Secretary of State Hillary Clinton specifically and publicly criticized this dimension of the Harper government's initiative. The communiqué papered over the cracks.

23. Statement by the Prime Minister of Canada, Stephen Harper, at the 2010 World Economic Forum, Davos, Switzerland, 28 January 2010. See also the article by Prime Minister Harper, "From Canada to Korea: Advancing Global Leadership through the G8 and G20," cited above.

24. Nicolas Sarkozy, adapted from an address to the 18th Ambassador's Conference, cited above.

25. For a fuller treatment of the United Nations, see Paul Heinbecker, *Getting Back in the Game: A Foreign Policy Playbook for Canada* (Toronto: Key Porter, 2010), from which some of this line of argument is derived.

26. UNHCR, "Table 22. Refugees, asylum-seekers, internally displaced persons (IDPs), returnees (refugees and IDPs), stateless persons, and others of concern to UNHCR by region, 2008–2009," www.unhcr.org/pages/4a0174156.html.

27. WFP Annual Report, 2010, available at http://documents. wfp.org/stellent/groups/public/documents/communications/wfp220666.pdf.

28. Deaths from measles, a major killer, declined by 74 per cent worldwide and by 89 per cent in Sub-Saharan Africa between 2000 and 2007.

29. See "Global Immunization Data," based on the latest

World Health Organization (WHO)/UNICEF global estimates for 2009 (October 2010).

30. For a fuller treatment of this subject, see Bruce Jones, *Making Multilateralism Work: How the G-20 Can Help the United Nations* (Washington, DC: Brookings Institution for The Stanley Foundation, April 2010), and Stewart Patrick, "The G-20: Shifting Coalitions of Consensus Rather Than Blocs," paper presented at the G20 Seoul International Symposium (September 2010).

31. This includes the staff of the World Bank, the IMF, and a constellation of related organizations, councils, tribunals, commissions, funds, and agencies; available at www. un.org (January 2010).

32. See "Monthly Summary of Military and Police, Contribution to United Nations Operations," available at www.un.org (January 2011).

33. Jonas Gahr Støre, "G20 sorely lacking in legitimacy," *New Straits Times*, 29 March 2010.

34. Jones, *Making Multilateralism Work*.

35. See Peggy Hollinger, *Financial Times*, 9 February 2011.

36. For a fuller treatment of the G20 and climate change, see Barry Carin, "Can the G-20 Save the Environment?," Centre for International Governance Innovation, prepared for the University of Calgary School of Public Policy (April 2011).

37. "UN Climate Change Conference in Cancún delivers balanced package of decisions, restores faith in multilateral process," press release, Cancún, 11 December 2010.

38. Robert B. Zoellick, president, World Bank Group, transcript of remarks at Cancun Summit on REDD+, 7 December 2010.

39. Remarks by the Right Honourable Paul Martin, former prime minister of Canada, keynote speaker to the Seoul International Symposium, "Toward the Consolidation Of G20 Summits: From Crisis Committee to Global Steering Committee," G20 Summit Site, COEX, Seoul, 27–29 September 2010.

40. See Barry Carin, Paul Heinbecker, Gordon Smith, and Ramesh Thakur, "Making the G20 Summit Process Work: Some Proposals for Improving Effectiveness and Legitimacy," CIGI G20 Papers, No. 2, June 2010.

41. Alan Beattie, "Successful Communications Strategies for G20 Summits," presented at the Conference on the New Dynamics of Summitry: Institutional Innovations for G20 Summits, Seoul, 27–29 September 2010.

42. For a fuller treatment of this subject see Heinbecker, *Getting Back in the Game*, on which this section draws.

43. See especially Smith and Heap, "Canada, the G8 and the G20," p 13.

44. John English, *Just Watch Me: The Life of Pierre Trudeau, 1968–2000* (Toronto: Alfred A Knopf, 2009), p. 373.

45. For a fuller treatment of this subject see Heinbecker, *Getting Back in the Game*, on which this section draws.

Selected Bibliography

Blanchard, James J. 1998. *Behind the Embassy Door: Canada, Clinton, and Quebec*. Toronto: McClelland and Stewart.

Bothwell, Robert. 2007. *Alliance and Illusion: Canada and the World, 1945–1984*. Vancouver: UBC Press.

Bow, Brian. 1992. *Canada and the United States*. Toronto: University of Toronto Press.

———. 2009. *The Politics of Linkage: Power, Interdependence, and Ideas in Canada–US Relations*. Vancouver: UBC Press.

Cellucci, Paul. 2005. *Unquiet Diplomacy*. Toronto: Key Porter.

Chapnick, Andrew. 2005. *The Middle Power Project: Canada and the Founding of the United Nations*. Vancouver: UBC Press.

Cooper, Andrew F. 2004. *Tests of Global Governance: Canadian Diplomacy and United Nations World Conferences*. Tokyo: United Nations University Press.

Doran, Charles. 1984. *Forgotten Partnership: US–Canada Relations Today*. Baltimore: Johns Hopkins University Press.

Gattinger, Monica, and Geoffrey Hale, eds. 2010. *Borders and Bridges: Canada's Policy Relations in North America*. Don Mills, ON: Oxford University Press.

Granatstein, J.L. 1992. *For Better or for Worse: Canada and the United States to the 1990s*. Toronto: Copp Clark Longman.

Granatstein, J.L., and Norman Hillmer. 1994. *From Empire to Umpire: Canada and the World to the 1990s*. Toronto: Copp Clark Longman.

Haglund, David G. 2000. *The North Atlantic Triangle Revisited: Canadian Grand Strategy at Century's End*. Toronto: Irwin.

Heinbecker, Paul. 2010. *Getting Back in the Game: A Foreign Policy Playbook for Canada*. Toronto: Key Porter.

Holmes, John W. 1981. *Life with Uncle: The Canadian–American Relationship*. Toronto: University of Toronto Press.

Jockel, Joseph T. 2007. *Canada in NORAD, 1957–2007: A History*. Montreal and Kingston: McGill-Queen's University Press.

Keating, Tom, and Larry Pratt. 1988. *Canada, NATO and the Bomb: The Western Alliance in Crisis*. Edmonton: Hurtig Publishers.

Kirton, John. 2001. "Guess Who is Coming to Kananaskis? Civil Society and the G8 in Canada's Year as Host," *International Journal* 57, 1 (Winter): 101–22.

Lennox, Patrick. 2009. *At Home and Abroad: The Canada–US Relationship and Canada's Place in the World*. Vancouver: UBC Press.

MacMillan, Margaret O., and David S. Sorenson, eds. 1990. *Canada and NATO: Uneasy Past, Uncertain Future*. Waterloo, ON: University of Waterloo Press.

Mahant, Edelgard, and Graeme S. Mount. 1999. *Invisible and Inaudible in Washington: American Policies toward Canada*. Vancouver: UBC Press.

McKenna, Peter. 1995. *Canada and the OAS: From Dilettante to Full Partner*. Ottawa: Carleton University Press.

Potter, Evan H. 1999. *Transatlantic Partners: Canadian Approaches to the European Union*. Ottawa: Carleton University Press.

Rochlin, James. 1994. *Discovering the Americas: The Evolution of Canadian Foreign Policy towards Latin America*. Vancouver: UBC Press.

Simpson, Erika. 2001. *NATO and the Bomb: Canadian Defenders Confront Critics*. Montreal and Kingston: McGill-Queen's University Press.

Smith, Gordon, and Daniel Wolfish, eds. 2001. *Who is Afraid of the State? Canada in a World of Multiple Centres of Power*. Toronto: University of Toronto Press.

Stairs, Denis. 1974. *Diplomacy of Constraint: Canada, the Korean War and the United States*. Toronto: University of Toronto Press.

———. 1999. "Global Governance as a Policy Tool: The Canadian Experience," pp. 67–85 in Raimo Väyrynen, ed., *Globalization and Global Governance*. Lanham, MD: Rowman and Littlefield.

Stevenson, Brian J.R. 2000. *Canada, Latin America, and the New Internationalism: A Foreign Policy*. Montreal and Kingston: McGill-Queen's University Press.

Taylor, Rupert, ed. 1995. *Canada in Action: Canada and the G7*. Waterloo, ON: Taylor Publishing.

Thompson, John Herd, and Stephen J. Randall. 2000. *Canada and the United States: Ambivalent Allies*. Montreal and Kingston: McGill-Queen's University Press.

Domestic Factors and Canadian Foreign Policy

Part 3 examines the relevance of domestic influences on Canada's international relations. Studies of foreign policy are often problematic, given the separate realms these issues occupy. The term *foreign* implies a context in which theories of international relations or global political economy might apply. The "policy" aspect, however, draws attention to public administration or public policy frameworks. In the first edition, the goal was to highlight these divergent trends by focusing on Kim Richard Nossal's and Cranford Pratt's dialogue in the Winter 1983–84 edition of *International Journal*. In this classic exchange, Nossal proposed a "modified statist" approach, which acknowledged that societal pressures had some impact on Canadian foreign policy.[1] Pratt's response, however, stressed the influence of a dominant class in Canada that was consistent with the objectives of elites in other states. Therefore, a counter-consensus was required to challenge these entrenched values.[2] As noted in the first edition, the importance of Pratt's work should not be underestimated. His discussion of dominant-class theory includes a wide range of variables related to the construction of knowledge, class, ideology, and political culture. The absence of ethical and normative considerations in Canadian foreign policy is also highlighted. The influence of Pratt on future scholars, such as Mark Neufeld, Sean McMahon (Chapter 8), and David Black (Chapter 28), is both important and obvious.

In contrast, the third edition focuses primarily on specific domestic issues in the formulation of Canadian foreign policy. Paul Gecelovsky, for example, argues that the prime minister has decisive control in the formulation of Canada's international relations, although this influence is dependent on the economic and political significance of specific issues. Gerald Schmitz also evaluates the challenges facing Parliament, especially in terms of parliamentary accountability, oversight, and investigation. Patrice Dutil, on the other hand, examines the relevance of the bureaucracy in matters of foreign policy, with an emphasis on institutional structures from a historical perspective. Anita Singh, who focuses on the impact of diasporas, explores the impact of the Indo-Canadian community on Canada's foreign relations. Finally, David Carment and Joseph Landry extend Singh's analysis of non-governmental actors to a broader discussion of the role of civil society on Canadian foreign policy.

PART 3

Despite the thoroughness of these chapters, some important domestic considerations were not included. The Winter 2008–2009 edition of *International Journal*, for example, highlighted the need to better understand the role of political parties in the formulation of Canadian foreign policy. Articles focusing on trade, climate change, and defence policy suggested that parties in Canada had considerable flexibility in this policy area due to the low priority given to these issues by Canadian voters.[3] This resulted in foreign relations that were often ad hoc, personality-driven, focused on tactical coalition-building, and in many cases shaped by US preferences.[4]

Although previous editions included a chapter on the role of the provinces in Canadian trade policy, there is no in-depth analysis of sub-federal influence in this volume, especially in relation to provincial implementation of international obligations. Article 27 of the 1969 Vienna Convention on the Law of Treaties, for example, states that signatories must not use domestic law as justification for violating international treaty obligations. Article XXIV: 12 of the General Agreement on Tariffs and Trade (GATT), which was later incorporated into the World Trade Organization (WTO), and Article 105 of the North American Free Trade Agreement (NAFTA), also outline the compliance of local and regional governments. These realities create additional constraints for Ottawa in the negotiation and implementation of international treaties. Finally, an additional weakness of Part 3 is its failure to include further critical analysis as well as its exclusion of a wide range of scholarship on the democratization of Canadian foreign policy. Having said that, other domestic issues are addressed, using both traditional and critical approaches, elsewhere in this volume.

Notes

1. Kim Richard Nossal, "Analyzing the Domestic Sources of Canadian Foreign Policy," *International Journal* 39, 1 (Winter 1983–84): 1–22.

2. Cranford Pratt, "Dominant Class Theory and Canadian Foreign Policy: The Case of the Counter-Consensus," *International Journal* 39, 1 (Winter 1983–84): 99–135.

3. Paul Gecelovsky and Christopher Kukucha, "Much Ado about Parties: Conservative and Liberal Approaches to Canada's Trade Policy with the United States," *International Journal* 64, 1 (Winter 2008–9): 29–45; Heather A. Smith, "Political Parties and Canadian Climate Change Policy," *International Journal* 64, 1 (Winter 2008–9): 47–66; and Brian Bow, "Parties and Partisanship in Canadian Defence Policy," *International Journal* 64, 1 (Winter 2008–9): 67–88.

4. See also Kim Richard Nossal, "'Opening Up the Policy Process: Does Party Make a Difference?," pp. 276–87 in Nelson Michaud and Kim Richard Nossal, eds., *Diplomatic Departures: The Conservative Era in Canadian Foreign Policy, 1984–93* (Vancouver: UBC Press, 2001).

13 Of Legacies and Lightning Bolts: An Updated Look at the Prime Minister and Canadian Foreign Policy

Paul Gecelovsky

Key Terms

Idiosyncratic Variable
Mandate Letters
Message Event Proposal

Plenipotentiary Power
Role or Positional Variable

Introduction

The purpose of this chapter is to examine the role played by the prime minister in the formulation of Canada's foreign policy. Other contributors to this volume have looked at various domestic factors which influence Canada's foreign policy, including Parliament (Schmitz), civil society (Carment and Landry), diasporas (Singh), and the bureaucracy (Dutil). What these contributors have overlooked, for the most part, is that the prime minister is the key person in deciding both the direction and content of Canada's foreign policy, and that the prime minister, when so choosing, may override the interests of other actors and have Canada pursue a foreign policy to his or her liking. The prime minister, in the making of Canada's foreign policy, is *primus* without *pares*, to borrow from Donald J. Savoie.[1] To demonstrate that the prime minister has no equal in setting the content and course of Canada's foreign policy, this chapter is divided into two sections. The first section examines the powers possessed by the prime minister, and the second looks at the constraints within which the prime minister operates. It will be shown that the former outweigh the latter significantly and that, furthermore, the constraints are only constraints if the prime minister allows them to stop him or her from acting. In short, the powers possessed by the prime minister are decisive.

Powers of the Prime Minister

The prime minister possesses a vast range of powers. The chapter focuses on only those powers possessed by the prime minister that are relevant to the formulation of Canada's foreign policy. The powers discussed in the chapter are divided between those possessed by the office of the prime minister, which is referred to as the **role or positional variable**, and the extent or degree to which a prime minister seeks to distinguish the international behaviour of her or his government from other administrations, which is often referred to as the **idiosyncratic variable**.[2]

In examining the role or positional variable, four main constitutional powers need to be addressed. The first power of office to be discussed concerns the power of appointment. The prime minister has the authority to name persons to various positions within the state including, *inter alia*, ministers, deputy ministers, ambassadors, and high commissioners. Who ultimately sits in the foreign minister's chair and for how long that person occupies that chair is, in large part, determined solely by the prime minister. While the department charged with maintaining Canada's foreign relations was created in 1909, it was not until 1946 that the prime minister relinquished the position of Secretary of State for External Affairs (SSEA) to another minister.[3] Louis St Laurent was coaxed out of retirement by then prime minister William Lyon Mackenzie King to become the first person to hold the external affairs portfolio who was not also the prime minister. King, it needs to be noted, believed that in giving up the position of SSEA to St Laurent, he was jettisoning the mundane chores of departmental administration and management while freeing up time to deal with the more important foreign policy concerns of the state; St Laurent was to do the housekeeping while King focused on diplomacy. Since the naming of St Laurent in 1946, successive prime ministers have appointed others to be responsible for the foreign affairs portfolio.

Appointing others to be responsible for Canada's international behaviour, however, does not mean that those holding the office of prime minister were not interested or influential in setting both the tone and course of Canada's foreign policy. It is the prime minister who establishes the parameters within which the foreign minister operates and who determines what leeway the occupant of the foreign minister's chair is given. This setting of the boundaries is accomplished through various means, including the prime minister's active involvement in any departmental matter of his or her choosing.

The prime minister may also discharge what Don Johnston, a former minister in the Trudeau government, has referred to as "lightning bolts."[4] That is, the prime minister is able to change the content and direction of Canada's policy at his discretion without consultation with a minister, cabinet, or departmental officials; what the prime minister says is policy. A lightning bolt was fired in March 2006 in the wake of the presidential elections in Belarus. It was apparent that the incumbent, Alexander Lukashenko, had won the election by brutally suppressing the opposition. As is usual, the Canadian government had to respond to the election of a foreign leader. Prime Minister Stephen Harper did not approve of the draft statement produced by Foreign Affairs. Paul Wells has reported that "Harper took one look at the proposed release, swore, took out a pen and paper and drafted his own version." The Harper version of the release replaced the typical phraseology "Canada notes with concern" with the more forceful "[the election] was not free or fair" and that "opposition workers and candidates were harassed and intimidated by the authorities." It continued: "I am shocked that a dictatorial and abusive regime such as this one can continue to exist in today's Europe." The statement was released by Harper without any input from Foreign Affairs and without any notification of its release given to the department. "Just put it out. Don't even tell Foreign Affairs. They can read it later. Maybe learn something," the prime minister is reported to have said.[5] The actions of Stephen Harper demonstrate that it is the prime minister who ultimately decides which issues or crises are important for Canada and how Canada will respond to those issues or crises.

It is not only through direct involvement in foreign policy matters that a prime minister establishes the boundaries for a foreign minister. Another way in which the prime minister can set the parameters for a foreign minister is through the appointment of more senior ministers to the foreign affairs troika. Since 1982, responsibility for Canada's foreign affairs has fallen to a triumvirate of ministers, including the minister of foreign affairs, the minister of international trade, and the minister of international development.[6] Within this triad of ministers, the minister of foreign affairs is usually the most senior, and lead, minister, followed by the minister of international trade and, finally, the minister of international development, who is the most junior. This is the situation at present with John Baird as minister of foreign affairs, Ed Fast as minister of international trade, and Christian Paradis as minister of international development and minister for La Francophonie.

There have been occasions, however, when the prime minister has appointed a more junior parliamentarian to the foreign minister portfolio. This occurred in 1989 when then Prime Minister Brian Mulroney was dissatisfied with the overly cautious approach to foreign policy exhibited by then Secretary of State for External Affairs Joe Clark. Mulroney replaced Clark with the more junior Barbara McDougall. Concurrent with this move, Mulroney moved Michael Wilson from finance to replace John Crosbie as minister for international trade. Monique Landry maintained her position as minister responsible for the Canadian International Development Agency, the third member of the triad. With these moves, Wilson rather than McDougall assumed the position of lead minister in the foreign affairs troika.[7] The main effects of this cabinet shuffle were that for the remainder of Mulroney's term in office, trade issues came to dominate Canada's foreign relations, and control over foreign policy effectively shifted to the prime minister and the Prime Minister's Office (PMO), with the foreign minister lacking any real freedom of action.

A third way in which the prime minister outlines the parameters of permissibility for foreign ministers is through the issuing of **mandate letters**.

Mandate letters are given to all ministers upon their being sworn into cabinet and also to those who have been assigned to a new portfolio as a result of a cabinet shuffle. A mandate letter will outline those issues and areas of importance on which the minister is to focus. The letters most often span only two or three pages and are prepared by officials in the Privy Council Office after they have consulted with relevant members of the PMO and the deputy minister(s) affected by the change. As Savoie has noted, there are two basic types of mandate letters. The first is the "Don't call us, we'll call you" letter, which, in effect, tells a minister to do nothing but maintain the status quo and stay out of trouble. The second type of mandate letter outlines the major challenges and the specific objectives with which the minister is to concern herself during her tenure.[8] The mandate letters effectively set the terms on which the minister is to serve in the appointed position.

After the July 2013 cabinet shuffle, it came to light that the Harper government compiled transition binders for all ministers. Included in the transition binders were each minister's mandate letter, as well as instructions on how to address Opposition questions during Question Period, and lists of stakeholders (including media outlets) and civil servants who were sympathetic and antagonistic to the government.[9]

A fourth manner in which the prime minister sets the boundaries for the foreign minister is through the appointment of senior civil servants. Since Pierre Trudeau came to office in 1968, prime ministers and their staff have increasingly involved themselves in the appointment of senior civil servants at the rank of deputy minister. All deputy minister appointments are vetted by the prime minister and the PMO as to the applicant's suitability for the position. All deputy ministers are also given mandate letters upon their appointment. This is done, in part, to ensure that the minister and deputy minister are both working from the same set of priorities and expectations, as determined by the prime minister.

A second constitutional power of the office possessed by the prime minister, in addition to the power of appointment and of relevance to our discussion, concerns the design of the administrative structures of government. The prime minister is the architect of government, as he or she has the authority to create, redesign, amalgamate, or eliminate departments. The power has been used most recently in March 2013 by Prime Minister Harper when it was announced that the Canadian International Development Agency was to be amalgamated with the Department of Foreign Affairs and International Trade to create the Department of Foreign Affairs, Trade and Development. This follows the move in February 2006, when Harper reconsolidated the Department of Foreign Affairs and International Trade, which had been separated into Foreign Affairs Canada (FAC) and International Trade Canada (ITCAN) by then prime minister Paul Martin in January 2004. The move by Martin undid the previous "consolidation and re-organization" initiatives of the Trudeau government in the 1980–83 period when Trudeau integrated sections of the Departments of Industry, Trade and Commerce, and Employment and Immigration, with the Department of External Affairs.[10]

While not of the same degree of importance as structural changes to administrative departments, the prime minister also has the authority to change the names of government departments. This power was exercised, in June 1989, by Prime Minister Mulroney when he changed the name of the Department of External Affairs, as it had been known since its creation in 1909, to External Affairs and International Trade Canada. Prime Minister Chrétien wasted little time in changing the name of the department when he renamed it the Department of Foreign Affairs and International Trade on 5 November 1993, only one day after assuming office. As noted above, Prime Minister Martin changed the name in 2004 to FAC and ITCAN, only to have it changed by Prime

Minister Harper to the Department of Foreign Affairs and International Trade, in 2006, and to the Department of Foreign Affairs, Trade and Development in March 2013. Concurrent with the changes in the name of the department is a change in the title of the minister's position—from secretary of state for external affairs from 1909 to 1993, to minister of foreign affairs after that time.

In addition to the constitutional powers of appointment and the design of administrative structures, the prime minister has the constitutional authority to mould the processes of decision-making within her or his own administration. While notable differences exist among prime ministers regarding their decision-making styles, one discernible trend has been a move to centralize foreign policy-making in the PMO. There was some movement in this direction under Trudeau; however, it was during Mulroney's tenure in office that this shift was more discernible, especially after the 1989 cabinet shuffle in which Barbara McDougall replaced Joe Clark as secretary of state for external affairs. This trend has accelerated further with the current Harper government, which has sought to control fully within the PMO not only decision-making but also communicating the results of those decisions to the Canadian public. Major policy decisions of the Harper government are taken by the prime minister and the PMO and then announced by the prime minister, leaving the various ministers to play a much diminished role in the government.

The final variable to be addressed concerns the **plenipotentiary power** possessed by the prime minister. The prime minister has the authority to negotiate and sign international agreements, a power first put to use in 1923 with the negotiating and signing of the Halibut Treaty with the United States. This bilateral treaty established that fishing for Pacific halibut would not occur during the winter spawning months (November to February) to help preserve the fish stock. More recently, the authority of the prime minister to negotiate, sign, and ratify treaties that concern those classes of subjects that are within the ambit of provincial authority has been called into question. Decisions of the Supreme Court of Canada have not fully or clearly articulated the extent of the prime minister's authority to act as an agent of the provinces in the international realm. The current state of affairs is that the prime minister may negotiate, sign, and ratify international treaties but he cannot force provinces to implement those agreements, or to be bound by the provisions of the ratified agreements. What the prime minister may do, however, is focus the public's attention on an issue and put that issue on the agenda of the provinces. A recent example of this concerns Canada's negotiating, signing, ratifying and, later, withdrawing from the Kyoto Protocol. Facing pressure from the provinces, industry, and even from within his party, then prime minister Chrétien moved forward with the ratification of the protocol. Chrétien went so far as staking the continuation of his government on the ratification of the legislation in the House of Commons by declaring Kyoto a motion of confidence. The Kyoto Protocol was ratified by Parliament in December 2002. Stephen Harper exercised his plenipotentiary power when in December 2011 Canada announced its formal withdrawal from the protocol. The ratification of and withdrawal from the Kyoto Protocol are clear demonstrations of the prime minister's plenipotentiary power.

Having looked at the four constitutional powers of the office of the prime minister that are relevant to our discussion regarding foreign policy-making (i.e., power of appointment, design of administrative structures, design of decision-making processes, and plenipotentiary authority), the chapter now moves to analyze the idiosyncratic component of prime ministerial authority. Juliet Kaarbo has outlined three components of **leadership style** which are relevant to this discussion. The first component is "the interest and experience the

prime minister has in a particular issue area."[11] In the post-World War Two era, only one leader has assumed the office of prime minister with extensive experience in international affairs: Lester B. Pearson. The others came into the office having travelled internationally but with scant experience in international diplomatic relations. Stephen Harper's international experience was limited to a few trips to Europe before he became prime minister. While most prime ministers come to office with little international experience, all have a sense of what is to be accomplished during the term in office.

A prime minister, however, cannot do everything that she wants to do and so needs to choose a few main policy objectives on which to focus the resources of the state. This "strategic prime ministership," as it has been termed by Thomas Axworthy, the former principal secretary to Pierre Trudeau, aids both the prime minister and the PMO in staying on track and in "saying no to hundreds of other requests" not related to the prime minister's strategic policy agenda.[12] While the prime minister's strategic policy agenda will be primarily shaped by domestic issues, prime ministers usually have a couple of foreign policy priorities that they seek to have met.

Canada's Israel policy is one area in Canada's foreign policy where Harper has had a direct and significant influence. Canada has moved from trying to play the role of helpful fixer or honest broker to a much more pro-Israel stance under Harper. This shift in policy is demonstrated by Canada's being one of the first governments to stop funding for Hamas after its 2006 electoral victory in Gaza, by "near categorical"[13] defence of Israel's military response to Hezbollah and Hamas attacks throughout 2006, and continued support for Israel during the December 2008 clash between Israeli and Hamas forces in Gaza and the June 2010 Israeli raid on the flotilla of ships from Turkey. Canada's unequivocal support for Israel continued through the 2011 G8 meeting, where Harper stood firm against the other members, including US President Barack Obama, insisting that no mention of Israel's 1967 borders be included in the final communiqué.

Prime Minister Harper has also stated publicly on a number of occasions that Canada "stands side-by-side with Israel," and that Canada would "continue to stand with Israel just as I have always said we would."[14] The strong Canadian support for Israel has come at a cost, and "we have the bruises to show for taking that stand," according to the prime minister. The "bruises" that Canada suffered refer to the vote lost in the fall of 2010 to Portugal at the United Nations for a non-permanent seat on the United Nations Security Council. This was the first time that Canada had failed in a bid for a seat on the Security Council. For Harper, those who claim that Canada has "lost influence" or "lost its balance" or "is no longer seen as an honest broker" are employing a "code for the view that Canada should go back to being ambivalent about our relationship with Israel," and this is something that a Harper government "will never do."[15]

Canadian support for Israel has been "outstanding."[16] Even Canadian Jewish leaders have been "surprised by the strength of Harper's defence of Israel" and they "feared it might undermine their advocacy efforts vis-à-vis the other political parties."[17] While there are many determinants influencing Canada's policy towards Israel, this shift in Canada's policy is due not to an assessment of Canadian interests in the region and globally but rather to Harper's support for Israel which is borne "out of conviction."[18]

For those persons who have had the opportunity to plan their retirement from the prime minister's chair, the ability to focus the resources of the state on a few priority issues has allowed them to better plan their legacies. Prior to his retirement in December 2003, Prime Minister Chrétien used his position as host of the G8 Summit in 2002 to ensure that discussions would not be overtaken by debates concerning the proper response to the acts of terrorism perpetrated against the United States on 11 September

2001, and that African concerns would have their "full place" at the Summit.[19] Knowing that the G8 Summit in Kananaskis was to be his last as host, Chrétien used this occasion to help build a legacy of compassion for his prime ministership.

A second component of leadership style concerns a prime minister's motivation to lead, or her task-orientation. Kaarbo discusses two broad forms of task orientation: *process* and *goal*. A process-oriented leader focuses on building relations among cabinet and caucus members and works to build consensus among party members. A goal-oriented leader comes to office to further a specific cause and/ or to promote an ideological position, and seeks to have her vision adopted.[20] There is little doubt that Prime Minister Harper is a goal-oriented leader who is motivated by the idea of the Conservative Party becoming the dominant party in Canadian politics in the twenty-first century. To this end, he has worked to exorcise all Liberal policies and programs from government. In terms of foreign policy, Harper has expunged from government websites, publications, and policies all mention of Liberal policies concerning human security, child soldiers, international humanitarian law, Responsibility to Protect, and gender equality. Kim Nossal has noted that "there is considerable evidence that, in foreign policy, the Conservatives sought policies that would distinguish themselves from their predecessors and encourage Canadians to let go of the past."[21] This rebranding exercise is part of an effort led by the prime minister to recast Canada and Canadian foreign policy in a more conservative light.

A prime minister's strategy for managing information is a third component of leadership style addressed by Kaarbo. Prime Minister Harper has demonstrated a desire for "iron clad message control."[22] At the prime ministerial level, this has been demonstrated by infrequent press conferences, limiting the number of questions asked by the media during press conferences, using media lists whereby reporters are required to sign up prior to a press conference if they want to pose questions to the prime minister, and not allowing photographers access to the prime minister to take pictures of him during speaking engagements. Staged pictures of Harper are then supplied to the media for publication and/or broadcast.

Upon coming to power in 2006, the Harper government instituted a system of message control to ensure continuity and consistency of message across all civil servants and Conservative caucus members and media. The **Message Event Proposal** (MEP) included, *inter alia*, Desired Headline, Strategic Objective, Desired Sound Bite, as well as information pertaining to the speaking backdrop, the ideal event photograph, and the speaker's wardrobe. Those addressing the public in any forum must fill out an MEP and submit it for scrutiny and approval by the Prime Minister's Office. The reach extended to all communications, as well as questions and answers being scripted beforehand for all presentations given by civil servants and caucus members, regardless of location or size of audience.

The Harper style of full control extends to the workings of cabinet and the Conservative caucus. In terms of cabinet, major policy decisions are made and communicated to the Canadian public by the prime minister, leaving ministers to reinforce the message of the prime minister and to ensure that his agenda is followed. This control even extends to Question Period, where ministers' responses are carefully scripted and rehearsed before the prime minister's approval is given. Whether driven by fear or by commitment, cabinet ministers in the Harper government have stayed on message and followed the policies outlined by the prime minister. Similarly, Harper's control over the Conservative caucus has been absolute, with no public dissension among the ranks tolerated. The prime minister has made it "clear," according to Lawrence Martin, that "if you stepped out of line, you stepped into a grave."[23] The

result of this has been that Conservative parliamentarians have toed the party line and, as Tom Flanagan has noted, "religiously follow[ed] the official talking points" set out by the prime minister and the PMO.[24]

At the bureaucratic level, the Harper Conservatives have sought to rein in any freedom given by previous governments to civil servants to speak publicly. All events have to be scripted and controlled via the MEP. Any deviations from the script, or any comments regarded by the government as critical of its performance or policies, will be responded to immediately and harshly. The removal of Paul Kennedy as the head of the Commission for Public Complaints Against the Royal Canadian Mounted Police; Peter Tinsley as the head of the Military Police Complaints Commission; Linda Keen as the head of the Canadian Nuclear Safety Commission; General Rick Hillier, as the head of the Canadian Armed Forces; Munir Sheikh as deputy minister of Statistics Canada; and Rémy Beauregard as president of the International Centre for Human Rights and Democratic Development, were all done, in large part, in response to comments or actions each made that were perceived by the Conservative leader as critical of his policies. They provided "evidence of a pattern: toe the government line or you're gone."[25]

For Harper, control over information and access is the "foremost priority" of his government.[26] The intense control over policy substance and communication by the prime minister is the Harper style of foreign policy-making. The level of control exercised by Stephen Harper far surpasses that of previous prime ministers.

Constraints on a Prime Minister

While the prime minister does possess an array of powers that enable her to dominate the policy-making process, a number of constraints may act to inhibit a prime minister from getting his or her way.

The first and most important constraint on a prime minister is time. The prime minister's schedule at the best of times is hectic, what with having to attend to cabinet business, Parliament, the legislative calendar, party caucus, party fundraising and other functions, and to government and patronage appointments. Added to this list is the amount of time taken up with consultations and meetings with personal staff, the principal secretary, the clerk of the Privy Council Office and individual ministers, as well as with provincial premiers, foreign heads of state, and business leaders. On top of this already crowded schedule, the prime minister must make time for constituency matters and for maintaining contact with members of the riding association. A prime minister, then, must be careful with her or his time as there are always issues and people who seek to have "just a few minutes of time." A prime minister who does not prioritize will soon fall victim to "political overload"—that is, "a pervasive sense of urgency and an accompanying feeling of being overwhelmed by events and the number of matters needing attention."[27] To avoid overload, a prime minister needs to be selective with the time and focus only on those issues on her or his strategic policy agenda.

In addition to time management, prime ministers have to be concerned with a number of issues that constrain freedom of manoeuvrability. Donald Smiley has referred to these as the *enduring axes* of Canadian politics. They are: French–English relations, regionalism, and Canada–US relations. The first two are of importance because they deal with national unity—always a primary concern for any prime minister. The first, moreover, is a foreign policy concern as Quebec, since the mid-1960s, has pushed for recognition abroad as an independent actor in foreign affairs. In relations with other states of importance to Quebec, especially other French-speaking states, the prime minister will be cognizant of Quebec's position on the issue(s) at hand—a position most likely at variance with that of the federal government—and the ramifications of the Canadian position on Quebec and on politics within that province.

In terms of Canada–US relations, the bilateral relationship affects all of Canada's international behaviour. This is not to argue that Canada's relationship with the US determines Canada's foreign policy but rather that the bilateral relationship is an important factor in decision-making. For example, John Holmes argued that it was "the fact of American policy"[28] that hampered Canada's recognition of the People's Republic of China as the government of China, a position that Canada had favoured since 1949 when Mao Zedong and the Chinese Communist Party first came to power. The "fact" to which Holmes was referring, and which prevented Canada from moving forward on recognition until 1970, was that communist states were seeking to expand their influence and needed to be "contained" in both their geographic boundaries and international influence. A similar "fact of American policy" is operative today, namely the "fact" that terrorism is perceived by American policy-makers as a serious threat to the American homeland, a threat from which the US needs to protect itself—and the protection of the US begins outside of its borders. To this end, Canada has instituted a number of measures, including legislation dealing with terrorism, a new Smart Border agreement with the US, and a restructuring of the civil service to create a Department of Public Safety and Emergency Preparedness. The point is that the prime minister needs to be aware that any action taken by Canada that might be construed as not being in line with the security concerns of both the American government and the prime minister will need to be weighed in terms of its costs and benefits to the bilateral relationship.

Moving attention away from the *enduring axes*, three additional constraints remain on a prime minister's power. Each of these remaining constraints derives from the workings of the Canadian system of parliamentary government: they are institutional factors. The first institutional constraint concerns whether the prime minister commands a majority in the House of Commons. The issue of support from the House is only problematic should the prime minister not command a majority in that body. Then the prime minister needs to be cognizant of the level of support within the House for her initiatives, in both domestic and foreign policy. In the case of a minority government, the prime minister's freedom of action might be somewhat circumscribed by the composition of the House. That being the case, the prime minister is not without some power over the House, as no party leader would want the government to fall over a matter of little importance to the Canadian public, and much of Canada's foreign policy falls within the ambit of minimal importance to Canadians. Foreign policy issues rarely dominate Canadian politics, and it is even rarer for a foreign policy issue to be more than a peripheral factor in a general election. For instance, the 1988 general election is often cited as an example of an election in which a foreign policy issue—whether Canada should sign a bilateral free trade agreement with the US—played a key role in determining the outcome. The major political parties were divided on the issue, with the Progressive Conservatives in favour of an agreement and both the Liberals and the NDP opposed to one. In their analysis of the election, Clarke et al. found that only 15.6 per cent of Progressive Conservative voters, 9.8 per cent of Liberal voters, and 6.5 per cent of NDP voters cast their ballot on the basis of their party's position on free trade.[29] For the overwhelming majority of voters, then, free trade was not the most important issue in the election, and people did not cast their ballots on the basis of their party's support for, or opposition to, a Canada–US free trade agreement.

A second institutional constraint on the prime minister derives from the role of Opposition parties in the House of Commons. The main role of Opposition parties is to find fault with the government and to provide an alternative choice for Canadians come the next general election. To this end, the Opposition parties use Question Period and other occasions to demonstrate the weaknesses of the current regime, and especially of the prime minister. Each Opposition party puts forward an alternative agenda, including a different foreign policy platform, to be implemented should one of them win the next general election and form the government. Other than putting forward an alternative to the present government and attempting to uncover ministerial misdeeds or departmental indiscretions, there is little that the Opposition parties can do to affect change in Canada's foreign policy.

A final institutional constraint on the prime minister comes from the need to involve the provinces in decision-making. Of particular relevance for our discussion is the constitutional responsibility of the federal government for the "regulation of trade and commerce" (sec. 91(2)), a federal power which has been circumscribed by the courts in interpreting the Constitution. The result is that responsibility for the regulation of trade has been effectively split between federal and provincial levels.[30] In this division of responsibility, the federal government still has a preponderance of power, including the authority to negotiate international trade agreements. But at the provincial level, the provinces have become much more active and aggressive in directly seeking new markets abroad for their goods. This means that the federal government needs to consult provincial actors in determining trade priorities and negotiating positions. In short, the workings of federalism and the need for federal–provincial cooperation in a range of foreign policy-related issues limits somewhat the range of possible choices for a prime minister.

Conclusion

In examining the various constraints under which a prime minister operates, it must be noted that none of them is decisive. None of the constraints discussed present an insurmountable challenge to the authority of the prime minister. All of the obstacles presented herein may be overcome by a prime minister who has the determination and desire to do so: it is a question of political will. A prime minister can use the powers of office to discharge lightning bolts to deal with unplanned events or crises and plan a legacy by focusing on a few key issues. In short, a prime minister who has the will can have his or her way.

Questions for Review

1. Do you agree that the powers possessed by the prime minister are decisive in directing Canada's foreign policy? Why or why not?
2. What other limits may be placed on a prime minister in determining Canada's foreign policy?
3. Discuss the three components of leadership style. Which is the most important? Why?
4. Some have argued that the adoption of the Message Event Proposal by the Harper government has stifled democracy in Canada. Do you agree? Why or why not?
5. Does a lack of experience in international affairs hamper a prime minister's capacity to direct Canada's foreign policy?

Suggested Readings

Kaarbo, Julie. 1997. "Prime Minister Leadership Styles in Foreign Policy Decision-Making: A Framework for Research." *Political Psychology* 18, 3 (September): 553–81.

Kukucha, Christopher J. 2008. *The Provinces and Canadian Foreign Trade Policy*. Vancouver: UBC Press.

Martin, Lawrence. 2010. *Harperland: The Politics of Control*. Toronto: Viking.

Rosenau, James M. 1966. "Pre-theories and Theories of Foreign Policy," pp. 27–92 in R.B. Farrell, ed. *Approaches to Comparative and International Politics*. Evanston, IL: Northwestern University Press.

Smith, Heather A., and Claire Turenne Sjolander, eds. 2013. *Canada in the World: Internationalism in Canadian Foreign Policy*. Don Mills, ON: Oxford University Press.

Notes

1. Donald J. Savoie, *Governing From the Centre: The Concentration of Power in Canadian Politics* (Toronto: University of Toronto Press, 1999).
2. James M. Rosenau, "Pre-theories and Theories of Foreign Policy," in R.B. Farrell, ed. *Approaches to Comparative and International Politics* (Evanston, IL: Northwestern University Press, 1966), 43.
3. From 1909 to 1993, the minister was known as the secretary of state for external affairs and, after 1993, the title became minister of foreign affairs.
4. As cited in Savoie, 319.
5. Paul Wells, *Right Side Up: The Fall of Paul Martin and the Rise of Stephen Harper's New Conservatism* (Toronto: McClelland and Steward, 2006), 296.
6. While the names of the various ministerial positions within the troika have all changed over the years, the troika has consistently comprised ministers responsible for foreign relations (i.e. political, security, and consular issues), international trade, and international development.
7. Charlotte Gray, "New Faces in Old Places: the Making of Canadian Foreign Policy," pp. 15–28 in Fen Osler Hampson and Christopher J. Maule, eds. *Canada among Nations 1992–93: A New World Order?* (Ottawa: Carleton University Press, 1992).
8. Savoie, 137.
9. Susan Delacourt and Bruce Campion-Smith, "Cabinet Shuffle 2013: New Ministers Given 'Enemy' Lists," *Toronto Star*, 15 July 2013.
10. Kim Richard Nossal, Stéphane Roussel, and Stéphane Paquin, *International Policy and Politics in Canada* (Toronto: Pearson, 2011), 239–42.
11. Juliet Kaarbo, "Prime Minister Leadership Styles in Foreign

Policy Decision-Making: A Framework for Research," *Political Psychology*, 18, 3 (1997), 564.

12. Thomas S. Axworthy, "Of Secretaries to Princes," *Canadian Public Administration* 31, 2 (Summer 1988), 247–64.

13. Brent E. Sasley and Tami Amanda Jacoby, "Canada's Jewish and Arab Communities and Canadian Foreign Policy," in Paul Heinbecker and Bessma Momani, eds., *Canada and the Middle East: In Theory and Practice.*(Waterloo, ON: Wilfrid Laurier Press and CIGI, 2007), 189.

14. Stephen Harper, "Prime Minister's Speech for Israel's 60th Anniversary," 8 May 2008. Available at www.pm.gc.ca/eng/media.asp?id=2097.

15. Stephen Harper, "Prime Minister Harper Addresses the 5th Action Party of the Canadian Jewish Political Affairs Committee (CJPAC)," 11 March 2011. Available at www.pm.gc.ca.

16. Ezra Levant, "Stephen Harper and Israel: Not Crass Political Calculation," *Toronto Star*, 29 May 2009. Available at www.thestar.com/news/canada/2009/05/29/stephen_harper_and_israel_not_crass_political_calculation.html.

17. Sasley and Jacoby,189.

18. Levant 2009; Sasley and Jacoby 2007; Darrell Bricker and John Ibbitson, *The Big Shift: The Seismic Change in Canadian Politics, Business, and Culture and What it Means For Our Future* (Toronto: Harper Collins, 2013), 248.

19. Robert Fowler, "Canadian Leadership and the Kananaskis G-8 Summit: Towards a Less Self-Centred Foreign Policy," in David Carment, Fen Osler Hampson, and Norman Hillmer, eds., *Canada among Nations 2003: Coping with the American Colossus* (Toronto: Oxford University Press, 2003), 219.

20. Kaarbo, 565.

21. Kim Richard Nossal, "The Liberal Past in the Conservative Present: Internationalism in the Harper Era," in Heather A. Smith and Claire Turenne Sjolander, eds., *Canada in the World: Internationalism in Canadian Foreign Policy* (Don Mills, ON: Oxford University Press, 2013), 30.

22. Lawrence Martin, *Harperland: The Politics of Control* (Toronto: Viking, 2010), 130.

23. Martin, 36.

24. Tom Flanagan, "'Something Blue....': Conservative Organization in an Era of Permanent Campaign," Paper presented at the annual meeting of the Canadian Political Science Association, Concordia University, June 2010, 9.

25. Tinsley, quoted in Martin, 234.

26. Martin, 273.

27. Donald J. Savoie, "The Federal Government: Revisiting Court Government," in Luc Bernier, Keith Brownsey, and Michael Howlett, eds., *Executive Styles in Canada: Cabinet Structures and Leadership Practices in Canadian Government* (Toronto: University of Toronto Press, 2005), 26.

28. John W. Holmes, *The Better Part of Valour: Essays on Canadian Diplomacy* (Toronto: McClelland and Stewart, 1970), 215.

29. Harold D. Clarke, Lawrence LeDuc, Jane Jenson, and Jon H. Pammett, *Absent Mandate: Interpreting Change in Canadian Elections*, 2nd ed. (Toronto: Gage, 1991), 145–48.

30. See Christopher J. Kukucha, *The Provinces and Canadian Foreign Trade Policy* (Vancouver: UBC Press, 2008).

14 Parliament and Canadian Foreign Policy: Between Paradox and Potential[1]

Gerald J. Schmitz

Key Terms

Arctic Sovereignty

Ballistic Missile Defences

Board of Internal Economy

Committee of Supply and Consideration of Supply

Confidence Motion

Democratic Deficits

Democratization

Expenditure Estimates

Foreign Policy Machinery

Green Paper

International Democracy Assistance

Legitimation

Liaison Committee

Liberal Internationalism

Minority Government

Multilateralism

Multilateral Trade Agreements

Omnibus Bill

Order-in-Council

Paradoxical Actor

Parliamentary Consent

Parliamentary Reform

Parliamentary Supremacy

Party Discipline

Power of the Purse

Private Members' Bills

Public Diplomacy

Representation

Second Reading

Speech from the Throne

Standing Committees

Statutory Enactment

White Papers

Whole-of-Government

Introduction: Parliament as a Paradoxical Actor

These are not happy times for those who believe in a robust parliamentary role in the shaping of Canadian public policy. Long-standing laments about the decline of parliamentary institutions have become louder in recent years. Supreme in theory, Parliament must approve all government legislation and spending. However, the weaknesses in actual parliamentary scrutiny and oversight of, much less control over, executive actions are a common refrain of both media commentaries and the academic literature (for example, Coyne 2013; the chapter on Parliament in Savoie 2013). Those weaknesses have contributed to the view that "Canada's parliament is a **paradoxical actor** with a split image; its powers and potential are belied by perceptions of little actual ability to effect change, especially in the traditionally executive-dominated areas of foreign and defence policy" (Schmitz and Lee 2005, p. 245).

At the same time it is a mistake to dismiss Parliament as an absent or "irrelevant" actor (Rempel 2002) in the making of Canada's international policies. Parliament has had an important if intermittent voice on foreign affairs, has occasionally asserted itself, and has the potential to become a more significant player, as will be explored in the last section of this chapter.

There are a number of structural and systemic reasons why Parliament's role has remained limited and constrained (Nossal, Roussel, and Paquin 2011). For one thing, parliamentarians are rarely called upon to enact legislation in the field of foreign affairs. **Parliamentary consent** is not required for Canadian governments to ratify international treaties and agreements, although any consequential changes in domestic law must pass through the normal legislative process. There is no example of such legislation having been rejected. The organization of the **foreign policy machinery** may require **statutory enactment** or amendment, though not always, as in the case of the Canadian International Development Agency (CIDA), created by **Order-in-Council** in 1968. Its merger into the renamed Department of Foreign Affairs, Trade and Development (DFATD), announced in the March 2013 budget, did require implementing legislation that was included in **omnibus Bill** C-60, passed by Parliament in June 2013. Generally these bureaucratic changes have taken place without prior parliamentary consultation. The exceptional case in which Parliament blocked the government's plans was in 2005 during the minority circumstances of the Martin government. Legislation to split the Department of Foreign Affairs and International Trade (DFAIT) into two separate departments provoked a backlash, and the Opposition parties had the numbers to defeat the

relevant bills at **second reading** in the House of Commons (Schmitz and Lee 2005).

Canadian governments have on occasion chosen to seek parliamentary views on international policy decisions, including the commitment of Canadian troops abroad, even when parliamentary approval is not strictly required. For example, the Harper **minority governments** looked for parliamentary support for the evolving military mission in Afghanistan, though, significantly, they created a high-profile extra-parliamentary panel chaired by former Liberal deputy prime minister John Manley to provide specific advice. The ultimate power to decide still rests with the cabinet, in which prime ministerial dominance has been especially apparent in matters of international affairs. As Nossal et al. (2011, p. 257) observe, "When prime ministers say 'Parliament will decide' issues of international policy they do not actually mean it, for prime ministers have always jealously guarded the prerogative to decide such matters. What they *really* use this formula for is as a refuge from unwanted foreign requests or from uncomfortable domestic political circumstances."

Another factor limiting parliamentary influence is that parliamentary debates on foreign policy have been infrequent and parliamentary votes have been even fewer. Partly this stems from the fact most parliamentarians have not developed expertise in this area, and from partisan and electoral calculations focused more on domestic issues. With the exception of the 1988 federal election in which the Canada–US Free Trade Agreement was a major point of contention, international issues have not garnered much attention during campaigns. That includes Canada's military role in Afghanistan from 2001 to 2011.

More generally, the **expenditure estimates** of the principal government departments and agencies charged with international affairs responsibilities rarely receive substantive scrutiny despite the theoretical **power of the purse**. The high degree of **party**

discipline within the Canadian political system also inhibits the ability of individual parliamentarians to advance independent positions, although this is more true of the House of Commons than of the unelected Senate.

Numerous reforms have been advanced to strengthen the hand of Parliament in matters of foreign and defence policy. Among those commonly advocated are: requirements for parliamentary debates and votes on key decisions including treaties and military deployments; expanded powers and research capabilities for the relevant parliamentary committees to conduct independent investigations and studies; more involvement of these committees in reviewing important government appointments; and better financial reporting to committees endowed with the resources necessary for serious ongoing expenditure oversight. Achieving enhanced accountability remains a complex question, however. In regard to defence policy in which the Crown prerogatives exercised by cabinet are especially strong, a detailed examination of the reforms proposed by Philippe Lagassé (2010, 2013) cautions that these proposed reforms could actually weaken accountability were they to dilute the responsibility of government ministers for executive actions or take away from Opposition parties' rightly adversarial role in critiquing and offering alternatives to existing policies.

The next sections examine the historical record of parliamentary activity in international affairs and the trends that have emerged up to the present day.

A Brief History of Parliamentary Involvement in International Affairs

Major international events have at times precipitated parliamentary debates on foreign policy, notably over issues of war and peace. One can go back to 1919 following the First World War when Conservative Prime Minister Robert Borden's submission of the Treaty of Versailles for House approval encouraged extensive discussion of Canada's role. Parliament's consent is not actually required for the deployment of Canadian forces or even a formal declaration of war, and has not always been sought. The Korean War of 1950, the first Gulf War that began in August 1990, and the coalition invasion of Afghanistan in 2001 are all cases where the Canadian military was sent into action without explicit prior parliamentary approval having been obtained. Nonetheless, Canada's involvement in such conflicts, in military alliances, as well as in numerous United Nations (UN) peacekeeping operations since the Second World War has led to vigorous parliamentary debates.

Beyond events-driven occasions, the means for more regular parliamentary input was gradually introduced. In 1947 External Affairs Minister (later prime minister) Louis St Laurent reported on Canada's foreign policy and invited debate in the context of the presentation of the Department of External Affairs' spending estimates to the House, sitting as the **Committee of Supply**, a practice continued by his successor Lester Pearson. Under **parliamentary reforms** introduced by the Trudeau government in 1968, the government's estimates were automatically referred to the relevant **standing committees**. In 1970 the Trudeau government also set out its foreign policy objectives in a series of formal statements or **white papers** under the rubric of *Foreign Policy for Canadians*. Parliament had little involvement in the development of these policies and there were complaints about fewer occasions for foreign policy debates in the House.

The role of House committees as a primary venue of foreign policy deliberation has grown from very limited origins. (Senate committees will be addressed separately.) In 1924, Prime Minister Mackenzie King's interest in International Labour

Organization (ILO) conventions led to the creation of the Standing Committee on Industrial and International Relations. That committee was replaced in 1945 by a Standing Committee on External Affairs, which in 1968 became the Standing Committee on External Affairs and National Defence (SCEAND). This committee in turn created several subcommittees, for example on international development assistance and, in the early 1980s, on Canada's relations with Latin America and the Caribbean. In 1980, the Trudeau government also established a number of parliamentary "task forces," one of which addressed North–South relations.

Committee activity was significantly boosted by the reforms begun in 1982 and expanded by the Mulroney government elected in 1984. SCEAND was divided into the Standing Committee on External Affairs and International Trade (SCEAIT) and the Standing Committee on National Defence and Veterans Affairs. Of equal importance, the committees were empowered to initiate their own studies without needing a reference from the House (in effect, the cabinet). SCEAIT took advantage to undertake a comprehensive review of Canada's official development policies and programs that resulted in a landmark 1987 report, *For Whose Benefit?* (Morrison 1998). Moreover, committees could now require the government to table in Parliament a comprehensive written response to their reports within 120 days from their presentation to the House. Standing committees could also now review Order-in-Council appointments falling within their purview (e.g., ambassadorial positions in the case of External Affairs), though without any power to reject them.

In addition, the Mulroney government created a new committee process for the purposes of foreign policy review. Rather than issue a white paper setting out its international policy directions, the government released a 1985 **green paper** entitled *Competitiveness and Security* to serve as a discussion document to be studied by a House of Commons and Senate Special Joint Committee on Canada's International Relations, which produced a major report, *Independence and Internationalism*, in 1986. The joint committee's main study was preceded by a series of public hearings held in 1985 on the questions of negotiating a free trade agreement with the United States and Canadian participation in President Reagan's Strategic Defense Initiative ("Star Wars"). The majority view was positive in regard to the former and negative on the latter. The committee process provided an important forum for testing public opinion on these key controversies. (The issue of Canadian involvement in American **ballistic missile defences** would recur in future years. The Martin government rejected any participation in 2005, a decision that has not been revisited.) The recommendations of the Special Joint Committee also led to the statutory creation of the International Centre for Human Rights and Democratic Development (later known as Rights and Democracy) in 1988, with all-party support and the strong backing of External Affairs Minister Joe Clark.

The Mulroney government made a number of important foreign policy announcements in the House of Commons and allowed sometimes lengthy Commons debates on these matters. Still, it was increasingly criticized by the Liberal official Opposition for taking too many decisions without adequate parliamentary and public consultation. Led by external affairs critic Lloyd Axworthy, the Liberal party issued a *Foreign Policy Handbook* prior to the 1993 election that promised a range of measures to "democratize" foreign policy development and decision-making.

The Chrétien government moved quickly to initiate its own parliamentary reviews, creating two special joint committees—one on foreign affairs and one on defence—for the purpose. Each process led to a subsequent government white paper. The report of the Special Joint Committee Reviewing Canadian

Foreign Policy was followed by the publication of *Canada in the World* in 1995. The Chrétien government also created a Canadian Centre for Foreign Policy Development and inaugurated an annual national forum on international affairs, though both proved to be short-lived. Major debates took place in the Commons on Canada's role in UN peacekeeping operations in the Balkans and participation in the NATO bombing of Serbian forces during the conflict over Kosovo. The Standing Committee on Foreign Affairs and International Trade (SCFAIT) was very active during the Chrétien years, encouraged by an activist foreign minister, Lloyd Axworthy. It should be noted, however, that several key early decisions of the Chrétien government—to ratify the North American Free Trade Agreement (NAFTA) and to implement the Uruguay Round **multilateral trade agreements** that established the World Trade Organization (WTO)—were made without much parliamentary discussion. Nor, a decade later, was there parliamentary debate prior to Prime Minister Chrétien's March 2003 announcement in the House of Commons that Canada would not participate in the American-led invasion of Iraq.

After long-time SCFAIT chair Bill Graham became foreign minister in 2002, he undertook a "Dialogue on Foreign Policy" as a mainly extra-parliamentary exercise to reach out to Canadians. The Dialogue was largely ignored after Paul Martin became prime minister and initiated a sweeping internal policy review that resulted in the 2005 *International Policy Statement: A Role of Pride and Influence in the World*. However, the ink was barely dry on that document when the Martin minority government was defeated.

The new Conservative government of Stephen Harper moved consciously in 2006 to distance itself from the policies of its Liberal predecessors without any formal review of its own. Indeed it has issued no foreign policy statements as such, preferring to proceed by actions rather than words. The most prominent international issues debated in the Commons since 2006 have revolved around Harper government priorities (such as the assertion of **Arctic sovereignty**) and major controversies (notably the role of Canadian troops in Afghanistan and the government's decision to withdraw from the Kyoto Accord on climate change).

The Role of the House of Commons and Its Committees

Canadian governments must maintain the confidence of a majority of elected members of the House of Commons at all times. Therefore the House is the primary chamber for holding the government of the day accountable for the conduct of international policy. Almost all members of the cabinet are also drawn from the Commons. Members of Parliament (MPs) have a variety of ways, both individually and collectively, to exercise this oversight role. They may speak in House debates on foreign policy matters, or they may interrogate the responsible ministers in the daily Question Period when the House is sitting, though this adversarial partisan forum has little impact on policy development. Behind closed doors, MPs may advance positions within their respective party caucuses and committees thereof. MPs are also called to debate and vote on government legislation. The chances of Opposition views and amendments influencing legislative outcomes are obviously greater during minority parliaments. As previously mentioned, the Commons killed the Martin government's 2004 attempt to split DFAIT into two separate departments.

Another avenue, albeit one that is rarely successful, is the use of **private members' bills** to try to influence policy. The minority government circumstances that prevailed from 2004 to 2011 did temporarily improve the opportunities for

Opposition MPs to get such bills studied and passed into law. A notable example was the 2008 *Official Development Assistance Accountability Act,* which made poverty reduction and human rights the central focus of Canada's foreign aid, as well as introducing some compliance reporting requirements. Despite negative votes by the Harper Conservatives, the bill was passed with Opposition agreement in the Commons—and at a time when there was still a Liberal majority in the Senate. Nossal et al. (2011, pp. 262ff) argue that although MPs are not foreign policy decision-makers, they can exert "indirect" influence through the important political functions of **representation**, **legitimation**, and education. MPs are supposed to represent the views and interests of their constituents. They may do so through raising these interests in the House and in committee, presenting citizen petitions to the House, and advocating on behalf of constituent concerns in regard to matters of immigration, asylum, consular and trade services, and the like.

The legitimation function provides a test that a majority of MPs support the government's international policies. As we have seen, even when not legally required, successive governments have often sought the benefit of such approval for policy decisions, if sometimes retroactively. There is only one instance—the Diefenbaker government's troubled bilateral Canada–US defence policy in 1963—in which issues related to foreign policy were a factor in the government's being defeated on a **confidence motion** in the Commons.

Legitimation can be seen in a more problematic light when it serves effectively to rubber stamp the government's foreign and defence policy decisions. For example, in the periodic parliamentary renewals of the NORAD continental defence agreement with the United States since the 1960s, non-renewal was never an option. In 2006 the Harper government put an end to these largely symbolic exercises by making the NORAD agreement permanent.

In several senses, the educative function provides the most scope for MPs to influence international policy. And it should be joined with what might be called the investigative function that, more than the study of government spending estimates or legislation, affords Commons committees opportunities to explore foreign policy subjects in detail.

Committee studies can be a means for MPs to improve their knowledge of foreign policy issues and understand and respond to public concerns. These studies involve both learning and listening that leads to more informed deliberation. In addition to requesting ministerial appearances and departmental briefings, committees can undertake independent research. They can receive oral testimony or written submissions from expert witnesses, interest groups, and the public at large. They may travel within Canada and abroad to broaden their perspectives, though any such travel must be authorized by the House, and budgets must be approved by both the Commons **Liaison Committee**, composed of committee chairs, and the **Board of Internal Economy** on which the parties' House leaders sit. Finally, committees may present reports to the House that include considerable analysis as a basis for making recommendations to the government.

The principal Commons foreign policy committee has been SCFAIT and its predecessors. In 2006, under the Harper government's reforms to the committee system, SCFAIT was split into two: the Standing Committee on Foreign Affairs and International Development (SCFAID) and the Standing Committee on International Trade. The latter has had a lower profile, though it became involved in the controversy over the Canada–Colombia free trade agreement about which civil society groups raised serious human rights concerns.

The leadership provided by the committee's chair and her relationship with members of all parties and with the responsible ministers are important factors in the foreign affairs committee's ability to work successfully. During the Chrétien years, SCFAIT was fortunate to have as its chair Bill Graham, a former professor of international law who not only had a great deal of expertise but also enjoyed a trusted stature among committee colleagues and with the relevant ministers. As a result, the committee was extremely active in pursuing in-depth policy studies, sometimes with the explicit encouragement of Foreign Affairs Minister Lloyd Axworthy and International Trade Minister Pierre Pettigrew. While cross-party consensus was not always possible, a determined effort was made to achieve common ground, a pattern continued by Graham's Liberal successors. SCFAIT also created two subcommittees—on International Trade, Trade Disputes, and Investment, and on Human Rights and International Development—the reports of which had to be considered and approved by the main committee before being presented to the House.

The following list indicates the range of international policy subjects addressed by SCFAIT over the decade 1994–2004. (Except for the first, all can be accessed online at www.parl.gc.ca.)

- Reform of the Bretton Woods international financial institutions, principally the World Bank and the International Monetary Fund (1995)
- The role of small and medium-sized enterprises in Canadian international commerce (1996)
- Canadian action to end child labour exploitation (1997)
- Canada and circumpolar cooperation (1997)
- The proposed OECD Multilateral Agreement on Investment (1997)
- Canadian policy on nuclear weapons (1998)
- Canada and the future of the World Trade Organization (1999)
- Review of the *Export Development Act* (1999)
- Canada and the Free Trade Area of the Americas (1999)

- Canada's role in the Kosovo conflict (2000)
- Issues in the Quebec City Summit of the Americas (2001)
- Canadian interests in the South Caucasus and Central Asia (2001)
- North American partnership and Canada–United States–Mexico relations (2002)
- The agenda of the G8 Summit in Kananaskis, Alberta (2002)
- A contribution to the Dialogue on Foreign Policy (2003)
- Canada's relations with countries of the Muslim world (2004)

In addition to lengthy analytical reports, the committee actively addressed specific regional and country situations (Iraq, Burma, Colombia, Sudan, Haiti, and others), as well as specific issues, from international assistance to United Nations bodies through short reports in the form of resolutions presented to the House for adoption. Typically, such reports called on the government to take timely action responding to particular events or urgent situations.

SCFAID remains the most important of Parliament's foreign policy committees and has continued to produce major reports, notably in 2007 on Canada's role in international democracy promotion and in 2008 on Canada's role in Afghanistan. However, before the latter report was released, the House had created a separate Special Committee on the Canadian Mission in Afghanistan which lasted until the 2011 election. The principal Commons committee overseeing defence matters is the Standing Committee on National Defence (SCOND), known as this since 2006 when Veterans Affairs was split off to form its own standing committee. As previously noted, national defence has been treated separately from foreign affairs in the House committee system since 1984. Many of the committee's subsequent studies touch on important international policy questions: Canada's role in military alliances (NORAD, NATO) and collective security more generally; the role of the Canadian Forces in UN peace operations; the deployment of Canadian military personnel and assets in external combat operations (during the First Gulf War, in the Balkans, in Afghanistan, and in Libya); and the defence of Canada's claims to Arctic sovereignty. SCOND has also addressed matters of internal defence policy, such as military procurement, that have significant international implications—notably the ongoing controversy over whether Canada should acquire the costly F-35 fighter aircraft (Vucetic and Nossal 2012–13).

One of the most contentious international defence issues of the past decade has concerned the treatment of Afghan detainees handed over to the Afghan government by the Canadian Forces. It was dealt with by the aforementioned temporary special committee, consuming most of its attention following explosive allegations in testimony before it by senior diplomat Richard Colvin in November 2009. He claimed the government knew, or should have known, that many transferred detainees were at risk of abuse and torture. This set off a firestorm of criticism from Opposition MPs over the inadequacies of the bilateral agreement governing such transfers and ministerial responsibilities related to Canada's international obligations. Opposition MPs then used their House majority to pass motions calling for a public inquiry (none was ever set up) and to demand uncensored access to all relevant documents. Prime Minister Harper's decision to prorogue Parliament at the end of 2009 was criticized as an evasive measure. Pressure intensified again in April 2010 when the Commons Speaker ruled that, as a matter of parliamentary privilege, MPs have the right to un-redacted documents. At the same time, he gave a deadline for an all-party solution that would not compromise security or confidentiality. After a partial deal was reached in May 2010 (the New Democratic Party refused its consent), a special

panel of MPs and an independent panel of jurists began reviewing the thousands of documents.

Notwithstanding all of this parliamentary activity, one can question how much sustained influence on foreign and defence policy development Parliament has actually had, or how often it has impacted government decisions in any significant way. Indeed, in regard to the Afghan detainees controversy, many documents have yet to be released in less-censored form, and SCOND did not take up the issue after the 2011 election. Overall, the role of MPs to date exhibits persistent weaknesses and prompts new concerns that deserve further elaboration. But first it is important also to consider the role played by their counterparts in the Senate.

The Role of the Senate and Its Committees

The Canadian Senate was designed to be a body based on regional representation which would act as a chamber of "sober second thought"—a brake on the passions of the elected House of Commons and a check on flawed or hastily passed legislation. Although money bills cannot be introduced in the Senate, all legislation must be approved by it before receiving royal assent and becoming law. Once appointed for life, Senators now hold office until age 75. This security of tenure, it is argued, allows them to rise above short-term partisan considerations and also to devote themselves to long-term studies of policy matters.

Fundamentally, however, as an appointed patronage body, often used by prime ministers to reward party supporters, the Senate faces a major problem of democratic legitimacy. The spending scandals that erupted during 2013 have further eroded its standing with the Canadian public and renewed pressures for systemic reform or, failing that, abolition.

That said, the Senate has performed some significant functions in international policy. A Committee on External Relations was first established in 1938 and has been in continuous existence, becoming the Standing Committee on Foreign Affairs and International Trade in 2006. Some of the in-depth studies undertaken by this committee have clearly influenced the policy environment. A notable example, under the chairmanship of Liberal Senator George van Roggen, were the committee's reports on Canada–US trade relations issued over a four-year period of study from 1978 to 1982. The committee came to the conclusion that it was in Canada's interest to negotiate a comprehensive free-trade agreement with the United States. Although the Trudeau government did not follow this advice, as Nossal et al. (2011, p. 260) point out, "the Senate committee made an important contribution to the shift in thinking about free trade that occurred in Canada in the mid-1980s, particularly the positive report of the Royal Commission on the Economic Union and Development Prospects for Canada (the Macdonald Commission)."

An interesting follow-up to this is that when the Turner Liberals strongly opposed the bilateral trade deal negotiated by the Mulroney government and hoped to use their Senate majority to stall its approval, Van Roggen resigned as chair in protest. One could argue that the Senate's role in the political battle over the Canada–US free-trade agreement helped to precipitate the 1988 election in which it was a central issue. Nevertheless, given the Senate's undemocratic nature, it was still widely seen to lack the legitimacy to thwart the will of the Commons. (Given the much-publicized scandals of 2013 and uncertain prospects for reform, it seems highly unlikely that the current Senate would obstruct legislation passed by the House.)

Defence policy questions were dealt with less regularly, sometimes through a subcommittee or a separate standing or special committee, until the creation in 2001 of the Standing Senate Committee on National Security and Defence (SCONSAD). Under the chairmanship of Liberal Colin Kenny, this committee achieved a significant public profile, aggressively pursuing issues of adequate defence spending, preparedness to counter external threats, and Canada's military role in Afghanistan, and producing reports that were sharply critical of both Liberal and Conservative governments.

An ongoing weakness, however, is that the government can simply ignore these reports. (Unlike with Commons committee reports, there is no requirement to make a formal written response.) A case in point on the foreign affairs side was that committee's extensive study of development assistance to Sub-Saharan Africa, conducted under the chairmanship of Hugh Segal, who had a considerable international policy background. The resulting controversial report (Standing Senate Committee on Foreign Affairs and International Trade 2007) that was strongly critical of existing patterns of aid and of CIDA's operations fell on deaf ears. Indeed, Segal was subsequently removed as chair by the Conservative leadership, raising questions about the degree of Senate committee independence from partisan control.

Individual senators have been prominent advocates on international issues—for example, former Progressive Conservative Senator Douglas Roche on nuclear disarmament and recently retired Liberal Senator Roméo Dallaire on the plight of child soldiers—owing mainly to their exceptional backgrounds. Senators have also contributed to several foreign and defence policy review exercises, as examined next.

Parliament and Foreign Policy Reviews

The idea of an overall examination of Canada's international policies emerged in the Trudeau era (although Canada–US relations were curiously exempted from its initial articulation), and the attention given to domestic national interest considerations in foreign policy formulation opened a space for more parliamentary and public discussion. Both House and Senate committees undertook hearings in 1968–69, notably on NATO and NORAD membership, and these may have persuaded a skeptical Trudeau to maintain the alliance status quo. Still, Parliament remained a secondary player, with Bland and Rempel (2004, p. 55) lamenting it "was hardly consulted during the so-called 1968–69 defence and foreign policy reviews."

That changed with the Mulroney government, which introduced reforms to empower backbench MPs and then handed the task of reviewing Canada's international relations to a special joint committee of the House and Senate. The committee held hearings across the country as well as in Ottawa, and heard from hundreds of witnesses over the course of a year. Its 1986 final report, *Independence and Internationalism*, did have at least one concrete result as already mentioned, namely the creation of Rights and Democracy (since abolished by the Harper government in 2012 without parliamentary consultation). However, most observers deemed the results to be unremarkable and underwhelming. Moreover, the process had the weakness that the work of the special committee, promptly disbanded after delivering its report, rapidly disappeared from view with no means of follow-up as the standing committees had not been involved.

A decade later the Chrétien government similarly bypassed the standing committees in creating two special joint committees to undertake separate foreign policy and defence reviews. (These parallel processes unfortunately never intersected, and neither gave much attention to the 1994 Rwandan genocide or the first terrorist attack on New York's World Trade Center the previous year.) Again, numerous witnesses were heard from and hearings were held from coast to coast, but the committees disbanded with their 1994 reports having a modest impact at best.

A senior DFAIT official involved with the 1985–86 review drew the lesson that: "Effectiveness will depend on Parliament's ability and willingness to hold the government responsible for implementing policy recommendations that arise from outside the bureaucracy. Ultimately, even limited democratization of foreign policy making cannot be effective without the strong leadership of the minister of foreign affairs who is responsible for making it happen" (Page 1994, p. 597). Joe Clark in the 1980s and Lloyd Axworthy in the 1990s were activist foreign ministers who clearly welcomed the participation of Parliament, even if officials did not. Nevertheless, the ambitious proposals of the 1993 Axworthy-authored *Foreign Policy Handbook* were scaled back in the course of the 1994 review. Indeed, a noted analysis of it and the subsequent Chrétien government white paper *Canada in the World* concluded that the "weakest sections . . . have to do with the engagement of Canadians on policy formulation and implementation" (Malone 2001, p. 575). The national forums on international policy ceased after a few years, and the Canadian Centre for Foreign Policy Development was quietly terminated by the Martin government in 2004. Axworthy's "human security" agenda sought to engage civil society actors—notably in efforts to ban landmines and to create the International Criminal Court—but owed little to parliamentary inspiration.

After SCFAIT chair Bill Graham became foreign minister, his 2003 "Dialogue on Foreign Policy" largely bypassed the committee he had led, which never took up the Dialogue's *Report to Canadians*. The Martin government then chose not to involve Parliament in the development of its 2005 *International Policy Statement* (IPS), although the relevant committees were invited to study it. SCFAIT did experiment with an electronic public consultation on the IPS and hold a few hearings on it, activities that were cut short by the defeat of the minority government. The Harper government subsequently removed the IPS documents from the departmental websites.

In short, given the episodic and ephemeral nature of government foreign policy review exercises, parliamentary participation in them has not had a deep or lasting impact on policy, nor has it contributed to creating a sustained parliamentary capacity for influencing the ongoing conduct of Canada's international relations.

Parliamentary Influence under the Harper Government

The Harper government has sought consciously to distance itself from the **liberal internationalist multilateralism** associated with its Liberal predecessors (Nossal 2013), declaring what it calls a "principled foreign policy" anchored in Canadian values and interests. The government has put less emphasis on the United Nations, has expressed strong support for Canada's armed forces and military alliances, and given unwavering support to Israel, eschewing any neutral "broker" role. These differences can be exaggerated. Although Harper had criticized the Chrétien government's refusal to participate in the 2003 invasion of Iraq, Canada never joined the US-led coalition. It was the Martin government that sent combat troops to Kandahar in 2005 and the Liberal Opposition that pushed for a special Commons committee on the Canadian mission in Afghanistan in 2008, subsequent to which the Harper government seemed anxious to end Canada's military role by 2011. The government's initial strong criticism of China on human rights grounds has been much moderated, with Chinese state investment being welcomed into the Canadian energy sector.

The Harper minority governments initiated no foreign policy reviews and were not marked by any dramatic moves. The government did encourage SCFAID's comprehensive study of Canada's role in **international democracy assistance** and broadly embraced the committee's 2007 report which, among other things, recommended a new Canadian entity for that purpose. After the 2008 **Speech from the Throne** promised its creation, the government appointed an expert panel (chaired by a prominent Liberal, Tom Axworthy), the 2009 report of which elaborated proposals for a well-funded agency. However, the government then dragged its feet, and when the highly publicized troubles afflicting the board of Rights and Democracy in 2010 created a negative atmosphere of partisan discord, the idea was abandoned (Schmitz 2013).

During these years, Opposition parties had a majority on committees, which influenced their agendas while having little discernible effect on government policy. Indeed, parliamentary and NGO critics charged that the government was not interested in their views or in wider public consultations. Controversial decisions to defund KAIROS, an interchurch coalition on international development, and the Canadian Council for International Cooperation, were protested to no avail. Canada's role in Afghanistan was the subject of several Commons debates, the last in 2008. However, it was greatly scaled back in 2011, with little parliamentary or public discussion of how, or even whether, to sustain Canadian engagement in Afghanistan's long democratic transition (Schmitz 2011). It could be argued that a partial exception was the 2009–10 controversy over the alleged abuse of Afghan detainees (see the section on the role of the House) in that testimony before a House special committee on the Afghan mission provoked vigorous debate, forcing the government's hand and leading to an important Speaker's ruling affirming MPs' right to obtain uncensored documents. Still, there has been no public inquiry, and the issue has had minimal parliamentary follow-up since the 2011 election, despite many documents remaining unreleased.

The Harper majority government has not shown any inclination to reach out to a diversity of views or to give parliamentary committees significant scope for independent inquiry, as was the case under the Mulroney majority governments. Indeed, indications are that committee agendas are more than ever controlled from the centre, with partisanship prevailing over the search for cross-party consensus that had been a hallmark of foreign affairs committee activity. This more partisan atmosphere seems to have affected the Senate as well.

It is troubling to think that there is less political space for committee members to explore new international policy directions, much less challenge existing ones, across party lines. After all, governments are always free to reject committee recommendations, and majority governments in particular should not feel threatened by committee work. If committee chairs and members have less independence to pursue inquiries, if their deliberations are more circumscribed or confined to scripted talking points, the educative and investigative functions of this parliamentary activity will surely suffer accordingly. Unless creative committee activity is valued and promoted, it will lose public visibility (SCFAID has never undertaken cross-country hearings) and have increasingly marginal influence in the policy process. This means that the government—and party leaders—must agree to allow committees the scope to undertake innovative work and to allocate sufficient resources for that purpose. Of course party positions on foreign policy issues will differ. But committees should never become mere echo chambers for familiar partisan divisions.

The Harper government has not sought parliamentary or public views prior to a number of foreign policy decisions. Although in a 2010 report, SCFAID members of all parties strongly supported a continued role for Rights and Democracy (Conservatives and Opposition members differed on what was responsible for its administrative troubles), the organization's termination was abruptly announced in the March 2012 Budget. This required repealing the 1988 statute passed during the Mulroney government, which was expediently done as a single sentence in the massive omnibus budget implementation bill without any referral to SCFAID. Such was the fate of a body that owed its existence to a parliamentary committee recommendation under a previous Conservative majority (Schmitz 2013). In 2013, the government announced the establishment within DFAIT of an Office of Religious Freedom, without the benefit of any public consultations or parliamentary hearings, notwithstanding the sensitive issues it might confront. After the March 2013 Budget announced that CIDA would be merged into DFAIT, legislation to create the consolidated department was adopted by the Commons in June 2013. If some welcomed the potential for more coherence among foreign policy, trade, and international development instruments, others worried that the Harper government's emphasis on private sector development and Canadian commercial interests (such as in the overseas mining sector) could weaken the priority given to poverty reduction as mandated in the ODA Accountability Act. Although SCFAID at least held several hearings on the matter, parliamentary influence on the government's direction seems likely to be slight.

Democratic Deficits and Prospects for Parliament's Potential Role

This chapter began with the image of Parliament as a paradoxical actor in which the theory of **parliamentary supremacy** and executive accountability is contradicted in reality by cabinet and, in particular, prime ministerial control over the policy agenda and decision-making, nowhere more so than in international affairs. Writing during a time of parliamentary review, David Taras (1985, p.16) observed that:

> The pressures brought by the domestication of foreign policy have had little impact on formal relations between the executive and Parliament in Canada. . . . The executive still has exclusive control over the levers of decision-making despite a change in attitude among parliamentarians, a shift in the domestic and international political climates, and some reform in Parliament's foreign policy machinery. Parliament's influence has depended on idiosyncratic variables; the right issue, the right minister, the right timing. There has been little consistency or constancy. At best, Parliament is a participant in the decision-making process, one among a number of institutions and forces that can have impact.

A Canadian Study of Parliament report released a year earlier (1984, p.12) had pinned its hopes for parliamentary committee influence in foreign affairs on: "An energetic and non-partisan chairman, a minister . . . willing to support and encourage the inquiry, a small but knowledgeable staff, objective and serious committee members, and the capacity to sustain an inquiry over the several years that might be necessary to complete it." Such ideal circumstances have been rare indeed. More often, Commons committees have been constrained, with unstable memberships that inhibit continuity. Moreover, even when ambitious reports have been produced, there has typically been little subsequent committee follow-up to press the government on implementing recommendations, including all-party ones. And the parliamentary scrutiny of the government's international spending estimates, although it provides opportunities to question ministers and senior officials, has been mostly a ritual exercise.

The efforts from the 1990s onward to "**democratize**" foreign policy and to address **democratic deficits** have disappointed proponents and led to further critical assessments (Cameron and Molot 1995, Potter 1996, Neufeld 1999, McCormick 2006). Government willingness to seek parliamentary and public support for its international positions and to go through the motions of consultation were seen as not having much effect on actual decisions. Parliamentary roles remained limited and parliamentarians also had to compete with a widening circle of NGOs and civil society actors wanting a voice in international policy deliberations (Stairs 2000). Historian John English (1998, p. 79), a member of the Special Joint Committee Reviewing Canadian Foreign Policy and subsequent SCFAIT subcommittee chair, recounted a telling anecdote from the "National Forum" that preceded the 1994 reviews:

> Someone asked the chair: "Who are those people at the back?" She replied sternly: "They are Members of Parliament. They may stay but they cannot speak." Although NGO representatives and academics were vocal, Canada's elected representatives were stifled. The ambiguity of public representation was clear.

The past decade has not witnessed any lasting advance in the ability of parliamentarians to exert policy influence, despite periods of significant committee activity. And except in tightly controlled circumstances, the current Harper government appears disinterested in parliamentary, public, expert, or other forms of consultation. The government has also slashed funding for **public diplomacy**.

Although the Martin government's ostensibly **whole-of-government** IPS was a wholly within-government exercise, it had promised annual updates to Parliament by the foreign affairs minister. That rather minimal step might have stimulated a more regular process of Commons debates and committee review. Years before, Lloyd Axworthy, in his first appearance as foreign minister before SCFAIT (1996), had optimistically envisaged the committee acting "to reinforce the role of Parliament in opening up foreign policy and bringing more Canadians into a dialogue of our role in changing times" through "an annual, revolving review of what is important on a year-to-year basis."

In principle, it is now commonly accepted that as Canadians increasingly have a stake in the world beyond Canada's borders, their involvement and that of their elected representatives should be actively encouraged in the development of policies that relate Canada to the world—that international

affairs cannot be left as a privileged preserve of executive power. Public engagement in international policy development might also aim to be more inclusive of the voices of women, youth, Aboriginal peoples, and minority communities that have often been under-represented.

Government attitudes towards Parliament will have to change, and the institutional mechanisms of parliamentary accountability, oversight, and investigation significantly strengthened, if Canadian foreign policy is to be developed and conducted as if parliamentary democracy truly matters. The potential to move beyond paradox awaits that possibility.

Questions for Review

1. What are the principal ways that Canadian parliamentarians can try to exercise oversight and influence in the making of foreign and defence policy?
2. How have these parliamentary roles changed over time?
3. What are the main differences between the House of Commons and the Senate in this regard?
4. How would you describe the relationship between the cabinet and Parliament in matters

of international affairs? Are there examples when Parliament has been successful in holding the government of the day accountable for its international policy decisions?
5. How are current trends affecting the ability of Parliament to play a significant international policy role?
6. Could strengthening the role of Parliament enhance Canada's international relations? If so, how?

Note

1. The author wishes to thank all those who spoke with him as background in the preparation of this chapter.

References

Bland, Douglas, and Roy Rempel. 2004. "A vigilant Parliament: Building competence for effective parliamentary oversight of national defence and the Canadian Armed Forces." Institute for Research on Public Policy, *Policy Matters* 5, 1 (February).

Cameron, Maxwell A., and Maureen Appel Molot, eds. 1995. *Canada Among Nations 1995: Democracy and Foreign Policy.* Ottawa: Carleton University Press.

Canadian Study of Parliament Group. 1984. *Parliament and Foreign Affairs.* Ottawa: Canadian Study of Parliament Group and Canadian Institute of International Affairs.

Coyne, Andrew. 2013. "Repairing the House: How to make Members of Parliament relevant again." *The Walrus* 10, 8 (October), 26–30.

English, John. 1998. "The Member of Parliament and foreign policy," pp. 74–79 in Fen Osler Hampson and Maureen

Appel Molot, eds. *Canada among Nations 1998: Leadership and Dialogue*. Toronto: Oxford University Press.

House of Commons Standing Committee on Foreign Affairs and International Trade (SCFAIT). 1996. *Evidence* (16 April). Ottawa: SCFAIT.

Lagassé, Philippe. 2010. *Accountability for National Defence: Ministerial Responsibility, Military Command and Parliamentary Oversight*. Montreal: Institute for Research on Public Policy Study No. 4 (March). Available at www.irpp.org/en/research/security-and-democracy/account-ability-for-national-defence.

———. 2013. "How Canada goes to war." *Ottawa Citizen*, 4 December.

Malone, David. 2001. "Foreign policy reviews reconsidered." *International Journal* 56, 4 (Autumn): 555–78.

McCormick, James. 2006. "Democratizing Canadian foreign policy." *Canadian Foreign Policy* 13, 1: 113–31.

Morrison, David. 1998. *Aid and Ebb Tide: A History of CIDA and Development Assistance*. Waterloo: Wilfrid Laurier University Press.

Neufeld, Mark. 1999. "Democratization in/of Canadian foreign policy: Critical reflections." *Studies in Political Economy* 58 (Spring): 97–119.

Nossal, Kim Richard. 2013. "The Liberal past in the Conservative present: Internationalism in the Harper era," pp. 21–35 in Heather A. Smith and Claire Turenne Sjolander, eds. *Canada in the World: Internationalism in Contemporary Canadian Foreign Policy*. Don Mills, ON: Oxford University Press.

Nossal, Kim Richard, Stéphane Roussel, and Stéphane Paquin. 2011. "The role of Parliament." Chapter 10 of *International Policy and Politics in Canada*. Toronto: Pearson Canada.

Page, Donald. 1994. "Populism in Canadian foreign policy: The 1986 review revisited." *Canadian Public Administration* 37, 4 (December): 573–97.

Potter, Evan. 1996. "Widening the foreign policy circle: Democratization or co-optation?" *Bout de papier* 13, 1 (Spring): 14–16.

Rempel, Roy. 2002. *The Chatter Box: An Insider's Account of the Irrelevance of Parliament in the Making of Canadian Foreign and Defence Policy*. Toronto: Breakout Educational Network.

Savoie, Donald J. 2013. *Whatever Happened to the Music Teacher? How Government Decides and Why*. Montreal and Kingston: McGill-Queen's University Press.

Schmitz, Gerald. 2011. "Ongoing dilemmas of democratization: Canada and Afghanistan." Chapter 13 of David Gillies, ed. *Elections in Dangerous Places*. Montreal and Kingston: McGill-Queens University Press.

———. 2013. "Canada and international democracy assistance: What direction for the Harper government's foreign policy?" Centre for International and Defence Policy, Occasional Paper No. 67. Kingston: Queen's University (August). Available at www.queensu.ca/cidp/publications/occasionalpapers.html.

Schmitz, Gerald, and James Lee. 2005. "Split images and serial affairs: Reviews, reorganizations and parliamentary roles," Chapter 14 of Andrew Cooper and Dane Rowlands, eds. *Canada among Nations 2005: Split Images*. Montreal and Kingston: McGill-Queen's University Press.

Stairs, Denis. 2000. "Foreign policy consultations in a globalizing world." Institute for Research on Public Policy, *Policy Matters* 1, 8 (December).

Standing Senate Committee on Foreign Affairs and International Trade. 2007. *Overcoming 40 Years of Failure: A New Road Map for Sub-Saharan Africa*. Ottawa: Senate of Canada (February). Available at www.parl.gc.ca/Content/SEN/Committee/391/fore/rep/repafrifeb07-e.pdf.

Taras, David. 1985. "From bystander to participant," pp. 3–19 in David Taras, ed. *Parliament and Canadian Foreign Policy*. Toronto: Canadian Institute of International Affairs.

Vucetic, Srdjan, and Kim Richard Nossal. 2012–13. "The international politics of the F-35 joint strike fighter." *International Journal* 68, 1 (Winter): 3–12.

15 The Institutionalization of Foreign Affairs (1909–2013)[1]

Patrice Dutil

"The Department of External Affairs is becoming more and more a branch office of a huge expanding bureaucracy."

–Charles Ritchie, Canadian Ambassador to the United States, 1962.[2]

Key Terms

Capacity

Undersecretary of State

Does bureaucratic structure matter? A number of people thought so in 2004 when the Martin minority government tabled two bills in the House of Commons (C-31 and C-32) to sever the Department of Foreign Affairs and International Trade (DFAIT) into two ministries. The approach was inspired by the concern that the two missions of the department were at odds, specifically that pure "trade" pursuits were undermined by diplomatic concerns or a distracting human rights agenda. Suddenly, the structure of a bureaucracy had become a hot political potato in the House of Commons, blogs, newscasts, and editorial pages. It mattered because the institutional shape of the department said something about its mission and about its expectations. The critics won and the bills were defeated in the winter of 2005.

The department's structure again became a political issue when the Harper government unexpectedly announced in 2012 that Canada would "pool" some of its services abroad with those of the British government. The idea was that a Canadian presence would be more likely in countries where Canada had been previously absent, and, at the same time, Canada would host British services. It was a simple, structural collaboration designed to save a few dollars, but quickly proved unpopular: many considered it inappropriate for Canada to underplay its image abroad. It smacked of an old-time colonial arrangement.

Structure again reared its head in the spring of 2013 when the government announced that the Canadian International Development Agency (CIDA) would be merged with DFAIT. The government argued that the amalgamation would create a better alignment of foreign relations, trade, and development projects that would give Canada's approach to the world more coherence and vigour. The critics—and there are always critics when it comes to Canada's approach to foreign policy—feared that Canadian aid would henceforth be subsumed by the hard-edged strategic and trade relation priorities of the much larger department. After all, CIDA had been, since its inception in 1968, somewhat of an arm's-length agency of the government so as to show that its pursuits in helping developing countries would not be politically motivated. Now this would change, and the government announced that the foreign affairs ministry would be called the Department of Foreign Affairs, Trade and Development (DFATD).

These three episodes of the past decade are illustrative of how policy actors concerned about Canada's relations with the world have debated the manner in which policy and service have been "institutionalized" by DFAIT's bureaucracy. *Institutionalize* in this case refers to the bureaucratic structures that were created to deliver reliable and stable foreign policy advice and service. Over the years, the government of Canada has moved from a highly personal approach to foreign policy (i.e., the prime minister) to one that entrusted a team of specialists—everybody from policy analysts in the Lester B. Pearson building on Sussex Drive in Ottawa to protocol officers, trade representatives, ambassadors, and consulate staff in provincial capitals around the world—to provide advice that was mindful of precedents and that was consistent, knowledgeable, and professional.

Prime ministers, who remain the key actors in the articulation of foreign policy, have grown to rely on it, but have often had trouble trusting the Department of External Affairs (as it was called for much of its history). While the department found its footing in its early years, Prime Minister Borden repatriated a young outsider, Loring Christie, a Canadian working in the United States government, to provide Borden directly with advice on foreign policy.[3] Borden's successor, Mackenzie King, encouraged a sophistication of the department but was often suspicious of the bureaucracy. John Diefenbaker never fully overcame his reservations

about the department. Even his successor, Lester Pearson, who had practically spent his entire career at External Affairs, either as an employee or as its minister, often had doubts about its advice. This had a lingering impact on even the youngest recruits. "Nobody, not even the undersecretary, was able to say if Canada had an overriding goal or goals in its foreign policy," remembered James Bartleman about his budding career in 1966.[4]

Then it got worse. When Pierre Trudeau came to power in 1968, he openly said to department officials that their ideas were as outdated as their methods and, like Borden many years before, hired a personal advisor (Ivan Head) to help him steer foreign affairs.[5] His Liberal successor, Jean Chrétien, was never comfortable with the organization and recruited his own diplomatic advisors, including James Bartleman, who left an account of this particular experience. Stephen Harper inherited that approach. It seems that only Louis St Laurent, Lester Pearson, and, to a great extent, Brian Mulroney, found a way to work effectively with the department.[6] The St Laurent years were described as a golden period, and the Mulroney period was febrile with activity around the globe.

Even the staff complained about the department. It was a mixed blessing that, while the department has continuously attracted brilliant minds, it also recruited writerly candidates. Many of them (vastly more of them than any other department) have written books and scholarly articles about their experiences, and the external afairs bureaucracy hardly ever comes off in a good light, even with the benefit of nostalgia. Allan Gotlieb's ambassadorial diaries of the 1980s often display frustration with the department's apparent inertia.[7] John Kneale and James Bartleman described the department in the 1990s as suffering "a deep malaise"[8] and as being "demoralized."[9]

Prime ministerial and staff suspicions aside, "External" and then "Foreign" developed an enviable reputation that endures in large part because of the way it was structured. People who study it and its role in defining Canada's international relations inevitably ponder why some decisions are made, are delayed, or indeed never made. In part, the answer lies in the philosophical predispositions of the political leadership that dominates a state. Secondly, answers are found in particular circumstances. For instance, crises provoked abroad necessarily focus thinking and prompt decision-makers to take a position they would not normally rush into. Thirdly, decision-making depends on a level of comfort and confidence that prime ministers and ministers have in the advice and feedback they receive from fellow politicians, Parliament, the media, and their constituents. Finally, it also depends critically on the advice they receive from the public service, and in Canada the staff in the Department of External Affairs, the Department of Foreign Affairs and International Trade, and ultimately the Department of Foreign Affairs, Trade, and Development has played a key role in advising and in executing the foreign policy of Canadian governments.

This chapter examines the structural evolution of this department since its incarnation in 1909. The purpose is to identify the key points of expansion and contraction in over 100 years of evolution and to demonstrate how the department "institutionalized" the government's priorities by translating key objectives into bureaucratic responsibilities. In this sense, the shape of the department took on the features required of it in response to what was expected from it by the prime minister, his cabinet, and the minister responsible. As government required more advice on more questions, it expanded certain divisions. Similarly, as Canadians travelled further and more often for both business and pleasure, the department extended its presence and ability to provide service. These changes reflected changing priorities, different sensitivities, and different preoccupations.

Building Capacity: 1909–1941

In terms of structure, Canada's external relations were nothing more than a concern of the prime minister and a handful of officials from the first summer of Confederation until the turn of the twentieth century. There were relatively few decisions to make, and those were often determined in London, where the British government spoke on behalf of the Commonwealth. With the 1900s, however, particularly over issues of trade and boundaries, the Laurier government felt the need for more rigour and better policy-making in dealing with other countries. It created a Department of External Affairs in 1909 that would be headed by a cabinet minister designated as Secretary of State for External Affairs (SSEA)—Charles Murphy. The whole "department" was so small that it fit neatly above a barber shop on Sparks Street. The undersecretary (or senior public servant for the department) was Joseph Pope, a man who had served Sir John A. Macdonald as personal secretary and then Sir Wilfrid Laurier as a senior official. Pope had long argued that Canada's external affairs needed continuous attention: "The present state of our external affairs can only be described by the one word 'chaotic,'" he wrote in his diary in the fall of 1908.[10]

In 1912, Prime Minister Robert Borden formally assumed the role of Secretary of State for External Affairs, and the undersecretary was made to report directly to the prime minister, a practice that would be sustained by the following four prime ministers (Borden, King, Meighen, Bennett) until 1946 (and, briefly, by John Diefenbaker in 1957). Pope would continue to manage the small department, but in a manner that increasingly seemed out of step with the policy demands of a government emerging from the searing experience of the First World War. He left his functions in 1924 after decades of selfless service, but the department he left behind had "not the shadow of a system, and things . . . [were] in a continual muddle."[11]

The first 30 years of the Department of External Affairs were marked by a very personal, informal, and indeed idiosyncratic style of administration. It depended almost exclusively on the personality of the undersecretary, and for most of those years that was Joseph Pope, and then Oscar D. Skelton, a Queen's University economist who was invited by Mackenzie King in 1925 to succeed the retiring Pope. Skelton, who was focused on building the department's **capacity** to investigate foreign policy issues and to advise the government on the best options for Canada, instituted a competitive hiring system for foreign service officers that included country-wide exams and interviews. Skelton personally recruited in the 1920s and 1930s some of the most highly-regarded public servants of the twentieth century. While the department developed an unparalleled reputation for its intelligent advice and energetic approach to files and issues, it was also known to be very poorly administered. This inevitably led to frustration, compounded by the fact that the department consistently had to manoeuvre in order to secure the attention of its busy minister, the prime minister of Canada, who insisted that most decisions be cleared with him first.

Canada's foreign policy in the 1930s was often confused and especially puzzling for the public servants who had to help define and act on it. Mackenzie King was a careful politician who did not like to act unless he had no choice. As an individual, King trusted few people, and certainly did not always trust the diplomats he had agreed to hire. Though its senior executives worked tirelessly, morale was reported as low. It was, as one employee put it, "a small, ramshackle Department where eccentricity was tolerated and where everyone was a generalist who flew by the seat of his pants."[12] One diplomat complained in the late 1930s that the department was in a "woeful state" as it was unable to be decisive in recruiting new people and overly conservative in

its approach to a host of issues.[13] O.D. Skelton—a brilliant thinker and strategist—could not administer the department beyond a "normal haphazard way."[14] Lester Pearson, who joined the department in 1928, described the office in the 1930s as "a hive of unorganized activity—the senior men are so busy that they haven't time . . . to delegate work to juniors who are, in consequence, not busy enough. I find, however, that very real and sincere attempt is being made to reorganize the Department . . . . I am not sanguine, however, that this scheme will achieve the decentralization essential for the speedy and effective conduct of departmental work."[15] This would be a recurring theme. "Lord, how I would like to be given the job of pulling External Affairs & the Foreign Service apart & putting it together again, with a few pieces left out," wrote Lester Pearson in 1935, during a posting in London.[16]

Waging War and Managing Peace: 1941–1951

O.D. Skelton died in harness in 1941 and was replaced by another imaginative policy advisor, Norman Robertson, who had joined the department in 1927. Upon Skelton's death, Escott Reid, who joined the department in 1938, wrote a long memorandum arguing for "a new conception" of DEA: "We must become a planning, thinking, creative body and not be content merely to solve day-to-day problems as they arise."[17] That opinion was widely shared, especially as Canada waged war on an unprecedented scale. Robertson launched a reorganization of the department to put it on a more professional footing that would respond to wartime demands. At a time when Canada's external relations—and the autonomy King so cherished—were tested by the shifting alliances brought about by global war, Robertson felt ill-suited to manage a large department. He often asked the prime

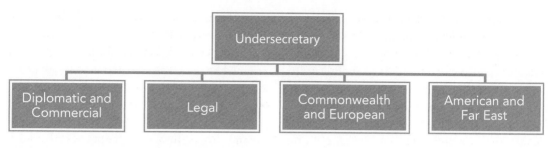

Figure 15.1 Secretariat of State for External Affairs, 1941

Source: John Hilliker, *Canada's Department of External Affairs, Vol 1: The Early Years, 1909–1946* (Montreal and Kingston: McGill-Queen's University Press and the Institute of Public Administration of Canada, 1990), p. 243.

minister to reassign him to a job that suited him better, but nevertheless oversaw a frenetic expansion and reorganization of DEA.

Robertson assumed leadership of a department that in 1940 had 44 officers and 328 support staff. Within three years 14 new foreign missions were opened. By 1944, the department had 72 foreign service officers and 474 employees, and administered 20 foreign delegations. It also acted as the principal liaison to the 20 embassies that were installed in Ottawa (there had been five before the war). The department's structure was formalized in 1941 (see Figure 15.1) with a clear hierarchy. Four assistant undersecretaries reported to the **undersecretary of state** for external affairs. Each of their divisions, in turn, brought together 10 sections.

But Robertson was not satisfied with the structure. As wartime demands intensified, he continued to expand its functions. Within a few years (see Figure 15.2), the department was headed by an

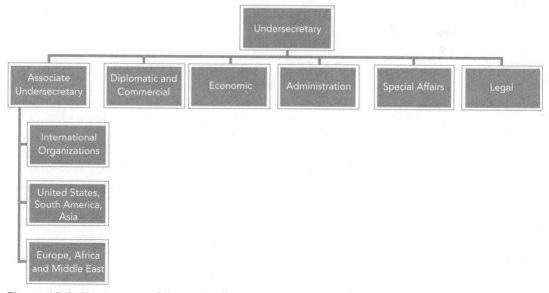

Figure 15.2 Department of External Affairs, 1945

Source: J.L. Granatstein, *"A Man of Influence": Norman A. Robertson and Canadian Statecraft, 1928–1968* (Ottawa: Deneau, 1981), p. 195.

undersecretary and an associate undersecretary. Reporting directly to the undersecretary were five divisions: diplomatic, economic, legal, special affairs, and administration. Three political divisions—one responsible for international organizations; a second for European, African, and Middle Eastern affairs; and a third for the United States, South America, and Asia—reported first to the associate undersecretary. Robertson also instituted a rudimentary training program for new recruits and appointed a full-time personnel officer to manage human resource issues.

That structure would be inherited by Lester Pearson when he became undersecretary late in 1946 (almost coinciding with Prime Minister King handing off external affairs to a minister, Louis St Laurent). Pearson was determined to improve the organization of the department by hiring more employees at a time when, according to Escott Reid, "a revolution took place in Canadian foreign policy," as Canada broke out of its traditional isolationism and asserted itself in the postwar world of the United Nations and the beginnings of the Cold War.[18] In 1948, Pearson's last full year as the top public servant, the first annual report was issued, outlining the progress of the department. It reported the department had 1,213 employees, including 216 foreign service officers.

As Canada joined the United Nations and its associated agencies and later confronted the Cold War through membership in the North Atlantic Treaty Organization, more and more men (there were very few women) were hired by the department to follow files, investigate issues, and prepare policy proposals. The rest of the 1940s and 1950s were years of "consolidation and strengthening both of the organization at home and of existing establishments abroad."[19] The department also emphasized the co-management of issues with the Department of Trade and Commerce, again both at home and abroad. Canada launched consular offices

in the United States, for instance, and the trade work previously carried on by the Department of Trade and Commerce in Chicago and San Francisco was assumed by the Consulates General. In countries where Canada had no established diplomatic missions, the consular functions of the Department of External Affairs were carried on by the Trade Commissioners. To facilitate the process, a committee on which both departments were represented was established to "consider common problems relating to Foreign Service, and to ensure the close co-ordination of effort abroad."[20]

In comparison with O.D. Skelton's long tenure, the leadership at DEA changed relatively often in the late 1940s. Pearson moved into politics in 1949 and immediately was named to cabinet by Prime Minister St Laurent as the secretary of state for external affairs. His deputy, Escott Reid, briefly assumed the mantle until Arnold Heeney was named to the post of undersecretary in March 1949 with the expectation that he would bring to the post the "emphasis on organization and administration in the Department which his predecessors at times tended to overlook."[21] Heeney, it was worth noting, earned a salary of $15,000 (about $152,000 in today's dollars, or about half what many deputy ministers earn in Ottawa today).[22] The money was well spent, as Heeney pushed forward on even greater expansion to organize external affairs to deal with Cold War concerns. A Defence Liaison Division was created to monitor Cold War developments. In 1950, a finance division was established to provide for a closer scrutiny of expenditures. Sections dealing with international conferences and supplies and properties were also set up, while the Archives unit and the Library were incorporated in a new Reports and Research section. The department was now spread across many buildings: the East Block still housed the most senior staff, but others were posted in the Langevin Block and other buildings in downtown Ottawa.

Cold War Department: 1951–1968

Working with an ambitious secretary of state for external affairs in Lester Pearson and a prime minister who wished Canada to be active on the world stage, Heeney built a larger bureaucracy (see Figure 15.3). As the undersecretary, he created more hierarchy to funnel decision-making. He maintained the role of deputy undersecretary and added three assistant undersecretaries. Escott Reid, as deputy undersecretary, was responsible for the United Nations, as well as the "American and Far Eastern Division."

An Office of Historical Research and Reports and a secretariat for "special studies" were created and made to report to Reid directly. Charles Ritchie, as assistant undersecretary, was responsible for defence liaisons, "information," and the European division. Jules Léger, the first French Canadian to attain this level of seniority in the department (he would later be named undersecretary in 1954), looked after the functional divisions: "America and Latin America" and the Commonwealth, in addition

to diplomatic concerns such as the "consular division," the "protocol division," and the "supplies and properties division," which reflected Canada's growing external presence. In 1953, Canada staffed 21 embassies, nine legations, six high commissioners' offices and eight consulates or consulates general. As the Cold War raged through the last half of the 1950s, Canada added 14 more embassies, 4 legations, 9 high commissioners' offices, and 13 consular offices in Asia, Latin America, and Eastern Europe. According to Escott Reid, there were 276 heads of missions and foreign service officers by the end of that decade (and no less than 37 of them had written books by 1989).[23]

An interesting feature in the breakdown of responsibilities was the policy concern of the United States. Responsibilities were shared in a way that left no doubt on what side Canada fought the Cold War, but the structure of Canada's external affairs department was confused. Indeed, the Far Eastern and Latin American divisions both included "American" concerns. One assistant undersecretary, for example, looked after his own American and Far East Division policy areas as well as an economic division and an

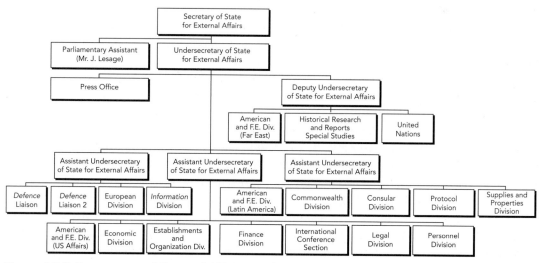

Figure 15.3 Department of External Affairs, April 1952

Source: Department of External Affairs, *Annual Report*, 1953.

establishment and organization division. In addition, he was responsible for administrative divisions such as finance, international conference management, legal, and personnel.

The senior management structure that featured a deputy undersecretary and three assistant undersecretaries reporting to the undersecretary of state was maintained through these years, concentrating responsibility in a remarkably small group of men who had worked alongside each other for decades. The leadership of DEA was drawn from within, never from outside. Earl Drake joined the department in 1953 and left an insightful account of his first impressions. "My first boss in External Affairs," he remembered, "was an Ontario Anglophone, stern, pedantic, bitter, and without a discernible spark of humour or humanity. He seemed to take a sadistic pleasure in criticizing everything I wrote and in rejecting every idea I put forward. I was terribly discouraged and ready to resign after the first six months." Drake then worked for Marcel Cadieux, a future undersecretary: "[W]orking for [him] was very satisfying but I feared that he was an exception, not the norm."[24]

External Affairs was evidently a place that demanded rigour but that frowned on freewheeling discussions, particularly among younger recruits. "When I see the tired, aging men who are my friends and who work in the Department I think it as well that I don't have to face that ordeal [of "buttoning up their nature"]," wrote Charles Ritchie. "There is something wrong here but it is the same thing that it has always been—overwork, the panic desire to escape before they get too old, and the fascination of being in the centre of things, these pulling in opposite directions. I know that dilemma and I have no desire to go through it all over again."[25] Nevertheless, the department kept a steady course through the 1950s as Arnold Heeney's structure seemed to respond to the needs of the government, and growth was steady, if uneven. In 1956, as

Canada's secretary of state for external affairs (Pearson) spearheaded the idea of a United Nations peacekeeping force to resolve the Suez Crisis, a communications division and a Middle East Division were created in the department in order to support Pearson's efforts.

If Louis St Laurent gave external affairs its "golden years," the department had reason to be despondent with his successor, John Diefenbaker, who was troubled by the external affairs bureaucracy. He saw in it the "Pearsonalities"—the lifelong friends of the adversary he faced in the House of Commons on most days: Liberal leader Lester Pearson. For a time, Diefenbaker hesitated in even naming a secretary of state, assuming the job himself for a few months like the prime ministers before 1947. Diefenbaker asked that a "financial adviser" and an "Inspection Service" be added to the bureaucratic structure in 1958, signalling that he wanted the government to keep closer oversight on how the department managed its funds. In 1960, a new division was created to monitor "Africa and the Middle East," a reflection of the prime minister's hostility to the apartheid regime in South Africa and his growing interest in the area. In 1963, a special branch was created to deal with Congo affairs, and an entire division was erected to cater exclusively to issues related to the United States (as relations with the Kennedy administration had grown turbulent).

The department also added personnel to respond to the demand for services. In 1961, for instance, it welcomed 66 new people, and in 1962 the passport division was formally added to the structure, showing that the processing of personal data had become an increasingly important activity as Canadians began to travel in unprecedented numbers.

The changes to the so-called Heeney structure grew more dramatic following the release, in April 1963, of the report of the Royal Commission on Government Organization (the Glassco Commission). The commission focused one of its studies (Report

21) on the Department of External Affairs, examining both its headquarters in Ottawa and its missions abroad. The commission made a number of recommendations that were well received by external, and a number of steps were taken to improve the department's performance. A revised and broadened training program for foreign service officers, which was conceived towards the end of 1962, was in full operation within a year. This included advanced French language training for certain foreign service officers at Laval University. Steps were also taken to improve existing departmental machinery to promote and facilitate the use of either the English or French language in departmental correspondence at the option of the author. In addition, a training unit was established in the personnel division to provide training for administrative staff proceeding abroad.

An Administrative Improvement Unit was established, and better management techniques were adopted. Human resource planning strategies were installed. Studies of the existing and future needs of the department for specialist staff were launched. The department also assumed more authority in deciding how it would allocate its resources, although this was done in close consultation with the staff of the Treasury Board.

The reforms developed even faster after the Pearson government took office in 1963 and the economy recovered. The *détente* in the Cold War made opening new missions in Eastern Europe possible, while decolonization in Africa, the Caribbean, and Asia demanded an appropriate response (and new missions) from Ottawa. The number of countries with which Canada maintained diplomatic relations had increased from 41 to 84. During this period, the number of Canadian diplomatic and consular posts abroad had risen from 53 to 77. Of these, 44 were embassies, 12 were high commissioners' offices, 6 were permanent missions to international organizations, and 15 were consulates or consulates general.[26]

In 1964, the department's recruiting was intensified for almost all classes. Increasingly, the bulging department was spread across Ottawa: the East Block still housed the most senior staff, but others were posted in the Langevin Block and other buildings in downtown Ottawa.

As the number of personnel grew, the department pursued an aggressive programme of acquiring real estate assets abroad to house embassies, consulates, and key personnel. In 1963 alone, it was engaged with the Department of Public Works in 16 projects concerned with the planning, construction, or alteration of chanceries, official residences, or staff quarters. In addition, the department pursued 47 furnishing schemes for accommodation either owned by the Canadian government or held by the government on long leases.

Perhaps the most important improvement in the department's organization was in the registry's records management. Progress in paperwork and records management was most noticeable during the year in the registry field. Last but not least, the department adopted a new filing system, designed to provide headquarters and personnel abroad with a uniform records-classification system.[27]

This was an important new development. Derek Burney, who joined in the summer of 1963, remembered the process of absorbing intelligence, and his recollection of the department in those days was indicative of where priorities lay and how knowledge was organized. "External Affairs still thrived on reporting," he wrote. "Dispatches of greater and less moment poured in daily from all parts of the globe to be analyzed, summarized, and, for the most part, filed by the responsible desk or division. Reports from major embassies got broader and more significant distribution in Ottawa and to her embassies. Instructions flowed from headquarters; replies and reports came from the embassies."[28]

Not least, the department launched a new attempt to improve its accounting by installing mechanisms to ensure better reporting of how money was spent, but progress was slow. In 1966, the department appointed an experienced officer as financial management advisor to develop a more sophisticated financial management program, and efforts were made to tie funding deliberately to individual programs so as to improve accountability and improve "long-term planning, budgetary reporting and control accounting systems."[29] An Organization and Methods Unit was established to "improve the department's management and operating procedures,"[30] the Supplies and Properties Division was strengthened and the Personnel Division was divided into a Personnel Operations Division and a Personnel Services Division. The Personnel Operations Division was to be "responsible for recruitment, establishment, training, research, and employee services, and the Personnel Services Division, with promotions, postings, and career planning." The administrative divisions of the department were regrouped under a single assistant undersecretary for administration. Perhaps the most important new measure was the introduction of more efficient and simplified accounting procedures, which were put into use at all missions abroad in 1964.[31] In 1967, an expert in computer techniques was lent to External Affairs by Treasury Board to ascertain ways in which computer services might be employed by the department; the possibility was

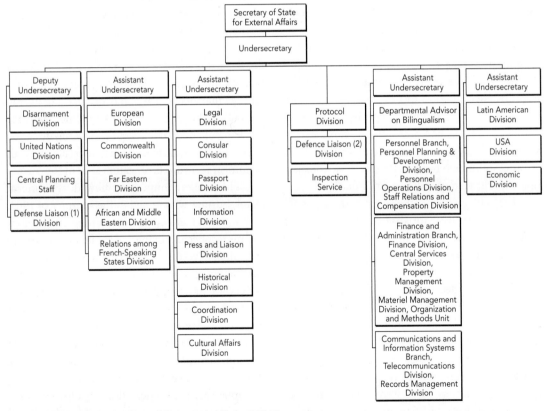

Figure 15.4 Department of External Affairs, 1968

Source: John Hilliker and Donald Barry, *Canada's Department of External Affairs, Vol. 2: Coming of Age, 1946–1968* (Montreal and Kingston: McGill-Queen's University Press and the Institute of Public Administration of Canada, 1995), p. 415.

explored of "computerizing" such routine work as the keeping of cumulative records of expenditures and the maintenance of detailed inventory listing of furnishings and equipment at headquarters and posts."[32]

By the time Lester Pearson ended his term as prime minister in April 1968, over 700 officers worked at External Affairs under a structure that was vastly expanded in terms of scope. There were still four assistant undersecretaries in addition to the deputy undersecretary. Two worked on recognizably "country files" while the two others focused on administrative issues and processes such as information, passport, personnel, and communications. Of interest here was the rise of a cultural affairs division, a reflection of the fact that Canada, in preparation for the *Man and His World* (Expo '67) exhibition, had recognized that its culture could be an instrument of diplomacy and useful in supporting its image around the world. In terms of country files, the files on Latin America and the US were brought into closer proximity, reporting to one assistant undersecretary (AUS). Indicative of its links with the Americas file, the economic division also reported to the same AUS. The rest of the globe was the purview of another AUS. The deputy undersecretary focused on more strategically pivotal files such as central planning, defence liaison, the United Nations, and disarmament.

New Priorities: 1968–1982

Even before he assumed the prime ministership, Pierre Trudeau was known to have been critical of External Affairs, but his arrival did not halt the modernization efforts of the department. Indeed, a major expansion of the department took place in the 1970s as Trudeau's search for a "Third Option" to develop relations with the world beyond the superpowers was made operational.

Two new sections were created in 1969 to help the department strategize. A manpower planning and forecasting section assumed the responsibility for advising senior management on the qualitative and quantitative requirements for human resources.[33] The second new section was the information systems division. Its communications and information systems branch consisted of three divisions—telecommunications, records management, and information systems. Typical of all bureaucracies in the 1970s, the department added dramatically more support staff and systems to improve its machinery of policy analysts and diplomats. Perhaps more important, the department assumed its own audit and accounting functions as a result of amendments to the Financial Administration Act in 1969, which assumed all the more importance when it was called to cut its budget in 1970.[34]

But there were other structural changes that reflected Canada's concern with the USSR and Canada's relations with its allies: arms control was added to the disarmament division in 1970, and a new division was created to concentrate on North American defence and NATO. Finally, a division was created to focus on the emerging movement to bring francophone nations into some sort of international alliance, and a new division was shaped to facilitate international policy on "scientific relations and environmental problems."

A Central Services Division was created to integrate a variety of common support services and to ensure adequate office space, furnishings, and equipment at headquarters, including general building alterations and maintenance. Another priority was knowledge management: as the department continued to grow, a Communications and Information Systems Branch was created, bringing the existing Records Management Division and Telecommunications Division under common direction.[35]

A departmental Training and Development Committee was formed early in 1970 to review and advise the senior committee on training and development policy, needs, priorities, budgets, and content of programs. The most welcome news, however was that the government approved the building of a new headquarters for External Affairs, and in 1973, the department moved into the Pearson Building on Sussex Drive, away from its historically proximate location near the Prime Minister's Office. John G. Kneale, who started work in the summer of 1973, wrote that the Pearson building "was a perfect physical expression of the idea that foreign policy is arcane, secret, and not for public consumption. There is no fresh air in the place, either intellectually or atmospherically. It is inbred. Those who work in the building must also eat in the building with one another, since the nearest restaurant or fast food place is a fifteen-minute walk away, and this too fosters an inward-looking, monastery-like environment."[36]

The explosion in branches in the Pearson building was even more dramatic the following year as new portfolios were unveiled to monitor issues and advise the government on issues as varied as "transport communications and energy," "commercial policy," "academic relations service," "security and intelligence liaison," "foreign travel and removal service," "materiel management," "property management," and "telecommunications." In 1971, a fifth assistant undersecretary was created, followed by a sixth in 1974 and a seventh in 1977 to help manage the rapidly growing department. The creation of a Consular Affairs Bureau reflected the new priority of managing these files in a consistent manner. The creation of a NATO and NORAD Division, which married two existing divisions, reflected the desire to integrate the two files.

In 1978, the senior ranks were transformed. Reporting to the undersecretary of state for external affairs were now five deputy undersecretaries and four assistant undersecretaries, as well as the Chief Air Inspector and the Inspector General. Reporting to this cadre were 26 branches that contained anywhere between one and six bureaus. The largest of these was the Passport Office.

The expansion of the department did not equate to better foreign policy advice, as far as the government was concerned, largely because most line departments were now establishing their own international affairs departments. The task of maintaining liaisons with departments to ensure consistent advice had always been a key—and exhausting—function of the department of external affairs. In the past, key relationships were particularly nurtured with the departments of finance, trade and commerce, and defence. As the department grew in numbers and size to respond to a growing international agenda, they also recognized that their concerns had international dimensions, making the task of ensuring consistent and knowledgeable advice all the more demanding.

The Trudeau government wanted a better coordination of policies affecting foreign relations and a better integration of the management, programming, and resource allocation processes for foreign operations. It also wanted to stem the tide of other departments setting up their own "external" activities and wished to see external affairs play a better role in coordinating the Canadian government's activities abroad. To this end, Trudeau named Allan Gotlieb to the position of undersecretary of state for external affairs on the understanding that the department would assert its role as a sort of central agency that would coordinate the government's actions abroad. A committee of deputy ministers on foreign and defence policy was established in 1980 to replace the Interdepartmental Committee on External Relations (ICER). The new committee of deputies, chaired by Gotlieb to demonstrate its elevated importance, had a mandate to review major policy and expenditures issues referred to it by cabinet committee, or prepared by departments for cabinet committee.[37]

International relations in the 1970s changed dramatically with the introduction of regular summits among leaders. The ease of air travel and, equally important, the sophistication of television broadcasts made summitry politically advantageous for political executives around the world. Prime Minister Trudeau travelled the globe regularly, as did many of the ministers. The Commonwealth became more active, and the Group of 7 nations began regular meetings in 1975, with Canada joining the following year. Summitry greatly reinforced the prime minister's role in foreign policy and ensured that he, rather than the secretary of state for external affairs, remained the most important actor.

The Integration of Trade and Diplomacy: 1982–1993

The department boasted over 5,000 employees (1,450 positions at headquarters, 1,250 employees in the field and another 2,375 locally hired people) and a budget of almost $400 million when the Trudeau Liberals were returned to government in 1980 and embarked on a revamping of the department.[38] In what turned

out to be the most dramatic reorganization, the Trudeau government amplified DEA's mandate in 1982 by entrusting it with the "trade" responsibility of the Department of Industry, Trade and Commerce (which simply became Industry Canada). The Department of External Affairs was given responsibility for trade policy and trade promotion along with the traditional area of foreign policy and functions related to immigration. The new trade policy units of the Department were mandated to work closely with the regional offices of the Ministry of State for Economic and Regional Development and the Department of Industry, Trade and Commerce/ Regional Economic Expansion. As a result of this reorganization, all foreign service officers from the Canadian International Development Agency, trade commissioners, and Canadian Government Office of Tourism employees would be fully integrated into the Department of External Affairs, along with the trade policy and trade promotion sections of the former Department of Industry, Trade and Commerce.

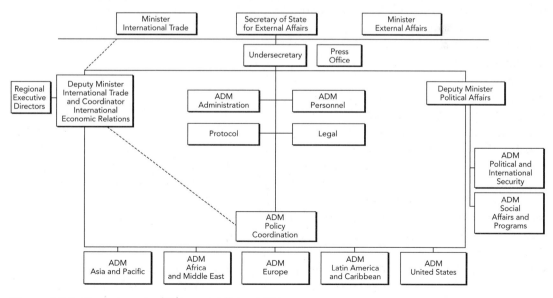

Figure 15.5 Department of External Affairs, 1984

Source: Department of External Affairs, *Annual Report*, 1985.

The 1982 reorganization announced a departure for the government of Canada's foreign policy. While the Cold War was waged in the form of arms races between the United States and the Soviet Union and various proxy wars in Asia, Africa, and South America, the government openly tied its foreign policy focus to trade. In the words of the department itself, the intention was to "give greater weight to economic factors in the design of foreign policy, to ensure that the conduct of foreign relations served Canadian trade objectives, to improve the service offered exporters in an increasingly competitive international marketplace and to ensure policy and program coherence in the conduct of Canada's whole range of relations outside of the world."[39]

Within months, the bare bones of a new structure were in place, but it would take years to fill out the department. External Affairs and Trade would be headed by the undersecretary, as before. Reporting to him (no woman has ever served as undersecretary) were deputy ministers: a deputy minister for international trade to manage trade and economic matters, and a deputy minister (political affairs) to oversee all other matters regarding Canadian policies and programs in the regions. The responsibility for all geographically formed policies and programs was invested in five new geographic branches, each headed by an assistant deputy minister (Africa and Middle East, Asia and Pacific, USA, Europe, and Latin America and Caribbean). These ADMs, in turn, were also responsible for the management both of the posts in their regions abroad and their branch at headquarters. The purpose of creating these five geographic branches was to provide clear accountability for regional and bilateral policies and operations, and to improve the development of coherent policies and programs across the full range of departmental activities.[40]

Changes continued in the department as the Mulroney government was installed in 1984. That year,

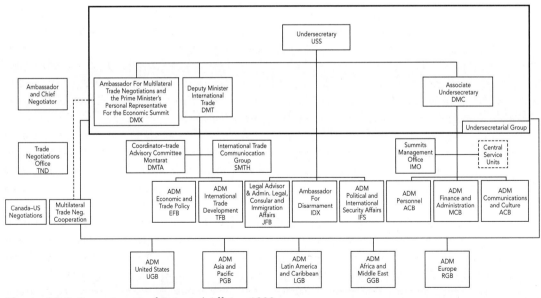

Figure 15.6 Department of External Affairs, 1988

Source: Department of External Affairs, *Annual Report*, 1989.

the Policy Development Secretariat, headed by a sixth ADM, was renamed the Policy Development Bureau and reorganized to include three divisions: political and strategic analysis, economic and trade analysis, and cabinet liaison and coordination. Its purpose was to lead a foreign policy review but also to monitor international economic and political developments and relevant long-term trends. It would play a critical role in coordinating policy responses and drafting speeches. The cabinet liaison division was mandated to manage cabinet submissions emerging from the department and to respond to cabinet submissions made by other departments. A year later, this division was moved into the Corporate Management Bureau.[41] By 1987, there were 13 assistant deputy ministers. Eight of them were responsible for a wide range of integrated portfolios: economic and trade policy; international trade development; legal, consular, and immigration affairs; an ambassador for disarmament; political and international security affairs; personnel; finance and administration; and finally, communications and culture. Five more were responsible for the traditional geographic portfolios.

DEA changed with the times. As the Cold War subsided and then disappeared in the early 1990s, new challenges emerged. The Mulroney government negotiated a free trade agreement with the United States, calling in no small part on the resources of the department. Derek Burney was hired out of the department to assume the role of principal secretary to the prime minister, and Allan Gotlieb, a former undersecretary of state for external affairs, played a key role as Canada's ambassador to the United States (he would continue to serve as ambassador under the Mulroney government). Its role was diminished in this case, as the negotiations were led by a specially designed team of mostly former Department of Finance officials. In 1990, Canada declared war on Iraq (its second declaration of war in history—the declaration of war on Hitler's Germany was the first) and was involved in the Balkan conflict that

ultimately led to the demise of Yugoslavia. In both those cases, it was the Department of National Defence that assumed the lead response, as it would again in the invasion of Afghanistan following the attack on a NATO partner on 11 September 2001.

Globalization and Retrenchment, 1993–

As part of a major reorganization of departments in 1993, DEA was renamed the Department of Foreign Affairs and International Trade (DFAIT). But with the mid-1990s also came a serious challenge to the budget of the department. The 1995 Statement *Canada and the World* announced that the department would create two new bureaus to deal with "global" change. Another a key aspect of the foreign policy of the 1990s was Canada's support for the campaign in favour of a larger "human security" agenda that included ending the enlistment of children in militias, removing anti-personnel landmines, and establishing an International Criminal Court. That policy agenda relied on Canada's "soft power" to convince key stakeholders to sign on and highlighted its importance. In this regard, DFAIT played a somewhat reluctantly supportive role to a minister who invested himself heavily in ensuring that the landmines agreement (the "Ottawa Treaty") was ratified.[42] The other marked conflict pitted Canada and the European Union, particularly Spain, over the Atlantic fisheries. DFAIT played an assistive role on this issue again, as the lead was assumed by Fisheries and Oceans, egged on by an energetic and motivated minister.

The austerity measures imposed on all aspects of government by the 1995 budget hit the department particularly hard. The DFAIT budget was slashed by 15 per cent in 1995–6, and similar reductions were imposed in the next two years. Programs were rationalized and hundreds of employees took up early retirement or agreed to leave government.[43]

In 2006–7, DFAIT undertook a strategic review of its operations. It committed to posting more people abroad and to focus on key strategic interests, including 25 "priority" countries: four countries and territories "of immediate interest" (Afghanistan, Haiti, Sudan, and the West Bank and Gaza) and five international organizations. At that time, Canada had 174 missions in 110 countries. Part of the impulse was to bring some balance to the ratio of Ottawa-based staff to staff overseas, which stood at 2:5 to 1 in 2007 (a far greater concentration of employees in the capital in comparison with other countries).

The grand structure of the late 1980s can be only dimly perceived today. Two deputy ministers now head the department, one for general policy and one focused on trade issues. (At the time of writing it was not clear to what rank the international development responsibility would be entrusted, but it is very likely to be at the deputy minister level, thus creating a rather odd structure with potentially three deputies answering to the minister.)

In contrast to the vast upper echelons of the 1980s, in 2012, eight assistant deputy ministers were responsible for a mixture of geographic, corporate, and policy concerns (see Figure 15.7). Four of the eight divisions are headed by an assistant deputy minister who is also charged with broad cross-sectional concerns and geographic bureaus. The ADM responsible for international security, for instance, is the political director of the department. The individual serving as ADM on global issues is the chief foreign policy officer. The chief security officer is the ADM in charge of consular services, and the chief trade commissioner is also the ADM for international business development. That division, perhaps not surprisingly, is focused on the new markets of the Far East and the Indian subcontinent. Another innovation brought in by the Harper government was the Office of Religious Freedom, placed in the global issues portfolio. The priority that has been accorded to developing free trade agreements with Europe and with India find their place as distinct branches within the Trade Policy and Negotiations Division. Passport Canada, the office that most likely touches the average Canadian, was spun off as an agency that reports to the deputy minister of foreign affairs. Strangely, the National Capital Commission (NCC), an agency of the Government of Canada that manages the physical presence of the government of Canada in the city of Ottawa, was entrusted to DFAIT in 2011 (not shown in the organizational chart below).

Perhaps most telling in the structure of DFAIT is the continued presence of a Transformation Office. This office was created in 2008 to lead the thinking over the shape the department is to assume in order to manage the issues of the future. The clear-cut structure of the past no longer responds to the fluid and complex issues of the twenty-first century, where traditional trade issues now mix with environmental, human rights, and broad political concerns on a wide plane. Canada belongs to many international groups and consequently places heavy "summitry" demands on the prime minister and cabinet that must be managed by the department, in concert with the Office of the Prime Minister and the Privy Council Office. Global issues require sophisticated communications practices and innovative approaches. While it is too early to tell what impact the amalgamation of CIDA and DFAIT into DFATD will have on either Canada's developmental efforts abroad or on its strategic relations or its trade priorities, there is no doubt that this new institutional approach will have lasting consequences. Figure 15.7 features a deputy minister position reserved to head up "development," but it is not clear if this will indeed be the final structure. Clearly, an entire bureaucracy devoted to development would also be reporting to this individual (its structure is unknown at the time of writing).

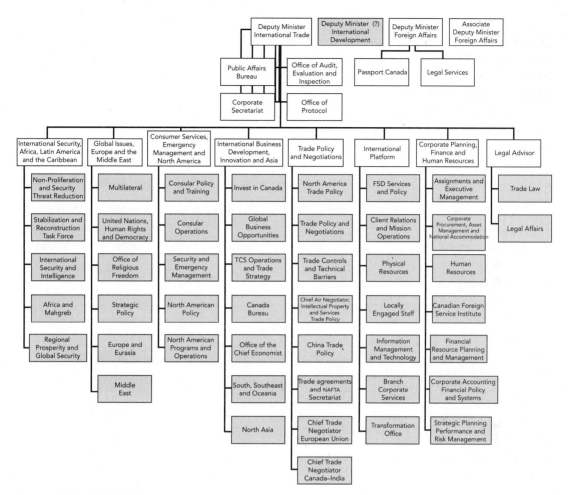

Figure 15.7 DFAIT 2012

Source: Originally retrieved from www.dfait-dfe.gc.ca.

Conclusion

The structure of the Department of External Affairs has grown consistently over its 100-year history, and it can be argued that form has often followed purpose. It has been mostly headed (there were exceptions, particularly in the 1980s) by career foreign service officers. With the exception of the 1982 integration of "trade" and the 2013 addition of international development, the growth of the bureaucracy was organic. While it has always reflected its policy pursuits along geographical lines, a greater concern over the past 40 years has been the integration of knowledge and operations over the century. First relying on exceptional minds that could scope the complexity of a handful of issues, it has evolved into a sophisticated institution that relies on systems to collect and then make sense of vast amounts of information.

The current incarnation of DFATD is the product of a slow and steady bureaucratic evolution.

Starting with a handful of men 100 years ago, men who were mostly concerned with Canada's relationship to Great Britain and the United States, it employs over 13,000 people today, deployed to all parts of the world as well as Ottawa. In 2012, it spent over $2 billion on a daily menu of activities that range from thinking about the loftiest questions of international politics, including war and peace, to routine matters of communications with Canadians at home and abroad, and managing real estate. The DFATD machine is important and thus continues to be the subject of constant tinkering that sometimes becomes controversial. How well its leaders manage to finesse the department's ability to do the right thing at the right time continues to be a subject of debate and ultimately will determine its success.

Questions for Review

1. What prompted the changes made to the structure of the department of external affairs over the past century?

2. To what degree does the bureaucracy shape foreign policy?

3. To what degree does the structure of the bureaucracy shape the sort of advice it offers to the government and the service it gives to the public?

Suggested Readings

Bartleman, James. 2004. *On Six Continents: A Life in Canada's Foreign Service, 1966–2002.* Toronto: McClelland and Stewart.

Bartleman, James. 2005. *Rollercoaster: My Hectic Years as Jean Chrétien's Diplomatic Advisor, 1994–1998.* Toronto: McClelland and Stewart.

Bothwell, Robert. 1988. *Loring Christie: The Failure of Bureaucratic Imperialism.* New York: Garland.

Burney, Derek. 2005. *Getting It Done: A Memoir.* Montreal and Kingston: McGill-Queen's University Press.

Donaghy, Greg, and Kim Richard Nossal, eds. 2009. *Architects and Innovators: Building the Department of Foreign Affairs and International Trade, 1909–2009.* Montreal and Kingston: McGill-Queen's University Press.

Drake, Earl. 1999. *A Stubble-jumper in Striped Pants: Memoirs of a Prairie Diplomat.* Toronto: University of Toronto Press.

English, John. 1989. *Shadow of Heaven: The Life of Lester Pearson, Vol. 1: 1897–1948.* Toronto: Lester and Orpen Dennys.

English, John. 1992. *The Worldly Years: The Life of Lester Pearson, Vol. 2: 1949–1972.* Toronto: Alfred Knopf Canada.

Gotlieb, Allan. 2006. *The Washington Diaries, 1981–1989.* Toronto: McClelland and Stewart.

Granatstein, J.L. 1981. *"A Man of Influence": Norman A. Robertson and Canadian Statecraft, 1928–1968.* Ottawa: Deneau.

Head, Ivan. 1995. *Shaping Canada's Foreign Policy, 1968–1984: The Canadian Way.* Toronto: McClelland and Stewart.

Hilliker, John. 1990. *Canada's Department of External Affairs, Vol. 1: The Early Years, 1909–1946.* Montreal and Kingston: McGill-Queen's University Press and the Institute of Public Administration of Canada.

Hilliker, John, and Donald Barry. 1995. *Canada's Department of External Affairs, Vol. 2: Coming of Age, 1946–1968.* Montreal and Kingston: McGill-Queen's University Press and the Institute of Public Administration of Canada.

Kneale, John G. 1993. *Foreign Service.* North York, ON: Captus Press.

Smith, Denis. 1988. *Diplomacy of Fear: Canada and the Cold War, 1941–48.* Toronto: University of Toronto Press.

Reid, Escott. 1989. *Radical Mandarin: The Memoirs of Escott Reid.* Toronto: University of Toronto Press.

Ritchie, Charles. 1983. *Storm Signals: More Undiplomatic Diaries, 1962–1971.* Toronto: Macmillan.

Notes

1. The author thanks Greg Donaghy, Head of the Historical Section of the Department of Foreign Affairs and International Trade, and David MacKenzie, Professor of History at Ryerson University, for their insightful comments and suggestions on an earlier draft of this text. Mathew Horvatin was a great help in research.

2. Charles Ritchie, *Storm Signals: More Undiplomatic Diaries, 1962–1971* (Toronto: MacMillan of Canada, 1983), p. 19.

3.   On Christie, see Robert Bothwell, *Loring Christie: The Failure of Bureaucratic Imperialism* (New York: Garland, 1988), and Margaret MacMillan, "Sir Robert Borden: Laying the Foundation," pp. 29–40 in Greg Donaghy and Kim Richard Nossal, eds., *Architects and Innovators: Building the Department of Foreign Affairs and International Trade, 1909–2009* (Montreal and Kingston: McGill-Queen's University Press, 2009). On Ivan Head, see John English, "Two Heads are Better than One: Ivan Head, Pierre Trudeau and Foreign Policy" in the same book, pp. 239–252. See also Head's own book: *Shaping Canada's Foreign Policy, 1968–1984: The Canadian Way* (Toronto: McClelland and Stewart, 1995).

4.   James Bartleman, *On Six Continents: A Life in Canada's Foreign Service, 1966–2002* (Toronto: McClelland and Stewart, 2004), pp. 11–12.

5.   Flora MacDonald, the Secretary of State for External Affairs under the short-lived Clark Government (1979–80), accused the department of "entrapping" her.

6.   See Mulroney's memoirs, as well as Nelson Michaud and Kim Richard Nossal, eds., *Diplomatic Departures: The Conservative Era in Canadian Foreign Policy, 1984–93* (Vancouver: UBC Press, 2001). Mulroney reaffirmed this view in the *Ottawa Citizen*, 17 February 2010.

7.   Allan Gotlieb, *The Washington Diaries, 1981–1989* (Toronto: McClelland and Stewart, 2006).

8.   John G. Kneale, *Foreign Service* (North York, ON: Captus Press, 1993), p. 2.

9.   James Bartleman, *Rollercoaster: My Hectic Years as Jean Chrétien's Diplomatic Advisor, 1994–1998* (Toronto: McClelland and Stewart, 2005), p. 27.

10.   Maurice Pope, ed., *Public Servant: The Memoirs of Sir Joseph Pope* (Toronto: University of Toronto Press, 1960), p. 212.

11.   John Stevenson to J.W. Dafoe, 31 August 1922, quoted in Carman Miller, "Sir Joseph Pope: A Pragmatic Tory," in Donaghy and Nossal, eds., *Architects and Innovators*, p. 25.

12.   Ritchie, *Storm Signals* (MacMillan, 1983), p. 19.

13.   Hume Wrong to R. Finlayson, 18 October 1935, cited in John English, *Shadow of Heaven: The Life of Lester Pearson, Vol. 1: 1897–1948* (Toronto: Lester and Orpen Dennys, 1989), p. 189.

14.   See J.L. Granatstein. "A Man of Influence": *Norman A. Robertson and Canadian Statecraft, 1928–1968* (Ottawa: Deneau, 1981) p. 184.

15.   Granatstein, p. 186

16.   English, *Shadow of Heaven*, p. 189. On Skelton, see Norman Hillmer, "O.D. Skelton: Innovating for Independence," pp. 59–73 in Donaghy and Nossal.

17.   Quoted in Denis Smith, *Diplomacy of Fear: Canada and the Cold War, 1941–48* (Toronto: University of Toronto Press, 1988).

18.   Escott Reid, *Radical Mandarin: The Memoirs of Escott Reid* (Toronto: University of Toronto Press, 1989), p. 241.

19.   1949 report, p. 81.

20.   Ibid.

21.   Letter from Pearson to Norman Robertson, cited in John English, *The Worldly Years: The Life of Lester Pearson Vol. 2: 1949–1972* (Toronto: Alfred Knopf Canada, 1992), p. 21. On Heeney, see Francine McKenzie, "A.D.P. Heeney: The Orderly Undersecretary," pp. 151–68 in Donaghy and Nossal.

22.   Reid, *Radical Mandarin*, p. 241.

23.   Ibid., p. 242.

24.   Earl Drake, *A Stubble-jumper in Striped Pants: Memoirs of a Prairie Diplomat* (Toronto: University of Toronto Press, 1999), pp. 17–18. On Cadieux, see Robert Bothwell, "Marcel Cadieux: The Ultimate Professional," pp. 207–22 in Donaghy and Nossal.

25.   Charles Ritchie, 26 June 1958 entry, p. 148.

26.   Paul Martin, Secretary of State for External Affairs, 1963 report (January 1964), p. 49.

27.   Ibid., p. 57.

28.   Derek Burney, *Getting it Done: A Memoir* (Montreal and Kingston: McGill-Queen's University Press, 2005), p. 10.

29.   1966 report (3 January 1967).

30.   1964 report, p. 55.

31.   Ibid., p. 53.

32.   1967 report, p. 66.

33.   1969 report, p. 78.

34.   1970 report, pp. 92–93.

35.   1968 report, p. 64.

36.   Kneale, *Foreign Service*, p. 2.

37.   1980 report, p. 83. See also Kim Richard Nossal, "Allan Gotlieb and the Politics of the Real World," pp. 272–288 in Donaghy and Nossal.

38.   1980 report, p. 82.

39.   1983–84 report, p. vii.

40.   Ibid.

41.   1984–85 report, p. 53.

42.   The combination of budget cuts and the expanding "human security agenda" provoked grave concerns inside the department. In part, this was a regret that Canada was pursuing an unfocused foreign policy agenda. It also betrayed a resentment that Axworthy seemed more comfortable with the advice he received from the Canadian Centre for Foreign Policy Development. The account of the tensions between the minister and the department is described by Daryl Copeland, an employee of DFAIT, in "The Axworthy Years: Canadian Foreign Policy in the Era of Diminished Capacity," pp. 152–72 in Fen Osler Hampson, Norman Hillmer, Maureen Appel Molot, eds., *Canada Among Nations 2001: The Axworthy Legacy* (Toronto: Oxford

University Press, 2002). See also Lloyd Axworthy's account of his years as minister, *Navigating a New World: Canada's Global Future* (Toronto: Vintage Canada, 2004), which hardly mentions DFAIT.

43. See Evan Potter, "Redesigning Canadian Diplomacy in an Age of Fiscal Austerity," in Fen Osler Hampson and Maureen Appel Molot, eds., *Canada Among Nations 1996: Big Enough to be Heard* (Ottawa: Carleton University Press, 1996).

16 The Indo-Canadian Diaspora and Canadian Foreign Policy: Lessons Learned and Moving Forward

Anita Singh

Key Terms

Diaspora

Homeland

Host State

Immigrant

Indians have immigrated to Canada since the 1900s as labour, refugee, and more recently, entrepreneurial and knowledge migrants. This 100-year history has created a diverse community of business-savvy, politically ambitious, and intellectually and economically wealthy Indo-Canadians. Further, Indo-Canadians have made inroads into many major economic sectors including agriculture, infrastructure, manufacturing, and higher education. My research into the Indo-Canadian community shows that this combination of factors has made for a community that is also well-organized, well-funded, and well-equipped to have an influence on foreign relations between the host state (Canada) and **homeland** (India) (Singh 2010). Further, this research shows that the Harper government, in an interest to improve its relationship with India, has created access points for the Indo-Canadian community to be involved in bilateral relations, benefiting from the **diaspora**'s overseas connections, business experience, intellectual prowess, and cultural similarities to repair the often tense relationship between the two countries.

This research falls within an academic tradition focused on role and influence of ethnic groups on foreign policy, spanning research on diaspora groups that support separatist and extremist activities in the homeland *to* interest groups that work within the political boundaries of their host states to influence bilateral relations. Within the latter, the Israel lobby is considered the penultimate example of scope and reach of influence (Mearsheimer and Walt 2006). My work on the Indo-Canadian community draws some parallels with the Israel lobby, showing how the community has organized its efforts towards stronger Canada–India ties. The research shows that the diaspora has been successful because its message and objectives are closely linked to national foreign policy objectives (Singh 2010).

This chapter reviews previous work on the influence of diasporas on foreign policy to advance this body of work in Canadian foreign policy. It uses the Indo-Canadian case study to help identify current gaps in the literature on diaspora group influence. To make this case, this chapter progresses in three sections. First, it provides a history of Canada–India relations and growth of the Indo-Canadian community. Second, it re-examines the findings of my previous research and the theory associated with diaspora groups and influence. Finally, it discusses the lessons learned and the theoretical implications of this research for this subject matter.

Old Friends, Old Enemies

Contemporary Canada–India relations began in 1947, after India gained independence. Thrown into the Cold War and its reconfigured alliances, the Canada–India relationship was founded on common characteristics such as democracy, multiculturalism and multilingualism, and Commonwealth heritage. Within this friendship, India became Canada's largest recipient of development funds, receiving over $2 billion in bilateral aid between 1947 and 1974. Canada also insisted that India join the Commonwealth to ensure that India could accrue economic benefits through its membership. However, for both countries, these commonalities led to assumptions about their strategic relationship. India saw Canada as a communication channel to the United States, while Canada saw India as a strategically important ally in the Cold War, particularly for gathering information on China. The events that followed—including but not limited to India's 1974 nuclear test—had a profound effect on the bilateral relationship until the 1990s.

Because there have been significant in-depth examinations of the history of Canada–India relations (Evans 2008; Thakur 1984; Kapur 1978; Touhey 2007; Delvoie 1998; Rubinoff 2002; Dobell 1990; Kumar and Narain 2005; Woo 2003), this chapter touches on three main issues between the two countries that antagonized their relationship. First, there was incongruence in how Canada and India understood the bilateral relationship. Canada saw India as a target for its development assistance, hoping that it would result in India becoming a Western ally, while India was fiercely resistant to any external

pressure on its domestic or foreign policy, as indicated by its leadership of the non-aligned movement.[1] Despite India's non-alignment, it had developed a relationship with the Soviet Union and took issue with the West's support of Pakistan, claiming that country was creating insecurity in the South Asian region. The interplay of these differing objectives resulted in tensions on several issues, such as Canada's support for UN Security Resolution 80 on Kashmir, their participation in the International Control Commission (ICC) on Vietnam,[2] the Suez Crisis, US–Pakistan relations, and the Bangladeshi War of Independence.

The second major issue between Canada and India was their nuclear relationship. In 1956, Canada provided India with nuclear technology (the CIRUS reactor) under the auspices of the Atoms for Peace program. Throughout their negotiations, India proved to be a difficult partner, pushing the boundaries of the agreement toward ambiguity rather than accepting defined safeguards and inspections. India's 1974 nuclear tests—which used Canadian technology—created a significant rift between the countries, with Canada claiming that India violated the terms of their agreement. The test was also an important insight into the philosophical differences between the two countries on the nuclear issue. While Canada has been a consistent supporter of the international nuclear regime, India argued that the regime was inherently unfair, as it bases "legitimacy" of nuclear ownership on timing—had India carried out its test before the cut-off date, it would have had full rights as a nuclear weapons state.

Third, the Canada–India relationship has been challenged by Khalistan (and to some extent Tamil) extremism supported by segments of the Indo-Canadian community. The Khalistan movement climaxed with the 1985 Air India terrorist attack, which killed over 300 Indo-Canadians, and was organized and executed from within Canada. Despite numerous warnings from both Canadian and Indian intelligence, little attention was paid to the warnings of growing extremism in the Indo-Canadian community. In addition, the aftermath of the bombing and its investigation was a series of missteps by Canadian authorities. In 2010, the RCMP's negligence and incompetence on the case was made public with the release of the final report on the Commission of Inquiry into the Investigation of the Bombing of Air India Flight 182 (Canada 2010).

The bilateral relationship in the 1990s was fraught with instability. With the end of the Cold War, India was adjusting to the realignment of its alliances, particularly with the loss of the Soviet Union. Yet its economic privatization and investment opportunities made it an attractive economic partner for the West. Just as Canada made its first overtures towards India, with a trip by 300 Team Canada representatives led by then prime minister Jean Chrétien, India conducted its second nuclear test in 1998 (Rubinoff 2002). The bilateral relationship did not recover from this second test until the election of Prime Minister Stephen Harper's Conservatives in 2006. While successive Canadian governments made reference to India's potential as a new ally in business and trade, the Conservative government had an active plan to engage with India, including the Foreign Investment Promotion and Protection Agreement (FIPA), the Comprehensive Economic Partnership Agreement (CEPA), the Nuclear Cooperation Agreement (NCA), and numerous memoranda of understanding in agriculture, science and technology, and higher education. In addition to these agreements, the Harper government made important efforts to gain face time with their Indian counterparts. In Harper's first term—between 2006 and 2010—Cabinet members made close to 20 trips to India.

Indo-Canadians

Indians first arrived in Canada in the early 1900s, largely to work in agriculture, industry, and on the railroads. Indians fulfilled a labour shortage caused by the Chinese Immigration Act of 1885, which legislated a $500 head tax for each Chinese immigrant. Within five years, 5,000 Indians had immigrated to British Columbia, and local concerns that Indians would take over factory, mill, and lumber-yard jobs resulted in legislation restricting Indian immigration and led to their disenfranchisement in 1907. Anti-Indian sentiment during the early part of the century pushed British Columbia's Indian community to organize politically. Gurdwaras built in Vancouver in 1908 and Victoria in 1912 served as religious forums and places of cultural and political assembly for all Indians. Sahoo and Sangha have described their multi-functionality as centres of fellowship that provided accommodation for newly arrived Indian immigrants. More important, they were "a rallying point for all members of the Indian community in their efforts to challenge racial discrimination and to gather money and support for the Indian independence movement" (Sahoo and Sangha 2010). In many ways, foreign policy activism within the Indo-Canadian community began with these early organizations.

Immigration reforms under prime ministers Pearson and Trudeau created the current "points-based" system for "independent-class" immigrants and introduced separate classes for refugee claimants, family reunification, and independent/professional migrants. In particular, these changes relaxed laws that traditionally prevented emigration from non-European states, balancing the ratios and patterns in terms of sex and ethnicity within the Indian community. According to the 2006 census, four per cent of the Canadian population, consisting of 1.2 million people, was from South Asia, a direct result of the Trudeau and Pearson immigration policies. Early decisions made in Canada's immigration history have permanently biased the diaspora's composition. For example, despite representing only two per cent of India's total population, over thirty per cent of Indo-Canadians come from Punjab. Further, the bulk of Canada's Indo-Canadian population is concentrated in the Greater Toronto Area (350,000) and in the Greater Vancouver Area (180,000), with other large Indo-Canadian populations in Calgary, Edmonton, Winnipeg, Ottawa, and Montreal.

One million South Asians constitute Canada's second largest **immigrant** community and are the largest annual source of immigration to Canada. Indo-Canadian population growth has been paralleled by the community's rapidly rising economic and political profile (Tremblay 2003). Tremblay argues that this homogenization makes it "inevitable that the community's lobbying efforts in favour of closer and more positive bilateral relations will expand and intensify." Margaret Walton-Roberts (2010) suggests that Indo-Canadian culture preserves strong family ties, reflected in "social linkages that are transnational in nature, since communities, families and individuals maintain and reinforce connectivity." These connections allow Indo-Canadians to become cultural, economic, and communication brokers between their old and new countries. Walton-Roberts continues, "Canada is home to a large Indian immigrant population, which should be an obvious and important resource in building trade links." As shown in the next section, the diaspora has been actively pursuing trade links through interest groups such as the Indo-Canada Chamber of Commerce (ICCC) and the Canada–India Foundation (CIF).

Theoretical Explanations for Diaspora Engagement in Foreign Policy

Foreign policy is largely considered the domain of the federal government, with decision-making authority resting in the executive branch. This being said, there has been significant debate on the influence of domestic inputs on the decision-making process. Academic work has focused on the role of the provinces (Feldman and Feldman 1984; Kukucha 2005, 2008; Nossal 1997), public opinion (Stairs 1977;

Potter 2002; Pratt 1983), business (Potter 2004), and of course domestic interest groups (Goldberg 1990; Carment and Bercuson 2008; Ross 2007). Largely, this literature on Canadian foreign policy has focused on the question of *whether* domestic groups matter in foreign policy. Equally important questions relate to the how and why of interest group activity: why do domestic groups form certain interests? How are these interests formed into a political strategy? Which strategies are the most effective when influencing policy-makers? Building on these earlier themes, my research has focused on ethnic interest groups within the Indo-Canadian community that have taken a particular interest in foreign policy—the Indo-Canada Chamber of Commerce (ICCC) and the Canada India Foundation (CIF). This section will focus on the theory behind interest group influence on government.

Organizational Structure and Membership

Paul Pross defines interest organizations as "groups of people associating together within the framework of a formal structure to share and promote a common interest" (1975, p. 2). However, this narrow definition confuses the differences between the organization, its functions, strategies, and membership. Further, this narrow definition inevitably excludes groups with a larger mandate or set of activities. Young and Everitt's definition has broadened the definition to "any organization that seeks to influence government policy but not to govern" (2004, p. 5). But even the authors acknowledge this broad definition is problematic, because it includes every informal, fledgling organization as well as more formal, well-established groups such as the Canadian Jewish Congress. Further, their definition does not differentiate between groups with selective or collective benefits, identity groups, sports organizations or political organizations.

Differentiating an *ethnic* interest group does provide some conceptual clarity. Membership within an ethnic lobby group is based on a shared history, language, religion, and immigration pattern rather than a formalized, fee-based membership that characterizes unions and other non-governmental organizations. Indo-Canadian groups, in particular, are a unique hybrid of identity-forming, political organization characterized by similar ethnic, economic, and foreign policy interests in its membership. This in-group identification then ascribes certain behaviours that determine political representation, and is translated into political demands, including improved relations with their home state (Fuchs 1959; Smith 2000; Saideman 2002). However, as Berry (1989, p. 5) argues, the "political reality is that most interest groups represent only a part—possibly a small part—of their potential membership." In order to be effective, diasporic interest groups get their power from the size and strength of the larger community, but do not require its sanction.

My research focused on the inter-organizational dynamics of Indo-Canadian interest groups—such as the Indo-Canada Chamber of Commerce and the Canada India Foundation. It examined the potential for cooperation or conflict when different groups emerge from the same community (Singh 2010). For example, the ICCC is very much a grassroots organization, with a non-restrictive and large membership. It has over 1,000 members in branches based out of Toronto, Ottawa, Montreal, Halifax, Winnipeg, Calgary, and Vancouver. In contrast, the CIF has a much more restrictive membership: new members are invited by a consensus of the executive board for "qualified members of the community in the policy-making and the legislative process" (CIF 2014). In addition, these groups also differ in their executive structures. The CIF is organized into three central decision-making structures: an executive branch that is in charge of administrative business;

a board of governors that handles organizational decisions; and thirty charter members—founding individuals who made large financial contributions to the organization. By contrast, the ICCC is much more hierarchically structured, with one president; several vice-presidents who oversee youth programming, finance, small business, and event portfolios; and numerous directors.

The research found that the membership qualifications and organizational models of the two organizations created niche areas within the foreign policy arena for each group to operate and advocate. As the most grassroots organization, the ICCC has garnered an important share of the federal government's attention as the Harper government sees the ICCC as the "go-to" organization for the Indian diaspora, often using it to communicate policy announcements and to gather perspectives from within the community. In contrast, the CIF's exclusivity has benefited its objectives by providing the organization ample space in the media and with minister-level decision-makers. Further, both organizations have worked actively to help both Canadian government and business navigate the Indian market by organizing networking opportunities, cutting through regulatory red-tape, and information-gathering. As Pradeep Sood argues, business is established through the existence of "common ground. . . . Being [Indo-Canadian] helps open the door" (Sood, personal communication 2010). However, the CIF's reliance on personal networks challenges its long-term success, since its ad hoc lobbying efforts have yet to produce formalized or more permanent channels for governmental access.

Homogenous Political Messaging and Objective

Literature on ethnic interest groups notes that a homogenous political objective is a necessary condition for successful ethnic lobbying (Fuchs 1959;

Haney and Vanderbush 1999; Ross 2009). Often, internal heterogeneity within an organization creates disagreement over the community's political objective. For example, Muslim lobby groups, such as the Canadian Islamic Congress (CIC), are an amalgam of ethnic groups from different regions, ethnicities, and religious sects. Studies of these lobby groups show that their heterogeneous composition divides their foreign policy interests, particularly on controversial issues such as the "war on terror" and the Israel–Palestine conflict (Ross 2009). This being said, even relatively homogeneous organizations can have cleavages within their central mandate. For example, Jonathan Smith's research on the Cuban–American community shows that the diaspora is almost unanimously committed to democracy in Cuba. Yet, the community disagrees over the form of and the means to achieve this democratic outcome (Smith 1998).

My work on the Indo-Canadian community shows that the existence of multiple interest organizations created a cooperative environment for advocacy rather than a divisive one. Cooperation between the groups is explained by two levels of homogeneity. First, while all organizations share an interest to improve Canada–India relations, each organization has tailored its efforts to support unique elements of Ottawa's India policy. Each organization has a self-appointed sector—the CIF on policy dialogue, the Canada–India Business Council (C-IBC) on business relations, and the ICCC on diaspora representation and Canada–India trade. For instance, the ICCC's diaspora focus has oriented its Canada–India trade policy towards individual Indo-Canadians interested in the Indian market. Its community-based round-tables, professional development seminars, and workshops have focused on information-gathering and networking in addition to their policy advocacy. By contrast, the C-IBC's trade mandate aims to remove the barriers to Indian trade for its clientele, and does not include a professional development or diaspora-centred services component. Nevertheless, their functions combine to produce mutually reinforcing pressures that facilitate overall improvements to the Canada-India relationship. These cooperative differences have been recognized by Ottawa, which has tailored its interactions with these organizations dependent on niche area.

Second, an ethnic group's objectives must evidence congruence and salience with government interests. Ethnic interest groups have a tendency to coalesce around the most difficult and salient issues facing their home state, as demonstrated by the Tamil protests on the Gardiner Expressway in Toronto, pro-Palestine boycotts of Israel, and Haitian earthquake relief organizations. However, successful advocacy efforts of ethnic interest groups must align their political message to pre-existing national interests, which eliminates potential opposition to their political objectives. Sean Carter's study shows how the Croatian diaspora in the US defined the 1995 "homeland war in 'American' terms, as democracy against dictatorship, the free-market against Communism, Western against 'an Other'" (2005, p. 62). Similarly, David Carment and David Bercuson argue "a Canadian foreign policy cannot be considered viable if it contradicts the preferences of ordinary Canadians" (2008, p. 5). Acknowledging this influence is particularly relevant for the study of the Indo-Canadian community. K.R.G. Nair states that "the present state of India–Canada economic relations is a shining example of unrealised potential particularly in view of the relative importance of the Indian diaspora in Canada's population" (2004). The Canadian government recognizes that there are multiple direct and indirect benefits to engagement with the politically charged and economically powerful Indo-Canadian diaspora. It does, however, confirm that there is a high level of congruence with respect to issues of interest between the Canadian government and Indo-Canadian interest groups.

A large reason for this engagement is the economic success of the Indo-Canadian community. Business-oriented diaspora groups provide a concentrated, organized point of contact within the community. Their knowledge of the Indian economy coupled with their overseas relationships makes them important contacts for a government attempting to increase its profile in India; working with the pre-existing diaspora organizations taps into already-established economic and trade relations. This engagement has successfully matched its definition of the national interest—increased economic and political engagement with India—with the long-standing political objectives of Indo-Canadian organizations. *Toronto Star* journalist Haroon Siddiqui notes that, in comparison with other diaspora groups, "segments of Chinese Canadians have spoken out about Tibet or the Falun Gong or for greater economic ties with China. Indo Canadians have helped improve [Canada's] economic, academic and political relations with India" (Siddiqui 2008).

Issue congruence only partly explains government openness and access. An important finding of this research shows that the Indo-Canadian community has played a role in creating issue salience. More specifically, issue congruence on non-salient policies is not likely to produce policy movement. In other words, diaspora organizations played a role in increasing the importance and relevance of the India file for the Harper government and the resultant desire to pursue relations with India. Ashok Kapur notes a difference between the Liberal and Conservative governments: "Indo-Canadians have been influential in consciousness-raising with the Conservative government and Harper and his cabinet colleagues" (Kapur, personal communication 2010).

In other words, the implementation of the government's India policy would not be possible without the community. In fact, the relationship that has developed between the Indo-Canadian community and the Canadian government is one of mutual deference, benefit, and reinforcement. The government has pursued initiatives that are beneficial to both business and community interests, such as the Foreign Investment Agreement, new trade consulates, and nuclear policies. At the same time, it has made sure to avoid decisions that could damage its relationship with the Indo-Canadian community and with the Indian government. For example, the Canadian government was careful to avoid any possible fallout from the issue of visas for retired members of Indian border services as a result of the negative response by Indo-Canadian groups. Indo-Canadian access to ministerial offices on this issue effectively confirmed the Indo-Canadian diaspora's symbiotic relationship with the government.

Ethno-politics and Ethnic Voting

Traditional examinations have emphasised an ethnic diaspora's ability to affect electoral outcomes. Particularly in the United States, academic work has argued that policy-makers are acutely sensitive to ethnic voters concentrated in swing states (Smith 2000, p. 53). These include Jewish communities in New Jersey, New York, Connecticut, and Pennsylvania (Keohane 1971), Cuban voters in Florida (Haney and Vanderbush 1999), Hispanic communities in California (Huntington 2004), and African American voters in the South. A recent examination of the 2000 American election has shown how both Republican and Democratic presidential candidates (George W. Bush and Al Gore) courted Muslim voters as an important demographic (Rose 2001). An extrapolation of this argument would suggest that the electoral concentration of the Indo-Canadian communities in the Greater Toronto Area, Ottawa, Vancouver, Calgary, and Edmonton would have an important foreign policy effect (Tremblay 2003).

In Canada, votes are often split between parties in largely ethnic ridings, regardless of whether opposing candidates are from the same or different immigrant group. This suggests that ethnic communities are not tied to a single party or platform (Black and Hicks 2006). Moreover, Canadian political parties have not differentiated themselves on foreign policy. Brian Bow and David Black note that the largest differences between parties are over "means and 'details'" (2008). While the Conservative and Liberal parties might differ on *how* to pursue improved relations between Canada and India, the differences are not so large as to suppose unified electoral support for one party or the other from the community. Finally, given the religious, ethnic, and nationalistic divisions *within* the Indian diaspora, it cannot be assumed that they vote as a unified entity (Haney and Vanderbush 1999, p. 53; Saideman 2002, p. 101). However, there are important alternatives to this perspective. Duane Bratt notes that "the Harper government has been trying to 'flip' the Indo-Canadian community into supporting the Conservative Party of Canada" (Bratt, personal communication 2010). Kim Nossal acknowledges that the Harper government is "extraordinarily sensitive to diaspora groups, given his overall goal of transforming Canadian politics permanently by wooing all of those 'ethnic' groups in Canada who for decades unthinkingly voted Liberal and avoided Conservatives" (Nossal, personal communication 2010).

Evidence from the Indo-Canadian community suggests that electoral explanations are only *part* of the equation. The nature of the Harper government's relationship with the Indo-Canadian diaspora is motivated by their economic, foreign policy, and cultural contributions, with the Indo-Canadian community ethnicity as a strategic characteristic (ethno-politics). Strategic approaches to gaining the Indo-Canadian vote were evident in the 2011 election. For example, in the riding of Brampton–Springdale, once represented by Liberal Ruby Dhalla,

the Conservative party made strong overtures to ensure votes from the Indo-Canadian community, including an appearance by Bollywood star Akshay Kumar at political rallies with the prime minister in the riding (Humphreys 2011). Further, by introducing an Indo-Canadian candidate to run against Dhalla, the Conservatives were able to split the Indo-Canadian vote.[3] Polling during the previous election in 2006 showed that ethnic communities are not immune to electoral strategies, suggesting that Conservative support from "visible minorities—who traditionally have overwhelmingly favoured the Liberals—[reached] just under 30 per cent, within striking distance of the Liberals' 38 per cent" (*The Globe and Mail* 2006). Further, since the 2006 federal election, the prime minister and the executive have wooed the Indo-Canadian community through large-scale public meetings and apologies for the *Komagata Maru* incident and the botched Air India investigation; foreign visits that include trips to holy sites such as the Golden Temple; and Bollywood connections with celebrities such as Akshay Kumar and Shiamak Davar as a mechanism to connect with the Indian diaspora in Canada.

"Ethno-politics" have been employed by other federal parties who have attempted to reach out to Indo-Canadian groups as well. During the 2011 election campaign, NDP and Conservative leaders were prominent features at Vaisakhi parades, temples, and events held by the Indo-Canadian community. For example, the late NDP leader Jack Layton addressed a Vaisakhi gathering in Vancouver describing his attention to beliefs in the Sikh religion, stating "*Vahiguru Ji Ka Khalsa! Vahiguru Ji Ki Fateh* [God's Khalsa, God's victory]! I have tremendous respect for the tenets of *Kirt Karna, Vand Shukna, Naam Japna*, and *Seva*, because working hard, sharing with others, having faith and community service are also important Canadian values." Similarly in 2006, Layton also focused on the major political issues from the Indo-Canadian community, calling on the

Conservative government to issue an apology on behalf of all Canadians for the *Komagata Maru* during a meeting with Surrey's Sikh community. After Harper's speech at the ICCC's annual event, Liberal leader Stéphane Dion spoke to the C-IBC to outline his vision of Canadian foreign policy. He promised $50 million "to create the 'South Asian Foundation of Canada' to promote closer ties between Canada and South Asian countries" (Campion-Smith 2008). In the face of this politicking, Indo-Canadian interest organizations have ensured that the Harper government continues to work in their favour by maintaining a largely non-partisan stance. As noted by a representative of the Canada India Foundation, their organization has members that belong to all federal political parties. Further, the three organizations have had conversations, roundtables, and meetings with all federal leaders.

In the course of articulating its India policy, the Harper government has focused on the business sector and members of organized interest groups. It has used selective, closed-door meetings with these elites to both gauge opinion within the community and work out action plans for the Canada–India relationship. Former Citizenship and Immigration Minister Jason Kenney has been an important figure in this effort. As noted by political observers, Kenney is one of the few cabinet members to have significant freedoms in his public role, and wields considerable influence in the PMO. It is this closeness to the Prime Minister's Office that has attracted the attention of Indo-Canadian organizations seeking meetings to discuss their interests. Arthur Rubinoff has observed that "Jason Kenney, a minister with a domestic portfolio, is actually a key player in the foreign policy field. This is unprecedented. He seems to be in charge of Canada's India policy" (Rubinoff, personal communication 2010). In exchange, Jason Kenney has maintained Conservatives' relationship with the Indo-Canadian community by addressing some of the pressing concerns from Indo-Canadian groups.

On a trip to India in 2010, for example, Kenney made common cause on immigration and visa issues by expressing concern over fraudulent immigration consultants: "The Indo-Canadian community has raised a number of important issues with me, including the need to take action against fraudulent immigration consultants, improve visa processing time, encourage immigration from Indian students to Canada, and build stronger connections between Indian and Canadian businesses" (Canada 2009).

Elite-Level Access

Generally speaking, the executive has been identified as the decision-maker for foreign policy in Canada (Nossal 1993). However, the introduction of domestic issues such as technology, aviation, national resource management, and climate change into the foreign policy space has opened Canadian foreign policy research to a multitude of areas where domestic groups play an important role. With this expansion of foreign policy issues, the domestic players involved have also expanded in scope and influence. For example, John Kirton and Blair Dimock recognize that access points have opened due to government interest as "proliferating channels of contact have been constructed, employed, and directed not by societal actors from below but by the state apparatus from above" (1983, p. 70). This is supported by Cranford Pratt's work, which argues that a "dominant class" bias is obvious in "the personal and financial links between the corporate sector and the two major parties, the links between the senior civil servants and the corporate sector, and the ideology which is largely shared by the dominant class and the senior bureaucracy" (1983, p. 135). Pratt's interpretation suggests foreign policy has opened to domestic groups but in a way that limits access to elite members of society. Similarly, Robert Presthus argues that lobby group influence is a product of elite accommodation, where interpersonal relationships and a "shared normative consensus" exist between the policy-makers and interest groups. It is this shared consensus that lends *elite* lobby groups disproportionate legitimacy, expertise, continuity, access, and power (Presthus 1973). Due to their government access, internal structures, and economically powerful membership, these organizations can engage in multiple types of activities, including policy formation, implementation, commercial exchanges, and selective services (Coleman and Jacek 1983).

Similar to Pratt's and Presthus's observations, the Indo-Canadian community has shown evidence that the effect of ethnicity—as a basis for policy influence—is greatly *magnified* when coupled with the community's socio-economic success. Thus, influential groups are those that have an ethnic connection to India and come from an elite socio-economic class. Both authors argued that business lobbies differ from grassroots organizations because the former belong to an "elite consensus" with the government, with financial resources and interests that complement government objectives. Similarly, in the Indo-Canadian community, a combination of ethnic affiliation and economic success determines corresponding influence in Canadian foreign policy. For example, in 2009, Ajit Someshwar, CIF charter member and former national convenor, was appointed to Finance Minister Jim Flaherty's Economic Advisory Council, one of eleven "business and academic heavyweights" (2010, personal correspondence). In closed-door meetings with the finance minister, the council was responsible for assessing (and correcting) Canada's response to the economic downturn, focusing "on the budget and deteriorating economy affected by the global economic meltdown" (2010, personal correspondence). Someshwar's appointment highlights two important aspects. First, it is noteworthy that an Indo-Canadian was included, because it suggests that the government recognizes the growing economic clout of the community. Second, it confirms the elite-centric perspective espoused by both Pratt and Presthus.

This demonstrates that Indo-Canadian organizations play two important roles. In addition to their personal success and lobbying accomplishments, the major strategies of the influential members of these organizations, and of the Indo-Canadian community more generally, have focused on profile raising in three areas: among the Canadian public, among Canada's politicians, and with overseas connections. This profile has had the effect of connecting to senior officials in Ottawa, accessing senior officials in India, and utilizing national media in both countries. Further, these activities have used unconventional and indirect methods to improve access to government. For example, the CIF's attention to "benign issues" such as education and philanthropy disarms officials that might otherwise reject interest group interjections into policy matters. Instead, the CIF successfully links the Indo-Canadian community with the betterment of Canadian society. This includes being politically active on more than just diaspora issues and Canada–India relations—it also includes mentoring, financial contributions, and volunteering. For example, members of the CIF recently established a "Tribute to Fallen Soldiers" memorial to honour Canada's war veterans at the Vishnu Temple in Richmond Hill. The event attracted representatives from all the federal political parties as well as national media coverage.

Second, Indo-Canadian organizations can publicize the fact that the Indo-Canadian diaspora has worked as effective cross-country brand ambassadors to address Canada's previous invisibility in India. Ryan Touhey explains, "the Diaspora is an accessible and inexpensive form of public diplomacy. The image of India in Canada is being sculpted by the Diaspora as it continues to flourish" (2010, personal correspondence). It is economic success that has rectified the negative image of India within the Canadian political establishment. For example, Ramesh Chotai, CIF chair, has built schools in his native Gujarat, naming them after key Canadian landmarks and individuals, such as the Pierre Elliott Trudeau Secondary School, and has rebuilt villages now named after Toronto's Bloor, Dundas, and Yonge Streets.

These elite-level relationships have helped develop international and transnational relationships. For its part, New Delhi has facilitated executive- and elite-level meetings, organized conferences, and engaged with its diaspora as a proxy to get the attention of the Canadian government. These overseas connections have also provided useful leverage points when attempting to influence the Canadian government, allowing diaspora organizations to engage in Track 2 diplomacy between the Canadian and Indian governments. The CIF's personal connections are also evident in its overseas political network, which is accessed when members travel to India. Developing this political network has been prioritized by the CIF, in contrast to the ICCC's and C-IBC's focus on economic connections. One example is the CIF's relationship with India's former president and architect of its nuclear programme, Dr. Abdul Kalam. After multiple meetings with CIF members in India, Kalam agreed to attend the CIF's 2008 inaugural gala as chief guest. He has since attended three CIF events, most recently for the 2010 Forum on Mining and Metals. Another example is the CIF's lobbying efforts towards improving Canada's relations with Gujarat, efforts which have been facilitated by the organization's relationship with the chief minister of Gujarat, Narendra Modi.

Lessons Learned and Moving Forward

Previous sections have examined aspects of the Indo-Canadian diaspora, their arrival in Canada, the growth of the community, and some of the activities of representative interest organizations. However, it also highlights some of the key factors that have not been addressed by previous work on diaspora influence on foreign policy.

Focus on Business Relationships

As discussed in the previous section, Canadian foreign policy has been broadened to include non-traditional areas of culture, national resources, finance, the economy, and trade policy. This broadening has been evidenced in Canada–India relations. Until the 1990s, security issues, such as Cold War alliances, nuclear security, and terrorist activity, defined the relationship. The shift to an economic focus through business, trade, and investment has created the space for diaspora involvement in foreign policy. In other words, Canada's economic interest in India created an ideal scenario for the Indo-Canadian community to have influence on the conduct of Canada–India relations.

One important example is the Canada–India Nuclear Cooperation Agreement (NCA). Given the history of negative relations between Canada and India—particularly with regard to nuclear politics—signing the NCA was possible because of a perceptual shift within the government. For Canada, India has been a nuclear pariah state, outside the behavioural norms of the non-proliferation regime. Thus, the lobbying of Indo-Canadian groups was directed towards creating the link between economic benefits and nuclear power, attempting to change perceptions from the security to the economic implications of the agreement. For example, the CIF's Energy Forum in 2009 highlighted the opportunities available through nuclear trade between the two countries. The discussions were not limited to nuclear relations; rather they examined all areas of energy cooperation and thus had the effect of normalizing nuclear power by comparing it to wind, electric, and fossil energy sources. In this vein, the discussions had the additional effect of normalizing India's nuclear program within the context of energy production (Bratt 2012, pp. 265–6).

Given the government's focus on economic relations, it was important for the community to reaffirm that the NCA is, in fact, a trade deal and not a security-related agreement. At its most basic level, the agreement allows businesses to place contracts for the trade of nuclear technology and material (particularly but not exclusively uranium). The deal is aimed at increasing India's nuclear energy supply so as to help meet the country's growing energy demands. India's ambitious nuclear goals are constrained by its lack of domestic uranium resources, as well as trade restrictions imposed by the nuclear Non-Proliferation Treaty. Indeed, without the help of imports, India's nuclear scientists estimate that the country would max out its nuclear energy production by 2020. The Indian government now estimates that it will spend $100 billion dollars on its nuclear industry in the next 10 years. For energy-starved and uranium-poor India, the deal provides the resources to fuel the economic growth of its massive population. For Canada, it links a crucial domestic industry to one of the largest nuclear markets in the world.

Further, the Indo-Canadian organizations were able to link the nuclear deal to other important improvements in Canada–India bilateral relations. Generally speaking, removal of trade barriers between the two states has an effect on the nuclear industry. Further, the Comprehensive Economic Partnership Agreement (CEPA)—an agreement to establish bilateral free trade—directly affects the success of nuclear trade. Both the ICCC and C-IBC have been committed to easing the difficulties arising from corruption—difficulties in acquiring land for business, and securing working visas and business licences, all of which are required for successful business in India, including in nuclear trade. Finally, my research has found that Indo-Canadian groups have not focused their attention on a single policy issue. Instead, the evidence shows that they are active on all issues related to Canada–India relations, and the NCA is one part of a much larger bilateral relationship. In this way, its role

of editing perceptions is probably one of the most important contributions of Indo-Canadian groups. By perpetuating an image of "new" India—democratic, pluralistic, technologically advanced, internationally powerful and nuclear-responsible—the Indo-Canadian community has legitimized and supported the development of Canada's nuclear relationship with India.

Positioning of the "Other" Government

Current diaspora literature has focused on the internal dynamics of the host state and its diaspora. Largely process-based, the literature has made significant strides in understanding how the configuration of government resources and interests provides the space for diaspora groups to enter the discussion of foreign policy. However, the literature remains particularly elementary on its understanding of the role of the foreign governments in determining how the influence of the diaspora group evolves within the host state. Current literature features a diaspora's homeland as a fixed entity, usually as a determinant for diasporic identity within the host state (Sheffer 1994, 61).

In the case of India, the Indian government has been a very active player in connecting with its overseas diaspora, particularly under prime ministers Vajpayee and Singh. The Ministry of Overseas Indian Affairs (MOIA) was created as a recommendation of the Report of the High Level Committee on the Indian Diaspora (2002). With its inception, the MOIA has developed tools to facilitate the engagement of its global diaspora, such as the Overseas Indian Facilitation Centre (OIFC), a centre to support business and investment ventures by diaspora. Another example is the Person of Indian Origin (PIO) and Non-Resident Indian (NRI) visas, which allow diaspora added benefits in India, such as the right to state services, to purchase real estate, and to engage in business activities without requiring special permits or allowances. A third example is the creation of forums for engagement, such as the Pravasi Bharatiya Divas, where overseas governments and diaspora members are invited to meet and engage with key players in India's key economic sectors.

Further, as seen with the Indo-Canadian community, the Indian government actively sought the community out in its relations with the Canadian government. Official ministerial level visits have purposely included Indo-Canadian groups in their roundtables, negotiations, and other conversations with Canadian groups. On many occasions, Indian government officials have held private meetings with diaspora groups and hosted diaspora missions coming from Canada, providing a level of access and communication unprecedented in relations between the state and its foreign diaspora. It will be important for future research to theorize and evaluate how the stance of the homeland affects the role and influence of the diaspora on host state foreign policy.

Intra-Diaspora Politics and Divisions

An additional challenge in the literature on diasporas and foreign policy has been a lack of understanding and consideration of the homogeneity within the community. The literature on diaspora influence on foreign policy has given little consideration to the development of divergent political interests within diaspora communities. In particular, sociological and cultural anthropological literature that focuses on the group identity notes that there is an important fluidity and heterogeneity that exists within diaspora communities. Several examples of these political divisions exist within the Indo-Canadian community.

The Generation Gap

An obvious gap exists between first-generation immigrants and second- and third-generation members in the diaspora community, but it has not been conceptually developed within the foreign policy literature. It is generally recognized that first-generation immigrants develop their diasporic identities based on their experiences of the homeland, which influences how diaspora groups politicize in their new host states. This is why the literature pays significant attention to the reason for dispersion from the homeland; the term *Diaspora* is originally derived as a reference to the Jewish migration experience. This forced dispersion, memories of the homeland, and a desire for eventual return shapes the political interests of first-generation diaspora (Sheffer 2003; Safran 1991; Clifford 1994). It is because of the limitation of this definition that more recent work has been keen to understand the implications of alternative reasons for migration that have created labour and economic diasporas, cultural diasporas, and trade diasporas (Cohen 1997). However, as Shuval argues, the expansion of this concept has created overlap between other theoretical and conceptual areas of ethnicity and immigration (2000). She differentiates, for example, between immigrants and diaspora, arguing that immigrants "have a certain temporal span and often last up to a third generation after which their self-identification as immigrants in most cases fades, even though they may retain an ethnic identity. A sense of diaspora can occur and re-occur after several generations when the group members are themselves no longer immigrants" (2000, 46).

Second- and third-generation diaspora differ significantly from earlier generations of diaspora for several reasons. The most important reason is that these generations do not have the same experience and relationship to the homeland as previous generations. These members of the community are raised, educated, and professionalized in Canada, imbibing many of the attributes of Canadian culture in their personal and professional lives. In particular, their relationship to the homeland is filtered through the culture,[4] religion, and linguistic traditions of the homeland as experienced by the first generation. Similarly, their relationship to the homeland is related to social bonds created within the community, which reinforce lessons from the homeland. Literature on political socialization has noted that for second-generation immigrants, political culture is developed through a balance of homeland tradition and ideology with a desire for assimilation (Zhou 1997).

Three important outcomes have developed within later generation immigrants. First, in many cases, the second- and third-generation members of the diaspora remain engaged in the community on the basis of arts, politics, culture, and/or religion. In this case, mainstream culture (such as Bollywood, the Indian movie industry) has had a major effect. However, other options include the assimilation of second- and third-generation diaspora to the culture of the host state, resulting in a distancing from the political identity and interests of the Indo-Canadian community and the homeland. The Indian government has recognized the tenuous grasp between second-, third-, and fourth-generation diaspora and the homeland. To strengthen this relationship, the government created a "Person of Indian Origin" (PIO) designation, which allows later generations to benefit from less stringent visa requirements, thereby facilitating economic, educational, employment, and financial transfers to India, without requiring work or study permits—despite an individual's not having been born in India.[5] A third possible outcome could result in homegrown extremism within younger members of the diaspora, where cultural acclimatization within the community has an inherent hostility towards the host state or the homeland. Examples include younger members of the Khalistan or Tamil separatist movements that currently exist in Canada.

Regional, Religious, and Ethnic Diversity

While the number of Indians in Canada grows, important homeland dynamics of regionalism,

language, and religion exist within the diaspora. These internal divisions have an effect on the politicization of the community, particularly in foreign policy. One example is the politics of the Punjabi community associated with the Khalistan movement. While there are several reasons for the growth of the Khalistan movement in Canada, it has had the effect of dividing attention in the Canada–India relations foreign policy space. The Indo-Canadian community provides a challenging yet interesting case study. The community does have inherent heterogeneity, since religious (Sikh, Hindu, and Muslim communities), linguistic, and even regional divisions predominant in India have developed within large diaspora communities overseas. In particular, the Sikh community see themselves as a distinct ethnic group, and form their own cultural, political and economic organizations. As well, supporters of the Khalistan movement are a distinct but powerful minority with control over many cultural and religious organizations (Nayar 2004; Tatla 1999). Particularly after the Air India bombing and during its legal battle, Indo-Canadians strongly condemned the actions of fundamentalists within the community, actions illustrated by the continued glorification of Khalistan terrorism during Vaisakhi celebrations and at gurdwaras in Canada. As the research shows, the influence of Indo-Canadian lobby groups has not been affected by these divisions. First, there are signs of growing cleavage within the Sikh community, with its internal support divided between separatist and pro-India factions. Second, the current Canadian government has not given Khalistan advocates the same policy-level access as other ethnic groups. Third, much of the Sikh community's current messaging is internally focused, attempting to keep members interested and active.

Twice-Removed Diaspora

Particularly within the Indo-Canadian community, a third example of heterogeneity within the community is the role of twice-removed diaspora and their role in the Indo-Canadian community. The British Slavery Abolition Act of 1833 introduced a system of indentured labour that dispersed Indians to various locations in the world. For close to 100 years,[6] this system resulted in the migration and development of Indian diaspora communities in the Caribbean, South Pacific, and Eastern Africa. These generational diaspora communities have developed various local cultures, linguistic evolution, and even local religious customs (Jayaram 2008). *Twice-removed diaspora* refers to a second wave of migration of Indian communities from these states to other countries. As with other Indian diaspora groups, the opening of Canadian immigration policy has resulted in a significant group of Indian diaspora from these countries. For example, Idi Amin's policy of Asian expulsion from Uganda in the 1970s resulted in many Indian–African refugees taking refuge in Western countries rather than returning to India (where often, there were few family ties left). Similarly, during Fiji's three military coups since 1986, large numbers of Indo-Fijians moved to Western Canada (Calgary, Vancouver, and Edmonton).

The influence of these groups in the realm of foreign policy is both direct and indirect. Directly, some members of twice-removed diaspora have re-assimilated into the larger political culture and interests of the larger Indo-Canadian community. The indirect influence of these communities lies in their interests to lobby the governments in relation to their most recent homelands. For example, during the coup d'état in Fiji in May 2000, Indo-Fijian communities in Calgary and Vancouver lobbied federal members of parliament to open immigration for refugee claims for Indo-Fijians affected by the coup.

Role of "Non-Aligned" Indo-Canadians

Largely, the focus of this research has been on interest groups that represent the Indo-Canadian community. However, the research must recognize the other organizations and individuals that indirectly contribute to Canada–India relations within specific sectors. For example, the Canada India Education Council is dedicated to supporting the establishment of post-secondary education facilities in India, knowledge translation between the two countries, and facilitation of transnational links between individual students and scholars in the two countries. Canada and India share a history of education innovation since the opening of the Shastri Indo-Canadian Institute in 1968.

In addition to these sector-specific efforts, the concept of "non-aligned" Indo-Canadians refers to the indirect impact of individuals on the Canada–India space. These are individuals that do not actively assert their interests in foreign policy but have influenced connections between the two countries. One example is cultural transmission through art between Canada and India. Internationally renowned artists such as Lisa Ray, Raghav Mathur, and Lata Pada have gained fame in both countries and, in their efforts, have drawn attention to cultural connections between the diaspora and the homeland. For example, Lata Pada, a trained Indian classical dancer based in Toronto, has a special connection to bilateral relations. She also has been an active member of the Air India Victims' Families Association, after losing her husband and daughters in the bombing of Air India Flight 182. In addition to being an outspoken member condemning the Canadian officials' response to the crash and the RCMP's lacklustre attempts to prosecute the perpetrators, Pada has used the stage to portray the personal effect of the crash in her art. Her piece "Revealed by Fire" was a tribute to her own loss in the terrorist attack, and it was staged in both Canada and India.

Conclusion

The Indo-Canadian community has emerged as one of the most organized, visible, and active diasporas in

Canadian politics. This chapter focuses on their influence on Canadian foreign policy, the effect of a growing diaspora and their involvement in various aspects of business, politics, and education. However, as addressed in the last section, academic investigations into understanding the role of immigrant and diaspora communities in Canadian society, culture, and foreign policy have had a limited scope of understanding.

Questions for Review

1. Other than the Indo-Canadian diaspora, what other immigrant communities could be effective ambassadors between Canada and their homelands? Why?

2. What are some of the explanations that differentiate radicalized diaspora groups and ethnic interest groups as outlined in this article?

3. What is the impact of the findings of this article when applied to other domestic groups in Canada that have an interest in influencing foreign policy (such as media, public opinion, business lobby groups, veterans' groups, or political parties)?

4. Diaspora groups have been significantly more effective at lobbying in the United States. What explanations could you give to explain their success in the US?

5. Heterogeneity within immigrant communities has a deleterious effect on the political impact of ethnic interest groups. What other factors negatively affect an interest group's impact on foreign policy?

Suggested Readings

Carment, David, and David Bercuson, eds. 2008. *The World in Canada: Diaspora, Demography, and Domestic Politics.* Montreal and Kingston: McGill-Queen's University Press.

Jayaram, N. 2008. "Heterogeneous diaspora and asymmetrical orientations: India, Indians and the Indian diaspora." *Diaspora Studies* 1, 2 (December): 1–21.

Mearsheimer, John J., and Stephen M. Walt. 2006. "The Israel lobby and U.S. foreign policy." *Middle East Policy* 13, 3 (September): 29–87.

Ross, Liat R. 2007. "Canadian Muslims and foreign policy." *International Journal* 63, 1 (Winter): 187–205.

Stairs, Denis. 1977. "Public opinion and external affairs: Reflections on the domestication of Canadian foreign policy." *International Journal* 33, 1 (Winter): 128–49.

Tatla, D.S. 1999. *The Sikh Diaspora: The Search for Statehood.* London: UCL Press.

Notes

1. While India maintained its non-aligned stance in the Cold War, its growing relationship with Russia was significant as it became increasingly reliant on Russia for its military investments during this time.

2. For a detailed account of Canada–India relations in the ICC on Vietnam, please see Ramesh Thakur's impressive monograph on this subject: *Peacekeeping in Vietnam: Canada, India, Poland, and the International Commission* (Edmonton: University of Alberta Press, 1984).

3. Parm Gill won the riding with 48.3 per cent of the vote over Ruby Dhalla's 27 per cent.

4. In this chapter, *culture* will largely refer to political culture, as there is inadequate space to discuss the larger sociological concept of culture in diaspora communities.

5. These 16 countries are the United States, Canada, United Kingdom, Netherlands, Italy, Ireland, Portugal, Switzerland, Greece, Cyprus, Israel, Australia, New Zealand, France, Sweden, and Finland.

6. The indenture system was an official policy in the United Kingdom until 1920.

Works Cited

Berry, Jeffrey M. 1989. *The Interest Group Society*. 2nd ed. Glenview, IL: Scott, Foresman.

Black, Jerome H., and Bruce M. Hicks. 2006. "Visible minority candidates in the 2004 federal election." *Canadian Parliamentary Review* 29, 2 (Summer): 26–31.

Bow, Brian, and David Black. 2008. "Does politics stop at the water's edge in Canada? Party and partisanship in Canadian foreign policy." *International Journal* 64, 1 (Winter): 7–27.

Bratt, Duane. 2012. *Canada, the Provinces, and the Global Nuclear Revival: Advocacy Coalitions in Action*. Montreal and Kingston: McGill-Queen's University Press.

Campion-Smith, Bruce. 2008. "Dion attacks PM's foreign policy." *Toronto Star*, 21 February.

Canada. 2010. *Commission of Inquiry into the Investigation of the Bombing of Air India Flight 182*.

Canada. Citizenship and Immigration. 2009. "Immigration minister's visit to highlight strength of Canada–India relationship; address issues raised by Indo-Canadian community." News release, 7 January. Available at http://news.gc.ca/web/article-en.do?m=/index&nid=429359.

Canada India Foundation (CIF). 2014. "Our Mandate." Available at http://www.canadaindia.org/about/mandate.

Carment, David, and David Bercuson, eds. 2008. *The World in Canada: Diaspora, Demography, and Domestic Politics*. Montreal and Kingston: McGill-Queen's University Press.

Carter, Sean. 2005. "The geopolitics of diaspora." *Area* 37, 1 (March): 54–63.

Clifford, James. 1994. "Diasporas." *Cultural Anthropology* 9, 3 (August): 302–38.

Cohen, Robin. 1997. *Global Diasporas: An Introduction*. Seattle: University of Washington Press.

Coleman, William D., and Henry J. Jacek. 1983. "The roles and activities of business interest associations in Canada." *Canadian Journal of Political Science/Revue canadienne de science politique* 16, 2 (June): 257–80.

Consulate General of India. Toronto. 2010. "Persons of Indian origin." Available at http://www.cgitoronto.ca/content/pio-0.

Delvoie, Louis A. 1998. "Canada and India: A new beginning?" *Round Table* 87, 345 (January): 51–64.

Den Tandt, Michael. 2005. "Liberals losing allure among minorities, poll suggests." *The Globe and Mail*, 30 November.

Dobell, William. 1990. "Canada and India: The Mulroney Years," *Journal of Asian and African Studies* 25, 3–4 (July): 131–45.

Esman, Milton J. 1987. "Ethnic politics and economic power." *Comparative Politics* 19, 4 (July): 395–418.

Evans, Paul. 2008. "Advancing Canada–India Relations: From Aspiration to National Strategy." Asia Pacific Foundation of Canada, 22 October. Available at http://www.asiapacific.ca/sites/default/files/filefield/PMEIndiareport.pdf.

Fearon, James D. 1994. "Domestic political audiences and the escalation of international disputes." *American Political Science Review* 88, 3 (September): 577–92.

Feldman, Elliot J., and Lily G. Feldman. 1984. "The impact of federalism on the organization of Canadian foreign policy." *Publius: The Journal of Federalism* 14, 4 (Fall): 33–59.

Fuchs, Lawrence H. 1959. "Minority groups and foreign policy." *Political Science Quarterly* 74, 2 (June): 161–75.

Goldberg, David H. 1990. *Foreign Policy and Ethnic Interest Groups: American and Canadian Jews Lobby for Israel*. Contributions in Political Science 256. New York: Greenwood Press.

Haney, Patrick J., and Walt Vanderbush. 1999. "The role of ethnic interest groups in U.S. foreign policy: The case of the Cuban American National Foundation." *International Studies Quarterly* 43, 2 (June): 341–61.

Harrison, Kathryn, and Lisa M. Sundstrom, eds. 2010. *Global Commons, Domestic Decisions: The Comparative Politics of Climate Change*. Cambridge, MA: MIT Press.

Horowitz, Donald L. 1985. *Ethnic Groups in Conflict*. Berkeley: University of California Press.

Humphreys, Adrian. 2011. "Riding profiles: 'Battle of the Indo-Canadians' in Brampton." *National Post*, 28 April. Available at http://news.nationalpost.com/2011/04/28/riding-profiles-battle-of-the-indo-canadians-in-brampton/.

Huntington, Samuel P. 2004. "The Hispanic challenge." *Foreign Policy* 141 (March-April), 30–45.

India, Ministry of External Affairs. 2002. *High Level Committee Report on the Indian Diaspora*. 8 January. Available at http://www.indiandiaspora.nic.in/contents.htm.

Indo-Canada Chamber of Commerce. 2012. Website. Available at http://www.iccconline.org/.

Jayaram, N. 2008. "Heterogeneous diaspora and asymmetrical orientations: India, Indians and the Indian diaspora." *Diaspora Studies* 1, 2 (December): 1–21.

Kapur, Ashok. 1978. "The Canada-India Nuclear Negotiations: Some Hypotheses and Lessons." *The World Today* 34, 8 (August) 311–20.

Keohane, Robert O. 1971. "The big influence of small allies." *Foreign Policy* 2 (Spring): 161–82.

Kirton, John, and Blair Dimock. 1983. "Domestic access to government in the Canadian foreign policy process 1968–1982." *International Journal* 39,1 (Winter): 68–98.

Kukucha, Christopher J. 2005. "From Kyoto to the WTO: Evaluating the constitutional legitimacy of the provinces in Canadian foreign trade and environmental policy." *Canadian Journal of Political Science* 38, 1 (March): 129–52.

———. 2008. *The Provinces and Canadian Foreign Trade Policy*. Vancouver: UBC Press.

Kumar, Ramesh C., and Nigmendra Narain. 2005. "Re-Engaging India: Upgrading the Canada-India Bazaar Relationship," pp. 169–84 in Andrew F. Cooper and Dane Rowlands, eds. *Canada among Nations 2005: Splitting Images*. Montreal and Kingston: McGill-Queen's University Press.

Mearsheimer, John J., and Stephen M. Walt. 2006. "The Israel lobby and U.S. foreign policy." *Middle East Policy* 13, 3 (September): 29–87.

Nair, K.R.G. 2004. "India–Canada Relations: A shining example of unrealised potential." New Delhi: Centre for Policy Research. Originally retrieved from www.asiapacificre-search.ca/caprn/cisp_project/2004/papers/nair.pdf.

Nayar, Kamala E. 2004. *The Sikh Diaspora in Vancouver: Three Generations Amid Tradition, Modernity, and Multi-culturalism*. Toronto: University of Toronto Press.

Nossal, Kim Richard. 1993. "The democratization of Canadian foreign policy?" *Canadian Foreign Policy Journal* 1, 3: 95–105.

———. 1997. *The Politics of Canadian Foreign Policy*. 3rd ed. Scarborough, ON: Prentice-Hall.

Potter, Evan H. 2002. "Canada and the new public diplomacy." *International Journal* 58,1 (Winter): 43–64.

———. 2004. "Branding Canada: The renaissance of Canada's commercial diplomacy." *International Studies Perspectives* 5, 1 (February): 55–60.

Pratt, Cranford. 1983. "Dominant class theory and Canadian foreign policy: The case of the counter-consensus." *International Journal* 39, 1 (Winter): 99–135.

Presthus, Robert V. 1973. *Elite Accommodation in Canadian Politics*. Cambridge: Cambridge University Press.

Pross, A. Paul, ed. 1975. *Pressure Group Behaviour in Canadian Politics*. Toronto: McGraw-Hill Ryerson.

Rose, Alexander. 2001. "How did Muslims vote in 2000?" *Middle East Quarterly* 8,3 (Summer): 13–27.

Ross, Liat R. 2007. "Canadian Muslims and foreign policy." *International Journal* 63, 1 (Winter): 187–205.

———. 2009. "The participation of Canadian Muslim pressure groups in the Canadian foreign policymaking process." Presented at the Canadian Political Science Association Conference, Ottawa, 27–29 May.

Rubinoff, Arthur G. 2002. "Canada's re-engagement with India." *Asian Survey* 42, 6 (November/December): 838–55.

Safran, William. 1991. "Diasporas in modern societies: Myths of homeland and return." *Diaspora: A Journal of Transnational Studies* 1, 1 (Spring): 83–99.

Sahoo, Ajaya K. 2006. "Issues of identity in the Indian diaspora: A transnational perspective." *Perspectives on Global Development and Technology* 5, 1: 81–98.

Sahoo, Ajaya K., and Dave Sangha. 2010. "Diaspora and cultural heritage: The case of Indians in Canada." *Asian Ethnicity* 11, 1: 81–94.

Saideman, Stephen M. 2002. "The power of the small: The impact of ethnic minorities on foreign policy." *SAIS Review* 22,2 (Summer–Fall): 93–105.

Sheffer, Gabriel. 1994. "Ethno-national diasporas and security." *Survival* 36, 1: 60–79.

———. 2003. *Diaspora Politics: At Home Abroad*. Cambridge: Cambridge University Press.

Shuval, Judith T. 2000. "Diaspora migration: Definitional ambiguities and a theoretical paradigm." *International Migration* 38, 5 (December): 41–56.

Siddiqui, Haroon. 2008. "Demographic changes fuel our foreign policy." *Toronto Star*, 24 February.

Singh, Anita. 2010. "Stephen Harper's India policy: The role and influence of the Indo-Canadian Diaspora." Unpublished dissertation. Halifax: Dalhousie University, Department of Political Science.

Smith, Jonathan C. 1998. "Foreign policy for sale? Interest group influence on President Clinton's Cuba policy, August 1994." *Presidential Studies Quarterly* 28, 1 (Winter): 207–20.

Smith, Tony. 2000. *Foreign Attachments: The Power of Ethnic Groups in the Making of American Foreign Policy*. Cambridge, MA: Harvard University Press.

Stairs, Denis. 1977. "Public opinion and external affairs: Reflections on the domestication of Canadian foreign policy." *International Journal* 33, 1 (Winter): 128–49.

Tatla, D.S. 1999. *The Sikh Diaspora: The Search for Statehood*. London: UCL Press.

Thakur, Ramesh. 1984. *Peacekeeping in Vietnam: Canada, India, Poland, and the International Commission*. Edmonton: University of Alberta Press.

Touhey, Ryan. 2007. "Canada and India at 60: Moving Beyond History." *International Journal* 62, 4 (Fall): 733–52.

Tremblay, Reeta C. 2003. "Canada–India relations: The need to re-engage." Paper prepared for the Asia Pacific Foundation of Canada's Roundtable on the Foreign Policy Dialogue and Canada–Asia Relations, 27 March.

Trilokekar, Roopa D. 2010. "International education as soft power? The contributions and challenges of Canadian foreign policy to the internationalization of higher education." *Higher Education* 59, 2 (February): 131–47.

Walton-Roberts, Margaret. 2010. "The Trade and Immigration Nexus in the India–Canada Context," pp. 145–72 in Benson Honig, Israel Drori, and Barbara Carmichael, eds. *Transnational and Immigrant Entrepreneurship in a Globalized World*. Toronto: University of Toronto Press.

Woo, Yuen Pau, Nizar Assanie, Pooja Sharma, and Rajesh Chadha. 2003. "Canada–India Trade: Retrospect and Prospects." *Canada-Asia Agenda*. NCAER, New Delhi and Asia Pacific Foundation of Canada.

Young, Lisa, and Joanna Everitt. 2004. *Advocacy Groups*. Vancouver: UBC Press.

Zhou, Min. 1997. "Segmented assimilation: Issues, controversies, and recent research on the new second generation." *International Migration Review* 31, 4 (Winter): 975–1008.

17 Civil Society and Canadian Foreign Policy

David Carment and Joe Landry

Key Terms

Diaspora
Foreign Policy Review
Human Security

Non-Governmental Organizations
Public Consultation

Civil Society and Foreign Policy in Recent Times

Canada's foreign policy posture has not evolved in a linear, straightforward path. Instead, its development has been characterized by many twists and turns, owing to the volatile nature of our democratic, parliamentary system which seeks to represent the wishes of a great number of individuals and groups with differing and often conflicting interests. Along with the capricious nature of the foreign policy positions taken by various governments over the past several decades, the level of civic engagement in the foreign-policy-making process has also had its ups and downs. These shifts often depend on a number of factors, including the ideology of the governing party; the level to which the government sees public engagement as being politically useful; the eagerness of the public to get involved in particular debates; and the ever expanding organizational capabilities of **non-governmental organizations** (NGOs) and other civil society groups.

While there are a number of prominent definitions of *civil society*, for our purposes it can be thought of broadly as "the sum of institutions, organizations, and individuals located between the family, the state, and the market, in which people associate voluntarily to advance common interests" (Anheier 2005, p. 9). Clearly this definition encompasses a great number of different groups; such entities must organize in order to effectively engage with policy-makers and other agents to promote change. Thus NGOs and non-profits can be thought of as the organizational infrastructure which allows civil society to interact with other dominant players in the policy-making realm. More formally, Sanjeev Khagram et al. note that NGOs are "private, voluntary nonprofit groups whose primary aim is to influence publicly some form of social change" (as cited in Ayres 2006, p. 493). Indeed, NGOs aim to affect a great variety of social issues, one of which is the foreign policy of our country, whether it be related to issues of security, development, environmental policy, diplomacy, and more.

Over the past several decades the number of registered non-profit organizations and NGOs in Canada has ballooned, along with their financial assets, scope, and political influence. Canada is known—both today and historically—as a country with a vibrant civil society. One 2005 study found that Canada's non-profit sector is among the largest in the world (Hall et al. 2005). Regardless of how dysfunctional and idiosyncratic it may appear to an outsider, Canada's foreign policy will, by virtue of its demography, **diaspora**, and domestic politics, reflect a diversity of viewpoints, interests, and values. At first glance one might be hard pressed to argue that civil society exerts any coherent influence on Canada's foreign policy-making. Yet to a very large degree, Canada's foreign policy choices are heavily constrained by domestic influences in general terms. Indeed, for the most part, Canada's foreign policy appears to be heavily influenced by domestic politics more than any other factor. Furthermore, as Canada's ethnic mosaic becomes more fragmented, the possibility exists that so too will our foreign policy.

This interpretation of foreign policy assumes that the credibility of a foreign policy depends on the likelihood that it will be carried out, which increases with domestic support for such a commitment (Carment and Bercuson 2008). Conversely, the more powerful the domestic groups that anticipate a resulting disadvantage, the less credible and sustainable will be the policy. Effective Canadian foreign policies depend on finding the right coalitions to support them, and in this regard civil society has an important role in shaping the scoped content and impact of foreign policy.

The casual observer might assume that when Canada takes action in a certain part of the world, or concentrates on a particular foreign policy issue, it may be due to pressure from interest groups lobbying for their own particular cause. Today, there is an increasing openness to invite such groups to lobby on foreign policy issues, and an increase in their influence on the foreign policy agenda is expected, even though groups are not formally organized and might not yet be fully capable of influencing the policy-making process. One outcome is a closer alignment of Canadian political parties allied with new immigrant communities, and the active participation of new Canadians in diplomacy, development, and trade would be expected.

From a historical perspective, civil society is an important element in creating space for policy dialogue in support of public policy initiatives. Several basic ideas regarding civil society activities in influencing the public are typically emphasized. The three most popular sentiments have typically been *empowerment* of local actors, *education* of people, and *dialogue* between governments and non-state actors. In addition, democratic principles are typically identified as important, as are law and order and human rights, including respect, accountability, and responsibility. Civil society organizations typically also make reference to the UN Charter, and documents on human rights, freedom of religion, and the responsibility to protect as physical representations of the principles at work within their organizations. Interestingly, these types of principles are also the foundation of much of the Canadian government's international policy. Democratic ideals, governance, security sector reform, electoral processes, accountability, and human rights all appear frequently in programming and funding initiatives announced by the federal government. In areas such as human rights, international law and a commitment to multilateralism tend to be general overriding themes.

Another historical trend is the increasing breadth of activities in which Canadian civil society organizations are involved. Programming by Canadian organizations reaches every corner of the globe and encompasses all aspects of foreign policy. Examples of this include aid programs undertaken by agencies such as the Canadian International Development Agency (CIDA)—training programs that teach specific skills, work to ensure the inclusion of women in the economic, social, and political development of a region, and manage natural resources and the environment. What this horizontal diffusion of foreign policy activities indicates is that Canada and Canadians continue to be involved in the global community, and that there is sustained and continuing interest in remaining involved.

Historically, then, the involvement of civil society in Canada's foreign policy activities has created a comprehensive and holistic approach that includes developmental as well as diplomatic, operational, and defensive work. These draw on historical traditions in Canada related to Pearson's peacekeeping initiatives, the focus on **human security**, and Canada's support for international law and institutions such as the United Nations as being the foundation upon which to build current and future civil society activities. While individual groups and organizations are involved in a variety of projects and issue areas, certain themes are relevant. One of the most important contributions of civil society is the quantity of grassroots work, local-level programs, and empowering programming that work with the support of Canadian institutions and individuals.

Many of these organizations see their own role as primarily one of support for "home-grown" solutions and initiatives. In essence, many civil society organizations see that the solutions to global problems are more likely to be found among those involved, and often these solutions require outside assistance to be realized. Education and development are often closely linked. Such links indicate that, for certain organizations, civil society and foreign policy have broadened to include many of the structural and systemic issues relating to global issues.

Today, however, the combination of the increasing power of political appointees, the lack of real and effective **public consultation**, and the absence of political leadership to engage the public have all contributed to a perception that civil society is no longer influential in foreign policy formation and implementation. Add to this some essential differences of opinion between new Canadians and Quebecers. For example, new Canadians from Eastern Europe, Asia, and Africa are, to a certain extent, adopting opinions about foreign policy that reflect the established English communities versus those opinions that are professed by the French demographic in the country (Carment and Bercuson 2008).

To some degree government policies have not yet embraced the values that new Canadians hold. Indeed such an approach may be undesirable because there are so many different values at play. For example, governmental institutions perceive the Cold War, the fall of the Berlin Wall, and the 1991 Gulf War as important international events that influence their mandate. On the other hand, many "established Canadians" hold to the belief that Canada is still a middle power internationally (Carment and Bercuson 2008). Some believe that Canada can still lead the world in norm-setting, big ideas, and soft-power concepts like human security, though that has certainly changed over the last seven years in which the Harper government has dismantled much of the foreign policy apparatus that underpinned these initiatives. Pinpointing an explicit set of values upon which to base a foreign policy may be near impossible now.

Consider that the current government has yet to hold a public **foreign policy review**. Historically, foreign policy reviews were considered an important mechanism through which government could engage civil society. Since Canadians were introduced to their first foreign policy review during a series of lectures at the University of Toronto given by Louis St Laurent, the review process has been considered a crucial element in a new government's contribution to public discourse. In his address, St Laurent spoke broadly of many problems facing Canada after World War II, but chief among them was the singular need for Canada to uphold the core values of freedom and liberty in the face of rising tyranny within the Eastern Bloc countries. In contrast, when Paul Martin's government released its International Policy Statement, the core tasks were efficiency and effectiveness in fixing the problems of a post-Cold War world confronted by failed and failing states, terrorism, and economic uncertainty.

Though facing vastly different tribulations, both leaders understood that identifying ends meant also showing to Canadians how these ends could realistically be achieved. Martin recognized that a pooling of resources and capabilities was an appropriate means to tackle the complex and interrelated problems facing Canada and the world. For St Laurent, international organizations such as the United Nations and the Commonwealth and later the North Atlantic Treaty Organization (NATO) were central to achieving his objectives.

Matching foreign policy means to foreign policy ends is no simple task. Any government contemplating a foreign policy review must consider how it will balance competing perspectives, how it will gather and evaluate relevant information to support the review process, and ultimately how it will engage the public in a discussion of those policy choices. No foreign policy review should purposefully divide a country; the policies a review espouses should speak to a combination of Canada's collective interests and capabilities. Further, a review is an important way to build bridges across departments, between the government and the people who elected them, and between the public and private spheres. Such cooperation and information sharing requires an overarching country strategy based on long-term objectives, strong leadership within and across government departments to enforce that strategy, and a full understanding of the costs and risks of pursuing a particular course of action. If a review is intended to establish parameters, identify means, specify objectives, and operationalize goals in a way that civil society can appreciate and value, it is understandable why some governments are ambivalent towards the review process. After all, a foreign policy review can be an extremely complex, time-consuming task, and it is an important, if not essential, way of holding Canada's elected officials accountable.

Engagement with civil society has been a hallmark of most foreign policy reviews. In 1970, the government of Pierre Elliott Trudeau produced *Foreign Policy for Canadians*; in 1995 Jean Chrétien released *Canada in the World*, which served to elucidate Canada's international priorities; and a decade later *A Role of Pride and Influence* was released and still stands as the most comprehensive foreign policy review put forward by the government of Prime Minister Paul Martin. In 1979, Joe Clark's minority government initiated a foreign policy review that was primarily driven by Flora MacDonald, the secretary of state for external affairs (Halloran et al. 2005). This exercise involved consultations with various government departments and resulted in two white papers being developed, one on defence issues and the other a more broad survey of Canadian foreign policy. In the end, the papers were never tabled due to the fall of the Clark government. From the mid-1980s to the early 1990s, the Progressive Conservative party was sharply criticized for its lack of transparency on foreign policy issues. In response, Prime Minister Brian Mulroney issued a foreign policy discussion paper in 1986 entitled *Competitiveness and Security*, which noted Canada's heavy dependence on trade and outlined strategic policies to improve the country's relationship with the United States.

The Trudeau and Mulroney eras are particularly notable, for it was during these periods that civil society organized itself through public debates over issues such as the NAFTA negotiations and the establishment of the Charter of Rights and Freedoms. It might be said that Canadians "woke up" to the idea that ordinary citizens could have a direct effect on government policy decisions (Ayres 2006, p. 495). The Liberal party under Jean Chrétien seized on this idea and public engagement became a key pillar of their platform for the 1993 election, with the party vowing to "democratize" Canada's foreign policy. This effort was not one-sided but rather driven by the ever-increasing organizational capacities of Canada's NGOs and civil society organizations. From 1993 to 2005, the Liberal government had a number of successful international policy initiatives that were heavily influenced and shaped by civil society actors in both Canada and abroad. Common examples include the Landmines Convention, the Responsibility to Protect, and the influential concept of "human security." Once the Conservative party led by Stephen Harper came into power in 2006, many of these perceived "Liberal" foreign policy initiatives were discarded in favour of a more ad hoc strategy focused on strengthening economic relationships and assisting Canadian business in entering emerging markets. Despite this, since the Harper government has been in power, no systematic, publicly accessible foreign policy review process has taken place. Instead, in its place, most foreign policy choices have occurred through changes in budgets that affect the structure and coherence of its departments and, in turn, support to civil society organizations, such as the decision to stop funding the Global Peace and Security Fund, the decision to merge CIDA with DFAIT, and the funding cuts to or dismantling of NGOs and think tanks such as KAIROS, the North–South Institute, the International Development Research Centre, and the Centre for Rights and Democracy.

In September 2012 a leaked document brought a draft "Canadian foreign policy plan" to the public eye. It focused on giving Canada access to China and other emerging markets around the world primarily for our own direct economic benefit (Weston 2012). While this document was not officially acknowledged as policy by the government, it paints a picture of what is to come for Canada's foreign policy in the future. Indeed, in November of 2013, the Harper government released a white paper laying out a foreign policy strategy that prioritized trade and the role of the private sector as the primary means to establish economic prosperity at home, echoing the key themes of the leaked 2012 document. However, the silence of the Conservative government on public engagement in either of these documents is perhaps the most salient feature of the shift that is currently occurring in the policy-making process.

In any case, it is clear that Canada's foreign policy has undergone significant transformations over the history of the country. The level of openness to civil society has been greatly affected by such shifts, reflecting the ideological differences between democratically elected governments, as would be expected. The following sections in this chapter will serve to further shed light on the sources and implications of these dynamic shifts.

Changing Values in a Changing Society

Consultations with civil society organizations in national and international forums have historically been important mechanisms to promote greater engagement, inclusivity, and transparency between governments and civil society on key foreign policy issues such as where and how to engage the world. Consultations would typically include academics and representatives from government departments and NGOs. The principal focus was to solicit civil society input on the implementation of Canada's foreign policy objectives. Such consultations might include briefings from representatives of the government followed by plenary discussions and open debate. With the exception of formal presentations, comments stemming from the consultations are typically not attributed. Prominent examples of such consultations include the Peacebuilding Consultations organized by the Liberal government when Lloyd Axworthy was foreign minister, and the Human Security Network consultations from about 10 years ago. These events were notable because

DFAIT operated with an open-door policy—everyone from student to practitioner was invited to participate and contribute.

Typically, consultations of this scope have a cross-regional nature and emphasize the role of civil society in their operational frameworks. The underlying rationale for these consultations was to help build leadership potential in regional and multilateral forums by providing continuity with the activities and priorities that can be carried forward. In addition, the goal was to look to civil society to help develop concrete, creative initiatives that focused on a specific issue. The goal was to use this common vision to move the issue forward in other bilateral and multilateral forums where there could be positive spillover effects.

A second goal was to further explore issues that were fully developed by the government, which lacked the capacity to do so. The idea was to develop a greater degree of consensus and understanding on specific issues so that, in the future, those consulted could work together to advance them in other forums.

A third goal was to project foreign policy principles where there was broad consensus. Examples include human rights, which requires developing thinking in regular meetings where experts and civil society work to exchange information and develop an articulated position on key issues.

While consultations can act as an enabler of foreign policy, they can also constrain the foreign policy decisions of governments, so governments work to shield themselves from such influences on particular issues in a number of ways. As long as the government is seen to be at least somewhat open to the viewpoints of Canadians, the public will often let the final policy decisions be made by those in power. For example, trade negotiations have not historically been sensitive to civil society pressure. The anti-free trade movement, which saw widespread application of neo-liberal, free market economic policies as a major barrier to social justice

and equality, came to a head in the late 1990s at the WTO summit in Seattle. Such protests were also prominent at the 2010 G20 summit in Toronto, causing widespread damage and the arrest of over 1,000 people.

Polling shows that Canadians are still hesitant about an unquestioned acquiescence to free trade agreements, with recent polls illustrating that a majority (59 per cent) of Canadians do not support the idea of a US-style free trade agreement with China (Ipsos 2012a). Similar numbers occur for other Asian countries including India, South Korea, and Japan (Asia Pacific Foundation of Canada 2013). On the other hand, more than 8 out of 10 Canadians support the idea of a free trade agreement with the European Union (EU) (Ipsos 2012b). This discrepancy signals that Canadians, rather than opposing free trade agreements wholly in principle, are discerning about who we trade with because of core values. Questions of human rights protection, value for money, and outsourcing of manufacturing jobs are just some of the key reasons for such a dichotomy of opinions. Nevertheless, the trend of governments through time has illustrated that such opinion polls and protests do not wholly influence a government's decision to pursue such agreements. Indeed, the 2012 leaked document referred to the need to trade with countries that had value systems much different from our own.

Another area where civil society pressure has a lesser impact is in decisions of military deployment. While Canada's initial involvement in the 2001 war in Afghanistan was initially supported by the majority of the population and by civil society organizations, it took nearly 10 years of increased opposition to the war for Canada to finally end its combat mission there, much longer than would have been expected if the pressure from NGOs and civil society actors had been more influential. This is somewhat surprising given that NGOs were seen—initially at least—to be a key component of our deployment to the Afghanistan theatre, under the guise of whole of government approaches to state-building. Indeed, the policy platform at the time emphasized the crucial role to be played by NGOs in the conflict zone—a process that had emerged over 20 years of crucial work they played on the ground in failed and failing states around the world. The fact that NGOs were not able to alter the approach taken by the Harper government over the latter half of the Afghanistan war speaks to their diminished influence.

Some other examples of issues that are sensitive to civil society pressure traditionally have included international treaty formulation and implementation, such as the Landmines Convention; propagation of uncontroversial norms, such as the Responsibility to Protect and human security; environmental policy initiatives, such as the signing of the Kyoto Accord; aspects of the humanitarian agenda, such as the Canadian response to the 2010 earthquake in Haiti; and regulation of Canadian companies to meet ethical standards of behaviour, both in Canada and abroad. For this analysis, two examples demonstrate how traditional civil society influences are evolving to bolster their effects on policy-makers in our changing society.

The first example is the Canadian government's response to the January 12, 2010 earthquake in Haiti, wherein Canada arguably provided a disproportionately large response due to the vast population of Haitian immigrants living in Canada. Immediately after the earthquake, Canada evacuated 4,620 Canadian citizens and permanent residents on 49 flights from Haiti (Government of Canada 2013). It also deployed approximately 2,000 personnel from the Canadian military, whose aim was to provide medical care; search and rescue aid; humanitarian assistance, including food and water delivery; security services; and engineering services. The Canadian Forces provided nearly 2.6 million liters of potable water, 1.5 million meals, and medical care for over 22,000 people in the aftermath of the disaster. In addition to this massive rescue operation, Canada also issued preferential immigration treatment to Haitian citizens. The special immigration measures that were used were both multi-level and multi-dimensional, in that they were enacted on both the federal and provincial levels and as a result of the unique humanitarian circumstances of this particular disaster (Citizenship and Immigration Canada 2010).

These immigration instruments were used primarily to allow Haitians who had been affected by the earthquake and who had close family ties in Canada to be able to enter the country swiftly and legally in order to secure their personal well-being. In this example, the relationship between the government and the Haitian community in Canada works two ways. The government aims to appease the concerns of diaspora communities in order to secure domestic political favour. At the same time these communities recognize their ability to sway decision-makers and often can act to pressure the government into taking certain actions. Both sides of this equation are important and self-reinforcing. The preferential treatment accorded to Haitian-Canadians following the earthquake therefore provides a useful example of civil society and state relations in action. To be sure, the earthquake in Haiti did not, however, represent the beginning of Canada's special relationship with Haiti; indeed, between 2006 and 2012, Canada provided more than $1 billion in aid to Haiti, making this small island nation the largest recipient of Canadian aid in the Americas (DFAIT 2013). Canada's special relationship with Haiti is predominantly driven by the large Haitian diaspora living in this country; political parties see these constituents as key to gaining political power, and the Harper government has been especially adept at currying favour with these groups. Ottawa and Montreal in particular are home to a number of active civil society groups based on a common Haitian ethnicity, and the community continues to grow. This example illustrates how certain issues can be affected by the changing makeup of Canada's civil society.

The next example of how civil society can influence certain issues relates to the conduct of mining and other extractive industries. Canada is home to some of the largest mining companies in the world, and these multinational companies (MNCs) have operations in every corner of the globe. Mining accounts for between 4 and 5 per cent of national GDP—nearly 15 per cent of Canada's national exports—making it one of the most valuable industries to the country (Hilson 2002). In many countries, however, labour laws and environmental regulations are not up to par with those in the West. As Canadian companies have expanded around the globe, examples of exploitation of both workers and the natural environment have become commonplace. Migration of workers and environmental degradation often upset the balance of local communities, having profound negative results (Hilson 2002). Indeed, communities around the world, in more than 10 countries as diverse as Colombia, Greece, and Nicaragua, have staged mass protests against Canadian mining firms' actions locally, and civil society groups in Canada have joined in the call to regulate these giant MNCs (Ortega Arango 2013). These clashes have often been violent and can be severely disruptive to the balance of the local communities being affected. In response, Corporate Social Responsibility (CSR) has developed as one of the most powerful new concepts in this fight, and MNCs are now expected to follow the same guidelines in developing countries as they would in Canada. In response to this civil society pressure, the government has not been quick to introduce or enforce any such legislation; rather, they have promoted lighter, voluntary initiatives, and have even co-opted CIDA into assisting transnational mining companies with their CSR activities. Critics argue that this shift in policy is merely a guise to give Canadian mining companies a competitive advantage over their rivals, as they have to expend less resources towards meeting acceptable CSR objectives due to the augmentation of government-funded projects in affected communities.

In order to transform the rhetoric surrounding the issue of corporate social responsibility into concrete and significant action, MNCs in resource extractive industries must implement risk analysis procedures and impact assessment mechanisms to evaluate their current practices and to guide their future decisions and actions. Such an action would prevent incidents such as the conflict that occurred in Indonesia when Canadian nickel mining company Vale's (formerly INCO) operations caused severe lowering of water levels in the local watershed, seriously affecting the ability of local people to conduct their day-to-day lives in a traditional fashion (Hilson 2002). Moreover, cancer rates increased and locals complained of dust and ash contaminating the air. Nevertheless, the company refused to admit wrongdoing or commission any type of study to determine what was causing the problems. This resulted in a great deal of tension building up, and protests similar to those mentioned earlier occurred. If Vale had succumbed to civil society pressure both from Canada and locally, these types of incidents could have been avoided. The process of improving land use policies and regulating large MNCs involves recognizing the potential positive and negative impacts of MNCs. The next step is then modifying corporate–community interactions in order to reduce harmful effects, including overt conflict, and to achieve improved impacts on the host community's economic, environmental, security, and political situation. It is important to emphasize that while companies are not expected to resolve complex issues such as conflict, governance, and human rights violations, the perception of companies as indifferent to issues that have the potential to exacerbate conflict can be very damaging. In fact, the risk of negative corporate publicity not only provides the rationale for corporate awareness and interest in conflict-related issues in the companies' sphere of development but also endorses the idea that demonstrating an awareness and an interest in this area can lead to positive public relations for a company.

Overall, these examples illustrate cases where civil society influence can have a major effect on government policy, none at all, or somewhere in between. These complex issues are not black and white, however, and often the effects of civil society pressure are felt to differing degrees. In certain cases it can be seen that governments merely adopt the minimal amount of civil society input, while in others it is civil society that drives an entire policy framework from the ground up.

Looking Forward: Democracy, Domestic Politics and Diaspora

The subject of "democratizing" Canadian foreign policy has been touched on briefly in the previous sections of this chapter, yet it is important to deconstruct what is really meant by this notion. It is clear that a major pillar of the 1993 Liberal election platform was this idea of opening up the foreign policy-making process to the public, yet exactly how this would or could be done remained unclear even well into their governing years. Indeed, Maxwell Cameron (1998) observes that "a volume commissioned to assess the Liberal record on this front in 1995 found little tangible evidence to suggest that the Liberal government was conducting foreign policy any more democratically than its predecessor, and considerable confusion—in both government and academic circles—about what it would actually mean to democratize foreign policy. The implication was that democratization was a failed promise of the Liberal government" (pp. 147–8).

Kim Nossal (1993) brought the same puzzle to the forefront, stating that technically, since Canada's parliament is made up of elected representatives, their foreign policy decisions are already democratic by right. On the other hand, if one were to pose the question of whether Canada's foreign policy is democratic, the answer from most would be "no" (cited in Cameron 1998, pp. 148–9). To reconcile this paradox, Nossal argues that politicians' "proposals for greater democratization in Canadian foreign policy are little more than techniques of elite management that have little to do with democracy" (p. 95). Rather, Nossal notes, politicians and policy-makers must define and pursue the interests of the community as a whole if true democracy is to be achieved in the policy-making process. If this is true, then what can make foreign policy more democratic, pragmatically?

One such attempt was the 1996 creation of the Canadian Centre for Foreign Policy Development (CCFPD) (Ayres 2006, p. 496), though it never lived up to its billing; it became a means for the foreign minister to float various trial balloons for public consideration rather than being a true consultative body. The practical measures undertaken to fulfill its rather broad mandate included conducting cross-country meetings and conferences which aimed to increase transparency and foster public engagement in the foreign policy-making process. In fact, the path ultimately taken by the CCFPD failed to live up to many of the recommendations made by Tim Draimin and Betty Plewes (1995), who had advocated for greater accessibility, transparency, and representativeness in foreign policy decision-making. Unfortunately for those academics, policy-makers, and engaged citizens who welcomed the establishment of this new mechanism for consultation, the centre shut down shortly after the departure of its creator, Minister Axworthy, before the Chrétien era had come to a close (Ayres 2006, p. 497). Whether the short-lived CCFPD represented an ideal mechanism for the democratization of Canadian foreign policy remains up for debate. Other processes have also been highlighted as examples of how civil society can effectively engage with policy-makers on vital issues.

Cameron (1998) uses a case study of the Ottawa process to demonstrate how such activities can occur in practice, beyond the usual rhetoric espoused by politicians. In brief, the Ottawa process, which culminated in the international treaty to ban landmines, was based on an unprecedented level of direct access on the part of NGOs to the international machinery of negotiation normally reserved for governments alone. Cameron states: "In the Ottawa Process, policy makers provided public reasons for their actions and exposed them to criticism from civil society by bringing an NGO coalition into the policy process, both as domestic partners and international allies. The result was one of the most significant Canadian foreign policy achievements in decades" (p. 163). To be sure, it took a foreign minister steadfastly focused on bringing civil society groups to the table in order to achieve this goal. Minister Axworthy was vocal in his recognition of the valuable role that NGOs could play in creating viable, effective policies.

If NGOs act as the infrastructure by which civil society affects policy choices, how exactly can these organizations do so? According to Louis Kriesberg (1997), there are five primary ways in which NGOs can affect policy choices: 1) helping to mobilize support for particular policies; 2) helping to widen public participation in international policy processes; 3) helping to sustain attention on critical global problems; 4) helping to frame issues and set the policy agenda; and 5) helping to carry out transnational policies. These five dimensions demonstrate that there are multiple ways by which democratic processes can influence foreign policy. While traditionally the Canadian government has utilized the foreign policy review process as the primary venue for soliciting participation from everyday citizens, technologies such as the Internet have completely revolutionized the way that citizens—through NGOs—can participate actively in the policy-making process. Along all of these dimensions it has become increasingly possible for civil society actors to provide input on and even steer the direction of particular policies. Moreover, this process is no longer limited to national borders. Global NGOs composed of individuals and groups who share the same passion for social change can now communicate, organize, and put forward their proposals to policy-makers.

There is both continuity and transformation in how civil society influences and shapes Canada's foreign policy. First, with respect to transformation, while Canada's political leadership has always had to fine-tune its foreign policy choices in relation to regional differences, these differences have clearly become sharper with time; in addition, today Canada's population changes are also influencing a shift in the locus of political power from Eastern Canada to Western Canada. A combination of non-native French speaker out-migration and a declining birthrate has reduced Quebec's share of the overall population to less than 30 per cent; Atlantic Canada's share of the population is also growing smaller. By the same token, Canada's cities, particularly Toronto, Calgary, and Vancouver, are becoming larger and more ethnically diverse, and their populations continue to grow at a rapid pace. Overall, as the Western provinces' share of political influence appears to be on the increase, the Eastern provinces' appears to be in decline, especially Quebec's. Conventional wisdom argues that an important distinction in this regard is premised on Quebecers' being essentially pacifist, anti-militarist, and isolationist.

Yet for all their potential importance these population and demographic shifts have not fully translated into major shifts in political influence for civil society either directly through parliamentary processes or indirectly through other means. For example, the distribution of seats in the House of Commons has not kept pace with an increase in the representation for urban centres. Rural constituencies still tend to have a greater clout than their numbers warrant. Similarly, Canada's newest immigrants have been relatively inactive on the political front in organizing themselves as lobbyists and the like. It is only now, in the last decade and a half, that immigration-based electoral politics has emerged strongly in a large number of Canada's cities. That influence can be readily seen in the changing nature of parliamentary representation, which has never been more ethnically diverse.

The most obvious change has arisen as the nation's chief source of immigrants from South and Southeast Asia, Africa, and South and Latin America bring with them their own distinct political, social, and economic agendas. For most of Canada's history, more than 90 per cent of its immigrants came from Western Europe. Since the 1990s, over 50 per cent of immigrants have come from Asia, while European immigration declined. Other less obvious changes are taking place as well. Canada's postwar baby boomers are now the retirees of the 2000s. While the agenda of their youth might have been to change the world for the better, now it is to keep their health and maintain their economic prosperity.

New Canadians also *stimulate* trade and investment because the information advantages they hold improve investment by reducing the transaction costs of entry into home markets for the banking and investment sector, and diaspora connections are important for overcoming obstacles to the transfer of resources. Questions of diaspora labour mobility and retention issues are also very important for the Canadian economy. More and more trade agreements include services issues with respect to the World Trade Organization's protocols on movement of natural persons, which has important implications for trade. The idea that diaspora relations can be easily harnessed by host governments to improve trade relations has been called into question by those who show that, in the case of trade between India and Canada (for example), there is no convincing evidence that Canada has managed to extract "ethnic surplus value" in the form of cultural and economic competencies.

On the development side, new Canadians with diaspora connections are now identified as key drivers of development, through remittances, the transfer of human and social capital, and through direct support for democracy processes and peacebuilding in fragile states. Health initiatives, brain circulation, and professional networks are all well documented. But aid also acts as a "pull factor" for potential migrations; bilateral aid might actually increase skilled-worker migration to specific donors by enhancing information about labour market conditions in donor countries. Regarding pull factors, host countries like Canada can ease this "brain drain" and contribute to development by creating policy frameworks conducive to flexibility in migration and investment in homelands.

Conclusion

This chapter has provided an introduction to the relationship between Canadian foreign policy and civil society. In doing so, several key themes have emerged. First, it is clear that civil society engagement has become increasingly important over time. At the same time, the form of engagement has varied through the years and depends on a number of key factors, including the ideology and policy-making preferences of the governing party, the specific characteristics of the issue of interest, and the organizational abilities of civil society groups, to name a few. Second, we have seen that domestic politics do influence policy decisions. This is true because in our democratic system politicians are acutely aware of the various interests of their constituents; if they are not, then they risk losing their positions as elected leaders. As Canada's civil society grows it is also increasingly influenced by demographic changes. Hence there is increasing pressure for better "representation," whether it is expressed through traditional democratic forums and reform or through diaspora connections. Third, as the political spectrum shifts, and if current trends hold, society may indeed be becoming more "conservative." But at the same time that does not mean civil society will be less influential over time; rather, the influence will be wielded in different ways than before as new groups affect the policy-making process in a less traditional manner. Along with this notion comes the idea that traditional forms of engagement—such as foreign policy reviews, community dialogues, and other channels for liaison with Canadians—are perhaps mainly driven by

political party preference rather than being a necessary feature of Canadian political society. Overall, despite the seemingly unpredictable nature of civil society and its impact on foreign policy-making, the relationship between the two is here to stay. To be sure, the size and capacity of civil society groups will continue to move forward unabated as it has for the past several decades. This revolution means that citizens are able to have their voices heard anywhere from in a local town hall all the way to the General Assembly of the United Nations—if the issue has enough salience. Whether the public engagement of the 1990s will return to Canadian political life remains to be seen, yet at this juncture in history it looks as though the tide is shifting to new, as of yet undiscovered, mechanisms for policy influence by the fluid regional and demographic transformations happening in Canada.

Questions for Review

1. Why are foreign policy reviews an important part of foreign policy-making?
2. What, historically, has been the role of civil society in Canadian foreign policy?
3. Identify three examples of civil society's role in Canadian foreign policy.
4. "Public consultation is an important means for

governments to assess the legitimacy of their foreign policy priorities." Do you agree with this statement?

5. "As Canada's demography changes by age and ethnicity, Canada's foreign policy must reflect these changes." Do you agree with this statement?

Suggested Readings

Ayres, Jeffrey M. 2006. "Civil society participation in Canadian foreign policy: Expanded consultation in the Chrétien years," pp. 491–507 in Patrick James, Nelson Michaud, and Marc J. O'Reilly, eds. *Handbook of Canadian Foreign Policy*. Lanham, MD: Lexington Books.

Cameron, Maxwell A. 1998. "Democratization of foreign policy: The Ottawa process as a model." *Canadian Foreign Policy Journal* 5, 3: 147–65.

Carothers, Thomas, and William Barndt. 1999. "Civil society." *Foreign Policy* 117 (Winter):18–29.

Draimin, Tim, and Betty Plewes. 1995. "Civil society and the democratization of foreign policy," pp. 63–82 in Maxwell A. Cameron and Maureen Appel Molot, eds. *Canada Among Nations 1995: Democracy and Foreign Policy*. Ottawa: Carleton University Press.

Nossal, Kim Richard. 1993. "The democratization of Canadian foreign policy?" *Canadian Foreign Policy Journal* 1, 3: 95–105.

Salamon, L.M., S.W. Sokolowski, and R. List. 2003. *Global Civil Society: An Overview*. Baltimore: Johns Hopkins Center for Civil Society Studies.

References

Anheier, Helmut K. 2005. *Nonprofit Organizations*. Abingdon, UK: Routledge.

Asia Pacific Foundation of Canada. 2013. *2013 National Opinion Poll: Canadian Views on Asia*. Available at www.asiapacific.ca/sites/default/files/filefield/national_opinion_poll_2013_-_may_29_-_final.pdf.

Ayres, Jeffrey M. 2006. "Civil society participation in Canadian foreign policy: Expanded consultation in the Chrétien years," pp. 491–507 in Patrick James, Nelson Michaud, and Marc J. O'Reilly, eds. *Handbook of Canadian Foreign Policy*. Lanham, MD: Lexington Books.

Cameron, Maxwell A. 1998. "Democratization of foreign policy: The Ottawa process as a model." *Canadian Foreign Policy Journal* 5, 3: 147–65.

Canadian Centre for Foreign Policy Development. 1998. *Annual Report*. Ottawa: Department of Foreign Affairs and International Trade.

Carment, David, and David Bercuson, eds. 2008. *The World in Canada*. Montreal and Kingston: McGill-Queen's University Press.

Citizenship and Immigration Canada. 2010. "Government of Canada introduces special immigration measures in response to the earthquake in Haiti." News release, 16 January. Available at http://news.gc.ca/web/article-en.do?m=/index&nid=506059&_ga=1.92059805.667167346.1414170704.

Department of Foreign Affairs and International Trade (DFAIT). 2013. "Haiti: After the earthquake."

Draimin, Tim, and Betty Plewes. 1995. "Civil society and the democratization of foreign policy," pp. 63–82 in Maxwell A. Cameron and Maureen Appel Molot, eds. *Canada Among Nations 1995: Democracy and Foreign Policy*. Ottawa: Carleton University Press.

Government of Canada. 2013. "Canada's response to the devastating earthquake." Available at www.canadainternational.gc.ca/haiti/engagement/earthquake-seisme.aspx.

Hall, Michael H., et al. 2005. *The Canadian Nonprofit and Voluntary Sector in Comparative Perspective*. Imagine Canada, Government of Canada, and Johns Hopkins University. Available at http://sectorsource.ca/sites/default/files/resources/files/jhu_report_en.pdf.

Halloran, Mary, John Hilliker, and Greg Donaghy. 2005. "The white paper impulse: Reviewing foreign policy under Trudeau and Clark." Presented at the 77th Annual Conference of the Canadian Political Science Association. Available at http://www.cpsa-acsp.ca/papers-2005/Halloran.pdf.

Hilson, Gavin. 2002. "An overview of land use conflicts in mining communities." *Land Use Policy* 19, 1 (January): 65–73.

Ipsos. 2012a. "Majority (59%) of Canadians don't support U.S.-style free trade agreement with China." 19 December. Available at http://www.ipsos-na.com/news-polls/pressrelease.aspx?id=5938.

———. 2012b. "Overall, eight in ten (81%) support a free trade agreement between Canada and the European Union." 16 September. Available at http://www.ipsos-na.com/news-polls/pressrelease.aspx?id=5772.

Khagram, Sanjeev, James V. Riker, and Kathryn Sikkink, eds. 2002. *Restructuring World Politics: Transnational Social Movements, Networks, and Norms*. Minneapolis: University of Minnesota Press.

Kriesberg, Louis. 1997. "Social movements and global transformation," pp. 3–18 in Jackie Smith, Charles Chatfield, and Ron Pagnucco, eds. *Transnational Social Movements and Global Politics: Solidarity Beyond the State*. Syracuse, NY: Syracuse University Press.

Nossal, Kim Richard. 1993. "The democratization of Canadian foreign policy?" *Canadian Foreign Policy Journal* 1, 3: 95–105.

Ortega Arango, Santiago. 2013. "Canadian mining companies subject of worldwide protests." CBC News: World, 3 April. Available at www.cbc.ca/news/world/canadian-mining-companies-subject-of-worldwide-protests-1.1368155.

Weston, Greg. 2012. "Secret document details new Canadian foreign policy." CBC News: Politics, 19 November. Available at www.cbc.ca/news/politics/story/2012/11/19/pol-foreign-policy-.html.

Selected Bibliography

Balthazar, Louis, Louis Bélanger, Gordon Mace, et al. 1993. *Trent Ans de Politique Extérieure du Québec 1960–1990*. Québec/Sillery: Septentrion and CQRI.

Bélanger, Louis. 1997. "The United States and the Formative Years of an Independent Quebec's Foreign Policy," *American Review of Canadian Studies* 27, 1: 11–25.

Brown, Douglas, and Murray Smith, eds. 1991. *Canadian Federalism: Meeting Global Challenges?* Kingston, ON: Queen's University Institute of Intergovernmental Relations.

Burney, Derek. 2005. *Getting it Done: A Memoir*. Montreal and Kingston: McGill-Queen's University Press.

Burton, B.E., W.C. Soderlund, and T.A. Keenleyside. 1995. "The Press and Canadian Foreign Policy: A Re-examination Ten Years On," *Canadian Foreign Policy* 3 (Fall): 51–69.

Copeland, Daryl. 2009. *Guerrilla Diplomacy: Rethinking International Relations*. Boulder, CO: Lynne Rienner.

De Boer, Stephen. 2002. "Canadian Provinces, US States and North American Integration: Bench Warmers or Key Players?" *Choices: Canada's Options in North America* 8 (November): 1–24.

Donaghy, Greg, and Kim Richard Nossal, eds. 2009. *Architects and Innovators: Building the Department of Foreign Affairs and International Trade, 1909–2009*. Montreal and Kingston: McGill-Queen's University Press.

Drake, Earl. 1999. *A Stubble-Jumper in Striped Pants: Memoirs of a Prairie Diplomat*. Toronto: University of Toronto Press.

English, John. 1992. *The Worldly Years: The Life of Lester Pearson, Vol. 2, 1949–1972*. New York: Knopf.

Gotlieb, Allan. 1991. *"I'll be With You in a Minute, Mr Ambassador": The Education of a Canadian Diplomat in Washington*. Toronto: University of Toronto Press.

———. 2007. *The Washington Diaries: 1981–1989*. Toronto: McClelland and Stewart.

Granatstein, J.L., and Robert Bothwell. 1990. *Pirouette: Pierre Trudeau and Canadian Foreign Policy*. Toronto: University of Toronto Press.

Halton, Dan. 2001. "International News in the North American Media," *International Journal* 56, 3 (Summer): 499–515.

Head, Ivan, and Pierre Trudeau. 1995. *The Canadian Way: Shaping Canada's Foreign Policy, 1968–1984*. Toronto: McClelland and Stewart.

Hilliker, John. 1990. *Canada's Department of External Affairs, Vol. 1: The Early Years, 1909–1946*. Montreal and Kingston: McGill-Queen's University Press.

Hilliker, John, and Donald Barry. 1994. "The PM and the SSEA in Canada's Foreign Policy: Sharing the Territory, 1946–1968," *International Journal* 50, 1 (Winter): 162–88.

———. 1995. *Canada's Department of External Affairs, Vol. 2: Coming of Age, 1946–1968*. Montreal and Kingston: McGill-Queen's University Press.

Jensen, Kurt F. 2008. *Cautious Beginnings: Canadian Foreign Intelligence, 1939–51*. Vancouver: UBC Press.

Kirton, John. 1978. "Foreign Policy Decision-Making in the Trudeau Government: Promise and Performance," *International Journal* 33, 2 (Spring): 287–311.

Kukucha, Christopher J. 2008. *The Provinces and Canadian Foreign Trade Policy*. Vancouver: UBC Press.

Lackenbauer, P. Whitney, ed. 2002. *An Inside Look at External Affairs During the Trudeau Years: The Memoirs of Mark MacGuigan*. Calgary: University of Calgary Press.

Lortie, Marc, and Sylvie Bédard. 2002. "Citizen Involvement in Canadian Foreign Policy: The Summit of the Americas Experience 2001," *International Journal* 57, 3 (Summer): 323–40.

McNiven, James D., and Dianna Cann. 1993. "Canadian Provincial Trade Offices in the United States," pp. 167–84 in Douglas M. Brown and Earl H. Fry, eds., *States and Provinces in the International Economy*. Berkeley: University of California Press; Kingston, ON: Institute of Governmental Studies Press and Institute of Intergovernmental Relations.

McRae, Rob. 2001. "Human Security, Connectivity, and the New Global Civil Society," pp. 236–49 in Rob McRae and Don Hubert, eds., *Human Security and the New Diplomacy: Protecting People, Promoting Peace*. Montreal and Kingston: McGill-Queen's University Press.

MacDonald, Laura C. 2002. "Governance and State-Society Relations: The Challenges," pp. 187–223 in George C. Hoberg, ed., *Capacity of Choice: Canada in a New North America*. Toronto: University of Toronto Press.

Mace, Gordon, Louis Bélanger, and Ivan Bernier. 1995. "Canadian Foreign Policy and Quebec," pp. 119–44 in Maxwell A. Cameron and Maureen Appel Molot, eds., *Canada among Nations 1995: Democracy and Foreign Policy*. Ottawa: Carleton University Press.

Matthews, Robert. 1983. "The Churches and Foreign Policy," *International Perspectives* January/February: 18–21.

Michaud, Nelson. 2002. "Bureaucratic Politics and the Shaping of Policies: Can We Measure Pulling and Hauling Games?" *Canadian Journal of Political Science* 35, 2 (June): 269–300.

Munton, Don, and Tom Keating. 2001. "Internationalism and the Canadian Public," *Canadian Journal of Political Science* 34, 3 (September): 517–49.

Nossal, Kim Richard. 1983–84. "Analyzing Domestic Sources of Canadian Foreign Policy," *International Journal* 39, 1 (Winter): 1–22.

———. 1984. "Bureaucratic Politics and the Westminster Model," pp. 120–7 in Robert Mathews et al., eds., *International Conflict and Conflict Management: Readings in World Politics*. Scarborough, ON: Prentice-Hall.

———. 1994. "The PM and the SSEA in Canada's Foreign Policy: Dividing the Territory, 1968–1993," *International Journal* 50, 1 (Winter): 189–208.

———. 1995. "The Democratization of Canadian Foreign Policy: The Elusive Ideal," pp. 29–43 in Maxwell A. Cameron and Maureen Appel Molot, eds., *Canada among Nations 1995: Democracy and Foreign Policy*. Ottawa: Carleton University Press.

———. 1996. "Anything But Provincial: The Provinces and Foreign Affairs," pp. 503–18 in Christopher Dunn, ed., *Provinces: Canadian Provincial Politics*. Peterborough, ON: Broadview Press.

Pearson, Geoffrey A.H. 1994. *Seize the Day: Lester B. Pearson and Crisis Diplomacy*. Ottawa: Carleton University Press.

Pratt, Cranford. 1983–4. "Dominant Class Theory and Canadian Foreign Policy: The Case of the Counter-Consensus," *International Journal* 39, 1 (Winter): 99–135.

Reece, David Chalmer, ed. 1996. *Special Trust and Confidence: Envoy Essays in Canadian Diplomacy*. Ottawa: Carleton University Press.

———. 2007. *Ambassador Assignments: Canadian Diplomats Reflect on Our Place in the World*. Markham, ON: Fitzhenry and Whiteside.

Rempel, Roy. 2002. *The Chatter Box: An Insider's Account of the Irrelevance of Parliament in the Making of Canadian Foreign and Defence Policy*. Toronto: Dundurn.

Riddell-Dixon, Elizabeth. 1985. *The Domestic Mosaic: Domestic Groups and Canadian Foreign Policy*. Toronto: Canadian Institute of International Affairs.

Skogstad, Grace. 2012. "International Trade Policy and the Evolution of Canadian Federalism: A Constructive Tension," pp. 203–22 in Herman Bakvis and Grace Skogstad, eds., *Canadian Federalism: Performance, Effectiveness, and Legitimacy*, 3rd ed. Don Mills, ON: Oxford University Press.

———. 2013. "Global Governance and Canadian Federalism: Reconciling External Accountability Obligations through Internal Accountability Practices," pp. 190–210 in Peter Graefe, Julie M. Simmons, and Linda A. White, eds., *Overpromising and Underperforming? Understanding and Evaluating New Intergovernmental Accountability Regimes*. Toronto: University of Toronto Press.

Skogstad, Grace, David Cameron, Martin Papillon, and Keith Banting, eds. 2013. *The Global Promise of Federalism*. Toronto: University of Toronto Press.

Stairs, Denis. 2001. "The Changing Office and the Changing Environment of the Minister of Foreign Affairs in the Axworthy Era," pp. 19–38 in Fen Osler Hampson, Norman Hillmer, and Maureen Appel Molot, eds., *Canada Among Nations 2001: The Axworthy Legacy*. Don Mills, ON: Oxford University Press.

Taras, David, ed. 1985. *Parliament in Canadian Foreign Policy*. Toronto: Canadian Institute of International Affairs.

Thordarson, Bruce. 1972. *Trudeau and Foreign Policy: A Study in Decision-Making*. Don Mills, ON: Oxford University Press.

Wolfe, Robert, ed. 1998. *Diplomatic Missions: The Ambassador in Canadian Foreign Policy*. Kingston, ON: Queen's University School of Policy Studies.

Security

Adam Smith famously wrote that government has three main responsibilities: 1) enforcing rules of conduct within society, 2) settling disputes between its members, and 3) protecting society from external attack. The primary purpose of a country's foreign policy, then, is Smith's last responsibility—the protection of its citizens. Canada is in an unusual circumstance. It has only the United States as a close neighbour and war between the two countries is inconceivable. In many respects Canada remains, in the words of Liberal Senator Raoul Dandurand at the League of Nations in 1924, "a fire-proof house, far from inflammable materials." Due to its favourable geographic situation, Canada has also felt an obligation to help build a more secure world. This section of *Readings in Canadian Foreign Policy* examines how Canada's foreign and defence policies are used to protect its territorial integrity and political independence as well as to contribute to international peace and security.

The first chapter in this section, by Kim Nossal, sets the table by providing an historical overview of Canadian defence policy. Nossal uses the concept of "defending the realm" to show how Canada has constantly redefined its military commitments beyond the Canadian territory. From 1867–1918, the realm comprised the British Empire, highlighted by Canadians fighting in the Boer War and World War I. The 1919–1939 interwar period was one of transition. During the Cold War era, 1945–1991, the realm was the "West" and led to the peacetime deployment of Canadian forces in Europe. The initial years of the post-Cold War era (1991–2001) saw another transition period, but the post-9/11 era (2001–present) has seen a significant narrowing of the realm. Nossal argues that despite high-profile military missions in Afghanistan and Libya, Canadians were retrenching back to the North American continent and possibly even to the Canadian territory. This can be seen through Canada's refusal to participate in either the 2003 Iraq War or American ballistic missile defence and how its deployment in Afghanistan became increasingly unpopular with the public.

The last remaining soldiers deployed to Afghanistan came home in March 2014. Afghanistan had been one of Canada's major foreign policy priorities for almost a decade. Its approach was multi-faceted, containing defence, development, and diplomatic aspects. Ottawa called it a "whole of government" strategy. This is why several chapters in this volume touch on Canada's role in Afghanistan. In

Chapter 7, Nicole Wegner uses a constructivist, gender-based approach to analyze the operation. Chapter 18, by Kim Nossal, places the Afghanistan mission into context by showing how it fits into the history of Canadian defence policy.

Beyond Afghanistan, and since the last edition of this book, Canada has also militarily intervened in Libya. This operation is discussed in Chapter 8 by Sean McMahon. In addition, Stéphane Roussel and Jean-Christophe Boucher, in Chapter 19, discuss both the Afghanistan and Libya missions as part of a larger study, relying heavily on public opinion polls, and on the attitudes of Quebecers on peace and security matters. Finally, in Chapter 20, Douglas Ross revisits a classic analysis of Canadian strategic thought by Dr. R.J. Sutherland from the early 1960s.[1] In the process, Ross shows the effect that the Afghanistan and Libya missions, and assessment of the potential for intervention into Syria, has had on Canadian defence policy. Other items that Ross looks at include the context of American defence policy, the possible military threat of China, Arctic security, and Canadian defence spending.

The Arctic has become a major potential flashpoint for conflict. Canada's Arctic region was securitized during the Cold War because the territory was the shortest distance between the United States and the Soviet Union. This led to the building of radar stations, the deployment of the Canadian Air Force, the creation of the Arctic Rangers, and strengthened defence cooperation with the United States in the region. Despite the end of the Cold War, the Arctic has taken on greater importance in Canadian foreign and defence policy, and this will continue to increase. This is because climate change has made travel through the Arctic, especially the contested Northwest Passage, easier due to melting ice. Not only will international shipping be enhanced due to climate change, but so will resource development, especially the exploration and production of oil and gas. In order to protect their national interests, other northern states (Russia, United States, Norway, Denmark) have mobilized their diplomats, international lawyers, and militaries. In Chapter 21, Rob Huebert, one of the foremost experts on the Arctic, outlines a strategy for Canada to respond to these challenges.

Note

1.   R.J. Sutherland, "Canada's Long Term Strategic Situation," *International Journal* 17, 3 (Summer 1962), 199–223.

18 Defending Canada[1]

Kim Richard Nossal

Key Terms

Human Security

Isolationism

Imperialism

Realm

For many countries, the focus of national defence is firmly fixed on defending the nation's territory, its sovereignty, and the interests of its citizens against intrusions or attacks by others in the international system. In this view, those "inside" the state are the proper focus of efforts to provide citizens with security and well-being. By contrast, those "outside" the state are unambiguously defined as the *other* and thus beyond the definition of altruism, to be assisted and defended only if it is in the state's interests to do so. Of course, this relentless pursuit of self-interest, defined purely in terms of the state and its citizens, is a core assumption of most theorizing about international relations.

In the Canadian context, however, defence policy makes little sense if it is examined using standard international relations (IR) theories. It is not that Canadians have been any less self-centred, selfish, and ungenerous towards outsiders in world politics. But unlike many others in the international system, Canadians face no serious threat of attack or armed intrusion by other countries. So why do Canadians spend approximately $20 billion per year to maintain a regular force of 68,000 personnel and a substantial capital equipment program (Perry 2013)? The key to understanding Canadian defence policy is that defence policy in Canada is not about defending *Canada*: rather, defence policy in a Canadian context can only be understood when it

is conceived as a policy designed to defend something more than just Canadian territorial integrity and the security and well-being of Canadians.

To make sense of Canadian defence policy, we need an ideational concept that goes beyond the restrictive definition of the sovereign state that is imposed on us by most contemporary IR theories. Rather, we need a concept that more closely reflects the way in which Canadians and their governors have conceptualized what—and who—is to be defended and made secure. I suggest that Canadians have conceived of defence policy as seeking to defend a broader definition of political community than just "Canada"; they have sought traditionally to defend a broader "realm," and it is only when Canadian security policy is seen as having been framed within this broader definition that it makes sense.

Realm is a word that long ago passed from common usage, perhaps not surprisingly given its intimate connection to a form of governance that has long been discarded in most places in the world. The commonest meaning of realm is the jurisdiction of a monarch, reflecting the word's etymological origins from the Old French *reaume*, derived from the Latin *regimen*—rule. While it has evolved a related meaning—a sphere or domain—it is still most commonly used in reference to the monarchy, sometimes with a hint of irony.

While this term is deeply rooted in nineteenth century government and linked to monarchical government, I use *realm* with an eye to both its meanings: a realm connotes a sphere or domain that is both a political space and an ideational construct of political identity and community that goes beyond the state as it is usually defined in international relations. In particular, as the term is used here, the realm refers to a political space defined by Canadians as including more than Canada—in other words, places and peoples that were (or are) defined as being "inside" rather than "outside."

This chapter provides a broad survey of the way in which Canadians have defined the realm to be defended since 1867. Mirroring what have been termed *dominant ideas* in Canada's international policies (Nossal, Roussel, and Paquin 2011: 117–53), I suggest that the definition of *realm* has shifted over the years. From 1867 to 1918, the realm for many (but not all) Canadians was expansive, including not only Canada but the broader British Empire of which Canada was a part—even though this expansive definition was deeply contested within Canada, with English-speaking Canadians and French-speaking Canadians having radically different perspectives on how the realm should be most appropriately defined.

From 1919 to 1939, the definition of realm was in transition, as Canadians responded to the grand shift in global politics occurring in the interwar period—in particular the rise of the United States and the emergence of the Axis challenge to the order established in 1919 that culminated in the Canadian decision to enter the war that broke out on 1 September 1939.

During the Cold War (1945–1991), how Canadians defined the realm reflected the rivalry between the United States and the Soviet Union and the threat that Soviet forces posed to both Western Europe and North America: in Canada's embrace of the North Atlantic Treaty of 1949 and the continentalization of air defence in 1957, the realm included both the countries of Western Europe and the United States.

In the post-Cold War era (1991–2001), the definition was again in transition. During this period the Canadian government experimented with alternative conceptions of security, expanding the definition of the *Canadian realm* to what some have suggested are post-modern limits. But in the era of world politics that began on 11 September 2001, the realm has once again been narrowing. In the post-9/11 era Canadians are no longer enthusiastic about expansive definitions of what should be defended, exemplified by the persistently tepid support for the struggle against global jihadism, the widespread opposition to Canadian contributions to American defence projects, and the unwillingness to intervene on behalf of others in the international system. To each of these eras we now turn.

Canada and the Imperial Realm: 1867–1918

Whatever definition of security embraced by Canadian policy-makers in the first decades of Canada's existence had to be framed within the context of the legal position of Canada as a self-governing dominion in the British Empire. As a polity created by an act of the British Parliament—the British North America Act of 1867—Canada was to be self-governing in matters of domestic policy, but matters of foreign and defence policy were to be left to the authority of the imperial government in London. The legal regime established in 1867 bound Canada and Canadians tightly to the structures of Empire.

However, for many—though not all—Canadians, the connection to the British Empire was not just simply a matter of formal allegiance to a legal order. More importantly, the connection was an emotional attachment to the *patria*, the land of their (or their parents') birth—even though English-speaking Canadians at the time tended to use the more maternal appellation, *Mother Country*. But the love for Britain demonstrated by many English-speaking Canadians in the late nineteenth century was not simply patriotism. Nor was it nationalism: most English-speaking Canadians, while they might have had a love for Canada as a nascent nation, did not embrace the core nationalist goal of establishing a separate and sovereign government to protect and nurture the nation (Berger 1970: 259–65; Holmes 1970: 28–31). Rather, **imperialism** was a hybrid identity that incorporated a simultaneous attachment to Canada, Empire, and *patria*. However, this identity did not always have a clear political articulation. As H. Blair Neatby (1969: 2) put it, most English-speaking Canadians were "bound to the old country by less clearly formulated sentiments [of] a natural affection for their Motherland."

As Canadian decision-makers in the last quarter of the nineteenth century sought to formulate a security strategy for the new dominion, the idea of Empire and its defence framed much of their decision-making. To be sure, Canadian defence in the late 1800s was still fixed on the United States, despite the Treaty of Washington of 1871 that had cleared away some of the irritants that had beset Anglo-American relations. But Canadian defence policy also focused on the defence of the British Empire.

The impetus to contribute to the defence of the Empire can best be seen in Canadian responses to the outbreak of the Boer War in October 1899. This was a conflict that involved the defence of the interests of British subjects; but the interests of Canada or Canadians were by no means directly affected by the outcome of the Imperial government's quarrel with the Transvaal. But this is not how public opinion in English-speaking Canada saw it. Rather, public opinion in English Canada was affected by what John W. Holmes (1970: 30) called the "hallucinations of Jubilee imperialism," with young men

flocking to recruiting centres to volunteer their services for the British cause. As Carman Miller (1993) has demonstrated so clearly, public support for a Canadian contribution of troops to fight in South Africa had been whipped up by an organized and coordinated campaign by the English-language press. As the editor of *The Globe*, a Liberal newspaper, said to Liberal Prime Minister Sir Wilfrid Laurier: "either send troops or go out of office" (Stacey 1977: 59–60). When a Liberal government member of parliament, Henri Bourassa, criticized the Imperial government for its war policies in South Africa in the House of Commons, he was hissed at by his fellow MPs, and called a traitor in the press (Levitt 1970: 35–43). But Bourassa was reflecting the strong opposition among French-speaking Canadians to sending Canadian troops to fight in South Africa. Despite this opposition, however, Laurier bent to pressure from English Canada and authorized the dispatch of troops to South Africa in response to an implicit request for military support from the imperial government in London.

The South African war demonstrated the degree to which the imperialist sentiments of English Canadians were basically incompatible with the dualistic nature of the Canadian polity. While Canadians of British extraction had no difficulty with the idea of loyalty to Canada and loyalty to Britain, such imperialist sentiment found little favour amongst French Canadians. As Bourassa put it in 1917: "French-Canadians are loyal to Great Britain and friendly to France; but they do not acknowledge to either country what, in every land, is considered the most exclusively national duty: the obligations to bear arms and fight. . . . The only trouble with the French-Canadians is that they remain the only true 'unhyphenated' Canadians. . . . Canadians of British origin have become quite unsettled as to their allegiance. . . . The French-Canadians have remained, and want to remain, exclusively Canadian" (Levitt 1970: 174). However, as long as the Empire—and therefore Canada—was at peace, this incompatibility could remain largely latent. It was when the Empire was at war that the contradictions broke into the open.

The degree to which English Canadians identified with the British Empire as the realm to which sacrifices of blood and treasure could and should be made is reflected in the willingness with which many Canadians went to war in August 1914. The declaration of war on Germany may have been issued by the King on the advice of his ministers in London, but for the vast majority of English Canadians, such legalities were quite irrelevant. The result would have been the same—willing participation on the side of the "Mother Country." Indeed, when the prime minister, Sir Robert Borden, asserted that "the 'national' interests of Canada and the 'imperial' interests of Canada during the Great War were demonstrably the same" (quoted in Brown 1992: 44), he would have been speaking for many English-speaking Canadians. (For French-speaking Canadians, by contrast, there was no such automatic identification of their interests with the European war.)

Shrinking the Realm: 1919–1939

The actual process of fighting the Great War fully exposed the internal contradictions within the Empire—and within Canada. The massive human and material costs posed a serious problem for all the dominions of the Empire: the Imperial government in London expected the empire to contribute young men and wealth for the successful prosecution of the war, but the various parts of the Empire were given no say over the conduct of the war. The enthusiasm that had been so evident in 1914 waned. By the end of 1916, volunteers for overseas duty had dramatically declined. The Conservative prime minister, Sir Robert Borden, had to decide whether

to introduce conscription. For French-speaking Canadians, who shared little of the emotional commitment to the war that had spurred voluntary recruitments in English Canada, the prospect of being forced to fight what many in Québec regarded as an English war posed a major threat to their interests, and they voted against Borden's Conservative-led coalition Unionist government in the elections of December 1917. For many English Canadians, the reaction of French-speaking Canadians to conscription was merely more evidence of Québec's abandonment of the Mother Country in its hour of need. There were violent clashes over the Easter weekend of 1918, as both sides gave vent to these divergent interests.

Involvement in the war diminished the enthusiasm for imperialism among many English-speaking Canadians and gave rise to a desire to control *all* elements of policy, domestic and external. It was a logical outgrowth of the autonomy in domestic policy achieved with Confederation in 1867, and was manifested in Borden's insistence on separate representation for Canada at the peace conference in Paris, and separate Canadian membership in the new international organization, the League of Nations, that had been created at Versailles. And it did lead directly to the Statute of Westminster, 1931, which granted sovereignty to all the self-governing dominions, thus bringing a formal end to the Empire.

The achievement of formal independence in 1931 did not suddenly extinguish those imperialist sentiments that had fuelled the enthusiasm for war in 1914. Imperial sentiment would linger throughout the interwar period. However, its political impact was more limited. For example, the Liberal government of Mackenzie King had no difficulty in turning down a request from the Imperial government in London for military assistance to be sent to the Gallipoli peninsula in September 1922, arguing that the Canadian Parliament would need to authorize any dispatch of troops abroad (Stacey 1981: 17–31). The Chanak affair demonstrated the degree to which definitions of the "realm"—among English-speaking Canadians in particular—had shifted as a result of four years of war fighting.

In the interwar period, Canadians adopted an **isolationism** that was in many respects comparable to the traditional isolationism of American politics and foreign policy (Haglund 2002–3). In the aftermath of a war that had cost over 60,000 Canadian lives, Canadians began to express that basic tenet of American isolationism: a deep resentment of European politics. The major concern was that the collective security provisions of the new League of Nations in Geneva would drag Canadians into another European war. More than one speaker in the debate on the Versailles treaty sounded the theme raised by MP Lucien Cannon: "I am not in favour of England ruling this country, but I would rather be ruled by England than by Geneva" (quoted in Veatch 1975: 29). For many Canadians, there was an additional impetus: the emotional remoteness from France inclined French-speaking Canadians to define themselves as a North American people rather than a European people (Waite 1983: 141).

Another major Canadian concern with collective security was that the arrangement seemed entirely one-sided. In North America, Canadians had no fear of the need to invoke the help of the League. The classic position was put by Raoul Dandurand, the Liberal leader in the Senate, at the League Assembly in 1924: "in this association of Mutual Assistance against fire, the risks assumed by the different States are not equal. We live in a fire-proof house, far from inflammable materials" (Riddell 1962: 462–65; Paquin 2009: 41–55). Such sentiments were reflected in King's isolationist policies during the 1920s and 1930s. While Canada relished its separate seat as a member of the League, the government tried as hard as possible to avoid any involvement in international commitments. The

reason was simple: King was always concerned to avoid the fate of Borden's Conservatives after the conscription crisis of 1917. King feared that Canada would be dragged into another European war, exposing the deep fractures between English- and French-speaking Canadians, and running the possibility that the Liberal Party would be consigned to the electoral wilderness in Québec, just as the Conservatives had been after 1917. From this concern, isolationism—and a feeble security policy (Eayrs 1964)—came naturally. In particular, the realm shrank as imperialist sentiment diminished and more and more English-speaking Canadians embraced the more limited definition of security common among French-speaking Canadians.

To be sure, sentiments of attachment to Britain were still clearly evident in the late 1930s, the legal and constitutional freedoms won in the Statute of Westminster notwithstanding. Supporting Britain in the Second World War was never in question for the majority of Canadians. As J.L. Granatstein and Robert Bothwell (1986: 125) put it, "support for Britain was first a moral duty, and a political duty, if it was at all, a long way after." They quote Stephen Leacock, who in the summer of 1939 summed up English-Canadian attitudes about the impending war in Europe this way: "If you were to ask any Canadian, 'Do you have to go to war if England does?' he'd answer at once, 'Oh, no.' If you then asked, 'Would you go to war if England does?' he'd answer 'Oh, yes.' And if you asked 'Why?' he would say, reflectively, 'Well, you see, we'd have to'" (Leacock 1939).

However, while many Canadians may have been isolationist and may have had a more restricted vision of the realm to be defended, there were fewer and fewer Canadians who viewed the rise of Adolf Hitler and Nazi Germany with indifference. When the Canadian government declared war on Germany on 10 September 1939, the country went into the Second World War relatively united.

The Realm in the Cold War: 1945–1991

The Second World War radically transformed Canadian definitions of the *realm*. After 1945, that realm was greatly expanded from the constricted definition of the isolationist interwar period. Instead, those who inherited the responsibility for defining Canadian foreign and defence policy in the mid-1940s had a markedly different calculation about Canadian defence and security than those of the interwar years.

First, the Liberal government of Prime Minister Louis St Laurent did not share Mackenzie King's almost pathological fear that international commitments would involve Canada in war, expose the contradictions between English- and French-speaking Canadians, and spell electoral disaster for the Liberals. On the contrary: St Laurent and many of his officials took the view that the primary "lesson of the 1930s" was that countries should be actively engaged in global politics in order to work for the maintenance of an international order that would prevent the recurrence of the events of the 1930s that led to the Second World War. This was the essence of Canada's postwar internationalism: a deep commitment to international institutions and to active involvement in international affairs (Keating 2002).

This activism manifested itself in a number of ways, including strong support for international institutions and a willingness to contribute Canadian resources to the creation and maintenance of international order. But it also involved a willingness to embrace an expansion of the de facto alliance that Canadians had entered into with the United States at the outset of the Second World War. After 1945, and the re-emergence of the enmity between the Soviet Union and Western countries that had lingered throughout the interwar period following the armed intervention by the United States and other Western states, Canada included, in the Russian civil war, Canadians expanded the definition of *realm* to include all the countries of Western Europe who joined in the North Atlantic alliance of 1949 (Reid 1977; Eayrs 1980; Holmes 1982: 98–122).

The North Atlantic Treaty and the organization that grew out of it represented one way in which Canada's definition of the defence realm expanded after 1945, for the alliance committed Canadians to a defence of Western Europe comparable to the defence of Britain and France in 1939–1940. It also reflected a willingness on the part of Canadians to identify themselves clearly as being part of the "West" in what was emerging as a global confrontation led by the two new superpowers. And while the negotiation of this alliance commitment was a governmental initiative, implemented by state officials, there can be little doubt that Canadians strongly supported the new alliance. The willingness to commit resources to NATO—not only the stationing of significant Canadian forces in Europe, but, more metaphysically, the readiness to fight a third European war in as many generations—suggests that the process of fighting the Second World War produced as radical a shift in Canadian sentiment as the process of fighting the First World War had.

The second expansion of the realm also grew out of the strategic shifts that had occurred with the "revolution of 1940"—the agreement between Canada and the United States establishing a joint mechanism for the mutual defence of North America (Haglund 1999)—and the subsequent emergence of a threat to the United States from Soviet intercontinental bombers. The decision of the Canadian government in the 1950s to continentalize air defence by entering into the North American Air Defense (NORAD) command was not only a pragmatic response to the defence requirements of the United States, but also a manifestation of the willingness of Canadians to draw their security perimeter and their definition of what was "inside" more widely than simply Canadian borders.

To be sure, the concrete Canadian commitments to NATO diminished over the long years of the Cold War (Nossal 2001). In the early 1960s, the Progressive Conservative government of John Diefenbaker was undecided on the wisdom of arming Canadian forces in Europe with nuclear weapons, raising broader questions about Canada's commitment to the alliance. The Liberal government of Pierre Elliott Trudeau came to office in 1968 wanting to withdraw Canadian forces from Europe, but, faced with both domestic and external opposition, opted in 1969 to dramatically reduce the number of forces stationed in Europe. Trudeau's desire for withdrawal was based on strategic calculations: a belief that stationing large numbers of Canadian troops in Europe was unnecessary for Canadian interests given the changes in the relationship between the US and the Soviet Union in the late 1960s. The Progressive Conservative government of Brian Mulroney (1984–1993) also sought to reduce the Canadian presence in Europe, but eventually backed away when faced with stiff opposition from other allies. Indeed, it was not until the Cold War was over that the Mulroney government finally closed Canada's bases in Europe.

But if Canadian governments exhibited diminishing levels of concrete support for NATO and NORAD in the last two decades of the Cold War, it can be argued that public support for the *idea* of a wider definition of the Canadian realm persisted throughout the 1970s and 1980s. While vocal opposition to Canada's strategic alignments in world politics emerged in the late 1950s and remained active through to the end of the 1980s, the majority of Canadians continued to embrace the idea that Canada should contribute to the defence of the West.

Expanding and Shrinking the Realm: 1991–2001

The end of the Cold War between 1989 and 1991 ushered in an era in Canadian foreign and defence policy markedly different from earlier eras. The dismantling of the Soviet Union had a dramatically disruptive effect on the thinking of some Canadians about security policy, since so much of the grand strategy of the Cold War era was structured around the existence of the Soviet Union as the enemy.

With the benefit of hindsight, we can now see that Canadian strategic thinking in the 10 years after 1991 was marked by a certain confusion. First, despite the end of the conflict that gave rise to the institutional arrangements of Cold War security policy, these institutions lingered long after the Cold War itself was over. The North Atlantic Treaty was designed to protect the states of Western Europe against an attack by the Soviet Union. However, with the disappearance of that threat, NATO did not simply fold its tent, its job done; rather, the alliance reinvented itself throughout the 1990s, expanding eastwards, embracing new members, and assuming new tasks that were more and more "out of area." Likewise, freed of the need to protect against an air-breathing threat from the USSR, NORAD did not wrap up its operations, but adapted to new tasks, including the interdiction of drugs being smuggled from Latin America and the Caribbean. The efforts to transform these two institutions to reflect the new realities of the post-Cold War environment received strong support from the governments of both Brian Mulroney and Jean Chrétien.

Second, with the disappearance of the Soviet Union and the sharp east/west divide that had marked the Cold War years, Canadian definitions of the realm were radically altered. To be sure, the Canadian government experimented with different conceptions of security during this period. For example, Lloyd Axworthy, Canada's foreign affairs minister from 1996 to 2000, welcomed the constant expansion of NATO, arguing that he could conceive of one day admitting Russia to NATO, forming a giant alliance that would stretch from Vancouver to Vladivostok. Likewise, Axworthy championed the idea of **human security** (Paris 2001), the notion that Canadians should be concerned about not only the security of states, but the security of all human beings, and that the Canadian state should occupy itself with improving the security of human beings under threat (Hillmer and Chapnick 2001; Nossal 2010).

But these attempts to redefine the realm appeared to have limited resonance among the Canadian public. The alliance formalized in 1949 was very easy to understand: the Soviet Union posed a threat to the countries of Western Europe, and the alliance was a means to deter a Soviet attack and to defend the countries of Western Europe should deterrence fail. After the Soviet Union ceased to be a threat, NATO transmogrified into an eminently post-modern construction: an alliance that existed without a clearly identifiable external threat to defend against. While Canadian public opinion polls demonstrate that NATO continues to command support, there is little evidence that Canadians expanded their definition of the realm along with NATO's eastward expansion. In the early 1950s, Canadians might have been willing to devote blood and treasure to defend Belgians and Dutch against potential predations from the Soviet Union; in the 1990s, it was unlikely that Canadians would apply that same logic to the new members of the alliance.

Likewise, Axworthy's effort to expand the realm of Canadian security to include human security had little resonance at a concrete level. It is true that during the 1990s the Canadian government used the Canadian Armed Forces (CAF) for a number of expeditionary missions designed to bring an end to intrastate conflicts in a variety of countries, including Yugoslavia, Somalia, Haiti, Rwanda, Sierra Leone, and East Timor. The CAF was also involved in one war during this period—the 78-day bombing of the Federal Republic of Yugoslavia in 1999—that was justified by the Canadian government as necessary to protect the human security of Kosovar Albanians. But while Canadians might have approved of the deployment of the armed forces for such missions, and while the rhetorical embrace of human security by their government appears to have generated some approval, there was little evidence that Canadians actually conceived of Kosovar Albanians, or Timorese, or Bosnian Muslims as being on the "inside" part of the "realm" of Canadian concern.

Thus the period from the end of the Cold War to the attacks of 9/11 reveals a paradoxical trend: while the formal and rhetorical Canadian definitions of the *realm* were expanding as a consequence of the enthusiasms of government officials—the expansion of NATO to include new members, the expansion of the "human security agenda"—the real and concrete definition of the realm actually shrank during the 1990s, with Canadians inclined to narrow their perimeter of concern. This narrowing can readily be seen in the response of Canadians to the activities of their government over the course of the 1990s: the absolute lack of concern expressed by Canadians as the Chrétien government dramatically reduced Canada's actual operations internationally (Nossal 1998–99; Cohen 2003); and the overwhelming silence of Canadians when they were confronted with unambiguous evidence of genocide in Rwanda, brutalities in Sierra Leone, violence in Chechnya, or human rights violations in a variety of other countries.

The Post-9/11 Era: The Narrowing of the Realm

In the years after 11 September 2001, we have seen another paradoxical trend emerge. On the one hand, the Canadian government acted in ways that appear to be a continuation of an expansive definition of the realm. Thus, for example, the Liberal government of Jean Chrétien responded to NATO's invocation of Article 5 of the North Atlantic Treaty—deeming that the attack on the United States had been an attack on all NATO members—by contributing to the

United States-led invasion of Afghanistan. His successor, Paul Martin, committed a Canadian battle group to Kandahar in 2005, and the new Conservative government of Stephen Harper, which came to power as the battle group took up position in Kandahar in early 2006, sustained Canada's commitment to Afghanistan until 2014.

Some might see Canada's contribution to what was widely called the **global war on terrorism** as yet another example of an expansive definition of what was to be defended that we saw in conflicts from the Boer War in 1899 to the war in Kosovo in 1999: in the global war on terrorism, the defence of Canada was conflated with a defence of the United States and, more broadly, the West. From 2001 until the end of the mission, approximately 30,000 Canadians served with the armed forces in Afghanistan; 158 members of the CAF lost their lives while on duty there, most killed by improvised explosive devices; over 2,000 were wounded, including 635 who were wounded in action, and an unnamed number who are still living with injuries or post-traumatic stress. The overall cost of the mission has yet to be calculated: estimates range from $18 billion to $28 billion. Certainly the commitment of Canadian blood and treasure to a 13-year war in a country physically remote from Canada that did not directly affect the interests of Canadians seemed to be a continuation of the same dynamic that led earlier generations of Canadians to embrace an expansive conception of defence; indeed Pigott (2007: 9–10) draws an explicit comparison between the Boer War and the Afghanistan mission.

But a closer look at Canadian attitudes towards national defence in the post-9/11 era suggests that Canadians' definition of what is to be defended actually continued to narrow over this period. First, a more careful reading of the immediate Canadian response to 9/11 reveals that the initial support for a military contribution to the emerging American-led global war on terrorism was actually quite short-lived (Nossal 2003). Second, there was very little support in Canada for all elements of the American strategy in the global war on terrorism, such as the attempt by the administration of George W. Bush to entwine Iraq in that struggle (Barry 2005; Richter 2005).

Third, the way in which Canada "returned" to Afghanistan after 2002—to Kabul with the International Security Assistance Force (ISAF) in 2003 and to Kandahar with a battle group in 2006—also suggests that factors other than a broad desire to include Afghanistan in the realm of Canadian defence were at work. The deployment to Kabul was driven in large part by the desire of Canada's allies, notably the United States, to have Canada fill a gap to allow the redeployment of American forces to the coming invasion of Iraq. And this certainly suited the Chrétien government, which had little desire in joining the "coalition of the willing" in Iraq, for the deployment to Kabul could be used to argue that Canada did not have sufficient forces to join the American operation in Iraq (Granatstein, 2007: 91n; Stein and Lang, 2007: 44–70). Likewise, most analyses of the Martin government's decision in early 2005 to dispatch a battle group to Kandahar under Operation Enduring Freedom focus on the government's desire to soothe American annoyance not only over Canada's refusal to support Operation Iraqi Freedom but also Martin's decision not to participate in the Ballistic Missile Defense System, discussed further below. In short, Canada's deployments to Afghanistan in 2001, 2003, and 2005 were driven by alliance politics rather than defence considerations.

Canadian public opinion on the Afghanistan mission persistently reflected the ambiguities underlying the mission. Polls after 2006 revealed that support for the mission was always less than 50 per cent, with a strong degree of opposition to the mission (Boucher and Roussel 2008; Fletcher et al. 2009; Nossal 2010). Moreover, these polling numbers remained remarkably consistent, even when the Kandahar mission produced large numbers of Canadian casualties (Nossal 2008; Boucher 2010), and even when the Conservative government of Stephen Harper tried articulating different justifications for the mission. As Fletcher et al. (2009: 931) put it: "The government's message was received; the public, however, was not persuaded. Something was missing." Eventually, Harper himself became an "Afghanistan skeptic": he negotiated with the Liberal opposition to secure approval for a parliamentary resolution withdrawing from Afghanistan in 2011 (Nossal 2009). This had the desired effect of removing Afghanistan as an issue in Canadian politics: Canada might have been at war, but the 2008 and 2011 elections were fought without any mention of the mission. Instead, the Harper government simply gave up trying to convince Canadians of the rightness of the mission, and simply ragged the puck waiting for the end of the combat mission in 2011, recognizing that Canadians were simply not buying the idea that Canadian blood and treasure should be expended making Afghanistan secure.

We can also see a shrinking conception of the realm in the post-9/11 era in the Canadian attitude to ballistic missile defence. While Canadians had been comfortable during the early Cold War with the continentalization of air defence against the Soviet bomber threat, this sentiment began to slowly evaporate, beginning in the 1970s. By the early 1980s, when the administration of Ronald Reagan outlined the Strategic Defense Initiative—a space-based missile defence system designed to thwart a nuclear attack by the Soviet Union—and invited Canada to participate, there was so much opposition to SDI in Canada that the Progressive Conservative government of Brian Mulroney decided in 1985 not to participate. By the post-Cold War era, when the United States was still experimenting with more limited ballistic missile programs—National Missile Defense and Theatre Missile Defense—to defend itself and its allies from

possible ballistic missile attacks from "rogue" states, the evanescence was complete. There was considerable public support for the Chrétien government's lack of enthusiasm for ballistic missile defence in the 1990s.

That lack of enthusiasm gelled into strong Canadian opposition in the post-9/11 era. The strength of that opposition can best be seen by looking at the policies of Paul Martin and Stephen Harper towards ballistic missile defence (BMD). Before they assumed the prime ministership, both Martin and Harper had publicly expressed their support for BMDs and had promised to accept the US invitation to join if they won power. Once in office, however, both Martin and Harper changed their minds. Martin announced in February 2005 that Canada would not participate (Fergusson 2005); when he came to power in February 2006, Harper did not move to revisit Martin's decision (Nossal 2007).

A further indication of the shrinking of the realm can be seen in Canadian responses to humanitarian crises in the post-9/11 era. While Canadians generally supported the involvement of Royal Canadian Air Force CF-18s in the NATO-led intervention in Libya in 2011 (Nossal 2013a), there was no support for Canadian intervention in the Syrian civil war that began in 2011, in the ongoing war in the Democratic Republic of Congo, or in the civil war that began there in December 2013. The relative indifference of Canadians generally has been mirrored by the Conservative Harper government, whose foreign policy has been appropriately characterized by Peter Jones (2014) as "bitter" and "small-minded" and increasingly abandoning the international stage (Smith and Turenne Sjolander 2013; Nossal 2013b).

Indeed, these cases all suggest that Canadian conceptions of the realm continue to narrow. Indeed, if present trends persist, Canadians will be in a situation where the defence "realm" will have shrunk to the borders of Canada itself—for the first time in Canadian history.

Conclusion

Making sense of Canadian defence policy requires an understanding of the fact that over the years Canadians have tended to define who and what is to be made secure in terms broader than the Canadian state. The term *realm* is a useful one to capture this dynamic, particularly because its etymological origins are apposite for an analysis of the Canadian experience in the nineteenth and early twentieth centuries, when Canadian sovereignty was still located with the government in London.

Now, it is true that those who make Canadian foreign and defence policy do not use the term now, and did not in the past. Even the most cursory examination of the historical record reveals that Canadian policy-makers have always framed their discourse in concrete terms—"Canada," or "the Empire," or "the West." But given the restrictive vocabulary of traditional IR theorizing that tends to limit discussions of strategic culture to the state, we need an ideational construct that permits an analysis that more accurately reflects the reality of identity as it has been manifested in the Canadian historical experience.

Questions for Review

1. Are public opinion polls a useful guide to the attitudes of Canadians about their country's role in world politics?
2. The narrowing of the "realm" after 9/11 has similar features to the narrowing of the definition of the realm after the First World War; can we call what we are seeing in the contemporary era *isolationism*?
3. What are the similarities and differences between the Canadian mission in Afghanistan (2001–2014) and the Canadian contribution to the Boer War (1899–1902)?

Suggested Readings

Dewitt, David B., and David Leyton-Brown, eds. 1995. *Canada's International Security Policy*. Scarborough, ON: Prentice-Hall Canada.

Eayrs, James. 1964–83. *In Defence of Canada*. 5 vols. Toronto: University of Toronto Press.

Middlemiss, D.W., and J.J. Sokolsky. 1989. *Canadian Defence: Decisions and Determinants*. Toronto: Harcourt Brace Jovanovich.

Morton, Desmond. 2003. *Understanding Canadian Defence*. Toronto: Penguin Canada.

Note

1. Originally published as "Defending the 'Realm': Canadian Strategic Culture Revisited," *International Journal* 59, 3 (Summer 2004): 503–20; revised and updated for this volume.

References

Barry, Donald. 2005. "Chrétien, Bush, and the War in Iraq." *American Review of Canadian Studies*, 35, 2: 215–45.

Berger, Carl. 1970. *The Sense of Power: Studies in the Ideas of Canadian Imperialism, 1867–1914*. Toronto: University of Toronto Press.

Boucher, Jean-Christophe. 2010. "Evaluating the 'Trenton effect': Canadian public opinion and military casualties in Afghanistan (2006–2009)." *American Review of Canadian Studies* 40, 2: 237–58.

Boucher, Jean-Christophe, and Stéphane Roussel. 2008. "From Afghanistan to 'Quebecistan': Quebec as the Pharmakon of Canadian Foreign and Defence Policy," pp. 128–56 in Jean Daudelin and Daniel Schwanen, eds., *Canada among Nations 2008: What Room for Manoeuvre?* Montreal and Kingston: McGill-Queen's University Press.

Brown, Robert Craig. 1992. "Sir Robert Borden, the Great War, and Anglo-Canadian Relations," pp. 28–46 in J.L. Granatstein, ed., *Towards a New World: Readings in the History of Canadian Foreign Policy.* Toronto: Copp Clark.

Cohen, Andrew. 2003. *While Canada Slept: How We Lost Our Place in the World.* Toronto: McClelland and Stewart, 2003.

Eayrs, James. 1964. *In Defence of Canada, Vol. 1: From the Great War to the Great Depression.* Toronto: University of Toronto Press.

———. 1980. *In Defence of Canada, Vol. 4: Growing Up Allied.* Toronto: University of Toronto Press.

Fergusson, James. 2005. "Shall We Dance? The Missile Defence Decision, NORAD Renewal, and the Future of Canada–US Defence Relations," *Canadian Military Journal* 6, 2: 13–22.

Fletcher, Joseph F., Heather Bastedo, and Jennifer Hove. 2009. "Losing Heart: Declining Support and the Political Marketing of the Afghanistan Mission," *Canadian Journal of Political Science* 42, 4: 911–37.

Granatstein, J.L. 2007. *Whose War Is It? How Canada Can Survive in the Post-9/11 World.* Toronto: HarperCollins.

Granatstein, J.L., and Robert Bothwell. 1986. "'A Self-evident National Duty': Canadian Foreign Policy, 1935–1939," pp. 125–44 in J.L. Granatstein, ed., *Canadian Foreign Policy: Historical Readings.* Toronto: Copp Clark Pitman.

Haglund, David G. 1999. "The North Atlantic Triangle Revisited: (Geo)political Metaphor and the Logic of Canadian Foreign Policy," *American Review of Canadian Studies* 29, 2: 211–35.

———. 2002–3. "Are We the Isolationists?" *International Journal* 58, 1: 1–23.

Hillmer, Norman, and Adam Chapnick. 2001. "The Axworthy Revolution," pp. 67–88 in Fen Osler Hampson, Norman Hillmer, and Maureen Appel Molot, eds., *Canada among Nations 2001: The Axworthy Legacy.* Toronto: Oxford University Press.

Holmes, John W. 1970. *The Better Part of Valour: Essays on Canadian Diplomacy.* Toronto: McClelland and Stewart.

———. 1982. *The Shaping of Peace: Canada and the Search for World Order, 1943–1957,* Vol. 2. Toronto: University of Toronto Press.

Jones, Peter. 2014. "Canada's Bitter, Small-Minded Foreign Policy," *The Globe and Mail,* 2 January, A13.

Keating, Tom. 2002. *Canada and World Order: The Multilateralist Tradition in Canadian Foreign Policy.* 2nd ed. Don Mills, ON: Oxford University Press.

Leacock, Stephen. 1939. "Canada and the Monarchy," *The Atlantic,* June, 735–44.

Levitt, Joseph, ed. 1970. *Henri Bourassa on Imperialism and Biculturalism, 1900–1918.* Toronto: Copp Clark.

Miller, Carman. 1993. *Painting the Map Red: Canada and the South African War, 1899–1902.* Montreal and Kingston: McGill-Queen's University Press.

Neatby, H. Blair. 1969. "Laurier and imperialism," pp. 1–9 in Carl Berger et al. eds., *Imperial Relations in the Age of Laurier.* Toronto: University of Toronto Press.

Nossal, Kim Richard. 1998–99. "Pinchpenny Diplomacy: The Decline of 'Good International Citizenship' in Canadian Foreign Policy," *International Journal* 54, 1: 88–105.

———. 2001. "The Decline of the Atlanticist Tradition in Canadian Foreign Policy," pp. 223–34 in George A. MacLean, ed., *Between Actor and Presence: The European Union and the Future of the Transatlantic Relationship.* Ottawa: University of Ottawa Press.

———. 2003. "Canadian Foreign Policy after 9/11: Realignment, Reorientation or Reinforcement?"pp. 20–34 in Lenard Cohen, Brian Job, and Alexander Moens, eds., *Foreign Policy Realignment in the Age of Terror.* Toronto: Canadian Institute of Strategic Studies.

———. 2007. "Defense Policy and the Atmospherics of Canada-U.S. Relations: The Case of the Harper Conservatives," *American Review of Canadian Studies* 37, 1: 23–34.

———. 2008. "The Unavoidable Shadow of Past Wars: Obsequies for Casualties of the Afghanistan Mission in Australia and Canada," *Australasian Canadian Studies* 26, 1: 91–124.

———. 2009. "No Exit: Canada and the 'War without End' in Afghanistan," pp. 157–73 in Hans-Georg Ehrhart and Charles C. Pentland, eds., *The Afghanistan Challenge: Hard Realities and Strategic Choices.* Montreal and Kingston: McGill-Queen's University Press.

———. 2010. "Rethinking the Security Imaginary: Canada and the Case of Afghanistan," pp. 107–25 in Bruno Charbonneau and Wayne S. Cox, eds., *Locating Global Order: American Power and Canadian Security after 9/11.* Vancouver: UBC Press.

———. 2013a. "The Use—and Misuse—of R2P: The Case of Canada," pp. 110–29 in Aidan Hehir and Robert Murray, eds., *Libya, the Responsibility to Protect and the Future of Humanitarian Intervention.* London: Palgrave Macmillan.

———. 2013b. "The Liberal Past in the Conservative Present: Internationalism in the Harper Era," pp. 21–35 in Heather A. Smith and Claire Turenne Sjolander, eds., *Canada in the World: Internationalism in Canadian Foreign Policy.* Toronto: Oxford University Press.

Nossal, Kim Richard, Stéphane Roussel, and Stéphane Paquin. 2011. *International Policy and Politics in Canada.* Don Mills, ON: Pearson Canada.

Paquin, Stéphane. 2009. "Raoul Dandurand: Porte-Parole de la Conscience Universelle," pp. 41–55 in Greg Donaghy and Kim Richard Nossal, eds., *Architects and Innovators: Building the Department of Foreign Affairs and International*

Trade, 1909–2009. Montreal and Kingston: McGill-Queen's University Press.

Paris, Roland. 2001. "Human Security: Paradigm Shift or Hot Air?" *International Security* 26, 2: 87–102.

Perry, David. 2013. "Defence Austerity: The Impact to Date." Conference of Defence Associations Institute, 1–9. Available at www.cdainstitute.ca/images/Defence_Austerity_ Budget_2013.pdf.

Pigott, Peter. 2007. *Canada in Afghanistan: The War So Far.* Toronto: Dundurn Press.

Reid, Escott. 1977. *Time of Fear and Hope: The Making of the North Atlantic Treaty, 1947–1949.* Toronto: McClelland and Stewart.

Richter, Andrew. 2005. "From Trusted Ally to Suspicious Neighbor: Canada-U.S. Relations in a Changing Global Environment," *American Review of Canadian Studies* 35, 3: 471–502.

Riddell, Walter A., ed. 1962. *Documents on Canadian Foreign Policy, 1917–1939.* Toronto: Oxford University Press.

Smith, Heather, and Claire Turenne Sjolander, eds. 2013. *Canada in the World: Internationalism in Canadian Foreign Policy.* Don Mills, ON: Oxford University Press.

Stacey, C.P. 1977. *Canada and the Age of Conflict: A History of Canadian External Policies, Vol. 1: 1867–1921.* Toronto: Macmillan Canada.

———. 1981. *Canada and the Age of Conflict: A History of Canadian External Policies, Vol. 2: 1921–1948: The Mackenzie King Era.* Toronto: University of Toronto Press.

Stein, Janice Gross, and Eugene Lang. 2007. *The Unexpected War: Canada in Kandahar.* Toronto: Viking Canada.

Veatch, Richard. 1975. *Canada and the League of Nations.* Toronto: University of Toronto Press.

Waite, P.B. 1983. "French-Canadian Isolationism and English Canada: An Elliptical Foreign Policy, 1935–1939," *Journal of Canadian Studies* 18, 2: 132–48.

19 The Myth of the Pacific Society: Quebec's Contemporary Strategic Culture

Stéphane Roussel and Jean-Christophe Boucher

Key Terms

Pacifism

Pearsonian Internationalism

Strategic Culture

Introduction

One of the enduring notions in Canadian foreign policy is that French-speaking Quebecers have a different attitude than other Canadians, resulting in a national division that has come to be known as "the two solitudes." This attitudinal distinction is said to be particularly important on matters related to defence and security policy. Historian J.L. Granatstein calls the phenomenon "the pacifist Quebec."[1] According to this view, Jean-Sébastien Rioux claims, "English and French-Canadians hold differing views on security and defence issues, with French-Canadians being more dovish, isolationist, and anti-militaristic than their Anglo counterparts. This world-view allegedly causes Quebecers to oppose increases in defence spending; to be against military interventions overseas; and to favour using the Canadian Armed Forces (CAF) only in humanitarian or peacekeeping roles."[2] In short, Quebecers are more pacifist, isolationist, and/or anti-militarist than their Canadian counterparts. Two sets of evidence are generally used in the literature to support that claim. The first is a list of historical events, usually centered on the two world wars, which are used to describe the defiance and the hostility of the

French-Canadians toward military institutions, and their reluctance to serve in the armed forces. The second is public opinion polls that allegedly show, one after the other, a considerable difference between the two linguistic groups (or, more precisely, between Quebec and other Canadian provinces). Quite aside from any political instrumentalization that one can make of such claims (from outright accusations that Quebecers are cowards and anti-Canadian, to a proclamation of the distinctiveness of Quebec's society), this dissimilarity in attitude is believed to be quite important in Canada's foreign policy decision-making. According to Granatstein, Quebecers are given a disproportionate influence in this process and are thus "deforming" Canada's foreign policy. This phenomenon is supposed to be at work in such events as the decision of the Chrétien government not to participate in the "coalition of the willing" against Iraq in March 2003 and Paul Martin's failure to support the US program on missile defence.[3]

This chapter offers a different interpretation of the nature of Quebecers' views on military issues and questions whether the historical record supports the idea that Quebecers are, in fact, "pacifists." Is it true that Quebecers are generally more distrustful or critical than other Canadians toward the use of the armed forces as an instrument of national and international problem-solving? Has this attitude changed over time? Is the conventional wisdom regarding Quebec still accurate to describe that province's contemporary public opinion? Is the criticism observed in 2003 on the Iraq issue the same as the one observed in 1910, 1917, or 1942? We will try to show that neither of the two main sets of data used to support the claim of the "pacifist Quebec" thesis is as convincing as it seems. If French-Canadians could be labelled as anti-militarist or isolationist (but certainly not pacifist) until the mid-twentieth century, things have changed since then. In fact, we argue that French-Canadians have expressed an internationalist attitude toward defence and security matters.

One of the key problems in the qualification of a society's attitude remains in the definition of the concepts. Such notions as "pacifism,"[4] "antiwar,"[5] "anti-militarism,"[6] "anti-imperialism," "isolationism,"[7] and "neutralism"[8] are generally left undefined and vague by authors. As a result, these central concepts are treated as if they were "naturally" linked to each other. In some cases, they are used as synonyms for each other. Worse yet, these concepts are generally associated (as a cause and/or a consequence) with other political attitudes, such as "anti-Americanism"[9] or, more commonly, "nationalism." Not surprisingly, this confusion obscures any attempt to understand the origin or the nature of Quebecers' stance toward defence and war issues. In fact, it allows commentators to explain any critical attitudes toward war or defence by the same vague clichés, as if Quebec's society was (and remains) homogeneous and unanimous over the last 250 years, no matter the context.

For our purposes,[10] the term **pacifism** is defined as an opposition on moral, legal, emotional, and/ or ideological grounds to the use of force (war in particular) to settle political differences.[11] *Anti-militarism* is defined as a rejection of or reluctance toward military institutions, ethos, and values. While historically associated with the labour movement of the early twentieth century, this concept, as we define it, includes those who are opposed to military institutions without necessarily rejecting violence as a political instrument. *Isolationism* is defined as an opposition to military commitment abroad in general, while *anti-imperialism* is defined as an opposition to military commitments that serve first and foremost the interests of a great power. However, we must note that neither *isolationism* nor *anti-imperialism* precludes military preparedness (including high defence spending) or involvement in a conflict if it serves the defence of the national territory or any other clear national interest. *Anti-Americanism* is a critical attitude toward what is perceived as US values, ethos, culture, and politics. In its moderate version, it represents a critical attitude toward *some* of these ideas, or toward *some* American leaders or even some decisions made by the US government.[12] In the latter case, however (and like some pacifism variants), the relevance of the concept itself remains debatable, since it encompasses situational attitudes.

Finally, the notion of internationalism, which is central in this chapter, is frequently defined as the opposite of isolationism. However, the chief aim of internationalism is to contribute to the peace and stability of the global system through policies premised upon functional and institutionalist principles. It calls for a reinforcement of international institutions (including international law) and organizations, and rests on the determination that international problems must be addressed by an active policy. In Canadian popular views, this set of ideas is strongly associated, sometimes wrongly, with Lester B. Pearson, minister of foreign affairs (1948–1957) and prime minister (1963–1968).[13]

Another concept that brings confusion is the word *Quebecer*. For the vast majority of authors addressing the "pacifist Quebec" question, the word designates, implicitly or explicitly, the French-speaking population living in the territory of the province of Quebec. This definition makes sense, in that the linguistic divide in that province is the most visible manifestation of a cultural and historical distinctiveness that might explain differences in the attitude toward war and defence. Nevertheless, this definition creates two concerns. First, it overlooks out-of-Quebec francophones and English-speaking Quebecers. Unfortunately, few data discriminate between these specific groups, and thus it is difficult to answer these questions. Therefore, they will, regrettably, not be included in this study. The second problem with the common definition of *Quebecer* is that a fair number of authors assume the existence of a straight relationship between the attitudes displayed by pre-1960s French-Canadians and post-1960s Quebecers. Such assumptions are commonsensical on the surface, since identity and culture (including **strategic culture**) extend some of their roots into history. Nevertheless, this connection must be verified. Again, however, a lack of comparative data makes this verification difficult, especially for the pre-1945 period, during which polls were almost nonexistent. Moreover, the context after the *révolution tranquille* is different enough to raise doubts. Thus, in this article, we are not making that assumption regarding attitudinal continuity in Quebec: we will consider various historical periods separately. We will *not* assume, for example, that the critical attitude displayed by French-Canadians toward the conscription in 1917–1918 is an expression of the same phenomenon as the demonstration against the invasion of Iraq by the US-led coalition forces some 85 years later. On the contrary, our main hypothesis, as expressed below, will question this assumption. This approach will allow us to provide alternative and separate interpretations for behaviours that *could* be interpreted as similar.

Heuristic considerations aside, we recognize, as do most commentators, that Quebecers hold a different attitude than other Canadians toward military issues and the use of force. *However*, the intensity and motivation explaining this opinion have evolved over time, such that Quebecers' preferences have changed since the "Quiet Revolution," if not since the end of the Second World War. If Quebecers are still circumspect with regard to the use of force, they have nevertheless lost their isolationist and anti-militarist reflexes. Although they openly support military operations to re-establish the rule of law or to assist endangered populations, they remain reluctant to use force as a means to resolve conflicts or solve other social and political problems, especially through an **international intervention**.

Lessons from the Past: Isolationism and Anti-militarism (1760–1945)

The image of Quebecers as pacifists, isolationists, and anti-militarists comes primarily from an interpretation of history; therefore, we must look at the past to understand the origins of today's perception. In the following overview of Quebec's relationship with military issues, we first try to show that, for roughly two centuries—from 1760 to 1945—French-Canadians generally saw military force in a critical light. It was during this period that the foundations of the "pacifist Quebec" were established. However, as Quebec's society evolved and was transformed by the Quiet Revolution, Quebecers have come to see military force from a different perspective. We argue that although attitudes may seem similar, Quebecers' position on military issues has evolved. From an anti-militarist and isolationist stance, Quebec's society has become more internationalist and deems the use of force legitimate, albeit only under specific considerations. Finally, we propose hypotheses to explain this gradual transformation, which took place between the 1970s and 1990s.

Rejecting Empire and the Military?

At first glance, the history of Quebec seems to support (and justify) the idea that its society is pacifist, anti-militarist, and isolationist. Although it is rarely mentioned today, the Conquest of 1758–1760, in which Nouvelle-France was defeated by British troops, was a violent and traumatizing experience that left deep scars.[14] Humiliated by the Conquest, French-Canadians turned their backs on military affairs and transformed their defeat into an "anti-militarist tradition."[15] In a relatively short period of time, the French-speaking population ignored the years when Nouvelle-France was a "vast military camp perpetually at war"[16] and adopted an attitude of indifference toward British–US bickering. Even though the Catholic Church, which saw its status confirmed by the Quebec Act of 1774, encouraged collaboration with the new political and economic masters of Quebec, French-Canadians showed a reluctance to defend the colony in the name of the King or for London's merchants. The departure of the French military elite, following the 1760 defeat, further weakened the interest of French-Canadians in military institutions, which would have an effect on subsequent generations of Quebecers.[17] The attitude of French-Canadians toward the military events of the late nineteenth century and first half of the twentieth century was mostly indifference. For the most part, French-Canadians refused to participate in British efforts to defend the colony from American invasions in 1775 and 1812, notwithstanding the romantic image of Canadian Charles-Michel de Salaberry and his men in the Châteauguay skirmishes of 1813. Likewise, in 1899, Henri Bourassa and Canadian nationalists opposed Canadian participation in the Boer War, arguing that they were

Canadians before being members of the British Empire.[18] Ten years later, they contested with the same passion the creation of a Canadian navy destined essentially to reinforce the British Royal Navy.

The pacifist myth is reinforced by Quebec's attitude during the two world wars. First, in May 1917, Robert Borden's Unionist government decided to introduce conscription measures in Canada. The opposition was fierce in Quebec, mainly from the nationalist and union elites, but also among the people generally. Riots broke out in Montreal and Quebec City, and on Easter Monday 1918 troops fired into the crowd, killing four and wounding scores of protestors.[19] One must note that the trigger for these uprisings were the conscription measures, not the participation in the war effort. Henri Bourassa, for example, initially supported participation in the First World War, but strongly opposed conscription measures. Nevertheless, the conscription crisis of 1917–1918 left an indelible impression on francophone and anglophone political elites in Canada. Events seemed to repeat themselves during the Second World War when, in 1942, Prime Minister William Lyon Mackenzie King proposed a plebiscite in order to disavow his promise not to implement conscription—a promise made to help Quebec's Liberals defeat Maurice Duplessis's *Union Nationale* in the 1939 election. Results from the 1942 plebiscite illustrate the two "solitudes" of Canada. While 80 per cent of English-speaking Canadians agreed to the federal government request, 85 per cent of French-speaking Canadians did not.[20] While Borden bluntly imposed his decisions on the French-Canadians, Mackenzie King proceeded much more carefully, and this second conscription crisis didn't leave the same historical legacy as the first.[21]

Up through the Cold War, the regular army in Canada remained fundamentally a British institution, one in which career opportunities for French-Canadians were limited unless at the price of assimilation. Francophone militia regiments in Quebec were essentially social clubs with little military ethos. In 1914, francophones constituted only 4 per cent of the first contingent formed to fight in Europe. It must be pointed out, however, that anglophones of Canadian origin were not doing significantly better, since 70 per cent of the volunteers were born outside the country. Similarly, less than 4 per cent of the Royal Military College graduates were francophones.[22] The creation of French-speaking battalions in October 1914, including the one which would soon be raised to regiment status—the Royal 22e Régiment—improved the situation, if only marginally. In this light, defiance toward a military institution perceived as "foreign" in nature is the first argument explaining the French-Canadian attitude. French-Canadians' attitude was essentially "anti-militarist"—rejecting the military institutions of the time—rather than "pacifist."

Furthermore, the motivation to fight on foreign battlefields remained weak. The defence of the British Empire was hardly a compelling notion for a population that had lived for generations in North America. The Canadian territory was not threatened. This was the central argument of Canadian nationalists, rallying behind Henri Bourassa. French-Canadian negative perception of military institutions was not counterbalanced by a feeling of insecurity from an external threat that would justify the existence of such institutions. Consequently, it seems more fitting to use the terms "isolationism" or "anti-imperialism" to qualify the French-Canadian attitude toward war during the 1760–1945 period. Quebec's political and religious elites essentially tried to discourage the Canadian government from participating in imperial wars and to prevent French-Canadians from joining foreign military ventures. In general, this position stemmed from the ability to make a distinction between Canadian and imperial interests, which by and large was lacking in the English-Canadian community.[23] Those Anglo-Canadians who had this ability, such as Oscar D. Skelton, undersecretary of state for external affairs in the Mackenzie King government, were more inclined to accept isolationistic logic.[24] In French Canada, this isolationism was mostly the manifestation of a desire to protect Canadian society from negative external influences. However, it is conceivable that for many French-Canadians, the perception that a war was an *imperial* one seemed the most important variable in determining the legitimacy of Canadian participation in armed conflicts. It must be noted that while isolationism/anti-imperialism and anti-militarism have common roots (both being a rejection of British institutions), they do not necessarily go hand in hand. For example, Henri Bourassa and some high representatives of the Catholic Church were not against the creation of military institutions or the Canadian participation in the Boer Wars or the First World War, but against the imperialist dimension that they represented. For French-Canadian nationalists, a Canadian armed force organized to protect the Canadian territory was perfectly acceptable.

The Military Record of a "Pacifist" Nation

Arguing that French-Canadians have, since the Conquest, shied away from the use of force is factually inconsistent. During the nineteenth century, French-Canadians participated in numerous armed conflicts. In November 1837, the Patriots of Lower Canada, under the leadership of Louis-Joseph Papineau and Dr. Jean-Olivier Chénier, took up arms in hopes of getting out of the constitutional quagmire in which the two provinces (Upper and Lower Canada) had been sinking for more than 20 years. In 1838, a series of violent incidents took place, which were promptly put down by British troops. Similarly, during the American Civil War (1860–1865), 10,000 to 15,000 French-Canadians (including Americans of French-Canadian origin) joined the Union army.[25] In 1868, 498 French-Canadian volunteers enrolled in the Papal Zouaves corps, hoping to defend the papal territory from the nationalist forces of Giuseppe Garibaldi. Members of this small group were treated like heroes by the Catholic Church and Quebec population.[26] Although this adventure appears quite burlesque, it nonetheless reveals a willingness on the part of the Quebecers to participate in wars on foreign territories. By contrast, French drafters trying to recruit volunteers to defend the Napoleon III Empire were not nearly as successful.[27]

In 1869, and most of all in 1885, the Northwest Métis (in what became Manitoba and Saskatchewan) did not hesitate to follow Louis Riel and take up arms in defence of his provisional provincial government. Also, some French-Canadians joined the *voyageurs* group formed to assist the expeditionary force sent to Sudan in the hope of rescuing the troops of the British General Charles Gordon, trapped inside Khartoum. This force was composed of francophones, anglophones, and Amerindians from the Montreal area. While the disaster of Khartoum stirred commotion in the imperialist Canadian elite,[28] in Quebec it was the hanging of Louis Riel in November that attracted attention. Finally, we must remember the enrolment of 63 French-Canadians in the International Brigades that fought during the Spanish Civil War (1936–1939). Half of those individuals served in the Mackenzie-Papineau Battalion (the "Mac-Pap").[29]

From this brief historical overview, three elements should be highlighted. First, French-Canadians have participated in numerous armed conflicts—sometimes in small numbers, as in Spain, and sometimes constituting a significant force, as in the American Civil War. The conscription crisis surrounding the two world wars often masks the fact that many francophones voluntarily enlisted and fought on European battlefields. To be sure, French-Canadians have had an essentially negative historical experience with the use of force and military institutions, and it is possible that this experience has to some extent conditioned their attitude toward military expeditions. However, it did not lead to a well thought out, structured discourse on the origins of war and on the condemnation of the use of force on moral, legal, or ideological grounds. More than that, on occasion—in 1837–1838, for example—the use of violence seemed like a viable and acceptable solution to most French-Canadians. Second, religious institutions played an important role, influencing the French-Canadian outlook on military matters. These institutions helped establish the legitimacy, or lack thereof, of military endeavours, with legitimacy dependent on the attitude of the protagonists toward the Catholic Church.

Culture Shift: Social and Cultural Transformations in Contemporary Quebec

Quebecers' attitude in the aftermath of the Second World War tended to reinforce the myth of a pacifist, isolationist, and anti-militarist society. During the Cold War, Quebecers showed a greater distrust than their English-Canadian compatriots toward foreign military commitments.[30] Quebec's skepticism against Canadian military commitments remained important during this period.[31] After the Cold War, this inclination seemed to endure. For example, in the first moments of the Gulf War in 1990, Quebecers' public opinion was significantly less supportive than English-Canadians toward Canadian participation in international invasion.[32] Similarly, Quebecers were opposed to a possible Canadian participation in the Iraq War.[33] Finally, one of the key issues championed by the Bloc Québécois in 2003–2006 was its opposition to Canadian participation in the anti-ballistic missile defence program proposed by Washington. Many authors see an element of continuity between Quebecers' attitude toward war in the nineteenth century and the public demonstrations of the early twenty-first century. However, this perceived continuity between the attitudes of French-Canadians before and after the *Quiet Revolution* is probably only an illusion. As shown, the historical record does not support the central claim of the pacifist society perspective.

The Quiet Revolution and Other Societal Changes

How can we explain this shift from an isolationist attitude to an internationalist one? We argue that Quebec's strategic culture has changed since the 1960s. Strategic cultures are sets of ideas (concepts, metaphors, images, symbols, etc.) shared by a given community, forming a coherent and persistent whole and helping to shape the group's attitude toward the use of force and the role of military institutions.[34] Because a strategic culture is moulded primarily by historical experience, it tends to remain stable over time. However, *stable* does not mean *immutable*. Sometimes this happens brutally, following a collective trauma (such as Pearl Harbor or the World Trade Center attacks on the United States), sometimes quite gradually, as the evolution of the socio-political context brings about new experiences and influences the reinterpretation of old lessons.[35]

The most prominent socio-political transformation in Quebec's contemporary society was the Quiet Revolution, in which Quebec experienced significant changes in nationalism, religious practices, attitudes toward military institutions, and the level of education within the population. First, French-Canadian nationalism (which would become Quebecers' nationalism) reinforced the idea that francophones should refrain from fighting on foreign battlefields to defend foreign—that is, English—interests (meaning British, American, or even English-Canadian interests). However, this

nationalism has changed, especially during the 1960s and 1970s, moving from a conservative framework of *survival* to a more *reformist* context—sometimes liberal, sometimes more critical and social democratic. This attitude, often interpreted as being pacifist, masks nationalistic values that have very little to do with a judgment on the legitimacy of the use of force to resolve political problems.

According to historian Michael Behiels,[36] this questioning was led by two groups. The first group, identified as *Citélibristes* (named after *Cité libre*, the movement's main publication), whose most popular member was Pierre E. Trudeau, was driven by the conviction of the universal value of liberalism. The second group, usually identified as *neo-nationalists*, also wished to modernize Quebec's state and society, but following a more social-democratic program. This group grew out of the *Bloc populaire* and the ideas published in *Le Devoir* and *L'Action nationale*. Neo-nationalism gradually evolved into a more endogenous vision: it was not enough for Quebec to protect and distinguish itself from English Canada anymore; there was a need to promote an identity and interests considered exclusive to Quebec. This logic brought about a desire for affirmation on the international scene and, consequently, the adoption of a more open attitude toward the world. Quebec's diminished reluctance regarding international military commitments can be seen as a result of this phenomenon.

A second important socio-political phenomenon that transformed the context in which Quebecers' public opinion has developed was the drastic diminution of the Catholic Church's influence on civil society in the 1960s. This was a remarkable phenomenon, since "from a society with staunch Catholic roots . . . Quebec has evolved into the most post-modern region of this continent."[37] The principal consequence of interest for us here is the fading importance of religious factors as a criterion of the legitimacy of foreign missions. The

Church cannot encourage or condemn the people's attitude in favour of a mission anymore.[38]

The third factor worth mentioning is the apparent reconciliation of Quebecers with the Canadian Armed Forces (CAF). In the last 60 years, the institution lost its "British" character to become a Canadian, rather than an imperial, entity. The Canadian Armed Forces also lost the reputation of being an "English" institution and was perceived as being more open to francophones.[39] The recent decision of the Harper government to reintroduce the CAF British tradition by, for example reinserting the term Royal in both the Canadian Navy and Canadian Air Force, was not perceived positively by Quebecers (nor other notable Canadian authors such as Granatstein), and it is not clear what effect this decision will have on Quebec's support of the Canadian Armed Forces. Moreover, the role played by CAF in several conflicts, such as Bosnia (1991–1995), the Rwanda genocide (1994), the Kosovo crisis (1999), and Libya (2011), have certainly demonstrated the importance of armed forces as an instrument of peacekeeping and peacemaking. Similarly, local events such as the Oka crisis (1990), involving a property dispute between a First Nation and a Quebec municipality; the Saguenay flood (1996); and the North American ice storm (1998) are all positive experiences of military intervention. Images from these experiences have replaced, in Quebec's collective memory, the images of repression associated with the conscription crises.

Finally, Quebec's increasing education level played a major role. One of the most tangible signs of the strategic culture shift in Quebec's society (though it is difficult to know whether this is a cause or an effect) is the emergence, since the mid-1990s, of a Quebec military history. For a long time, Quebec maintained a distant relationship with its military past. Academic works on the subject were rare prior to the mid-1990s, and the public as well as the political elite ignored commemorations. The

contrast with the current situation is salient, as many authors contend.[40] In short, the Quebec society that emerged after the 1960s looked less and less like the French-Canadian society that had been struggling to survive in North America since the Conquest. This transformation is felt in the way Quebecers now view military issues.

There is no doubt that Quebec's society has changed since the Quiet Revolution of the 1960s. If this change is particularly striking in the political, social, and economic spheres, what effect has this revolution had on the public's attitude toward defence and security issues? There are many indications that Quebec has evolved from a conservative and isolationist society to a more progressive and internationalist one. In his study of Quebecers' attitudes between 1945 and 1960, James I. Gow already saw a tendency toward internationalist ideas.[41] During the period of the Quiet Revolution, this tendency grew, and probably continues to evolve.

Quebec's Public Opinion Regarding Defence and Security Issues Since 1990

Overall, public opinion polls demonstrate a shift toward internationalist values from an earlier isolationist position. Since the beginning of the 1990s, the publication of more than 60 public opinion polls representing Quebecers' views on defence and security issues makes it possible to follow the development of Quebec's society. Although enlightening, Canadian public opinion polls should always be used with great caution, especially if they pertain to foreign policy issues. First, there is no systematic examination of public attitudes toward international issues in Canada. Public opinion polls are sparse, and rarely does a pollster ask repeatedly the same question on the same issues across time. Second, data on public attitudes regarding Canadian military participation have not been collected for *all* military missions in the last 30 years. For example, we lack data on Canadian participation in most UN peacekeeping missions across the 1970s and the 1980s. Third, methodological considerations have changed in time. Many pre-1980 polls do not publish results by provinces. Many polls present significant margins of errors, which make comparative analyses troublesome (since we must add the margins of errors for the two compared data sets). Hence, we are quite limited by the data provided by pollsters, meaning that any conclusions using these results should be pondered carefully.

The "pacifist society" discourse insists on the premise that a majority of French-speaking Quebecers are opposed to international Canadian military commitments, and that when Quebecers do support such missions, it is generally with great reluctance. The dominant image is one of a massive schism between the two communities, recalling the polarized society of the 1942 plebiscite.[42] However, as shown in Figure 19.1, a quick overview of public opinion polls reveals that Quebecers are generally in favour (i.e., by more than 50 per cent) of missions conducted under the auspices of the United Nations (UN).[43] This support tends to shrink slightly when these missions are led by other organizations or by ad hoc coalitions, as shown in Figure 19.2.

One of the most surprising findings revealed by these public opinion polls is a phenomenon of "strategic convergence" between the French- and the English-Canadian communities. Far from corresponding to the results of the 1942 plebiscite, polls conducted after 1990 show that the margin separating the two communities is rarely over 10 per cent, regardless of the issue. As illustrated in Figure 19.2, between 1990 and 2006, there were only four cases where the difference between Quebecers and rest of Canada exceeded 10 per cent: the Gulf War of 1991; the "War on Terror" following 9/11; the participation of Canada in a possible Iraq War in 2003; and the involvement of Canadian troops in southern Afghanistan (Kandahar). For all other cases, the average margin between the two linguistic groups is less than 6 per cent, with the margin of error accounted for. Another dimension of the "strategic convergence" between Quebec and the rest of Canada is that both groups tend to move in the same direction, reacting similarly to the same events, even if sometimes we observe temporal lag in reaction. Therefore, when we observe a favourable opinion on a certain mission on the part of French-Canadians, we generally find a corresponding

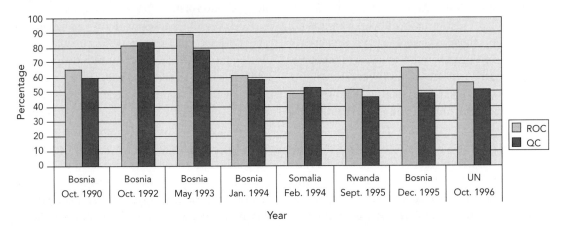

Figure 19.1 Evolution of ROC and Quebec Public Opinion Regarding Canadian Participation in UN Missions (1990–1996)

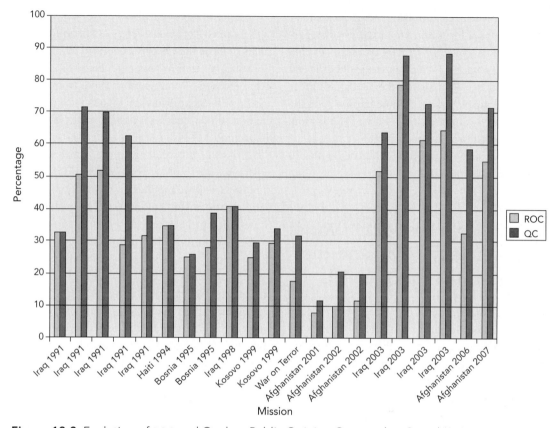

Figure 19.2 Evolution of ROC and Quebec Public Opinion Opposed to Canadian Participation in Non-UN Missions (1991–2007)

movement in English public opinion—and vice-versa. In brief, not only are the opinions expressed by Quebecers and English-Canadians more comparable than conventional wisdom would have us believe, but also both opinion curves follow the same pattern in time. In light of these results, we can say only that Quebecers are more vocal in their opposition to Canadian interventions abroad; we cannot claim that they are fundamentally different from other Canadians on defence and security issues.[44] What we perceive in Quebec's public attitude toward military interventions after 1990 is a clear identification of the principles of liberal or **Pearsonian internationalism**. In fact, on the face

of it, Quebecers appear to adhere to internationalism more so the Canadian federal government.

So how can we explain the difference—though minimal—that persists between Quebec and other Canadians despite strategic convergence? As Figure 19.2 indicates, the largest differences between Quebec and other provinces occur during conflicts where American interests are at stake (Iraq 1991; Iraq 2003; the "War on Terror" 2001; and Afghanistan 2006–2012), while they disappear on conflicts where these interests are less apparent (Haiti, Bosnia, Kosovo, and Libya). Even if the hypothesis remains fragile, it is tempting to identify at least one element of historical continuity: until

1945, the principal legitimizing factor for military interventions abroad from a French-Canadian perspective was that those interests were serving Canadian rather than British interests; since the end of the Cold War (if not since the 1960s), a similar trend is taking place, but this time in relation to the United States. This conclusion raises the question, which is no less controversial than Quebecers' alleged "pacifism," of an "anti-American" reflex in Quebec public opinion.[45]

Canada in a Post-9/11 World: Afghanistan, Libya, and the Militarization of Quebec's Society

The international environment after 9/11 offers the right conditions—a war in southern Afghanistan, a military intervention in Libya, and a federal government willing to increase substantially Canada's military expenditures and emphasize Canadian military history (War of 1812, "Re-royalization" of the Canadian Armed Forces)—to examine, albeit anecdotally, Quebec's specificity in regards to defence and security issues. The Canadian government decision to take part in the international effort in Kandahar, Afghanistan, from 2006 to 2011 remains a defining event in Canada's military history since the Korean War. By itself, the Canadian presence in southern Afghanistan since 2006 offers all the essential elements necessary to study Quebec's hypothesized pacifism: overseas intervention, no obvious and direct Canadian national interests, combat operations using ground forces (the first time since the Korean War in 1950) and significant military losses. Taken collectively, these factors would theoretically point toward a strong Quebec opposition and an explosive political situation that would potentially strain Canadian national unity. In effect, the

reflex regarding the "pacifist Quebec" was still alive in the mind of many observers. In the summer and fall of 2008, on the eve of the deployment of Roto 4, mainly composed of soldiers from the Royal 22e Régiment, some commentators (both from French and English Canada) foresaw a harsh reaction when the first soldier bearing a French name was killed in action.[46]

However, as we shall argue, the Kandahar experience does not support the "Pacifist Quebec" hypothesis and exemplifies, to the contrary, a contemporary strategic culture that has evolved and come to accept, even expect, the use of force under the right conditions. Figure 19.3 below represents the evolution of Quebec, Alberta, and the rest of Canada (ROC) public opposition toward Canada's engagement in Afghanistan from 2006 to 2011.

First, analyzing public opinion polls published between March 2006 and December 2011 on the attitudes of Quebec, Alberta, and other provinces (ROC without Quebec and Alberta) toward Canadian participation in combat operations in Kandahar shows that Quebecers remained robustly opposed to Canada's mission in Kandahar since its inception. Considering the data illustrated by Figure 19.3, from March 2006 to December 2011 (when the combat mission ended), an average of 65 per cent[48] of Quebec's population disagreed with Canada's presence in Afghanistan and would have preferred an early withdrawal. Compared with the ROC, Quebecers appear to be more critical than other Canadians by an average of 15 per cent. However, we must note that ROC attitude remained quite ambiguous in its support of the Afghan intervention, maintaining an average of 47.7 per cent opposing the mission. Alberta, for its part, stayed generally supportive across the time period with an average of 38 per cent opposing Canada's deployment in Kandahar. Nevertheless, the image of a fundamental split between the francophone and anglophone communities does not appear to

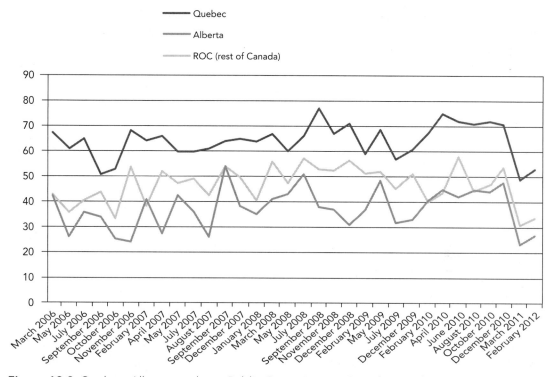

Figure 19.3 Quebec, Alberta, and ROC Public Opposition to Canada's Involvement in Afghanistan (2006–2012)[47]

materialize. In truth, Canadian public opinion seems to move along a continuum ranging from Quebec to Alberta and indicating a regional divide more than a linguistic one.[49] Accordingly, ROC looks as if to be caught between two hard places, dovish Quebec and hawkish Alberta.

Yet, despite Quebec's strong objection regarding Canadian involvement in southern Afghanistan, this perception did not translate into an activist and militant movement that could have forced the federal government to reconsider its policy. In hindsight, Quebecers' opposition remained passive with little or no political consequences for Ottawa, and remained a non-factor in the three federal elections of January 2006, October 2008, and May 2011. This missed opportunity for the "pacifist" Quebec thesis

tends to reveal that the Belle province's relation with defence and military issues is complex and is more than what is conventionally assumed. In our minds, two main factors associated with Quebec's shifted strategic culture account for this passive opposition.

First, Quebec's political and public opinion elites remained largely sympathetic to the Canadian mission in Kandahar, Afghanistan. Most adopted an internationalist stance toward the Afghanistan mission, wishing for a better equilibrium between combat and humanitarian objectives, but still supporting Canada's presence in Southeast Asia. Politically, Conservative, Liberal, and even Bloc Québécois leaders in Quebec advocated for an active military participation in Afghanistan. On this, the Bloc Québécois' position is extremely telling; although it always demanded that Ottawa refocus its actions toward diplomatic, reconstruction and foreign aid, it still maintained that security was an essential aspect of any endeavour in Afghanistan and that Canada's international responsibility required its participation in the international effort.[50] Likewise, most print[51] and electronic media have been supportive or nuanced in their coverage of the Canadian military engagement in southern Afghanistan. Following this general consensus from Quebec's elites, pacifist movements in Quebec lacked the political clout to actively bring their position into an effective force. Consequently, although Quebecers remain circumspect toward *how* the Kandahar mission is handled (opinion unambiguously asserted by Figure 19.3), this attitude is dormant and did not become a real political issue. Case in point: as much as Quebecers opposed "combat" operations in Afghanistan from 2006 to 2011, they actually supported Canada's mission to train Afghan police and military personnel from 2012 to 2014. As one can observe in Figure 19.3, public opinion polls conducted in March 2011 and February 2012 show there is a sharp decline in public opposition in Canada.

Second, since 2006, Quebecers associated themselves favourably with the province's military personnel rotating in and out of Kandahar. Unlike historical military adventures of the past, where the Canadian Armed Forces seemed uncomfortable in a French environment and where Quebecers had a hard time relating to its British tradition, Quebec's own Valcartier (the province's main military base near Quebec City) regiments, most notably the Royal 22e Régiment and the 12e Régiment blindé du Canada, symbolized Quebecers' ideals and acceptance of a certain (although young) military history. This "connection" with Canadian military institutions is lived with a sense of ambivalence in which Quebecers still oppose the Kandahar mission but support its military personnel deployed abroad.

This love–hate relationship toward Canada's participation in the international mission in Kandahar is splendidly epitomized by the personal experience of one of Quebec's main pacifist advocates, Francis Dupuis-Déri, professor of political science at Université du Québec à Montréal (UQAM). Dupuis-Déri is well-known in the province's pacifist circles and media. Throughout Kandahar's deployment, he has been an active critic publicly and in the media of Canada's participation in the international mission in Afghanistan. Incidentally, Professor Dupuis-Déri's sister serves as a captain in the Canadian Armed Forces. In June 2007, he published an opinion letter in *Le Devoir* entitled "Lettre à ma sœur militaire qui part en Afghanistan" ("Letter to my military sister leaving for Afghanistan"),[52] in which he condemns and denounces Canada's presence in Southeast Asia while wishing the best for his family member. In this letter, all the ambiguity and the ambivalence of Quebec's public opinion toward the Kandahar operation is symbolized: the objections are based on philosophical grounds without being transferred to the institution and the members of the Canadian Armed Forces. We could argue that this nationalistic, even emotional, connection with francophone regiments of the Canadian Armed Forces has moderated Quebec's hostile manifestation toward the overall Afghan policy.

Contrary to what was expected, even in the midst of mounting military losses, Quebec's public opinion remained consistently unsympathetic towards Canada's participation in the international effort in Afghanistan. Surprisingly, Quebecers' attitudes seemed to crystallize with the first week of the Kandahar deployment in 2006, and no issues (either negative or positive) have changed it significantly through the years. In light of this, nothing changed Quebec's attitude until the end of combat operations in southern Afghanistan in 2011. What is interesting, however, is that a different Canadian involvement in Afghanistan after 2011, one that focused on training and support to Afghan institutions, was not met with the same opposition in Quebec. With respect to Canada's intervention in Kandahar, Quebecers appeared to oppose *what* the Canadian Armed Forces were doing in Afghanistan, not necessarily *why*.

Quebec's nuanced attitude toward military issues, one that emphasized an internationalist perspective, was further exemplified during Canada's participation in NATO's intervention in Libya in 2011. Figure 19.4 presents the public opposition in Quebec, Alberta, and ROC to Canada's engagement in Libya in 2011. Canada's action in Libya during the spring of 2011 was a response to United Nations Security Council Resolution 1973, which imposed a no-fly zone and authorized member states to "take all necessary measures" to protect civilians under attack by Qaddafi's regime. Although the Harper government publicly asserted that Canada's participation in international efforts was not an endorsement of the Responsibility to Protect principle,[53] the mission embodied values in accordance with liberal internationalism: a well-defined international mandate, engagement of Canada's allies (US, France, and UK), clear presence of liberal ideals such as the protection of civilians, and minimal military involvement from the United States. As we can observe in Figure 19.4, Quebecers, as did other Canadians, overwhelmingly favoured military operations in Libya. Opposition was minimal in Quebec, with only 25 per cent of respondents opposed to the intervention in May 2011. Other Canadians essentially agreed, with only 28 per cent of Albertans and 20 per cent of ROC opposing Canada's intervention. A month later, in June 2011, as the objectives of the mission oscillated between protecting civilians and regime change, public opposition rose in Canada with Quebecers (37 per cent) and ROC (30 per cent) re-evaluating their position on the issue. Almost half of Albertan (47 per cent) respondents indicated that they objected to military intervention in Libya. Similar to the intervention in Kosovo in 1999, Quebecers were undoubtedly sympathetic to the use of force. In hindsight,

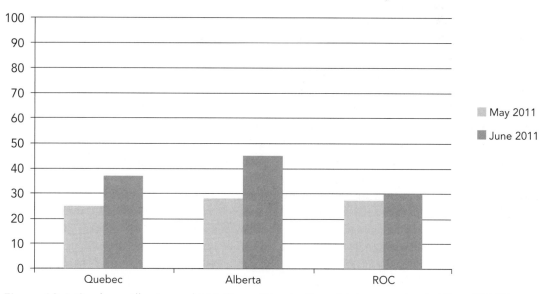

Figure 19.4 Quebec, Alberta, and ROC Opposition to Canada's Intervention in Libya (2011)[56]

there is a clear militarization of Quebec's society.[54] In this context, Quebecers seem to adhere to the tenets of offence-oriented liberalism,[55] subscribing to the notion that the use of force is acceptable when the goals are circumscribed to liberal ideals such human rights, freedom, and the like.

Conclusion

The conventional wisdom about Quebec's attitude toward the use of force and the role of military institutions must be seriously nuanced. It is a historical fact that Quebecers experienced a very different relationship with the use of force than did English Canadians, and this experience probably explains lingering differences in attitudes between the two linguistic groups. Remnants of the old isolationist attitude may still be observed among Quebecers from time to time. Nevertheless, remaining differences between the two solitudes are certainly much smaller and much less important than the majority of Canadians (including Quebecers themselves) would like to think. Contemporary Quebecers are, from a certain perspective, more attached to the classical Pearsonian model in Canadian foreign policy (usually called *liberal internationalism*) than are many English-Canadians. The key features of Quebec's "strategic culture" are: 1) a central role in UN undertakings; 2) the use of military force for peacekeeping operations rather than for combat missions; and 3) the primacy of Canadian interests—all values consistent with the image that Canadians as a whole have of their own foreign policy.

The upending of conventional wisdom regarding Quebec's attitude toward the use of military force—an upending for which we argue in this article—has important policy implications. First, it reveals as an exaggeration the claim that Quebec is hijacking Canadian foreign policy: if Quebecers are not so different from other Canadians, there is no point in accusing them of pursuing their own foreign policy agenda. Moreover, focusing on Quebec's opposition to a given mission simply leads to ignoring other pockets of opposition in Canada. Second, emphasizing the differences between Quebec and the rest of Canada tends to result in ignoring other potential regional differences within Canada. Furthermore, it tends to place the responsibility for those differences on Quebec, seeking (for example) an explanation in Quebec's alleged pacifism rather than in other regions' "war-proneness." Finally, the claim for a different attitude can also be used by sovereignist political leaders to support the rationale for independence, as Bernard Landry, then head of the PQ, did during the debate on the possible Canadian contribution to the American-led alliance against Iraq in 2003.[57]

Quebecers have started to revisit their military past through different lenses than their parents and grandparents did. Their recent contribution to the strategic debate is likely to grow, and, as guardians of Pearsonian orthodoxy, they could force a debate on alternatives to liberal internationalism—such as (neo) continentalism—in Canadian foreign policy. As we contended elsewhere,[58] an element of support exists for the hypothesis of the rise of a new strategic culture in Canada, labeled "neocontinentalism" or "neoconservatism," based on principles that are radically different than those of liberal internationalism: a moral clarity (opposed to the relativism of the internationalist), a clear support for US international initiatives against rogue states and terrorism, a defiance toward international institutions, and a lower threshold for the use of force. If this hypothesis is confirmed, Quebec's liberal internationalism stance is a more a promise of a new debate with English Canada rather than a convergence between the two linguistic groups.

Questions for Review

1. What is Quebec's contemporary strategic culture?

2. What are the principal factors explaining the transformation of Quebecers' attitude toward military issues?

3. How would you characterize Canadian public opinion on international military intervention?

4. In your own opinion, does (or should) public opinion influence Canadian decision-makers on foreign affairs?

Suggested Readings

Granatstein, Jack L. 2007. *Whose War Is It? How Canada Can Survive in the Post-9/11 World.* Toronto: HarperCollins.

Haglund, David G. 2006. "Québec's 'America Problem': Differential Threat Perception in the North American Security Community." *American Review of Canadian Studies* 36, 4: 552–67.

Lachapelle, Guy. 1995. "La guerre de 1939–1945 dans l'opinion publique: Une comparaison entre les attitudes des Canadiens français et des Canadiens anglais." *Bulletin d'histoire politique* 3, 3–4: 201–26.

Massie, Justin, and Jean-Christophe Boucher. 2013. "Militaristes et anti-impérialistes: Les Québécois face à la sécurité internationale." *Études internationales* 44, 3 (septembre): 359–85.

Roussel, Stéphane, and Charles-Alexandre Théorêt. 2004. "A 'Distinct Strategy'? The Use of Canadian Strategic Culture by the Sovereignist Movement in Québec, 1968–1996." *International Journal* 59, 3 (Summer): 557–77.

Waite, P.B. 1983. "French-Canadian Isolationism and English Canada: An Elliptical Foreign Policy, 1935–1939." *Journal of Canadian Studies* 18, 2 (Summer): 132–48.

Notes

1. J.L. Granatstein, *Whose War Is It? How Canada Can Survive in the Post-9/11 World* (Toronto: HarperCollins, 2007), Chapter 6.

2. Jean-Sébastien Rioux, *Two Solitudes: Quebecers' Attitudes Regarding Canadian Security and Defence Policy* (Calgary: CDFAI, 2005), 1. See also Antoine Robitaille, "Quebecers: A Pacifist People?," *Inroads* 14 (2003): 62–75, and Serge Mongeau, "La tradition antimilitariste au Québec," pp. 81–89 in Mongeau, ed., *Pour un pays sans armée* (Montreal: Écosociété, 1993).

3. J.L. Granatstein, "Quebecers are at the Helm," *Ottawa Citizen*, 1 November 2005, A-15. See also his *Who Killed the Canadian Military?* (Toronto: HarperCollins, 2004), 193–94), and his "Multiculturalism and Canadian Foreign Policy," in David Carment and David Bercuson, eds., *The World in Canada: Diasporas, Demography, and Domestic Policy* (Montreal and Kingston: McGill-Queen's University Press, 2008), 87–88; Janice Gross Stein and Eugene Lang, *The Unexpected War: Canada in Kandahar* (Toronto: Viking Canada, 2007), 73 and 170. For an opposite view, see Pierre Martin, "All Quebec's Fault, Again? Quebec Public Opinion and Canada's Rejection of Missile Defence," *Policy Options* 26, 4 (2005): 41–44; Justin Massie,

Jean-Christophe Boucher, and Stéphane Roussel, "Hijacking a Policy? Assessing Quebec's 'Undue' Influence on Canada's Afghan Policy," *American Review of Canadian Studies* 40, 2 (2010): 259–75.

4. Granatstein, *Whose War Is It?*; Robitaille, "Quebecers: A Pacifist People?"

5. David Carment and David Bercuson, "Conclusion: Putting Canada's Diversity into Canadian Foreign Policy," in Carment and Bercuson, eds., *The World in Canada*, 211.

6. Mongeau, "La tradition antimilitariste"; J.L. Granatstein, "Multiculturalism and Canadian Foreign Policy," in Carment and Bercuson, 87.

7. Robert Comeau, "L'opposition à la conscription au Québec," in Roch Legault and Jean Lamarre, eds., *La Première Guerre mondiale et le Canada* (Montreal: Méridien, 1999), 109; P.B. Waite, "French-Canadian Isolationism and English Canada: An Elliptical Foreign Policy, 1935–1939," *Journal of Canadian Studies* 18, 2 (1983): 132–48.

8. Granatstein, *Whose War Is It?*, 141.

9. David G. Haglund, "Québec's 'America Problem': Differential Threat Perception in the North American Security Community," *American Review of Canadian*

Studies 36, 4 (2006): 552–67; David G. Haglund, "The Parizeau-Chrétien Version: Ethnicity and Canadian Grand Strategy," in Carment and Bercuson, 92–108.

10. For an in-depth analysis of concepts such as pacifism, isolationism, internationalism, anti-militarism, and anti-imperialism as applied to Quebec, see Justin Massie and Jean-Christophe Boucher, "Militaristes et anti-impérialistes: Les Québécois face à la sécurité internationale," *Études internationales* 44, 3 (2013): 359–85.

11. Definition inspired by Marcel Merle, "Pacifisme," in Thierry de Montbrial and Jean Klein, eds., *Dictionnaire de stratégie* (Paris: Presses universitaires de France, 2000), 396–403. Of course, this definition does not capture all the distinctions between different forms of pacifism, from a general condemnation of the use of force in all circumstances to a specific condemnation, motivated by opposition to a particular war (such as the war in Vietnam) or a particular weapon system (for example, nuclear weapons). Nevertheless, in the context of this article, this nuance is unnecessary.

12. Jocelyn Coulon, "Le nouvel antiaméricanisme," *Argument* 7, 2 (2005): 49.

13. Kim Richard Nossal, Stéphane Roussel, and Stéphane Paquin, *International Policy and Politics in Canada* (Toronto: Pearson Education, 2011), 135–41.

14. See Guy Frégault, *La Guerre de la Conquête* (Montreal: Fides, 1955).

15. Béatrice Richard, *La mémoire de Dieppe: Radioscopie d'un mythe* (Montreal: VLB, 2002), 34.

16. Ibid.

17. Roch Legault, *Une élite en déroute: Les militaires canadiens après la Conquête* (Montreal: Athéna, 2002), 161–67.

18. Carman Miller, *Painting the Map in Red: Canada and the South African War, 1899–1902* (Montreal and Kingston: McGill-Queen's University Press, 1993), 27–30.

19. Gérard Filteau, *Le Québec, le Canada et la guerre 1914–1918* (Montreal: Éditions de l'Aurore, 1977), 158–63; see also Comeau, "L'opposition à la conscription au Québec."

20. Paul-André Linteau, René Durocher, Jean-Claude Robert, and François Ricard, *Histoire du Québec contemporain: Le Québec depuis 1930* (Montreal: Boréal, 1986), 138. For Canada, the total of "yes" votes would be 2,943,514 against 1,643,006. In contrast, the Quebec vote would be 993,663 "no" against 376,188 "yes." These figures come from C.P. Stanley, *Armes, hommes et gouvernements: Les politiques de guerre du Canada, 1939–1945* (Ottawa: Department of National Defence, 1970), 441.

21. Marc-André Cyr, "De l'engagement à la révolte: Les Canadiens français et les guerres mondiales," *Argument* 10, 2 (2008).

22. Serge Bernier, *Le Royal 22e régiment, 1914–1999* (Montreal: Art Global, 1999), 15–16 and 18. See also Granatstein, *Who Killed the Canadian Military?*, 102–3.

23. Of course, even in English-Canadian circles, the relationship between nationalism and imperialism took many forms and should not be considered a clear dichotomy. See, for example, the excellent study by Carl Berger on Canadian imperialism between 1867 and 1914: Carl Berger, *The Sense of Power* (Toronto: University of Toronto Press, 1970).

24. P.B. Waite, "French-Canadian Isolationism and English Canada: An Elliptical Foreign Policy, 1935–1939," *Journal of Canadian Studies* 18, 2 (1983): 132–48.

25. Robin W. Winks, *Canada and the United States: The Civil War Years* (Montreal and Kingston: McGill-Queen's University Press, 1998), 178–84; Jean Lamarre, *Les Canadiens français et la Guerre de Sécession* (Montreal: VLB, 2006), 25, 45–51.

26. Antoine Robitaille, "Pacifisme des Québécois—Vous avez oublié les zouaves!," *Le Devoir*, 25 September 2006.

27. Stéphane Paquin, "Les relations internationales du Québec avant la Révolution tranquille," in Paquin, ed., *Histoire des relations internationales du Québec* (Montreal: VLB, 2006), 14.

28. C.P. Stanley, *Canada and the Age of Conflict: A History of Canadian External Policies, Vol. 1: 1867–1921* (Toronto: Macmillan Canada, 1977).

29. See Jean-François Gazaille, "Les Canadiens français dans la guerre d'Espagne: Des héros très discrets," in Robert Comeau and Serge Bernier, eds., *Dix ans d'histoire militaire en français au Québec: Actes du 10e colloque en histoire militaire* (Montreal: Lux, 2005), 77–83. See also Caroline Désy, *Si loin, si proche: La Guerre civile espagnole et le Québec des années trente* (Quebec: Presses de l'Université Laval, 2003).

30. C.P. Stacey, *Canada and the Age of Conflict: A History of Canadian External Policies, Vol. 2: 1921–1948, The Mackenzie King Era* (Toronto: University of Toronto Press, 1981), 416–17.

31. James Ian Gow, "Les Québécois, la guerre et la paix, 1945–1960," *Canadian Journal of Political Science* 3, 1 (1970): 88–122, at pp. 104–11.

32. Jocelyn Coulon, *La dernière croisade: La guerre du Golfe et le rôle caché du Canada* (Montreal: Méridien, 1992), 108.

33. Claire-Andrée Cauchy, "La plus grosse manifestation de l'histoire du Québec," *Le Devoir*, 17 February 2004, A-1.

34. Stéphane Roussel and David Morin, "Les multiples incarnations de la culture stratégique et les débats qu'elles suscitent," in Stéphane Roussel, ed., *Culture stratégique et politique de défense: L'expérience canadienne* (Montreal: Athéna, 2007), 17–42.

35. "Conclusion," in *Neorealism Versus Strategic Culture: A Debate*, ed. John Glenn, Darryl Howlett, and Stuart Poore (London: Ashgate, 2004), 224–25.

36. Michael Behiels, *Prelude to Quebec's Quiet Revolution: Liberalism Versus Neo-Nationalism, 1945–1960* (Montreal and Kingston: McGill-Queen's University Press, 1985).

37. Michael Adams, *Fire and Ice: The United States, Canada and the Myth of Converging Values* (Toronto: Penguin Canada, 2003), 82.

38. At the end of the 1960s, some authors were already arguing that diminishing religious fervour, and the increase in the average income and of the level of education, would affect Quebec's public opinion toward war and peace issues. See Gow, "Les Québécois, la guerre et la paix," 90–91.

39. Massie and Boucher, "Militaristes et anti-impérialistes," 380–81; David Morin, "Le côté obscur de la force: L'unité nationale victime collatérale de la 'nation guerrière,'" *Études internationales* 64, 3 (2013): 444–45.

40. Béatrice Richard, *La mémoire de Dieppe*, 34–42; Jean-Pierre Gagnon, "Dix ans de recherche, dix ans de travail en histoire militaire: Que peut-on dire de ces dix ans?," pp. 7–20 in Comeau and Bernier, eds., *Dix ans d'histoire militaire en français au Québec*; Yves Tremblay, "Entre l'arbre et l'écorce: Douze ans d'histoire militaire officielle au Québec," *Bulletin d'histoire politique* 15, 3 (2007): 63–80.

41. Gow, "Les Québécois, la guerre et la paix"; see also Gérard Bergeron, "Le Canada français: du provincialisme à l'internationalisme," pp. 99–130 in John S. Gillespie, ed., *The Growth of Canadian Policies in External Affairs* (Durham, NC: Duke University Press, 1960).

42. Guy Lachapelle, "La guerre de 1939–1945 dans l'opinion publique: Une comparaison entre les attitudes des Canadiens français et des Canadiens anglais," *Bulletin d'histoire politique* 3, 3–4 (1995): 201–26.

43. No major polls were conducted by principal Canadian pollsters after 1996. This "blind spot" in our data is concordant with the fact that Canada has not made a major contribution to UN peacekeeping operations in the last 10 years.

44. Access to public opinion polls used by the authors is available upon request.

45. Haglund, "Québec's 'America Problem'" and "The Parizeau-Chrétien Version"; Jean-Frédéric Légaré-Tremblay, "Le soleil à l'ombre de Gulliver," *Argument* 7, 2 (2005): 40–47.

46. Bruce Campion-Smith, "NATO fails to round up new troops; Delay could endanger soldiers on front line; Deployment from Quebec may erode support further," *Toronto Star*, 14 September 2006, A10.

47. These data were collected from polls conducted by Angus Reid Strategies and Strategic Counsel. Data is available from the authors upon request.

48. Standard deviation of this result is 6.34 per cent. Considering a margin of error of approximately 6 per cent for Quebec's graphs, this fluctuation is not important, and we can argue that Quebec's public opinion remains quite constant across the time period.

49. We have made the same argument in Boucher and Roussel, "From Afghanistan to 'Quebecistan': Quebec as the pharmakon of Canadian foreign and defence policy," pp. 128–58 in Jean Daudelin and Daniel Schwanen, eds., *Canada Among Nations 2007: What Room for Manoeuvre?* (Montreal and Kingston: McGill-Queen's University Press, 2008).

50. Bloc Québécois, "Le Canada en Afghanistan," position paper, available at www.blocquebecois.org/dossiers/mission_afghanistan/accueil.asp.

51. One notable exception is *Le Devoir*, which has kept an anti-Afghanistan stance.

52. Francis Dupuis-Déri, "Lettre à ma soeur qui part en Afghanistan," *Le Devoir*, 15 June 2007.

53. Jean-Christophe Boucher, "The responsibility to think clearly: The realist internationalism of the Harper government (2006–2011)," in Heather A. Smith and Claire Turenne Sjolander, eds., *Canada and the World: Internationalism in Canadian Foreign Policy* (Don Mills, ON: Oxford University Press, 2012).

54. *Études internationales* (44, 3 [September 2013]) devoted an entire issue to the subject. See Massie and Boucher, "Militaristes et anti-impérialistes."

55. Samantha Power, *A Problem from Hell* (New York: Harper-Perennial, 2003); Anne-Marie Slaughter, *A New World Order* (Princeton, NJ: Princeton University Press, 2004); G. John Ikenberry, *Liberal Leviathan* (Princeton, NJ: Princeton University Press, 2011); John Charvet and Elisa Kaczynska-Nay, *The Liberal Project and Human Rights: The Theory and Practice of a New World Order* (Cambridge: Cambridge University Press, 2008); Tim Dunne and Trine Flockhart, eds., *Liberal World Order* (Oxford: Oxford University Press, 2013).

56. Abacus Data National Poll, "Canadians split over mission in Libya" (data collected from 23 June to 24 June 2011); Ipsos-Reid, "Assessment of NATO's military intervention in Libya" (data collected from 6 April to 21 April 2011).

57. Robitaille, "Quebecers: A Pacifist People?," 62.

58. Justin Massie and Stéphane Roussel, "The Twilight of Internationalism? Neocontinentalism as an Emerging Dominant Idea in Canadian Foreign Policy," pp. 36–52 in Heather A. Smith and Claire Turenne Sjolander, eds., *Canada in the World: Internationalism in Canadian Foreign Policy* (Don Mills, ON: Oxford University Press).

20 Canadian International Security Policy in the 21st Century: Closing the Book on the Sutherland Era? Not at All.

Douglas Alan Ross

Key Terms

Crisis Stability

Non-nuclear Counterforce Coercion

For the last 25 years, Canada's international security policy has experienced an incremental hollowing out in its capabilities base. Both the military and foreign aid have been in relative decline since the Mulroney cabinet's 1987 white paper on defence and the end of the Cold War. In the summer of 2013, Prime Minister Harper terminated the Canadian International Development Agency (CIDA). Canada's defence spending has been scaled back because Mr. Harper's ambitious capital re-equipment program for the Department of National Defence (DND), announced in 2006 ($490 billion over 20 years), is being postponed or stretched out so that urgently needed replacement supply ships, new surface combatant ships, Arctic offshore patrol ships, and icebreakers are all stalled or progressing extremely slowly in their respective procurement pipelines at greatly inflated costs with gravely inadequate managerial oversight.[1]

The Royal Canadian Navy (RCN) must ask flight crews to risk their lives on each mission in the 50-year-old Sea King helicopters they attempt to fly.[2] The remaining Aurora long-range patrol aircraft are also extremely high mileage, and their anti-submarine warfare (ASW) equipment and avionics have not kept pace with new technologies. The four second-hand British submarines of the RCN have spent more time under repair than at sea since they were purchased and have required very expensive repairs and overhaul work.[3] Even when fully operational, they will not be able to transit or patrol the sea lanes of the Arctic archipelago as American, British, French, and most likely Soviet and now Russian nuclear hunter-killer submarines have been doing for decades. If nuclear propulsion for Canadian submarines remains off limits, then air independent propulsion (AIP) engines should be considered to enable under-ice operations. As to replacement of the CF-18s, Peter MacKay, as minister of national defence, erred badly in committing to the F-35 without an open bidding process. The erosion in military capabilities raises a fundamental question about Canada's contribution to world order. Is it a game worth playing at all if our only role is a very minor one? Will Canadians ever again be prepared to commit a responsible level of resources to the common defence effort of the Western powers? If they are not, what is the minimum that simply *must* be done?

What are the international security threats that require prompt and sustained attention?

On the left, observers think a renewed commitment to traditional peacekeeping or responsibility to protect (R2P) intervention under United Nations (UN) auspices would be appropriate, but Prime Minister Harper's Ottawa is unlikely to go down that path given the PM's evident unhappiness with the organization. The inability to foster stability or democratic governance in Afghanistan after 10 years of collaborative international effort there does not augur well for future humanitarian interventions. While the Canadian role in the Libyan intervention in 2011 was significant, it clearly had as much or more "strategic" interest (deposing Muammer al-Qadhdhafi's regime) driving it as any humanitarian concern for preventing a massacre. On the right, commentators would like to see a full commitment to American plans for continental anti-ballistic missile (ABM) defence, and perhaps a reorientation in Canadian defence planning toward the Pacific and East Asia in support of the American "pivot" from Europe and the Middle East to the western Pacific and northeast Asia. However, direct Canadian participation in the American ABM defence of North America is unlikely given its great expense, uncertainty as to its effectiveness, and the probable impact it could have in perpetuating more unstable nuclear rivalries between the US and Russia and the US and China, regardless of *actual* system effectiveness. Supporting the "pivot" toward Asia is unlikely too, because of the cost and the long lead-time before either the RCN or the Royal Canadian Air Force (RCAF) will be able to deploy properly equipped forces to the region. Frigates without helicopters, repaired submarines of doubtful reliability, and a shrinking number of high-mileage/high maintenance fighter and anti-submarine warfare (ASW) patrol aircraft are unlikely to be of much help—even if Ottawa wished to support containment of China.

For Canada, more than for most countries, spending on defence is largely discretionary—but not entirely so. This has been made possible primarily by geographical remoteness from Eurasia (with three ocean barriers plus an "Arctic desert" to deter any conceivable territorial attack), and, secondarily, by an "involuntary security guarantee" from the United States—a notion first explicitly articulated by Canada's greatest strategic thinker, defence scientist R.J. Sutherland, in the summer of 1962.[4] The temptation to divert military spending toward domestic programs (or debt reduction) is perennial and unavoidable, especially if officials in Ottawa perceive no real threat to the country by virtue of its geographic isolation and the double coverage of both the conventional force and nuclear deterrent "umbrellas" that are permanently extended over Canadian territory by the United States—the world's last superpower and our somewhat befuddled, politically polarized "hegemonic" neighbour.

What are the fundamental constraints in light of which a twenty-first-century international security policy can be constructed? Are there any parallels in Canadian history to the strategic environment now facing leaders in Ottawa? What is the range of options that Canadian policy-makers can reasonably consider given our present very limited and declining military capabilities? This chapter suggests some answers to these questions by studying what a previous strategic analyst, Dr. Sutherland, outlined in his prognosis for Canadian international security policy in the early 1960s. From there we will consider the arrested, partial renewal of Canada's armed forces under seven years of Stephen Harper's leadership, the evolving contemporary military balance that is characterized by an intermingling of conventional and nuclear deterrence, and the rising intensity of Sino-American military rivalry now that China has emerged as the most challenging "peer competitor" the US has ever faced.

Sutherland's Half-century-old Insights

Fifty years ago, Dr. R.J. Sutherland (originally an economist and statistician, later head of the DND's Defence Research Board) contemplated what the world might look like and what Canadian foreign and defence policies might resemble by the year 2000. His assessment was written in 1962 just prior to the Cuban missile crisis—another time of rising tensions and imminent crisis. Nevertheless, Sutherland's frame of mind was, on the whole, rather positive. In retrospect, his forecast of Canada's future and the course of world events was remarkably prescient.

As Sutherland thought would be the case, "all-out thermonuclear war" was avoided—not by nuclear disarmament but something approaching institutionalized mutual deterrence. That outcome is the best nuclear "end state" that can be attained, according to those "defensive realists" who believe in the possibility of more or less *well-managed deterrent forces in perpetuity.* Mutual Assured Destruction (MAD) is here to stay, they suggest.[5] Secondly, Sutherland was correct to suggest that the Soviet Union eventually would become a status quo power—even if it is now in the form of a demographically and geographically reduced post-Soviet Russia. Moscow, despite its authoritarian residue and corruption, is a supporter of the global market economy status quo. Thirdly, China's rise, he forecast, will be more "ominous" if it achieves "great power without affluence." That was perhaps his most prophetic comment. Fourthly, he foresaw that Western Europe would come closer together in many respects toward a coordinated if not exactly unified confederal structure. And indeed, a common EU defence policy concept is at least now imaginable, just as Anglo-French nuclear missile submarine patrols are now planned jointly to ensure constant "on station" deterrent capability for the two

European nuclear arsenals. Finally, as a pragmatic, skeptical, and rather classically minded realist, Sutherland appreciated that the UN would be no closer to becoming a world federal government in 2000 than it was in 1962.[6] Right again.

With respect to Canada, he stressed that the geographic "invariant" of Canada's strategic situation meant that the foundation of defence and security planning "for as far ahead as one can possibly foresee" would be based on maintaining a sound cooperative defence relationship with governments in Washington. Any marked deviation from "reasonable" Canadian efforts to prevent Canadian territory, waters, and airspace becoming a threat to the US would call into question "Canada's right to existence as an independent nation." He did not expect that this would ever happen, because the area of common security interest between Canadians and Americans was and would remain so large: "in the final analysis the security of the United States is the security of Canada."[7]

By 2000, Sutherland thought Canada would fall from its status in 1962 as the seventh- to ninth-ranked military power in the world to some lower status, but he still thought Canadians could aspire to status and influence comparable to that of the UK, France, Germany, Italy, and Japan. In this respect his forecast was sadly incorrect; Canadians are still not "near the top of the international batting order." France and Britain became modest nuclear weapon states (NWSs), and Germany after unification became the economic powerhouse of the European Union. Italy, with almost double Canada's population, and Japan, with four times, are both able to field substantially larger military forces, although in Italy's case its recent economic travails threaten to undo its more elevated security status. The Japanese, despite American prodding, have refused to consider creating their own independent nuclear deterrent, but they are widely acknowledged to have a "near-nuclear weapon state" status.[8] All such concern for geo-political status, though, Sutherland emphasized, was beside the point. The vital interest of Canadian international security policy would remain the promotion of the healthy functioning of the Canadian–American relationship and the accumulation of as much respect, access, and influence in Washington that Canadians could muster.

Canada's long-term relations with Africa and Asia would be determined by Canadian interests not sentiments, but relations with Americans and Europeans would be shaped by both in unpredictable ways. Any idea that the NATO relationship could be used by Canadians to offset or reduce American influence was naive, he believed, and doomed to "disappointment." A NATO role should be conceived as a further opportunity to state Canadian interests and perspectives when the big decisions are being made by our great power allies at the "top table." Sutherland forecast correctly that the onrush of military technological innovation was "revolutionary" and that it condemned everyone to living in a "dangerous and dynamic" world indefinitely. It was not just the nuclear weapons revolution that had permanently changed international relations. *All technological innovation* was likely to cause continuing instability in world politics because so much of it was being driven by the search for military advantage.

Sutherland did not foresee a major investment in military capability in the Arctic. While he thought it possible that Arctic waters might become "a natural deployment area for Polaris-type [nuclear missile-launching] submarines," it probably would take the advent of more effective anti-submarine warfare (ASW) technologies to drive such a move. This was prophetic too. American ASW capabilities did improve through the 1970s and 1980s, and Soviet sea-based nuclear missile submarine deployments were more and more confined to an Arctic Ocean "bastion" where they could be defended by shore-based naval aviation and echelons of hunter-killer submarine escorts and other protectors.

Sutherland went on to note that the straits of the Canadian archipelago might well be used as a transit route from the Arctic basin to the North Atlantic by Soviet (now Russian) submariners in order to bypass NATO's ASW sub-surface acoustic detection network deployed from Greenland to Iceland to Norway. He did not speculate that American nuclear attack submarines also eventually might use the Canadian straits from south to north to enter Arctic waters secretly to track and trail (and in a crisis destroy) Soviet (or Russian) missile-launching submarines (SSBNs).[9]

Dr. Sutherland died before long-range submarine-launched ballistic missiles (SLBMs) were deployed by the Soviet navy in Arctic waters, or before the Soviet navy had acquired long-range, nuclear-armed, land-attack cruise missiles that could be launched from submarines or bombers. Thus, he made no mention of any practical effort to control or block *all* such submarine movements via a Canadian naval mine-laying capability for the Arctic straits.[10]

Notwithstanding the fact that Sutherland saw Canada's Arctic territory as "a sort of strategic desert" between the American military "strong points" in Alaska and Greenland, Sutherland saw anti-bomber defences as a continuing part of the US–Canada defence relationship. Early warning (EW) of, and some active air defence against, "air-breathing" attack on American strategic nuclear weapons sites or command and control "nodes" was and would remain an *essential, unavoidable,* and *permanent function* that must be carried out by the Canadian military to protect Canada's sovereign control over the Arctic.[11] Failure to do so would lead to the Americans doing it for themselves, and that, Sutherland thought, would be a bad idea: Canada's "legal claim to the Arctic islands" was, he suggested, still "not beyond question."

In the distant future, he foresaw a possible need for such an EW and active air defence capability against long-range aircraft coming from China across the Pacific.[12] Perhaps that will one day be proven correct; but one can still hope that such an eventuality might be avoided. The intended reach of Chinese military aircraft is still limited to the zone within the two "island chains" in the western Pacific, and the regional military assets of Russia and India. It is not intercontinental. To date, only the Americans and the Russians are intent on building a new generation of long-range bombers able to carry nuclear bombs or air-launched cruise missiles (ALCMs).

For Sutherland, limited anti-bomber defences increased *strategic stability*, but only so long as they did not get so numerous that they threatened to facilitate a first strike on the adversary's nuclear arsenal or leadership. Anti-bomber defences had to be strong enough to defeat small surprise attacks but too weak to have a credible role in destroying the small residual retaliatory force that might survive a premeditated American surprise missile and bomber attack on the Soviet nuclear arsenal.

The advent of effective ABM interceptors would be developed eventually, he thought. So long as their numbers were not excessive and so long as they were tasked with protecting retaliatory ballistic missile sites or American leadership and military "command, control, and communications" (C3) they would not be destabilizing. But if such active air and missile defences became part of an extensive "area defence" of the continental US and its major cities, they would then become a challenge to Soviet (now Russian) retaliatory credibility. ABM development and deployment, he noted correctly, would tend to energize the development of new generations of bombers and bomber-delivered stand-off weapons in the normal course of ongoing strategic rivalry.[13] And so it has.

Precisely because Sutherland embraced the idea that the nuclear powers should not try to create doubt or ambiguity as to the effectiveness of the assured destruction threat of their adversary, he would not have found merit in American plans to develop **non-nuclear counterforce coercion** capabilities since the late 1980s. Anxiety about the vulnerability of the Russian nuclear arsenal emerged in Moscow in the mid-1990s but has become especially intense since the unilateral American abrogation of the ABM Treaty in 2002 and the ensuing American effort to deploy land- and sea-based ABM capabilities. Russian fears are now being compounded by the possible American development of conventional prompt global strike (CPGS) capability, which many Russian analysts believe that "when combined with global missile defense" could provide the US with "a means of seeking to dominate the world politically and strategically."[14]

Sutherland's views on nuclear strategy and arms control were original and incisive. He is known to be one of the originators of the "first-strike/second-strike" distinction, and one of the key strategic thinkers in Ottawa who saw that the *stability* of the Soviet–American nuclear balance was in everyone's interest—this at a time when American strategists were still promoting a war-winning approach to the nuclearized East–West rivalry. Stable mutual deterrence was what Sutherland hoped would evolve between the US and the USSR, even if such stability was based on a simultaneously shared capacity to annihilate most cities in both countries.

In the bomber age of the 1950s, the US enjoyed strategic superiority over Soviet nuclear forces because of superior aerospace technologies. Sutherland thought that the deployment of ICBMs and SLBMs by both the Soviets and the Americans would guarantee beyond any possible doubt that there was a *mutual* ability to inflict "assured destruction" at unacceptable levels. Certainty about nuclear war's horrific lethality was the key. Building nuclear weapons suitable for retaliation made sense, while deploying weapons intended and able to execute surprise attacks because they were accurate with low-yield warheads was actually a very bad idea likely to destabilize East–West relations by causing an intense nuclear arms race.

Sutherland was aware that threatening to commit a horrendous act of mass murder was less than rational if it guaranteed that your own country would be wiped out as well. This led him to argue (as did some French strategists) on behalf of the need for Western leaders to appear somewhat irrational: "we must convince [an opponent] that if the situation arose we would act without counting the cost; in other words, that we would be a little bit crazy." Nuclear deterrence could not prevent nuclear exchanges, but so long as the "rationality of irrationality" seemed plausible, it could prevent enemy state leaders' nuclear war gambling.[15]

Sutherland and other strategic analysts at the Defence Research Board or in the Department of External Affairs thought through the developing sinister logic of mutual assured destruction and found it to be acceptable as a lesser evil. In their view, the MAD acronym could be more usefully expanded to mutual assured deterrence. What they presumably feared most was the messianic tendency, that persisted well into the 1960s, for some American strategists to advocate a war-winning, "counter-force" nuclear strike capability, or the equally dangerous idea apparently popular among some Soviet strategic planners who favoured a decisive *surprise attack* capability. Soviet long-range aviation never did adopt "fail safe" operations that were intended to reduce the intra-crisis vulnerability of a given bomber force, most likely because Soviet strategists during the first half of the Cold War always intended to use them as part of a phased surprise attack campaign. Thus, the risk of a relatively small, bomber-only surprise attack had to be acknowledged and addressed in Canadian and American planning for continental air defence. As Sutherland noted, the "Achilles heel" of any strategic bomber force is that "its bases are few, easy to find, and very vulnerable to nuclear attack."[16]

Those comments remain apt for the present strategic context: with shrinking arsenals under START and now NewSTART, far fewer bombers are operational in both Russia and the US, so that each country's entire force is correspondingly more vulnerable. Bombers then (and bombers today that carry small, stealthy ALCMs) were and remain far harder to detect than ballistic missiles that give off huge infrared emissions visible to satellites immediately upon launch. Later in their trajectory they are clearly detectable by the giant ballistic missile early warning radars in Alaska, Greenland, and the UK that became operational in 1963 and were upgraded after 2000. Now the EW radars are supplemented by ABM tracking radars and layers of satellite-based sensors, as well as large, sea-based X-band radars that are movable to different zones of potential conflict to guide ABM interceptors toward their targets.

The air-breathing threat in the form of bombers and later highly accurate ALCMs has been the weapon of choice for those envisaging nuclear war-fighting, either as a limited preventive war "counter-force" assault or as the opening surprise salvo of an all-out nuclear war. In the summer of 1961, in response to fears about a Soviet takeover of West Berlin, three American strategic analysts working for Kennedy's national security adviser developed a plan for a bombers-only surprise attack on all Soviet intercontinental-range nuclear delivery systems. With 55 bombers attacking 80 targets (46 nuclear bomber bases, 26 bomber staging bases, and the only 8 ICBM sites), and with quite inadequate Soviet air defence radars and interceptors that could not cope with low-altitude penetration tactics, the US planners estimated that there would be virtually no US aircraft lost and that further strikes could then proceed if need be on other military assets (presumably nuclear missiles and medium-range bombers aimed at Western Europe or Japan). Probable Soviet casualties were estimated at "only" 500,000 to 1 million collateral civilian deaths.[17] After some weeks of study by the US joint chiefs, and the National Security Council, President Kennedy and his secretary of defense, Robert McNamara, shelved the study after learning that the authors of the plan estimated that the eventual resulting American loss of life ranged from zero to 75 per cent of the population.

A bombers-only surprise strike was the sort of "nuclear Pearl Harbor" raid that Sutherland feared could befall the US and lead to either the loss of most American retaliatory striking power or US political and military leadership, or both. Therefore, North American air defence plans "were designed with an eye to the most dangerous case . . . a relatively small surprise attack against SAC [strategic air command] bases" (both bomber and missile).[18] So long as the Russians (or any other potentially hostile "peer competitor") possess bombers capable of striking at American strategic systems, a viable EW and active air defence system *must* be kept operational. For this reason, Canadian–American air defence cooperation can never shrink to zero because it would place at risk the "assured second-strike capacity" of the American nuclear deterrent force. Any suggestion that Canadian failure to participate in American plans for continental ABM defence might lead to termination of NORAD is thus not supported by strategic analysis. The only alternative would be ceding bases for American air defence and missile defence forces across Canada— in the manner of Iceland perhaps.

Sutherland concluded his long-term forecast by noting that any concept of complete neutrality disconnected from any sort of defence cooperation with the US was a strategic and political impossibility. However, a form of *strategic isolationism* was nonetheless conceivable for some future Canadian government. It would be conditional, though, on maintaining an effective early warning and modest air defence capability across the Canadian North indefinitely— probably on a fully integrated, binational basis as it

has existed since 1957–58. A coastal navy would be needed that could perform anti-submarine warfare (ASW) activities to deter forward deployment of ballistic missile or cruise missile-launching submarines, as would some land and air capabilities for deployment in the North to assert sovereign control in peacetime and during any great power crisis confrontation. Sutherland's preference was for a much more activist international security posture in which Canadians would be full partners with their American and NATO allies in dealing with major defence threats and broader international security issues. To maximize Canadian influence with American and other allied policy-makers, Canada had to be "a paid up member of the Western club and . . . on terms of special intimacy with the United States."[19]

Were Sutherland still with us, he would no doubt be nonplussed by the relative decline in Canada's capabilities and the overall attitude of neglect toward military-strategic affairs. The issue for Canadians, he thought, "is whether we will be a powerful and effective ally or a weak and reluctant one," and "whether our role in world affairs will be one of dependence upon the United States or whether we will be effective members of a larger community."[20] "Weak and reluctant" seems to be the choice Canadians have made, some deliberately and some without any awareness of what they were doing, but in all cases repeatedly in election after election. In 2003, Andrew Cohen published a book lamenting the loss of a Canadian foreign and defence policy with any real weight or consequence.[21] He attributed much of the national decline to the issue of Quebec separatism, to related public boredom with endless constitutional wrangling, to globalization and the hollowing out of the Canadian manufacturing sector, to the collapse of any vision of how to promote international order at the highest levels of government, or any interest in and understanding of international affairs and foreign policy among the educated public across the country. As a sympathetic liberal, Cohen failed to mention one key element in Canada's national psychology that might be the most important factor in building support for an effective, capable military and an astute diplomatic corps directing a wise international security policy: fear. Great fear of war's catastrophe afflicted Canadians from 1939 to the Cuban missile crisis. Thereafter it diminished gradually, and so too, not coincidentally, did the political will in Canada to make a difference in world affairs.

We will consider what options remain available for Ottawa in the conclusion, but first a summary of some of the more salient and troubling aspects of the geo-strategic environment now facing Ottawa. The looming confrontation in the Western Pacific between the Chinese and American militaries is at the top of the list. Fear and anxiety may be returning soon to Canadian thinking about world affairs, and that may catalyze the kind of responsible policy-making and careful cultivation of national military capability that Mr. Cohen hoped for, and which Mr. Sutherland thought was normal.

The Twenty-first-century Geostrategic Context

Far more than was the case 50 years ago, both strategic and tactical military operations depend on speed and range, but now also on stealth and exceptional precision in targeting. Conventional and nuclear warfare are no longer discrete "rungs" on the escalation ladder separated by deep trepidation about "crossing the nuclear threshold." The idea of a nuclear taboo might still be widely recognized, and the first use of even a few nuclear weapons in anger would be an earthshaking international event after seven decades of a nuclear peace. But this increasingly fragile nuclear peace does not preclude *conventional* attacks on *nuclear* deterrent forces. At least in terms of American strategy, conventional

and nuclear warfare have overlapped ever since the US Navy adopted its Maritime Strategy in 1986 and became publicly committed to "counterforce nuclear coercion" by having American attack submarines tasked with sinking adversary missile submarines early on in any major war with the USSR. Conventionally armed torpedoes from American attack submarines would thin out or eliminate completely the Soviet sea-based nuclear deterrent if war in Europe had come during the late 1980s. The intent then was to take away progressively "with each passing day" what should be the most reliable retaliatory part of the adversary's nuclear arsenal (the Soviet "boomer" nuclear-armed missile submarine fleet). Russian bombers and land-based missiles that would be the residue of the strategic nuclear forces then would have been far more susceptible to the threat of a full-scale disarming first-strike—or, more plausibly, continuing attrition by conventional bombing or cruise missile strikes.[22]

John Mearsheimer criticized this strategy as unduly provocative, entailing as it did both a deliberate effort to convince the Soviets that they would be stripped of their nuclear deterrent if the war in Europe continued, and an intentional manipulation of risk by imposing an additional threat of *inadvertent escalation* once central nuclear weapons systems were involved in the fighting. Furthermore, to have any impact on a still conventional war in Europe, American SSNs would have to surge into the Barents Sea and track and trail Soviet missile submarines immediately, from the very outset of fighting—if the US Navy were to have any hope of halting the fighting on land. Diplomats would have no time to try to forge compromises to kick-start military de-escalation of the fighting.

Now fast forward 30 years. With the arrival of robotic weapon systems for the battlefield and aerial warfare married to new stealth aircraft design and materials, as well as sensor-queued targeting (via networked satellites, aerial reconnaissance drones, and ground-force or surface-ship forward-based radar and other sensing), conventional weapons are now able to destroy many well-protected nuclear systems or tactical command and control as well as strategic leadership targets.[23] US qualitative superiority in robotic warfare goes far beyond its experience with propeller-driven drone surveillance and assassination tactics in Afghanistan, Pakistan, Yemen, and elsewhere. On 10 July 2013, Northrop Grumman's Unmanned Combat Air System (UCAS, designated the X-47B) made its first landing on board a moving aircraft carrier deck after repeated, exquisitely precise "touch and go" approaches in May. The X-47B is a tailless, highly stealthy, jet-engined strike platform with a wingspan twice that of an F-16. It will be able to bring significant glide bombs or stand-off missiles to time-urgent, heavily defended targets at no risk to Navy personnel.[24] The US Navy hopes to have the first UCAS aircraft enter service by 2019. The US Air Force *already* operates a highly stealthy jet-powered robotic UCAS, the RQ-180, which is thought to be able to enter any "contested" or "denied" airspace with impunity for intelligence-gathering, targeting, or electronic and/or cyberwarfare attack. Funded as a classified or "black" program, this UCAS is twice as large as the X-47B and has performed so well that the Air Force now wants to retire many of its large intelligence, surveillance, and reconnaissance drones known as "Global Hawk." The latter, while able to cruise and loiter at near U-2 altitudes, cannot enter airspace defended by the most modern Russian or Chinese surface-to-air missiles. Given its far greater size and range, the RQ-180 is being used by the US Air Force as a "global strike enabler."[25]

Such robotic aircraft will be able to penetrate deep into adversary airspace and will either facilitate (or execute) attacks on air- and missile-defence radars, long-range early warning OTH (over the horizon) radars, satellite downlink sites, all "soft" command and control locations, and, of course,

either fixed site or land-mobile nuclear missile systems. In destroying the adversary's air defence network (or simply blowing large gaps in it), corridors would be opened for older non-stealthy aircraft to deliver highly accurate stand-off glide bombs that are far cheaper than cruise missiles and will soon have glide ranges from 100 to 150 kilometres, thanks in part to Australian foresight and development spending.[26]

Additionally, the US research and development effort in ABM technologies has continued unabated under President Obama. There has been no let-up in the development effort from the Bush years, and in fact, much progress has been made on several fronts—most notably the development and testing success of the Aegis ship-based system and its evolving SM-3 interceptor missile (22 successful intercepts in 28 attempts). The US Missile Defense Agency (MDA) has also scored successes in development and testing of the PAC-3 system "that provides low-tier, terminal air and missile protection for a small area," as well as in the development of THAAD (terminal high altitude area defence) that "adds an upper layer of protection to the terminal architecture while also offering the capability to . . . intercept in the exoatmosphere" (10 intercepts in its last 10 tests). Its biggest setbacks so far have been in the development of MDA's ground-based missile defence (GMD) technology, a program which saw failures in October 2012 and July 2013 (overall only 8 of 16 test "successes" since 1999, many of them flawed or meaningless). GMD is "designed to protect the U.S. homeland from an international ballistic missile attack from North Korea or Iran."[27] GMD is the most difficult technology to perfect because incoming warheads will be travelling far faster than targets intercepted by the other systems, and it will have to cope with decoys, multiple independently targeted re-entry vehicles (MIRVs), manoeuvring warheads, and other attack force "penetration aids." Activation of a fully integrated "system of systems" (i.e., full interlinking of all ABM components whether tactical, mid-course, or terminal) of ABM battle management and command and control (BMC2) is hoped to be realized by 2020.

American superiority in such robotic flight and precision strike technologies, and ABM technologies as well, has made both the Russian and Chinese governments quite cautious about proposals for nuclear arms control and disarmament since 9/11. Simply put, they fear that the elimination of their nuclear deterrent forces would just widen American military dominance over them and all other states.[28] In response, the Russians, under both Vladimir Putin and Dmitri Medvedev, have committed to acquiring "more than 400 new missiles" by 2022. Huge Topol-M ICBMs are being converted to multiple warhead versions. A new RS-Yars 24 with 4 to 6 warheads each is being built and deployed. The first Borei-class missile submarine, *Yuri Dolgorukiy*, will accept missiles in mid-2014 and will be followed by seven other missile submarines equipped with new Bulava SLBMs. Details of another new ICBM under development, the Rubezh, have yet to be confirmed. It might be road-mobile or rail-mobile, but it is said to be a "missile-defence killer" according to Deputy Prime Minister Dmitry Rogozin.[29] Russia's long-range nuclear bomber force (63 TU-95 and 13 TU-160) is being equipped with new Kh-101 ALCMs. The Tupolev design bureau is "expected" by US officials to begin work on a new "blended wing-body, stealthy, subsonic aircraft" in 2020.[30]

Some American analysts think Chinese strategists also might be thinking of a "limited" nuclear-use option if their intermediate-range, conventionally armed ballistic missile barrage capability fails to deter or halt US naval and air force encroachment on newly deployed Chinese military positions in the waters and airspace off its east coast. Accordingly, the "extended nuclear deterrent" protection offered to countries such as Japan, South Korea, Taiwan, and others may become increasingly hollow and

incredible in years to come. According to one American analyst, "limited use of low-yield nuclear weapons will become the new normal and give rise to a second nuclear age whose dangers and uncertainties will dwarf those of the first."[31]

Equally troubling for Chinese military strategists and policy advisers is the flat refusal of American policy-makers to consider adoption of a No First Use approach to nuclear strategy. For the Chinese, an American adoption of such an approach is the essential first step needed before Beijing can enter into bilateral nuclear arms control talks. So long as the US refuses to rule out the threat of limited first use of nuclear weapons in scenarios of "extended deterrent" protection of allies (most notably Japan and South Korea), Chinese officials say they cannot respond.[32]

From the perspective of Chinese strategists, American actions since 2011 are seen as a direct challenge to Beijing's plans to expand its control (and reinforce its new territorial sea claims) over all the waters inside the "first island chain" that comprises the Ryukyus down to Taiwan, Taiwan itself, and then all the waters west of the islands angling south to the northern part of Luzon and the rest of the Philippine archipelago. Chinese officials say these waters belong to China for historic reasons and that their archaeological explorations over the past 30 years have validated the claim of regular visits by Chinese ships and crews (although not continuous occupation) for many centuries. They refuse to acknowledge the relevance of the UN Convention on the Law of the Sea in settling competing territorial claims by the Philippines, Vietnam, and Indonesia, to name but three.

Chinese arms control analysts have complained often in recent years about American proposals to develop conventional prompt global strike (CPGS) capabilities and base them on American submarines and aircraft carriers. Such complaints were originally related to fears of CPGS systems being aimed at China's small nuclear force. Now, however, they are directly related to the Obama administration's "pivot toward Asia-Pacific" that was announced in late 2011, confirmed in the administration's strategic defence guidance statement of January 2012,[33] and embodied in an earlier acceptance by the US Department of Defense of a new doctrinal concept of "AirSea Battle" (ASB). ASB is intended to guide the US Navy and Air Force in developing the ability to defeat the "anti-access, area denial" strategy that has guided the Chinese military buildup of the past 15 years.

ASB has raised grave concerns because it frontally challenges the vast regional military buildup that has been pursued by both the Second Artillery Corps of the Chinese army and the Chinese navy. This buildup was triggered by the 1996 humiliation China suffered when its missile "blockade" of Taiwan had to be lifted after two American carrier task force groups came to the island's assistance and implicitly threatened to destroy the Chinese missile launch sites.

The Chinese 15-year long buildup in regional conventional strike capability has been simply staggering in its scale. It has included short- and medium-range ballistic missiles with conventional warheads (estimated at 1,000 to 1,200 already deployed); several hundred supersonic cruise missiles of 200-km range (intended to overcome fleet missile air defences on American Aegis-class cruisers); 60 fast-attack catamarans with 8 anti-ship cruise missiles (ASCMs) each (perhaps able to challenge or destroy in saturation barrages the newly deployed, very fast, shallow draft, stealth-enhanced US Navy littoral combat ships); ASCM-equipped destroyers and frigates in large numbers and in several classes; far quieter diesel-electric submarines equipped with ASCMs; long-range land attack cruise missiles (LACMs, with a range of 1,500 to 2,000 km) able to attack Guam, Okinawa, other US island bases as well as ports and local naval forces in Japan and the Philippines; medium-range ballistic missiles derived from the DF-21 nuclear MRBM armed with new conventional manoeuvring re-entry vehicle (MaRV) warheads and terminal infrared

radar, or laser guidance for targeting American aircraft carriers. All of these missiles and their launch sites or ship or aircraft platforms benefit from new satellite-based command, control, and communications. In addition, the number of modern fourth-generation fighter aircraft has increased 10 times from 50 to some 500 in a little over a decade, and they are well-armed with air-to-air missiles and air-launched ASCMs able to attack American ships. Some analysts estimate that by 2020 Chinese generals may have over 1,000 fourth- and fifth-generation (stealthy) aircraft to throw into any major battle with US forces.[34] A kinetic-kill anti-satellite capability (ASAT) has also been developed that was tested in 2007 at higher intercept altitudes than similar American test launches in 1985 and 2008.

As the Canadian strategic analyst David McDonough assessed this buildup: "With this arsenal, Beijing can potentially prevent the United States from operating out of forward bases from Okinawa to Guam and curtail its access to the Taiwan Straits, whether by coercive demonstration shots near the adjacent waters of naval bases like at Yokosuka, more direct attacks at home-ported carriers, runways, or unsheltered aircraft at air bases in Kadena or Guam, or by hitting logistical or command and control nodes to inflict operational paralysis."[35]

The American planned response to this strategic challenge under the AirSea Battle doctrine is to be able to launch a "blinding attack" against land- and sea-based missile launchers, ISR and other communication platforms, satellites, and ASAT launch sites, and Chinese command and control. The US attack is to be done via "interoperable air and naval forces that can execute networked, integrated attacks in depth to disrupt, destroy, and defeat enemy anti-access area denial capabilities."[36] Commenting on this strategic approach, Amitai Etzioni noted several American and Australian defence specialists who think this will raise a very serious risk of nuclear escalation by the Chinese military since they will not be able to distinguish between an effort to win the conventional AirSea Battle in China's coastal waters that overlap to an extent onto the mainland, and *an intentional preventive war attack aimed at destroying all of China's strategic nuclear deterrent assets.* The deeper that US forces would be striking into the interior of the People's Republic of China (PRC) territory, the more it would appear as a disarming counterforce strike that was being carried out by conventional means: nuclear counterforce coercion by conventional means. With respect to their own nuclear deterrent force, leaders in Beijing would be confronted with rising pressure to "use it, or lose it." But against what targets would they use their weapon: US aircraft carriers, island air force bases, satellite assets, American naval bases in the region, Honolulu or San Diego? The PRC nuclear warhead inventory is now estimated at some 250 weapons and it continues to grow.

To achieve a conventional deep-strike capability, the US Navy is contemplating modification of its newest Virginia-class hunter–killer submarines so as to include a number of conventionally armed, medium-range ballistic missiles in vertical launch tubes ahead of the submarine "sail."[37] The air force has also been pressing for acquisition of a distinctively different boost-glide hypersonic conventionally armed scramjet missile that would be fired to hypersonic speed by a chemical rocket on a trajectory distinctly different from any submarine-launched missile, at which point the scramjet would take over propulsion. The missile would have a range of up to 600 nautical miles and could cover that distance in 10 to 12 minutes, sufficient to hit many time-urgent relocatable targets (such as land-mobile ballistic missiles). This technology is still far from mature, however, and its development might take quite some time.[38] Two tests in January 2014 of a Chinese Mach 10 "hypersonic glide vehicle" warhead have suggested to American analysts that China's evolving strike capabilities are nearly at par with American

development efforts, and may be applied to both anti-ship ballistic missile attacks and range extension of existing and new Chinese ICBMs.[39]

As of early 2012 the US Navy had 42 Los Angeles class, 3 Seawolf, and 8 Virginia-class attack submarines (SSNs), and was said to be adding 2 Virginia-class boats per year. Each Virginia SSN can carry 12 vertical launch SLCMs and 26 torpedoes. The LA-class SSNs will be retiring faster than new SSNs will be commissioned. Between 1995 and 2007, the Chinese navy *added* 38 submarines to its fleet. As of 2012, only five of its submarines were nuclear-powered.[40] But it should be understood that many of its new diesel-electric submarines are inherently quieter than American SSNs, and therefore might have "first shot" in submarine duels.

Leadership in Moscow and Beijing doubt the US will to move toward global nuclear disarmament. To get the NewSTART treaty passed by the Congress, the Obama Administration had to promise more than $80 billion in funds for modernization of the nuclear weapons manufacturing complex in the US. The administration also promised a new strategic bomber. Some 80 to 100 highly stealthy bombers will have a targeted initial operational capability by 2024–26 and will carry a new ALCM. It will also be "crew optional" or fully robotic.[41]

To all intents and purposes, the Americans and the Chinese have been in an arms race for a decade, and the rivalry shows every sign of intensifying, not diminishing. Canada is far from immune to the threat of a Sino-American military collision in the western Pacific.

Canadian Engagement in "the Pivot" and the Arms Race, and the Associated Risks

Regrettably, Canada is at risk of becoming caught up in this struggle without an effectively equipped navy or air force and therefore with little or no access to nor influence over American decision-making. As Sutherland emphasized, capabilities secure access and the possibility of consultation and influence. Military incapacity or irrelevance can only lead to utter strategic marginalization.

During his last year in the defence portfolio, Peter MacKay responded positively to American overtures to reallocate resources to the Pacific region away from the Atlantic. In July 2012, Ottawa sent its largest ever contingent of ships and personnel to the biannual RIMPAC (Rim of the Pacific) naval exercise, and "for the first time Canadians . . . occupied senior leadership positions within the predominantly US operation."[42] The previous March, the prime minister announced that "Canada had signed an agreement strengthening military ties with Japan," while in June, Mr. MacKay, at a security forum in Singapore, declared a strategic interest in "the Pacific community of nations" and announced "a logistics agreement" with the government of Singapore that would aid in Canadian military activities in the region.[43] But projecting forces to the South China Sea that are technologically obsolete would be militarily disastrous and strategically inconsequential: no useful influence would be derived from it. Creating new capabilities could take almost two decades at great cost—far greater than any Conservative or Liberal government is likely to be willing to fund.

On the US side of the Sino-American military rivalry, it is primarily a qualitative arms race; on the Chinese side, it is a more heavily quantitative competition. Unfortunately, the military establishments on both sides seem to see a future conflict as entirely conceivable. And both Washington and Beijing may be prepared to raise the spectre of nuclear escalation either to try to get their way or to try to escape humiliation. The Chinese military evidently hope to deter a confrontation by building so many ships, submarines, aircraft, and missiles that they will be able to saturate and overwhelm any American theatre-based air and missile defences—and thereby discourage any further deployments to the Western Pacific. The Americans on the other hand are attempting to convince Chinese leaders that there is no way to catch up to American high technology weaponry, or to overcome US superiority in electronic warfare, cyber-espionage and cyberwar capability, anti-submarine warfare, submarine-against-submarine warfare, or military competition in space. Beijing's defeat is thus inevitable, they imply, and the pursuit of this competition is pointless and costly. But for Beijing to accept the American argument, it would have to relinquish its claims to the East and South China Seas and to the fisheries and energy resources in them. A failure to stand up now to the US also might mean that it will ultimately lose Taiwan, as John Mearsheimer has suggested. Chinese leaders thus probably believe they are in a legitimately "defensive" position and that they therefore hold the "balance of resolve" in their contest with the Americans.

From Washington's perspective, if the US disengages, it will be abandoning its allies in the northwest Pacific to the detriment of its credibility as a guarantor of key allies' security. Abandonment might drive Japan and possibly South Korea as well to try to acquire nuclear weapons at a time of intense dispute if not open conflict with Chinese authorities over disputed islands and territorial sea boundaries. Furthermore, a retreat of US forces in such a conflicted context might destabilize the Korean peninsula by prompting North Korean adventurism. In light of such considerations, American leaders are unlikely to back down from this developing confrontation. In light of such risks, John Mearsheimer has found discussion of the "rise of China" to be "categorically depressing."[44] The Chinese are likely to be just as determined to secure regional hegemony in east Asia as was the US in the western hemisphere in the nineteenth century.

To summarize, the execution of military operations is now extraordinarily fast, and such operations are managed by "network-centric," computerized "battle-management" systems. But the preparation time for the development, procurement, and effective deployment of new weapon systems and their integration into the C4ISR complex (command, control, communications, computers, intelligence, surveillance, reconnaissance) continues to lengthen.

While China and the US seem at present to be on a collision course, Prime Minister Harper's Ottawa is apparently queuing up to join the fray in some fashion—but with a quite obsolete military "kit." Only Canada's long-range and tactical air military transport have been suitably modernized with the acquisition of four large C-17 jets and many new C-130J tactical transport since 2006. What would be needed to meet Chinese forces is not battle-hardened ground troops and equipment appropriate for "stability operations" in Afghanistan or Africa, but state-of-the-art, ultra-quiet submarines; long-range, fast, stealthy strike fighters; and Aegis-equipped air-defence and ABM-capable destroyers or cruisers.

If officials and political leaders in Ottawa really were thinking of a serious role in deterring (or defeating) Chinese territorial expansion, a new fighter aircraft is urgently needed—one whose development is already complete and in serial production. It would also be useful to have an aircraft with long-range, high-sprint speed, two engines for operating in hostile environments over the Pacific or the Canadian Arctic environment; a very powerful Active Electronically Scanned Array (AESA) radar and other advanced avionics; as well as a large weapons load; a straightforward mid-air refueling ability; and an ability to prosecute electronic warfare and cyberattacks on adversary aircraft and ground targets. That is not the F-35, which, while very stealthy, has a very small weapons load, limited range, poor top speed, a single-engine of unproven durability, and low manoeuvrability. Stealth-enhanced F/A-18F and G Super Hornets (as purchased by Australia and modified with conformal

fuel tanks) or F-15 Silent Eagles (as purchased by the Saudi government) are likely to be far more durable and versatile platforms over the next 30 years and more cost-effective. The RCAF officer class has a clear preference for the F-35's superior electronic warfare/cyberwarfare capability, but the aircraft may well become vulnerable to ever-advancing Russian and Chinese radar technologies able to find and target the F-35 or to continuing rapid progress in long-range infrared detection.[45]

Sutherland might have had some inkling that one day a situation like this would develop, and perhaps that is why he suggested that medium powers such as Canada would necessarily have to *specialize* rather than attempt to participate in all aspects of the alliance's grand strategy agenda. If so, where does this leave a "weak and reluctant" Canada? Perhaps doing a better job at keeping the home fires burning—but little else?

The Canadian Challenge: A Question of Irrelevance?

Canada's Cold War levels of spending on defence and foreign aid averaged between 5 and 6 per cent of GDP during the 1950s (the Korean conflict and the initial buildup of air and ground forces in NATO Europe); averaged some 3 per cent in the 1960s (Canadian nuclear weapon deployments under both NATO and NORAD programs of nuclear "sharing"); fell below 3 per cent through the 1970s (termination of the nuclear roles and considerable shrinkage of forces in Europe and North America); dropped further to 1.8 per cent in the 1980s; and continued to edge down to a bit above 1 per cent from 1998 to 2005.[46] Over the period 1990 to 2003, the average annual change in the budget of the Department of National Defence (DND) was minus 1.7 per cent.[47]

After 2006, Prime Minister Stephen Harper called for a major renovation of the defence industrial base and extensive capital re-equipment of the Canadian Forces (CF). New long-range strategic air transport and tactical transport planes were acquired from Boeing and Lockheed Martin. New Leopard tanks were purchased from Germany. At the same time, the costs of the Canadian military intervention in Afghanistan grew considerably, so DND spending went from some $16 billion to some $22 billion by 2011.

Canada's Afghan intervention under three prime ministers was costly: the deaths of 158 soldiers and over 600 wounded in combat, as well as many thousands permanently psychologically scarred—or suicidal.[48] That too might have contributed to popular indifference to Canadian military decline. The economic cost of the Afghan counterinsurgency war was some $20 billion over a decade, and that does not include aid transfers to Afghanistan—the largest recipient of Canadian aid during the Harper years.[49] But Canada's Afghan intervention never commanded strong national public support; the country remained divided about the appropriateness of "the mission." Only the national political elite developed a consensus that overseas deployment of some 2,800 troops was required in light of Canadian rejection of participation in the Anglo-US intervention in Iraq and then rejection of Bush's plans for continental ABM defence. The last Canadian trainers are to leave Afghanistan in February 2014. A viable government in Kabul that will be independent of the Taliban appears unlikely.[50] NATO's defeat in Afghanistan will not help build support for renewing the Canadian military.

In the wake of Afghanistan and the great recession of 2008–9, Canadian defence spending seems headed for 1.08 per cent of GDP by 2015, according to one informed estimate, and perhaps the onset of a new "decade of darkness."[51] Harper and Jim Flaherty, former minister of finance, wish to balance the federal budget by election year 2015.[52] Defence and foreign aid remain the only readily compressible part of federal spending—the same method of "deficit fighting" used by Chrétien and Martin. This will guarantee that the "gold coin" of military capability will not be available to Canadian governments and diplomats attempting to shape the international security issues of the day in coming years.

Canada remains among the top 15 countries who together spent 80 per cent of the world's budget on defence in 2012—but only barely.[53] In a list based on purchasing power parity, Australia and Canada have not made the top 15 since at least 2006.[54] The Harper government's intention is to continue to shrink the Canadian forces and stretch out its capital renewal. Militarily this simply means that Canada will not have sufficient military capability to warrant G8 status, and in five years' time it might not have sufficient capability to be worthy of G20 status.

Meanwhile, the figures from East and South Asia are disturbing. From 2009 to 2012, the average annual increase in spending by China was 15 per cent, by India 9 per cent, by South Korea 6 per cent—while Russian spending increased by 9 per cent per year and Saudi Arabia by 10 per cent per year over this period.[55] From 2003 to 2012, China's "military spending rose by 175 per cent in real terms . . . the largest increase for the period among the top 15 spenders."[56] Naval modernization generated an increase of 130 per cent in Vietnam's spending and a 73 per cent increase over the same period in Indonesia's spending.

US defence spending has been falling in absolute and relative terms since well before the impact of the 2011 Budget Control Act (referred to as *sequestration*) by virtue of cuts in spending on operations in Iraq and Afghanistan. But the sequestration cuts that are being inflicted (some $50 billion per year from original budget plans) will drastically reduce US fighting abilities: in 2000, there were 13 ground divisions in the marines and army, but by 2021, sequester may cut them to 9; in 2000 there were 1,666 fighter and attack aircraft available, but by 2021 there may be just 1,157; in 2000 there were 330 major combatant ships and 10 aircraft carriers, but by 2021 there may be just 221 ships and only 7 carriers.[57] Replacement plans for American ballistic missile submarines might have to be put on hold for a decade, partly because the Obama administration is determined to speed up the development of its next strategic bomber—primarily for potential use in the Western Pacific.

In NATO Europe the budgetary situation is worse. From 2001 to 2010, European defence spending fell 23 per cent to €194 billion. From 2010 to 2013, a further estimated drop of 10 per cent has occurred. Combined spending on military research and development in Brazil, Russia, India, and China (BRIC) was "nearly equal" to that of the UK, France, and Germany in 2008. By 2013, BRIC spending on R&D had climbed to *twice* that of the big three European defence spenders.[58]

With political deadlock in the US Congress and sequestration imposing potentially huge cuts to American military capabilities over the rest of the decade, the American role in global affairs is likely to be substantially reduced. To accomplish one of their central goals—the preservation of the openness of the global ocean commons—they are going to need help, and American military figures have acknowledged this in various proposals for creating a US Navy-led multinational fleet of Aegis-based destroyers and cruisers.[59] Given the rate of Chinese construction of ballistic missiles, cruise missiles, ships, and submarines, that help might be essential. It might also be simply strategically pointless. Offensive cruise missiles and ballistic missiles are far less expensive to build in massive numbers than are ABM interceptors and the vulnerable multi-layered sensing and targeting systems that make them work. The "cost-exchange ratio" favours the offence.

There seems to be no recognition in Ottawa of the imminence of the threat of Sino-American

military collision. Under the Harper government's procurement process, new supply ships and surface combat ships might not be available until 2030. And the Canada First buildup contained no reference to purchasing very expensive Aegis-class or ABM-equipped destroyers or frigates.

Obama's "pivot" was preceded by a subdued role in the Libyan intervention earlier in 2011. After re-election in 2012, Obama and his secretary of state, John Kerry, refused European pressure to intervene in the Syrian civil war and settled for the negotiated elimination of Syria's chemical weapons capability. Regarding Iran's nuclear weapons program, the US showed a willingness to compromise regardless of the level of protest from Israel and Saudi Arabia. The Saudis went so far as to "leak" their plans to acquire a "shared" nuclear deterrent from warheads in Pakistan the moment they think Tehran is racing to assemble its first atomic devices.[60] Perhaps Washington thinks the Saudis are bluffing? Perhaps the administration thinks it has more important security obligations elsewhere and that Israeli nuclear deterrence will suffice to constrain Iranian behaviour? A decline in the US presence in the Middle East may lead to some disturbing proliferation surprises.

Conclusion:
Would Sutherland Suggest a Better Effort in Continental Security and Defence?

It is a consolation that the CF-18 replacement will most likely be exempt from any requirement to source production in Canada. But a full-scale search for the next fighter aircraft will take far too long, given the sorry, shrinking state of the old CF-18 fleet. Near-term relief via the purchase of low-mileage, second-hand fighter aircraft from the US seems an obvious step. Such aircraft could enter into service quickly and allow Canadian pilots to fill any gaps that might be created in Alaska or on the mainland west coast of the US by American deployments down toward the East and South China Seas. A similar interim fix for the helicopter-less frigates, the acquisition of new supply ships, and the replacement of the Aurora long-range (ASW) patrol aircraft also might be feasible.

Ottawa might be able to lease several squadrons of fighter-interceptors—perhaps retired Navy Super Hornets or F-15C Eagles (the latter are already teamed effectively with F-22s based in Alaska), because of the F-15's speed, great electrical power, far greater radar range (when equipped with AESA radar), as well as a large weapons load. Then DND could go through a full, formal acquisition process but not have Canadian defensive capabilities in North America impaired while acquisition and construction proceeded. So long as the leased aircraft came with advanced AESA radar and current avionics, Canadian pilots would be able to look after much of the continent if need be—and particularly its western and northern approaches. Eventually Ottawa might even consider whether it wished to join any policing containment of Chinese regional expansion. An alternative must be found to being drawn in to some foolish and dangerously provocative "high noon" shoot-out in and above the waters of the Taiwan Strait with obsolete military assets. The risk of such a conflict extending deep into China with potentially catastrophic nuclear escalation would be substantial.[61]

The key point to remember is that the Canadian government must keep fulfilling the basic requirement for the Canadian end of the "involuntary security guarantee" bargain. So long as that is done well, sovereignty will be assured, American deterrent assets and leadership will be protected from long-range surprise attack, and Canadians will be working jointly on the same page of the NORAD continental defence handbook. Canada's declaratory international security policy orientation for the next several decades is yet to be determined. It is a blank slate waiting to be filled. Sino-American war is not inevitable, but it must be seen as a credible risk. To date, Mr. Harper's most important issue on the Canada–China relations "file" is how much investment room should be allocated to China's state-owned energy enterprises. The military rise of the PRC seems to be "off his radar screen" entirely, and so too any awareness of the refurbishment of Russian nuclear strike capability towards North America. That too must change if Ottawa is going to be able to counsel restraint to American policy-makers in the tense and unstable future now developing.

Questions for Review

1. How was the strategic threat to North America in the 1950s different from the present military context?

2. Why is China a greater potential threat to American strategic preponderance than the Soviet Union ever was?

3. Are contemporary Chinese leaders' regional territorial ambitions in any way analogous to Soviet territorial gains and ambitions after World War II?

4. How does a strengthened air defence under NORAD contribute to **crisis stability** between Washington and Moscow?

Suggested Readings

Fergusson, James G. 2010. *Canada and Ballistic Missile Defence, 1954–2009*. Vancouver: UBC Press.

McDonough, David S. 2012. *Canada's National Security in the Post-9/11 World*. Toronto: University of Toronto Press.

McDonough, David S., and Douglas A. Ross, eds. 2005. *The Dilemmas of American Strategic Primacy*. Toronto: Royal Canadian Military Institute.

Mearsheimer, John J. 2001. *The Tragedy of Great Power Politics*.

New York: W.W. Norton.

Richter, Andrew. 2002. *Avoiding Armageddon: Canadian Military Strategy and Nuclear Weapons, 1950–63*. Vancouver: UBC Press.

Notes

1. See Michael Byers and Stewart Webb, "Blank cheque: National shipbuilding procurement strategy puts Canadians at risk," report by the Canadian Centre for Policy Alternatives and the Rideau Institute (December 2013), available at www.policyalternatives.ca/publications/ reports/blank-cheque. See also Steven Chase, "Shipyards have 'blank cheque' from Ottawa," *The Globe and Mail*, 12 December 2013.

2. Daniel LeBlanc, "New setback puts chopper deal 10 years behind schedule," *The Globe and Mail*, 4 January 2014.

3. HMCS *Chicoutimi* is being returned to the navy in 2014 after 10 years of repairs. HMCS *Corner Brook* is undergoing repairs and refit after "slamming into the ocean floor off Vancouver Island." Of the four submarines, only HMCS *Victoria* is fully operational and able to fire weapons. Murray Brewster, "Navy sub back at sea a decade after fatal fire," *National Post*, 7 January 2014. CF officers' visions of distant water deployments seem far-fetched at best.

4. R.J. Sutherland, "Canada's long term strategic situation," *International Journal* 17, 3 (Summer 1962): 199–223, esp. 202; cited hereafter as Sutherland, "LTSS."

5. The most notable nuclear optimist in the American international relations debate was the late Kenneth Waltz, whose last published paper advocated encouraging Iran to acquire nuclear weapons. See Waltz, "Why Iran should get the Bomb," *Foreign Affairs* 91, 4 (July/August 2012). Another defensive realist, Stephen Van Evera, suggests there is no rational alternative to traditional conceptions of mutual deterrence. See his *Causes of War* (Ithaca, NY: Cornell University Press, 1999), Chapter 8. Sutherland's views seem to have anticipated Van Evera's judgment that "we must learn to live in a MAD world because all escapes from it are infeasible and undesirable. . . . Efforts to escape MAD will be swamped by powerful technical forces running the other way. Escapes are undesirable because they would raise large risks of war. All alternate military orders are more dangerous than MAD" (p. 243). Van Evera lists two caveats: all state elites in the system must be deterrable, that is to say, not governed by a crazed leader or a Stalin, Hitler, or Pol Pot (who are not perturbed by mass death), and secondly, all states must block the spread of nuclear weapons technology to anonymous users such as terrorists or criminal elements who are inherently immune to retaliation (p. 249).

6. Ibid., 199–201.

7. Ibid., 202–3.

8. Academics such as John Mearsheimer and senior American policy analysts such as Fred Iklé have long recommended that both Japan and Germany should acquire independent nuclear capabilities. See Mearsheimer, "Back to the future: Instability in Europe after the Cold War," *International Security* 15, 1 (Summer 1990), esp. 19–20, 32–40.

9. Sutherland, "LTSS," 216. The first under-ice submarine transit to the North Pole was made by the US Navy's *Nautilus* in August 1958. For a review of current Arctic policy issues as seen in Ottawa, see Chapter 21 by Rob Huebert.

10. This creative idea was later proposed for consideration by the late David Cox of Queen's University, one of Canada's foremost analysts of continental defence in the 1970s and 1980s.

11. For a most helpful historical summary of NORAD's mission evolution, with maps and images, see Lt.-Gen. Tom Lawson and Capt. Michael Sawler, "NORAD in 2012—ever evolving, forever relevant," *Canadian Military Journal* (last modified 16 May 2011). Available at www.journal.forces.gc.ca/vol12/ no3/page5-eng.asp.

12. Canadian air defence cooperation would be needed by Americans because any long-range bombers taking off from Manchuria would transit northwestern and central BC before entering the continental US on a shortest Great Circle route toward their most likely targets: military assets, political leadership, and military command and control, or urban industrial centres.

13. Sutherland, "LTSS," 214.

14. See James Acton quoting Anatoly Antonov, former head of Security and Disarmament in the Russian Ministry of Foreign Affairs, in "Conventional prompt global strike and Russia's nuclear forces," p. 1, at the Carnegie Endowment website; available at http://carnegieendowment.org/files/ Acton_NVO_trans.pdf.

15. Quoted by Andrew Richter, *Avoiding Armageddon: Canadian Military Strategy and Nuclear Weapons, 1950–63* (Vancouver: UBC Press, 2002), 65–66. Richter's careful, thorough reconstruction of Sutherland's and other Canadians' views definitively established the strategic analytical independence of postwar Ottawa from American strategic thought on nuclear weapons and strategy. See also Richter, "Strategic theoretical parasitism reconsidered," *International Journal* 55, 3 (Summer 2000), 401–26.

16. Sutherland, "LTSS," 210.

17. See Fred Kaplan, "JFK's first-strike plan," *The Atlantic* 288, 3 (October 2001), 81–86. Because of the quite inadequate

Soviet air defence radars and interceptors that could not cope with low-altitude penetration tactics, the US planners estimated that there would be virtually no US aircraft lost and that further strikes could then proceed on nuclear missiles and bombers aimed at Western Europe or Japan.

18. Sutherland, "LTSS," 210–11.

19. Ibid., 218.

20. Ibid., 223.

21. Andrew Cohen, *While Canada Slept: How We Lost our Place in the World* (Toronto: McClelland and Stewart, 2003).

22. For a critique of the "dangerous," escalatory and ill-advised adoption of such counterforce coercion methods, see John Mearsheimer, "A strategic misstep: The Maritime strategy and deterrence in Europe," *International Security* 11, 2 (Fall 1986), esp. 14–17.

23. The explicit threat of new American force deployments in the Western Pacific is heavily focused on long-range precision conventional strikes using the latest electronic warfare and cyberwar capabilities being introduced to US Navy and Air Force squadrons in the region.

24. Amy Butler, "Again and again: Carrier and civil aviation could eventually take lessons from UCAS landing trials," *Aviation Week and Space Technology*, 5 August 2013. Its first computerized landings were so remarkably accurate that Lockheed Martin may incorporate this new autonomous landing capability in its carrier-based F-35s so as to greatly speed up pilot training for the badly lagging F-35 development effort.

25. Amy Butler and Bill Sweetman, "Return of the penetrator," *Aviation Week and Space Technology*, 9 December 2013. The Global Hawk can loiter for up to 24 hours some 1,400 miles from its base, providing electronic, optical, radar, and other sensing data and targeting information, but it does not possess "all-aspect, broadband radar cross section reduction" better than that of the F-22 and the F-35—as does the RQ-180.

26. Australia commissioned Boeing independently to design and build 100-km-plus, highly accurate glide bombs for its new F/A-18F and G Super Hornets. This technology is an extension of the JDAM revolution in ordnance in which adjustable fins or "strakes" and a GPS guidance system kit are attached to old-inventory iron bombs with from 500 to 2,000 lbs. of explosive yield. The "new" precision-strike weapon costs less than $25,000 per kit unit and has a glide range of some 28 km. From 1998 to August 2013, 250,000 kits were delivered by manufacturers, most to the US Air Force. Allies pay more. It is an amazingly inexpensive way to turn "dumb" bombs into smart cruise missiles. Given that they are far smaller than a cruise missile, and so inexpensive that they can "saturate" air defences, such weapons are much harder to destroy and defeat.

27. Amy Butler, "Sensory input," *Aviation Week and Space Technology*, 12 May 2013. GMD was formerly expanded as ground-based mid-course defence technology.

28. For an exceptionally informative review of Chinese security specialist comments on American strategy and nuclear arms and their "self-contradictory character," see Lora Saalman, "China and the U.S. nuclear posture review," *The Carnegie Papers* (Washington: Carnegie Endowment for International Peace, 2011), available at http://carnegieendowment.org/files/china_posture_review.pdf.

29. Bill Sweetman, "Russian renaissance," *Aviation Week and Space Technology*, 11 November 2013. The Rubezh may have a fully functioning manoeuvrable re-entry vehicle warhead and might be capable of depressed trajectory launches that considerably reduce warning time for missile defence radars.

30. Ibid.

31. See "Nuclear Weapons," preface to the review of Russian nuclear force modernization, *Aviation Week and Space Technology*, 11 November 2013, 48–49. Comment by Barry Watts of the Center for Strategic and Budgetary Assessments.

32. With the country's minimum deterrent nuclear posture (a deployed force able to deliver only some 60 warheads on North America), Chinese officials argue that their deterrent credibility depends importantly on opacity and ambiguity. To act on US requests for more transparency in China's plans for nuclear force modernization and expansion would be highly detrimental to national security—given existing American nuclear superiority, conventional strike superiority, stealth superiority, and especially its growing and non-treaty-constrained ABM capability: Saalman, 17. Deployed missiles able to reach the US are thought to include 32 DF-4 and DF-5A (ensiloed, 13,000-km range, single 3.3 MT warhead) and some 28 DF-31A in three brigades (mobile, 11,000-km range, single warhead of 200 to 300 kt) that use solid fuel. See Konstantin Kakaes, "Modest Dragon," *Aviation Week and Space Technology*, 11 November 2013; also Hans M. Kristensen and Robert S. Norris, "Chinese nuclear forces, 2013," *Bulletin of the Atomic Scientists* 69, 6 (November/December 2013), at bos.sagepub.com/content/69/6/79.full#ref-8. China has no long-range bombers. Its three Jin-class SSBNs, undergoing sea trials, are not expected to receive missiles until 2014.

33. United States, Department of Defense, *Sustaining U.S. Global Leadership: Priorities for 21st Century Defense*, January 2012, available at www.defense.gov/news/defense_strategic_guidance.pdf.

34. See David S. McDonough's exhaustive and insightful review of the literature on this massive buildup in his "America's pivot to the Pacific: Selective primacy, operational access, and China's A2/AD challenge," Calgary Papers in Military and Strategic Studies, Occasional Paper Number 7 (Calgary: Centre for Military and Strategic Studies, University of Calgary, 2013), 18–24.

35. Ibid., 18.

36. General Norton Schwartz's comments in May 2012, as quoted by Amitai Etzioni, "Who authorized preparations for war with China?," *Yale Journal of International Affairs* 37 (Summer 2013), 39.

37. Elaine M. Grossman, "Pentagon unveils new plan for conventional submarine-based ballistic missiles," Global Security Newswire, 27 January 2012. Available at www.nti. org/gsn/article/pentagon-unveils-new-plan-conventional-submarine-based-ballistic-missiles/. Congress vetoed giving Trident II D-5 missiles a conventional capability in 2010 because of a perceived threat to crisis stability.

38. Guy Norris, "Stealthy strike," *Aviation Week and Space Technology*, 4 November 2013.

39. Bradley Perrett, Bill Sweetman, and Michael Fabey, "High speed hit," *Aviation Week and Space Technology*, 27 January 2014.

40. Joseph Henrotin, "L'évolution de la flotte de sous-marins américains à l'horizon 2030," *Défense et sécurité internationale* 78 (février 2012); and "The dragon's new teeth," *The Economist*, 7 April 2012.

41. The bomber specified is "not much more than half the size of the B-2." It is limited to carrying hard target weapons below 5,000 pounds. Bill Sweetman, "Take your partners: New bomber team leaves Northrop Grumman in the cold," *Aviation Week and Space Technology*, 4 November 2013.

42. Lee Berthiaume, "Canada joins Pacific exercise, 1400 troops," *National Post*, 17 July 2012.

43. Ibid.

44. John Mearsheimer, "The rise of China will not be peaceful at all," *The Australian*, 18 November 2005. Available at http://mearsheimer.uchicago.edu/pdfs/P0014.pdf. As he noted: "Why should we expect the Chinese to act differently than the U.S. did? Are they more principled than the Americans are? More ethical? Less nationalistic? Less concerned about their survival? They are none of these things . . . which is why China is likely to imitate the U.S. and attempt to become a regional hegemon."

45. See Anton Bezglasnyy and Douglas Alan Ross, "Strategically superfluous, unacceptably overpriced: The case against Canada's F-35A Lightning II acquisition," in *Canadian Foreign Policy* 17, 3 (September 2011), 239–50; see also Michael Byers and Stewart Webb, "Canada's F-35 purchase is a costly mistake," *Canadian Foreign Policy* 17, 3 (September 2011), 217–27, and Kim Richard Nossal, "Late learners: Canada, the F-35, and lessons from the New Fighter Aircraft program," *International Journal* 68, 1 (Winter 2012–13): 167–84.

46. Mark Collins, "Canada's declining defence budget as percentage of GDP," Canadian Defence and Foreign Affairs Institute, *The 3Ds Blog*, 11 June 2012, available at www.cdfai.org/the3dsblog/?p=1197.

47. Robert Hartfiel and Brian Job, "Raising the risks of war: Defence spending trends and competitive arms processes in East Asia," Working Paper No. 44 (Vancouver: Institute of International Relations, Liu Centre, University of British Columbia, March 2005), p. 7, available at www.ligi.ubc.ca/ sites/liu/files/Publications/Hartfiel_Job_WP44.pdf.

48. Up until 2010, 610 soldiers had been wounded in combat, with another 1,244 injured off the battlefield. After 2010, casualties and injuries were declared "secret." Among the 30,000 Canadian veterans who served in Afghanistan, the suicide rate is some 45 per cent higher than that of the general population. See Jason Fekete, "Johnston urges more PTSD care for soldiers," *National Post*, 13 December 2013; John Ivison, "Much of the cost of war comes after," *National Post*, 5 December 2013; Gloria Galloway, "Mentally ill soldiers fear being discharged," *The Globe and Mail*, 6 December 2013.

49. According to the Parliamentary Budget Office, the cost of the war was some $18.5 billion to 2011. The Harper government persistently refused to provide clear cost data.

50. For a review of the many inherent weaknesses of the Karzai regime—the widespread use of torture and the endemic corruption in the Afghan National Police, and the ineffectualness of the Afghan National Army, especially in Kandahar province—see the former long-time *Globe and Mail* correspondent in Afghanistan, Graeme Smith, *The Dogs are Eating Them Now* (Toronto: Knopf-Random House, 2013).

51. Lee Berthiaume, "Harper government's defence spending cuts raise spectre of another 'decade of darkness.'" *National Post*, 20 March 2013. This was the assessment of Lt.-Col. (ret'd) Brian MacDonald in reaction to a study by the Conference of Defence Associations.

52. Bill Curry, "Ottawa plans $3.7 billion surplus," *The Globe and Mail*, 13 November 2013. Expenditures for 2012 were lower than expected because of systematic underspending by various departments, especially DND. Flaherty hoped to be able to offer a tax cut in 2015.

53. Stockholm International Peace Research Institute (SIPRI) figures, as per Sam Perlo-Freeman, Elisabeth Sköns, Carina Solmirano, and Helen Wilandh, "Trends in world military expenditure, 2012," SIPRI Fact Sheet, April 2013, available at http://books.sipri.org/files/FS/SIPRIFS1304.pdf. Canada was fourteenth on the list, just ahead of Australia.

54. At market exchange rates (MER) in 2006, Canada was thirteenth of fifteen in defence spending, but was passed by Turkey, Iran, and Pakistan when assessed by PPP methods. See the SIPRI Military Expenditure Database at www.sipri. org/research/armaments/milex/milex_database. US share of global defence spending was 46 per cent in 2006, and 48 per cent in 2008.

55. Perlo-Freeman et al., "Trends in world military expenditure, 2012," SIPRI Fact Sheet, April 2013, p. 3.

56. Ibid.

57. Michael Bruno, "Hamburger Hill: Upcoming fights in Congress will look a lot like old ones," *Aviation Week and Space Technology*, 28 October 2013. Estimates by the

Bipartisan Policy Center. In 1988, Reagan's last year in office, the numbers were: 23 army and marine divisions; 2,789 fighter/attack aircraft, and 15 carriers, with 558 other principal surface combatant ships.

58. Amy Svitak, "Seizing the day," *Aviation Week and Space Technology*, 5 August 2013.

59. McDonough, America's pivot to the Pacific," 27.

60. Mark Urban, "Saudi nuclear weapons 'on order' from Pakistan," BBC News, 7 November 2013, available at www.bbc.co.uk/news/world-middle-east-24823846.

61. Thomas J. Christensen, "The meaning of the nuclear evolution: China's strategic modernization and U.S. China security relations," *Journal of Strategic Studies* 35, 4 (August 2012): 447–87.

21

Canadian Arctic Sovereignty and Security in a Transforming Circumpolar World

Rob Huebert

Key Terms

Climate Change
Human Security
International Law of the Sea

Security
Sovereignty

Introduction

Canadian Arctic policy is faced with some of the most intriguing, yet complex, challenges in its history. Perhaps the greatest current challenge for Canada is the worldwide realization that the Arctic is melting, and so it is more accessible than ever before. Consequently, Canada must prepare for the outside world's entry into the Arctic. With international challenges to Canadian control of the region now emerging, Canada can no longer afford to ignore its Arctic. The objective of this chapter is to achieve an understanding of Canadian Arctic **sovereignty** and **security** in the context of a fundamentally changing Arctic. First, it examines sovereignty and security. The chapter then examines the forces that are transforming the very fabric of the Arctic, specifically **climate change**, resource development, and geopolitical forces.

Part I: Understanding Sovereignty and Security

Sovereignty

Sovereignty is the theoretical cornerstone of the international legal state system. There are three main elements of sovereignty: a defined territory, an existing governance system, and a people within the defined territory.[1] A state must have a functioning government system that is able to make final decisions that are enforced upon the people within its geographic territory. Each of these variables might appear to be straightforward, but the reality is that all three are difficult to achieve within the Arctic.

The most common problem with determining sovereignty is the existence of an accepted governance system. The sovereignty of a state is said to be threatened when parties compete to govern. In such cases, until one side is defeated, either militarily or politically, or a negotiated settlement is reached whereby the competing bodies agree to share power as a single entity, there is no one sovereign body. The process for determining sovereignty is complicated by the fact that even after the competition for power is internally settled, the international community must also recognize the new governing body.

In the Canadian Arctic there is no question about the existence of an accepted governance system. This system may be evolving as power devolves to the territories, but as long as this is done on a peaceful basis, all sovereign states have the right to allocate their powers to political sub-units within their borders. Within the borders of the Canadian Arctic, the northern Canadian population has completely accepted the government's right to govern. Thus the federal government does not diminish the sovereignty of the Canadian state by transferring powers to its three northern territories: the Northwest Territories, Nunavut, and Yukon.

This transfer leads to the issues surrounding the second variable of sovereignty, which requires that a people are contained within the defined geography of a state. Consequently, there is no sovereignty in a case where there is no local population, such as in Antarctica. But there are no limits as to how small a population can be. The Canadian Arctic contains a small number of individuals, but it contains enough to give Canada sovereignty over all of the land territory of its Arctic. The only land area in Canada where Canada's sovereignty is challenged is Hans Island, a small uninhabited island.

The third variable—defined boundaries—has the greatest relevance for the discussion of Canadian Arctic sovereignty. For a boundary to have validity, the international community needs to agree on its boundaries. The number of states that need to agree before a boundary is said to be accepted remains unclear. The growing complexity of ocean boundaries is extremely pertinent to sovereignty in the Arctic. The United Nations Convention on the Law of the Sea (UNCLOS), which was finalized in 1982 and came into force in 1996, codified existing customary international law and created several new maritime zones.[2] In general, the farther that the zone moves out from the land territory of the state, the less control the state has over the activities within the zone. Thus the first main zone—the territorial sea—gives the coastal state almost complete control over all activities within it. The one important exception is that the state cannot interfere in the innocent passage of foreign vessels in these waters. Moving closer to shore, the Exclusive Economic Zone (EEZ) extends 200 nautical miles from the coastline of the state. The coastal state has control over all living and non-living resources in this zone. Therefore, only the coastal state can fish, drill for oil or gas, or grant permission to a foreign state or organization. However, in the EEZ, the coastal state has no control over international shipping that is not engaged in resource exploitation. UNCLOS created a third zone of control. A state can extend its control over the ocean soil and subsurface beyond the EEZ if it can show that it has an extended continental shelf. If a state can prove that it meets the criteria required for a continental shelf, and if this shelf extends beyond 200 nautical miles, then a state can claim control of the seabed and its resources for an additional 150 nautical miles (and in some instances even beyond that). A state with this zone has control of all activities that occur on or beneath the seabed. This control is currently understood to mean that the state has authority over activities such as oil and gas development. However, the state has no control over activities in the water column such as shipping, fishing, or even scientific research.

Two other maritime zones depend on geography and history. If a state has a body of water that directly joins two other international bodies of waters, and if it has been used in the past by international shipping, then the joining body of water, or strait, is used for international navigation. The coastal state has the right of control of all activity within this international strait except international shipping, as all foreign vessels enjoy the right of passage. This control specifically allows all vessels to travel in their normal mode of transportation. Thus submarines could remain submerged as they transit an international strait.

Internal waters are the last maritime zone of significance for the Arctic. Bodies of waters such as lakes and rivers that lie entirely within the land mass of a state normally fall into this category. The host state enjoys complete control over these waters, including foreign shipping. There may be a small number of instances where a state may designate a specific body of water that lies outside its land boundaries as internal waters. Generally these exceptions occur where there has been historical acceptance of treating them like a lake or river: this designation was codified by UNCLOS as historical bays. Some countries, however, such as Canada, have attempted to extend this designation beyond bays.

A challenge to Canadian Arctic sovereignty must involve a dispute with one of the three elements of sovereignty. There is no challenge to the Canadian governance system, and there is an identifiable population that completely accepts the authority of the Canadian government. As a result, the element of sovereignty that is challenged is the recognition of Canada's borders, specifically its Arctic maritime borders. Can Canada exercise control of its Arctic borders?

Security

The concept of security has undergone a transformation in both theoretical and practical terms since the end of the Cold War. Historically, security was framed in a context that focused on the military ability of a state to either defend itself against the military actions of other states or to enforce its will on another state. If a state was powerful enough it acted alone, or it could develop alliances with other states. The critical element of security was the ability of states to utilize their economic capabilities to build militaries that could both enforce and protect their will.[3] The use of deadly force was the ultimate means of providing for the security of the state.

The development of nuclear weapons changed the nature of security because the deterrence of nuclear war rather than the waging of war became the ultimate security objective of states during the Cold War period. It was still necessary, however paradoxically, to avoid war by preparing for war. Security was linked to the ability to build a nuclear weapon capability sufficient enough to deter the opposing side from attacking. National security was still viewed as the core responsibility of the state which could only be achieved through military force.

As the Cold War came to an end, the consensus on the nature of security was challenged. First, the end of the Cold War ended the nuclear balance that had threatened the existence of the entire international system. With the collapse of the USSR, the core military rivalry with the United States ended and the need for military forces appeared to dramatically diminish. This led many to begin questioning whether the traditional definition of security, with its focus on the military and the state, remained valid. This led to the development of **human security**, which expanded the conceptualization of security.[4] Human security was an attempt to move security away from state-based analysis. It was recognized that in many instances the state was the cause of insecurity of some or all of its peoples—that is, repressive regimes such as Pinochet's military dictatorship in Chile or the Khmer Rouge in Cambodia. The movement from defensive military use to the construction of international norms and institutions, such as treaties and agreements, supported this new concept of human security and created an environment whereby the affected parties could enjoy security. Efforts were made to construct international means of bringing justice to those who suffered at the hands of the state. Substantial effort was given to create means for outlawing the use and construction of certain weapons systems, such as anti-personnel landmines.

A second and related challenge to traditional security occurred when some academics and policy-makers began to look to the dangers posed by environmental degradation.[5] The physical security of an individual in Bangladesh or the Seychelles who lost their home due to rising sea levels from melting ice caps as a result of climate change was just as tenuous as someone in a war zone. Supporters who sought to extend the meaning of security pointed to the physical dangers that pollution and environmental degradation posed to the well-being of people both within and beyond the state. As in the case of human security, greater security did not come from military action. Instead, international cooperation was required at both the individual and state levels. Conceptual extensions of security, similar to advances made by environmental security specialists, have further extended the term "security" to include economic security, cultural security, and so on. In all cases, there was a desire to expand the definition of security beyond a focus on the state and the military.

What conclusions can be reached prior to discussing Canadian Arctic sovereignty and security? If Canadian Arctic sovereignty is threatened, then the Canadian government does not control a specific geographic territory. Sovereignty is about controlling the actions of others within the boundaries claimed by the Canadian government. From this perspective, Canada's challenge lies in the maritime nature of its boundaries of the area in dispute. International laws pertaining to maritime sovereignty are different than those for sovereignty over a land mass. Specifically, UNCLOS clearly establishes the various degrees of control over maritime zones, the rule of thumb being that the farther away from the coastline, the less control the coastal state enjoys.

The most important question that follows from the exercise of sovereignty is, why exercise it in the first place? What do states gain by pursuing and then defending national sovereignty? States defend their sovereignty for the principal reason of securing their core interests and values in a specific region. Traditionally this was done through the use of military force. But it is now recognized that some threats to a state's security, such as environmental security, cannot be addressed by military action. The underlying point is that whatever those steps are to be, they are undertaken with the objective of protecting the security of the state's citizens.

Part II: Canadian Concepts of Arctic Sovereignty and Security

Throughout much of the Cold War, the effort to have policy reflect the terms *Arctic sovereignty* and *Arctic security* was frustrated by the tendency of Canadian policy-makers, media, and academics to assume that the two terms were separate and distinct concepts. During the Cold War, Arctic security meant defence against the Soviet Union. Canada left the maritime dimensions of Arctic security entirely in American hands while allowing them to pay for much of it. Arctic sovereignty was associated with diplomatic disputes with the United States and with reacting to American actions that were perceived to threaten Canada's claim over the region, most notably the waterways of the north. In this manner Arctic security and Arctic sovereignty were viewed as separate policy concerns. However, sovereignty and security are interconnected: they cannot and should not be separated. The Canadian government attempts to defend Canadian Arctic sovereignty for the purpose of protecting the security of its citizens as well as the security of the core values and interests of Canadians.

The issue of Canadian Arctic sovereignty is complicated by its maritime dimension. Within the **international law of the sea**, the right to make final decisions about what activities occur within its maritime zones is not absolute but is modified by the waterway's nature. With the exception of Denmark's assertion of ownership of Hans Island, no other actors in the international system challenge Canada's right to control its Arctic land mass. However, international challenges do emerge over Canada's claim to its Arctic maritime space. The United States disagrees on the boundary dividing the Beaufort Sea. Likewise, Denmark disagrees on division of the Lincoln Sea (though only in two small regions). Canada might also disagree with the United States, Russia, and Denmark about its anticipated claim over its continental shelf boundaries in the Arctic Ocean. Canada's most well-known Arctic sovereignty issue is over the control of international maritime traffic in the Northwest Passage. Canada claims that the waterways that comprise the Northwest Passage are internal waters, and, therefore, the Canadian government has the right to control who can enter these waters and under what conditions. The American and the European Union position is that these waters are part of an international strait, which means that it is not Canada but the international community, in this case through the International Maritime Organization (IMO), which has the final, authoritative decision-making power over international shipping in the Northwest Passage.

Ultimately, whether it is dividing the Arctic Ocean seabed, determining the boundaries of Canadian sections of the Beaufort and Lincoln Sea or shipping in the Northwest Passage, the issue is control. What are the Arctic maritime boundaries that Canada can control and what can it do within these boundaries? This is where the issue of Arctic security connects with Arctic sovereignty. If sovereignty is being pursued for the purpose of protecting the security, safety, and well-being of Canadians, then not only is it worth the effort, but it is an absolute necessity.

If Canadian Arctic sovereignty is control, then Canadian Arctic security is about responding to threats. The threats to Canadian Arctic security are nebulous, multi-dimensional, and evolving.

Throughout the Cold War, Arctic security was exclusive to the threat posed by the USSR to the national survival of Canada and the United States. When the Cold War ended and concerns about traditional threats to national security receded, scientists soon discovered that the Canadian Arctic was the end location for a wide number of pollutants that originated elsewhere on the globe (including seemingly improbable sources such as India and the Philippines). The transboundary migration of toxic substances—persistent organic pollutants such as pesticides and fertilizers, for example—contaminated the food supply and negatively impacted the health of northern Canadians.[6] It was soon realized that the environmental security of the Canadian north needed protection. Issues regarding threats to the law and order of the Canadian north are arising. Recently, foreign criminal elements have made unauthorized entries into the Canadian Arctic. In the summer of 2007, a group allegedly associated with the Norwegian Hell's Angels made it as far as Cambridge Bay on a small boat.[7] Other threats in the Canadian Arctic involve economic, societal, and cultural issues. It also appears that traditional security threats are re-emerging as each Arctic nation has begun rebuilding its northern military capabilities.

Canadian policy-makers need to protect Canadian Arctic sovereignty in order to provide for Canadian Arctic security. The Canadian government needs to have control over its north so that it can take action to protect against a wide number of threats that will increasingly come from beyond Canadian northern boundaries. As it is impossible to protect Canadian Arctic security without protecting its Arctic sovereignty and vice versa, the two concepts are completely interlinked.

Part III: The Changing Arctic

The Arctic is fundamentally changing. At least three unique and extremely powerful forces are leading to this transformation: climate change, resource development, and geopolitical transformation. Any one of these factors by itself would create a serious transformation in the Arctic. The reality that three such forces are at work only underlines the magnitude of the changes that are now occurring in the Canadian Arctic.

Climate Change

Climate change is warming the Arctic at a considerable rate, a fact that has garnered the attention of the world. It was only as recently as the 1990s that few even knew of climate change, let alone understood its magnitude. Among the many changes taking place, the most important impact of climate change in the Arctic is the melting of sea ice, which is receding at an accelerated and unprecedented rate.

The melting sea ice means that Canadian Arctic waters will be more open and therefore more accessible. This accessibility will lead to the entry of an increasing array of interests into the region. The Canadian government's ability to control what happens in its Arctic region will be tested with this entry of newcomers who will seek to exploit and benefit from a more accessible Arctic. Thus the melting sea ice will be at the root of the challenges to Canadian Arctic sovereignty and security. Debates about the expected impact of climate change are considerable. Scientists studying the issue have been continually surprised by the rapid rate of change.[8]

Regardless of when the ice will melt, two important elements must be stressed. First, the processes that are leading to the melt are speeding up. The recognition that while the processes are not fully understood they are becoming more pronounced underlies the information that is emerging from the current studies. This suggests that the physical nature of the Arctic will be transforming even more rapidly than previously thought.

So what is happening? The Arctic Climate Impact Assessment (ACIA) study remains the definitive work on the subject, although it will soon require an update. Its 2004 report was commissioned by the Arctic Council when it became clear that processes not yet understood were redesigning the physical nature of the entire Arctic region. In 2000, the Arctic Council directed two of its working groups, the Arctic Monitoring and Assessment Programme (AMAP) and Conservation of Arctic Flora and Fauna (CAFF), along with the International Arctic Science Committee (IASC), to undertake an extensive and exhaustive study of the impact of climate change on the Arctic. This brought together the world's leading experts, who produced a peer-reviewed, scientific document and a more concise summary document. Its findings, which were both troubling and overwhelming, emphasized the magnitude of the problem:

1. The Arctic climate is now warming rapidly and greater changes are projected.
2. Arctic warming and its consequences have worldwide implications.
3. Animal species' diversities, ranges, and distribution will change.
4. Many coastal communities and facilities face increasing exposure to storms.
5. Reduced sea ice is very likely to increase marine transport and access to resources.
6. Thawing ground will disrupt transportation building and other infrastructure.
7. Indigenous communities are facing major economic and cultural impacts.
8. Elevated ultraviolet (UV) radiation levels will affect people, plants, and animals.
9. Multiple influences interact to cause impacts to people and ecosystems.[9]

This study had its limitations; one was its scale. The report made assessments of the entire Arctic, as opposed to assessing specific areas of the Arctic. It subsequently became apparent that the changes occurring in the Arctic vary depending on local conditions. Thus the original observation that the ice is receding has now been tempered by the recognition that it recedes at different rates throughout the Arctic. Specifically, the Russian side of the Arctic has experienced the greatest rate of ice decline, followed by the central Arctic and then the Northwest Passage.[10] The Passage's slower melting rate is due to a series of geophysical forces that include prevailing ocean currents, the location of the many islands of the Arctic archipelago, and so forth. However, while it might lag behind the other regions, it is still melting.

Historically, the extreme climate and extensive ice cover prevented the outside world from entering the Canadian Arctic. This is now changing as the Arctic is melting. With a diminishing ice cover, the Arctic is becoming more accessible, which in turn will make it easier for the world to come. But just because accessibility is eased does not mean there is necessarily a reason to arrive. The outside world needs a reason to take advantage of the improved accessibility. The second major set of forces that cause change in the Arctic serve to provide the world with its reason for coming to the Arctic: resource development.

Resource Development

Notwithstanding the melting, the Arctic will remain a unique and dangerous place to operate in. Regardless of the warming climate, the Earth's tilt means that for significant periods of time, the Arctic will remain in darkness. This darkness alone complicates any activities that will take place in the region. Related to this is the reality that unless the overall temperature of the earth reaches levels in which more southern latitudes are literally baking, some ice will reform during the Arctic winters. So while the Arctic Ocean will be ice-free in the summer months it will never be completely ice-free year-round, as is the case with the other oceans.

So if that is the case, why come north? The reason is that melting sea ice allows for greater accessibility to and exploitation of the Arctic's marine resources. In terms of oil and gas, the Arctic is estimated to contain approximately 25 per cent of the world's remaining undiscovered oil and gas deposits. The US Geological Survey estimates that 13 per cent of oil and 30 per cent of natural gas remains in the Arctic.[11] If correct, the Arctic is the world's last major source of oil and gas.

When discussing the development of Arctic resources in Canada in 2009, it is clear that its defining features are vast and potentially tempered by uncertainty. It is becoming increasingly apparent that the Arctic is indeed a treasure trove of resources. However, until the beginning of the 2000s, the market price of most of these resources did not make their exploitation economically viable. But, at the beginning of this decade, there was both an ongoing rise in most commodity prices as well as improvements in the technology that would allow for their extraction. Exxon, British Petroleum (BP), and Shell have now all expanded their exploration for oil and gas in the Arctic.

New technologies for resource development further facilitate the changes in the Arctic. Non-Arctic states have entered into the region and assumed leadership roles in advancing new technologies for use in the Arctic. The best known example is the construction of ice-capable commercial vessels. Historically, Finnish and Russian companies were the leaders in ship design and construction of ice-capable vessels, but they are now increasingly challenged by South Korean companies that have invested heavily in building ice-capable vessels.

But it is necessary to remember that all of this currently remains speculative due to the uncertainty that surrounds almost all aspects of northern resource development. The quantity of oil and gas in the Canadian Arctic is unknown; the technology to exploit these resources is in a state of rapid development, and which resources are usable and when they will even be used is further unknown.

Resource exploration and development is further complicated by sliding commodity prices, which demonstrates that it is impossible to expect regularity in the market.

Where does this leave the issue of Canadian Arctic sovereignty and security? The pursuit of resources will be the incentive for outside interests to enter the Canadian Arctic. However, international law gives Canada the sovereign right to control the development of these resources. Thus the Canadian government has the right to control all shipping that comes into Canadian Arctic waters for the purposes of resources, if it chooses to do so. The challenge remains controlling vessels that want to use Canadian Arctic waters as a passageway. If Canada loses its dispute with the Americans and Europeans as to the international legal status of the Passage, then they will not be able to unilaterally control those vessels. On the other hand, if the Canadian position that these waters are internal Canadian waters perseveres, then it will also be able to control that shipping.

As the Arctic's resources are developed, Canada needs to continue strengthening its ability to enforce its rules in the Arctic. Canada has the right to control all economic activity on its Arctic lands and in its Arctic Ocean, with the exception of Arctic shipping to a distance of 200 nautical miles from its coastline. But having the right and ability to do so are two separate things. In order for Canada to actually control economic activity in its Arctic, the Canadian government must act to improve both its ability to know what is happening in the north as well as its ability to control any activity that takes place there. While successive Canadian governments have recognized the necessity to protect Canadian security and sovereignty in the region, they generally have been unwilling to allocate the funds to develop the means to acquire the necessary assets.[12] In particular, there were two high-profile incidents, one in 1969 and the other in 1985,

involving US travel through the Northwest Passage. Each incident created a crisis in Canadian–American Arctic relations.

Geopolitical Change

As if climate change and resource development were not enough forces for change, the geopolitical forces that have re-emerged after the end of the Cold War are literally redrawing the map of the Arctic. New international laws allow the Arctic nations to extend their control over the Arctic seabed. It is possible that almost all of the Arctic Ocean's seabed may come under the control of one of the Arctic states. At the same time most Arctic nations are beginning to strengthen the ability of their armed forces and coast guards to operate in the north. Thirdly, non-Arctic states have begun to show interest in Arctic operations. The net effect of these factors is a growing international recognition of the importance of the Arctic, concurrent with increasing international action in the region.

The media increasingly reports about a race for resources in the Arctic, with continuous references to efforts to "carve" up the Arctic. The reality is that there is no division of the Arctic—yet. Currently, the five Arctic states with coastlines on the Arctic Ocean are about to extend their control of the soil and subsoil of the seabeds extending from their continental shelf. At the heart of this extension is the right to the minerals, oil, and gas that might be found on and in this extension.

This extension might give Canada one of the largest new territories in the Arctic, and is occurring under the terms of UNCLOS. This Convention is one of the most comprehensive and complex international agreements that has received almost universal agreement. UNCLOS created new zones of control over ocean space. Prior to the Convention, international law recognized only the right of a state to extend control of its adjacent ocean space to a distance of 12 nautical miles. However, UNCLOS has created different zones of control by allowing coastal states control of resources up to a distance of 200 nautical miles in an area called the EEZ. Under the terms of Article 76, if a state also sits on an extension of the continental shelf that goes beyond 200 nautical miles, it can also claim control of the resources on the soil and subsoil to an additional distance of 150 nautical miles and, in certain instances, even beyond this. Unlike the EEZ, which all coastal states can claim, states must prove that they have an extended continental shelf. They have 10 years to engage in the research necessary to prove this. Canada, Denmark (for Greenland), Russia, and the United States are now all engaged in research programs to determine the extent of their continental shelf. When they have completed their research, each country must submit their findings to an international body named the Commission on the Limits of the Continental Shelf (CLCS). The CLCS reviews and passes judgment on the technical and scientific merits of the country's submission. If the CLCS accepts the submission and if the state's neighbours have submitted overlapping claims, then the dispute must be resolved at that stage. The Convention provides that all such disputes must be resolved peacefully and also provides a variety of means for achieving resolution. Article 280 of Section XV of the Convention allows the state parties to a dispute to use "any peaceful means of their own choice" to resolve a dispute caused by the Convention. The overlapping claims thus created by Article 76 will be such a dispute.

The parties to such a dispute can also use Article 284 of Section XV of the Convention to use a conciliation process established within Annex V of the Convention. If either of these processes are not acceptable, then Article 287 requires the parties to the dispute to select from four options: 1(a) the International Tribunal for the Law of the Sea; 1(b) the International Court of Justice; 1(c) an arbitral tribunal constituted in accordance with Annex VII of the Convention; or 1(d) a special arbitral tribunal

constituted under Annex VIII of the Convention. If the parties are not able to agree to the specific means of settlement, then the fourth means is to be employed. The five Arctic states that are making continental shelf claims, which were agreed upon in May 2008 in a meeting held in Ilulissat, Greenland, will have to resolve any differences peacefully and through the mechanisms established by the UNCLOS.[13]

However, the United States, unlike Russia, Canada, and Denmark (for Greenland), has neither signed nor ratified the treaty.[14] Successive presidents since George H. W. Bush have attempted to accede to the treaty but have been prevented by a small minority of Republican senators. The American constitutional system requires all international treaties to be passed by a two-thirds Senate majority. Since the early 1990s, this minority of Republican senators has been able to consolidate over 33 senators who have refused to accede to UNCLOS. Their primary motivation is an ideologically based opposition to the United Nations. However, with the recent American election, and the defeat and retirement of some of the senators in question, the anticipation is that President Obama will eventually achieve success. The US has recognized the importance of being party to the treaty to protect its interest in the north. In anticipation of their accession they have begun mapping their extended continental shelf. They conducted an expedition with Canada in the Beaufort Sea in 2008 and plan to continue mapping its continental shelf in 2009.

Following its ratification of UNCLOS, Canada seriously began to map its continental shelf. The 2004 budget allocated $69 million for the mapping of both the Arctic and the Atlantic seabed, with the bulk of the funds expected to be spent in the north. The 2008 budget provided an additional $20 million. This investment has enabled Canadian scientists to carry on with a robust agenda that should be completed by 2010, giving Canada the necessary time to prepare its submission to the CLCS.

The media has focused on the potential disputes that might develop from any overlapping claims. Until all of the states have submitted their claims, it is impossible to know whether any disputes will arise or, if they do, how serious they will be. Currently, Canada, the United States, Denmark, and Norway have already issued diplomatic demarches against the 2001 Russian submission. After submitting their claim in 2001, the Russians were advised by the CLCS to further develop the science behind their claim, so it is possible that a revised Russian claim might not be challenged. But this would require the Russians to reduce their claimed area. This seems unlikely.

The Russians have responded to Norway's claim of an extended continental shelf in somewhat aggressive terms. In the summer of 2008, the Russian Navy resumed surface naval patrols. Specifically, two Russian warships sailed into the region that Norway has claimed around Spitsbergen Island.[15] The Russians and the Norwegians have a longstanding dispute about the island, which is undoubtedly being intensified by Norway's claim to extend its continental shelf. Under international law, the Russians have the right to sail warships into the EEZ and over the continental shelf. So by sailing into the disputed region they did not break international law. But it is hard to avoid the conclusion that the Russians were sending a message to the Norwegians by sailing into the disputed area.

This is not the only action that the Russians have taken to support their claim. Using a minisubmarine, they dropped the Russian flag at the North Pole in summer 2007. The other Arctic states widely dismissed this as a meaningless act. Then Canadian minister of foreign affairs Peter MacKay stated, "This isn't the 15th century. You can't go around the world and just plant flags" to claim territory.[16] Yet questions remain as to why the Russians would take such potent symbolic action.

The Russians are attempting to justify their claim

that the North Pole should be the delimitation point dividing their claim from Canada and Denmark (and possibly the United States). Their initial submission to the CLCS in 2001 shows that they intend to claim up to the North Pole. While such an approach appears logical on a map, it has no basis in international law. The Russian effort is based on the sector theory. This theory was first put forward by Canadian Senator Pascal Poirier in 1907 as a means of extending Canadian Arctic claims. Poirier suggested that each of the states on the Arctic Ocean should extend their boundaries northward until they meet at the North Pole. Such a suggestion was never supported by the Canadian government, or by international law. One of Canada's leading experts on international law in the Arctic, Donat Pharand, provided the definitive examination on the issue and came to the conclusion that such an approach is simply not valid.[17] However, the Russians are attempting to revive it. The Soviets never repudiated the principle after considering it in the 1930s. If it was accepted, this approach would benefit the Russians.

Canada and Denmark claim that the Lomonosov Ridge connects to the North American/Greenland land mass. If it does, then they can make an extended claim similar to that of Russia's. This means that they too can go to the North Pole. If this is the case, then Canada, Denmark, and Russia can claim the entire Arctic Ocean as part of their extended continental shelf. In any other part of the globe the normal means of dividing such an overlapping claim would be to determine the equidistant point (the halfway mark) between the competing states. This point would be determined by drawing a line between the most northern Canadian, Danish, and Russian land points and then determining where the halfway mark of this line is. It is probable that this point is found somewhere on the Russian side of the North Pole. Thus the pole and its surrounding area would be either Danish or Canadian, depending on the precise measuring of the ridge. The support this method gains on

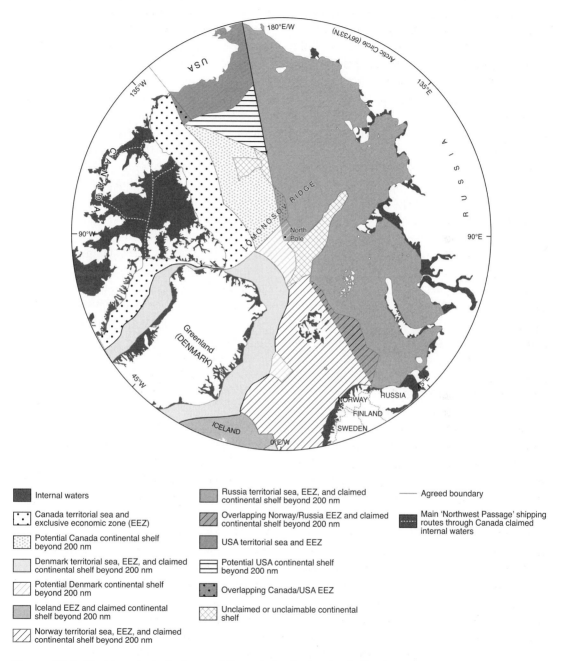

Figure 21.1 Maritime Jurisdiction and Boundaries in the Arctic Region

Source: International Boundaries Research Unit, Durham University. Accessed June 22, 2009, www.dur.ac.uk/bru/resources/arctic.

the Russian side can only be determined once all three states have made their submission to the CLCS.

Shortly, Canada may have to decide whether it will challenge Russia's claim. If it challenges this claim, this will be the first time that Canada engages in a territorial dispute with Russia since Russia and the United Kingdom resolved the land boundary between Alaska and Yukon in 1825. At the meeting in Ilulissat, Greenland, the Russian government promised that all disputes arising over the Arctic continental shelf would be dealt with in a cooperative spirit and in a peaceful manner.[18] However, recent events point to an increasingly assertive (and possibly aggressive) Russia. Georgia was temporarily invaded and partially occupied by Russia over a territorial dispute. Ukraine had its gas supplies temporarily suspended as it battled with the Russians over a pricing contract. It is difficult to imagine a Canadian–Russian Arctic dispute escalating to the point of conflict, but it is easy to believe that Russia could be assertive in support of its claim. Thus Canadian officials should not shy away from challenging Russia's extended continental shelf claim, but they should be prepared for Russia to adopt "hardball" policies.

The situation facing Canada and the United States is even more confounding. Canadian scientists have dedicated substantial effort to determine the extent of the continental shelf in the Beaufort Sea. Canada faces two problems once it submits its coordinates. First, Canada and the United States have a substantial boundary disagreement as to how to divide the territorial sea and the EEZ in the Beaufort Sea. The disagreement stems over the interpretation of the 1825 Treaty between Russia and the UK, which provided for the drawing of land boundaries between Alaska and Yukon, but made no reference to maritime boundaries. As a result, the Canadians and the Americans dispute how to draw the boundaries for their territorial sea and the EEZ in the Beaufort. The United States contends that the border needs to be drawn at a 90 degree angle to the coastline. The Canadian position is that the maritime boundary is an extension of the land boundary. This disagreement creates a triangle-shaped disputed zone of approximately 6,250 square nautical miles, which may contain substantial oil and gas resources.

This dispute could significantly impact the determination of the Canadian continental shelf in the western Arctic. The starting point of the continental shelf will probably be determined by the tip of the top point of the farthest extent of the EEZ. The disagreement over the boundary dividing the EEZ and territorial sea may lead to a problem in dividing the extended continental shelf.

Further complicating this situation is the fact that the US is not a party to UNCLOS. The Americans cannot formally submit a claim for their continental shelf until they accede to the Convention. As mentioned earlier, the hope is that the American Senate will pass the Convention in the American Congress. Statements by Secretary of State Hillary Clinton suggest that this will be an important priority for the new administration.[19]

Canada faces substantial uncertainty and challenges in determining the limits of its extended continental shelf. Such uncertainty makes it difficult for Canadian officials to prepare for their diplomatic campaign if there is an overlap with the other Arctic claimant states. Canadian efforts to determine its continental shelf may show that Canada's claim is limited geographically and does not extend into either the American, Russian, or Danish areas. It is also possible that Canadian efforts may result in considerable overlap with its three Arctic neighbours. It is doubtful that this issue will be resolved any time before 2020.

Ultimately the issue is one of control. The entire purpose of Canada's effort to determine the coordinates of its Arctic continental shelf is to allow for its future control of the development and exploitation of any resources that might be found. This control will give Canada the right to set the rules as to how the resources are to be developed. It will also give Canada the right to decide if it even wants to develop the resources. It might be that a future Canadian government may decide that it is simply better to leave the resources in the ground, but this will be for Canadians to decide. Consequently, the issue of control of this territory is important.

The Northwest Passage

The other issue that has perplexed Canadians in the Arctic is the Northwest Passage. This has been one of the major irritants in Canada–US relations since 1969. The Canadian position is that the passage is internal Canadian waters, which gives Canada absolute control over all activities within it. The American position is that the passage is a strait used for international navigation. If the Canadian position is correct, then Canada has the right to control all elements of shipping in the passage, including the right of controlling who comes into the passage and who cannot. If the American position is correct, then Canada has only the right to control international shipping in regard to international rules and standards, and has a limited ability to stop shipping.[20]

Canadian scholars suggest that it might, or even should, be possible to work out a deal with the United States on this issue. Some writers have suggested that it should be feasible to work out a deal similar to the St. Lawrence Seaway Agreement in which both states arrange for the joint management of the passage.[21] Others have suggested that as long as Canada can show that it is serious about asserting proper control and therefore maintaining the security of the region, the Americans should respond by not overly asserting their position. In other words, American agreement not to challenge Canada would be exchanged for Canadian protection of the region.

In theory this approach makes sense. However, such hopes were severely damaged in the last days of the George W. Bush administration amidst reports that the United States had been working on

a national Arctic Policy since 2007. To the surprise of most observers, the Bush administration released its policy on 9 January, 2009, literally less than two weeks before the January 20 presidential inauguration of Barack Obama. This National Security Presidential Directive reaffirmed in the strongest terms the American commitment to accede to the UNCLOS to ensure that American interests in the Arctic were protected. However, the Americans also presented one of the most direct statements of their position on the Northwest Passage.

> Freedom of the seas is a top national priority. The Northwest Passage is a strait used for international navigation, and the Northern Sea Route includes straits used for international navigation; the regime of transit passage applies to passage through those straits. Preserving the rights and duties relating to navigation and overflight in the Arctic region supports our ability to exercise these rights throughout the world, including through strategic straits.[22]

The enunciation of the American policy makes it difficult to see how any agreement can be reached unless the new Obama administration moves to repel or replace this directive. But any such movement seems very unlikely. The policy directive does not state anything that is new; it only puts the American position in very stark and direct terms. The Canadian position is further complicated by a policy statement issued by the EU in December 2008. In this statement, the EU was equally clear on its position on the Northwest Passage: while acknowledging the particular environmental needs of the waterways of the Arctic, the EU also affirms that the principle of freedom of navigation through the passage must be maintained.[23]

From a Canadian position it has always been difficult to understand both the American and European positions on the Passage. There have been only three instances where vessels transiting the passage have specifically not sought the Canadian government's permission to do so: the *Manhattan* in 1969 and 1970, and the *Polar Sea* in 1985. All other transits have occurred with the explicit agreement of Canadian authorities. Thus when both the US and the EU maintain that the Northwest Passage is a strait used for international navigation, they speak of a principle and not an existing reality.

What motivates the Americans and the Europeans to oppose the Canadians on this issue? Why do they seem so intent on denying Canada the right to control shipping in what are obviously unique waterways that have not been used for international shipping? Two reasons provide the answer as to why they persist in this position regardless of the damage it might do to their relationship with Canada: the fear of setting a precedent and the anticipation of a substantially larger number of transpolar shipping transits.

The Americans are not necessarily referencing only the Northwest Passage in their discussion about freedom of navigation in their Arctic policy paper. Rather, they are worried about the Straits of Hormuz, Gibraltar, Malacca, and others that are used for international navigation worldwide. The Americans' primary concern is to ensure that the Northwest Passage does not establish a precedent which weakens the principle of free passage through international straits. The driving force behind the Americans' concern in these other straits is both strategic and economic. The Americans are determined to ensure that countries such as Iran do not acquire the right to limit or to restrict their navy's travel through such waters. The second and related objective of the US is to ensure that commercial traffic continues to have the right of unfettered passage. It is once again feared that a country such as Iran may stop oil tankers from entering or exiting the Strait of Hormuz to load off the coast of Saudi Arabia and Kuwait.

The EU has similar interests in ensuring that its naval and commercial vessels also retain navigational freedoms through these waters. But the EU also seems to be interested in the potential future use of the Arctic as a major shipping route. The Commission of the European Communities stated in a 2008 document that:

> EU Member States have the world's largest merchant fleet and many of those ships use transoceanic routes. The melting of sea ice is progressively opening opportunities to navigate on routes through Arctic waters. This could considerably shorten trips from Europe to the Pacific, save energy, reduce emissions, promote trade and diminish pressure on the main transcontinental navigation channels. . . . It is in the EU's interest to explore and improve conditions for gradually introducing Arctic commercial navigation, while promoting stricter safety and environmental standards as well as avoiding detrimental effects. By the same token, Member States and the Community should defend the principle of freedom of navigation and the right of innocent passage in the newly opened routes and areas.[24]

This commercial interest is the basis for the European Union's interest to protect its future Arctic shipping interests.

Where does this leave Canada? Even with a melting Arctic, shipping in the region will still remain extremely challenging. The Canadian side of the Arctic will likely be the last region to experience the elimination of year-round ice. First-year ice will reform in the winter months, limiting shipping to only those vessels that are ice-capable. The summer months will become increasingly ice-free, but communication will remain difficult until additional communication and global positioning satellites are positioned in orbits that accommodate the high latitudes. It is difficult to expect that the northern straits will be similar to all other straits in terms of accessibility, navigation, and communication. The great challenges to navigation well into this century will require different and more powerful forms of regulations and controls than any other waterway. It is clear that in these cases, Canada must retain some form of control.

In addition to the challenges that Canada faces in its attempts to retain control over the Northwest Passage, it is also necessary to consider the unintended results of the American and European position on the Northwest Passage. If the Passage becomes an international strait, the security of the North American Arctic will be compromised in terms of air security and maritime security. Under international law, an international strait also accords the right of overflight to all states. This means that the Russians, who recently reinstituted their long-range Tu-95 (Bear) bomber air patrols in the Arctic, would have the right to overfly the passage if it was eventually determined to be an international strait. This overflight ability allows them to come much farther into North American airspace than ever before. Canada would also be denied the right to stop vessels that it might consider a security risk unless it could demonstrate that the vessel in question was breaking international rules and laws. The problem for the north is that given the widely unpopulated regions that exist, if a vessel was attempting to smuggle any illicit product into the country, it would only have to appear to be following international rules. Canada would not have the right to conduct mandatory inspections or to deny passage if it did not have solid evidence against the vessel.

In the future, countries that might not be friendly to the United States or Canada would also have the right of navigation without being required to ask the Canadian government for permission to transit. What would it mean for Canadian security to have a hostile navy sailing through the passage? Of course states such as Iran have to deal with hostile US and UK navies sailing through the Strait of Hormuz. Thus it is possible to argue that Canada would be in a situation similar to that of Iran. But if that is the case, Canada and the United States would have to ensure that if and when that happens they could provide security for the North American Arctic. Maintaining North American Arctic security is both simple and effective if Canada is understood to have control over the waterway. The same cannot be said if the classification of the Passage changes. It is thus somewhat troublesome to note that the policy positions of Canada's allies will increase the threat to Canadian Arctic security.

Strategic Developments

What are the new strategic realities that are taking shape in the Arctic? What do these developments mean for Canada? It is difficult to fully delineate this issue as these new realities are only now starting to take shape. The Arctic states are beginning to rebuild their northern military capabilities. The major driving force is the recognition that new economic development in the Arctic is going to increase the activity level in the region, but no one can fully anticipate what this new economic activity will look like. It is expected to be substantial. As such, Arctic nations are beginning to prepare so that they are able to respond to new contingencies.

Concern is particularly rising among some Arctic states that Russia is beginning to militarily redeploy to the Arctic. But this concern has yet to translate into a fear that the Russians are an actual threat, especially as none of the Arctic states are willing to acknowledge this potential military threat. Instead, the concern is to ensure that should Russian actions become more threatening, the Arctic states will have the ability to respond if necessary.

An equally nebulous concern is the impact that climate change is expected to have. Most Arctic states have issued statements that the increasingly accessible melting Arctic is expected to facilitate new economic activities. The full nature of these activities is not yet understood. As such, the concern is to be sufficiently prepared. This desire for preparation focuses the attention of most decision-makers—Canadian included—on surveillance and enforcement capabilities. Most officials want improved means of knowing what is happening in the Arctic, and they want to have the ability to respond if unlawful action occurs.

These concerns are accompanied by the growing recognition that the Arctic remains a very expensive region to operate in. As the Arctic states prepare plans to revitalize their security abilities in the Arctic, most recognize that it remains a challenging operational environment. Given the lack of existing infrastructure, any effort to improve both surveillance and enforcement capabilities remains costly. The current economic crisis has only heightened concerns over how an improved Canadian Arctic capability is to be achieved.

A general agreement was reached at the end of the Cold War that the strategic significance of the Arctic had ended and that the need to be concerned about traditional security threats was eliminated. The Soviet northern fleet, with its vast number of nuclear-powered attack and nuclear missile carrying submarines (SSNs and SSBNs), were immediately retired. The collapse of the USSR was so total that the threat posed by these submarines changed overnight from a threat of nuclear war resulting in the destruction of North America (and even the world) to one of a potential Arctic environmental disaster as these vessels were left to rust in northern Russian harbours with the inherent risk of a massive radionuclear spill or accident. It took the direct intervention of the G8 and Norway to provide the Russians with both the funds and the technology to properly dispose of these submarines. The United States Navy also disposed of its older class of submarines, including the Sturgeon class, which was considered to be their best submarine for under-ice operations. Furthermore, the Seawolf class submarines, which were to be the new class of American SSNs, were

scaled back to three vessels. A new and cheaper submarine, the Virginia class, was selected instead, despite the fact that it was not given the same degree of under-ice capability as the Seawolf.[25] The other Arctic nations also reduced the northern element of their own forces. From 1989 to approximately 2002, the northern military capabilities of all the Arctic states were substantially reduced.

There were some important exceptions. One of the most important, which received little attention, was the American decision to place one of two ballistic missile interceptor ground bases in Fort Greely, Alaska, in 2002. This base is now operational, meaning that missiles designed for interception are now in the ground and ready to engage incoming missiles. The location is presumed to be well suited for a missile attack on the US from Asia. Currently, the Americans are supplementing their two bases with additional maritime mobile systems, such as placing anti-ballistic missiles on board ships, and negotiating to place other interceptor sites in countries such as Poland. But with its secured silos placement, Fort Greely ensures that the Arctic will remain a strategic concern for the United States well into the future.

The Canadian effort to maintain military control over its Arctic ended almost as soon as the Cold War ended. Any meaningful military exercises were stopped, and even the sovereignty patrols of the navy and air force were either stopped or reduced to only symbolic levels. The only current land force presence in Canada's Arctic is the Canadian Rangers units. It was not until 1999 that members of the CF seriously reconsidered their role in the Arctic. This was, to a certain degree, the result of the initiative of individual officers who had become concerned about what they perceived to be a changing Arctic security environment.[26] These concerns led to the creation of an interdepartmental (federal and territorial) security work group named the Arctic Security Intergovernmental Working Group

(ASIWG), as well as an internal Department of National Defence (DND) review of its Arctic capabilities. After the terrorist attacks of 9/11, the entire Canadian government began to take security issues much more seriously. In 2002, Canada resumed military training operations in the north.

The short-lived Martin government sought to improve Canada's Arctic security. Its 2005 International Policy Statement, focusing on the expected rise of activity in the north, stated that "[t]he demands of sovereignty and security for the Government could become even more pressing as activity in the North continues to rise,"[27] meaning that Canada will need to increase its ability to act in the north. The Martin government was also developing a domestic policy statement that would provide a Government of Canada position on the north. This statement was an attempt to move away from the traditional approach of department-specific policy and was further aimed to provide a Government of Canada Arctic policy. Referred to as the Northern Strategy, it was to be built on seven pillars or subsections, one of which was "Reinforcing Sovereignty, National Security and Circumpolar Cooperation."[28] However, the document was not finalized before the government's defeat in the 2006 federal election.

The Harper government has increasingly recognized the significance of maintaining a strong presence in the Arctic and has vigorously begun to improve Canada's northern abilities. Northern Watch is a research program dedicated to developing a Canadian-built and designed system that will provide surveillance of the subsurface, surface, and airspace of the Arctic. It is not yet ready for operational status and is still being developed. Canadian scientists have also developed a more advanced program of satellite imagery systems designed to provide space-based surveillance of surface vessels in the Arctic. At the lower end of the technology spectrum, both the Martin and the Harper governments increased the size and the training of the Rangers

units based in the north. The Rangers are a northern militia unit whose primary task is to provide surveillance in the north at the local level. The Rangers are volunteers comprising primarily indigenous peoples, and are particularly skilled observers who can live off the land. All of these initiatives will enable the Canadian government to know who is in its Arctic region and what they are doing, which is the first step in controlling activity in the Canadian north. The Harper government has also made a series of promises to considerably expand Canada's northern capability, including: six to eight Arctic offshore patrol vessels that will be able to sail in first-year ice that is up to one metre thick; a replacement for the Coast Guard's largest and oldest icebreaker, the *Louis St. Laurent*; the construction of a deep-water replenishment site at Nanisivik; new replenishment vessels that will have the capability to operate in first-year ice for the navy; new long-range patrol aircraft to replace the Aurora (CF-140); and the establishment of a northern military training base in Resolute Bay. The 2007 throne speech also emphasized the protection of Arctic sovereignty and security and promised to establish a world-class research station in the Canadian north.[29] If these promises are implemented, Canada will have significantly improved its ability to control activity in its Arctic. However, most of these commitments have not yet moved from promise to reality. There are now signs that the government is backtracking on some of its promises. The program to build the new replenishment vessels, for instance, has been postponed because domestic builders submitted bids that were too high for the government. It remains uncertain what will happen with this program. Likewise there is little discussion of when construction of the Arctic Offshore Patrol Vessel or ice-breaker will begin.

Other Arctic nations are also reviving their military capabilities. From a strategic position, nuclear-powered submarines remain the principal weapon platform. In 2004, both the Russians and then the

Americans took action to rebuild their under-ice capabilities.[30] The Russians have also begun to consider rebuilding their surface fleet capability. Recently the naval commander-in-chief announced the plan to build up their forces to six carrier battle-groups.[31] This announcement has also been accompanied by an increase in operations in the region. The Russians' Arctic sovereignty flights were suspended in 1992, but resumed in the summer of 2007.[32] Using its long-range Tu-95 (Bear) patrol and bomber aircraft, the Russians are now sending out patrols over the Arctic and as far as the Sea of Japan and Cuba. The Russians also resumed Arctic patrols by their surface naval vessels in 2008.[33] As a Russian navy official stated, "[t]he Russian Navy has restored the presence of combat ships of the Northern Fleet in the Arctic region, including in the region of Spitsbergen."[34] The two vessels, the destroyer *Severomorsk* and cruiser *Marshal Ustinov*, also made a point of sailing through several regions that are the subject of ongoing diplomatic disputes between Russia and Norway.

Norway has refocused its entire defence policy on the north. In a series of recent statements, the Norwegian Defence Minister Anne-Grete Strøm-Erichsen has made it clear that Norway recognizes that resources and climate change are bringing new actors to the north. To this end, the most recent Norwegian Defence Policy Review makes it clear that "the Armed Forces play an important role by virtue of their operational capabilities with the emphasis on maintaining a presence and upholding national sovereignty in the North."[35] As a result Norway has been rebuilding its ability to operate in its Arctic region. It has a slightly easier task than the other Arctic states in that its Arctic waters seldom freeze because of the impact of the Gulf Stream. It is in the process of taking possession of five new frigates that are Aegis-capable and also have a very sophisticated anti-submarine capability.[36] The Norwegians have also announced that they will be moving air assets to northern bases and increasing the defence budget. Lastly, they have

also signed a contract to buy 48 F-35 Joint Strike Fighter aircraft in November 2008.[37]

The American military, despite possessing the most vigorous Arctic security apparatus, has also rediscovered the Arctic. While it did decommission older nuclear-powered submarines, the United States maintained and added new submarines to its navy throughout the 1990s and 2000s. The American Coast Guard has been arguing that it needs to build new icebreakers. Right now, there are three icebreakers, but two of them are reaching the end of their operational life.[38] The US also maintains a very strong air wing in Alaska, with three wings of National Guard F-15s (22 aircraft/wing) as well as a number of AWACs (large aircraft that carry advance radar and electronic systems designed to give a very detailed surveillance picture of the region around the aircraft). They are now replacing the F-15 with the newer F-22 Raptors. To support these activities, the numbers of serving personnel remained at about 26,000 in 2005.[39]

In an effort to come to terms with the changing Arctic, the Americans have been engaged in a policy development process since 2008. The US executive branch, led by the Department of State and the National Security Council, reviewed its policies in the Arctic region. The core issues examined by this review were:

1. national security and homeland security;
2. international governance;
3. extended continental shelf and boundary issues;
4. international scientific cooperation;
5. shipping;
6. economic issues, including energy; and
7. environmental protection and conservation of natural resources.[40]

The Bush Administration released the above policy on 9 January 2009 as National Security

Presidential Directive 66. The document makes it clear that national security considerations are the first priority of the United States when it comes to the Arctic. This directive presents five points in its national security and homeland security interests in the Arctic:

1. The United States has broad and fundamental national security interests in the Arctic region and is prepared to operate either independently or in conjunction with other states to safeguard these interests.

2. The United States also has fundamental homeland security interests in preventing terrorist attacks and mitigating those criminal or hostile acts that could increase the United States' vulnerability to terrorism in the Arctic region.

3. The Arctic region is primarily a maritime domain; as such, existing policies and authorities relating to maritime areas continue to apply, including those relating to law enforcement. Human activity in the Arctic region is increasing and is projected to increase further in coming years. This requires the United States to assert a more active and influential national presence to protect its Arctic interests and to project sea power throughout the region.

4. The United States exercises authority in accordance with lawful claims of United States sovereignty, sovereign rights, and jurisdiction in the Arctic region, including sovereignty within the territorial sea, sovereign rights and jurisdiction within the United States exclusive economic zone and on the continental shelf, and appropriate control in the United States contiguous zone.

5. Freedom of the seas is a top national priority. The Northwest Passage is a strait used for international navigation, and the Northern Sea Route includes straits used for international navigation.[41]

Where, then, does this leave Canada in regard to protecting its Arctic security? First, the strategic environment is in flux as Arctic states are improving their northern military capabilities. All of the main Arctic states contend that this is only being done to provide the ability to respond to the expected increase in activity in the Arctic. But it is interesting to note that both Norway and Russia are increasing their Arctic capabilities with weapon systems that are clearly designed to fight and not to act in a Coast Guard-type capability. The Americans are also looking to further develop the strategic nature of their forces. Canada does not face a direct military threat in the Arctic, but the indicators are becoming somewhat worrisome. Why would Canada's neighbours dedicate increasingly substantial resources for the harder edge of their security forces in the region unless they were beginning to see a need? Canada will need to maintain a careful watch on events as they unfold.

Conclusion

The Arctic is changing in so many different ways and with such complexity that it almost seems impossible to comment on how best to protect Canadian Arctic sovereignty and security. Clearly Canadian officials are going to have to make some hard decisions sooner rather than later to ensure that Canada can control its section of the Arctic for the protection of Canadian interests and values.

So how is this to be done? First it needs to be recognized that there is no one set solution to the problem. The rapid and complicated transformation of the Arctic is an ongoing process. Thus the government needs to be thinking in terms of process rather than result. The challenges of the Arctic require government action that transcends any one department. It is currently trendy to use terms such as *whole of government* when talking about efforts to break down departmental silos. The Arctic definitely requires that such silos be broken down. But Canadian Arctic policy needs to go even beyond this. The territorial governments must also be included, as well as the various northern Aboriginal peoples' organizations. But perhaps most important, this process must have direct access to the prime minister. Canadian Arctic policy develops when the prime minister is interested. If not, other priorities quickly refocus the bureaucracy. Thus the creation of a Cabinet committee that is chaired by the prime minister would be one means to ensure that attention on the Arctic is maintained. There might be other means, but the main point is that the prime minister must be continually engaged in the process.

Once the attention of the prime minister is institutionalized, there are three major sets of actions that the Canadian government must follow in order to establish and then maintain control. To a certain degree, both the Martin and the Harper governments already began the process, but the critical point will be sustainability. Historically, Canadian governments have promised a wide array of policy actions only to renege on them when other political and economic issues have arisen. The issue, then, is developing a flexible long-term program that will be maintained. Ultimately, this program needs to provide for the ability to:

1. know what is happening in the Canadian north;
2. enforce Canadian rules and laws; and
3. cooperate with Canada's circumpolar neighbours.

One of the greatest political challenges now is the artificial divide that seems to be developing between Liberal and Conservative Arctic policy. A disturbing trend is emerging whereby the Conservatives are focusing on providing Canada with enforcement and surveillance capabilities while the Liberals traditionally focus on diplomatic initiatives. In keeping with their policy position, the Conservatives eliminated the position of Circumpolar Ambassador and have contentedly followed the diplomatic initiatives of the other Arctic states. Throughout the entire Chrétien era, no discussion was ever undertaken regarding building up Canadian Arctic capabilities. This debate is being increasingly cast in unilateral versus multilateral terms. The Conservatives are perceived as focusing on Canada's military while the Liberals are viewed as focusing on the diplomatic requirements for establishing control. The reality is that both sets of action are required. Canada needs to have strong surveillance and enforcement capabilities to control the new activities that will increasingly be taking place in the Arctic. These capabilities will primarily be the responsibility of the DND, but it also requires the involvement of the Coast Guard and Royal Canadian Mounted Police.

At the same time, Canada cannot act in isolation in the Arctic. It needs to work with its Arctic neighbours in order to develop the international frameworks that will provide both the international rules necessary to protect the Arctic as well as a spirit of cooperation in the region. The new accessibility of the Arctic will bring new actors and activities to the region and it will therefore be necessary to develop a regional set of rules and arrangements for these new activities. These include a coordinated approach to search and rescue, as well as pollution response for environmental accidents that will inevitably occur. It would also be beneficial for the entire region if agreements were reached on future economic activity. A regional approach to the expanding Arctic fisheries would head off differences before they arise over the issue of fishing new stocks as they move north. Likewise a regional approach could be a means of avoiding the sovereignty challenges surrounding the issue of international shipping. If the Arctic nations could agree on the standards for ship construction and operation and crew requirements in Arctic waters, then Canada could possibly achieve the control it seeks over the expected shipping in Canadian northern waters.

The greatest international challenge facing Canada may be the reality that two of its Arctic neighbours are the United States and Russia. The United States is Canada's most important trading partner and ally, and the former USSR, at various times throughout Canada's recent history, was both an important ally and a most dangerous enemy. Throughout the Cold War period, both the United States and Russia's importance and significance to Canada was amplified by their geographic location as Arctic neighbours. Now that the Arctic is warming and becoming more accessible the dynamics of this relationship are about to become even more important.

Canada must work with both the US and Russia in the region, but the problem is that they have very different Arctic visions. The Russians see the Arctic as the key to their future economic prosperity, understanding that the undeveloped oil and gas resources in their Arctic region will provide them with the economic capability to regain their great power status. They are also aware that, from a strategic perspective, the north is their primary access to the world's oceans. During the past few years, the Russians have clearly become more assertive in their foreign policy, including their policy in the Arctic. This does not mean a return to the Cold War, but it does signify that the period of complete cooperation of the 1990s has ended. Canada can still expect to work with the Russians, but this needs to be tempered by a more realistic framework. The Russians will not cooperate simply for the benefit of cooperation. Rather, it will be increasingly necessary for Canada to show the Russians why cooperation is in their interest. At the same time, when Canadian interests do not intersect with Russian interests, the Canadian government needs to be prepared for an increasingly assertive Russian response. Such an incident would occur if Canada decides to claim any part of the Arctic continental shelf that has been claimed by the Russians.

If this happens, the Russian government's reaction will set the tone for future Canadian–Russian relations. If the reaction is tempered and diplomatic, Canada should seize the moment by trying to further engage the Russians in other means of cooperation. If the reaction is more belligerent, then Canada may need to garner support from its other Arctic neighbours in order to maintain its claim.

Canada's Arctic relationship with the United States will also continue to develop. The Americans are increasingly aware of the transformations that will increase the Arctic's importance. Canada's key challenge will be to minimize, if not resolve, the various disputes over boundaries and sovereignty in the North American Arctic. The issues of control of international shipping through the Northwest Passage and the division of the Beaufort Sea are challenging. However, the two states must find ways to prevent these issues from contaminating future cooperation. Ultimately, the two states must find ways to cooperate in the Arctic since it is in their mutual interest to do so. Both states need to ensure that the new activities in the Arctic are controlled in such a manner that environmental protection remains a core requirement. At the same time, it is also in the interests of both states to ensure that those who call the north home benefit fully from the forthcoming activities.

Thus Canada needs to pay special attention to its relationship with Russia and the United States. While many of the issues can be addressed in a bilateral fashion, the time has arrived for Canada to renew its efforts to strengthen the multilateral forums in the region. The Arctic Council, which Canada will soon chair, is at the centre of this. Canada can serve the interests of the region and itself by dedicating its time as chair to strengthening the council. First, Canada needs to avoid directly undermining the council. For example, the Ilulissat meeting in May 2008 of the five Arctic continental shelf claimant states should have taken place within the Arctic Council. While Iceland, Sweden, and Finland do not have claims, each state will be affected by what happens within the areas claimed by others. Likewise, the permanent participants also have interests in these regions. Yet these members of the council were excluded from this very important meeting. Second, Canada should lead the way in creating a more powerful support system for the council. Relying on each member state to simply volunteer support is not working. Canada should establish some form of a permanent support body. Third, Canada should also take the initiative to work out a series of regional agreements to deal with issues such as standards for international shipping, fishing, tourism, environmental protection, and so on. Canadian interests are best served by the creation of such agreements now, and not later when many other competing interests will seek to be included.

Ultimately, Canada needs to recognize what it wants its Arctic to look like in the emerging future. The time when lip service could be paid to the north is over. The forces of transformation are creating a new era in which the world will be coming to the entire Arctic region. Canada can choose to simply react to the new changes or it can take the lead and recognize that there are both dangers and opportunities. The dangers can be mitigated by thoughtful preparation. The opportunities can best be taken advantage of by allocating the necessary resources to promote and protect Canadian interests and values.

Questions for Review

1. What are the different variables that make up the concept of sovereignty?
2. What distinguishes human security from traditional security?
3. How do the concepts of sovereignty and security apply to Canada's Arctic?
4. Explain the three forces that are changing the Arctic.

Suggested Readings

Fossum, John Erik, and Stéphane Roussel, guest eds. 2010. *The Arctic is Hot, Part 1. International Journal* 65, 4 (special issue – Autumn).

Griffiths, Franklyn, Rob Huebert, and P. Whitney Lackenbauer. 2011. *Canada and the Changing Arctic: Sovereignty,* *Security, and Stewardship.* Waterloo, ON: Wilfrid Laurier University Press.

Huebert, Rob. 2009. *Canadian Arctic Sovereignty and Security in a Transforming Circumpolar World. Foreign Policy for Canada's Tomorrow,* No. 4. Toronto: Canadian International Council.

Notes

1. Alan James, *Sovereign Statehood: The Basis of International Society* (London: Allen and Unwin, 1986).
2. R.R. Churchill and A.V. Lowe, *The Law of the Sea*, 3rd ed. (Manchester: Manchester University Press, 2002).
3. For the best collection of articles that address the entire discussion on the nature of security see: *Strategy in the Contemporary World*, 2nd ed., ed. John Baylis, James Wirtz, Eliot Cohen, and Colin S. Gray (Oxford: Oxford University Press, 2007); and *Contemporary Security Studies*, ed. Alan Collins (Oxford: Oxford University Press, 2007).
4. *Human Security and the New Diplomacy: Protecting People, Promoting Peace*, ed. Rob McRae and Don Hubert (Montreal and Kingston: McGill-Queen's University Press, 2001).
5. Thomas Homer-Dixon, *Environment, Security and Violence* (Princeton, NJ: Princeton University Press, 1999).
6. *Northern Lights Against POPs: Combatting Toxic Threats in the Arctic*, ed. David Downie and Terry Fenge (Montreal and Kingston: McGill-Queen's University Press, 2003).
7. The story of their association with the Hell's Angels and drugs are alleged activities since they were never proven to have engaged in such actions. CBC, "'Wild Vikings' land in Cambridge Bay jail," CBC News, 30 August 2007.
8. See *Arctic Climate Impact Assessment (ACIA), Impacts of a Warming Arctic* (Scientific Report) (Cambridge: Cambridge University Press, 2004); and Rhéal Séguin,

"Scientists predict seasonal ice-free Arctic by 2015," *The Globe and Mail*, 12 December 2008.

9. ACIA, Impacts of a Warming Arctic, 1011.

10. Anne Casselman, "Will the opening of the Northwest Passage transform global shipping anytime soon?" *Scientific American*, 10 November 2008. Available at www.sciam. com/article.cfm?id=opening-of-northwest-passage.

11. Kenneth J. Bird et al., "Circum-Arctic resource appraisal; estimates of undiscovered oil and gas north of the Arctic Circle," U.S. Geological Survey Fact Sheet 2008-3049 (2008). Available at http://pubs.usgs.gov/fs/2008/3049/.

12. For a more complete history of the development of Canadian policy see Rob Huebert, "Canada and the changing international Arctic: At the crossroads of cooperation and conflict," pp. 77–106 in Frances Abele et al., eds., *Northern Exposure: Peoples, Powers and Prospects for Canada's North* (Montreal: IRPP, 2009).

13. "The Ilulissat Declaration," Arctic Ocean Conference, Ilulissat, Greenland, 27–29 May 2008. Available at www. oceanlaw.org/downloads/arctic/Ilulissat_Declaration.pdf.

14. UN Division for Ocean Affairs and Law of the Sea, "Chronological lists of ratifications of, accessions and successions to the Convention and the related Agreements as at 3 October 2014." Available at www.un.org/Depts/los/reference_files/chronological_lists_of_ratifications.htm.

15. Barents Observer, "Russia sends Navy vessels to Spitsbergen," 15 July 2008. Available at www.barentsobserver.com/russia-sends-navy-vessels-to-spitsbergen.4497720-58932.html.

16. Doug Struck, "Russia's Deep-Sea Flag-Planting at North Pole Strikes a Chill in Canada," *Washington Post*, 7 August 2007. Available at www.washingtonpost.com/wp-dyn/content/article/2007/08/06/AR2007080601369.html.

17. Donat Pharand, *Canada's Arctic Waters in International Law* (Cambridge: Cambridge University Press, 1988).

18. "The Ilulissat Declaration."

19. Sylvie Lanteaume, "US 'committed' to ratifying Law of Sea Convention: Clinton," 6 April 2009. Available at www. spacedaily.com/reports/US_committed_to_ratifying_Law_of_Sea_Convention_Clinton_999.html.

20. Donat Pharand, "The Arctic waters and the Northwest Passage: A final revisit," *Ocean Development and International Law* 38, 1-2 (January 2007).

21. Brian Flemming, *Canada–US Relations in the Arctic: A Neighbourly Proposal* (Calgary: Canadian Defence and Foreign Affairs Institute, December 2008); Donald McRae, "Arctic Sovereignty? What is at Stake," *Behind the Headlines* 64, 1 (January 2007).

22. White House, National Security Presidential Directive/NSPD 66 and Homeland Security Presidential Directive/HSPD 25—Arctic Region Policy, 9 January 2009.

23. Commission of the European Communities, Communication from the Commission to the European Parliament and the Council: The European Union and the Arctic Region

24. Commission of the European Communities, The European Union and the Arctic Region, 8.

25. Rob Huebert, "Renaissance in Canadian Arctic Security?" *Canadian Military Journal* 6, 4 (2005–2006): 17–29.

26. Department of National Defence, *Canada's International Policy Statement: A Role of Pride and Influence in the World—Defence* (Ottawa, 2005): 17.

27. Canadian Arctic Resource Committee (CARC), *Northern Perspectives* 30, 1 (Winter 2006): 2. Available at www.carc.org/pubs/v30no1/CARC_Northrn_Perspctves_Winter_2006.pdf.

28. Government of Canada, "Protecting Canada's future," Speech from the Throne, 19 November 2008. Available at http://pm.gc.ca/eng/news/2008/11/19/speech-throne-protecting-canadas-future.

29. "SSN-774 Virginia-class New Attack Submarine [NSSN] Centurion," Globalsecurity.org, 5 September 2008. Available at www.globalsecurity.org/military/systems/ship/ssn-774.htm.

30. "Russian navy promises new nuclear subs with new strategic missiles," Bellona, 6 October 2008. Available at www.bellona.org/news/news_2008/new_nuke_subs.

31. Defense Strategies, "Russia plans to deploy 6 carrier battle-groups by 2025," 23 December 2013. Available at http://defensetiger.blogspot.ca/2013/12/russia-plans-to-deploy-six-carrier.html.

32. BBC News, "Russia restarts Cold War patrols," BBC News, 17 August 2007. Available at http://news.bbc.co.uk/2/hi/europe/6950986.stm.

33. Russian Federal Ministry of Defence, "Russian Navy Resumes Presence in Arctic Area," News Details, 14 July 2008. Originally retrieved from www.mil.ru/eng/1866/12078/details/index.shtml?id=47433.

34. Associated Foreign Press, "Russian navy boasts combat presence in Arctic," Canada.com, 14 July 2008. Available at www.canada.com/topics/news/world/story.html?id=3572ff95-9a88-4dd8-944f-58af497c3fa6.

35. Norwegian Ministry of Defence, *Norwegian Defence 2008* (Oslo, 2008). Available at www.regjeringen.no/upload/FD/Dokumenter/Fakta2008_eng.pdf.

36. Endre Lunde, "Norway's new Nansen Class frigates: Capabilities and controversies," *Defence Industry Daily*, 7 June 2006. Available at www.defenseindustrydaily.com/norways-new-nansen-class-frigates-capabilities-and-controversies-02329/.

37. Doug Mellgren, "Norway picks US fighters to replace aging fleet," Foxnews.com, 20 November 2008. Available at www.foxnews.com/printer_friendly_wires/2008Nov20/0,4675,EUNorwayJointStrikeFighter,00.html.

38. These numbers were provided directly to the author by a senior American military official in an open briefing in Alaska on 10 March 2005.

39. Ronald O'Rourke, *Coast Guard Polar Icebreaker Modernization: Background, Issues, and Options for Congress—CRS Report for Congress* RL 34391 (Washington: Congressional Research Service, 26 February 2008). Available at https://www.uscg.mil/history/docs/CRS/2008CRSIcebreakerRL34391.pdf; and Committee on the Assessment of U.S. Coast Guard Polar Icebreaker Roles and Future Needs, National Research Council, *Polar Icebreakers in a Changing World: An Assessment*

of U.S. Needs (Washington, DC: National Academies Press, 2007). See http://books.nap.edu/catalog.php?record_id=11753.

40. Margaret F. Hayes, Director, Office of Oceans and Polar Affairs, Department of State, "Arctic Policy—Speech to Arctic Parliamentarians on Aspects of U.S. Arctic Policy," Fairbanks, Alaska, 13 August 2008.

41. White House, NSPD 66 and HSPD 25, 2–3.

Selected Bibliography

Axworthy, Lloyd. 1997. "Canada and Human Security: The Need for Leadership," *International Journal* 52, 2 (Spring): 183–96.

Barry, Donald, and Duane Bratt. 2008. "Defense Against Help: Explaining Canada–U.S. Security Relations," *American Review of Canadian Studies* 38, 1 (Spring): 63–89.

Bell, Stewart. 2004. *Cold Terror: How Canada Nurtures and Exports Terrorism Around the World.* Toronto: Wiley.

Bland, Douglas L., ed. 2004. *Canada Without Armed Forces?* Montreal and Kingston: McGill-Queen's University Press.

Bland, Douglas L., and Sean M. Maloney. 2004. *Campaigns for International Security: Canada's Defence Policy at the Turn of the Century.* Montreal and Kingston: McGill-Queen's University Press.

Bratt, Duane. 1999. "Nice-Making and Canadian Peacekeeping," *Canadian Foreign Policy* 6, 3 (Spring): 73–84.

———. 2006. *The Politics of CANDU Exports.* Toronto: University of Toronto Press.

Buckley, Brian. 2000. *Canada's Early Nuclear Policy: Fate, Chance, and Character.* Montreal and Kingston: McGill-Queen's University Press.

Cameron, Maxwell A., Robert J. Lawson, and Brian W. Tomlin, eds. 1998. *To Walk Without Fear: The Global Movement to Ban Landmines.* Don Mills, ON: Oxford University Press.

Carroll, Michael K. 2009. *Pearson's Peacekeepers: Canada and the United Nations Emergency Force, 1956–67.* Vancouver: UBC Press.

Clearwater, John. 1998. *Canadian Nuclear Weapons: The Untold Story of Canada's Cold War Arsenal.* Toronto: Dundurn.

Coates, Ken S., P. Whitney Lackenbauer, William R. Morrison, and Greg Poelzer. 2008. *Arctic Front: Defending Canada in the Far North.* Toronto: Thomas Allen.

Dallaire, Roméo. 2003. *Shake Hands with the Devil: The Failure of Humanity in Rwanda.* Toronto: Random House.

Dawson, Grant. 2007. *"Here is Hell": Canada's Engagement in Somalia.* Vancouver: UBC Press.

Dewitt, David B., and David Leyton-Brown, eds. 1995. *Canada's International Security Policy.* Scarborough, ON: Prentice-Hall.

Edgar, Alistair D., and David G. Haglund. 1995. *The Canadian Defence Industry in the New Global Environment.* Montreal and Kingston: McGill-Queen's University Press.

English, Allan D. 2004. *Understanding Military Culture: A Canadian Perspective.* Montreal and Kingston: McGill-Queen's University Press.

Ehrhart, Hans-Georg, and Charles C. Pentland, eds. 2009. *The Afghanistan Challenge: Hard Realities and Strategic Choices.* Montreal and Kingston: McGill-Queen's University Press.

Gammer, Nicholas. 2001. *From Peacekeeping to Peacemaking: Canada's Response to the Yugoslav Crisis.* Montreal and Kingston: McGill-Queen's University Press.

Granatstein, J.L. 2004. *Who Killed the Canadian Military?* Toronto: HarperCollins.

———. 2007. *Whose War Is It? How Canada Can Survive in the Post-9/11 World.* Toronto: Harper Collins.

Granatstein, J.L., and David Stafford. 1990. *Spy Wars: Espionage and Canada from Gouzenko to Glasnost.* Toronto: Key Porter Books.

Griffiths, Franklyn, Rob Huebert, and P. Whitney Lackenbauer. 2011. *Canada and the Changing Arctic: Sovereignty, Security, and Stewardship.* Waterloo, ON: Wilfrid Laurier University Press.

Hayes, Geoffrey, and Mark Sedra. 2008. *Afghanistan: Transition under Threat.* Waterloo, ON: Wilfrid Laurier University Press.

Hillier, Rick. 2009. *A Soldier First: Bullets, Bureaucrats and the Politics of War.* Toronto: Harper Collins.

Jockel, Joseph T. 1994. *Canada and International Peacekeeping*. Washington: Center for Strategic and International Studies.

———. 1999. *The Canadian Forces: Hard Choices, Soft Power*. Toronto: Canadian Institute of Strategic Studies.

Laxer, James. 2008. *Mission of Folly: Canada and Afghanistan*. Toronto: Between the Lines.

Legault, Albert. 1999. *Canada and Peacekeeping: Three Major Debates*. Clementsport, NS: Canadian Peacekeeping Press.

Legault, Albert, and Michel Fortmann. 1992. *A Diplomacy of Hope: Canada and Disarmament, 1945–1988*, trans. Derek Ellington. Montreal and Kingston: McGill-Queen's University Press.

Mackenzie, Lewis. 1993. *Peacekeeper: The Road to Sarajevo*. Vancouver: Douglas and McIntyre.

Morrison, Alex, ed. 1992. *A Continuing Commitment: Canada and North Atlantic Security*. Toronto: Canadian Institute of Strategic Studies.

Morton, Desmond. 1999. *A Military History of Canada: From Champlain to Kosovo*. Toronto: McClelland and Stewart.

———. 2003. *Understanding Canadian Defence*. Toronto: Penguin.

Nossal, Kim Richard. 1994. *Rain Dancing: Sanctions in Canadian and Australian Foreign Policy*. Toronto: University of Toronto Press.

Plamondon, Aaron. 2009. *The Politics of Procurement: Military Acquisitions in Canada and the Sea King Helicopter*. Vancouver: UBC Press.

Rempel, Roy. 2006. *Dreamland: How Canada's Pretend Foreign Policy Has Undermined Sovereignty*. Toronto: Dundurn.

Roach, Kent. 2003. *September 11: Consequences for Canada*. Montreal and Kingston: McGill-Queen's University Press.

Sloan, Elinor C. 2005. *Security and Defence in the Terrorist Era: Canada and North America*. Montreal and Kingston: McGill-Queen's University Press.

Smith, Graeme. 2013. *The Dogs are Eating Them Now: Our War in Afghanistan*. Toronto: Knopf.

Spooner, Kevin A. 2009. *Canada, the Congo Crisis, and UN Peacekeeping, 1960–1964*. Vancouver: UBC Press.

Stein, Janice Gross, and Eugene Lang. 2007. *The Unexpected War: Canada in Kandahar*. Toronto: Viking.

Windsor, Lee, and David Charters. 2010. *Kandahar Tour: The Turning Point in Canada's Afghan Mission*. Toronto: Wiley and Sons.

Trade and Other Economic Issues

Until the last two decades only a small number of academics focused on Canada's foreign trade and economic policy. The end of the Cold War, the negotiation of the Canada–United States Free Trade Agreement (CUFTA), the North American Free Trade Agreement (NAFTA), the creation of the World Trade Organization (WTO), the prominence of the G7/8-G20, the stagnated Doha Round, and the failure of the Multilateral Agreement on Investment (MAI) all contributed to increased interest and awareness in this policy area. The nature of trade and investment also changed during this period. Specifically, Canada faced new challenges related to the relevance of non-traditional issues, such as services, subsidies, labour, and the environment. The increasing fluidity of financial capital and the intrusiveness of these commitments into areas of domestic policy space also made it increasingly difficult for federal and provincial officials to respond to these changes.

Recent events continue to highlight the need to better understand Canada's role in the global political economy. The ongoing global financial crisis, the rise and fall of the Canadian dollar, the signing of the Canada–European Comprehensive Economic and Trade Agreement (CETA), participation in Trans-Pacific Partnership (TPP) negotiations, and the pursuit of other trade agreements with South Korea and India (among others), all make it clear that Canada is potentially vulnerable to international economic developments. In some cases, however, the Canadian government continues to assert its influence in response to these challenges. As Paul Heinbecker notes in Chapter 12, Canada has a long history of leadership in the G8 and G20 forums, and most recently hosted both summits in 2010. In 2013, Canada's minister of international trade, Ed Fast, also presented the Global Markets Action Plan, calling for a new strategy to align Canadian trade, development, and foreign policy objectives to advance commercial interests in various markets. Four prominent authors with extensive background in trade and economic policy will address many of these issues in Part Five.

Michael Hart begins with a provocative argument designed to move Canada to a "post-mercantilist trade and productivity agenda." First published for the C.D. Howe Institute, this chapter highlights declining trade and productivity performance in Canada. Hart makes it clear that the only option is to adapt existing trade and investment practices to better adjust to ever deepening global integration. The solution is not more international agreements. Instead, Hart argues, Canada should act unilaterally and remove barriers and restrictions hampering trade, including procurement practices, subsidies, anti-dumping and countervailing regimes, supply management, excessive regulatory rules in specific sectors, and restrictions on foreign ownership. This will ensure an increase in trade and productivity for Canada but will also increase the likelihood of successfully completing other ongoing trade negotiations, such as the TPP.

Stephen McBride, on the other hand, questions Canada's handling of the global economic crisis. He begins by noting various academic perspectives of Canada in the international community and Ottawa's tendency to adopt both bilateral and multilateral approaches to economic policy. During the ongoing crisis, however, the federal government initially adopted a perspective of denial, which was soon followed by an attempt to minimize the significance of these developments for Canada. When Canada did act, it was to pursue bilateral solutions related to procurement and the automobile industry. Canadian options were also limited due to the entrenched neo-liberal approach to economic policy in Canada. As a result, McBride argues, the financial crisis highlighted Ottawa's limited options in matters of foreign economic policy, especially when dealing with the much stronger United States. He does, however, offer hope that other Canadian governments, of a "different ideological persuasion," might pursue different options to respond to economic problems in the future.

Elizabeth Smythe adds to the discussion by focusing on changes to Canada's foreign and domestic investment policies. The first shift in focus resulted from an increase in Canadian foreign investment abroad to non-OECD countries, which created pressure on Ottawa to seek greater protection for investors abroad. Initially, Canada pursued new investment rules within the framework of the WTO, but stiff opposition from developing states limited the possibility of creating an extensive investment regime in that forum. In addition, the last decade represented a shift in the origin of investment in Canada, especially in the resource sector, from countries with vastly different legal and corporate governance models, most notably from Asia. After allowing the two controversial takeovers of Nexen and Petronas, the Harper government indicated that further deals would be denied. Ultimately, investment remains a highly sensitive policy issue in Canada, although Ottawa has demonstrated greater autonomy in influencing domestic rules and regulations, as opposed to similar objectives at the international level.

Finally, Duane Bratt explores the potential emergence of an "energy triangle" for Canadian exports. In doing so, Bratt challenges the long-standing "continental" reality of trade in this sector where, historically, over 99 per cent of Canada's oil, gas, and electricity was shipped to the United States. Not surprisingly, a great deal of infrastructure, in the form of pipelines and electricity lines, was created over the years to facilitate the export of Canadian energy. Despite this, Bratt points to the emergence of China as a challenger to this continentalist legacy. China's increasing demands for energy and increasing pressure from environmental groups in the United States each increase the possibility of shifting Canadian exports. Ongoing challenges, however, include a lack of infrastructure, as well as the time and geographic distance, to transport and ship oil and gas to China. Added to this are domestic concerns associated with Chinese foreign investment in the Canadian oil and gas industry.

22 Breaking Free: A Post-mercantilist Trade and Productivity Agenda for Canada

Michael Hart

Key Terms

General Agreement on Tariffs and Trade (1948)   World Trade Organization (1995)

Notwithstanding Canada's many advantages, we remain very concerned about the continuing instability of the global economy of which we are a part. The problems afflicting Europe—and for that matter the United States—are not only challenging today but, in my judgment, threaten to be even greater problems in the future.

Having said that, each nation has a choice to make. Western nations, in particular, face a choice of whether to create the conditions for growth and prosperity, or to risk long-term economic decline.

In every decision—or failure to decide—we are choosing our future right now. And, as we all know, both from the global crises of the past few years, and from past experience in our own countries, easy choices now mean fewer choices later. Canada's choice will be, with clarity and urgency, to seize and to master our future, to be a model of confidence, growth, and prosperity in the twenty-first century.

— Prime Minister Stephen Harper, Davos, Switzerland, January 2012

The prime minister's call to world leaders at the 2012 World Economic Forum in Davos, Switzerland,[1] provides much food for thought. His words echoed similar calls in the 1940s to deal with a world economy devastated first by global depression and then by a Second World War.

Today's circumstances might not be as dire as they were then, but there is much to be learned from the response of world leaders at that time: the construction of a global economic regime that stood the test of time in underpinning much of the growth and prosperity that followed. Then as now, the interconnected nature of national economies was an important part of the challenge facing world leaders, and global trade rules were an integral part of the response.

The system of trade rules and procedures worked out and applied in the period from the founding of the **General Agreement on Tariffs and Trade** (GATT) in 1948 through the establishment of the **World Trade Organization** (WTO) in 1995 embodied both sound economic goals and sensible political procedures to achieve them. That system of rules suited well the political economy of the postwar years. By the end of the first decade of the twenty-first century, however, the regime appeared to be proving inadequate to the challenges facing the global economy. To that end, Prime Minister Harper's call to action suggests a need for some new thinking about trade policy to take account of changing patterns of production and cross-border exchange, which largely reflect the positive impact of the GATT-based trade regime.

As a share of global production, trade in goods alone quadrupled in volume over the second half of the twentieth century. The last 20 years of the century, in particular, saw a quantum leap in global integration. Trade historian Douglas Irwin calculates, for example, that US merchandise *exports* as a share of merchandise *production* grew from 15 per cent in 1970 to nearly 40 per cent in 1999, even though the share of merchandise trade to gross domestic product (GDP) grew much more modestly, largely because of the growth of services production as a share of GDP (Irwin 2005, 8).

In Canada, the exports of goods in 1999 represented 125 per cent of the value of goods production, consistent with the higher level of imports in Canadian exports and the much more export-intensive nature of production in Canada. The comparable figure for 1970 was 65 per cent, suggesting a similar rise in the export intensity of the economy. The growth of Canada's export intensity reached its zenith, however, in 2000. Since then, trade as a share of Canadian economic activity and as Canada's share of world exports (see Figure 22.1) have both steadily declined, as trade with the United States and most other traditional markets has stagnated. Mark Carney, the governor of the Bank of Canada, recently observed that, "[s]ince 2000, Canada's export growth was almost 5 percentage points slower than global export growth on average per year. Our share of the world export market fell from about 4.5 percent to about 2.5 percent and our manufactured-goods export market share has been cut in half. Consistent with this drop, employment in Canada's manufacturing sector has fallen by more than 20 percent, representing nearly half a million jobs" (Carney 2012). Carney concluded that three factors have contributed to Canada's export malaise: waning competitiveness due to changes in the exchange rate, wages, and relative productivity; the failure of Canadian firms to adapt with sufficient dispatch to changing global demand; and a lack of focus by Canadian firms on the best markets.

Canada's experience is not unique. Mature trade relationships have weakened globally while new economic relationships remain fragile. Efforts to address the growing pains of emerging global trade patterns at the WTO have proven disappointing and mired in the thought patterns and negotiating habits of an earlier era. Bilateral and regional efforts have been more interesting, but even they have been hampered by mandates that look too much to the past rather than to the future, including in Canada.

Many of the assumptions upon which the trade regime was built have become difficult to sustain. Rather than the original system of rules designed to govern trade in goods among 23 autonomous national economies, the much more ambitious WTO was designed to address frictions emerging from the exchange of goods, services, capital, and intellectual property rights among 155 increasingly interdependent economies, with a further 33 countries in the process of negotiating their accession. More and more firms are now located in more than one jurisdiction—often in many more. In addition to the multilateral GATT/ WTO regime, governments have negotiated hundreds of complementary bilateral and regional arrangements.

Ultimately, the global trade regime will need to be rethought at the multilateral level and brought into line with the reality of a much more integrated and interdependent world. Canada can exercise leadership in working toward that objective, but there is also much that Canada can do on its own to bring its policies and practices into line with new realities.[2]

Canada's declining trade performance has been matched by an equally anemic productivity performance. In many ways, trade and productivity are inextricably linked; together, they are the key determinants of prosperity. The transformation of Canadian trade, productivity, and investment

Per cent change in share of world exports, 2000 to 2010

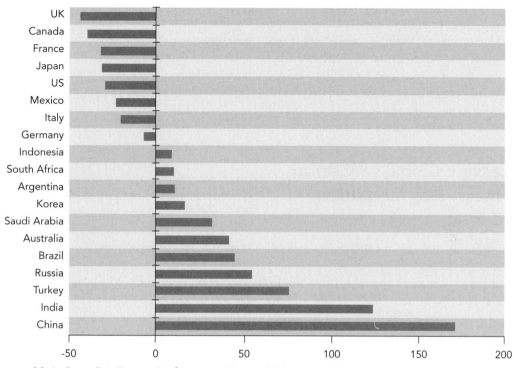

Figure 22.1 Canada's Export Performance Second Worst in G20

Source: Carney (2012, p. 4).

patterns in the 1980s and 1990s flowed not only from more liberal terms of access to the US market, but also from domestic policy measures as well as new technologies and industrial strategies. The boost to Canadian productivity that flowed from the reforms of the 1980s, however, had worked its way through the economy by the end of the 1990s. Since then, both trade and productivity have stagnated.

To revitalize Canadian trade and improve Canada's productivity performance, Canadians will have to be prepared to address remaining barriers to greater global engagement. A concerted effort to address the effect of dated, dysfunctional, and intrusive border administration, the remnants of the inward-looking regulatory state, the haphazard process leading to cross-border regulatory convergence,

and the frail institutional capacity to govern integration will be critical to improving trade with the United States. More strategic, cooperative policymaking to address investment, intellectual property rights, labour, services, and other economic transactions will be an important determinant of Canadians' ability to reap greater benefits from deeper global integration, particularly with the rapidly developing economies of Northeast and Southeast Asia.

Although the trade policy of the past might have reached the point of diminishing returns, the challenges that remain are amenable to resolution through a combination of domestic reforms and intergovernmental negotiations. In this chapter, I argue that progress on these issues requires a better understanding of the nature of modern production and exchange, the changing patterns of Canadian trade and investment, and the barriers, both domestic and international, to gaining greater advantage from deepening global integration. Following a discussion of these factors, I conclude with an overview of the trade and productivity-related policy issues that need to be addressed and the benefits that should flow from their successful resolution.

The New Global Industrial Context: Fragmentation and Integration

Starting in the late 1970s, traditional international exchange gradually gave way to a much more integrated kind, with more and more cross-border transactions taking place within firms, among related parties, or within integrated networks. Global competition, scientific and technological breakthroughs, and increasing consumer sophistication shortened the product cycle and placed a premium on quality, manufacturing fluidity, and innovation. As a result, many more goods now traded internationally are parts and components, as firms have sliced up the value chain and located discrete activities in the most congenial locations. Production has been reorganized to serve much wider markets, the range of goods and services that are exchanged internationally has widened considerably, and capital and technology move more freely to create value in optimum locations. The vertically integrated firms of the first four postwar decades have given way to much more flexible, horizontally organized enterprises and networks.[3]

Three basic catalysts were critical to the acceleration of this new phase of globalization: the steady, GATT-based liberalization of trade and investment among industrialized countries after the Second World War, the more recent but rapid industrialization and liberalization of the post-Soviet and more advanced developing countries, and the impact of technological breakthroughs that have brought down the costs of transportation, communication, and information processing. The impact of these three factors proved mutually reinforcing and cumulative.

The effective market today is global, as is the organization of production. The United States in the nineteenth century—and the European Union and, to a lesser extent, Canada in the closing years of the twentieth century—saw a need to forge rules and governance structures consonant with the emergence of larger markets and more widely integrated production strategies. These efforts focused on divergent regulatory regimes that artificially segmented markets and frustrated the achievement of the benefits of wider markets and more efficient production structures. Today, although both markets and production have gone global, governance remains largely national or regional in scope and reach.

East Asia has emerged as the prime site for locating labour-intensive assembly and related activities. The process of increasing value through disaggregation and rebundling is in many ways the key to understanding the rapid growth of that region. No other countries embraced the benefits of these new production patterns more enthusiastically than those in East Asia. They provided the means by which economic reforms initiated in the late 1970s could be harnessed to bring development to large parts of Asia and its huge labour pool. More recently, India has become the favoured place for services inputs, to take advantage of its wealth of information technology professionals and English-speaking, well-educated workers. Its contribution began with low-value-added activities, such as back-office transactions and call centres, but it has expanded steadily to include software programming, engineering, design, accounting, legal and medical advice, and a broad array of other professional services.

Systematic data on the extent of this fragmentation and integration are difficult to find, in part because official statistics cannot capture the full value of cross-border service links or the input of services provided through proprietary and other networks, whether done in-house, outsourced locally, or outsourced internationally. Statistical agencies have yet to devise a reliable and systematic way of counting the value of, for example, US design, engineering, and marketing in a computer assembled in China from components manufactured in various locations in East Asia. In a world in which tariffs are increasingly unimportant, customs officials are less interested in the origin or foreign-value-added of a particular transaction, and are content to record a product's final transaction price and country of export. The data they supply to statistical agencies often severely overstate the value contributed by the last country of export and undervalue the diverse inputs from other countries (Maurer 2011). A decade ago, Alexander Yeats, by analyzing data for selected industries and extrapolating the results more widely, estimated that a third or more of world trade was made up of parts and components (2001, 108–43); the proportion has grown since then.

From a policy perspective, governments are particularly interested in the intersection of firm-specific and location-specific value. Firms are now less constrained in their choice of location by geography and policy, and seek to enhance value by spatially dispersing a wide range of discrete activities. Governments, in the interest of attracting value-added activities to their location-specific jurisdictions, now compete in promoting policy settings that are congenial to increasingly mobile slices of production by removing barriers and providing positive incentives. In this quest, they are learning that, although the trade agreements of the past might have been critical to providing the framework of rules that initially promoted fragmentation and integration, they are no longer sufficient.

Canada–US Cross-border Integration

The integration that increasingly characterizes the global economy has a longer history at the bilateral Canada–US level. In an earlier era, proximity disposed Canadians to develop trade and investment dependence on the US market and US capital, on which both the exploitation of Canada's storehouse of raw materials and the establishment of miniature-replica branch plants depended. Indeed, Canada continues to exhibit a high level of both production and consumption dependence on the US economy.

Cross-border integration's earliest modern manifestation involved the automotive industry. A unique set of circumstances at the time, including common ownership and integrated labour unions, disposed auto firms to develop cross-border production patterns, to which the Canadian and US governments responded with an auto pact that removed policy disincentives to integration. Much of what is now commonplace was pioneered in the Canada–US auto sector: in-house fragmentation and outsourcing on a continental, rather than a national, basis, followed by out-of-house cross-border fragmentation. The successful introduction of lean, just-in-time production techniques, developed in Japan and introduced in North America in the 1980s, further accelerated this fragmentation process.

Since the implementation of the Canada–US and North American Free Trade Agreements, fragmentation and integration have become routine throughout North American industry, including in the agriculture, manufacturing, and services sectors. High levels of both two-way intra-industry trade and foreign direct investment (FDI)—Canada is the second-leading destination of US direct investment while the United States is the prime destination of Canadian direct investment—indicate that cross-border integration, rationalization of production, and deepening interdependence of manufacturing industries are continuing. Proximity of the two countries' industrial heartlands and their well-developed infrastructures, transparent legal systems, and similar regulatory regimes have all contributed to the highly integrated nature of the two economies. In turn, this integration has contributed to high trade levels.

Today, both cross-border and global supply chains depend critically on relationships that extend well beyond arm's-length transactions between customers and suppliers. Cross-border rationalization has allowed Canadian industry to become more specialized and has contributed importantly to productivity and the growth of value-added sectors. Discussion of Canadian international economic patterns often focuses on trade in goods, and emphasizes exports. A more realistic picture emerges, however, if one looks at imports and exports of both goods and services, inflows and outflows of investment capital, sales by foreign affiliates, and exports of goods as a share of domestic shipments. As Howard Lewis and David Richardson point out, "it is becoming increasingly meaningless, if not outright impossible, to think of trade as something separate from cross-border investment, or of exporting as something separate from importing products and innovative ideas. All are tied together in the extended family of global commitment" (2001, 11). As such, Canada's involvement in the global economy is much more diversified, and the full importance of international exchange becomes clearer. It also makes clear why, as the US economy moves further up the value chain, the Canadian economy does too, increasing trade opportunities for foreign exporters to North American markets and investment opportunities in overseas economies.

The Evolving International Trade Policy Context

The conclusion of the Uruguay Round of GATT negotiations in 1994 and the entry into force of the multilateral WTO in 1995 marked the culmination of an extraordinarily productive decade of parallel regional trade liberalization and rules making. Consider the following developments.

- In 1994, Canada, the United States, and Mexico implemented the North American Free Trade Agreement (NAFTA), itself built on the 1989 Canada–US Free Trade Agreement.
- In Europe, the 1993 Maastricht Treaty transformed the European Common Market into the European Union (EU) on the basis of a much deeper and more intrusive set of economic and political commitments. With the reunification of East and West Germany in 1993 and the addition of Sweden, Austria, and Finland in 1995, Western Europe could boast a single market comparable in size to that of the United States.
- The implosion of the Soviet bloc in 1989 paved the way for the Eastern European satellites and the periphery of the USSR to pursue autonomous and more liberal trade policies. The first group—some of which were already members of the WTO—pursued membership in the EU, while the latter sought membership in the WTO.[4]
- In Asia, the members of the Association of Southeast Asian Nations (ASEAN) embarked on efforts to expand membership and deepen commitments, China continued its remarkable progress toward becoming a more open and market-oriented economy, and India showed early signs of a willingness to abandon its statist and closed economic policies.
- In Latin America, the long infatuation with import-substitution industrialization appeared to be coming to an end with a new generation of leaders prepared to make serious efforts at internal reform and external liberalization.

The period since 1995, however, has been much less productive—more a matter of consolidation than of innovation. Membership in the WTO has expanded (from 125 to 155 at the end of 2011), and the initiation of hundreds of cases of dispute settlement has provided important confirmation of WTO members' commitment to the rule of law. On the other hand, the Doha Round of multilateral trade negotiations, launched in 2001, reached a stalemate by 2005 and has been on life support ever since.[5] Bilateral free trade agreements and negotiations have proliferated, but the majority of the 319 agreements in force among WTO members at the end of 2011 extend well-established commitments to smaller countries reluctant to make them without the support of a major economy.

The stalemate at the Doha Round suggests that, among other problems, the bargaining techniques that worked so well for more than 50 years are proving less well suited to the new architecture and the much more comprehensive and intrusive ambit of international trade rules. Nevertheless, the GATT trade relations system, now encompassed in the WTO, remains an enduring idea, and continues to be at the centre of the modern trade relations system. A report prepared by the secretariats of the WTO and the Organisation for Economic Co-operation and Development (OECD) for the 2010 G20 Summit, for example, concluded that, for the first time in modern history, the 2008–9 recession had not resulted in a surge in protectionism (WTO and OECD 2010). Whatever the problems of deeper integration, the political appetite for short-term protectionist responses proved more a matter of rhetoric than of action, a tribute to the effect of the existing body of rules on governments' capacity for protectionist mischief (see Hart and Dymond 2010).

Most government-to-government negotiations involve finding a politically acceptable balance among competing domestic interests. The mercantilist bargaining technique—trading concessions on market access—that dominated postwar negotiations satisfied this need by maximizing export opportunities for some domestic economic sectors while minimizing import exposure for others. This is less feasible in a world of proliferating bilateral and regional negotiations. As defined originally in GATT Article XXIV for trade in goods and later in Article V of the General Agreement on Trade in Services, such negotiations must involve deeper commitments by extending, for example, tariff-free trade to substantially all sectors of the economy. To that end, regional arrangements such as the EU and NAFTA are built on an architecture of positive, rather than negative, prescriptions, and in which mercantilist bargaining played a much less prominent role. Both are much more ambitious in their coverage than the WTO, and both reflect the much more integrative nature of exchange within the territories covered by the rules. In the case of the EU, treaties have helped to forge more integrative business strategies. In the case of North America, the agreements reflect the extent to which businesses were already pursuing more integrative strategies. In both instances, the architecture and bargaining strategy of the old trade policy were insufficient.

Emerging Patterns of Canadian Trade and Investment

Canada's historic decision in 1985 to negotiate a free trade agreement with the United States was well grounded in the patterns of Canadian trade and economic development in the postwar years, and sought to remove public policy impediments to Canadian firms' ability to participate more effectively in a much larger and more integrated North American market. In response to the agreement, cross-border trade and investment grew rapidly, underpinning strong growth in the Canadian economy. NAFTA, which incorporated Mexico into the mix, consolidated the gains of the earlier bilateral agreement.

Canada's 1985 decision was consistent with broader societal recognition that economies do best when public policies and private initiatives are aligned. Public policies that provide an open, enabling, competitive market environment, that work with, rather than against, market-based preferences, and that limit direct government intervention to market failures have a much higher success rate in democratic societies than do *dirigiste* policies. As a result of that decision, the Canadian economy is much more open and productive today than it was 30 years ago, although as outlined further below, there remain pockets of protection reflecting the policy preferences of an earlier era.

Canada's choice also reflected recognition of the dynamism of the US economy, the waning prospect of the EU's ever emerging as anything more than a specialized, limited regional market for Canadian suppliers, and frustration with the slow pace of multilateral trade negotiations at the GATT in Geneva. At the time, there was also some hope that stronger Canada–US ties would create an enhanced platform from which Canadian firms could pursue emerging markets in Latin America and Asia. The Latin American market did not develop as many had hoped, despite some early hopeful signs and efforts to build stronger institutional ties. The Asia-Pacific market, on the other hand, took off with a dynamism that few had anticipated.

The dynamism of the US economy, so evident in the 1990s, slowly waned, however, as the United States faced a growing list of domestic and international problems and its political leaders seemed unprepared to take the tough decisions needed to put the economy back on track. For Canada, the initial surge in bilateral trade and investment reached its peak in 2000. Since then, bilateral trade and investment have stagnated—Figures 22a and Figure 22b show the declining US share of Canada's trade profile—as a result of factors that include the US housing and financial crises, the thickening of the border following the terrorist attacks of 11 September 2001, the lingering recession of 2008–9, and the

globalization of production. Although bilateral trade improved strongly in 2011 and continues to do so in 2012, it is unlikely to regain the dominant role it enjoyed in the 1990s. Nevertheless, despite the decline in the US share in Canadian exports, the US market still outweighs Canada's next-largest market, the EU, by a factor of almost nine and that of China by a factor of twenty. As Bank of Canada governor Mark Carney (2012) points out, sustained Canadian recovery depends upon US recovery, which all signs suggest will take longer than after previous recessions, as will growth in other mature markets. The rapidly expanding markets of China, India, and other Asian countries are well worth the pursuit, but the US market will remain the bread and butter of the Canadian economy for the foreseeable future.

Canada's spotty trade performance over the past few years, however, reflects not just a decline in bilateral trade with the United States. The 2008 global financial crisis and the resulting recession took a serious toll on international trade in general, and although Canada's GDP growth recovered in 2010, trade—largely reflecting anemic demand in Canada's primary markets—continues to underperform. The direction of Canadian trade has also changed. Conventional trade statistics provide an indication of this change, but they cannot capture the full impact of changing international trade patterns. China, for example, appears the most prominent new player in Canadian and US markets, but East Asia as a whole has become an increasingly prominent player. The evolution of the global economy—particularly the rise of value-chain production networks—has driven East Asia (including China) and North America into an interdependence that is stronger than with any other parts of the globe: transatlantic trade links are now of a distinctly lower order than transpacific ones. Thus, although Canadian firms' continued attention to their US customers reflects their experience that the United States is their most profitable market, they nevertheless have been quietly expanding their

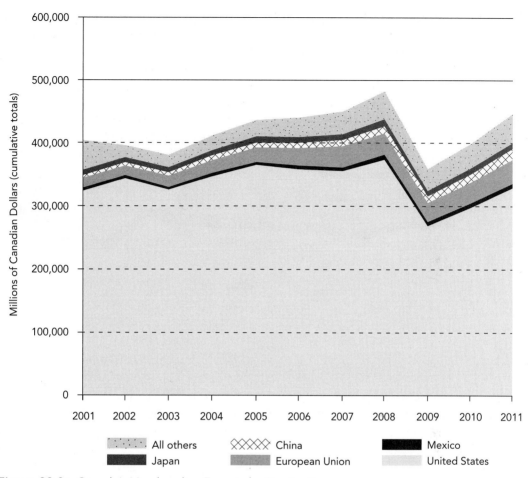

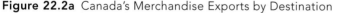

Figure 22.2a Canada's Merchandise Exports by Destination

Source: Compiled from Statistics Canada, Canadian International Merchandise Trade Database. Available at www5.statcan.gc.ca/cimt-cicm/home-accueil?lang=eng.

presence elsewhere, particularly in Asia. Indeed, as a study for the Department of Foreign Affairs and International Trade shows, Canadian firms are over-performing in China and other Asian markets and underperforming in more mature markets, including in the United States (Vesselovsky 2009). The principal reason is that demand in Asian markets for competitively priced Canadian goods—particularly resources—is rising rapidly. Accordingly, while Canada needs to continue to press the United States to resolve

remaining bilateral issues, under current circumstances Canadian business leaders and policy-makers also should consider alternative and complementary opportunities beyond North America.

The figures for Canadian direct investment abroad and foreign investment in Canada, however, have been more encouraging than trade figures over the past decade (see Table 22.1). While bilateral investment flows between Canada and the United States have continued to grow steadily, the growth

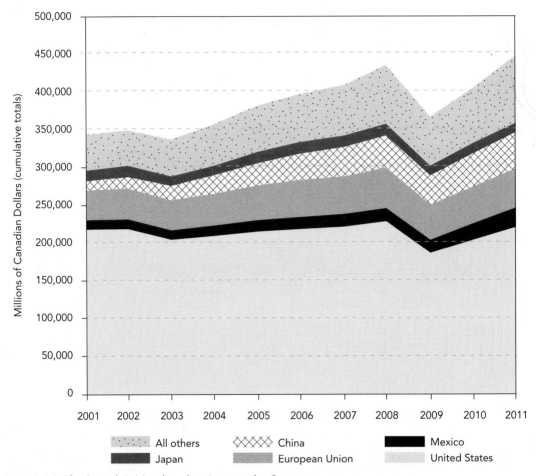

Figure 22.2b Canada's Merchandise Imports by Source

Source: Compiled from Statistics Canada, Canadian International Merchandise Trade Database. Available at www5.statcan.gc.ca/cimt-cicm/home-accueil?lang=eng.

of such flows between Canada and East Asia has been remarkable, though absolute numbers remain modest. Two-way investment flows with the EU have also increased significantly, but with an important difference: much of the investment flow across the Pacific is trade-creating, involving either value-chain production in Asia or investment in resources exploitation in Canada; transatlantic investment, on the other hand, tends to be a substitute for trade in that Canadian and EU firms locate in each other's markets only in order to serve those markets.

The growing role of Canadian firms as players in the global economy is indicated by the rise in sales by the affiliates of Canadian-based multinational firms (see Table 22.2). Although there has been some systematic analysis of the extent to which Canadian firms are engaged in the more complex world of value chains and production networks, analysts have yet to gain a firm grasp of the full implication of this new phenomenon in the organization of international trade and production (see, for example, Goldfarb and Beckman 2007; Ridgeway 2007; Hart

Table 22.1 Canada's foreign direct investment (FDI) position (millions of current Canadian dollars)

FDI in Canada	2001	2005	2009	2010	2011
All countries	340,429	397,828	572,842	585,107	607,497
United States	219,927	251,477	299,340	318,412	326,055
Europe	100,747	116,138	185,029	174,210	184,211
Asia/Oceania	15,390	21,416	67,578	66,714	69,310
South/Central America	997	3,168	13,303	17,421	18,785
Canadian FDI Abroad					
All countries	399,253	452,195	629,717	639,911	684,496
United States	188,481	202,398	255,397	253,417	276,145
Europe	99,240	123,239	178,110	176,826	181,885
Asia/Oceania	28,617	30,664	46,086	58,889	66,065
South/Central America	22,536	20,717	34,323	36,253	37,849

Source: Statistics Canada, CANSIM Table 376-0051—International investment position, Canadian direct investment abroad and foreign direct investment in Canada, by country; 2011 figures preliminary.

Table 22.2 Canadian foreign affiliate sales (millions of current Canadian dollars)

	2001	2005	2007	2009	2010
All countries	364,554	401,507	476,926	472,626	462,201
United States	223,798	223,770	240,519	240,277	228,690
European Union	75,258	87,594	92,324	84,584	73,247
Rest of the World	65,498	90,143	144,083	147,765	160,264

Source: Statistics Canada, CANSIM Table 376-0061—Foreign affiliate trade statistics, Canadian operations abroad, by countries.

and Dymond 2008; Sydor 2011). Ministerial speeches and other federal government initiatives suggest an increased awareness of the influence of this phenomenon on Canadian trade interests, but there is scant evidence that Ottawa is factoring this awareness into the design and delivery of Canadian economic policy and practice.

The Emerging Policy and Research Agenda

Canada's evolution as a trading nation has contributed significantly to making Canadians better off both as consumers and as producers in at least three important ways. First, Canadians employed in export-oriented sectors have been consistently better educated and better paid than the national average. Second, greater access to internationally competitive goods and services has allowed Canadians to stretch their earnings further. And, third, specialization has increased as markets have expanded in response to the increased openness fostered by trade agreements. Maintaining and expanding Canadian engagement in the global economy, however, will require more than a continuation of the policy orientation of the years since the Second World War. The trade stagnation of the past decade suggests that Canadians need to reconsider their priorities in determining how best to use government resources and policies to facilitate and strengthen the country's trade and economic performance.

As already noted, the period since 1995 has been largely one of consolidation rather than of innovation. Multilateral negotiations are moribund and offer little prospect of meaningful breakthroughs in the foreseeable future. The enthusiasm for bilateral negotiations with relatively minor—and seemingly randomly selected—partners has been good for those partners and for some Canadian firms and sectors, but has had little impact on Canadian trade and economic performance as a whole. The expansion of Canada's network of foreign protection investment agreements, double-tax agreements, air services agreements, and similar instruments has improved the policy framework within which competitive Canadian firms can pursue outward-oriented opportunities, while improvements in trade-facilitating infrastructure, such as the Pacific Gateway, have made important contributions to Canada's global engagement. Yet Canada–US relations have been marked by numerous initiatives but limited achievements. Domestically, Canada has taken a few steps to reform trade-inhibiting laws and policies, but Canadians would benefit from a bolder approach.

Home-grown Impediments

In order to tackle the challenges posed by changing global trade and production patterns, Canadian firms will have to ensure that their domestic operations are as competitive as possible. Canada's productivity performance over the past decade was among the worst in the OECD. A recent analysis of this dismal record (Deloitte 2011) identifies six key issues: business-leader risk aversion; inefficient and insufficient private sector support for innovation; lack of risk capital for start-up companies; chronic underinvestment in machinery and equipment; sheltering of the Canadian economy; and increasing competition for human

capital. The study concludes that the "courage to lead must come from within the highest levels of business, government, and academia" (44–45).

To remain competitive at home and abroad, Canadian firms must innovate and make better use of human resources and scarce capital. In the words of Bank of Canada Governor Mark Carney (2012), "the more Canadian businesses refocus, retool and retrain, the more they can take advantage of opportunities in Canada and around the world." Deloitte reports that "Canada offers one of the highest levels of support for R&D [research and development] in the OECD . . . [but] Canada yields the lowest business expenditure in R&D per dollar of government support" (Deloitte 2011). The record is particularly poor among small and medium-sized enterprises (SMEs). Canadian firms would also benefit by paying greater attention to the commercialization of Canadian R&D by transforming innovative ideas from universities into commercially successful enterprises in Canada.

Although the heavy lifting to improve Canada's productivity performance will be the work of the private sector, and although there are many ways in which Canadian public policy creates a business environment that promotes private investment in productive, efficient, and competitive economic activity, there remains considerable scope for improvements in public policy. Such improvements should be pursued not only on their own merit but also because of the important contribution they can make to improving Canada's productivity performance, to strengthening the competitive position of Canadian firms in the global economy, and to ensuring greater prosperity for individual Canadians. At a time when governments are looking for ways to reduce their expenditures, many such domestic reform initiatives should also improve governments' fiscal positions, both by reducing direct expenditures and by strengthening the tax base.

Progress in reducing conventional tariff and

non-tariff barriers to trade and investment flows has now reached the point that, with a few exceptions, the Canadian economy is open to broad international competition, as are most markets of interest to Canadian suppliers and investors. Canadian trade and investment patterns thus increasingly reflect the market choices of Canadian consumers, investors, and traders and are less and less the result of Canadian and foreign trade and investment policies. There remain, however, pockets of high tariffs, such as those sheltering supply-managed dairy and poultry products and a few consumer products such as clothing and footwear. Eliminating these tariffs would reduce existing drag on the economy by allowing markets to determine areas of comparative advantage in these sectors.

To its credit, the federal government has recognized that access to competitively priced inputs is essential for business success. Both the 2009 and 2010 budgets provided for the reduction and elimination of tariffs on essential imported inputs and capital goods. In addition, many "nuisance" tariffs—for example, on products no longer produced in Canada or rates that had fallen below 2 per cent—have been eliminated. Indeed, fluctuations in exchange rates alone are now more important to profitability than remaining low tariffs. Nevertheless, a surprising number of tariff lines continue to defy explanation. For example, maintaining tariff protection as possible "payment" to be used in future trade negotiations makes little sense; conventional access to most foreign markets is already good, so continuing to hobble some sectors of the Canadian economy on the slim mercantilist premise that some of this protection can be traded for improved access to other markets at some point in the future does more harm than good.

Removing protection from the supply-managed dairy and poultry sectors would require a thorough review of the costs and benefits of supply management and a willingness to consider appropriate transitional arrangements. More generally, the time has come for the federal government to consider seriously more thorough tariff reform. In addition to the benefits that would accrue from lowering the costs of agricultural and industrial inputs and consumer costs, tariff elimination should lead to significant savings in customs administration. Ottawa would no longer need to administer a complex tariff regime, including valuation provisions, differential rates arising from the growing number of free trade agreements with minor partners, and onerous rules of origin. Border officials would be freed to deal with more pressing security-related concerns rather than collecting a residual tax. The contribution of this tax to government revenue has shrunk to negligible levels, an amount that would be recouped readily from savings and from enhanced tax revenue in a stronger economy.

Antidumping (AD) and countervailing duty (CVD) measures are equally anachronistic and in need of serious cost-benefit analysis. Canada invented antidumping duties in 1904 as a way of defending its import-substitution industries from the alleged harm arising from dumped imports by larger, more efficient US competitors. It introduced CVDs in 1977 in response to new-found US zeal for rooting out the subsidy practices of other countries through its own CVD investigations.[6] Economists have long pointed to the economically nonsensical arguments used to justify these measures and to the costly procedures required to implement them. Unfortunately, both these trade remedy measures were enshrined in the original GATT rules. Even more regrettably, detailed constructions of rules governing these trade remedies were embedded within the WTO, and have now been adopted by an increasing number of developing countries in the perverse belief that they are integral to full WTO participation. In the Canada–US free trade negotiations, Canada made the case, with limited success, that neither measure was compatible with an integrated market. The years since have demonstrated the strength of that case and extended it to a wider range of trading relationships. The incidence of new AD and CVD cases between Canada and the United States declined rapidly after the initial free trade agreement entered into force (Hart and Dymond 2007). Now, as markets integrate, most businesses refrain from attacking their competitors in another jurisdiction because, while they might be competitors in one product line, they might be suppliers, customers, or strategic partners in others. More generally, production networks and value chains can be disrupted easily by ill-conceived antidumping or countervailing duty investigations affecting any of the production nodes. Again, Canada can provide global leadership by dismantling these instruments of an earlier era of industrial policy and relying on competition law and simpler safeguard procedures to address any egregious cases of injurious price discrimination or seriously harmful import surges.

Canada also maintains a variety of other trade-impacting policies that remain as reminders of an earlier era of regulatory zeal and nationalist foolishness, including ownership restrictions in the telecommunications, energy, and transportation sectors, subsidies to favoured sectors, government procurement preferences, restrictive banking regulations and tax policies that coddle some economic activities and shackle others, and competition policies that limit mergers and acquisitions and growth. Such policies, which are from an era that assumed that products and firms had clear national identities and would benefit from policies to promote national champions, are also at odds with facilitating Canadian participation in global value chains and North American integration. For example, although the Harper government has eliminated some ownership restrictions and raised review thresholds, Canada continues to impose severe restrictions on foreign ownership and control in selected sectors of the economy. There is no apparent reason the standard rules of investment protection agreements should not be applied to FDI in protected industries. Most FDI today originates with multinational corporations and is often part of larger regional or global business strategies. Canadians gain no benefits from cutting themselves off from these developments in selected sectors.

The presumed benefit of linking ownership to the achievement of a range of regulatory objectives appears to be a holdover from the era when there were many more regulated industries—particularly so-called natural monopolies such as telephone, electricity, urban transit, and similar activities—and the belief that such restrictions were needed to ensure effective public regulation. Over the years, both economic theory and practice have demonstrated the benefits of competition, privatization, and foreign investment even in these industries, as well as the capacity of governments to regulate in the public interest without regard to ownership or control. Canadians would be better off if these lessons were applied across all sectors of the economy.

Similarly, subsidies ostensibly help some industries but penalize others. No matter how welcome to individual firms, regions, or industries any particular government grant or "investment" might appear, each involves a transfer of resources from one group of taxpayers to another. Any jobs "created" or "saved" by such programs rely on reduced opportunities for other, often more productive and competitive firms or sectors. It might be theoretically possible for governments to make choices that, over time, prove wise and beneficial, but experience is less than overwhelming in validating the superiority of political over business judgment for market-based activities: factors that are persuasive to governments are rarely so to private capital. In the long run, Canadians would be better off and would gain greater benefits from their engagement in the global economy if there were fewer politically motivated investments of public funds in market-based activities.

Government procurement preferences—purchases made by governments for their own use—are another remnant of activist industrial policy. An early exemption in the GATT's national treatment provisions gave governments the scope to favour local suppliers. In response, governments began to use procurement as a tool for industrial development. It was not until the 1970s that industrialized countries accepted that procurement preferences could have perverse effects and concluded a modest GATT agreement to discipline their use. That agreement has since expanded in scope but remains largely one among the industrialized countries. In Canada, some federal government purchases are subject to the agreement's discipline, but not those of provincial governments. As Canadians learned from the use of preferences in recent US federal stimulus programs, preferences make little sense in a world of geographically dispersed production. Accordingly, both the federal and provincial governments should phase these out gradually and place their civilian procurement programs on the same market criteria as private firms: price and quality.[7]

Public finance experts have long maintained that tax efficiency is critical to the competitiveness and productivity of the corporate sector, and in recent years the federal and provincial governments have made significant progress in reducing corporate tax rates. As a result, Canada has moved from the least to the most tax-competitive member of the G7. More could be done, however, to ensure that Canada's tax regime places Canadian-based firms in the best competitive position to tackle global markets, particularly in light of the fact that other jurisdictions are moving in the same direction. Tax neutrality is among the most important considerations in maintaining an efficient and effective

corporate tax regime. Using the tax regime to favour some sectors over others leads to distortions in the allocation of scarce resources and to sub-optimal economic performance. Canada's tax regime continues to favour manufacturing and extractive industries over the services sector, thus penalizing investment in some of Canada's most outward-oriented firms. The tax regime also favours small firms over large, a policy that discourages SMEs from growing into globally competitive players.

Over the past 30 years, the regulatory role of government in society has grown exponentially, even as economically oriented regulations have been reduced or eliminated. Every year, the federal and provincial governments initiate or amend some 5,000 regulatory requirements affecting Canadian citizens (Hart 2006, 2009). Most of these new regulations are related to matters of health, safety, and the environment, and ostensibly are grounded in evidence-based science. In fact, many are based on irrational fears that serve little purpose other than to satiate the bureaucratic hunger for information or to accommodate what British blogger John Brignell (2008) calls the "march of the zealots." The result has been a massive intrusion of the state into matters involving private choices and responsibilities, with a large and energetic bureaucracy administering an expansive body of laws and regulations predicated on the belief that governments can shield their citizenry from the vicissitudes and risks of life. This development involves not only the direct costs of administering regulations, but also the much larger indirect costs of compliance, a burden that falls disproportionately on the corporate sector, particularly SMEs. Canada might be one of the easiest jurisdictions in which to start a business, but it has become among the most expensive in which to maintain it. Although there might be little social appetite for a major reduction of risk-based regulations, there are good reasons to review the continued application of some of them. At a minimum,

Canadian governments need to consider systematic reviews of existing regulations to consider their continued utility; introducing mandatory review and sunset provisions into new or amended regulatory requirements; and aligning regulatory requirements to the greatest extent possible with international norms and those of Canada's major trading partners, particularly the United States, as discussed further below.

All of these reforms of Canadian policies and practices, in addition to providing a more open and less discriminatory business environment, reducing consumer costs, and enhancing productivity, would have the added benefit of reducing government expenditures. Literally thousands of officials in Ottawa and around the country are engaged in administering tariffs, trade remedies, supply management, subsidy programs, investment restrictions, procurement preferences, regulatory requirements, and other holdovers from the past. For a government looking for ways to reduce charges on the public purse, that most of these programs retard rather than promote Canadian productivity, efficiency, and economic growth should be sobering news. Their elimination should not only strengthen the Canadian economy, but also lead to savings and a stronger tax base.

The Canada–US Agenda

Beyond Canadian domestic policy, the area of potentially greatest immediate benefit lies in addressing impediments to trade with the United States. Cross-border trade remains the indispensable foundation of any Canadian policy to strengthen benefits from international engagement. The policy attitude since the implementation of NAFTA, however, has been that such improvements as might be desirable in facilitating Canada–US trade and investment can be tackled on the basis of incremental improvements in discrete policies and programs, many of them by Canadians on their own. But this approach

is slow and fails to take advantage of the synergies that might exist in dealing with related issues, particularly those of interest to the United States, and thus provide scope for trade-offs. If the purpose of many of these programs is to strengthen US confidence in Canada as an economic and security partner, full bilateral engagement is critical. Additionally, given the forces of proximity and consumer and producer preferences, deepening integration is inevitable; without bilateral engagement, however, it will happen on a basis that favours US default positions rather than jointly agreed programs.

Reaping the full benefits of deepening cross-border economic integration will require that Canada and the United States jointly address three fundamental, and interrelated, issues: reducing the impact of the border; accelerating and directing the pace of regulatory convergence or alignment; and building the necessary institutional capacity to implement and administer the results of meeting the first two challenges.

Border administration. Since 1996, six different bilateral or trilateral initiatives have sought to improve border administration. Some progress has been made, but it has been much slower than desirable (see Hart 2010; Schwanen 2011a). The latest bilateral effort—*Beyond the Border: A Shared Vision for Perimeter Security and Economic Competitiveness*—announced by Prime Minister Harper and President Barack Obama in February 2011, produced a bilateral action plan aimed at making the border more open, predictable, and secure. Unlike earlier initiatives, the action plan outlines specific "deliverables" and the time frame within which they are to be completed. To date, progress has been encouraging.[8] The federal government has consulted widely with and received strong endorsement from the business sector and other interested parties for a bold, comprehensive approach to these discussions. If Ottawa proceeds on the basis of what it has learned from the consultations and what is set out in the action plan, and if the US government shares some of this vision and is prepared to follow through, the prospects for a breakthrough on this difficult file could be more promising than was the case with earlier initiatives.[9]

Regulatory cooperation. At the same time as the prime minister and president announced their border initiative in February 2011, they also announced a regulatory cooperation initiative. Similar to the border initiative, officials have prepared an action plan containing "deliverables" and timelines aimed at identifying areas ripe for early agreement to forge greater regulatory alignment.[10] The main cautionary note suggested by the past decade of similar initiatives is the need for strong political leadership. In its absence, bureaucratic ducks on both sides of the border will nibble this initiative to death. Inertia is a powerful force in bureaucracies, particularly for those engaged in administering established regimes; determined leadership is required at the top to overcome.

Institutional capacity. Integral to any progress in addressing the governance of deepening integration is the need to build sufficient institutional capacity and procedural frameworks to reduce conflict and provide a more flexible basis for dynamic rule-making and adaptation for the North American market as a whole. It might well be necessary to overcome traditional Canadian and US aversion to bilateral institution building and to look creatively to the future. Although the EU model of a complex supranational infrastructure might not suit North American circumstances, Canadians and Americans can learn from the EU experience. Much can be achieved on the basis of existing networks of cooperation, with the addition as necessary of specific joint or bilateral commissions in instances where existing networks are inadequate. More would be achieved, however, if Canada and the United States were to commit to establishing a limited number of bilateral institutions with a mandate to provide their two national governments the necessary advice and information to effect a more integrated approach to regulation and border administration.

Policy Priorities beyond North America

Ironically, Canada's self-image as a trading nation and its record of active and constructive engagement in international trade negotiations might stand in the way of rethinking the objectives of contemporary export trade policy. Officials remain busy pursuing a wide range of activities, from trade negotiations to export financing. To be sure, there remain problems amenable to resolution through such activity. World agricultural markets, for example, remain deeply distorted by misguided subsidy, border, and other measures; the markets of many developing countries are less open than those of developed countries; and the spread of trade remedy measures to an ever-increasing number of countries is a blight on the international trade regime. However, while these policies might affect the interests of individual Canadian firms, their impact on the Canadian economy as a whole is often marginal. Much of this activity, therefore, now serves what might be characterized as retail trade policy, responding to the interests and complaints of individual Canadian firms rather than to the broader interests of the Canadian economy.

Most modern industries, from automobiles to electronics and banking, have developed sophisticated global and regional supply and distribution networks, and would be hard pressed to identify the national origin of their inputs or even of some of their final products. Individual firms are not averse to using the extensive trade and investment promotion services offered at Canadian missions around the world, but few would be prepared to pay for them, suggesting that their importance has become marginal to their interests. In these circumstances, it might be time for the federal government to reconsider the benefits Canadians derive from such services. Many domestic services to Canadians, from access to national parks and museums to passports and mail delivery, are now provided on a cost-recovery basis, so why should trade-promotion services not be offered on the same basis or be reduced or even eliminated where they are of little benefit? Cost recovery would ensure that these resources are deployed where they are most needed and appreciated, rather than at posts with attractive amenities but little prospect for new trade and investment.

The Doha Round of multilateral trade negotiations effectively has been put on ice. The diminishing role of the WTO as a negotiating forum, however, does not mean that Canada should be indifferent to other developments at the WTO. As noted earlier, the rules and procedures embedded in the WTO and its constituent agreements provide an essential basis for the conduct of world trade. Canada should exercise leadership in ensuring that the WTO is fully

engaged in the important task of managing the existing regime and in preparing the ground for possible future negotiations on a more realistic basis than was evident during the Doha Round.

In recent years, Canada's instrument of choice for pursuing trade diversification and strengthening trade and investment with new, typically small partners has been the bilateral free trade agreement (see Table 22.3). This is an admirable policy impulse, and signals the extent to which free trade, rather than protection, has become the default position in Canadian trade policy. Bilateral negotiations have the advantage of being more nimble than multilateral ones and provide greater scope for experimentation. Nevertheless, experience shows that it is difficult to conclude such agreements with minor partners; more to the point, there is no evidence that such agreements serve strategic objectives or have

Table 22.3 Post-NAFTA Canadian bilateral and regional trade initiatives

Status/Country/Group	Total Merchandise Trade 2011 (CAD millions)	Status/Country/Group	Total Merchandise Trade 2011 (CAD millions)
Initiated/Signed		Initiated, but not concluded	
Israel (1995/97)	1,382	Singapore (2001)	2,360
Chile (1996/97)	2,730	South Korea (2004)	11,703
Costa Rica (2000/02)	637	Dominican Republic (2007)	297
Colombia (2007/08)	1,561	Caricom (2007)	2,400
Peru (2007/08)	4,925	European Union (2009)	92,123
Jordan (2007/09)	85	India (2009)	5,162
Panama (2008/10)	235	Ukraine (2010)	287
EFTA (1996/2009)	11,535	Morocco (2011)	419
Honduras (2001/Legal review)	236	Japan (2012)	23,727
Initiated, but now suspended		Study Launched	
Guatemala (2001)	513	Turkey (2011)	2,394
El Salvador (2001)	166	Thailand (2012)	3,514
Nicaragua (2001)	371	China (2012)	64,966
Interest indicated		Trans-Pacific Partnership (2011)	
Suspended		Free Trade Area of the Americas (2005)	

Source: Author's compilation based on Burney et al. (2012), Table 1, and Statistics Canada, Canadian International Merchandise Trade Database. Available at www5.statcan.gc.ca/cimt-cicm/home-accueil?lang=eng.

any discernible impact on subsequent bilateral trade and investment patterns. Negotiations with Israel, Chile, Costa Rica, Colombia, Peru, Jordan, and Panama all concluded successfully within a reasonable time period, but negotiations with the rump of the European Free Trade Area (Norway, Switzerland, Iceland, and Liechtenstein) took 13 years to conclude in the face of politically significant opposition from the shipbuilding industry. Negotiations with South Korea—a market that is at least large enough to warrant some serious attention—have faced well-organized opposition from the auto sector and remain in limbo. Negotiations with other minor partners, such as Singapore, the Dominican Republic, Central American countries, and Ukraine, seem to be facing a similar fate. In the absence of strong support from the business community as a whole, such negotiations are easily derailed by entrenched import-competing interests concerned about the loss of a cherished remnant of the interventionist past. As a result, federal ministers determine that the amount of political capital needed to conclude such agreements is out of all proportion to their economic and commercial, let alone political, benefits. The result is a willingness to initiate, but not to conclude, such negotiations. This misuse of resources signals a lack of seriousness that is unlikely to advance long-term Canadian trade and investment interests. Should Canada proceed with some or all of the domestic reforms outlined above, such agreements would become easier to conclude and implement, as should be the case with those that serve largely as statements of political interest rather than as instruments of commercial policy.[11]

In any event, rather than the seemingly random initiation of bilateral trade negotiations, Ottawa should proceed with negotiations only on the basis of clear business support, extensive consultations, and a clearly articulated rationale—in short, it should pursue agreements that are geared to the most pressing issues in the bilateral relationship. It makes little sense, for example, to negotiate a full-fledged free trade agreement when the principal issue between Canada and the other country is, say, investment protection and where the most appropriate instrument would be a revamped foreign investment promotion and protection agreement. Ottawa should also take a broader view of such negotiations—for example, it should consider such issues as education exchanges as part of relationship building.

In 2009, Canada entered into negotiations with the EU to conclude a comprehensive economic and trade agreement (CETA), with the hope of concluding negotiations by 2012. This initiative marks but the latest attempt by Canada to forge stronger ties with Europe, dating back to the 1970s. Over the years, however, Canada's quest has been hampered by two inconvenient realities: indifference by business communities on both sides of the Atlantic and indifference by the European political class. The latter impediment apparently was overcome in 2009, but there is no evidence that the two business communities have become enthusiastic supporters of the initiative, in part because, over the years, they have forged mutually beneficial investment ties and are hard put to identify issues that require negotiations on the scale of a CETA. Undoubtedly, there are irritants in the relationship that might be resolved through negotiations, but most that have been identified are EU complaints about Canadian practices, ranging from supply management to geographical indications for European wine, cheese, and similar products to provincial procurement practices. Some of these issues should be cleaned up on their merits; others would place Canadian producers at a disadvantage. None, however, adds up to a comprehensive agreement that would make much difference to bilateral trade and investment.[12]

Transpacific Prospects

There is more scope for potentially useful breakthroughs across the Pacific than across the Atlantic.

The EU represents a mature market with limited potential for growth; indeed, even more than in the United States, political leaders in Europe are finding it extremely difficult to cope with the fallout from the 2008 financial crisis, and the fiscal position of most EU members is even more parlous than that of the United States. Asia, on the other hand, represents the future. The growth of China alone over the past 30 years has been astounding. India is now catching up. ASEAN members and South Korea have become established markets. All are important components of the world of value chains and production networks. Yet, while acknowledging the importance of Asia to its future, Canada remained conspicuously absent from the Trans-Pacific Partnership (TPP) initiative, choosing instead to continue to rely on the increasingly sclerotic Asia-Pacific Economic Cooperation (APEC). The APEC forum, established in 1993, sought to stimulate transpacific ties through a range of government initiatives. Rather than negotiating a regional accord, governments opted for "concerted unilateralism" as the key to more liberal trade and investment conditions, reflecting Asia's preference for ambiguity and consensus rather than structure and rules. This government-led initiative soon ran out of steam. In its place, private businesses forged their own ties and opened markets by means of production networks and value chains. To capture a share of this activity, governments throughout East Asia, often unilaterally, took the steps necessary to welcome foreign investors and become players in this world of integrated or networked production. Even India, long one of the world's most reluctant liberalizers, introduced reforms that encouraged firms to locate slices of activity there, particularly the services dimension of global production networks.

Governments on the eastern and southern fringes of the Pacific have now begun to catch up to the reality of this Asian dynamism by looking at ways to consolidate business ties with stronger governance provisions. New Zealand and Australia led the way with bilateral overtures and arrangements, followed by the TPP initiative launched by Chile, New Zealand, and Singapore in 2002. At the 2011 APEC Summit, Prime Minister Harper, perhaps mindful of the pessimistic discussions a week earlier at a G20 meeting in Cannes, France, dominated by Europe's problems, signalled Canada's interest in becoming a party to the TPP talks, as did Japan and Mexico, bringing the potential number of participating governments to 12. To date, China has not indicated any interest in joining, but it is watching developments closely (Dawson 2012).[13]

Canada's expression of interest in the TPP marked a further step in a significant, if recent, reorientation of Canadian public policy. In its first five years in office, the Harper government showed a preference for strengthening ties with Europe and Latin America, but five years of frustration have shown the limits of this preference. In its place, Ottawa has turned toward Asia, particularly China, no longer emphasizing the human rights concerns that seemed high on the agenda prior to the 2011 election, but focusing instead on strengthening trade and investment ties. High-level visits to the region have proliferated, as have expressions of interest in negotiating the intergovernmental instruments that would strengthen bilateral and regional ties.

At one level, Canada is well positioned to increase trade across the Pacific. Both South and East Asia are hungry for energy, protein, and other resources, and Canada is potentially a much more reliable and stable supplier than those in Africa, Latin America, and the Middle East. More needs to be done, however, to improve transportation infrastructure on the West Coast and to remove regulatory bottlenecks. For Canadian businesses affected by the global recession and looking worriedly toward their customers and suppliers in the United States and, to a lesser extent, Europe, Asia provides the most dynamic opportunity in more than a decade. Some firms, of course, have already decided to put resources into developing or expanding their presence in Asia. Others might be thinking about it, and need to hear from their colleagues about both good and bad experiences. Those that have shied away from China and other Asian markets might have done so for reasons that made sense a few years ago but look less compelling today. Those waiting for the federal government to prepare the way and reduce the risk premium are likely to fall further and further behind as more nimble and adventurous firms make the connections and establish the relationships so vital to developing Asian markets.

Complementary agreements have also proven their value in gaining and defending access and in strengthening institutional ties. These begin with such instruments as foreign investment protection, aviation, and double tax agreements. Canada has negotiated a new foreign investment agreement with China, but also needs to ensure that other ancillary agreements are consonant with the new reality—a new air agreement was negotiated in 2005, but the double tax agreement dates to 1986.

At this stage in Asia's economic development, government-to-government contacts remain an important part of enhancing economic ties. Such contacts range from ministerial visits and government-led business delegations to on-the-ground government representation. Recent visits to China by the prime minister and the trade and foreign affairs ministers mark a new beginning, but they will need to be repeated on a regular basis to achieve higher levels of awareness of Canada in both official and business circles. Accordingly, effective Canadian representation in the region will be essential; leaving posts vacant for extended periods of time, as now happens, sends a poor message.

Consultations with Canadian Business

In the 1980s, the Mulroney government established a horizontal and sectoral business advisory system to obtain confidential advice on the free trade negotiations with the United States, the GATT multilateral trade negotiations, and the NAFTA negotiations. The system responded effectively to a long-standing business desire to be engaged more closely and systematically in developing and implementing Canada's trade agenda, providing the federal government with valuable insights on business trade priorities, and ensuring business support for Ottawa's agenda. Since then, however, the system has been replaced by public online consultations on specific issues—for example, negotiations with the EU and spasmodic "multi-stakeholder" meetings involving business, labour, and non-governmental organizations. The result is that those businesses that are engaged in international trade and investment believe they have been deprived of an effective and coordinated voice in the setting of Canadian trade policy priorities.

In developing and implementing a future-oriented trade agenda, Ottawa should convene a small group of 15 to 20 senior business leaders engaged in international trade and investment to provide advice on the structure, organization, and agenda of a consultative trade policy mechanism. The minister of trade should further ask the House of Commons Standing Committee on Foreign Affairs and International Trade to resume the highly effective, democratic role it played as a consultative forum and lightning rod for broader public comments on Canada's trade agenda.

Conclusion

The world has become increasingly intertwined in response to demands by producers and consumers alike for the best products, services, capital, and ideas, in the process creating jobs and wealth across many sectors and accelerating the forces of mutually beneficial global integration. The trade policy of the postwar years, grounded in well-established international trade theories and pursued on the basis of the politically pragmatic strategy of mercantilist bargaining, proved critical to underwriting the first stages of modern global integration. The framework of rules and institutions developed during that period worked well to facilitate and govern a process of market-led integration.

The rules and institutions of the postwar regime are no longer well suited, however, to the global trade and production patterns that have emerged over the past few decades, in part thanks to the success of the earlier regime. The development of much more fragmented production strategies, the ability to disperse production much more widely around the world, the emergence of new security threats, and the reality of a much wider range of cross-border transactions all point to the need to look at a new set of policy issues that threaten to disrupt the beneficial process of integration and specialization.

The effects of these new trade and production patterns and the limits of traditional trade negotiations and instruments are reflected in the relative decline of Canada's trade performance over the past decade. Canada weathered the 2008–9 recession better than most other OECD economies, thanks to prudent fiscal management and other reforms. Its trade performance, however, remains underwhelming, in part because of anemic demand in its major markets and in part because of self-imposed barriers to greater engagement in global markets.

In these circumstances, the federal government should pursue a trade strategy that leads to a much more open economy and recognizes that reforms begin at home. It should begin by dismantling a range of policy instruments—from tariffs and trade remedy measures to subsidies and government procurement preferences—that reflect an earlier reality. As a happy by-product, such reforms would strengthen Canada's productivity performance, reduce charges to the public purse, make a major contribution to restoring fiscal balance, and reduce cost differences between Canada and the United States. In an age when

governments face rising education, health, and other social costs, savings from the elimination of programs that raise consumer costs and undermine the ability of Canadians to compete and create wealth in the global economy should be compelling.

Traditional trade negotiations have become much less important, in part because the trade negotiations of the past created a solid framework of rules and commitments by all major traders to keep their markets open. Remaining pockets of protection are more likely to be eliminated through smaller and more focused negotiations than the grand multilateral rounds of the past. Canada needs to tailor its approach to such negotiations more strategically, focusing scarce resources on issues and markets that are likely to make a material difference to Canadian producers and consumers.

On the Canada–US front, the continued presence of a heavily administered border, similar but differentiated regulatory regimes, and inadequate institutional capacity to solve problems now undermines the ability of firms and individuals alike to reap the full benefits of deepening cross-border integration. In a world where firms have many more choices about what to produce and where, the smaller partner in a deeply integrationist relationship is particularly vulnerable to the impact of border delays and regulatory differences. In these circumstances, the federal government would be well advised to continue to invest in efforts to bring the framework of rules governing cross-border exchange into line with commercial and economic reality.

Beyond North America, Canada needs to focus its limited resources where they are likely to make a difference. Changes in both Canadian and global trade and production patterns indicate that engagement with East Asia should be a priority. To that end, Ottawa should avail itself of both existing and emerging opportunities to strengthen transpacific relations, from the TPP initiative to new institutional links and agreements.

Questions for Review

1. What are the factors that made the postwar trade and economic regime one of the most successful experiments in intergovernmental cooperation?

2. Why is the postwar trade and economic regime no longer adequate to the demands of twenty-first-century global commerce?

3. What are Canadian interests in developing a more complete and satisfactory multilateral trade and economic regime?

4. What are the factors that are leading to the diversification and specialization of the Canadian economy?

5. What interests do China and other major emerging economies have in negotiating a more modern global trade regime?

6. Why do many countries prefer bilateral to multilateral trade agreements?

7. How can Canada best position itself to tackle the emerging trade and investment agenda?

Suggested Readings

Blustein, Paul. 2009. *Misadventures of the Most Favored Nations: Clashing Egos, Inflated Ambitions, and the Great Shambles of the World Trade System.* New York: Public Affairs.

Hart, Michael. 2006. *Steer or Drift? Taking Charge of Canada–US Regulatory Convergence.* C.D. Howe Institute Commentary 229. Toronto: C.D. Howe Institute.

Hart, Michael. 2012. *Ambiguity and Illusion in China's Economic Transformation: Issues for Canadian Policy Makers and Business Leaders.* Canadian Council of Chief Executives (February). Available at ceocouncil.ca/wp-content/uploads/2012/02/Ambiguity-and-Illusion-in-China-Michael-Hart-February-2012.pdf.

Irwin, Douglas A. 2005. *Free Trade under Fire.* 2nd ed. Princeton, NJ: Princeton University Press.

Maurer, Andreas. 2011. "Trade in Value Added: What Is the Country of Origin in an Interconnected World?" Background paper. Geneva: World Trade Organization. Available at www.wto.org/english/res_e/statis_e/miwi_e/background_paper_e.htm.

Sally, Razeen. 2008. *Trade Policy, New Century.* London: Institute of Economic Affairs.

Notes

This paper builds on a body of work pursued together with the late Bill Dymond, and published in various earlier pieces either individually or under both names, including by the C.D. Howe Institute. Helpful comments on earlier drafts of this paper were provided by Gilles Leblanc, Daniel Schwanen, and Philip Stone, by the Institute's anonymous reviewers, and in discussion by the Institute's Trade Policy Council.

1. "'Major transformations' coming to Canada's pension system, Harper tells Davos," *National Post*, 26 January 2012. Available at http://news.nationalpost.com/2012/01/26/major-changes-coming-to-canadas-pension-system-harper-says-in-davos-speech.

2. For an overview of the evolution of the postwar trade system and the challenges to it posed by increasing global economic interdependence, see Hart and Dymond (2000, 2008). Good summaries of the achievements of the postwar trade regime can be found in Sally (2008) and Schenk (2011).

3. See Cattaneo, Gereffi, and Staritz (2010) and Sydor (2011) for further discussion of emerging global production patterns and their impact on trade and investment. Arndt and Kierzkowski note that "fragmentation is not a new phenomenon; nor is outsourcing.... In the modern era, however, both have acquired *international* dimension and complexity and probably represent one of the most important distinguishing features of contemporary globalization" (2001, 2).

4. Poland, the Czech Republic, Slovakia, Hungary, Romania, Latvia, Estonia, Lithuania, and Slovenia have acceded to the EU. Poland, Czechoslovakia, Hungary, Romania, and Yugoslavia had all been members of the GATT. Since 1995, Latvia, Estonia, Lithuania, Ukraine, Bulgaria, Moldova, Albania, Macedonia, Croatia, Georgia, Armenia, the Kyrgyz Republic, Montenegro, and Russia have acceded to the WTO; Azerbaijan, Uzbekistan, Belarus, Bosnia-Herzegovina, Kazakhstan, Tajikistan, and Serbia are in the process of acceding.

5. This chapter is not the place to discuss the many reasons for the failure of the Doha Round, but they range from 1) developed countries being sufficiently satisfied with the current trade regime to find the need for major new concessions politically underwhelming to 2) developing countries being dissatisfied with major demands that would affect developed country interests but having very little willingness to make political reforms that would make their demands more compelling. See Blustein (2009) and Jones (2010) for overviews of the Round's many problems.

6. US CVD procedures date back to 1890, but they had been used sparingly. Their utility was rediscovered by the Washington trade bar in the 1970s in the *Michelin Tires from Canada* case. That case was followed by a flood of new cases, some involving Canadian products, such as ground fish, glass beads, and optic liquid sensors, a development that spurred Canadian business interest in an agreement with the United States that would curb this new appetite for protection. Ottawa had authority to impose CVDs, but lacked detailed procedures to put this authority into effect until remedial regulations were introduced in 1977.

7. A case in point is Ottawa's 19 October 2011, announcement of a major warship acquisition project worth $35 billion. Three Canadian firms applied and two received major contracts; no foreign firm was invited to apply. Watson (2011) estimates that Canadians will pay a 20 per cent premium for this exercise in industrial policy.

8. The detailed action plan, announced in December 2011, is available at http://actionplan.gc.ca/grfx/psec-scep/pdfs/bap_report-paf_rapport-eng-dec2011.pdf. The website includes the details of consultations with Canadians and provides information on the work of the Regulatory Cooperation Council.

9. In a press interview, Alan Bersin, commissioner for the US Customs and Border Protection Agency, offers some comfort to those who are optimistic that the US government is taking the initiative seriously enough to warrant cause for cautious optimism; see "US–Canada: a relationship 'unique in world history,'" *Financial Post*, 20 October 2011.

10. See "Terms of Reference for the United States–Canada Regulatory Cooperation Council, June 3, 2011"; "What Canadians Told Us: A Report on Consultations on Regulatory Cooperation between Canada and the United States"; and "Regulatory Action Plan" at the Perimeter Security and Economic Competitiveness website, available at www.actionplan.gc.ca/en/content/perimeter-security-and-economic-competitiveness.

11. Some of Canada's bilateral negotiating activity flows from the demise of the Free Trade Area of the Americas initiative. Canada devoted considerable resources to making this initiative a success, but learned that Canadian enthusiasm was not enough to offset the many problems that led to its demise, including US and Brazilian reluctance to proceed. Nevertheless, it served the useful purpose of leading many governments in Latin America to examine their trade policies in depth and to strengthen their intellectual and negotiating capacities on the trade front. For Canada, the initiative provided a solid base on which to build stronger bilateral ties, some of which have resulted in the desire to underpin these with a bilateral trade agreement.

12. Before initiating negotiations, both Canada and the EU commissioned studies to estimate the potential impact of an agreement; only with heroic assumptions could the analysts generate numbers that were not embarrassing. See European Commission and Canada (2008) and Guerin and Napoli (2008). For opposing views of the CETA initiative, see Hart and Dymond (2002) and Schwanen (2011b).

13. Canada was formally invited to join the talks in June 2012.

References

Arndt, Sven W., and Henryk Kierzkowski, eds. 2001. *Fragmentation: New Production Patterns in the World Economy.* Oxford: Oxford University Press.

Blustein, Paul. 2009. *Misadventures of the Most Favored Nations: Clashing Egos, Inflated Ambitions, and the Great Shambles of the World Trade System.* New York: Public Affairs.

Brignell, John. 2008. "March of the Zealots." Available at www.numberwatch.co.uk/zealots.htm.

Burney, Derek, Thomas d'Aquino, Leonard Edwards, and Fen Osler Hampson. 2012. *Winning in a Changing World: Canada and Emerging Markets.*

Canada. 2012. Department of Foreign Affairs and International Trade. "Pocket Facts." 2 March. Ottawa.

Carney, Mark. 2012. "Exporting in a Post-Crisis World." Remarks to Greater Kitchener-Waterloo Chamber of Commerce, 2 April. Available at www.bis.org/review/r120403e.pdf.

Cattaneo, Olivier, Gary Gereffi, and Cornelia Staritz, eds. 2010. *Global Value Chains in a Post-crisis World: A Development Perspective.* Washington, DC: World Bank.

Dawson, Laura. 2012. *Can Canada Join the Trans-Pacific Partnership? Why Just Wanting It Is Not Enough.* C.D. Howe Institute Commentary 340. Toronto: C.D. Howe Institute.

Deloitte. [2011.] "The Future of Productivity: An Eight-step Game Plan for Canada." 24 November. Available at http://media.deloitte.ca/flash/future-of-productivity/pdf/ca_en_future-of-productivity_full.pdf.

European Commission and Canada. 2008. "Assessing the Costs and Benefits of a Closer EU–Canada Economic Partnership."

Available at http://trade.ec.europa.eu/doclib/html/141032. htm.

Goldfarb, Danielle, and Kip Beckman. 2007. "Canada's Changing Role in Global Supply Chains." Ottawa: Conference Board of Canada.

Guerin, Selen Sarisoy, and Chris Napoli. 2008. "Canada and the European Union: Prospects for a Free Trade Agreement." Working Document 298. Brussels: Centre for European Policy Studies. Available at www.ceps.eu/book/canada-and-european-union-prospects-free-trade-agreement.

Hart, Michael. 2006. *Steer or Drift? Taking Charge of Canada–US Regulatory Convergence.* C.D. Howe Institute Commentary 229. Toronto: C.D. Howe Institute.

———. 2009. *Potholes and Paperwork: Improving Cross-Border Integration and Regulation of the Automotive Industry.* C.D. Howe Institute Commentary 286. Toronto: C.D. Howe Institute.

———. 2010. *A Matter of Trust: Expanding the Preclearance of Commerce between Canada and the United States.* C.D. Howe Institute Commentary 309. Toronto: C.D. Howe Institute.

Hart, Michael, and William Dymond. 2000. "Post-Modern Trade Policy: Reflections on the Challenges to Multilateral Trade Negotiations after Seattle." *Journal of World Trade* 34, 3: 21–38.

———. 2002. "A Canada-EU FTA Is an Awful Idea." *Policy Options* (July-August): 27–32.

———. 2007. "Free Trade and Dispute Settlement: Time to Declare Victory." *Policy Options* (October): 45–51.

———. 2008. *Navigating New Trade Routes: The Rise of Value Chains, and the Challenges for Canadian Trade Policy.* C.D. Howe Institute Commentary 259. Toronto: C.D. Howe Institute.

———. 2010. "The Great Recession and International Trade." *Policy Options* (June): 84–87.

Hart, Michael, with Bill Dymond and Colin Robertson. 1994. *Decision at Midnight: Inside the Canada–US Free Trade Negotiations.* Vancouver: UBC Press.

Irwin, Douglas A. 2005. *Free Trade under Fire*, 2nd ed. Princeton, NJ: Princeton University Press.

Jones, Kent. 2010. *The Doha Blues: Institutional Crisis and Reform in the WTO.* New York: Oxford University Press.

Lewis, Howard, III, and J. David Richardson. 2001. *Why Global Commitment Really Matters.* Washington, DC: Institute for International Economics.

Maurer, Andreas. 2011. "Trade in Value Added: What Is the Country of Origin in an Interconnected World?" Background paper. Geneva: World Trade Organization. Available at www.wto.org/english/res_e/statis_e/miwi_e/background_paper_e.htm.

Ridgeway, Art. 2007. "Data Issues on Integrative Trade between Canada and the US: Measurement Issues for Supply Chains." In Dan Ciuriak, ed. *Trade Policy Research 2006.* Ottawa: Department of Foreign Affairs and International Trade.

Sally, Razeen. 2008. *Trade Policy, New Century.* London: Institute of Economic Affairs.

Schenk, Catherine R. 2011. *International Economic Relations since 1945.* London: Routledge.

Schwanen, Daniel. 2011a. "Beyond the Border and Back to the Future: Seizing the Opportunity to Enhance Canadian and US Economic Growth and Security." *Backgrounder* 141. Toronto: C.D. Howe Institute.

———. 2011b. "Go Big or Go Home: Priorities for the Canada-EU Economic and Trade Agreement." *Backgrounder* 143. Toronto: C.D. Howe Institute.

Statistics Canada. 2001. *Canadian International Merchandise Trade,* Cat. 65-001-X1B. Ottawa.

Sydor, Aaron, ed. 2011. *Global Value Chains: Impact and Implications.* Ottawa: Public Works and Government Services.

Vesselovsky, Mykyta. 2009. "New Horizons for Canada: The Return to a Multi-Polar World." In *Canada's State of Trade: Trade and Investment Update, 2009.* Ottawa: Department of Foreign Affairs and International Trade. Available at www.international.gc.ca/economist-economiste/performance/state-point/state_2009_point/2009_7.aspx?lang=eng&view=d.

Watson, William. 2011. "Hope they float." *Financial Post,* October 20. Available at http://opinion.financialpost.com/2011/10/19/william-watson-hope-they-float.

WTO and OECD (World Trade Organization and Organisation for Economic Co-operation and Development). 2010. *Report on G20 Trade and Investment Measures,* September 2009 to February 2010. Geneva: WTO.

Yeats, Alexander. 2001. "Just How Big Is Global Production Sharing?" In Sven W. Arndt and Henryk Kierzkowski, eds. *Fragmentation: New Production Patterns in the World Economy.* Oxford: Oxford University Press.

23 Canada's Policy Response to the Global Financial Crisis

Stephen McBride

Key Terms

Bilateralism

Denial

Exhortation

Middle Power

Minimalism

Multilateralism

Neo-liberalism

Principal Power

Satellite

This chapter evaluates Canada's response to the global financial and economic crisis and seeks to locate it in the context of traditional assessments of Canada's foreign policy role. Thus we begin by reviewing the standard images of Canada as a middle power; a principal but not great power; and as a **satellite** of various empires, most recently the US. In examining the response to the crisis a number of themes are identified: **exhortation, denial, minimalism**, and **bilateralism**.

The Foreign Policy Context

Traditional descriptions of Canadian foreign policy focused on three images: Canada as a **middle power** (or "honest broker"), a **principal power**, and a satellite of the United States (see Cooper 1997). These different images highlighted some of the ambiguities in Canadian foreign policy and have continued to play out during the period since the global financial and economic crisis developed.

Canada made significant efforts to construct a role as a "middle power." Some analysts considered that over time Canada achieved this goal and actually made the transition to being, if not a great power, then at least a "principal" power. Others detected a growing subservience to the United States that rendered those categories pure imagery. They saw the roots of Canadian subservience as lying in the close and growing integration of the Canadian and US economies, though this view is perhaps modified by the condition of the US—if its hegemony seems in decline in various periods, this might open more opportunities for countries like Canada.

Political factors, of course, also played a role. After the election of the Progressive Conservative government led by Brian Mulroney in 1984, Canada pursued a strategy of close political alliance and closer economic integration with the United States. Under the previous Liberal governments of Pierre Trudeau, Canadian efforts to maintain a sense of distance from the United States had at least limited substance, expressed through initiatives like the Foreign Investment Review Agency, the Third Option, and the National Energy Program. The shift from Trudeau to Mulroney has been represented as a redefinition of Canada's middle-power role—from an approach partially exercised in a "counter-consensus" direction to one that was "limitationist," reflecting "an orientation more in keeping with existing power and privilege in Canadian society and in the global order" (Neufeld 1995: 22). Another trend saw a heightened emphasis on economic priorities in Canada's foreign policy. This was symbolized by the addition of international trade to the external affairs ministry, and its renaming as the Department of Foreign Affairs and International Trade (DFAIT) (see Doern, Pal and Tomlin 1996: ch. 10). The subsequent merger of the Canadian International Development Agency (CIDA) with DFAIT to form a new Department of Foreign Affairs, Trade and Development raised similar concerns that economic considerations would dominate over aid and development, though this was not a unanimous view (see Schwartz 2013). The predominance of economic priorities within Canadian foreign policy was reinforced in 2013 with the release of the *Global Markets Action Plan*, which entrenched "the concept of 'economic diplomacy' as the driving force behind the Government of Canada's activities through its international diplomatic network. . . . [A]ll diplomatic assets . . . will be marshalled on behalf of the private sector in order to achieve the stated objectives within key foreign markets" (Canada 2013:11).

The focus on markets, the private sector, and global economic integration could be taken as evidence of the neo-liberalization of foreign economic policy, along with Canadian foreign policy generally.

More traditional activities may have faded in importance. Pointing to declining levels of official development assistance (ODA), unavailability of military resources for conducting peacekeeping operations, and a preference for pursuing trade over human rights concerns, critics have argued that Canada has changed its priorities. Similarly, Canada's record in international environmental negotiations over issues such as climate change has drawn widespread adverse comment.

Much of the discussion of Canada as a middle power has focused on the country's role in security and humanitarian contexts. But there are some common threads with discussions of Canada as an economic middle power. As a middle power, Canada's greatest influence was exercised multilaterally through membership in international institutions and organizations. Its foreign policy was functionalist, deliberately focusing on issues in which it has had the greatest potential to exert influence internationally. Multilateralism and functionalism went together. Canada's interests as a middle power and foreign policy objectives were based largely on its need for cooperation in the international system (Holmes 1967: 13).

In economic terms, the middle-power approach assumes that rules and norms have a significant impact on interstate relations and that Canada had the potential to play an important role in multilateral and bilateral arrangements. Strong multilateral regimes became a means of enhancing economic welfare and peace in an interdependent global system and of reducing US domination of the economy (Cutler and Zacher 1992: 3). The most effective medium was a cooperative and rules-based system whereby Canada's strength is derived, it is said, not from traditional sources such as military capabilities or economic status, but instead from its ability to generate ideas. More recently, Keating (2010) has noted mixed signals regarding Canadian governments' attachment to multilateralism.

Indeed, Canada's traditional commitment to multilateralism and the establishment of regime-based norms was always questioned. Historically, Canada has pursued bilateral as well as multilateral agreements (Cutler and Zacher 1992: 4; see also Cooper 1997: ch. 2; Keenes 1995). One analysis of Canada's postwar international trade policy argued that the Canadian commitment to international economic regimes was never absolute (Finlayson and Bertasi 1992). Christopher Thomas (1992) examined the bilateral trade regime with the United States in terms of Canada's growing disillusionment with the

General Agreement on Tariffs and Trade (GATT) and the need to reinforce the economic relationship with its largest trading partner. Such initiatives mirrored a long history of "creeping continentalism" in security as well as economic policy, from the wartime Hyde Park Declaration through the Defence Production Sharing Agreement of 1958 to the 1965 Auto Pact (Black and Turenne Sjolander 1996: 14).

Eventually, thinking about Canada as a middle power spawned another interpretation: that Canada made the transition to being a "foremost" (Eayrs 1975), "major" (Lyon and Tomlin 1979; Gotlieb 1987) or "principal" power (Dewitt and Kirton 1983). John Kirton has argued that the Asian financial crisis of 1997–99 affirmed Canada's position as a principal power: "In the diplomacy behind the Hong Kong reform package, Canada acted as an equal member of the G-7 concert" (Kirton 1999: 607). Canada's diplomacy during that financial crisis questioned traditional interpretations of Canadian foreign policy. Kirton argued that it demonstrated that Canada was a global player, rather than one that played a more restricted, niche-based, regional focus (624). Echoes of such ambitions can be seen in the current crisis as Canada has exhorted other countries to follow austerity policies while lauding its own fiscal rectitude in the 1990s and its stable banking sector.

Others have posited a more modest role. Michael Webb (1992) held that small and medium-sized countries were ineffective in multilateral settings, which is why Canada turned to a bilateral agreement with the United States—not from strength but rather from weakness. Some considered that the closing of the Cold War ended the conditions in which middle powers found space in which to act (David and Roussel 1998).

In contrast to arguments suggesting middle- or principal-power status, there is an interpretation of Canada as a dependent, satellite state. In this view Canada's capacity for independent and autonomous action in international affairs had been much reduced

by its successive membership in the British and US empires. Canada went from colony to nation to colony, so "what for some marked the emergence of a middle power in world politics was, for others, merely a transfer of dependent orbit, with Canada consigned to the periphery—or at best the 'semiperiphery' of the world economy" (Nossal 1997: 60–61; see also Hawes 1984; Clarkson 1968; Lumsden 1970).

David Dewitt and John Kirton (1983: 28), who have advanced the idea of Canada as a principal power, labelled this perspective as the "peripheral-dependence" perspective because it stresses Canada's cultural, political, and economic dependence on a more powerful international actor. It also highlights the reliance of Canada on the US market for international trade, and the predominance of US investment in Canada.

Growing nationalism in the late 1960s and 1970s suggested, even to supporters of the satellite interpretation, that this situation might be reversed. The so-called Third Option represented a desire to "lessen the vulnerability of the Canadian economy to external factors, in particular the impact of the United States" (Sharp 1972). Despite the Third Option's lack of success, nationalist hopes were aroused periodically, as with the nationalist measures taken by the Trudeau government of 1980–84.

Indeed, it could be argued that by the 1970s, Canada was close to achieving, or had achieved, middle-power status as measured by autonomy from the United States, but that later events, like the federal government's decision on the free trade agreement with the United States, abdicated much of Canada's economic and cultural sovereignty and returned the country to a satellite-like status (Clarkson 1991). Efforts at greater autonomy, such as the attempt at a third national policy and the Third Option trade initiative, lasted only as long as the global balance of power was conducive to the more autonomous role. The election of President Reagan signalled a much more aggressive US stance, and that of Prime Minister Mulroney signalled the end of any Canadian attempt to retain autonomy in the face of the new US stance. Once this shift happened, the most important international agreements became the bilateral ones with the United States. Canada's involvement in multilateral economic regimes was primarily designed to support US preferences and policies—"Multilateralism was always first and foremost a product of American hegemony" (Black and Turenne Sjolander 1996: 27). In sum, Canada's multilateral involvement "provides direct reinforcement for United States foreign policy doctrines and limits [Canada's] dissent from U.S. positions to marginal aspects. Bilaterally [Canada] assigns the highest importance to themes of harmony and commonality in the 'special relationship' . . . and encourages a flow of transaction from the United States into Canada" (Dewitt and Kirton 1983: 28). As we shall see, the theme of bilateralism has certainly been a feature of Canada's reaction to the 2008 economic crisis. However, we also note the continued interdependence between bilateralism and multilateralism in the North American context (Macdonald 2010). Various multilateral initiatives, such as the proposed Comprehensive Economic and Trade Agreement with the European Union and the Trans-Pacific Partnership (TPP) negotiations, coexist with the bilateral impulse of successive Canadian governments.

Canada in North America: Triumph of Economism

The policy record of the Mulroney years—the Canada–US Free Trade Agreement (CUFTA), the pursuit of deregulation, the elimination of some of the key elements of the welfare state and the embrace of a more hawkish foreign policy—signalled to some that Mulroney had "closed down the Canadian dream" of autonomy and independence (Martin

1993: 272–73). Yet even under Mulroney, it has been argued that there were examples of an independent course being followed—on the Strategic Arms Limitation Treaty, and on Central America, Cuba, and South Africa (Clarkson 2002: 387–8).

Following Mulroney, foreign policy once again exhibited ambiguity and contradiction in which, however, economic considerations loomed largest. The Chrétien and Martin years were characterized by a concerted pursuit of export-led growth typified by large "Team Canada" trade missions. Although much of Canada's trade liberalization agenda was in step with that of the US, particularly with respect to hemispheric free trade in the Americas, other aspects of Canadian foreign policy deviated from the "US friendly" version articulated by the Mulroney government.

Of course, in the case of trade, Canada–US relations are not always harmonious. Though many argue that Canada's heavy reliance on the US as an export market, combined with the CUFTA and North American Free Trade Area (NAFTA), put Canada in a vulnerable position vis-à-vis the US (Cohen 2003: 38–39), Canada nonetheless has vigorously engaged in numerous trade disputes with the US through both the World Trade Organization (WTO) and NAFTA. The ongoing softwood lumber dispute is perhaps the best known of these disputes (Zhang 2007), but many others have taken place in areas surrounding agriculture, steel, fisheries, and magazines. However, these are disputes over specific applications of internationally and bilaterally agreed rules and in defence of specific private interests. On the need for a rules-based system and the content of those rules there are no significant differences between Canada and the US.

Proponents argue that the overall trading relationship between Canada and the US runs quite smoothly when one considers its size (Cohen 2003: 39). According to the US Department of State, bilateral trade disputes between the two countries occur in about 2 per cent of total trade (US Department of State 2008). Yet this ignores pressures which have been brought to bear since the Canada–US Free Trade Agreement and NAFTA were signed, and which have led to some of the dispute settlement procedures of those agreements falling into disuse (McBride 2012). Chapter 19 of both agreements allowed an appeal of US determinations on dumping and subsidy issues to a binding binational panel of trade experts. A report commissioned by the Canadian–American Business Council demonstrated that the US government had sought to delegitimize the Chapter 19 process, originally a feature of the Canada–US agreement, by a variety of means. These included changing the language of Chapter 19 when NAFTA was negotiated, underfunding the US section of the NAFTA Secretariat, making political and protectionist appointments to the US roster of prospective NAFTA Chapter 19 panellists, delaying adjudication wherever possible, attacking the integrity of NAFTA panellists involved in adverse decisions (Herman 2005), rewriting US laws to escape adverse rulings, and adopting administrative practices, such as refusing to accept that practices ruled inadmissible in one case should not be used in other cases. The effect of this strategy is to deprive exporters of finality with respect to Chapter 19 decisions, thus rendering the process unattractive to many (Baker and Hostetler LLP 2004: 1–5). So the absence of current disputes may reflect inadequate mechanisms to resolve them rather than an absence of grounds for them.

The lack of balance in the economic relationship with the US created vulnerability for Canada, especially in a post-9/11 environment where the Unites States' security concerns trumped trade. Canadian exports to the United States accounted for approximately 85 per cent of Canada's total exports, while exports from the US to Canada represented only 25 per cent of US exports (Cohen 2003:38). In the early 2000s, even long-time supporters of continental free trade made the case for trade diversification: "However, it may now be necessary for Canada to consider a second policy direction, one that would attempt to confront the U.S. export dependency that is at the root of the present uncertainties facing Ottawa. . . . The Canadian government should take a more proactive role in analyzing Canada's strengths and weaknesses in export trade, including the prospects for developing new overseas markets. In the past decade, exports from Canada and other countries were drawn into the United States due to the extraordinary vitality of the U.S. economy. The current U.S. slowdown may provide Canada an opportunity to diversify export trade in a way that would strengthen the country's economy and, ultimately, its polity" (Winham and Ostry 2003).

Many argued that the events of 9/11 necessitated some degree of greater integration with the US and that Canadian foreign policy should be articulated more within a "North American" context. Organizations such as the C.D. Howe Institute and the Canadian Council of Chief Executives (CCCE) promoted further policy integration between Canada and the US in both military and economic matters. In rather stark contrast to this US-oriented approach, others, such as the Council of Canadians (COC), Canadian Centre for Policy Alternatives (CCPA), and Polaris Institute were deeply skeptical of further integration in either area.

A parliamentary report (House of Commons 2002) suggested that Canada must conduct cost-benefit analysis in order to determine in what areas "more integrated policies make sense, as well as where Canadian policies—on foreign, defence and security, and trade issues, and in affected domestic fields—ought to be different from, or even at odds with, those of its North American partners" (14). However, the report went on to say that "this analysis must take into account cross-border effects, given how costly disruptions to established continental connections could be, potentially raising the 'price of difference' to unacceptable levels" (14).

The latter part of this recommendation was very much in keeping with the Canadian government's trade-focused and pro-liberalization foreign policy trajectory, which either viewed the trade-off of some degree of sovereignty as an acceptable cost to securing open markets and unrestricted borders, or insisted that these trade-offs were an "expression of sovereignty." Thus trade trumps other foreign policy objectives. Andrew Cohen argued, "Today trade is the brightest face of Canada's internationalism. As a soldier, Canada is ill-equipped; as a donor, Canada is underfunded, and ineffective; as a diplomat, Canada is becoming less influential and less imaginative. As a trader though, Canada is a success, and getting stronger . . ." (Cohen 2003:109).

Canadian business was the chief architect of deep integration with the United States and tirelessly promoted the original free trade agreement with the US and its NAFTA successor. But the push for a new "grand bargain" (Dobson 2002) gave way in the face of US indifference to a more incremental approach.

The Crisis

Whatever the ultimate cause of the financial and economic crisis that became headline news in the fall of 2008, its immediate impact was felt in the US finance and banking sector. From there its effects spread to other banking systems which, it transpired, were either interlocked with the US system or had been similarly deregulated and exposed to high-risk investments. The impact of actual or threatened bank collapse and a consequent credit crunch were quickly transferred to the "real" economy, with resulting bankruptcies and lay-offs.

The crisis was deep and global and it became a real issue whether the world was in for a repeat of the Great Depression of the 1930s or whether this could be averted by a coordinated policy response by the world's leading states. It is clear that the world economy experienced its most significant crisis since the 1930s and escaped, if it proves to have done so, because of major policy interventions falling well outside the box of the **neo-liberal** orthodoxy that has long informed economic policy-making and was arguably part of the reason for the crisis itself.

Canada's Response

Canada's response to the crisis can be analysed using a number of descriptors. One is **exhortation** for others to follow Canada's example of relatively strong banking regulation and 1990s fiscal conservatism. Other descriptors—**denial** and **minimalism**—highlight its government's lack of speed and urgency in the face of the crisis. Other responses built on the traditional and, as noted previously, interconnected themes of **bilateralism** and **multilateralism** in Canadian foreign policy, in particular the desire to strengthen the bilateral relationship with the United States while simultaneously exploring opportunities for diversifying beyond it.

Denial

Many accounts of the crisis begin by noting the role of deregulation of banking and finance in the US. The reforms reduced state regulation to minimal levels and instead increasingly relied on self-regulation by the industry. These moves "permitted banks and investment companies to overexpose themselves to risky mortgage-backed financial instruments . . . (and) . . . the expansion of unregulated mortgage-brokers with their subprime mortgages increased the fragility of the housing market" (Hudson 2009: 57–58). It was, as many have noted, a crisis waiting to happen. The shocks in the US were severe. The five largest investment banks—Bear Stearns, Merrill Lynch, Lehman Brothers,

Goldman Sachs, and Morgan Stanley—were all hit hard, and either failed or were subject to government reorganization. The Washington Mutual Bank failed in September 2008, and other banks and insurance companies were on the verge of collapse. In response, the US government introduced a $700 billion Troubled Asset Relief Program (TARP) to purchase bank equity and buy out bad loans. Other measures included the nationalization of Fannie Mae and Freddie Mac, institutions which held half of US mortgages, complemented by other initiatives to restore liquidity and provide assistance to financial institutions (Loxley 2009: 60–70). Similar measures were taken in other countries, and world attention was focused on the developing crisis in the autumn of 2008.

But not in Canada. Or, at least, the government of Canada was not focused on the looming crisis. The first pattern in Canada's response to the crisis was one of official denial. In part, the denial rested on the argument that the Canadian banking system was better regulated and not as exposed to the meltdown as banks in many countries. There is obviously some truth to this claim, although deregulatory measures in the 2006 budget did bring a version of sub-prime mortgages to Canada, including zero down payments and extended amortization periods first to 35 and later to 40 years (McKenna 2013: B1), until a policy reversal in 2008 banned the practice (McNish and McArthur 2008). Moreover, the federal government has ended up guaranteeing some $900 billion through CMHC mortgage insurance schemes (McKenna 2013: B1). It is also true that the federal government has subsequently pumped very large sums into supporting financial institutions, amounting to an estimated $114 billion (Macdonald 2012; see also Russell 2012: 26-7), and that a number of Canadian banks have had to write down billions of dollars in bad loans. But Canada did not nationalize banks as was the case elsewhere (Loxley 2009: 70-1), and the Canadian Bankers Association (CBA)

(2012) dismissed claims that the funding supports were "bailouts" designed to prevent bank failure. Rather, the CBA argued, they were liquidity measures designed to ensure the continued flow of credit to businesses and consumers.

Not surprisingly, the prospect that Canada faced an economic crisis was downplayed by the ruling Conservatives during the federal election campaign, which concluded with the election of another minority Conservative government on 14 October 2008. On 4 October, Prime Minister Stephen Harper followed his earlier (Laghi, Leblanc, and Clark 2008) opinion that "If we were going to have some kind of crash or recession we would have had it by now" by criticizing the US Congress for "panicking" after deciding on a $700 billion bailout package: "I think if we don't panic here, we stick on course, we keep taking additional actions, make sure everything we do is affordable, we will emerge from this as strong as ever" (CanWest News Service 3 October 2008: A2). Perhaps more surprisingly, the government continued to deny the severity of the economic situation in the immediate post-election period. Indeed, when the government presented a fiscal and economic update to Parliament on 27 November, it turned out to contain a series of provocations to the opposition parties—suspension of the right to strike for federal civil servants until 2011, suspension of the right of female federal employees to achieve remedies on pay-equity issues, privatization of some Crown assets, and elimination of subsidies to political parties. More importantly, in an international context where many governments were engaged in drastic action to address the economic crisis, Finance Minister Jim Flaherty declined to introduce a stimulus program at that point in time and opted for a neo-liberal business-as-usual approach consisting of low taxes and a prediction of a small budget surplus (Valpy 2009: 9–10). The effect was to launch the country into a short but bitter constitutional crisis as a coalition of opposition parties representing a majority of seats in the House of Commons unsuccessfully attempted to oust the minority Conservative government (see Russell and Sossin 2009).

In the course of the constitutional crisis the government demonstrated its determination to stay in power at all costs, and arguably did so as a result of a Governor General's decision that violated Canada's constitutional order in a number of respects (Heard 2009). Notwithstanding the economic crisis, government leaders, including the prime minister, used rhetoric that inflamed traditional regional and linguistic–cultural divisions.

Minimalism

With the benefit of hindsight we can see that the Canadian government made bold claims regarding the vigour of its response to the crisis by way of fiscal stimulus (Flaherty 2012), while also preaching the virtue of fiscal austerity at home and abroad. Austerity measures designed to achieve a balanced budget by 2015 were implemented. Overall, the pattern seemed to be one of restoring neo-liberal normality as quickly as possible while gleaning political credit by claiming that stimulus measures had averted a deep recession.

Early signs of a business-as-usual approach on the part of the Canadian government included an emphasis on tax cuts rather than spending as a way of producing a stimulus. As late as 20 November 2008, these were defended as an adequate response to the crisis. Certainly the tax cuts were significant, amounting to 2 per cent of GDP (Blackwell 2008). Moreover, they were conceived as permanent—that is, to remain in place after any recession had ended. Finance Minister Flaherty contrasted them with any temporary spending stimulus package that, in his view, gave only a transitory economic boost (Blackwell 2008).

By the time of the 27 January 2009 budget, the federal government was prepared to admit that the global crisis had reached Canada and that the economy was in recession (albeit one that had come later and was shallower than elsewhere). In that budget the government claimed it would provide a stimulus of $30 billion, or 1.9 per cent of GDP (Canada Department of Finance 2009: 10). There were grounds for thinking the actual stimulus might be less. For example, the figures assumed that provinces and municipalities would step forward with matching funds for infrastructure programs. To the extent that they did not, the stimulus could fall to 1.5 per cent (Canada Department of Finance 2009: 30). Moreover, critics claimed that, in attempting to come close to the International Monetary Fund (IMF), Organisation for Economic Co-operation and Development (OECD), and other international recommendations of a stimulus of 2 per cent of GDP, the government had jumped "through a variety of creative hoops . . . but the reality is that the proposed federal stimulus amounts to just 0.7% of GDP in 2009–10" (Macdonald 2009: 5). Moreover, almost 35 per cent of the stimulus came in the form of broad-based and corporate tax cuts, measures with poor stimulative multipliers compared to spending programs (Macdonald 2009: 5). By the CCPA's calculations, only 4 per cent of the budget tax cuts were directed to low-income Canadians, arguably the group most likely to spend any moneys received, and thus help stimulate the broader economy (CCPA 2009: 3). The spending component of the stimulus package was explicitly declared to be temporary in order to enable a quick return to balanced budgets (Canada Department of Finance 2009: 12). Thus program spending, 13 per cent of GDP in 2007–8, was projected to rise to 14.7 per cent in 2009–10, before falling back to 13.1 per cent in 2013–14 (Canada Department of Finance 2009: 29). Later figures (Flaherty 2012: 238) projected program expenditures to fall to 12.7 per cent of GDP by 2016–17. Clearly the role of government in the economy was to revert to the status quo once the immediate crisis was over. Much of the apparent pressure on the Canadian budget was self-induced: "the policy preference for tax cuts has helped to diminish government revenues and in so doing has also contributed to the narrative of 'belt-tightening' for the public sector. Having helped manufacture a sizeable deficit, Minister Flaherty has made . . . the deficit into . . . a major public issue and used it to justify austerity measures" (Stoney and Krawchenko 2013: 39). Spending and tax cuts were dwarfed by up to $200 billion made available to fill gaps in credit markets and "improve access to financing for Canadian households and businesses" (Canada Department of Finance 2009: 15).

Exhortation

Just as Canada's early domestic stance on the crisis was minimalist, so too was its reaction in international circles. Early manifestations of crisis in 2007 were met with Bank of Canada refusal to ease monetary conditions or resort to economic stimulus. At the IMF meeting of finance ministers and central bank governors in October 2007, the conclusion was drawn that the private sector was responsible for developing solutions to rectify the credit crisis. Reportedly, Canada was one of the strongest advocates of leaving it to the private sector (Baragar 2009: 88).

A year later, in advance of a G20 meeting of finance ministers and central bankers, the *National Post* reported that Canada was opposing efforts by European states to make significant reforms in the global financial architecture—crafting financial regulations to bind all countries and having them enforced by a stronger IMF. Canada, together with the US and Australia, emphasized domestic regulation and, according to John Kirton, Canada was on "the minimalist end of the spectrum and is probably even more minimalist than the United States" (Vieira and Callan 2008: FP1). The subsequent G20 leaders' summit adopted a compromise declaration that emphasized better international oversight of large financial institutions, greater transparency of financial products, and monitoring of executive salaries (*Montreal Gazette* 16 November:A4), and a more detailed communiqué was issued after the London G20 in April 2009.

In general, it is fair to say that the G20 Finance Ministers' Communiques record the transition in prescriptions from the 2008–9 period to the period 2010 and on. In the 2008–9 period, the ministers highlighted the need for coordinated demand-stimulus, in conjunction with reduced interest rates, financial institution recapitalization, and regulation of the financial sector. From around 2010 onwards, there was a shift towards fiscal consolidation, deficit reduction, reduction of debt-to-GDP ratios, structural labour market reforms, and measures to buttress investor confidence.

Canada certainly played a role in pushing this transition and in maintaining pressure for a fiscally conservative approach. As host for the Toronto G20 summit in 2010, Stephen Harper opened the meeting by balancing stimulus and fiscal consolidation goals:

> Financial consolidation plans must be credible. They must lay out easily understood objectives, and member countries must be accountable for achieving these objectives. Specifically, we should agree the deficits will be halved by 2013. We should also agree that government debt to GDP ratios should be stabilized by 2016 at the least, or put on a downward path. (Harper 2010a)

He was able to conclude the meeting by noting that:

> . . . [W]e have arrived at firm targets for advanced economies on debt reduction and reducing debt-GDP ratios. The targets are a 50 per cent deficit reduction by 2013 and a debt-to-GDP ratio that should be at least stabilized or

on a downward trend by 2016. Now, that said, all leaders recognized that fiscal consolidation is not an end in itself. There will be a continued role for ongoing stimulus in the short term as we develop the framework for strong, sustainable and balanced growth. (Harper 2010b)

Reporting on Canada's position at the St Petersburg G20 meetings in 2013, the *Financial Post* reported that:

Even before Russian president and host Vladimir Putin greeted leaders at the opulent Constantine Palace on Thursday, Harper had already thrown a challenge to other G20 nations. His government is committing to a debt-to-GDP ratio of 25% by 2021 and encouraging others to follow suit with their own targets—despite earlier G20 pledges this year to favour growth-oriented policies over austerity . . . . Harper has consistently staked his ground in the debt-reduction camp. He was a key driver behind a commitment made at the Toronto G20 summit in 2010 to reduce debt around the world and has made deficit reduction his top domestic priority leading up to the 2015 federal election. (Ditchburn 2013)

Bilateralism and the Pursuit of Special Status

In considering Canada's role in NAFTA, Stephanie Golob (2008) has made the argument that just as Canada entered NAFTA to protect its already existing bilateral free trade agreement with the US, its conduct inside the agreement has continued to exhibit bilateralism rather than trilateralism. Although the formation of the Security and Prosperity Partnership (SPP) in March 2005 appeared to herald greater attention to trilateral

relations, it has languished as Canada has continued a more traditional approach, seeking to be viewed as an "insider" in Washington while seeking to privilege Canadian over Mexican interests.

To some extent this view must be qualified by Canada's conduct in multilateral forums since the crisis—being positioned in the austerity camp at the G20 rather than the US's favoured stimulus camp, for example, and its engagement in trade diversification negotiations such as those with the EU, together with vigorous lobbying of Washington on issues such as the Keystone pipeline project—deemed central to Canada's economic interests.

Still, the bilateral approach has also been highlighted. In an exchange of opinion pieces in *The Globe and Mail* in May 2009, Andrés Rozental, a former deputy foreign minister of Mexico and chairman of the Mexican Council on Foreign Relations, and Robert Pastor, co-director, Center for North American Studies at American University, penned an appeal for Canada "to accept Mexico as a true partner. If it does, the North American concept will be reinvigorated and become an example of progressive co-operative integration, rather than a failed experiment to be disdained and discarded." The current reality, they argued, was that "the three countries of North America have reverted to two bilateral relationships—U.S.–Canada and U.S.–Mexico—rather than approaching our common challenges together" (Rozental and Pastor 2009). In response, John Manley, former deputy prime minister and finance minister of Canada, and later president and CEO of the CCCE, together with Gordon Giffin, former US ambassador to Canada, asserted the case for bilateralism: "Our friends seem skeptical that Canada and the United States share a 'special relationship.' We assert that this is a unique bilateral relationship, a model in international relations built over many decades based upon similar values and democratic institutions and common heritage. . . . By contrast, the trilateral relationship began with

NAFTA in 1994. It is an economic arrangement with none of the deep historical and other connotations of the Canada–U.S. partnership. While the United States does have two borders, the similarity ends at that statement. . . . If the concept of a real North American Community is ever going to be realized, it will be because leadership has been shown by the northern partners" (Manley and Giffin 2009). The tendency towards bilateralism can be seen at work in Canadian reactions to the buy-America components of the US stimulus package and in the "me too-ism" of the bailouts of the automobile industry. Similarly, Canada's imposition of complex application procedures and visa fees for Mexican visitors infuriated its NAFTA partner (Blanchfield 2013).

The post-crisis US stimulus package contained provisions barring foreign suppliers from participation in funded projects. As most of the money in question was to be spent by state and municipal governments, which are not part of either WTO or NAFTA government procurement provisions, US officials considered the measures compliant with trade agreements. Canadian politicians and officials reacted by pleading for exemptions and, alternately, for President Obama to veto the legislation, or Canada would take action under trade treaties (*The Globe and Mail* 9 April 2008). Business organizations worried that protectionist measures could spread and start a trade war on a 1930s scale. It soon became apparent that threatening action under trade treaties was an empty gesture since the US was correct that state and municipal procurement was excluded. The Canadian tactic then switched to calls for reciprocal procurement liberalization. Under these proposals, Canadian companies would have access to procurement in the US, and Canadian provinces and municipalities, some of which had adopted calls for retaliatory action against US companies, would be open to bids from US companies. There was broad provincial agreement and some support, too, from highly integrated companies with cross-border

supply chains (CBC News 29 September 2009). A bilateral deal was concluded on 5 February 2010.

The crisis of the tightly integrated North American auto industry meant that Canada had a strong interest in making sure it participated in any industry bailout lest a US package privilege auto production in that country. Expressed willingness to participate does not obscure the fact that it was the US which devised the package, leaving Canadians as "ultimately passive observers, who can only cross our fingers and hope that the Obama administration's plans save Canadian autoworkers' jobs" (Ibbitson 2009: A19).

Over the course of 2008–9 it became clear that Canada's contribution would be set by and proportionate to the package established by the US. Similarly, conditions attached to the deal in the US reduced labour costs, amounting to $10 per hour, and changes in work organization would resonate north of the border (Vieira and Van Praet 2009). When the US had determined the size of the bailout to General Motors (GM) for instance, the Canadian contribution ($10.5 billion, one-third of which would be paid by Ontario) became clear.

Conclusion

Canada seems to have played a limited role in handling the global economic crisis, though it certainly exerted its influence in support of the most conservative solutions on offer. It is possible that Canada's low profile reflects the lesser degree to which it was affected by the crisis. In any case, in terms of classic views of Canada as a middle or principal power, there seems little to substantiate such roles. Indeed, as the G20 replaces the G7 or G8 as a key international forum, Canada may find its voice correspondingly lessened.

The combination of denial, minimalism, exhortation, and bilateralism may also reflect the limited options available to a country that has increasingly prioritized economic factors in its foreign policy while also emphasizing, in practice if not in theory, bilateralism with a much stronger partner rather than the multilateral approach traditionally favoured by Canadian governments. The choices made in the past, notably free trade and ever tighter economic integration with the United States may indeed, as Lawrence Martin commented about the Mulroney government, have foreclosed the possibility of Canadian autonomy and independence (Martin 1993: 272–73). Still, this comment may be exaggerated or limited in its temporal or spatial applicability, as indicated by a series of highly publicized rejections of foreign investments (McClearn 2012). Notwithstanding such apparent exceptions, it is difficult in conditions of neo-liberal globalization, augmented by continental integration, to imagine a Canadian government resorting to economic nationalist measures such as the National Energy Program, or controls, or routine rejections of foreign investments. Of course, one of the explicit purposes of NAFTA was to end the possibility of this type of measure within that trade area. As Bruce Doern and Brian Tomlin put it, for the Mulroney government this was a "desirable loss of sovereignty" (Doern and Tomlin 1991: 258).

The fact that Canada, for the past 25 years, has had neo-liberal governments reluctant to depart from pre-existing certainties about the superiority of market solutions only increases the difficulty of imagining alternatives and, more concretely, of estimating how many degrees of freedom a country like Canada would have in implementing them. Perhaps we will not really know until such time as Canada has a government prepared to at least examine whether the choices made in the neo-liberal period continue to serve the county's interests. For example, a future government might consider whether the collapse of the Chapter 19 process under NAFTA, the procedure that was supposed to guarantee Canadian exporters a fair hearing in the face of US protectionist pressures, means that the calculus of costs and benefits of that agreement should be revisited. It could be that NAFTA, given its costs in national autonomy in areas like energy, no longer provides anything additional to what is available under the WTO, the autonomy costs of which are lower. A future government might revisit the climate change-environmental file and reach different conclusions; or might consider whether the Canadian military might be more usefully employed in peacekeeping or conflict resolution situations than as a bit-player in US military operations; or it might re-evaluate the idea that one size fits all in free trade and investment agreements with developing countries; and so on.

The argument that Canada is heavily constrained by global structural forces undoubtedly has some strength. But it is also true that much Canadian policy, including its response of denial, minimalism, exhortation, and bilateralism to the recent economic crisis, while driven by the government's neo-liberal ideology, seems to have offered some scope for manoeuvre, space that might be exploited also by a future government of different ideological persuasion.

Questions for Review

1. Are the traditional lenses for viewing Canadian foreign policy—middle power, principal power, satellite—helpful in understanding Canada's response to the global economic crisis?

2. Are bilateralism and multilateralism alternative or complementary strategies?

3. What is the evidence for suggesting that economic self-interest has now become the dominant motivation in Canadian foreign policy?

4. Do you think that Canada's resort to exhortation and praising its own record is likely to be effective in influencing others?

Suggested Readings

Baragar, Fletcher. 2009. "Canada and the Crisis," pp. 77–106 in Julie Guard and Wayne Antony, eds. *Bankruptcies and Bailouts*. Halifax: Fernwood.

Clarkson, Stephen, ed. 1968. *An Independent Foreign Policy for Canada?* Toronto: McClelland and Stewart.

Keating, Tom. 2010. "Multilateralism: Past Imperfect, Future Conditional." *Canadian Foreign Policy Journal* 16, 2: 9–25.

Macdonald, Laura. 2010. "A Fine Balance: Multilateralism and Bilateralism in Canadian Policy in the North American Region." *Canadian Foreign Policy Journal* 16, 2: 111–24.

Stoney, Christopher, and Tamara Krawchenko. 2013. "Crisis and Opportunism: Public Finance Trends from Stimulus to Austerity in Canada," pp. 33–58 in Carlos Fanelli and Bryan Evans, eds. *Great Recession Proof? Shattering the Myth of Canadian Exceptionalism*. Ottawa: Red Quill Books.

References

Baker and Hostetler LLP. 2004. *Duties and Dumping: What's Going Wrong with Chapter 19?* Washington, DC: Canadian-American Business Council and Center for Strategic and International Studies.

Baragar, Fletcher. 2009. "Canada and the Crisis." In Julie Guard and Wayne Antony, eds. *Bankruptcies and Bailouts*. Halifax: Fernwood.

Black, David, and Claire Turenne Sjolander. 1996. "Multilateralism Re-constituted and the Discourse of Canadian Foreign Policy." *Studies in Political Economy* 49 (Spring): 7–36.

Blackwell, Richard. 2008. "No further stimulus in the works, Flaherty says." *The Globe and Mail*, 29 November, B6.

Blanchfield, Mike. 2013. "Mexican Ambassador wants 'road map' for end of visa rules." Available at www.theglobeand-mail.com/news/world/were-really-mad-at-canada-over-visa-restrictions-mexico/article14326868/.

Canada. Department of Finance. 2009. *Canada's Economic Action Plan: Budget 2009.* Ottawa: Department of Finance.

Canada. Department of Foreign Affairs, Trade and Development (DFATD). 2013. *Global Markets Action Plan.* Ottawa: DFATD. Available at http://international.gc.ca/global-markets-marches-mondiaux/plan.aspx?lang=eng.

Canadian Bankers Association. 2012. "Canadian Bankers Association statement regarding Canadian Centre for Policy Alternatives (CCPA) bank report." 30 April. Available at www.cba.ca/en/media-room/65-news-releases/618-canadian-bankers-association-statement-regarding-canadian-centre-for-policy-alternatives-ccpa-bank-report.

Canadian Centre for Policy Alternatives (CCPA). *Federal Budget 2009: CCPA Analysis.* Ottawa: CCPA.

CanWest News Service. "Harper criticizes U.S. economic policy while unveiling help for apprentices." 3 October 2008. Available at www.canada.com/topics/news/features/decisioncanada/story.html?id=bc22b1f3-a93c-41b0-a97a-d05d4f3409eb.

Clarkson, Stephen, ed. 1968. *An Independent Foreign Policy for Canada?* Toronto: McClelland and Stewart.

———. 1991. "Disjunctions: Free Trade and the Paradox of Canadian Development," pp. 103–26 in Daniel Drache and Meric S. Gertler, eds. *The New Era of Global Competition: State Policy and Market Power.* Montreal and Kingston: McGill-Queen's University Press.

———. 2002. *Uncle Sam and Us: Globalization, Neoconservatism, and the Canadian State.* Toronto: University of Toronto Press.

Cohen, Andrew. 2003. *While Canada Slept: How We Lost our Place in the World.* Toronto: McClelland and Stewart.

Cooper, Andrew F. 1997. *Canadian Foreign Policy.* Scarborough, ON: Prentice-Hall.

Cutler, A. Claire, and Mark W. Zacher. 1992. "Introduction," pp. 3–16 in A. Claire Cutler and Mark W. Zacher, eds. *Canadian Foreign Policy and International Economic Regimes.* Vancouver: UBC Press.

David, Charles-Philippe, and Stéphane Roussel. 1998. "'Middle Power Blues': Canadian Policy and International Security after the Cold War." *American Review of Canadian Studies* 28, 1–2 (Spring and Summer): 131–56.

Dewitt, David, and John Kirton. 1983. *Canada as a Principal Power: A Study in Foreign Policy and International Relations.* Toronto: Wiley.

Ditchburn, Jennifer. 2013. "Harper challenges G20 leaders to follow Canadian example on debt reduction." *Financial Post*, 5 September. Available at http://business.financial-post.com/2013/09/05/harper-challenges-g20-leaders-to-follow-canadian-example-on-debt-reduction/.

Dobson, Wendy. 2002. "Shaping the Future of the North American Economic Space: A Framework for Action," *The Border Papers.* C.D. Howe Institute No. 162, April.

Doern, G. Bruce, and Brian W. Tomlin. 1991. *Faith and Fear: The Free Trade Story.* Toronto: Stoddart.

Doern, G. Bruce, Leslie A. Pal, and Brian W. Tomlin. 1996. *Border Crossings: The Internationalization of Canadian Public Policy.* Toronto: Oxford University Press.

Eayrs, James. 1975. "Defining a New Place for Canada in the Hierarchy of World Power." *International Perspectives* (May/June): 15–24.

Finlayson, Jock A., and Stefano Bertasi. 1992. "Evolution of Canadian Post-War International Trade Policy," pp. 36–46 in A. Claire Cutler and Mark W. Zacher, eds. *Canadian Foreign Policy and International Economic Regimes.* Vancouver: UBC Press.

Flaherty, James. 2012. "Jobs, Growth and Long-term Prosperity: Economic Action Plan 2012." Ottawa: Government of Canada.

Golob, Stephanie R. 2008. "The Return of the Quiet Canadian: Canada's Approach to Regional Integration after 9/11," pp. 83–100 in Brian Bow and Patrick Lennox, eds., *An Independent Foreign Policy for Canada? Challenges and Choices for the Future.* Toronto: University of Toronto Press.

Gotlieb, Allan. 1987. "Canada: A Nation Comes of Age." *The Globe and Mail*, 29 October, A7.

Guard, Julie, and Wayne Antony, eds. 2009. *Bankruptcies and Bailouts.* Halifax: Fernwood.

Harper, Stephen. 2010a. Statement at the Opening Plenary session, G20 Summit, Toronto, 27 June. Available at http://pm.gc.ca/eng/news/2010/06/27/statement-prime-minister-canada-opening-plenary-session-g-20-summit-toronto.

———. 2010b. Statement on the closing of the G20 Summit, Toronto, 27 June. Available at http://pm.gc.ca/eng/news/2010/06/27/statement-prime-minister-canada-closing-g-20-summit.

Hawes, Michael K. 1984. *Principal Power, Middle Power, or Satellite?* Toronto: York Research Programme in Strategic Studies.

Heard, Andrew. 2009. "The Governor General's Suspension of Parliament: Duty Done or a Perilous Precedent?," pp. 47–62 in Peter Russell and Lorne Sossin, eds. *Parliamentary Democracy in Crisis.* Toronto: University of Toronto Press.

Herman, Lawrence L. 2005. "Making NAFTA Better: Comments on the Evolution of Chapter 19." Ottawa: Centre for Trade Policy and Law, Occasional Papers in International Trade Law and Policy 57.

Holmes, John. 1967. "Canada's Role in International Organizations." *The Canadian Banker* 74, 1 (Spring): 115–30.

House of Commons. 2002. "Partners in North America: Advancing Canada's Relations with the United States and Mexico." Ottawa: Standing Committee on Foreign Affairs and International Trade.

Hudson, Ian. 2009. "From Deregulation to Crisis." In Julie Guard and Wayne Antony, eds. *Bankruptcies and Bailouts.* Halifax: Fernwood.

Ibbitson, John. 2009. "When it comes to the Canadian economy, Obama may as well be PM." *The Globe and Mail*, 20 May, A19.

Keating, Tom. 2010. "Multilateralism: Past Imperfect, Future Conditional." *Canadian Foreign Policy Journal* 16, 2: 9–25.

Keenes, Ernie. 1995. "The Myth of Multilateralism: Exception and Bilateralism in Canadian International Economic Relations." *International Journal* 50, 4 (Autumn): 755–78.

Kirton, John. 1999. "Canada as a Principal Power: G-7 and IMF Diplomacy in the Crisis of 1997–9." *International Journal* 54, 4 (Autumn): 603–24.

Laghi, Brian, Daniel Leblanc, and Campbell Clark. 2008. "Harper Unfazed by Market Crisis." *The Globe and Mail*, 15 September. Available at http://www.theglobeandmail.com/news/politics/harper-unfazed-by-market-crisis/article1061165/?page=all.

Loxley, John. 2009. "Financial Dimensions: Origins and State Responses." In Julie Guard and Wayne Antony, eds. *Bankruptcies and Bailouts.* Halifax: Fernwood.

Lumsden, Ian, ed. 1970. *Close the 49th Parallel, Etc: The Americanization of Canada.* Toronto: University of Toronto Press.

Lyon, Peyton, and Brian Tomlin. 1979. *Canada as an International Actor.* Toronto: Macmillan of Canada.

Macdonald, David. 2009. "Too Little Too Late." Ottawa: *ccpa.*

———. 2012. "The Big Banks' Secret: Estimating Government Support for Canadian Banks During the Financial Crisis." Ottawa: CCPA.

Macdonald, Laura. 2010. "A Fine Balance: Multilateralism and Bilateralism in Canadian Policy in the North American Region." *Canadian Foreign Policy Journal* 16, 2: 111–24.

Manley, John, and Gordon Giffin. 2009. "A table for two, not three." *The Globe and Mail*, 15 May.

Martin, Lawrence. 1993. *Pledge of Allegiance: The Americanization of Canada in the Mulroney Years.* Toronto: McClelland and Stewart.

McBride, Stephen. 2012. "The Scope and Limits of a Public–Private Hybrid: Dispute Settlement under NAFTA Chapter 19." *New Political Economy* 17, 2: 117–35.

McClearn, Matthew. 2012. "Is Canada Closed to Foreign Investment?" *Canadian Business*, 19 November. Available at http://www.canadianbusiness.com/business-strategy/is-canada-closed-to-foreign-investment/.

McKenna, Barrie. 2013. "After decades of loosening mortgage credit, Ottawa tangles in a mess of its own making." *The Globe and Mail*, 12 August 2013, B1.

McNish, Jacquie, and Greg McArthur. 2008. "Special Investigation: How high risk mortgages crept north." *The Globe and Mail*, 12 December.

Neufeld, Mark. 1995. "Hegemony and Foreign Policy Analysis: The Case of Canada as a Middle Power." *Studies in Political Economy* 48 (Autumn): 7–29.

Nossal, Kim Richard. 1997. *The Politics of Canadian Foreign Policy.* Scarborough, ON: Prentice-Hall.

Rozental, Andrés, and Robert Pastor. 2009. "A case for the three amigos." *The Globe and Mail*, 1 May.

Russell, Ellen. 2012. "No More Swimming Naked: The Need for Modesty in Canadian Banking." Ottawa: *ccpa.*

Russell, Peter, and Lorne Sossin, eds. 2009. *Parliamentary Democracy in Crisis.* Toronto: University of Toronto Press.

Schwartz, Daniel. 2013. "Should international aid serve Canada's commercial interests? Mixed views on merging CIDA with Foreign Affairs." *cbc* News. Available at www.cbc.ca/news/canada/story/2013/03/27/f-cida-dfait-merger.html.

Sharp, Mitchell. 1972. "Canada–U.S. Relations: Options for the Future." *International Perspectives* (Special Edition), 17 October.

Stoney, Christopher, and Tamara Krawchenko. 2013. "Crisis and Opportunism: Public Finance Trends from Stimulus to Austerity in Canada," pp. 33–58 in Carlos Fanelli and Bryan Evans, eds. *Great Recession-Proof? Shattering the Myth of Canadian Exceptionalism*. Ottawa: Red Quill Books.

Thomas, Christopher. 1992. "Reflections on the Canada–US Free Trade Agreement in the Context of the Multilateral Trading System," pp. 47–61 in A. Claire Cutler and Mark W. Zacher, eds. *Canadian Foreign Policy and International Economic Regimes*. Vancouver: UBC Press.

U.S. Department of State. 2008. "U.S. Relations with Canada." Fact sheet: Bureau of Western Hemisphere Affairs. Originally retrieved from www.state.gov/r/pa/ei/ bgn/2089.htm.

Valpy, Michael. 2009. "The 'Crisis': A Narrative," pp. 3–18 in Peter Russell and Lorne Sossin, eds. *Parliamentary Democracy in Crisis*. Toronto: University of Toronto Press.

Vieira, Paul, and Eoin Callan. 2008. "Canada set to fight Europe over financial cure." *Financial Post*, 5 November, FP1.

Vieira, Paul, and Nicolas Van Praet. 2009. "Canada Pushed to match U.S. Auto Aid." 9 December. Originally retrieved from www.driving.ca/news/story.html?id=1052163.

Webb, Michael. 1992. "Canada and the International Monetary Regime," pp. 153–85 in A. Claire Cutler and Mark W. Zacher, eds. *Canadian Foreign Policy and International Economic Regimes*. Vancouver: UBC Press.

Winham, Gilbert, and Sylvia Ostry. 2003. "The second trade crisis." *The Globe and Mail*, 17 June.

Winnett, Robert. 2009. "G20 summit: Foreign Office 'relegates' countries." *The Telegraph*. Available at www.telegraph.co.uk/finance/financetopics/g20-summit/4983689/G20-summit-Foreign-Office-relegates-countries.html.

Zhang, Daowei. 2007. *The Softwood Lumber War: Politics, Economics, and the Long U.S.–Canada Trade Dispute*. Washington, DC: Resources for the Future.

24 Canada and the Negotiation of Investment Rules: Open for Whose Business?

Elizabeth Smythe

"Canada is open for business again. We want to reassure investors that Canada's energy sector offers outstanding opportunities to do business."

—Prime Minister Brian Mulroney's speech to the Economic Club, New York City, 10 December 1984.

"To be blunt, Canadians have not spent years reducing the ownership of sectors of the economy by our own governments, only to see them bought and controlled by foreign governments instead . . . When we say that Canada is open for business we do not mean that Canada is for sale to foreign governments."

—Prime Minister Stephen Harper, 7 December 2012 press conference after the approval of the takeover of Nexen Energy by China National Offshore Corporation (CNOOC).

Key Terms

Expropriation

Foreign Direct Investment

National Treatment

State-owned Enterprises

World Trade Organization

Introduction

As these two statements 28 years apart indicate, **foreign direct investment** (FDI) and ownership remain sensitive issues, as they have been for much of Canada's history. Public concern has often coincided with high profile takeovers of Canadian corporations by foreign (initially US, but more recently Chinese) firms.[1] In particular, the $15.1 billion friendly takeover of Nexen energy by the China National Offshore Oil Corporation (CNOOC) prompted the prime minister's comments in November 2012. Like trade, investment has been tied to concerns about our sovereignty. Since the 1980s, the landscape of Canadian policy on FDI and of international rules on foreign investments has been altering and shifting in response to change.

This chapter examines the policy project of liberalization of Canada's domestic regulations on foreign investment and its quest for international investment rules that liberalize access for Canadian investors abroad and enhance protection of their assets. It discusses the reasons why this project, espoused by both Liberal and Conservative governments in Canada, has not had a smooth trajectory in the context of domestic concerns about sovereignty and security and the ongoing changes in the sources and nature of incoming and outgoing FDI. As a result of these changes, divisions have arisen within the Canadian corporate elite and the governing party over what kind of investment is welcome, and in which sectors, creating, some argue, mixed messages to the rest of the world. At the same time efforts to develop multilateral investment rules have had limited success, and as Canada's outward investment interests shift, it has opted for aggressive pursuit of regional and bilateral trade and investment agreements. This chapter examines the role of evolving interests and ideas in shaping Canadian investment policy.

We begin with a discussion of how Canada's investment interests have been re-defined over time.

Canada's Evolving Investment Interests: From Screening to Liberalization and Protection of Investors

Interests usually imply a material basis for action or policy related to the benefit or gain an actor will derive. In the case of policy on FDI and international investment agreements, investment flows and the interests of powerful economic actors provide a key to understanding the source of Canadian negotiators' interests in investment rules.

For much of the post-World War II period, Canada was a capital importer, or what is often termed a *host* to foreign direct investment. FDI refers to a cross-border relationship where a resident (individual or corporation) of one country makes a long-term financial commitment within another country, either establishing a new corporation or acquiring or taking over an existing firm. High inflows of FDI such as those Canada experienced in the postwar period resulted in high levels of foreign (largely US-based) ownership in major sectors of the economy. This spurred a national debate about sovereignty and FDI and a series of policies from the late 1960s to manage incoming FDI. Given that the Canadian government wanted new investment, the policy involved protecting a small number of what were seen to be key sectors from foreign ownership while managing incoming FDI by reviewing projects and providing conditional market access to investors (often called *screening*) in return for commitments ensuring local economic benefits and backward linkages to the domestic economy. From the mid-1970s to the mid-1980s, the Foreign Investment Review Agency (FIRA) handled negotiations with investors.

Internal and external pressures in the 1980s undermined this definition of Canada's investment interests. The US administration, powerful American corporations, some provinces, and Canadian business interests became increasingly hostile to Canadian FDI policies. Federal officials had concluded, even before a change of government in 1984, that screening put Canada at a disadvantage because international competition for investment, as many economies liberalized, was intensifying.[2] Continued high levels of foreign ownership and the persistence of a nationalist critique, however, meant that wholesale abandonment of the policies was also politically costly.

Inward and outward FDI increased rapidly in the late 1990s, as the following table indicates, but the balance shifted as outward FDI began growing more rapidly. By 1997, Canada became a net capital exporter (host as well as home to FDI) (see Figure 24.1). Initially the United States was the overwhelming destination for outward FDI, followed by other Organisation of Economic Co-operation and Development (OECD) economies. At the same time, Canada remains host to a large stock of FDI ($607.5 billion in 2011) of which about 51 per cent is US-based (down from 66 in the 1990s).[3] Investment from the EU has

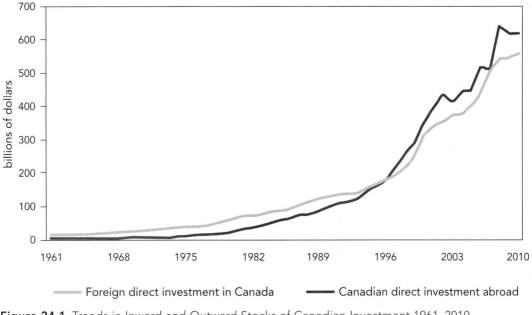

Figure 24.1 Trends in Inward and Outward Stocks of Canadian Investment 1961–2010

Source: Statistics Canada (2012), Canada's International Investment Position.

increased steadily in recent years to account for just over 30 per cent of inward FDI stock.

The destination of outward FDI has also changed, as Figure 24.2 indicates. By 2012, $310 billion, just over one-third of the $637.3 billion stock of Canadian FDI, was located in the United States, which, along with the rest of the OECD, accounts for about 74 per cent. Canadian FDI in non-OECD countries, which was insignificant two decades ago, has grown.

In regions such as Latin America, Canadian FDI more than doubled from 8.7 per cent to 18.5 per cent between 1988 and 1999.

As Figure 24.3 indicates, much of this investment is concentrated in a few sectors, the largest of which—finance and insurance—is tied to offshore financial centres and tax havens. The second largest is mining and energy extraction. The rapid decline of Canadian FDI share in manufacturing is notable.

Similarly, as Figure 24.4 indicates, inward FDI

has also seen a significant shift. Over time, the share of the stock of FDI in manufacturing has declined, while that of mining and oil and gas began significantly increasing in 2004.

While Canada had sought to protect its right to screen incoming FDI and limit access to certain sectors, given the rapid growth of outward FDI in the 1990s, negotiating rules to protect Canadian outward investment appeared to be in Canada's interests. Such rules involve seeking to ensure that Canadian investors, when operating abroad, are not subject to discrimination (i.e., that they are given **national treatment**) in comparison to domestic investors or have performance conditions imposed on them such as local sourcing or export obligations (called *performance requirements*). Most critical is to ensure that Canadian investors are not subject to uncompensated and arbitrary **expropriation** of their assets by host governments. While sovereign governments are free

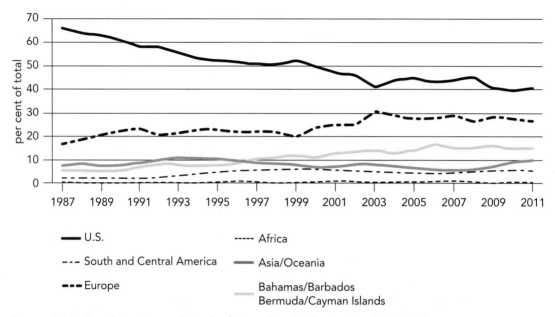

Figure 24.2 Trends in Outward Stock of Canadian FDI by Region 1987–2011

Source: Conference Board of Canada (2013), Outward Foreign Direct Investment (FDI) Performance Index

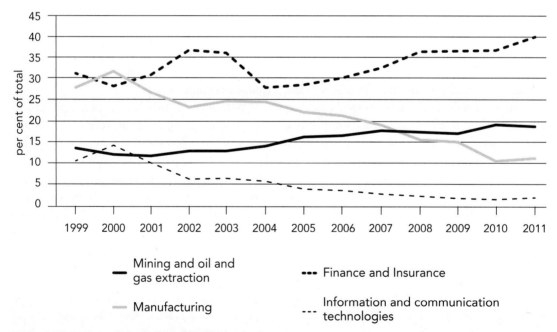

Figure 24.3 Canadian Outward FDI by Industry

Source: Conference Board of Canada (2013), Outward Foreign Direct Investment (FDI) Performance Index

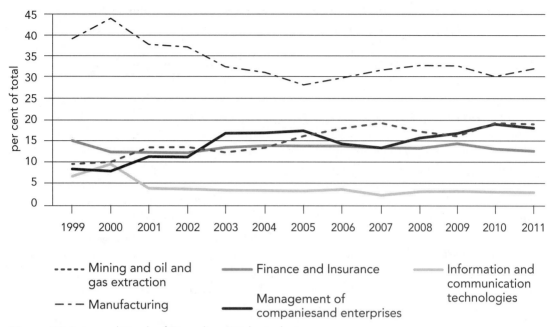

Figure 24.4 Inward Stock of Canadian FDI by Industry

Source: Conference Board of Canada (2013), Inward Foreign Direct Investment (FDI) Performance Index. Available at www.conferenceboard.ca/hcp/details/economy/inward-fdi-performance.aspx.

to expropriate assets under domestic law, international norms call for foreign investors to be compensated promptly and adequately, which normally means fair market value.

A large proportion of Canadian outward, and the majority of inward, FDI was with the United States, though it has been decreasing as a proportion over time. Clearly the complex nature of integrated global production today and the ebbs and flows of highly mobile capital, often sensitive to exchange and interest rates, require some way to attach meaning and significance to flows. To understand how investment interests are defined we need to look both at ideas about investment and the context in which negotiations take place. Canada's definition of its interests has involved a complex mix of what trade negotiators call *offensive* and *defensive* interests.

In the 1970s, Canada sought to preserve its ability to screen and regulate FDI in the face of rules

designed to limit host state policy discretion (defensive). When developing countries called for a New International Economic Order at the United Nations (UN) in the early 1970s, including negotiations on a Code of Conduct for Transnational Corporations, the United States tried to counter it by establishing norms of national treatment and high levels of protection for foreign investors through the negotiation of the OECD's Declaration on International Investment and Multinational Enterprises in 1975. At the OECD, Canada was on the defensive, seeking to balance the right of a host state to regulate incoming FDI with fair and non-discriminatory treatment of foreign investors; Canada fought hard to weaken the agreement or opt out.[4] While the US was unable to attain a binding agreement at the OECD, the organization has since become an important institution in furthering norms of national treatment and transparency and de-legitimizing host state regulation of FDI through its Committee on Investment and Multinational Enterprise.

Canadian officials in the 1980s viewed FDI inflows as necessary to ensure economic growth and competitiveness. No longer protected by high tariffs, Canada—as a host state—had to compete aggressively for FDI by providing an attractive investment climate. The "right" climate was seen by corporate interests as one with low taxes, limited state regulation, and liberalized access for foreign investors. Officials saw enhanced market access, national treatment of foreign investors, and transparent regulation as important norms. Binding codes of corporate conduct, which implied an active regulatory role for states or international organizations, were *not* seen as legitimate. Rather voluntary guidelines for conduct similar to the OECD's Guidelines on Multinational Enterprises were preferred.

Investment flows were viewed as a report card on the Canadian economy, similar to the way in which the changing value of the Canadian dollar vis-à-vis the US dollar is perceived. Canada's share of global FDI inflows measured Canada's attractiveness as a location for FDI, an attractiveness which had to be promoted while outward FDI was viewed negatively. Protection of outward FDI was, therefore, not a priority.

Canada's more limited policy of investment screening was still a target in bilateral trade negotiations. US demands reached their high water mark with the negotiation of Chapter 11 of the North American Free Trade Agreement (NAFTA) in 1993, which afforded a high level of protection to foreign investors against any direct expropriation or other measures (i.e., domestic regulations) that could be tantamount to expropriation. Canada's NAFTA investment interests were driven not by a desire to protect the limited Canadian investments in Mexico but rather, as the trade minister indicated in 1992, "to ensure that Canada remained an attractive location for investors wishing to serve the North American market."[5] Within multilateral organizations, the US sought to limit host state performance requirements imposed on foreign investors at the General Agreement on Tariffs and Trade (GATT) first by lodging a complaint against FIRA and then by the negotiation of Trade-Related Investment Measures (TRIMs) in the Uruguay Round. The US then set its sights on a NAFTA-like "high standards" multilateral investment agreement that would afford foreign investors strong protection against host state regulations to be negotiated at the OECD—the ill-fated Multilateral Agreement on Investment (MAI).

As outflows of Canadian FDI increased in the 1990s they were viewed more positively as necessary to maintaining Canada's competitiveness in increasingly globalized systems of production, and Canadian negotiators became more interested in protecting outward investment. The question was how and where to negotiate rules that would achieve this goal. Canada had been focused on bilateral negotiations to secure access to the US market and then trilaterally in NAFTA to preserve that access and ensure that Canada remained an attractive investment location. In both cases, the US played the role of *demandeur* on investment rules.

One option to protect Canadian non-OECD investment was to negotiate bilateral agreements following the pattern of the United States and Germany, major capital exporters. In 1991, Canada began negotiating with host economies to provide protection and legal recourse for Canadian investors abroad. Despite efforts in 1998 to more clearly identify Canada's interests and priorities for these FIPAs based on investment flows, future investment opportunities, and business demands, the FIPAs being negotiated could not be clearly linked to those interests as they are also driven by requests from host countries seeking to show a welcoming face to foreign investors, assuage multilateral institutions such as the World Bank, or as a part of "photo op" diplomacy and agreements for a visiting prime minister to sign.[6]

Table 24.1 Foreign investment protection agreements

Country	Brought into Force
Argentina	1993
Armenia	1999
Barbados	1997
Costa Rica	1999
Croatia	2001
Czech Rep.	2012
Ecuador	1997
Egypt	1997
Hungary	1993
Jordan	2009
Latvia	2011
Lebanon	1999
Panama	1998
Peru	2007
Philippines	1996
Poland	1990
Romania	2011
Russian Federation	1991
Slovak Republic	2012
Thailand	1998
Trinidad and Tobago	1996
Ukraine	1995
Uruguay	1999
Venezuela	1998

Table 24.2 FIPAs being negotiated or concluded but not yet in force

FIPAs Being Negotiated	FIPA Concluded
Albania	Bahrain
Burkina Faso	Benin
Ghana	Cameroon
Guinea	China
India	Côte d'Ivoire
Indonesia	Kuwait
Kazakhstan	Madagascar
Moldova	Mali
Mongolia	Nigeria
Tunisia	Senegal
Vietnam	Serbia
	Tanzania
	Zambia

Canada's 2005 international market access priorities, outlined in *Opening Doors to the World*, included India, Brazil, and China—which had replaced Japan as Canada's second largest bilateral trading partner. Canada has concluded negotiations with China on a FIPA (discussed further below) and is negotiating an FTA with India. Brazil is important as a trading partner, a destination for investment (over 40 mining operations) and source of FDI (seventh largest, over $15.8 billion). Yet Canada's efforts at closer cooperation, including a role in the regional trade agreement Mercosur, have been stymied by, among other issues, allegations of Canadian spying on Brazilian authorities.[7] Clearly there is no one-to-one relationship between the negotiation of agreements and investment patterns.[8] Instead, a complex mixture of economic and political interests play a role.

A new pattern emerges post-2005 with the aggressive negotiation of bilateral and regional trade agreements, many of which include chapters on investment. In its negotiation of FTAs and FIPAs Canada is following a trend that other countries had begun—a reflection of the diminishing prospects for concluding multilateral negotiations and the failed efforts over seven years to launch negotiations on investment rules at the **World Trade Organization** (WTO). Why Canada's initial preferred strategy was to develop binding rules at the WTO is the subject to which I now turn.

Canada Investment Rules and the WTO

The WTO case reflects the evolving nature of Canadian international economic policy, especially changes in economic interests and official thinking about FDI and the challenges in pursuing these interests within the context of a changing WTO. The case also helps in understanding recent efforts to secure Canadian investment interests through a more aggressive policy of negotiating bilateral and regional agreements.

Along with agriculture, divisions at the WTO over the so-called "Singapore issues," which included investment, are widely seen as having contributed to the failure of the WTO ministerial meeting in Cancún, Mexico, in 2003.[9] A proposal to launch negotiations on an investment agreement was so controversial that it was finally dropped altogether from the WTO agenda in July 2004. The European Commission, negotiator for the EU, is often blamed for pushing the Singapore issues, particularly investment. With the EU identified as the main *demandeur*, little attention has been paid to Canada's role. In fact, Canada was one of the most active advocates of launching negotiations on investment rules at the WTO over the seven-year period of discussions.[10]

Negotiating at the WTO made sense given Canada's support for multilateral trade rules. As a net exporter of FDI since 1997, Canada's interests are best served by pursuing rules to enhance investors' access to foreign markets and protect them against arbitrary or discriminatory treatment by host states. However the issue was divisive, as reflected in the compromise forged in Singapore in 1996 to launch a study of, but not negotiations for, an investment agreement. The failure of the MAI negotiations at the OECD, and the cases launched under the investment chapter (Chapter 11) of the NAFTA, made many WTO members wary. Even Canadian business has waxed and waned about the priority placed on investment rules.

Efforts to launch investment negotiations at the WTO must be seen within the context of the US initiative to negotiate a binding MAI within the OECD. Canada had not supported the OECD as the best venue to negotiate investment rules. Broader coverage of countries where Canadian FDI was growing, the WTO's credentials as a trade negotiating forum, and its strengthened dispute resolution capacity made it the preferred venue. Canada, along with the European Commission and Japan, worked to build a consensus to negotiate investment for the first WTO ministerial meeting in Singapore in December 1996. The United States opposed WTO negotiations because the completion of an MAI at the OECD was its priority. Given the limits of the TRIMs negotiated in the Uruguay Round, the US was pessimistic about the prospects at the WTO. Despite US opposition, Canada, the EU, and Japan persisted.

Canada presented a proposal in April 1996 to begin an educative work program at the WTO that did not presuppose future negotiations, a recognition that immediate attempts to launch negotiations were doomed to failure.[11] India spearheaded efforts to stop the inclusion of investment and a number of other new issues on the WTO agenda. The final Singapore declaration established a working group to examine the relationship between trade and investment but the work "shall not prejudice whether negotiations will be initiated in the future."[12] The European Commission, Japan, and Canada tried to use the working group established in 1997 to build consensus on the need to include investment in the agenda of a future round of negotiations. Outlining its experience with FIPAs and NAFTA, Canada argued a WTO focus on "investment rights and obligations [to] deepen trade agreements" offered more consistent rules than bilateral investment treaties."[13] At no time in the following six years did Canada outline any obligations of foreign investors in host countries beyond obeying domestic laws. Investor security was the priority. On the other side, opposing new negotiations, was India supported by Pakistan, Egypt, Morocco, Cuba, and the Association of Southeast Asian Nations (ASEAN) group. After 18 months, only a few areas of consensus in the Working Group on Trade and Investment (WGTI) had been identified, including the idea that FDI could provide benefits for economic development and that trade and investment were closely linked. There was no agreement on the need for new rules. External events had an impact on discussions, however.

The first was the collapse of OECD negotiations on the MAI in December 1998, the failure of which provided support to opponents of investment rules within the WTO. The MAI failure also meant that the transnational coalition of critics of the MAI—which included a number of Canadian labour, environmental, cultural, and other groups—would now turn their full attention to the WTO and the upcoming meeting in Seattle that would attempt to launch a new round of negotiations including investment rules. The MAI also provided Canadian officials with a lesson on the need to consult more broadly with domestic groups beyond traditional business and producer interests seen to have a stake in trade agreements.

Chapter 11 of NAFTA and its provisions on expropriation also provided critics of strong standards of investment protection with ammunition. By March 1999, US investors had filed four cases against the Canadian government under Chapter 11 of NAFTA. The Ethyl case was filed on 15 April 1997 when a Virginia-based company claimed compensation, arguing that a Canadian law banning imports of the gasoline additive MMT, for environmental reasons, was tantamount to expropriation of their assets. Since that time many more cases have been filed against the NAFTA partners and led to attempts by officials to address the problem. Chapter 11 had an impact at the WTO. As one developing country delegate indicated, by 1999 everyone knew about Chapter 11.[14]

With the failure of the December 1999 Seattle ministerial the WGTI largely spun its wheels. A similar situation prevailed outside the WTO. Despite having been enthusiastic about the inclusion of investment rules at the newly launched Free Trade Area of the Americas (FTAA) negotiations in 1998 and growing FDI in Latin America, Canada put forward no substantive proposals on investment until August 2001, and then only on the concept of "minimum standard of treatment."[15]

As a result of a presentation by the United Nations Conference on Trade and Development (UNCTAD) on the concept of "policy space for development," the emphasis in the WGTI shifted to whether investment rules would limit developing country "policy space." The *demandeurs* were going to have to make a case that FDI rules to protect investors could be flexible, meaning offering flexibility and technical assistance[16] to members. Canada and other proponents recognized that the model of a "top-down" NAFTA/MAI-type of agreement, involving broad commitments to standards of national treatment and market access, was unacceptable. Their alternative was the model of a bottom-up, positive list approach of the General Agreement on Trade in Services.

[At t]he November 2001 Ministerial meeting in Doha, Qatar[17] developing countries requested language to ensure that a consensus would be required to launch negotiations and not merely to establish the modalities of negotiations. This reflected a growing unease among many developing country members with the whole process of WTO decision-making and its lack of transparency. The Declaration, including the text on investment, also clearly placed development, at least at the level of rhetoric, front and centre in the Doha Round. Thus proponents now had to show how negotiations could further development objectives.

On the question of FDI flows, claims made about the link between investment agreements and increased FDI inflows to developing countries by the *demandeurs* were increasingly challenged even by researchers at the World Bank and UNCTAD. Finally, on the question of a NAFTA-like investor–state system of dispute resolution, Canada stated the obvious:

that such a system would be "inappropriate." What had once been a model for an investment agreement in 1997 was now "inappropriate." By the final meeting in 2003, no consensus among members to negotiate an investment agreement had emerged.

Proponents of negotiating rules were supported by some developing countries and states in transition. However, an equally large group of countries were opposed, and some important developing countries, including China and Brazil, were on the fence. China had collaborated with opponents in a WGTI submission, arguing that corporations also had obligations that an investment code should address. Beyond a 1999 EU paper, which argued that existing weak and unenforceable guidelines for MNCs, such as the OECD's, were more than adequate to ensure corporate social responsibility, proponents, including Canada, had not addressed the issue at all. While many small and least developed countries remained marginal to the process, opponents such as India worked hard in the summer of 2003 to organize their opposition in a series of meetings.

The level of disagreement on the Singapore issues going into Cancún was reflected in the July and August 2003 General Council meetings. Canadian Trade Minister Pierre Pettigrew was appointed facilitator for the Singapore issues by the Mexican chair, despite Canada's having been an active proponent of negotiating investment rules and other Singapore issues. The disagreement on the Singapore issues became quickly evident. On 12 September, a group of 30 developing countries plus Bangladesh—representing the 30 least developed countries—sent a letter to Pettigrew opposing negotiations on the Singapore issues and raising concerns about the capacity to both negotiate and implement potential commitments.[18] A draft ministerial text approving negotiations (which appeared the next day), considering the level of opposition, was stunning. It also tied the start of negotiation on investment to agreements in agriculture and also

meant that many of the proponents of investment negotiations, such as the EU, Japan, and Korea, would have to give way there in order to see talks start. The Mexican foreign minister sought a resolution of the impasse, but the EU was reluctant to unbundle the issues. When the African Union countries declared they would not accept negotiation on *any* of the four issues, and Korea (backed by Japan) insisted on all four, the chair called the meeting to an end, citing the impasse. The subsequent decision of the EU to drop all four issues, and the July 2004 WTO General Council decision to proceed only on trade facilitation, marked the end of the seven-year campaign on investment.

The failure at Cancún seemed to surprise only the Canadian officials. Despite extensive consultations with critics, evidence of well-organized developing-country opposition, and critiques of mainstream economists that investment negotiations at the WTO were a bad idea,[19] Canadian officials had persisted in seeing it as worthwhile.

Open for Business: What Kind of Business, and Whose Investment? The Canadian Government and Investment Liberalization

Despite the trend to liberalization in Canada, limitations on incoming investment in a small number of sectors and screening of large takeovers (acquisitions) remain in place, even though the latter process provided few impediments to foreign investment. They reflect continued political sensitivity about takeovers, even as governments continued to promote Canada as an investment location. Domestic screening came to the fore again in 2006 as the result of a number of economic forces, including commodity prices and exchange rates which led to a wave of takeovers or attempted takeovers of iconic Canadian corporations including Hudson's Bay, Inco, Dofasco, and Falconbridge. These generated public disquiet, media attention, and concern among some corporate executives. Many referred to it as the "hollowing out" of corporate Canada.

Yet the Conservative government's economic policy statement of 2006 reflected the continued negative view of FDI restrictions, declaring that "[p]olicy restrictions on foreign investment in Canada have contributed to our economy's relative decline in foreign direct investment flows."[20] Despite a reluctance to reverse the trend to further liberalization of Canadian investment regulation, pressures continued and the minority Conservative government responded by appointing a panel in November 2006, headed by former Bell executive Lynton (Red) Wilson, to review whether changes were needed to the Investment Canada Act. The report *Compete to Win*, released in June 2008,[21] recommended an increased threshold for reviews of takeovers, changing the net-benefit-to-Canada test to one where government must prove a takeover does not provide such benefit, and removing restrictions on FDI in certain sectors such as uranium mining.[22] Despite the creation of the review, pressures on the government continued and in April 2008, then industry minister Jim Prentice stopped the attempted takeover of Alliant Techsystems, the owner of the RADARSAT2 Satellite, by US-based firm MacDonald, Dettwiler and Associates after a well-coordinated public campaign and opposition outcry forced the government to intervene.

A number of changes recommended by the Wilson report were adopted by the government and incorporated into amendments to the Investment Canada Act in March, 2009, including gradually increasing the threshold for review of foreign takeovers from $295 million to $1 billion, eliminating an estimated two-thirds of the transactions reviewed. But in 2007 the Conservative government also added amendments to the Investment Canada Act which included a national security review of takeovers. This adding of a very open-ended set of criteria to the process led some to criticize the mixed message regarding liberalization and the potential for the politicization of controversial takeovers.[23]

As a result of the changes proposed investments could be subject to a national security review even if it did not exceed the threshold for the net benefit review, whether the investment is proposed or already implemented, and even in cases in which a minority interest is acquired in a Canadian business (i.e., where there is no acquisition of control of a Canadian target). As in the case of other countries, there is no definition of what could be "injurious to national security," and there is a distinct possibility that the test could be used to target certain types of sovereign investment.[24]

Concerns with national security reflected the changing nature of FDI and Canada's emergence once again as a potential host to foreign investment, particularly in its resource sectors. Canada's increasing dependence on resource industries for economic growth and exports and the increased significance of **state-owned enterprises** as investors in this sector has created dilemmas for the government. This dilemma is a reflection of the changing nature of FDI globally. As the UNCTAD World Investment report (WIR)[25] has noted, 2012 was the first time that developing economies absorbed more FDI than developed economies. It has also noted the increased role that state-controlled entities, sovereign wealth funds, and state-owned enterprises (SOEs) are playing as sources of FDI, especially from non-OECD countries. The top 100 transnational corporations in 2012 include 18 state-owned enterprises. SOEs are increasing in size and taking on the roles of national champions. Many have been established in the past decade in developing countries, including the BRICS, and are aggressively investing in developed countries. As the WIR points out, their criteria for investment may not be based solely on financial returns but might incorporate other strategic industrial objectives. Prime Minister Harper's comment at the start of this chapter reflects the dilemma that Canada faces, especially in the case of global oil and gas companies—a trend to increased state ownership and the dominance of such firms outside North America.

At the same time, the Canadian economy has seen, since the crash of 2008 and the slow recovery of the US economy, a re-orientation of its trade and investment interests toward other regions, especially Asia. The share of total exports going to the US continues to decline. At the same time, the growing importance of resources to the economy and trade balance is reflected in the increased value and volume of energy products in exports, up 23 per cent by value in 2011 alone. Crude oil has been particularly important. Even given the impact of higher prices, oil exports increased 13 per cent in volume from the previous year.[26]

Challenges to the government's investment liberalization regime occurred in 2010 with the $38.6 billion hostile bid for Potash Corporation by the Australian mining company BHP Billiton. While Potash had been privatized and moved its headquarters to Chicago, much of its production was Saskatchewan-based. That and its key role in the Canpotex export cartel led the conservative (Saskatchewan Party) premier of Saskatchewan to oppose the sale. In November, the federal government denied the bid, citing a lack of overall benefit to Canada.[27] Even more troubling for the Harper government over the next three years was the growing trend to takeovers of Canadian firms being launched by state-owned enterprises. This culminated in June 2012 in the largest such takeover bid, when the China National Offshore Oil Corporation (CNOOC) announced its $15 billion bid for Nexen Energy. Shortly before in June, the Malaysian state

oil company Petronas had announced a $5.5 billion friendly takeover of Progress Energy, which had the potential to expand liquefied natural gas exports to Asia. However, this deal was initially rejected by the industry minister in October 2012, and the CEO of Petronas vowed to improve the offer and meet the net-benefit screening test.[28] Thus the fall of 2012 set the stage for a public debate about whose and which type of investment is welcome in Canada, a debate that revealed divisions both within the corporate elite and within the Harper (now a majority) government. Issues raised included whether approvals of such bids would open the door to even more SOEs or send a negative message to foreign investors. Of equal concern was the lack of reciprocity in terms of market access for Canadian investors, especially in China, and the close links to government and the opaque and rather different legal and corporate governance norms.

The response to the dilemma was laid out on 7 December 2012 in the press conference with the prime minister quoted at the beginning of this chapter.[29] While approving both the Nexen and Progress takeovers, the prime minister made it clear that "all investments are not equal," raising the question, given that SOEs have different objectives from privately owned firms, can such "foreign state control of Canadian business be of net benefit to Canada?" His answer is not likely except in very exceptional circumstances.

The government had already articulated guidelines as part of its security assessment for state-owned enterprises, which focused on transparency, disclosure, and evidence of a Canadian presence in corporate management and governance. In addition to these criteria, any such takeovers would be assessed in light of the extent of a foreign government's control or influence over the firm and the degree or control such an SOE would have over the Canadian business being acquired. While the threshold for private transactions would continue to be raised to $1 billion, the review threshold for SOEs would remain at $350 million.

Despite government efforts to continue to clearly welcome investment, the mixed messages have continued according to some critics, most particularly in the telecommunications sector, one of those where historically foreign investors had been denied access. In the name of increased competition the government had, in 2009, allowed foreign investment by smaller companies for up to 10 per cent of the mobile phone market, going so far as to overrule the Canadian Radio-television and Telecommunications Commission (CRTC) and allowing an Egyptian-based investor to back a new entry, WIND Mobile, into the sector. Yet two years later in the fall of 2012, once again in the name of national security, Industry Minister James Moore vetoed the sale of Allstream by the Manitoba Telephone System to the same Egyptian investor for $520 million. Minister Moore pointed out that Allstream "operates a national fibre-optic network that provides critical telecommunications services to businesses and governments, including the Government of Canada,"[30] but would not elaborate on national security concerns. A former Conservative minister, now a corporate executive, Jim Prentice has argued that such actions are now deterring foreign investment in Canada. Evidence that that is indeed the case is limited. On the other hand, the government has in the same time period continued to pursue bilateral and regional investment agreements. However, once again, in the case of investment, the ground appears to be shifting and Canada's definition of its interests is facing challenges.

Investment Protection— Bilateral and Regional Agreements Post-2004

How have governments addressed the interests of Canadian investors, given the failure to launch WTO investment negotiations and the slowing momentum of multilateral trade negotiations? In the absence of a comprehensive WTO agreement, Canada maintained its program of **Foreign Investment Protection Agreements**, which is logical given that outward investment in regions of South and Central America and Asia was increasing. In 2004, a revised new draft agreement based on the NAFTA model (including investor–state dispute resolutions, however, with some changes regarding expropriation) was developed, despite Canada's previous assertion at the WTO that aspects of its investor–state dispute process might not be appropriate for some developing countries. The more recent wave of FIPAs and new bilateral trade agreements which cover investment reflect a much closer tie to the interests of investors and regions where Canadian investment is growing.

As Tables 24.1 and 24.2 indicated, most FIPAs are with smaller economies where Canada has generally played the role of a capital exporter; these FIPAs did not generate much public concern. However, the announcement of the conclusion of a FIPA with China in February 2012 and the formal signing of it in September did. Chinese investment in Canada reached $14.6 billion as of 2010. While Canadian investment in China was up 39 per cent in 2010, the reality is that with $4.8 billion invested in China, in this relationship Canada has become a host to Chinese FDI, almost all of which is in the resource sector, and much of which comes from SOEs. Given the nature of the Chinese regime and the many restrictions on market access that remain for foreign investors, critics have argued that the agreement, unlike many other FIPAs and FTAs, lacks reciprocity. The national treatment guaranteed to Canadian investors in China is only post-establishment and thus does not address access. In the event of a dispute between China and a Canadian company operating there, Chinese procedures and provisions may not afford the same level of transparency that has become the norm of investor–state procedures elsewhere.[31] A court challenge to the agreement by the Hupacasath First Nation claiming that the agreement violated the government's duty to consent was dismissed in 2013, and an NDP motion to stop the agreement was defeated by Conservatives and Liberals in the House of Commons. There remains, however, even among some Conservatives, a level of unease regarding investment relations with China (CBC).[32]

Table 24.3 indicates that Canada is negotiating and has concluded many trade agreements. In each case, investor protection and market access have been important elements. Agreements, such as Peru's, include variations on NAFTA permitting investors to sue governments in cases where corporations claim state regulation constitutes expropriation. Not all negotiations have gone smoothly; some, such as those with Korea, have raised questions about the balance of benefits to Canada, while the agreement with Colombia involved concerns about human rights which held up a similar bilateral agreement in the US Congress. The table also reflects, with the exception of the EU, a clear emphasis on the Americas, where much of Canada's growing mining and financial investment is located, and on Asia, where economic growth has been strong. These agreements suggest that Canada has joined a process that was already well under way by a number of other actors including the United States and the EU. In fact, a 2009 Canadian trade strategy document entitled *Seizing Global Advantage* laid out the urgency of Canada's joining the trend.

> [G]overnments are increasingly competing against one another to help their businesses and investors gain an edge in the race for market share, technological advantage, foreign investment and other global value chain opportunities. Canada must do the same.[33]

The primacy of commercial interests in the process of negotiations is clear, as is the emphasis on investment protection. While some FTAs have side agreements on labour and the environment, they remain, as do Canada's pronouncements on corporate social responsibility, limited largely to best efforts,[34] with little capacity for enforcement even as civil society groups in Canada and elsewhere continue to raise concerns about the behaviour of Canadian firms abroad, especially in extractive industries.

Table 24.3 Free trade agreements

Agreements in Force		Agreements under Negotiation
Country	Date	
Panama	2013	CARICOM
Jordan	2012	Central America 4
Colombia	2011	European Union (CETA-agreed in principle 2013)
Peru	2009	India
European Free Trade Assoc.	2009	Japan
Costa Rica	2002	Korea
Chile	1997	Singapore
Israel	1997	Trans-Pacific Partnership
NAFTA	1994	Ukraine
		Modernization of FTA with Costa Rica

On 18 October 2013, after four years of negotiation, Prime Minister Stephen Harper announced in Brussels that Canada and the EU had reached agreement in principle on a major Comprehensive Economic and Trade Agreement (CETA) with the European Union. The details provided at the time of writing are limited to a general summary of the agreement, which has not been finalized. Investment came into the negotiations in 2011 after the EU had gained competence over its member states to negotiate in this area as a result of the Lisbon Treaty. While no formal text of the investment chapter has been released, as a result of concerns about the investment provisions on the part of the European Parliament, a confidential draft of the negotiating text was leaked by a member in 2012. Analysts note that it reflects a mixture of offensive and defensive interests of each actor in terms of access of investors to the other's market and a process of investor–state arbitration, not unlike NAFTA.[35] The EU has sought increased access to sectors protected from FDI, such as banking, uranium mining, and hydroelectric projects. It has also sought a higher threshold for screening EU corporate acquisitions of Canadian firms. Canada, on the other hand, has sought to ensure that decisions on screening cannot be subject to investor–state dispute resolution. While the final mixture of trade-offs is unknown at this time, critics have largely focused on other issues, such as the EU's use of geographic indications and increased European cheese imports, stronger patent protection, and opening public procurement to foreign bidders. The relatively strong EU labour and environmental standards, along with similarities of legal frameworks, has led to a different reaction than to that of the Canada–China FIPA. Nonetheless, some civil society critics have expressed concern that, once again, investor–state arbitration and dispute resolution may limit the ability of Canadian governments to regulate in the public interest without incurring costly financial penalties.[36]

Conclusion

We began with the question of why Canada's investment liberalization project, both in domestic policy and international investment rules, has had a rocky ride despite a strong consensus on the project across governments and among the business elite. We also sought to link policy changes to a changing landscape in terms of sources and types of investment, and Canada's changing interests as both a source of, and destination for, FDI. Initially in the early part of this decade, the growing importance of Canadian capital exports to non-OECD countries led to demand for higher levels of protection for Canadian investment abroad. The initial goal was to negotiate such rules at the WTO. Multilateral institutions like the WTO were viewed more positively because of their potential to offset bilateral asymmetry with the United States and allow Canada to reconcile offensive and defensive interests. The WTO was also preferred because of its more universal membership and its dispute resolution system. Because of strong developing country member opposition to launching negotiations, this effort became an exercise in persuasion. Officials interested in protecting Canadian investors in developing countries had to couch these interests in the language and ideas of development and make a compelling case that investment rules would facilitate development. This was necessary because states were being asked to accept limits to their domestic regulations in return for the hope that investment inflows would increase. Proponents, such as Canada, could offer little else because, as liberal states, governments do not control private capital flows. But the MAI and the increasing controversy over the Singapore issues at the WTO 2003 ministerial finally led many business organizations to drastically downgrade as a priority the negotiation of investment rules at the WTO.

Canadian officials' ambitions had been shaped by the high levels of investment protection NAFTA accorded. They preached the NAFTA model's virtues at both the OECD and the WTO. By 1999, it was clear that Canada itself faced conflicts between the high levels of protection afforded investors in NAFTA through recourse to investor–state dispute mechanisms and the right of host states to regulate in the public interest. In fact, while the expectation was that many investor–state disputes under NAFTA would likely target Mexico, the reality is that most have targeted Canada. That experience coloured the views of many states on the wisdom of such high levels of investment protection. As the multilateral effort failed, Canada moved to regional and bilateral agreements as a way to protect Canadian investors' interests abroad.

Even as Canadian officials were seeking to protect Canadian investment in non-OECD countries as outward investment shifted in that direction, changes were emerging globally in the sources and types of foreign direct investment, posing challenges to an investment liberalization project that both Liberal and Conservative governments and the corporate elite had strongly supported. The past decade has seen strong growth in outward FDI from larger non-OECD countries, especially in Asia. A portion of this investment has been via SOEs from states that have very different political regimes and legal and corporate governance frameworks. That much of this investment has targeted resource industries, especially oil and gas, poses challenges. This has been one of the few sectors of growth in the Canadian economy as the aftermath of 2008 continues to bring slow or no growth in North America and Europe. Higher growth in Asia makes it an important target for Canadian trade and investment. Yet the wave of investments and takeovers by SOEs has raised unease both in the public and among the corporate elite. Fearing a wave of such takeovers, the government opted to permit the Nexen and Petronas deals and signal that further such takeovers will be unwelcome. Provincial premiers, the oil industry, and some Conservatives see a need for clearer rules, and claim that these ad hoc decisions are sending mixed messages to foreign investors. Others complain that the decisions to approve them were a sellout of the Canadian economy.

The plethora of FIPAs and FTAs in which Canada is now enmeshed have strong investment protection, in particular provisions on expropriation, both direct and indirect, which allow for investor–state arbitration and dispute resolution. Despite their purpose in protecting Canadian investors abroad they have already proven costly to Canada and have been rejected by some states, such as Australia, in their trade agreements. Other organizations, such as Oxfam,[37] question the morality of imposing such measures on many developing countries who need space for development policy but are often negotiating in relationships of profound asymmetry. Canadian governments, moreover, have shown little or no interest in strengthening corporate codes of conduct or addressing some of the major concerns that have been raised about the role of Canadian firms abroad, especially in the extractive industries of developing countries.

As this chapter has indicated, investment remains a sensitive policy issue in Canada and in our external relations. Even as governments and policymakers seek to advance what are perceived to be the interests of Canada as both an exporter and importer of capital, the nature of global capital flows and corporate actors has shifted, creating a need to redefine Canada's interests. Such redefinitions, however, are contentious and divisive and will continue to pose policy challenges even if Canada is *open for business.*

Questions for Review

1. How has the changing landscape of inward and outward direct investment shaped the policy debate about foreign investment in Canada?

2. Should Canada be negotiating high levels of protection of Canadian investors abroad via investor–state dispute resolution? Should we follow Australia's rejection of that approach, stated by their prime minister in 2011, that if "businesses are concerned about sovereign risk in Australian trading partner countries, they will need to make their own assessments about whether they want to commit to investing in those countries."

3. Should we as Canadians be concerned about acquisitions of Canadian energy companies by state-owned enterprises?

4. Compare the acquisitions of Nexen by CNOOC and Potash Corporation by BHP Billiton. Did the government make the right decision in accepting one and rejecting the other?

Suggested Readings

Dashwood, Hevina S. 2007. "Canadian Mining Companies and Corporate Social Responsibility: Weighing the Impact of Global Norms." *Canadian Journal of Political Science* 40, 1 (March), 129–56.

Hale, Geoffrey. 2008. "The Dog That Hasn't Barked: The Political Economy of Contemporary Debates on Canadian Foreign Investment Policies." *Canadian Journal of Political Science* 41, 3 (September): 719–47.

Krzepkowski, Matt, and Jack Mintz. 2010. "Canada's Foreign Direct Investment Challenge: Reducing Barriers and Ensuring a Level Playing Field in Face of Sovereign Wealth Funds and State-Owned Enterprises." University of Calgary School of Public Policy, *SPP Research Papers* 3, 4 (October).

North, Liisa, Timothy David Clark, and Viviana Patroni, eds. 2006. *Community Rights and Corporate Responsibility: Canadian Mining and Oil Companies in Latin America.* Toronto: Between the Lines.

Rocha, Manuel Pérez, and Stuart Trew. 2014. "NAFTA at 20: A Model for Corporate Rule." *Foreign Policy in Focus* (15 January). Available at http://www.commondreams.org/views/2014/01/15/nafta-20-model-corporate-rule.

Sauvant, Karl P. 2009. *FDI Protectionism is on the Rise.* Policy Research Working Paper 5052. World Bank Poverty Reduction and Economic Management Network, International Trade Department (September).

Smythe, Elizabeth. 2003. "Just Say No! The Negotiation of Investment Rules at the WTO." *International Journal of Political Economy* 33, 4 (Winter): 60–83.

Tomlin, Brian, Norman Hillmer, and Fen Hampson. 2008. *Canada's International Policies: Agendas, Alternatives, and Politics.* Part I. Don Mills, ON: Oxford University Press.

UNCTAD. 2013. *World Investment Report 2013. Global Value Chains: Investment and Trade for Development.* New York and Geneva: United Nations.

Notes

1. The Chinese takeover bid for Noranda in early 2005 set off alarm bells in Ottawa and led to amendments to the Investment Canada Act. See "Security concerns spur reviews on foreign investment," *The Globe and Mail*, 18 June 2005, B5.

2. External Affairs Canada, *Trade Policy for the 1980s* (Ottawa: External Affairs, 1983).

3. Department of Foreign Affairs and International Trade, *State of Trade* (Ottawa: DFAIT), April 2012, Chapter 6, pp. 98–104. Analysts Torbjörn Fredriksson and Zbigniew

Zimny, "Foreign Direct Investment and Transnational Corporations," in *Beyond Conventional Wisdom in Development Policy: An Intellectual History of* UNCTAD *1964–2004* (New York and Geneva: United Nations, 2004), have likened changing international views on investment issues to a swinging global pendulum.

4.   For a discussion of Canada's role in the UN and OECD negotiations in the 1970s, see Elizabeth Smythe, *Free to Choose: Globalization, Dependence and Canada's Changing Foreign Investment Regime* (Ph.D. dissertation, Carleton University, 1994), Chapter 6.

5.   House of Commons, Standing Committee on External Affairs and International Trade, "Statement of the Hon. Michael Wilson," 17 November 1992.

6.   Andrea Bruce, *Assessing the Impact of Canada's Foreign Investment Promotion and Protection Agreements* (MA thesis, Norman Paterson School of International Affairs, Carleton University, 1999).

7.   Stephanie Nolen, "Spying allegations throw cold water on Canada's trade and business plans in Brazil," *The Globe and Mail*, 8 October 2013; see also Government of Canada, "Canada–Brazil Relations," available at www.canadainternational.gc.ca/brazil-bresil/bilateral_relations_bilaterales/index.aspx.

8.   A leaked memo to the Cabinet dated 22 October 2002 ("Memo to Canadian Cabinet Sets Out Proposed Changes to Canadian Foreign Investment Protection Agreements," *Investment Law and Sustainable Development Weekly News Bulletin*, 13 December 2002) claims that Canadian business had been lobbying hard for FIPAs with Brazil, India, and China. In other cases, officials claim a number of developing countries, such as Peru, approached Canada to sign bilateral agreements. Often, developing countries are seeking to attract new FDI and qualify for investment insurance from various export development agencies.

9.   This case is based on interviews with Canadian and WTO officials in 2003 and on the reports of the Working Group on Trade and Investment (2002–3). For further discussion, see Elizabeth Smythe, "Just Say No! The Negotiation of Investment Rules at the WTO," *International Journal of Political Economy* 33 (Winter 2003): 60–83.

10.   Elizabeth Smythe, "Your Place or Mine? States, International Organizations and the Negotiation of Investment Rules," *Transnational Corporations* 7, 3 (December 1998): 85–120. See also Hon. Sergio Marchi, Minister of Trade, statement at the OECD Ministerial Meeting, 27 April 1998.

11.   R.B. Ramaiah, "Towards a Multilateral Framework on Investment?" *Transnational Corporations* 6, 1 (April 1997): 116–35.

12.   The Singapore issues were trade facilitation, transparency in government procurement, competition policy, and investment. All four involve domestic regulation. WTO

Singapore Ministerial Declaration (Geneva: WTO, 1996), paragraph 20.

13.   Submission from Canada to the Working Group on Trade and Investment, 11 December 1997 (WT/ WGTI/ W/19).

14.   Comment by WTO delegate in Geneva to the author in 2003. There have been so many controversial cases that the Department of International Trade now has a section of its website devoted to them, available at www.international.gc.ca/trade-agreements-accords-commerciaux/topics-domaines/disp-diff/gov.aspx?lang=eng.

15.   The heavily bracketed, leaked version of the FTAA investment chapter, which appeared on the Internet in 2001, was largely based on a US, NAFTA-like proposal.

16.   Submission from Canada to the WGTI, March 2001, "Foreign Investment Barriers: A Report by the Canadian Chamber of Commerce in Partnership with Industry Canada" (WT/ WGTI/W/97).

17.   Fatoumata Jawara and Aileen Kwa, *Behind the Scenes at the* WTO: *The Real World of International Trade Negotiation Lessons from Cancun*, updated ed. (London: Zed Books, 2004).

18.   Seri Rafidah Aziz (Malaysia) and Arun Jaitley (India), *Letter to Hon. Pierre Pettigrew*, 12 September 2003.

19.   Jagdish Bhagwati, *Financial Times*, 22 October 1998.

20.   Department of Finance, *Advantage Canada* (Ottawa 2006).

21.   Competition Policy Review Panel, *Compete to Win* (June 2008).

22.   Julian Beltrame, "Allow more foreign investment, bank mergers in Canada: Panel of experts says," Canadian Press, 26 June 2008.

23.   Karl Sauvant, *FDI Protectionism is on the Rise*, Policy Research Working Paper No. 5052, Poverty Reduction and Economic Management Network, International Trade Department, World Bank (September 2009). See also Subrata Bhattacharjee, "National Security with a Canadian Twist: The Investment Canada Act and the New National Security Review," *Columbia* FDI *Perspectives*, No. 10 (30 July 2009).

24.   Sauvant, 11.

25.   UNCTAD, *World Investment Report*, 2012; *Global Value Chains: Investment for Trade and Development* (Geneva and New York, 2013).

26.   Department of Foreign Affairs, Trade and Development Canada, *State of Trade* (2012).

27.   Shawn McCarthy, Steven Chase, and Brenda Bouw, "Tories reject BHP bid for PotashCorp," *The Globe and Mail*, 3 November 2010.

28.   See Carrie Tait and Shawn McCarthy, "Petronas sweetens progress pot to win Ottawa's okay," *The Globe and Mail*, 21 November 2012; Shawn McCarthy and Jacquie McNish, "Protect Canadian ownership of oil sands firms, executives urge," *The Globe and Mail*, 25 September 2012; and Nathan VanderKlippe, Shawn McCarthy, and Jacquie McNish,

"Harper draws line in the oil sands," *The Globe and Mail*, 9 December 2012.

29. Statement by the Prime Minister of Canada on Foreign Investment Ottawa, 7 December 2012, available at www.pm.gc.ca/eng/news/2012/12/07/statement-prime-minister-canada-foreign-investment.

30. Christine Dobby, "Memoirs of a stranded asset: Inside Ottawa's ill-fated Allstream review," *Financial Post*, 12 October 2013.

31. For the text of the Agreement between the Government of Canada and the Government of the People's Republic of China for the Promotion and Reciprocal Protection of Investments, see www.international.gc.ca/trade-agreements-accords-commerciaux/agr-acc/fipa-apie/china-text-chine.aspx. For legal analyses of the text, see Catherine Walsh and Michael G. Woods (Heenan Blaikie), "The Canada–China Foreign Investment Promotion and Protection Agreement, Part II: Investor–State Dispute Settlement Provisions," available at www.tradeready.ca/the-canada-china-foreign-investment-protection-and-promotion-act/; and Gus Van Harten, "Taking apart Tories' Party Line on China–Canada Treaty," *The Tyee*, 5 November 2012, available at http://thetyee.ca/Opinion/2012/11/05/Van-Harten-FIPA.

32. CBC News, as a result of an access-to-information request, reported on opposition inside the party and industry associations. See CBC News: Politics, "3 Conservative MPs raised concerns about CNOOC–Nexen deal," 29 January 2013, available at www.cbc.ca/news/politics/3-conservative-mps-raised-concerns-about-cnooc-nexen-deal-1.1386871.

33. Department of Foreign Affairs and International Trade, *Seizing Global Advantage*, 2009.

34. The government created the position of Corporate Social Responsibility counsellor in 2008; the counsellor reports to the trade minister and is equipped with limited powers of investigation.

35. For an analysis of the investment provisions see Armand de Mestral and Stephanie Mullen, *The Investment Provisions of CETA*, CETA Policy Brief Series, Canada Europe Transatlantic Dialogue, October 2013.

36. Canadian Union of Postal Workers, *Transatlantic Statement Opposing Excessive Corporate Rights (Investor–State Dispute Settlement) in the EU–Canada Comprehensive Economic and Trade Agreement (CETA)*, 5 February 2013, available at www.cupw.ca/index.cfm/ci_id/14446/la_id/1.

37. Oxfam International, *Signing Away the Future: How Trade and Investment Agreements between Rich and Poor Countries Undermine Development* (2007), Oxfam briefing paper, 1.

25 The Energy Triangle: Canada, the United States, and China

Duane Bratt

Key Terms

Continentalism   Ethical Oil
Emerging Energy Superpower   State-owned Enterprises

Continentalism is a prominent approach in the Canadian foreign policy literature, "based on the assumption that the destiny of Canada (both the society and the state) is inextricably tied to that of the United States, and that it is in Canada's national interest to align itself openly with its southern neighbour to guarantee its access to the American market and keep a functional and friendly relationship with Washington."[1] Historically, Canadian foreign policy around energy, with the notable exception of nuclear energy,[2] has been exclusively continentalist. Each and every year, over 99 per cent of Canadian oil and gas and electricity exports went to the United States. Foreign investment in Canada's oil and gas sector was dominated by American firms. An elaborate infrastructure of electricity lines and oil and gas pipelines ran north-south between the two countries. Energy relations between Canada and the United States, except for the tensions over the Trudeau government's imposition of the National Energy Program (NEP) in the early 1980s,[3] were warm and uncontroversial. The passage of the Canada–United States Free Trade Agreement (CUFTA) in 1988 ensured Canadian access for oil and gas exports to the US market in return for a guaranteed proportionality of Canadian production for export to the US. The CUFTA created, in effect, a common oil and gas market between Canada and the United States.[4] In his study of multilateralism, Tom Keating has acknowledged that "the energy sector has played a prominent role in Canadian foreign policy in the past, most often in regard to bilateral relations with the US."[5]

Recently, a new country—China—has come on the scene, a development that has changed the dynamics of Canada's energy foreign policy (at least in the oil and gas sector). There have been increases in both exports to China and foreign investment from China, and there are hopes that this will greatly expand in the years to come. In addition, new infrastructure such as pipelines and new ports are being proposed for construction in Canada for the purpose of exporting oil and gas to China.

This chapter explores Canada's continentalist approach to oil and gas policy to determine whether it will become more international. It highlights the drivers for a less continentalist approach, including the rise of China (especially its increasing demands for energy resources), increasing US energy self-sufficiency, and the appearance of US environmentalism. However, it also highlights the challenges that Canada has encountered in altering its continentalist energy paradigm, including geographic distance, infrastructure, nationalism over Chinese foreign investment, and Canadian domestic politics.

The chapter's first section describes the possible shift away from continentalism with a focus on export statistics, market access through new pipeline infrastructure that reaches ocean ports, and increased Chinese foreign investment in the energy sector. The second section explains this shift in three ways: 1) China as an emerging superpower and its increased demand for energy resources; 2) growing United States energy self-sufficiency; and 3) Canada's desire for market diversification and Harper's new China policy (see Burton's chapter in this volume). The chapter conclusion explains the resilience of the continentalist approach in Canada's energy foreign policy.

Describing the Shift

Trade Statistics

Canada is a trading nation. About a third of Canada's gross domestic product (GDP) is based on trade. Reflecting the continentalist approach, the United States has been Canada's number one trading partner for decades. However, recently China has become more important, surpassing Japan and the United Kingdom to become Canada's second largest trading partner. As Table 25.1 shows, however, Canada has a large trade deficit with China. Ottawa

believes increasing oil and gas exports to China would help alleviate the bilateral trade deficit.

Canada is the world's sixth largest oil producer and third largest natural gas producer. Given the relative small size of the Canadian domestic market, much of this oil and gas is exported. Table 25.2 shows that the United States currently imports 99 per cent of all Canadian oil and gas exports. This demonstrates the historic continentalist position when it comes to energy policy. China, which is Canada's second largest export market, bought only $0.5 billion of oil and gas in 2012. If there is a move to a more internationalist approach to energy policy, there needs to be a substantial increase in oil and gas exports to China.

Market Diversification and Access

Market diversification for Canada's oil and gas products has become critical. In 2013, then natural resources minister Joe Oliver told Canada's provincial energy ministers that "the US market remains an important market for Canada, but it is not going to be growing at the pace that it had been growing." Therefore, it "is a strategic imperative" for Canada to establish "the conditions necessary" to diversify its markets.[6] In a 2011 speech, Oliver had declared that it was in Canada's "national interest" to gain "access to Asian markets for our energy products, for our oil and gas."[7] But market access remains a significant problem. How does Canada get its products to the United States, China, and other markets? The oil sands, where the

---

Table 25.1 Canadian merchandise trade (2012)

	Exports	Imports	Balance
United States	$338.7 billion	$233.9 billion	$104.8 billion
China	$19.4 billion	$50.7 billion	–$31.3 billion
Rest of the World	$96.3 billion	$177.4 billion	–$81.1 billion
Total	$454.4 billion	$462.0 billion	–$7.6 billion

Source: Industry Canada, "Trade Data Online." Available at www.ic.gc.ca.

Table 25.2 Canadian oil and gas extraction exports (2012)

United States	$82.6 billion
China	$0.5 billion
Rest of the World	$0.4 billion
Total	$83.5 billion

Source: Industry Canada, "Trade Data Online." Available at www.ic.gc.ca.

majority of Canada's oil reserves are located, are in a remote northeastern corner of Alberta. The cheapest, safest, and most efficient way of transporting oil is via pipelines. A report from the Canada West Foundation made it clear that "Western Canada needs additional pipeline capacity to absorb expected production growth and to reach critical markets: Asia, the US Gulf Coast and eastern North America."[8] But building new pipelines has become a domestic and international political problem, seen in the efforts to build three new pipelines: 1) the Keystone XL pipeline, a north–south route to US refineries along the Gulf of Mexico in Texas and Louisiana; 2) the Northern Gateway pipeline, an east–west route from Edmonton to the Pacific Ocean coast (Kitimat, BC) for export to China and other Asian markets; and 3) the Energy East pipeline, a west–east route to the Atlantic Ocean coast (Saint John, NB) for export to India, China, and other markets.

Keystone XL

The Keystone XL pipeline would follow a 1,900-km route and would transport 830,000 barrels of crude a day from the Alberta oil sands and the shale fields in North Dakota to US refineries along the Gulf Coast. Part of the pipeline, from Cushing, Oklahoma, to the Gulf of Mexico, has already been built. TransCanada, based in Calgary, would build the pipeline at an estimated cost of $5.3 billion.

Advocates of the Keystone XL pipeline emphasize the economic benefits that would accrue to both Canada and the United States. In Canada, the project would create 3,500 jobs and generate an additional $617 billion in GDP.[9] In the US, construction of the pipeline would directly create 9,000 American jobs and another 7,000 spin-off jobs. The operation of the pipeline would create an additional 1.8 million person-year jobs over a 22-year period and would add $172 billion to America's GDP by 2035.[10] An additional benefit is that it would deliver new sources of heavy oil from the Canadian oil sands and the North Dakota Bakken fields to the refineries along the US Gulf Coast. Currently those refineries are operating well below capacity and need new sources of crude.

Obviously the Canadian energy industry, the Alberta provincial government, and the federal government are all enthusiastic supporters of the Keystone XL pipeline. But there is also support for the pipeline inside the US. The energy sector is obviously in favour, but so are labour unions and the US Republican Party. Public opinion polling shows strong support for the Keystone XL pipeline in the US. Princeton University did a survey in July 2013 and found more than two-thirds of Americans wanted the project approved.[11]

Environmentalists are the strongest critics of the Keystone XL pipeline, with two primary environmental objections. The first is pipeline safety and the fear of damaging oil spills. The second is the environmental destruction associated with developing the oil sands. In particular, it is noted that the oil sands release a high rate of greenhouse gas emissions (GHG). Environment Canada predicts that GHG emissions from the oil sands will have increased from 48 Mt in 2010 to 104 Mt in 2020.[12] Environmentalists hope that if they can reduce the transportation of oil sands products, such as by blocking the building of the Keystone XL pipeline, the development of the oil sands will simultaneously be reduced. Canada withdrew from the Kyoto Protocol in 2011, and even though Canada was not close to meeting its commitments under the protocol, the withdrawal was seen by environmentalists, many of them in the US, as the Harper government's endorsement of the "dirty oil" from the oil sands.

As part of its strategy to ensure completion of the Keystone XL pipeline and therefore maintain its preferential access to the US market, Ottawa started using the **ethical oil** rhetoric that had been popularized by conservative commentator Ezra Levant.[13] The "ethical oil" thesis argues that the oil sands environmental degradation has been greatly exaggerated by environmentalists. During a March 2013 speech in Chicago, then natural resources minister Joe Oliver pointed out that "total GHG emissions from oil sands production represent 0.1 percent . . . of global emissions," which is "just one-fortieth of coal emissions in the United States." Oliver also mentioned that "between 1990 and 2010, oil sands emissions per barrel have dropped by 26 percent."[14]

More importantly, if Americans do not want oil sands products, the alternative is to import oil from unstable and/or undemocratic countries such as Saudi Arabia, Venezuela, Sudan, Nigeria, or Russia. Not only are these countries substantially less environmentally responsible than Canada, they also have questionable commitments to human rights. Levant's polemic was designed to counteract anti-oil sands polemics,[15] but it took on more significance when political leaders such as Oliver and Environment Minister Peter Kent started to use the same language to defend the Keystone XL pipeline. In a speech in Washington in April 2013, Oliver said "the US can choose Canada—a friend, neighbour and ally—as its source. Or it can choose to continue to import oil from less friendly, less stable countries with weaker—perhaps no—environmental standards."[16] Oliver was even more explicit when he stated that "strengthening our bilateral energy collaboration would displace oil from Venezuela and the Middle East with a stable continental supply and thereby enhance the energy security of North America."[17] Stephen Harper went even further when, during an event in New York sponsored by the Canadian American Business Council, he warned that Canada would not "take no for an answer. We haven't had that [from the US], but if we were to get that, that won't be final. This won't be final until it's approved and we will keep pushing forward."[18] It also appears that Ottawa will address some of the environmental concerns that the Americans have about the Keystone XL pipeline in order to secure its approval. In September 2013, Harper promised, in a private letter to President Obama, to work with the US on reducing oil sands emissions in return for the approval.[19]

US President Barack Obama delayed making a decision in early 2012 because of the potential impact that a decision, whether to approve or deny, would have on the 2012 election. In spring 2013, the US State Department issued a report that did not reject, on environmental grounds, the building of the pipeline.[20] At the time of writing in early 2014, Obama has yet to make a decision on whether to approve the Keystone XL pipeline. He has a tough decision because his Democratic Party is deeply divided on the Keystone XL pipeline, with two of its base groups on opposite sides. Environmentalists oppose the pipeline, but labour unions support it. As Obama has admitted, "the politics" of the Keystone XL pipeline "are tough."[21]

Northern Gateway

The proposed Northern Gateway pipeline is to be built by Enbridge at an estimated cost of $7.9 billion. The 1,177-km long pipeline would move 525,000 barrels of oil a day from Edmonton to Kitimat, BC. A marine terminal will be built in Kitimat that would include 2 tanker berths, 3 condensate storage tanks, and 16 oil storage tanks. As many as 220 tankers a year would deliver the oil through the Douglas Channel along the BC coast to markets in China and other parts of Asia.

The Northern Gateway pipeline is strongly supported by the energy sector and the Alberta government. Greg Stringham, vice-president of the Canadian Association of Petroleum Producers, believes that the pipeline is critical "for market access of the West Coast."[22] Alberta Energy Minister Diana McQueen similarly saw the project as a way for the landlocked province to diversify its energy products away from the United States in order to get a better price from China.[23] Alberta is expected to reap $67 billion over 30 years in revenue from the Northern Gateway pipeline.[24]

Opposition to the Northern Gateway pipeline comes from Native bands across northern BC and from environmentalists. The BC government was initially opposed to the Northern Gateway Pipeline.[25] In July 2012, BC Premier Christy Clark laid out five conditions that the province needed in order to support the Northern Gateway pipeline.

1. Successful completion of the environmental review process. In the case of Enbridge, that would mean a recommendation by the National Energy Board Joint Review Panel that the project would proceed;

2. World-leading marine oil spill response, prevention and recovery systems for BC's coastline and ocean to manage and mitigate the risks and costs of heavy oil pipelines and shipments;

3. World-leading practices for land oil spill prevention, response, and recovery systems to manage and mitigate the risks and costs of heavy oil pipelines;

4. Legal requirements regarding Aboriginal and treaty rights are addressed and First Nations are provided with the opportunities, information, and resources necessary to participate in and benefit from a heavy oil project; and,

5. British Columbia receives a fair share of the fiscal and economic benefits of a proposed heavy oil project that reflects the level, degree and nature of the risk borne by the province, the environment and taxpayers.[26]

Although Victoria has yet to formally endorse the Northern Gateway pipeline, it appears that four of the five conditions have been met or will be met. In December 2013, the National Energy Board (NEB) Joint Review Panel gave technical approval for the Northern Gateway pipeline, albeit with 209 environmental, safety, and financial conditions.[27] A month earlier, after over a year of frosty relations between the two provinces, and especially the two premiers, Alberta and BC reached a rapprochement on BC's five conditions. Even on the contentious condition concerning the fair share of economic benefits, the two provinces agreed that they would not receive any of the increased royalties and taxes that Alberta would get from completed pipeline projects, but that BC could negotiate directly with the energy industry over transit rights such as a pipeline toll.[28] The remaining condition for supporting the pipeline is negotiating approval from Aboriginal groups. In June 2014, Ottawa accepted the NEB report giving the project federal approval. However, Natural Resources Minister Greg Rickford highlighted the fact that "consultations with aboriginal communities are required under many of the 209 conditions that have been established and as part of the process for regulatory authorizations and permits. The proponent [Enbridge] clearly has more work to do in order to fulfill the public commitment it has made to engage with aboriginal groups and local communities along the route."[29] The Northern Gateway pipeline requires support from all the Aboriginal bands whose land the pipeline would pass through. The federal cabinet's approval did not mollify Aboriginal concerns. Art Sterritt, executive director of British Columbia's Coastal First Nations, warned of legal challenges and civil disobedience if Enbridge "dare[d]" to "put shovels in the ground. First Nations and our allies will protect our rights and the interests of future generations. We will never allow oil tankers into our territorial waters."[30] A series of court challenges from Native groups is expected. This is because there is a constitutional duty to consult that requires federal and provincial governments "to respect . . . decisions, [so] that negative impacts on these rights and uses are avoided, minimized or mitigated and rights are accommodated."[31] Failure to properly do so will lead to legal challenges. This was confirmed in a unanimous Supreme Court ruling in late June 2014 stating that, in parts of Canada where land claims treaties were never signed between Native Canadians and the Crown, Natives still owned their ancestral lands and could control all economic activity. This is the case over much of interior British Columbia, including most of the proposed Northern Gateway route.[32] Jim Prentice, a former cabinet minister in Harper's government (including Minister of Indian Affairs) and current Progressive Conservative Premier of Alberta, warned a Calgary business audience that "there will be no way forward on West Coast access without the central participation of First Nations of British Columbia."[33] But, already, Native leaders such as Art Sterritt have maintained that "no amount of consultations" will result in Native support for the pipeline.[34]

Environmentalists, who are more numerous and powerful in BC than in the rest of Canada, remain very hostile to the Northern Gateway. They fear a pipeline and/or tanker spill. Chris Genovali, executive director of Raincoast Conservation Foundation, warned that the federal government should prepare to deal with "potentially the biggest environmental battle we've ever seen in Canada."[35]

Energy East

On August 1, 2013, TransCanada Corporation announced that it was converting and expanding an underutilized 3,000-km natural gas pipeline system running from Alberta to Montreal so that it could carry heavy oil. It would also expand the pipeline by 1,400 km so that it stretched as far as Saint John, New Brunswick. The $12 billion project would enable Alberta heavy oil to get to refineries in Montreal and Saint John as well as to the Atlantic Ocean for shipping overseas. Regulatory approval from the NEB would be sought in 2014, and the expansions would come into operation in late 2017 (Quebec) and 2018 (New Brunswick).

The Energy East pipeline would serve three main purposes. First, it would be a hedge in the event that neither the Keystone XL nor Northern Gateway pipelines are built. Second, it gets landlocked Alberta's heavy oil to a coast for shipping to China and other parts of Asia. This would require tankers to take a more circuitous route using the Panama Canal to go from the Atlantic to Pacific Oceans. This additional distance increases the shipping cost to $7 for shipping from Alberta to New Brunswick, up from $5 for shipping from Alberta to British Columbia.[36] However, the eastern route is much shorter if Canada wants to enter the Indian market. Third, it would displace more expensive imported oil from Saudi Arabia, Nigeria, and Libya with domestic oil.

Opposition to the Energy East pipeline comes from various environmental groups who have general concerns about the oil sands and pipeline safety and specific concerns about the safety of reconfiguring a natural gas pipeline to transport heavy oil. However, it is more likely that it will be built when compared to Keystone XL or Northern Gateway. Unlike Keystone XL, the Energy East pipeline does not require the support or approval of a foreign government, and unlike Northern Gateway, Energy East has the support of all the relevant domestic governments: federal government, key opposition parties, and the premiers of Alberta, Quebec, and New Brunswick. For example, Prime Minister Harper claimed that "we're not just expanding our market for energy projects, which we need to do, but we are also at the same time making sure that Canadians themselves benefit from those projects and from that energy security."[37]

The Canada West Foundation, using data derived from the Canadian Energy Research Institute (CERI), calculated that if Keystone XL, Northern Gateway, and the expansion of the Trans Mountain pipeline (from Edmonton to Vancouver) were all approved (excluding the Canada East pipeline), Canada's GDP would increase by an incredible $1.3 trillion. Most of the economic benefits (jobs, royalties, taxes, and spinoff activities) would accrue to Alberta, but there would still be benefits across the other provinces.[38] This increased economic activity would result from oil sands products getting to the international markets of the US, China, and other parts of Asia, allowing Alberta to ramp up production in the oil sands. It would also address the discounted rate that much of Alberta oil receives. This is reflected in both the so-called bitumen bubble, which is the price gap between the North American standard of West Texas Intermediate (WTI) and Western Canadian Select (WCS), as well as the gap between the Canadian and global price for oil.

Foreign Investment

As Table 25.3 shows, the largest supplier and destination of Canadian foreign direct investment remains the United States, and China is only a marginal player. The situation is the same when we examine the energy sector. Canadian oil production is controlled 59 per cent by Canadian companies; 41 per cent are majority foreign owned. Natural gas production is also majority owned by Canadian companies (54.4 per cent) compared to majority foreign owned (45.6 per cent). The top 20 energy companies operating in Canada are split 50–50 between Canadian owned and majority foreign owned (see Table 25.4 for a list). Of the 10 that are foreign owned, seven are American.[39] According to a report from CIBC, Chinese **state-owned enterprises** (SOEs) own only 7 per cent of oil sands reserves, and all SOEs own only 10 per cent.[40]

This pattern of heavy US investment in the Canadian energy sector was challenged when the China National Offshore Oil Corporation (CNOOC) attempted a $15.1 billion purchase of Nexen. There is a $330 million threshold under the Investment Canada Act, so Industry Canada was required to review the CNOOC Nexen deal. The biggest issue facing Canada was the fact that CNOOC was a state-owned enterprise. The fear was that CNOOC would have a competitive advantage over public companies by having a lower cost of capital through state subsidies and access to cheap loans. In addition, it was believed that CNOOC, and consequently Nexen, takes orders from the Chinese government, and this worry was exacerbated by the fact that China is not a democracy. It was also noted that there would be a lack

Table 25.3 Canadian foreign direct investment (2011)

	Inward FDI		Outward FDI	
	$ millions	Percentage	$ millions	Percentage
United States	326,055	53.7	276,145	40.3
China	10,905	1.8	4,463	0.6
Rest of the World	270,537	44.5	403,888	59.1
Total	607,497	100	684,496	0.6

Source: Asia Pacific Foundation, "Investment Statistics." Available at www.asiapacific.ca/statistics/investment.

Table 25.4 Top 20 oil and gas producers in Canada

Majority Canadian-Owned	Majority Foreign-Owned
Canadian Natural Resources Limited	Husky Energy (Taiwan)
Suncor	Shell (UK)
Cenovus Energy	ConocoPhilips (US)
Encana	Imperial Oil (US)
Penn West	Devon (US)
Pengrowth	Apache (US)
Canadian Oil Sands Ltd	Exxon (US)
Crescent Point	Chevron (US)
Talisman	Murphy (US)
ARC Resources	TAQA North (UAE)

Source: Nathan VanderKlippe, "Canada's energy sector: Foreign vs domestic," *The Globe and Mail* (4 December 2012).

of reciprocity in China; for example, if the roles had been reversed, the Chinese government would never have allowed Nexen to purchase CNOOC. Finally, national security concerns were raised about SOEs. The Canadian Security Intelligence Service (CSIS), in its annual report released in September 2012, noted that some "SOEs and private firms with close ties to their home governments have pursued opaque agendas or received clandestine intelligence support for their pursuits" in Canada. CSIS feared that this could lead to "illegal transfers of technology . . . espionage and other foreign interference activities," which would "represent a threat to Canadian security interests."[41] CSIS left out, at least publicly, the names of the SOEs that it suspected of committing industrial espionage, but the implication was that it was Chinese firms. However, former CSIS officials such as Ray Boisvert could be more explicit. Boisvert, a former deputy director, argued that "state-owned enterprises have the same marching orders or essentially the same mandate or mission as China's intelligence services, which is to serve the interests of the party and the state."[42]

On the other hand, there were also individuals who were not terribly vexed by the fact that CNOOC was an SOE. After all, other SOEs operate in the oil sands (Kuwait National Petroleum, Norway's Statoil, and France's Total) without much attention. CNOOC already had $3 billion worth of Canadian energy assets, and other Chinese SOEs (Sinopec and PetroChina) had minority investments in a number of oil sands projects. The argument was made that CNOOC operates, and would continue to operate, as a private company. Margaret Cornish, a Canadian trade lawyer based in Beijing, argued that Chinese SOEs are similar to other large publicly traded multinationals. They are listed on international stock exchanges, have disclosure requirements, and are driven by the profit motive. This is especially true of Chinese energy SOEs, of which Cornish maintained that "their organization and strategies reflect and respond to those of their global rivals rather than the Chinese state."[43]

Beyond the SOE issue, which was absolutely paramount, Ottawa was concerned about the CNOOC-Nexen deal for a number of reasons. First was the overall size of the deal, which, at $15.1 billion, would represent one of the largest foreign takeovers in Canadian history. Second, Nexen was Canada's twenty-fourth largest oil and gas company, and this raised fears that the deal, along with the Malaysian Petronas's $6 billion purchase of Canadian natural gas producer Progress Energy Resources Corp., could be the beginning of the de-Canadianization of the oil patch. If these two transactions were allowed, what would happen if a foreign firm, possibly another state-owned oil company such as PetroChina or Sinopec, went after one of Canada's really big energy firms such as Canadian Natural Resources, Suncor, Encana, or Cenovus? Third, there was a need to attract additional investment, foreign or domestic, to exploit the oil sands. For example, CERI estimated, in its reference case scenario, that the oil sands would require $216 billion in new investment between 2011 and 2030.[44]

Fourth, Canada was an international proponent of liberalizing investment rules. In the late 1990s, Canada went from being a net importer of capital to a net exporter. Cognizant of that shift, Canada had promoted investment agreements to protect the interests of investors in a variety of international forums: the ill-fated Multilateral Agreement on Investment, at the World Trade Organization, in comprehensive economic negotiations with India and the European Union, and in negotiating bilateral foreign investment promotion and protection agreements (FIPAs) (see Smythe's chapter in this volume). Canada had already blocked the $39 billion hostile takeover of PotashCorp by the Australian mining giant BHP Billiton in 2010. Did Canada want a reputation as a mercantilist when it came to FDI—exporting of capital: good, but importing of capital: bad?

Another complicating feature was that 12 per cent of Nexen's assets were in the United States. This meant that the US would have to approve those portions of the deal. There was no guarantee that that would occur because, in 2005, the US government had stopped CNOOC's proposed takeover of Unocal on national security grounds.

Ottawa used the net-benefits test to determine whether it would allow the CNOOC takeover of Nexen. On the one hand, CNOOC offered a package of benefits specifically designed to satisfy the test. For example, it would keep the head office in Calgary, seek to retain Nexen's management team and number of employees, maintain Nexen's commitment to corporate social responsibility, list its shares on the Toronto Stock Exchange, and invest an additional $5–8 billion in oil and gas development in North America.[45] CNOOC also maintained that Canada and Alberta would still regulate the resource and collect royalties and taxes. A further net benefit consideration was the fact that Nexen was underperforming and had been on the market for a while, but no

North American firm wanted to touch it. CNOOC, for its part, was willing to pay a hefty premium to acquire Nexen: $27.50 a share for a company that had been trading at $17.30.[46] A final point was that only 25 per cent of Nexen's assets were in Canada; it is a global company. However, companies in the past had made promises to Industry Canada that were eventually broken, either explicitly or using loopholes to get around the regulations. For example, Vale S.A. and U.S. Steel both failed to keep their investment and employment commitments after they bought Inco and Stelco. In determining what constitutes a "net benefit," the fact is that the rules are quite vague. This was notwithstanding the promise by then industry minister Tony Clement in 2010 to clarify the rules after the PotashCorp takeover was blocked. Thus, there was plenty of room for Ottawa to make up its mind on the CNOOC-Nexen deal.

Canada–China relations were also a consideration for the Harper government. This will be analyzed in more detail later in the chapter, but it needs to be mentioned now that CNOOC would never have approached Nexen during Harper's anti-China phase. But now, with relations warming and both the Canadian and Alberta governments encouraging China to invest in the oil sands, CNOOC felt that it could move to acquire Canadian energy firms. Canada–China relations would take a significant step back if Ottawa denied the CNOOC-Nexen deal. This was especially important because the Canada–China Foreign Investment Promotion and Protection Agreement had recently been ratified.

In the domestic political calculations, the opposition Liberal party was largely in favour (including interim leader Bob Rae and future leader Justin Trudeau), but the NDP was firmly opposed. Provincial support from Alberta was also present, unlike the takeover attempt of PotashCorp, which was strongly opposed by the Saskatchewan government. However, there was some opposition within the Conservative caucus as a few MPs from Alberta, mainly Rob Anders and Ted Menzies, opposed the takeover. Public opinion also suggested Canadians were leery of the deal. In an Angus Reid poll taken in October 2012, 58 per cent of Canadians wanted the government to block the takeover and only 12 per cent would allow it. Alberta, at 22 per cent, had the highest support for the deal, but even there, 63 per cent said that they wanted the government to block it. Fear of SOEs drove the opposition. Forty-eight per cent of Canadians agreed with the sentiment that SOEs have a competitive advantage over public companies, and only 19 per cent opposed. In addition, 78 per cent of Canadians said that foreign governments should not control resources on Canadian soil.[47] Even corporate Canada opposed the deal, with only 42 per cent of Canadian corporate executives supporting the deal while 50 per cent opposed it.[48]

Finally, in December 2012, after several delays, Stephen Harper announced a compromise decision on the acquisitions of Nexen and Progress Energy Resources by CNOOC and Petronas respectively. Industry Canada would allow the foreign takeovers, but it would also close the door on future SOE takeovers in the oil sands. Harper stated that the government would "approve foreign investments that are of net benefit to Canada," but warned that "purchases of Canadian assets by foreign government through state-owned enterprises are not the same as other transactions." Therefore, "the Government of Canada has determined that foreign state control of oil sands development has reached the point at which further state control would not be of net benefit to Canada." In the future, the takeover of Canadian oil sands firms by SOEs would be approved only in "exceptional circumstances." As far as SOE investment in general is concerned, Harper promised that Ottawa "will strengthen scrutiny" under the Investment Canada Act "of proposals by foreign state-owned enterprises to acquire Canadian businesses." This would involve a three-pronged test:

1. the degree of control or influence a state-owned enterprise would likely exert on the Canadian business that is being acquired;
2. the degree of control or influence that a state-owned enterprise would likely exert on the industry in which the Canadian business operates;
3. most importantly, the extent to which the foreign government in question is likely to exercise control or influence over the state-owned enterprise acquiring the Canadian business.

Harper added that "the onus to show these investments are of net benefit to Canada rests with the investor." Further emphasizing the point that Canada was open to investment, but not SOE investment, Harper laid out a two-tier strategy. The review threshold for private takeovers would rise to $1 billion, but the threshold for SOEs would remain at $330 million.[49]

CNOOC, as well as the Chinese government, was obviously "very pleased" by the decision,[50] but so were most Canadian energy executives. Marcel Coutu, CEO of Canadian Oil Sands Ltd., and Hal Kvisle of Talisman Energy both supported the decision and acknowledged that it was "very balanced."[51] However, there were also critics of the decision. Most were typical opponents of all foreign investment, such as the Canadian Auto Workers union.[52] However, critics also included two of Alberta's most senior ministers (Finance Minister Doug Horner and Energy Minister Ken Hughes), who were worried that the new foreign investment rules would reduce the amount of capital available for the oil sands.[53] Then Alberta Premier Alison Redford echoed the views of her ministers when she said, on the eve of a trip to China in September 2013, that Harper's rules around SOE investment in the oil sands were part of the reason for her visit. "There is no doubt" that "there was some concern that this might signal a change of policy from the federal government on foreign investment by state-owned enterprises. And we've always taken the view that we welcome that investment."[54] The Alberta government, and, for that matter the Chinese, want greater clarity beyond Ottawa's promise to examine on a case-by-case basis what types of foreign investment would be approved by Industry Canada. Opposition to the Nexen takeover also extended to much of the Canadian public. A December 2012 Ipsos Reid poll found that 68 per cent of Canadians believed the government should block the sale of Canadian firms to all foreign investors. The opposition to foreign takeovers rose to 74 per cent in the case of foreign state-owned enterprises.[55]

Explaining the Shift

Why has Canada tried to shift away from a continentalist approach in its energy policy? First is the rise of China, which has been one of the key events of the twenty-first century. China is the world's most populated state and comprises the third largest land mass. Since 2010, China has become the second largest economy in the world with an $8.2 trillion GDP.[56] China has had annual GDP growth rates of more than seven per cent annually over the past thirty years. China is also extending its political reach. As Robert Kaplan has argued, "on land and sea, abetted by China's favorable location on the map, Beijing's influence is expanding—from Central Asia to the South China Sea and from the Russian Far East to the Indian Ocean."[57] China has also been strengthening its ties with African countries through trade, investment, and foreign aid. Militarily, China has the largest army in the world, with 1.6 million soldiers, is a nuclear weapons state, and is rapidly increasing its military spending ($166 billion in 2012).[58] It is also making efforts to expand and modernize its navy with the goal of denying the US Navy access to the East China Sea and other Chinese coastal waters.

China's rise is contrasted with a perceived American decline. The US continues to possess the world's strongest military and economy, but shows growing indications of weakness. The wars in Iraq and Afghanistan, with a high cost in blood and treasure and an outcome that is ambiguous at best, have sapped some of its strength. The Iraq war has also cost the US some of its political prestige around the world. Finally, the US was hit hard by the 2008 financial crisis and subsequent recession. The US has a budget debt of over $17 trillion, and in 2012 alone it had a $1.1 trillion budget deficit.[59] To finance this debt, the US has a very large balance-of-payments deficit, with China holding almost $1.3 trillion in US treasury bills as of May 2014.[60]

At the same time, arguments about the US being replaced have been heard before. During the Cold War, some believed that the Soviet Union would eventually pass the US, and in the 1980s the same thing was said about Japan. Yet, each time, the US's intrinsic advantages—an open economy, rule of law, its universities, its diversity, its cultural attraction, and more—have allowed it to beat back its potential competitors. This can be seen in competing assessments of American and Chinese soft power. *Soft power* was a term coined by American political scientist Joseph Nye to refer to a state's ability to persuade others to follow its lead by being an attractive example.[61] For example, a 2009 report by the Center for Strategic and International Studies assessed Chinese soft power efforts in Southeast Asia, Africa, and Latin America. Although much of Chinese activity towards these developing countries has been economic, "Beijing has also promot[ed] regional economic integration and security arrangements, emphasiz[ed] the role of the United Nations, participat[ed] in humanitarian missions, provid[ed] concessionary loans and debt relief, increase[d] cultural and academic exchange programs, and engage[ed] local communities through skilled diplomats."[62] Despite these efforts, China still trails the United States in soft power. In surveys of international public opinion, the United States retains a much more favourable image than does China.[63]

Even if China does not replace the US as the world's leading power, Canadians need to be aware that it is a rising power and possibly a future global superpower. Canada needs to establish better economic relations with China, particularly in the oil and gas sector, and hedge against US relative decline, especially since Chinese demand for energy continues to skyrocket. The International Energy Agency (IEA) recognizes that global demand for oil will continue to rise, but this increase is not uniform. The largest increase in demand for oil is in China, India, and the rest of the developing world, but there will also be a corresponding drop in oil consumption in North America and Western Europe. Between 2011 and 2020, Chinese oil demand will increase by more than 3 million barrels a day and Indian oil demand will increase by about 1 million barrels a day. By 2030, Chinese oil demand will increase by over 6 million barrels a day and Indian oil demand will increase by over 4 million barrels a day.[64] China uses 10.9 million barrels of oil a day and has to import 6.3 million barrels. In September 2013, China surpassed the US to become the world's largest importer of oil.[65]

While the debate about American relative decline continues to wage, there is no doubt about the changing nature of American energy requirements, which is the second explanation for Canada's attempted shift away from continentalism. The International Energy Agency forecasts that the United States will become the world's largest oil producer by around 2020. This is due to a combination of dropping demand and the discovery of new domestic supplies. A game changer in the American energy sector has been the expansion of shale oil and natural gas using hydraulic fracturing (fracking) extraction technology. As a consequence, the

US will be importing less oil. Currently, the US consumes about 15 million barrels of oil a day. In order to meet this need, it currently imports between 8 and 9 million barrels a day, although this is expected to drop to 6 million barrels a day by 2020. Canada is the largest single supplier, sending over 2.4 million barrels a day to the US. Other major suppliers to the US market include Saudi Arabia and Venezuela. The US will continue to need to import oil in successively decreasing amounts until it becomes a net exporter in around 2030.[66]

The third explanation for this attempted shift from continentalism to a more internationalist approach has been the rise in importance of energy as an instrument of Canadian foreign policy. Just after being first elected in 2006, Prime Minister Stephen Harper began touting Canada as an **emerging energy superpower**. At a speech in London, Harper told his audience: "We are currently the fifth largest energy producer in the world. We rank 3rd and 7th in global gas and oil production respectively. We generate more hydro-electric power than any other country on earth. And we are the world's largest supplier of uranium."[67] By deliberately invoking the term *superpower*, Harper meant that Canada was more than just a major exporter of energy, and was interested in using energy as a key tool in Canadian foreign policy. Harper has continued to use the term "emerging energy superpower." Most notably, during a trip to China in 2012, Harper stated that Canada is "an emerging superpower. We want to sell our energy to people who want to buy our energy. It's that simple. . . . It is increasingly clear that Canada's commercial interests are best served through diversification of our energy markets. To this end, our government is committed to ensuring that Canada has the infrastructure necessary to move our energy resources to those diversified markets."[68]

A related element has been the changing nature of Canadian–Chinese relations under the Harper government. The conventional view is that the Harper government, since coming to power in 2006, has consistently steered away from China. A typical statement came from Professor Andrew Lui, who wrote that the Harper government had made a "deliberate geopolitical shift away from China."[69] This was clearly true in the initial years of Harper's mandate when he vocally criticized China's human rights record, saw several members of the Conservative caucus visit Taiwan, awarded honorary Canadian citizenship to the Dalai Lama, boycotted the 2008 Olympics in Beijing, and refused to visit China until 2009. In a memorable quote during his first year as prime minister, Harper, discussing his criticism of China's human rights record, said, "I think Canadians want us to promote our trade relations worldwide, and we do that, but I don't think Canadians want us to sell out important Canadian values. They don't want us to sell that out to the almighty dollar."[70] It was for these reasons that, several years later, Mei Ping, China's ambassador to Canada, commented that the Harper government's China policy was "short-sighted and out-of-date." Ottawa, he felt, "lacked a strategic view in its dealings with China," and had "overestimated Canada's influence and seemed to believe that Canada matters a lot for China."[71]

However, in recent years, there has been a slight rapprochement towards China. In 2009, both Foreign Minister Lawrence Cannon and Trade Minister Stockwell Day visited China. Later in the year, in December 2009, Harper himself finally went to China—a trip marked by Chinese Premier Wen Jiabao's telling Harper that by waiting "too long" to visit, he had created serious "problems of mutual trust."[72] In 2010, Chinese President Hu Jintao reciprocated Harper's visit through a state visit of his own. Of particular relevance for this chapter have been the efforts by Canadian politicians and

industry officials to try opening the Chinese market for oil and gas exports. For example, former Alberta Premier Alison Redford made three trips to China between October 2011 and September 2013.

Conclusion

This chapter tests the thesis of economic continentalism using a key sector of the Canadian economy. It shows how difficult diversification away from the United States can be. Canada's geography, infrastructure, culture, history, and political ties are north–south. Even if the Keystone XL pipeline is not built, the vast majority of Canadian oil and gas exports will still go to the United States through existing pipelines and by rail.

Even though China is now the second largest economy in the world and is desperate for energy resources, Canada finds itself constrained from realizing the economic benefits. There is a lack of infrastructure to get energy products to China. While there are proposals on the table to address this deficiency—Northern Gateway and Energy East pipelines—there remains significant domestic opposition from environmentalists and Native groups. China has tried to force the issue by investing in Canada's energy sector, but this too has raised domestic opposition, seen in the fight over the CNOOC-Nexen deal and the role of Chinese SOEs.

In short, while Canadian policy-makers and even members of the energy sector might desire moving away from continentalism in the energy sector, they seem unable to reduce the existing barriers. At the same time, there remain significant incentives to continue to pursue continentalism. Thus, for the foreseeable future, continentalism will remain the dominant approach to Canada's energy foreign policy.

Questions for Review

1. What are the drivers for Canada's attempted shift away from continentalism in its energy policy?

2. What are the constraints for Canada's attempted shift away from continentalism in its energy policy?

3. How accurate is the "ethical oil" thesis?

4. Should Canada maintain a continentalist approach to its energy policy?

Suggested Readings

Bratt, Duane. 2009. "Tools and Levers: Energy as an Instrument of Canadian Foreign Policy," pp. 209–31 in Robert Bothwell and Jean Daudelin, eds. *Canada among Nations 2008: 100 Years of Canadian Foreign Policy.* Montreal and Kingston: McGill-Queen's University Press.

Cornish, Margaret. 2012. *Behaviour of Chinese SOEs: Implications for Investment and Cooperation in Canada.* Toronto: Canadian International Council: Toronto (February).

Holden, Michael. 2013. *Pipe or Perish: Saving an Oil Industry at Risk.* Calgary: Canada West Foundation (February).

Levant, Ezra. 2010. *Ethical Oil: The Case for Canada's Oil Sands.* Toronto: McClelland and Stewart.

Lui, Andrew. 2013. "Sleeping with the Dragon: The Harper Government, China, and How Not to Do Human Rights," pp. 90–107 in Heather A. Smith and Claire Turenne Sjolander, eds. *Canada in the World: Internationalism in Canadian Foreign Policy.* Don Mills, ON: Oxford University Press.

Nikiforuk, Andrew. 2008. *Tar Sands: Dirty Oil and the Future of a Continent.* Vancouver: Greystone.

Notes

1. Heather A. Smith and Claire Turenne Sjolander, eds., *Canada in the World: Internationalism in Canadian Foreign Policy* (Don Mills, ON: Oxford University Press, 2013), 265.

2. For an examination of Canadian foreign policy and nuclear energy see Duane Bratt, *The Politics of CANDU Exports* (Toronto: University of Toronto Press, 2006).

3. See Stephen Clarkson, *Canada and the Reagan Challenge: Crisis and Adjustment, 1981–85*, updated ed. (Toronto: Lorimer, 1985), 55–82.

4. Duane Bratt, "Tools and Levers: Energy as an Instrument of Canadian Foreign Policy," pp. 209–31 in Robert Bothwell and Jean Daudelin, eds., *Canada Among Nations 2008: 100 Years of Canadian Foreign Policy* (Montreal and Kingston: McGill-Queen's University Press, 2009).

5. Tom Keating, *Canada and World Order: The Multilateralist Tradition in Canadian Foreign Policy*, 3rd ed. (Don Mills, ON: Oxford University Press, 2013), 240.

6. Quoted in Carrie Tate, "Ministers cast eye toward Asia," *The Globe and Mail*, 28 August 2013.

7. Quoted in Peter O'Neil, "Oil industry's 'nation-building' Northern Gateway pipeline won't be stopped by protesters," Joe Oliver," *National Post*, 6 December 2011.

8. Michael Holden, *Pipe or Perish: Saving an Oil Industry at Risk* (Calgary: Canada West Foundation, February 2013), 18.

9. Canadian Energy Pipeline Association, "Pipeline projects worth trillions to Canadians," 18 September 2013, available at www.cepa.com/pipeline-projects-worth-trillions-to-canadians.

10. TransCanada Corporation, "Jobs & Economic Benefits: Keystone XL means jobs," available at http://keystone-xl.com/about/jobs-and-economic-benefits/.

11. Paul Koring, "Keystone XL support grows in U.S., poll finds," *The Globe and Mail*, 18 July 2013.

12. Environment Canada, *Canada's Emission Trends 2012* (August 2012), available at www.ec.gc.ca/Publications/253AE6E6-5E73-4AFC-81B7-9CF440D5D2C5/793-Canada's-Emissions-Trends-2012_e_01.pdf.

13. Ezra Levant, *Ethical Oil: The Case for Canada's Oil Sands* (Toronto: McClelland and Stewart, 2010).

14. Joe Oliver, "Canada's Energy Future: The United States, and Beyond," speech given to the Chicago Council on Global Affairs, 5 March 2013, available at http://www.nrcan.gc.ca/media-room/speeches/2013/1883.

15.   For example, Andrew Nikiforuk, *Tar Sands: Dirty Oil and the Future of a Continent* (Vancouver: Greystone, 2008); and William Marsden, *Stupid to the Last Drop: How Alberta is Bringing Environmental Armageddon to Canada (and Doesn't Seem to Care)* (Toronto: Knopf, 2007).

16.   Quoted in Paul Koring, "Canada best source for oil for U.S., Oliver says," *The Globe and Mail*, 25 April 2013.

17.   Natural Resources Canada, "Minister Oliver Reinforces Importance of Canada–U.S. Energy Relationship," news release, 24 April 2013.

18.   Quoted in Joanna Slater, "Harper stands firm on Keystone," *The Globe and Mail*, 27 September 2013.

19.   Shawn McCarthy and Jeff Jones, "Harper asks Obama for joint oil strategy," *The Globe and Mail*, 7 September 2013.

20.   United States State Department, *Keystone XL Project—Environmental Impact Statement* (March 2013).

21.   Quoted in Michael D. Shear, "Obama Tells Donors of Tough Politics of Environment," *The New York Times*, 4 April 2013. Available at www.nytimes.com/2013/04/05/us/politics/obama-donors-keystone-pipeline.html?_r=0.

22.   Jeffrey Jones and Brent Jang, "For Canada's oil industry, ruling brings hope—and hurdles," *The Globe and Mail*, 20 December 2013.

23.   James Wood and Chris Varcoe, "Gateway benefits outweigh risks: Panel," *Calgary Herald*, 20 December 2013.

24.   Ibid.

25.   Interestingly, the BC government is not opposed to a 750-km natural gas pipeline being proposed by TransCanada and Progress Energy Canada Ltd. There are two reasons for explaining its support of the natural gas pipeline but opposition to the Northern Gateway oil pipeline. First, the BC government believes that natural gas pipelines are safer than oil pipelines. Second, the natural gas pipeline is transmitting from within BC, as opposed to from the Alberta-based oil sands. This means that BC gets the royalty money.

26.   British Columbia, Department of the Environment, *Requirements for British Columbia to Consider Support for Heavy Oil Pipelines* (July 2012), available at www.env.gov.bc.ca/main/docs/2012/TechnicalAnalysis-HeavyOilPipeline_120723.pdf.

27.   National Energy Board, *Report of the Joint Review Panel for the Enbridge Northern Gateway Project* (2013).

28.   James Wood, "Alberta, BC salvage deal on Gateway pipeline," *Calgary Herald*, 6 November 2013, available at www.calgaryherald.com/news/Alberta+salvage+deal+Gateway+pipeline/9127739/story.html.

29.   Government of Canada, "Government of Canada Accepts Recommendation to Impose 209 Conditions on Northern Gateway Proposal," news release, 17 June 2014, available at http://news.gc.ca/web/article-en.do?nid=858469.

30.   Quoted in Laura Payton and Susana Mas, "Northern Gateway pipeline approved with 209 conditions," CBC News, 17 June 2014, available at www.cbc.ca/news/politics/northern-gateway-pipeline-approved-with-209-conditions-1.2678285.

31.   Government of Saskatchewan, *First Nations and Métis People Consultation Policy Framework* (June 2010), available at http://www.gov.sk.ca/adx/aspx/adxGetMedia.aspx?mediaId=1164&PN=Shared.

32.   Sean Fine, "Supreme Court expands land-title rights in unanimous ruling," *The Globe and Mail*, 26 June 2014, available at www.theglobeandmail.com/news/national/supreme-court-expands-aboriginal-title-rights-in-unanimous-ruling/article19347252/.

33.   Quoted in Shawn McCarthy and Nathan VanderKlippe, "Prentice issues energy warning," *The Globe and Mail*, 28 September 2012.

34.   Quoted in Shawn McCarthy, Gloria Galloway, and Brent Jang, "*neb* clears path for Northern Gateway," *The Globe and Mail*, 20 December 2013.

35.   Ibid.

36.   James Wood and Reid Southwick, "Politicians hail new markets, revenues for province, Canada," *Calgary Herald*, 2 August 2013.

37.   Jane Taber, "Harper hails pipeline as N.B. seeks to halt exodus of workers," *The Globe and Mail*, 9 August 2013.

38.   Holden, *Pipe or Perish*, 23.

39.   All statistics are from Nathan VanderKlippe, "Canada's energy sector: Foreign vs domestic," *The Globe and Mail*, 4 December 2012.

40.   Shawn McCarthy and Jacquie McNish, "Oil patch seeks foreign takeover rules," *The Globe and Mail*, 26 September 2012.

41.   Canadian Security Intelligence Service (CSIS), *Public Report 2010–2011* (Public Works and Government Services: Ottawa, 2012), 19.

42.   Quoted in Shawn McCarthy, "CNOOC an arm of Beijing, security experts warn," *The Globe and Mail*, 18 October 2012.

43.   Margaret Cornish, *Behaviour of Chinese soes: Implications for Investment and Cooperation in Canada* (Toronto: Canadian International Council, February 2012), 10.

44.   Canadian Energy Research Institute, *Canadian Oil Sands Supply Costs and Development Projects* (2011–2045), Study No. 128 (March 2012).

45.   CNOOC Limited, "CNOOC Limited Receives Industry Canada Approval on its Proposed Acquisition of Nexen Inc.," press release, 8 December 2012, available at www.cnoocltd.com/encnoocltd/newszx/news/2012/2181.shtml; and Shawn McCarthy, Mark MacKinnon, and Pav Jordan, "Takeovers and promises: CNOOC's deal for Nexen includes a pledge to spend billions more," *The Globe and Mail*, 13 December 2012.

46.   Christopher Swann, "Bid a tricky question," *The Globe and Mail*, 27 September 2012.

47.   Angus Reid, "Most Canadians Would Block Proposed Takeover of Nexen," 16 October 2012.

48.   Richard Blackwell, "The Nexen divide," *The Globe and Mail*, 1 October 2012.

49. Office of the Prime Minister, "Statement by the Prime Minister of Canada on foreign investment," 7 December 2012, available at www.pm.gc.ca/eng/media.asp?id=5195.

50. CNOOC Limited, "CNOOC Limited Receives Industry Canada Approval."

51. Carrie Tait, Shawn McCarthy, and Nathan VanderKlippe, "Alberta fears chill in oil sands investment," *The Globe and Mail*, 11 December 2012.

52. Jim Stanford, "Canadian energy doesn't need foreign capital," *The Globe and Mail*, 8 December 2012.

53. Tait et al., "Alberta fears chill in oil sands investment."

54. James Wood, "Redford sets off on China mission to boost trade," *Calgary Herald*, 6 September 2013.

55. Mark Kennedy, "Foreign buyouts lack public support," *Calgary Herald*, 19 December 2012.

56. International Monetary Fund, *World Economic Outlook* (October 2013), available at http://www.imf.org/external/pubs/ft/weo/2013/02/pdf/text.pdf.

57. Robert D. Kaplan, "The Geography of Chinese Power," *Foreign Affairs* 89, 3 (May/June 2010), 22–41.

58. Stockholm International Peace Research Institute, "SIPRI Military Expenditure Database" (2013), available at http://www.sipri.org/research/armaments/milex/milex_database/milex_database.

59. United States, The White House, Office of Management and Budget, *The Budget—Historical Tables*, available at www.whitehouse.gov/omb/budget/Historicals.

60. United States, Department of the Treasury, Federal Reserve Board, *Major Foreign Holders of Treasury Securities*, 16 July 2014, available at www.treasury.gov/resource-center/ data-chart-center/tic/Documents/mfh.txt.

61. Joseph S. Nye, Jr., *Soft Power: The Means to Success in World Politics* (New York: Public Affairs, 2004).

62. Denise E. Zheng, "China's Use of Soft Power in the Developing World: Strategic Intentions and Implications for the United States," in Carola McGiffert, ed., *Chinese Soft Power and its Implications for the United States: Competition and Cooperation in the Developing World* (Washington, DC: Center for Strategic and International Studies, 2009), 2.

63. Pew Research, "America's Global Image Remains More Positive than China's," *Global Attitudes Project*, 18 July 2013, available at www.pewglobal.org/2013/07/18/americas-global-image-remains-more-positive-than-chinas/.

64. International Energy Agency (IEA), *World Energy Outlook 2012*, available at http://www.iea.org/publications/freepublications/publication/world-energy-outlook-2012.html.

65. CBC News: Business, "China overtakes U.S. to become world's biggest oil importer," 10 October 2013.

66. IEA, *World Energy Outlook 2012*.

67. Stephen Harper, "Address by the Prime Minister at the Canada–UK Chamber of Commerce," London, 14 July 2006, available at http://pm.gc.ca/eng/news/2006/07/14/address-prime-minister-canada-uk-chamber-commerce.

68. Stephen Harper, "Statement by the Prime Minister of Canada in Guangzhou, China," 10 February 2012, available at http://pm.gc.ca/eng/node/24923.

69. Andrew Lui, "Sleeping with the Dragon: The Harper Government, China, and How Not to Do Human Rights," pp. 90–107 in Heather A. Smith and Claire Turenne Sjolander, eds., *Canada in the World: Internationalism in Canadian Foreign Policy* (Don Mills, ON: Oxford University Press), 92.

70. CBC News: World, "Won't 'sell out' on human rights despite China snub: PM," 15 November 2006.

71. Mei Ping, "Return to Realism and Restart the Relationship," pp. 132–42 in Fen Hampson and Paul Heinbecker, eds., *Canada Among Nations 2009–2010: As Others See Us* (Montreal and Kingston: McGill-Queen's University Press, 2010), 137.

72. Quoted in Lui, 101.

Selected Bibliography

Acheson, Keith, and Christopher Maule. 1999. *Much Ado about Culture: North American Trade Disputes*. Ann Arbor: University of Michigan Press.

Anastakis, Dimitry. 2005. *Auto Pact: Creating a Borderless North American Auto Industry, 1960–1971*. Toronto: University of Toronto Press.

——. 2013. *Autonomous State: The Struggle for a Canadian Car Industry from OPEC to Free Trade*. Toronto: University of Toronto Press.

Anderson, Michael A., and Stephen L. Smith. 1999. "Canadian Provinces in World Trade: Engagement and Detachment," *Canadian Journal of Economics* 32, 1 (February): 22–38.

Barry, Donald, and Ronald C. Keith, eds. 1999. *Regionalism, Multilateralism, and the Politics of Global Trade*. Vancouver: UBC Press.

Bow, Brian. 2009. *The Politics of Linkage: Power, Interdependence, and Ideas in Canada–US Relations*. Vancouver: UBC Press.

Bratt, Duane. 2012. *Canada, the Provinces, and the Global Nuclear Revival: Advocacy Coalitions in Action*. Montreal and Kingston: McGill-Queen's University Press.

Brown, Douglas M., and Earl H. Fry, eds. 1993. *States and Provinces in the International Economy*. Berkeley: University of California Press; Kingston, ON: Queen's University Institute of Governmental Studies Press and Institute of Intergovernmental Relations.

Browne, Dennis, ed. 1998. *The Culture/Trade Quandary: Canada's Policy Option*. Ottawa: Renouf Publishing/ Centre for Trade Policy and Law.

Cameron, Maxwell A., and Brian W. Tomlin. 2000. *The Making of NAFTA: How the Deal was Done*. Ithaca, NY: Cornell University Press.

Clarkson, Stephen. 2008. *Does North America Exist? Governing the Continent after NAFTA and 9/11*. Toronto: University of Toronto Press.

———. 2009. *A Perilous Imbalance: The Globalization of Canadian Law and Governance*. Vancouver: UBC Press.

Courchene, Thomas J., ed. 1999. *Room to Manoeuvre? Globalization and Policy Convergence*. Montreal and Kingston: McGill-Queen's University Press.

Cutler, A. Claire, and Mark W. Zacher, eds. 1992. *Canadian Foreign Policy and International Economic Regimes*. Vancouver: UBC Press.

Doern, G. Bruce, and Brian W. Tomlin. 1991. *Faith and Fear: The Free Trade Story*. Toronto: Stoddart.

Doern, G. Bruce, Leslie A. Pal, and Brian Tomlin, eds. 1996. *Border Crossings: The Internationalization of Canadian Public Policy*. Don Mills, ON: Oxford University Press.

Drache, Daniel, ed. 2008. *Big Picture Realities: Canada and Mexico at the Crossroads*. Waterloo, ON: Wilfrid Laurier University Press.

Froese, Marc D. 2010. *Canada at the WTO: Trade Litigation and the Future of Public Policy*. Toronto: University of Toronto Press.

Grinspun, Ricardo, and Yasmine Shamsi, eds. 2007. *Whose Canada? Continental Integration, Fortress North America and the Corporate Agenda*. Montreal and Kingston: McGill-Queen's University Press.

Hale, Geoffrey. 2012. *So Near Yet So Far: The Public and Hidden Worlds of Canada–US Relations*. Don Mills, ON: Oxford University Press.

Hale, Geoffrey, and Monica Gattinger, eds. 2010. *Borders and Bridges: Canada's Policy Relations in North America*. Don Mills, ON: Oxford University Press.

Halle, Mark, and Robert Wolfe, eds. 2007. *Process Matters: Sustainable Development and Domestic Trade Transparency*. Winnipeg: International Institute for Sustainable Development.

Hart, Michael. 1995. *Decision at Midnight: Inside the Canada–US Free-Trade Negotiations*. Vancouver: UBC Press.

———. 2002. *A Trading Nation: Canadian Trade Policy from Colonialism to Globalization*. Vancouver: UBC Press.

Hart, Michael, and William Dymond. 2001. *Common Borders, Shared Destinies: Canada, the United States and Deepening Integration*. Ottawa: Centre for Trade Policy and Law.

Helliwell, John F. 1998. *How Much Do National Borders Matter?* Washington, DC: Brookings Institution Press.

———. 2002. *Globalization and Well-Being*. Vancouver: UBC Press.

Hoberg, George, ed. 2002. *Capacity for Choice: Canada in a New North America*. Toronto: University of Toronto Press.

Kaiser, Karl, John J. Kirton, and Joseph P. Daniels, eds. 2000. *Shaping a New International Financial System: Challenges of Governance in a Globalizing World*. Aldershot, UK: Ashgate Publishing.

Kirton, John J., and Virginia W. MacLaren, eds. 2002. *Linking Trade, Environment, and Social Cohesion: NAFTA Experiences, Global Challenges*. Aldershot, UK: Ashgate Publishing.

Krikorian, Jacqueline D. 2012. *International Trade Law and Domestic Policy: Canada, the United States, and the WTO*. Vancouver: UBC Press.

McBride, Stephen. 2005. *Paradigm Shift: Globalization and the Canadian State*. 2nd ed. Halifax: Fernwood Publishing.

McDougall, John N. 2006. *Drifting Together: The Political Economy of Canada–US Integration*. Peterborough, ON: Broadview Press.

Madar, Daniel. 2000. *Deregulation, Trade and Transformation in North American Trucking*. Vancouver: UBC Press.

Muirhead, B.W. 1992. *The Development of Postwar Canadian Trade Policy: The Failure of the Anglo-European Option*. Montreal and Kingston: McGill-Queen's University Press.

Ostry, Sylvia. 1997. *The Post-Cold War Trading System: Who's on First?* Chicago: University of Chicago Press.

Plumptre, A.F.W. 1977. *Three Decades of Decision: Canada and the World Monetary System, 1944–75*. Toronto: McClelland and Stewart.

Schmitz, Andrew, ed. 2005. *Trade Negotiations in Agriculture: Case Studies in North America*. Calgary: University of Calgary Press.

Stairs, Denis, and Gilbert R. Winham, eds. 1985. *The Politics of Canada's Economic Relationship with the United States*. Toronto: University of Toronto Press.

Stone, Frank. 1992. *Canada, the GATT and the International Trade System*. 2nd ed. Montreal: Institute for Research on Public Policy.

Studer, Isabel, and Carol Wise, eds. 2008. *Requiem or Revival? The Promise of North American Integration*. Washington: Brookings Institution Press.

Urmetzer, Peter. 2005. *Globalization Unplugged: Sovereignty and the Canadian State in the Twenty-First Century*. Toronto: University of Toronto Press.

Watson, William. 1998. *Globalization and the Meaning of Canadian Life*. Toronto: University of Toronto Press.

Winham, Gilbert. 1992. *The Evolution of International Trade Agreements*. Toronto: University of Toronto Press.

Wolfe, Robert. 1998. *Farm Wars: The Political Economy of Agriculture and the International Trade Regime*. New York: St Martin's Press.

Social Considerations: The Need to Do More?

National interests are usually narrowly defined to only two dimensions: 1) protecting a country's territorial integrity, physical security, and political independence; and 2) enhancing a country's economic prosperity. However, Canadian policy-makers have often added a third dimension: the promotion of Canadian values. This third dimension has been featured prominently in every comprehensive foreign policy announcement for the last four decades. The 1970 white paper identified six areas of national interest, and three of them—social justice, quality of life, and a harmonious natural environment—are directly related to the promotion of Canadian values. The 1985 green paper similarly identified justice, democracy, and the integrity of the natural environment as key priorities of Canadian foreign policy. The 1995 white paper highlighted "the projection of Canadian values and culture by promoting universal respect for human rights, the development of participatory government and stable institutions, the rule of law, sustainable development, the celebration of Canadian culture, and the promotion of Canadian cultural and educational industries abroad." The 2005 International Policy Statement stated that Canada will make a difference globally by promoting sustainable development, respecting human rights, and building genuine development.[1]

This final section of *Readings in Canadian Foreign Policy* provides a greater analysis of Canada's efforts at promoting social dimensions in its foreign policy. Canada has a tendency, in order to differentiate itself from the American superpower, to see itself as a *moral* superpower. Typical of this sentiment is a report by Canada25, a non-partisan organization of politically active Canadians aged 20 to 35, entitled *From Middle to Model Power: Recharging Canada's Role in the World.*[2] This is neither a recent phenomenon, nor necessarily one that is appreciated by other countries. For instance, former US Secretary of State Dean Acheson once referred to Canada as the "stern daughter of the voice of God."[3] There are also prominent domestic critics of the idea of asserting a cultural role in Canadian foreign policy. For example, Denis Stairs has been skeptical of the idea that Canadian foreign policy is (or should be) driven by virtue instead of national interests. Attempting to project Canadian values, however defined, can lead to "misunderstanding the true origins of their behaviour" and can cause "significant damage to the effectiveness of their diplomacy."[4]

The problem of climate change caused by the emission of greenhouse gases into the atmosphere has been at the centre of Canada's international environmental policy. On 17 December 2002, Canada ratified the Kyoto Protocol and committed to reducing its greenhouse gas emissions by 6 per cent of 1990 levels. Unfortunately for environmentalists who support action on climate change, Canada never even come close to meeting its Kyoto target and so became the first country to officially withdraw from the Protocol in December 2012. In December 2009 states met in Copenhagen, Denmark, at the Fifteenth Conference of Parties Meeting. The hope had been that states would be able to negotiate commitments for the period beginning 2012. However, the conference resulted in a weak non-binding statement. Canada had been targeted in the press as a laggard and had been condemned broadly for its climate change policy. The Alberta oil sands, a major source of greenhouse gas (GHG) emissions, but also a major source of wealth, has become a particular target of domestic and international opponents. Prime Minister Harper argued that Canada would align its climate change policy with the United States and in January 2010 notified the United Nations that the Canadian target for 2020 would be a 17 per cent reduction of emissions from a 2005 baseline "aligned with the final economy-wide emissions target of the United States in enacted legislation," thus directly linking Canada's position with that of the United States.[5]

Nowhere is the problem of climate change most visible than in the melting sea ice and warming temperatures of the Arctic region. In Chapter 26, Heather Smith uses the Arctic to frame her analysis of climate change and Canadian foreign policy. Smith argues that the Harper government's focus has been to claim stewardship of the Arctic to maximize its economic potential and to "securitize" it from external threats. In the process, Canada has turned a blind eye to its "contribution to the looming environmental tragedy." Rob Huebert (Chapter 21) also discusses the implications of climate change on the Arctic, but not in the same way, or in the same detail, as Smith does.

Former Canadian Prime Minister Lester Pearson chaired the Pearson Commission on International Development in 1969. One of the commission's key recommendations was setting a target for developed countries of 0.7 per cent of their gross national product (GNP) to be put towards official development assistance (ODA). While several countries have consistently met that target (the Netherlands, Sweden, Denmark, and Norway), most developed countries have not come close. Canada is no exception. While it did increase ODA throughout the 1970s and early 1980s, Canada never came close to the 0.7 per cent target. Additionally, in the last 20 years there has been a steady decline in Canada's level of foreign assistance. In 1986–87, Canada's ODA/GNP ratio was 0.5 per cent, but after years of sustained budget cuts by the Mulroney and Chrétien governments, it dropped to 0.23 per cent by 2003–4.[6] As Ottawa's financial situation improved, it began to reinvest in foreign assistance. Both the Martin and Harper governments gradually increased foreign aid. However, the 2008–9 recession, and the resulting large federal budget deficits, led to a return of reducing foreign aid. For example, the 2012 federal budget cut foreign aid by 7.5 per cent over a three-year period.

The debate over the size of the ODA/GNP ratio is an interesting one, but there are other debates. For example, a basic question is why Canada gives between $2.5–3.5 billion a year in ODA. Many Canadians assume that foreign assistance is provided for altruistic reasons, such as helping the poorest people in the poorest countries. Cranford Pratt has argued that development assistance is a policy tool that combines all three of Canada's international objectives: physical security, economic prosperity, and the promotion of Canadian values.[7] This link remains a cornerstone of Canadian aid policy. The 2005 International Policy Statement asserts that "failure to achieve significant political, economic, social and environmental progress in the developing world will have an impact on Canada in terms of both our long-term security and our prosperity."[8]

The Harper government did more than just reduce foreign aid. Recent international development ministers argued that its ODA program should also benefit Canadians, especially through private-sector initiatives. More significantly, in 2013 the Canadian International Development Agency (CIDA) was disbanded and its aid programs assigned to the new super ministry that would be called the Department of Foreign Affairs, Trade and Development (DFATD). The purpose of this structural change was for development to be better aligned with Canada's other foreign policy interests.

These changes were all about increasing the effectiveness of foreign aid. This topic is tackled by Stephen Brown in Chapter 27. After all, developed countries have spent hundreds of billions of dollars on foreign assistance for decades, and yet there remain over a billion people in abject poverty. Brown notes that "since Chrétien's final years in office, and increasingly so under Harper, the government has presented its policy initiatives as ways of improving the effectiveness of Canadian aid." This has led to the "the untying of aid, the questioning of impact and search for results, the issue of aid volume, the 'focus on focus' (fewer recipient countries and economic sectors), and the coherence between aid policy and policies in other areas."

In Chapter 28, David Black conducts a case study of Canada's development policy by looking at Canadian–African relations. There have been political, security, and economic dimensions in Canada's relationship with Africa: the fights within the Commonwealth against South African apartheid that were led by John Diefenbaker and Brian Mulroney; the deployment of Canadian peacekeepers to the Congo, Rwanda, and Ethiopia–Eritrea; and the activities of Canadian mining and oil companies on the African continent. However, the major feature of the relationship has been Canadian development assistance to Africa. Some prominent examples include Canada's leadership on the New Partnership for African Development (NEPAD) at the 2002 G8 Summit in Kananaskis and the efforts of Stephen Lewis as UN Special Envoy for HIV/AIDS in Africa.[9] Black argues that under the Harper government "there are signs of a clear shift not only from the high profile emphasis on Africa articulated in the latter years of the Chrétien government, but from 50 years of broad bipartisanship in policies toward the continent." Its development focus has shifted away from Africa to Latin America, Canadian peacekeepers have abandoned Africa for the military conflict in Afghanistan, and diplomatically there have been the closing of Canadian missions on the continent. All of these trends, for Black, suggest not just a reduction in attention towards Africa, but a significant decline in the influence of humane internationalism.

A final social consideration in Canadian foreign policy is the promotion of human rights. The international promotion of human rights has been a broad foreign policy goal of successive Canadian governments. This is because "Canadians expect their government to be a leader in the human rights field by reflecting and promoting Canadian values, including respect for diversity, on the international stage."[10] Canada's human rights efforts began in the immediate aftermath of World War II as a direct consequence of the horrors of the Holocaust. Canada participated in the Nuremburg Tribunals, which tried Nazi officials for war crimes. In addition, Canada was an original signatory to the Universal Declaration of Human Rights, and it was a Canadian, John Humphrey, who was the principal drafter of the Declaration. Canada also signed and ratified many of the subsequent UN-sponsored protocols. Despite this initial flurry of activity, "it was not until the mid-1970s," as a major study on human rights and Canadian foreign policy concluded, "that Canada was prepared to assign staff and resources to the task of promoting international respect for human rights."[11] Kim Nossal similarly has noted that this commitment to human rights was "neither sustained nor widespread. But there has been a historical empathy with those whose human rights have been violated and a desire to give expression to these symbolic interests."[12]

Since the mid-1970s, Ottawa's rhetoric, both at home and abroad, was increasingly used to promote human rights. In 1977, External Affairs Minister Don Jamieson stated that "Canada will continue to uphold internationally the course of human rights, in the legitimate hope that we can eventually ameliorate the conditions of our fellow man."[13] Parliament's Special Joint Committee on Canada's International Relations declared in 1986 that "the international promotion of human rights is a fundamental and integral part of Canadian foreign policy."[14] The Mulroney government, following in the footsteps of John Diefenbaker in 1960–61, took a leadership position on the opposition to South African apartheid. Mulroney even publicly challenged his core allies (Ronald Reagan in the United States and Margaret Thatcher in the United Kingdom) to use economic sanctions to generate change. The 1995 foreign policy review by the Jean Chrétien government proclaimed that human rights were a "fundamental value" and "a crucial element in the development of stable, democratic and prosperous societies at peace with each other." It added that Canada would "make effective use of all of the influence that our economic, trading and development assistance relationships give us to promote respect for human rights."[15] During his tenure as Canada's foreign affairs minister (1996–2000), Lloyd Axworthy made human rights a central plank in his human security agenda. Axworthy's work on human rights was reflected in, among other things, his initiatives on the protection of children in armed conflict, the Ottawa Process on landmines, and in his support for the establishment of an International Criminal Court (ICC). The International Policy Statement from the Paul Martin government identified "promoting respect for human rights" as a key foreign policy priority.[16]

Ottawa has also tried to go beyond statements and speeches and attempted to institutionalize its promotion of human rights. Human rights offices in both DFAIT and CIDA were created and human rights training programs were established for Canadian officials. Canadian embassies were required to submit reports on states' human rights records. Human rights also became one of CIDA's six program priorities in making decisions on Canadian development assistance. Critics maintain, however, that the promotion of human rights remains secondary to Canada's security and economic concerns.

Axworthy's legacy was also clear in Canada's role in the development of the concept of the Responsibility to Protect (R2P). At the core of R2P was a need to re-evaluate concepts of state sovereignty and humanitarian intervention. Motivated by atrocities in Rwanda, Yugoslavia, and Kosovo, the 2001 International Commission on Intervention and State Sovereignty (ICISS) promoted a new approach in which governments had an obligation to respect the sovereign rights of other states as well as a responsibility to protect their own citizens. The criteria for involvement, however, would exclude intervention based on political oppression or the removal of democratically elected governments. As such, the ICISS process was endorsed by numerous non-governmental interests, in Canada and internationally, that were concerned about the potential abuse of R2P for less altruistic foreign policy objectives. In the aftermath of 11 September and the subsequent American invasion of Iraq, Prime Minister Martin also made it clear at the 2005 World Summit that R2P did not exist as a tool for US unilateralism.

Canada's foreign policy has also engaged questions of human rights in China (also see Chapters 11 and 25). For the most part Canada has attempted to address these issues using "quiet" or "soft" diplomacy. Pierre Trudeau, for example, recognized the communist People's Republic of China in 1970 and famously met with Mao Zedong during a state visit, but was reluctant to raise questions concerning human rights. In contrast, Brian Mulroney's China Policy was extremely critical of Deng Xiaoping's violent response to student protesters in Tiananmen Square in 1989. The Chrétien government, on the other hand, took a more subdued approach on human rights in China, despite its commitment to Axworthy's human security objectives. This was due to Chrétien's efforts to increase Sino-Canadian trade and investment through several Team Canada trade missions to China in the 1990s. The Chrétien government also failed to co-sponsor a UN resolution on China's human rights record during this period but instead established the Canada–China Bilateral Human Rights Dialogue in 1997. In a series of nine annual meetings, Chinese and Canadian officials discussed a wide range of human rights issues, and during this period China signed the International Covenant on Civil and Political Rights (ICCPR) and the International Covenant on Economic, Social and Cultural Rights (ICESCR). The current Harper government, on the other hand, has taken a noticeably tougher stance on human rights in China, especially on Tibet. Harper also waited five years to officially visit China and has continually rejected any attempts to link trade and human rights. Recently, Harper and the rest of the government have toned down their criticism of China's human rights record to focus on economic relations.

Historically, human rights have received considerable attention in Canada's foreign relations. This is not to suggest, however, that Canadian policies in this issue area are beyond reproach. Critics, for example, have highlighted the selective and economically marginal sanctions that Canada ultimately adopted against South Africa. Axworthy, despite his many successes, was often criticized as opportunistic and willing to capitalize on the work of other state and non-governmental interests, most notably the International Criminal Court and landmine initiatives. The Martin government also struggled with its commitment to R2P, especially its failure to take a strong stand against atrocities committed by *Janjaweed* militias against the Fur people in Sudan. Although the current Harper minority deserves credit for its action in Haiti, concerns have also been raised regarding the treatment of Afghan detainees and massive cuts to official development assistance.

Recent issues have focused on the question of Canada's responsibility to its citizens abroad. Traditionally, this has been viewed in terms of evacuating Canadians from natural disasters (like the 2010 earthquake in Haiti) or war zones (like the 2008 Lebanese–Israeli war), or providing consular services for Canadians accused of crimes in foreign lands (like William Sampson in Saudi Arabia). However, since 11 September 2001, the issue has been expanded to human rights violations of Canadian citizens by foreign governments (especially the US and its allies) as part of the war on terror. For example, Maher Arar was arrested at New York's JFK airport in September 2002 and was subsequently deported to Syria where he was imprisoned and tortured until his release in October 2003. Meanwhile, Omar Khadr was captured as a teenage "unlawful combatant" by American forces in Afghanistan and resided at the US military prison in Guantanamo Bay for almost a decade before being transferred to a Canadian prison.

Notes

1. Department of External Affairs, *Foreign Policy for Canadians* (Ottawa: Department of External Affairs, 1970), 14–16; Department of External Affairs, *Competitiveness and Security: Directions for Canada's International Relations* (Ottawa: Department of External Affairs, 1985), 3; Canada, *Canada in the World: Government Statement* (Ottawa: Canada Communications Group, 1995); Canada, *Canada's International Policy Statement: A Role of Pride and Influence in the World* (Ottawa: Government of Canada, 2005), 20.

2. Canada25, *From Middle to Model Power: Recharging Canada's Role in the World* (Toronto: Canada25, 2004).

3. Dean Acheson, "Canada: Stern Daughter of the Voice of God," in Livingston Merchant, ed., *Neighbours Taken for Granted* (Toronto: Burns and MacEachern, 1966), 134.

4. Denis Stairs, "Myths, Morals, and Reality in Canadian Foreign Policy," *International Journal* 58, 2 (Spring 2003): 239.

5   Environment Canada, "Canada's Submission to the UNFCCC of its Quantified Economy-Wide Emissions Target" (2010). Originally accessed at www.climatechange.gc.ca/cdp%2Dcop/default.asp?lang=En&n=C4BD2547-1#p4.

6. Canadian International Development Agency, *Statistical Report on Official Development Assistance: Fiscal Year 2003–2004* (Ottawa: CIDA, 2005), 1.

7. Cranford Pratt, "Competing Rationales for Canadian Development Assistance," *International Journal* 54, 2

(Spring 1999), 306–23.

8. Canada, *Canada's International Policy Statement: A Role of Pride and Influence in the World—Development* (Ottawa: CIDA, 2005), 6–7.

9. For Lewis's reflections on Africa, the UN, and HIV/AIDS see Stephen Lewis, *Race against Time: The 2005 Massey Lectures* (Toronto: Anansi, 2005).

10. Foreign Affairs, Trade and Development Canada, "Canada's International Human Rights Policy" (21 December 2009). Available at www.international.gc.ca/rights-droits/policy-politique.aspx.

11. Robert O. Matthews and Cranford Pratt, "Conclusion: Questions and Prospects," in Matthews and Pratt, eds., *Human Rights in Canadian Foreign Policy* (Toronto: University of Toronto Press, 1988), 294.

12. Kim Richard Nossal, *The Politics of Canadian Foreign Policy*, 3rd ed. (Scarborough, ON: Prentice-Hall, 1997), 114.

13. Canada, External Affairs Minister Don Jamieson, "Human Rights: One of the Most Complex Foreign Policy Issues," *Statements and Speeches* (March 16, 1977), 7.

14. DFAIT, "Human Rights and Canadian Foreign Policy" (September 1998).

15. DFAIT, *Canada in the World: Canadian Foreign Policy Review* (1995).

16. DFAIT, Canada's *International Policy Statement: A Role of Pride and Influence in the World* (2005).

26 Choosing Not to See: Canada, Climate Change, and the Arctic

Heather A. Smith

Key Terms

Arctic Sovereignty
Climate Change

Indigenous Peoples
Discourse

In August 2008, Canadian Prime Minister Stephen Harper stated: "Canada takes responsibility for environmental protection and enforcement in our Arctic waters. This magnificent and unspoiled ecological region is one for which we will demonstrate stewardship on behalf of our country, and indeed, all of humanity."[1]

"Our Arctic waters." "Our country." "We" take responsibility and "we" are the "stewards." Constructions of ownership and acts of boundary-drawing are deeply embedded in this statement. *We* and *our* are words that function to exclude and simultaneously claim a space as Canadian. The statement also tells us that *we* are committed to the environmental well-being of the Arctic and *we* will care for the Arctic on behalf of humanity.

The unfortunate reality is that when we consider the political **discourse** crafted by the Conservative government of Stephen Harper on the Arctic, we are encouraged to regard Canada as an Arctic power, to focus on sovereignty and security, and to consider the melting Arctic as an opportunity for economic development. In spite of claims of stewardship, these discourses encourage us to be blind to the realities of **climate change**, to disregard the problematic nature of sovereignty in an era of global environmental change, and to turn a blind

eye to our contribution to the looming environmental tragedy. The government discourse is also shaped in a way that allows the government to appear to be the champion of **indigenous peoples**, even to the point of co-opting part of their discourse with reference to climate change. However, the government discourse actually obscures alternative views of the Arctic and climate change and discourages us from looking beyond government statements to see the impact on indigenous peoples. As the government, and some academics, debate the finer points of international law regarding the Northwest Passage, envision future terrorist plots with their origins in the Arctic, and ponder the riches that await us, the Arctic melts.

This article begins by examining the dominant themes in the discourse relating to the Arctic as articulated by members of the Canadian Conservative government. In this section I focus on the themes of sovereignty, security, resource development, and climate change. I then turn my attention to an analysis of how the government discourse works to deflect our attention away from the realities of climate change, obscures the Canadian contribution to the problem of climate change, and discourages us from seeing the peoples most affected by climate change in the Arctic. The article ends with reflections on the implications of a government discourse that is built on antiquated and indeed dangerous understandings of the world in which we live.

Key Themes in the Conservative Arctic Discourse

Canadian government speeches and policy statements about the Arctic are an interesting mix of romantic invocations of the north coupled with aggressive claims of ownership. For example, when announcing the building of a new polar-class icebreaker in 2008, Harper described the initiative as a "major **Arctic sovereignty** project" and then went on to wax poetic about the Arctic and Canadian identity, stating: "The True North is our destiny, for our explorers, for our entrepreneurs, for our artists. And to not embrace its promise now at the dawn of its ascendency would be to turn our backs on what it is to be Canadian."[2] Former Minister of Foreign Affairs Lawrence Cannon has made similar statements that link Canadian identity to the Arctic, romanticize the Arctic, and make power and ownership claims.[3] And while leaders muse about the true north (verbally planting flags with their references to the English version of Canada's national anthem), and declare Canada to be an Arctic power, the 2010 policy statement on the Arctic concludes with a statement that would have been appropriate in the Cold War era, as its tone is nothing if not aggressive: "When positions or actions are taken by others that affect our national interests, undermine the cooperative relationships we have built, or demonstrate a lack of sensitivity to the interests or perspectives of Arctic peoples or states, we respond . . . we will never waiver in our commitment to protect our North."[4]

In the midst of all the verbal swaggering, government speeches and policy statements inevitably tell us that there is a growing awareness about the Arctic and provide us with a shopping list of reasons for our interest in the Arctic. The 2009 northern strategy, for example, tells us that "international interest in the North has intensified because of the potential for resource development, the opening of new transportation routes, and the growing impacts of climate change."[5] In response to these opportunities and challenges, the federal government is crafting policy with four priorities, or pillars, in mind: "exercising our Arctic Sovereignty; promoting social and economic development; protecting our environmental heritage; improving and devolving northern governance."[6] And while the four pillars may be presented as equally important in the 2009 northern strategy, the 2010 statement on Canada's Arctic foreign policy leaves little doubt that sovereignty is the most significant priority. It states that "in our Arctic foreign policy, the first and most important pillar toward recognizing the potential of Canada's Arctic is the exercise of our sovereignty over the Far North."[7]

The discussion of sovereignty in the 2009 northern strategy notes that sovereignty includes an enhanced presence in the north as well as the protection of Arctic waters. Sovereignty also involves mapping the Arctic to support claims to the continental shelf. As a bit of a throwaway at the end of this section there is reference to the human dimension, although it is not clear whether it is the human dimension of sovereignty. This section is part of the sovereignty discussion, in which we are told that Canada works with indigenous groups associated with the Arctic Council, but what constitutes the human dimension is unclear.[8] It may well be the case that the use of the term *human dimension* was simply an effort to use language being used by Inuit leaders, in which case it is a weak effort to co-opt language and placate critics.

In the 2010 statement on Canada's Arctic foreign policy, we are told that the exercise of sovereignty in the Arctic happens daily through "good governance and responsible stewardship."[9] Central to Canada's sovereignty claims is the resolution of international boundary disputes and recognition of Canadian sovereign rights over the continental shelf. Ultimately, we are told that "protecting national sovereignty, and the integrity of our borders, is the first and foremost responsibility of a national government. We are resolved to protect Canadian sovereignty throughout our Arctic."[10]

Sovereignty, in the context of the government discourse on the Arctic, as noted earlier, is essentially about control, ownership, and the protection of what we consider to be our territory. While the promotion and protection of Canadian sovereignty includes numerous multilateral diplomatic and international legal initiatives, the securitization of the Arctic is noteworthy. Security is not a pillar or priority in the government documents, but realist constructions of security are deeply embedded in the Arctic discourse as sovereignty claims are used in ways that prop up and reinforce the securitization of the Arctic. For example, speeches made by Canadian politicians, as well as the two respective policy statements on the Arctic, have a tone that is reminiscent of the Cold War, when state leaders engaged in defensive and aggressive rhetoric to articulate and support their visions of security for their states. Canadian policy on the Arctic is rife with statements about protecting both our national interest and our borders. All that is within Canadian territory can and will be controlled by "more boots in the Arctic tundra, more ships in the icy water and a better eye in the sky."[11]

What is not clear, however, is exactly who and what is threatening Canada. As Michael Sheehan notes, "to 'securitize' an issue . . . [is] to challenge society to promote it higher in its scales of values and to commit greater resources to solving the related problems."[12] The power of securitizing an issue and a region is that through the act of securitizing we are also told by the government, and some academics, what to fear and, implicitly, what not to fear. So what then are the problems we want solved? We are told by the government that "this increased Canadian capacity demonstrates Canada's presence in the region and will also ensure that we are better prepared to respond to unforeseen events."[13] It is further suggested by the government and some academics that future potential problems could include environmental emergencies, and terrorists, criminals, and illegal migrants entering Canada through the Arctic.[14] Thus the federal government constructs a future "other" threatening Canada's borders as a means to justify increased military commitments to the Arctic region. The future others, however, are in fact secondary to more immediate concerns because the securitization of the Arctic is about establishing some sort of presence in the Arctic, "not only to demonstrate to foreign governments that Canada is prepared to defend its sovereignty but to *force* those states to recognize Canadian claims."[15] What the Canadian government really seeks to protect, through military means, is the economic potential of the Canadian Arctic.

Canada's Arctic warrior rhetoric is motivated not simply by future unseen threats but also by future opportunities. Merging economy and security, the prime minister himself has articulated the value of the Arctic: "Its economic and strategic value has risen exponentially over the years. The rising global demand for energy and mineral resources has sparked a so-called 'cold rush' of countries to the Arctic region, and with the retreat of the ice pack, record numbers of ships are plying our Northern waters. Canada must therefore move quickly to affirm and protect its sovereignty over the archipelago, including the navigable waterways within it, and the undersea extensions of our continental shelf."[16] The promotion of social and economic development, another pillar of Canada's Arctic foreign policy, is treated as a means to support and enhance the well-being of all northerners, yet the focus is clearly on resource development. The 2009 northern strategy, for example, celebrates the north's "immense store of minerals, petroleum, hydro and ocean resources" and provides us with maps of potential oil and mineral reserves—thus solidifying visually the Arctic as a space and place of resource wealth.[17] Consistent with the northern strategy, the 2010 statement on Canada's Arctic foreign policy highlights the vast oil reserves in the Arctic and, interestingly, equates sustainable development with oil and gas, stating that "[a]s an emerging clean energy superpower, Canada will continue to support the responsible and sustainable development of oil and gas in the North."[18] Of course, the race for wealth is as much about potential futures as opposed to current realities, but the Canadian government is willing to bet on potential opportunities where oil and gas are concerned. The opportunities arise, of course, because of climate change.

One of the most intriguing elements of the way in which the Conservative government constructs the Arctic discourse is the relative marginalization of climate change in the whole equation. Sometimes the impact of climate change is mentioned as a challenge facing the Arctic, or, as in the case of the northern strategy, climate change is given a passing scientific reference. Passing references to climate change are also included in ministerial and prime ministerial speeches. For example, in a speech given in March 2009, Cannon stated that "the government has focused global efforts on both the impacts of climate change in the region and efforts to adapt to them."[19] He states elsewhere that Canada will "work through appropriate multilateral mechanisms like the United Nations Framework Convention on Climate Change to address these challenges."[20] In July 2009, Cannon framed climate effects as resulting from activities outside of the Arctic region, stating that "in the North, climate change, melting ice and rising contamination levels result from activities that take place thousands of kilometres away from the region but still have a disproportionate impact on its environment."[21]

In the statement on Canada's Arctic foreign policy, the treatment of climate change is more substantive than in the 2009 document. Similar to Cannon's statement above, the source of climate change is located outside the region, and indeed Canada, and we are told that what happens in the Arctic will have global repercussions and require a global solution. The now-common Conservative statements on climate change are applied to the case of the Arctic: Canada is committed to contributing to the global effort by taking action to reduce Canadian emissions. Canada will work with its North American partners. Canada will be "constructively engaging with our international partners to negotiate a fair, environmentally effective and comprehensive international climate change regime."[22] Canada will also continue to support work on adaptation.

The difficulty with this treatment of climate change is that it hides more than it reveals. As part of discussions of the Arctic, the Canadian government and some scholars treat climate change primarily as a catalyst for change. Climate change is the source of the melting ice; climate change is caused by someone else; climate change is external to future plans for oil and gas exploration—but Canada is committed to working on efforts to combat climate change. What would happen if the government actually shared the severity of current and projected impacts of climate change in the Arctic? What if it told Canadians what it meant by contributions to global efforts? What would happen if the people who were most immediately affected by climate change had a real voice? What then would we say about the Canadian government discourse on the Arctic?

Why Don't We See Climate Change?

The Arctic discourse as framed by the Conservative government minimizes the depth and breadth of climate change impacts. There is a common recognition of melting sea ice both by the government and scholars working in this area, but the melting sea ice is typically the jumping-off point for discussions of new transportation routes, increased access to resources, and the enhanced need to protect Canada's northern borders. However, the reality is that climate change impacts in the Arctic are not limited to thinning and melting sea ice.

The Arctic climate impact assessment, one of the most substantive regional impact assessments to date, details the range and depth of climate change impacts. First and foremost, central to the assessment is the observation that the Arctic is one of the regions most vulnerable to climate change impacts. "Arctic average temperature has risen at almost twice the rate as the rest of the world in the past few decades."[23] As a result, tree lines are expected to shift northwards, fires are expected to be more common, and new species can be expected in the Arctic. The melting sea ice that is a cause for celebration for some, in terms of access to new resources, will have and is having a devastating impact on the habitat of polar bears, seals, and seabirds, "pushing some species toward extinction."[24] Coastal communities will be faced with coastal erosion and rising sea levels. The relocation of communities is expected (and indeed planned and under way in some cases). Thawing permafrost will also disrupt current transportation routes, and as "frozen ground thaws, many existing buildings, roads, pipelines, airports, and industrial facilities are likely to be destabilized, requiring substantial rebuilding, maintenance and investment."[25] The assessment also highlights the fact that indigenous peoples are facing devastating cultural and economic impacts. Traditional ways of knowing and traditional ways of life are being undermined by rapid environmental change. Finally, the impacts being felt in the Arctic and the future predictions are not isolated events but are caused by global emissions; there will be broader implications. Glacial melting will contribute to sea-level rise and the loss of Arctic snow and ice may contribute to further global warming. As we know, the Arctic is not a neat, tidy, unique space distinct from the rest of the world. We know that climate change is also affecting the rest of Canada and the world. However, the actions of current and past Canadian governments on climate change have never signalled any sense of the urgency of climate change.

If we consider the commitments of the Conservative government in any depth we see that this is a government that does not seem to be terribly concerned about climate change. When the Conservatives came to office they publicly denounced Canadian commitments to the Kyoto Protocol, saying they were unachievable. Canadian negotiators have routinely been accused of trying to undermine international negotiations. The Conservative government frames the issue of climate change as global and routinely argues that Canada only emits a small percentage of global emissions, conveniently overlooking per capita emissions and historic contributions to current levels of greenhouse gases. Ottawa demands that large emitting states such as China take on emissions-reductions targets, while Canada is more than 25 per cent above its Kyoto target. Canada's current target ties Canadian action to the American target but also requires that the American target be legislated. And while we wait to see if the Obama administration can secure an environmental victory on climate change, Canada promotes itself as an energy superpower. Nowhere in the Conservative climate change policy, or in the discussion about climate change in the Arctic, is there recognition that we are part of the problem.

In fairness, previous Canadian governments were not great climate change leaders either. Consecutive governments have failed to take substantive action. The US administrations also have weak records. Given all the evidence of current impacts, one has to wonder whether there is some kind of climate change denial or whether perhaps it is argued that, given that it is happening, we might as well make the best of it. If we "make the best of it," does climate change become an opportunity?

Climate change is an opportunity from the perspective of the "global culture of carboniferous consumption."[26] It is an opportunity if we assume that we can continue our current consumptive lifestyles unfettered. But perhaps if we listened to those in the Arctic whose lives and cultures are under siege, we might be prompted to revisit some of those assumptions about opportunities.

The indigenous peoples of the Arctic are not a homogenous entity, and there are debates within communities about the balance between development and traditional environmental ways of being and knowing. However, if we consider indigenous voices' perceptions of the effects of climate change and traditional environmental knowledge, we are challenged to consider the way in which our Western gaze shapes our understanding of the Arctic.

As noted in the chapter on indigenous perspectives on climate change in the scientific report of the climate impact assessment, traditional environmental knowledge is a contested term, but at minimum it includes recognition of the spiritual nature of knowledge and assumptions of how indigenous peoples are connected to the land, and it encompasses "the various systems of knowledge, practice, and belief gained through experience and culturally transmitted among members and generations of a community."[27] Indigenous ways of knowing do not subscribe to the compartmentalization and categorization common to Western ways of knowing. In the words of Dene elder Bella T'selie: "Scientists like to talk about things apart. We think in holistic terms and cannot think about things separately. Dene spirituality is in traditional knowledge. Dene ways are very formal. We cannot separate spirituality in Dene, but scientists think this is ridiculous."[28]

Inuit elders, like Dene elders, have observed changes in their landscape. The weather has become unpredictable and as a result, their knowledge of the world in which they live has no longer become reliable. As noted by elder N. Attungala of Baker Lake, "Inuit have a traditional juggling game. The weather is sort of like that now. The weather is being juggled; it is changing so quickly and drastically."[29]

As the weather is juggled because of activities outside of the Arctic, the peoples of the north become the equivalent of the canaries in the global environmental coal mine, and their leaders have called for inclusion in ongoing state-based discussions about the future of the Arctic. As Sheila Watt-Cloutier stated at the Copenhagen climate change meetings in 2009: "The people whose lives depend upon the ice and snow for cultural survival must be a central component of all our plans. We must not permit the discussion of northern development to be conducted only in terms of sovereignty, resources, and economics. The focus must be on the human dimension, human communities and protection of human cultural rights."[30]

A substantive inclusion of indigenous peoples and their ways of knowing into the dialogue related to the Arctic would fundamentally disrupt the dominant narrative currently articulated by the Canadian Conservative government. Indigenous peoples remind us that we are not just stewards—masters of our domain—but are connected to, and are part of, the land. We are not just isolated consumers of oil and gas. We are connected to each other through environmental processes that disregard attempts to draw lines between us and them. Our actions affect others in real and tangible ways. Perhaps the power of this knowledge helps us to understand the exclusion of indigenous peoples from the Canadian-sponsored meeting of Arctic Ocean states that saw American Secretary of State Hillary Clinton leave in protest, in part over the exclusion of indigenous peoples.

Conclusion

So what happens when we consider the Conservative government discourse on the Arctic in light of the realities of the climate change impacts in the Arctic? What happens when we expose the limited and ineffective nature of Canadian climate change policies? How does our understanding of the Arctic change if we include the voices of indigenous peoples?

We see that the assumptions of control and domination that are so central to the idea of sovereignty in the Conservative discourse on the Arctic are naive and dangerous. They are naive because they entail some sort of control over the future of the Arctic, when in fact we cannot control the environment. Climate change impacts will not be linear and are not limited to melting sea ice. All of the Arctic, indeed all of the world, will be affected by climate change. Plans for oil-and-gas drilling will be disrupted by environmental changes that will also disrupt infrastructure and transportation routes.

We also see that climate change impacts are not simply about the future; they are taking place now. Our past consumption is affecting the Arctic environment and well-being of indigenous peoples now. The Arctic is not simply a space of future opportunities. Action is needed now. And the action that is needed now is not more boots on the tundra. The militarization and securitization of the Arctic does not address the problem of climate change.

The way the Conservative discourse securitizes the Arctic serves only to divert our attention from our own complicity in environmental degradation. We are encouraged by the Conservatives and some scholars to be fearful of the arrival of illegal migrants or terrorists in the Arctic. These intangible and future threats justify military spending and rhetorical swaggering while simultaneously downplaying the ways in which we are the creators of our own insecurities. Canadians and consecutive Canadian governments have chosen to not take climate change seriously. Rather than blame those outside of Canada for climate change, as does Lawrence Cannon, we need to look within our own borders and ask: how are we responsible?

When we include the voices of indigenous peoples, we are made aware of the human dimension of climate change. The Arctic is more than a map of potential resources; it is someone's home. So when the Conservative government tells us we will care for the Arctic for all of humanity, perhaps we should question the credibility of this statement. We are not taking care of the Arctic for all humanity; we are taking care of the Arctic for ourselves. We are protecting our consumptive lifestyles and turning a blind eye to the juggling game in which we are involved.

Questions for Review

1. What are the core components of Stephen Harper's "Arctic discourse"?
2. Do these differ from the Conservative government's actual Arctic foreign policy? If so, why? If not, why not?

3. How are indigenous perspectives on climate change different from Western conceptions?
4. What theoretical perspectives from Part One best reflect Smith's argument?

Suggested Readings

Battiste, Marie, and James Youngblood Henderson. 2000. *Protecting Indigenous Knowledge and Heritage: A Global Challenge.* Saskatoon, SK: Purich Publishing.

Beier, J. Marshall, ed. 2009. *Indigenous Diplomacies.* New York: Palgrave.

Purdy, Margaret, and Leanne Smythe. 2010. "From Obscurity to Action: Why Canada Must Tackle the Security Dimension of Climate Change." *International Journal* 65, 2, (Spring): 411–33.

Smith, Heather. 2009. "Unwilling Internationalism or Strategic Internationalism? Canadian Climate Change Policy under the Conservative Government." *Canadian Foreign Policy/ La politique étrangère du Canada* 15, 2: 57–77.

Notes

1. Office of the Prime Minister, "Prime Minister Harper announces measures to strengthen Canada's Arctic sovereignty and protection of the northern environment," 27 August 2008. Available at http://pm.gc.ca/eng/news/2008/08/27/prime-minister-harper-announces-measures-strengthen-canadas-arctic-sovereignty-and.

2. Office of the Prime Minister, "Prime Minister Harper announces the John G. Diefenbaker icebreaker project," 28 August 2008. Available at http://pm.gc.ca/eng/news/2008/08/28/prime-minister-harper-announces-john-g-diefenbaker-icebreaker-project.

3. See, for example, Foreign Affairs, Trade and Development Canada, "Address by Minister Cannon at the news conference for the Arctic Ocean foreign ministers' meeting," 29 March 2010. Available at www.international.gc.ca/media/aff/speeches-discours/2010/2010-15.aspx?lang=eng; "Notes for an address by the Honourable Lawrence Cannon, Minister of Foreign Affairs, at the Center for Strategic and International Studies, on Canada's Arctic foreign policy," 6 April 2009. Available at www.international.gc.ca/media/aff/speeches-discours/2009/387040.aspx?lang=en; and "Minister Cannon outlines Canada's Arctic foreign policy," 11 March 2009. Available at www.international.gc.ca/media/aff/news-communiques/2009/386927.aspx?lang=eng.

4. Foreign Affairs and International Trade Canada, "Statement on Canada's Arctic foreign policy: Exercising sovereignty and promoting Canada's northern strategy abroad," 2010, 28. Available at www.international.gc.ca/arctic-arctique/assets/pdfs/canada_arctic_foreign_policy-eng.pdf.

5. Government of Canada, *Canada's Northern Strategy: Our North, Our Heritage, Our Future,* 2009, 5. Available at www.northernstrategy.gc.ca.

6. Ibid., 2.

7. "Statement on Canada's Arctic foreign policy," 4.

8. *Canada's Northern Strategy,* 9–13.

9. "Statement on Canada's Arctic foreign policy," 5.

10. Ibid., 9.

11. *Canada's Northern Strategy,* 9.

12. Michael Sheehan, *International Security: An Analytical Survey* (Boulder, CO: Lynne Rienner, 2005), 52.

13. "Statement on Canada's Arctic foreign policy," 6.

14. Ibid., 9. See also Adam Lajeunesse, "The Northwest Passage in Canadian policy," *International Journal* 63, 4 (Autumn 2008): 1037–52; Margaret Purdy and Leanne Smythe, "From obscurity to action: Why Canada must tackle the security dimensions of climate change," *International Journal* 65, 2 (Spring 2010): 411–33; and Rob Huebert, "Renaissance in Canadian Arctic security?" *Canadian Military Journal* 6, 4 (Winter 2005–06), 17–29.

15. Lajeunesse, "The Northwest Passage," 1041.

16. "Harper announces measures to strengthen Canada's Arctic sovereignty."

17. *Canada's Northern Strategy,* 16.

18. "Statement on Canada's Arctic foreign policy," 11.

19. Cannon speech, 11 March 2009.

20. Cannon speech, 6 April 2009.

21. Foreign Affairs, Trade and Development Canada, "Notes for an address by the Honourable Lawrence Cannon, Minister of Foreign Affairs, on the release of the Government of Canada's Northern Strategy," 26 July 2009. Available at www.international.gc.ca/media/aff/speeches-discours/2009/387436.aspx?lang=en.

22. "Statement on Canada's Arctic foreign policy," 19.

23. Arctic Climate Impact Assessment (ACIA), *Impacts of a Warming Arctic (Overview Report)* (Cambridge: Cambridge University Press, 2004), "Executive summary," 8. Available at http://amap.no/acia.

24. Ibid., 10.

25. Ibid., 11.

26. Simon Dalby, "Geopolitical identities: Arctic ecology and global consumption," *Geopolitics* 8, 1 (Spring 2003): 198.

27. Henry Huntington and Shari Fox, "The changing Arctic: Indigenous perspectives," in Arctic Climate Impact Assessment, *Scientific Report* (Cambridge: Cambridge University Press, 2005), 64. Available at http://www.acia.uaf.edu/PDFs/ACIA_Science_Chapters_Final/ACIA_Ch03_Final.pdf.

28. Ibid., 78.

29. Ibid., 82.

30. Sheila Watt-Cloutier, "Reclaiming the moral high ground," *Nunatsiaq Online,* 21 December 2009.

27 Aid Effectiveness and the Framing of New Canadian Aid Initiatives

Stephen Brown

Key Terms

Aid Effectiveness

Millennium Development Goals

Official Development Assistance

Policy Coherence

Tied Aid

At the end of the twentieth century, foreign aid appeared to be in almost terminal decline, both in Canada and in other Western countries. During the 1990s, Canada's **official development assistance** (ODA) dropped from $3.0 billion in 1990–91 to $2.6 billion in 2000–1. Relative to the size of the Canadian economy, the decline was even more dramatic. The government cut aid disbursements almost in half during this same period, from 0.45 per cent to 0.25 per cent of gross national income (GNI) (Canada 2009: 10). The optimism that accompanied the end of the Cold War quickly evanesced. Disillusioned with the lack of tangible results, Canada and most other donors slashed their aid budgets as part of deficit-cutting strategies, turning their backs on long-standing commitments to reaching 0.7 per cent of GNI. After 30 years of aid growth, it felt like the end of an era.

The new century ushered in a radical reversal of this trend. The **Millennium Development Goals** (MDGs) adopted at the United Nations in 2000 epitomized the new thinking. Donors recognized that massive efforts were required to reduce poverty drastically over a 15-year period, including through increased spending to improve access to health and education. At the beginning of the twenty-first century, at UN conferences and G8 summits, Western donors renewed and reiterated their commitments to providing higher levels of aid, to target poverty reduction, and to focus especially on Africa, the continent where needs are the greatest. They also sought to improve **aid effectiveness** so as to provide not only more but also better aid. For the first few years, Canada was an enthusiastic participant in this trend. By 2005, Canadian ODA disbursements had bounced back to 0.35 per cent of GNI (OECD 2009), though this remained only half the international target.

A year after the adoption of the MDGs, the al Qaeda terrorist attacks of 11 September 2001, profoundly shaped the context in which foreign aid operated. The new mindset of the "war on terror" and the linked US-led invasions of Iraq and Afghanistan recast how Canada and other donors framed and oriented their aid programs. Almost overnight, security concerns gained central importance, often eclipsing focus on the MDGs. Within the context of these contradictory international trends, Canada began to rethink its place in the world and especially its relationship with the United States.

Successive Canadian prime ministers each brought a new direction to foreign aid, usually building on predecessors' achievements. For instance, Jean Chrétien reversed the decline in aid flows and designated Africa a priority. Paul Martin integrated aid more closely with other foreign policy "instruments" (known as the *whole-of-government approach*) and took steps to focus on a smaller number of countries. Stephen Harper sought to concentrate and integrate aid even further, notably focusing resources on Afghanistan but also replacing Africa with the Americas as the priority region for aid.

This chapter analyzes the main trends in Canadian development assistance policy since 2000–1, the pivotal "international moment" that pulled ODA simultaneously in two new directions: a preoccupation with the immediate and medium-term needs of the poor that were embodied in the MDGs and with donor countries' own security concerns in the post-9/11 era.[1] It argues that shifts in Canadian aid policy reflect the government's broader foreign policy concerns, especially a preoccupation with prestige (the quest for a personal legacy under Chrétien and for Canada's place among peers and in the post-9/11 world under Martin and Harper) and most recently with commercial self-interest, with a new geographical focus on Latin America and the Caribbean, as well as the promotion of mining interests. Though these forms of self-interest are not new or unique to Canada, the Canadian government has generally framed these changes as improvements in aid effectiveness and thus as being of benefit to poor countries. With the notable exception of the gradual untying of aid, however, the impact of most Canadian initiatives on effectiveness would be unclear or even detrimental. Couching these changes in aid effectiveness terms, the Canadian government is increasingly seeking to instrumentalize the Canadian International Development Agency (CIDA) and

Canadian aid programs to reflect non-development-related interests.

The chapter is organized as follows. Its first section analyzes the politics of aid effectiveness by examining in turn the main components in the effectiveness discussions that have been part of Canadian aid policy initiatives in recent years: the untying of aid, the search for results, the "focus on focus" (fewer recipient countries and economic sectors), and the coherence between aid policy and policies in other areas (including the 2013 absorption of CIDA into the Department of Foreign Affairs and International Trade, DFAIT). It then explores the motivations that underpin recent Canadian aid policy initiatives. The conclusion summarizes the main argument and speculates on the effect of global changes on Canadian foreign aid in the years to come.

The Politics of Aid Effectiveness

Virtually every time the Canadian government announces changes in aid policy, it evokes the need for aid to have greater impact, regardless of who is in power.[2] At first blush, this might appear impossible to be anything but a good thing. After all, it is hard to oppose effectiveness. Upon further examination, however, the concept's malleability permits its use to justify any new initiative, preventing it from having any fixed connotations. *Effectiveness* becomes a substitute for *good policy*, which in turn is really the government's preferred policy, enhanced by an aura of supposed objectivity and benevolence, underpinned by cost-effectiveness and international legitimacy.

Aid effectiveness is currently one of the most important buzzwords in aid circles. In recent years, the term has acquired two distinct meanings. First, in the late 1990s, the World Bank published an influential report entitled *Assessing Aid: What Works, What Doesn't, and Why* (World Bank 1998).

Based on econometric analysis, it argued that aid produces growth only in countries with a "good" policy environment and "sound" fiscal, monetary, and trade policies, without which, it inferred, aid is wasted (further argued in Burnside and Dollar 2000). Though the methodology and reasoning were roundly criticized (Lensink and White 2000), this strand of aid effectiveness came to signify the ability to produce economic growth (notably not a synonym for *development*) when combined with the "right" policies in recipient countries.

Simultaneously, a different meaning emerged among donor countries, more specifically the member countries of the Development Assistance Committee of the Organisation for Economic Co-operation and Development (OECD/DAC), where donors discuss and try to coordinate aid policy. Concerned not only with policies in recipient countries, as the World Bank had been, they considered how *donor* aid policies could improve the effectiveness of their contributions. The 2005 Paris Declaration on Aid Effectiveness, supplemented by the 2008 Accra Agenda for Action, formalized as basic principles the centrality of harmonization among donors, alignment with recipient country ownership, and the predictability of aid flows, among others. In other words, aid's effectiveness depended not on the "correct" neo-liberal policy environment in recipient countries, but rather on strengthened commitment and cooperation of donors among themselves and with recipient countries.[3] The 2011 Busan Partnership for Effective Development Co-operation expanded the concept to "development effectiveness" in order to include the non-aid dimensions of development, but that term's meaning was even less well defined than *aid effectiveness* (Kindornay 2011).

As a member of the DAC and part of the DAC-led process in defining the principles of aid effectiveness, the Canadian government often invoked these principles to outline the basic philosophy of Canadian assistance. However, the government continued to use the World Bank's approach and present its neo-liberal justifications in its policy documents for directing aid to certain countries (Canada 2002, 2005)—even after most other donors had abandoned the logic behind that argument, along with that particular use of the term *effectiveness*. Lacking any robust empirical evidence to support this approach, Canada embraced what was essentially a political or ideological preference for countries with minimal state intervention in their economy and great openness to international finance and investment.

More recently, however, the government and especially successive Cabinet ministers responsible for aid have invoked *effectiveness* to justify any changes the government makes, even if they contradict the basic consensus principles. Canada's version of aid effectiveness is clearly "a distinct, more narrow version" of the internationally endorsed agenda that concentrates on internal organizational issues and accountability to Canadian taxpayers (Lalonde 2009: 169; see also Brown and Jackson 2009). Some Canadian initiatives, such as completely untying aid (i.e., not requiring that funds be spent on Canadian products and services), are fully in line with aid effectiveness principles. Others, such as frequently changing priority countries and sectors, are less so. This raises the question of effectiveness for what and for whom, to be further addressed below.

This chapter does not seek to assess Canada's progress in the actual implementation of the international "aid effectiveness agenda," which is examined in Lalonde (2009) and OECD (2011). Rather, it analyzes recent Canadian policy initiatives and the extent to which they can be justified by the aid effectiveness rationale, by which I mean whether they improve the quality of aid from the point of view of beneficiaries in recipient countries. The rest of this section thus examines the recent evolution of the four main components of Canadian aid policy changes—focus, **tied aid**, results, and **policy coherence**—and their links to aid effectiveness.[4]

Focus, Focus, Focus

Given Canada's relatively paltry generosity when compared to its peers and its lack of commitment to increasing aid flows, it is logical that the government prefers instead to emphasize improving effectiveness, increasing Canada's prestige and the benefits that accrue to Canada, all discussed below.[5] As part of its effectiveness mantra, the government constantly repeats the word *focus*. Greater focus, both geographical and thematic, is assumed but never demonstrated to improve effectiveness. The constant shifting in priority countries, continents, and sectors, however, unambiguously decreases effectiveness.

Canadian aid has been very widely dispersed since the early 1970s (Morrison 2000: 26). Canada is the only donor country to belong to the Commonwealth, the Francophonie, and the Organization of American States. Membership has its privileges, but also obligations—or at least an interest in providing assistance to developing country members in Asia, francophone and anglophone Africa, Latin America, and the Caribbean. Canada's aid is also spent in a broad range of sectors. The donor consensus, however, is to focus on a smaller number of both countries and sectors in order to increase effectiveness. Canada's donor peers, like its domestic critics, have often criticized CIDA programming for being excessively scattered (OECD 2002, 2007). Successive Canadian governments have taken steps to concentrate not only on a subset of countries, but also on a handful of sectors.

In 2002, the Chrétien government announced its intention to bolster its relationship with "a limited number of the world's poorest countries," emphasizing how this would improve the impact of Canadian ODA (Canada 2002: 11). Of the nine countries selected for "enhanced partnerships," two-thirds were in sub-Saharan Africa.[6] Unable to achieve this degree of concentration, the Martin government announced in 2005 that Canada would increase the impact of its aid by dedicating two-thirds of its bilateral aid to 25 "development partners" (Canada 2005).[7] To the existing nine countries, it added eight sub-Saharan African ones, two Latin American ones, five Asian ones, and one European one.[8] In 2009, the Harper government radically redrew the list, retaining the original core of nine, adding the West Bank/Gaza, and four new countries in the Americas, while dropping 12 of the 16 additions from 2005, including all eight African ones.[9] It announced that 80 per cent of bilateral aid would be directed to those 20 priority countries. In 2014, it designated 7 new "countries of focus," most of which were in sub-Saharan Africa and Asia, and dropped 2, for a total of 25 countries to which 90 per cent of bilateral aid would flow.[10]

Successive governments also announced a focus on a limited number of sectors. In 2001, CIDA adopted social development priorities in health and nutrition, basic education, HIV/AIDS, and children, all of which were meant to include the promotion of gender equality. These aligned well with Canada's commitment to the Millennium Development Goals. In the 2002 development policy statement, the minister added rural development and agriculture, as well as the private sector (Canada 2002: 14–16). In Martin's 2005 policy statement, the list was redrawn to focus on good governance, health, basic education, private sector development, and environmental sustainability, again with gender as a cross-cutting theme (Canada 2005: 11). In 2009, the government announced three "priority themes": increasing food security, stimulating sustainable economic growth, and securing the future of children and youth. This unexpected announcement created confusion in the Canadian development community, as *themes* are not quite the same as *sectors* and could in fact encompass numerous sectors. For instance, the future of children and youth would certainly include health and education but arguably also a variety of efforts in technical training, job creation, and peacebuilding, to name but a few. To these "priority" themes the government added three "crosscutting" ones: environmental sustainability, equality between men and women, and governance (FATDC 2013), further muddying the waters as to what was to be included and, more to the point, excluded.

Though one could endlessly debate the merits of individual country recipients and sectors, two facts put into perspective the question of focus. First, despite consensus among donors on the need to focus on fewer recipients and sectors, the theoretical argument that this approach increases aid effectiveness has serious weaknesses, and claims to that effect lack empirical evidence (Munro 2005). If all donors adopt such focus without coordinating their efforts, this also creates new risks, including the overconcentration of aid in certain recipient countries and the relative neglect of others. Furthermore, Canada's decision to focus only on certain sectors or themes contradicts its commitment—in previous aid policy statements (Canada 2002, 2005), the government's own Aid Effectiveness Agenda (FATDC 2013), and, under the Paris Declaration—to recipients' ownership of their development strategy and donor alignment with recipients' national priorities.

Second, even if increased focus were in fact beneficial, significantly changing the list of priority countries and sectors every few years—even in the name of effectiveness—increases aid volatility and thus actually reduces aid effectiveness.[11] According to a report by the Auditor General of Canada (2009: 21), "the lack of clear direction," in large part due to frequently changing priorities and senior staff, including presidents and ministers, "has confused CIDA staff, recipient governments, and other donors, effectively undermining the Agency's long-term predictability." For instance, it is clearly not conducive to aid effectiveness to designate Benin and Burkina Faso priority countries in 2005, delist them in 2009, and then reinstate them in 2014.

"Focusing on focus" rather than on more substantive issues, such as the origins of and solutions to poverty and inequality, serve as a convenient justification for a given government's own preferences, while providing a veneer of selflessness and assuaging peer pressure.

Tied Aid: The Long Goodbye

Tied aid is a practice that involves making ODA conditional on the purchase of goods and services from the donor country. Tied aid adds on average an extra 15–30 per cent to costs because it prevents funds from being used to buy the best value for money in a competitive market (Jepma 1991: 15). This benefits the donor country, but provides no advantage to the recipient. Tied aid is thus antithetical to the notion of aid effectiveness.

The most unambiguous advance in Canadian aid policy since 2000 is the progressive, albeit slow, untying of aid. In 2002, the government recognized that tied aid was "at odds with trends towards trade liberalization and the dismantling of investment barriers" and that tying its aid benefited Canada rather than developing countries. At the time, Canada tied more of its ODA than the majority of its peers. At least 50 per cent of aid to African and least-developed countries and two-thirds of aid to other countries had to be spent in Canada. No more than 10 per cent of the cost of emergency food aid could be used to purchase food in countries other than Canada. Under pressure from G8 and DAC partners, Canada initially agreed to untie certain categories of aid to least-developed countries only, but not food aid (Canada 2002: 19–23).

After a tsunami devastated the coastal areas of many Asian countries in 2004, the Canadian response highlighted the shortcomings of tied food aid. Rather than buy rice available in nearby Asian countries, the government shipped Canadian surplus wheat, which cost more, took longer to arrive, and was less suited to local diets. The government responded to widespread criticism by reducing the tied component of its food aid to 50 per cent.

In 2005, Canada signed the Paris Declaration on Aid Effectiveness, which committed the government to untying aid, though with no specific deadline for eliminating the practice altogether (OECD 2005: 6, 9). In 2008, the government announced its intention to untie fully all aid by 2012–13 (CIDA 2008). This has eliminated the ineffectiveness caused by tying procurement to the donor country and has brought Canada in line with the international norm, though only slowly and rather belatedly.

An Unhealthy Obsession with Results

The need to focus on results has long been a concern for the DAC (see OECD 1996) and CIDA itself (reflected in its use of "results-based management" tools since the 1990s). However, an overemphasis on immediately visible results often has a negative effect on aid effectiveness (Vollmer in press). Canada's new fixation, bordering on obsession, is linked to both the Conservative leitmotif of accountability and the need to justify massive expenditures in Afghanistan, which had rapidly become by far the largest recipient of Canadian aid, as well as aid to Africa (see criticisms in Canada 2007a, b; 2008). The focus on results also reflects the skepticism of the Conservative Party and an important part of its constituency towards the actual desirability of foreign aid, as well as the party's wish to demonstrate to taxpayers that their money is being well spent.

Unfortunately for donor governments seeking to claim credit, development assistance results are not always tangible or quick. For instance, "qualitative changes in gender relations" are difficult to monitor and measure (Edwards and Hulme 1996: 968). Likewise, aid to the governance sector cannot be immediately assessed by quantifiable indicators—or if it is, they can only capture some components of results. Others can take a generation to bear fruit with any certainty. Even then, causality is difficult to establish. Long-term development successes are not attributable to a single source, especially when donors work closely with each other or a recipient government. As a growing proportion of aid funds are channelled to development programs and sector-wide approaches, rather than individual projects (in line with current thinking on aid effectiveness), the task of attributing results becomes more difficult. Moreover, foreign aid is but one contribution to the development process in a given country. Others include domestic policies and planning, national and international investment, international trade policies, and resource endowments.

CIDA's inability to claim direct credit for some of its endeavours leaves it vulnerable to unfair accusations of failure. The lack of demonstrable results imputable to Canada does not mean that Canadian aid was wasted. However, by embracing and fetishizing immediately visible results, Canada biases its assistance towards short-term, stand-alone project assistance in sectors where results can be tangible and quick, exemplified by Canada's three signature projects in Afghanistan: repairing the Dahla Dam and the connected irrigation system in Kandahar province, supporting the education sector, and eliminating polio.

This can easily backfire and further discredit Canadian aid when high-profile projects fall behind schedule or fail to meet their targets, as has been the case (Watson 2013; A. Woods 2009). Moreover, this type of assistance is at odds with the principles of the aid effectiveness agenda, which emphasizes the long-term integration of development efforts with recipient government institutions, based on recipient needs and strategies, rather than scoring quick points for individual donors' pet projects. It also contradicts the state-building objectives that underpin assistance to "fragile states" such as Afghanistan, whose future depends far more on its own government's gaining legitimacy among Afghans than on the Canadian government's doing so. In sum, a fixation on short-term visible results emphasizes "accountancy" more than it does actual "accountability," which requires a longer time horizon (Edwards and Hulme 1996: 968).

A more productive approach would also acknowledge the inherent uncertainties in development assistance, especially in conflict zones, and adopt aid modalities that try to mitigate these problems over the medium to long term. Rather than pandering to public pressure and aiming for "quick wins" for Canada, the government could educate the Canadian public about the challenges of development, the importance of strengthening local institutions, and the real principles of effectiveness in the longer term.

The Quest for Policy Coherence

The question of coherence among different government departments and policies has been on the donor agenda for well over a decade (OECD 1996; Pratt 1999). The Chrétien government mentioned it in its 2002 development policy statement (Canada 2002: 17–18), but it was under Paul Martin that it became an important practice. Initially known as the "3-D approach" (referring to diplomacy, defence, and development), it was later expanded to include commerce and other areas and renamed the "whole-of-government approach," which featured prominently in the Martin government's international policy statement.

Though in principle, coherence and consistency (much like aid effectiveness) can only be seen as a good thing, their impact on development goals is not necessarily positive. In essence, it depends on what becomes the overriding concern. If other departments, such as foreign affairs, international trade, and defence, were to line up behind development goals, this could help a donor government

achieve aid objectives. Notably, the interests of developing countries themselves could be better reflected in donor policies, at home and at the international level. For example, the lowering or elimination of tariff barriers and other protectionist measures would promote developing country exports and could raise incomes more than foreign aid does. Likewise, the use of donor troops to stabilize countries emerging from civil war could improve the impact of aid.

In practice, however, evidence from other donor countries suggests that policy integration leads to the subordination of development objectives to donors' foreign policy and defence priorities, not the other way around (Smillie 2004: 15), which reduces rather than increases aid effectiveness. For many donors, the war on terror has profoundly influenced their aid disbursements, with the goal of enhancing their own security in a global trend towards the increased "securitization" of foreign aid (N. Woods 2005). Such was clearly the case for Canada's involvement in Afghanistan, which commanded a disproportionate amount of CIDA's attention and resources. Canadian ODA to that country ballooned from a paltry US$7 million in 2000 to US$345 million in 2007, representing about 8.5 per cent of total Canadian ODA.[12] In spite of unprecedentedly high expenditures, it became clear that achieving aid effectiveness was especially difficult in a war zone like Kandahar. Despite attempts to link Canadian defence, diplomatic, and development initiatives in Afghanistan, none of the three Ds appeared to produce any clear progress, be it the defeat of the Taliban insurgency in Kandahar province, the strengthening of the Afghan state with a legitimate government, or the improvement of the lives of millions of impoverished Afghans.

Without this form of policy coherence, CIDA would have been able to function with greater autonomy (Brown 2008a) and have a greater impact on development by spending its funds in countries where they could be used more effectively, rather than being used—and ineffectually at that—to shore up Canada's and other donors' strategic priorities in Afghanistan. Even so, it might be too early to call for the end of the whole-of-government approach, since it might prove more effective for promoting development in countries in the midst of complex crises unrelated to the war on terror, such as Haiti and Sudan (Baranyi and Paducel 2012).

The Canadian government signalled its desire to integrate policy even further when it merged CIDA into DFAIT in 2013, creating the megalithic Department of Foreign Affairs, Trade and Development (DFATD). The government argued the amalgamation would "maximize the effectiveness of the resources available to deliver development and humanitarian assistance" (Canada 2013b: 241). Whether it will actually "put development on equal footing with trade and diplomacy," as Minister of International Cooperation Julian Fantino (2013) stated at the time, will depend on the mix of motivations that underpin policy coherence. As argued in the next section of this chapter, they are unlikely to do so.

Morphing Motivations

States are not monolithic unitary actors, and it is generally not possible to discern clear overarching motivations. As Ilan Kapoor (2008: 78) points out, one should avoid "presupposing a homogeneous nation-state and fully rational and controlled policy-making." Just as individuals can have mixed motives, so too can states. Moreover, different actors within government (CIDA, DFAIT, Prime Minister's Office) or within a government department or agency (CIDA President's Office, Policy Branch, country desk officers) can differ widely in their approaches to ODA.

Analysts have long recognized that the simultaneous pursuit of political, commercial, and development objectives hampers aid efficiency (Canada 1987: 7; Morrison 2000: 15). The recent aid policy changes discussed above illustrate shifts in the government's thinking about ODA and the motivations that underpin them, even if the initiatives do not necessarily have a large impact on the actual day-to-day implementation of Canadian aid outside Afghanistan, especially not in the short term. Most CIDA employees try to keep their heads down and carry on with their jobs, regardless of new policy initiatives. In other words, though self-interested motivations characterize recent Canadian aid policy *changes*, one should not infer that those motives underlie Canadian foreign aid as a whole.

Traditionally, the motivation debate has been set up as a tug-of-war between self-interest ("realism," epitomized by Morgenthau 1962) and selflessness ("humane internationalism," such as Lumsdaine 1993). Though self-interest has become more important (Brown 2007; Pratt 2000), the desire for prestige (as suggested by Nossal 1988), in particular Canada's international reputation, initially explained changes at CIDA during the early years of the Harper government better than did more tangible commercial or even national security interests—including the emphasis placed on Afghanistan. However, starting in 2011, promoting Canadian commercial interests gained in importance.

Throughout the 1990s, under Prime Minister Jean Chrétien, Canada's ODA declined steadily. Assistance to Africa was especially hard hit: By 2000, it was less than half its previous level (Brown 2013: 182). It is thus a particularly noteworthy achievement—and compelling evidence of Canadians' capacity for collective amnesia—that Chrétien managed to reinvent himself in the early 2000s as a vociferous proponent of development assistance in general and aid to Africa in particular. Chrétien's sudden about-face in the final years of his mandate, including the renewal of aid itself and increased attention to Africa, was closely linked to his own concerns for personal legacy, a generous imprint he could make in Canada and on the global stage—though he was more successful at home than internationally (Black 2005, 2006; Brown 2008b).

Chrétien's successor, Paul Martin, focused less on personal credit than on trying to improve Canada's global presence, notably mending its relations with the United States, which had suffered under Chrétien, most recently because of Canada's refusal to take part in the US-led invasion of Iraq. Martin's international policy statement was tellingly titled *A Role of Pride and Influence in the World*, which played to both the domestic and the international audience. The priority the Liberals and later the Conservatives accorded to Afghanistan reflected a concern to prove that Canada could make important contributions to the NATO alliance, including by sending Canadian soldiers to Afghanistan, assuming lead responsibility in Kandahar province, and making Afghanistan a top-priority recipient of Canadian ODA.

The Conservative government of Stephen Harper, first elected in 2006, has not yet released any official documents outlining its approach to foreign aid. For that reason, any analysis of aid policy initiatives is only slightly more exact than reading tea leaves. One must glean information from relatively brief press releases and vague public statements made by politicians, none of which has provided any in-depth rationale or justification for changes. As such, the making of aid policy under Prime Minister Harper has been done "by stealth" and is being drip fed to Parliament, CIDA/DFATD employees, and the Canadian public.

Still, some statements by top officials strongly suggest that international prestige has been a crucial consideration for the Conservative government as well. For example, in 2007, the government indicated that Canada would concentrate efforts in countries where Canada could be among the top five donors, demonstrating a clear desire to have a place at the table with major donors (Canada 2007c: 262)—assuming of course that there are actually five seats at the metaphoric and literal table. At the time, International Cooperation Minister Josée Verner noted that, in some cases, increasing expenditures only slightly would place Canada there, suggesting that the government was more interested in impressing voters and donor peers than it was in actual impact (Brown 2008a).

After Bev Oda replaced Verner as CIDA minister in 2007, prestige abroad became less central—though it still characterized the desire for signature projects in Afghanistan. As Kapoor (2008: 87) notes, "Nationalist symbols permit donors to be identified, thanked, or envied; they also enable it to stake its territory, and perhaps to gloat." Signature projects mark Canada's international presence and enhance its national credibility, but—as mentioned above—they also contradict widely held principles of aid effectiveness. For that reason, they can actually detract from Canada's reputation among other donors and development workers in Canada and abroad. According to Nilima Gulrajani (2009: A13), "In the world of international aid, Canada is reputed as a money-grubbing flag planter rather than effectively and selflessly serving the world's poor." A discredited Canada makes it harder for the Canadian government and individual Canadian officials to influence donor debates within the OECD/DAC and in donor coordination groups on the ground in recipient countries. Harper's hastily assembled 2010 Maternal, Newborn and Child Health Initiative did little to restore the Canadian government's credibility (Black 2013), while recent aid budget cuts are likely to further hurt Canada's international reputation.

With the shift in focus from Africa to the Americas, first announced by Harper at the 2007 G8 summit, the government's motivation ostensibly started to move away from rather symbolic prestige concerns and towards more concrete economic and specifically commercial self-interest. The new list of

20 "countries of focus" released in 2009 operationalized this new regional priority when, as mentioned above, it dropped many poor African countries and added wealthier ones in Latin America and the Caribbean, notably ones of particular trade interest to Canada.[13] Soon after, the government listed for the first time "alignment with Canada's foreign policy" as an explicit, official criterion for selecting core recipients (FATDC 2013). Bev Oda announced new tripartite funding arrangements with Canadian NGOs and mining companies in 2011 (Brown 2014), while her successor, Julian Fantino, continued to emphasize the importance of supporting the private sector and ensuring that Canadians themselves benefit from foreign aid (Brown 2013: 187–88). This new trend caught the attention of the OECD, which reminded the Canadian government that "there should be no confusion between development objectives and the promotion of commercial interests" (OECD 2012: 11). Nonetheless, the government increasingly linked aid to commercial interests. The following year, it declared its intention to "leverage development programming to advance Canada's trade interests" (Canada 2013a: 14), illustrated in 2014 by the addition of several new "countries of focus" of great interest to the Canadian extractive industry, including the Democratic Republic of the Congo, Mongolia, and Myanmar/Burma.

A concern for personal or national prestige, however, should not be overemphasized in the analysis of policy shifts.[14] Pressure from the donor community, notably within the OECD/DAC, has played an important but under-recognized part in shaping Canadian aid policy, as was the case with Canada's renewed emphasis on Africa in 2001–2 (Black 2006). Chrétien and Martin generally followed the donor consensus, at times contributing to it. Harper, on the other hand, seemed at times to relish breaking with it and distancing himself from global norms (and Liberal priorities), especially eschewing the focus on Africa in favour of the Americas.

In this tale, one significant effort sought to push the Canadian government in the opposite direction. The ODA Accountability Act was passed by Parliament in 2008 as a private member's bill. It aimed to ensure that all Canadian aid would contribute directly to poverty reduction, take into account the perspectives of the poor, and be consistent with international human right standards. However, its provisions lack teeth. According to the government's interpretation, Canadian ODA is already in compliance with the new law, even if one can at best expect a very indirect, long-term contribution of certain aid activities to poverty reduction. The new law may thus have no discernible effect on aid (Halifax Initiative 2009). Certainly, the government would prefer to ignore the act's attempt to reorient aid, much to the consternation of Canadian development NGOs. Tellingly, none of the government's announcements since the law was passed have made any reference to the act as providing guidance on aid policy.

Conclusion: What Would Lester Do?

Prior to 2001, observers such as Cranford Pratt (2000) noted with concern that the government was increasingly justifying Canadian aid on the basis of global security, rather than the need to fight poverty and inequality. Most lamented the decline of Pearsonian idealism and a global justice imperative. This trend intensified after the al Qaeda attacks on the United States in 2001, impelling the government to focus on specifically Canadian security, rather than global security (Brown 2007). As mentioned above, Canada is not exceptional in the "securitization" of its foreign aid and the increased focus on self-interest rather than poverty eradication (N. Woods 2005).

At the same time, since 2000, a counter-trend has been manifesting itself in the global aid regime.

Epitomized by the MDGs' underlining of the urgency of the fight against poverty, emerging donor norms dictated increased aid volumes, especially to sub-Saharan Africa, and much greater attention to social spending. This new trend also underscored the importance not only of policies in recipient countries but ways that Canada and other donors themselves could improve their aid delivery, embodied in the Paris Declaration on Aid Effectiveness.

Since Chrétien's final years in office, and increasingly so under Harper, the government has presented its policy initiatives as ways of improving the effectiveness of Canadian aid. Some efforts, particularly the untying of aid, were clear contributions to that goal, even if Canada was one of the last holdouts in this area. Other efforts, such as concentrating aid in fewer countries and sectors, have not shown evidence of a positive or negative effect on aid effectiveness—and raise some concerns and potential new risks for developing countries. Moreover, the frequency of changes in priority countries and sectors have in themselves undermined the effectiveness of Canadian aid. Other policies and practices, especially the emphasis on signature projects in Afghanistan and the redefining of core sectors and countries every few years, are political decisions and preferences that directly or indirectly contradict stated Canadian policies on local ownership, the predictability of aid flows, the centrality of long-term relationships with recipients and other internationally accepted principles of aid effectiveness. The heavy concentration of Canadian ODA in Afghanistan, despite severe security-related impediments to effective aid, epitomized politically motivated aid priorities. Finally, the adoption of a whole-of-government approach to foreign policy could theoretically enhance aid effectiveness. However, to date, policy coherence has instead undermined it by generally subjecting development priorities to donor self-interest rather than the other way around.

Throughout this period, new Canadian policies and priorities usually reflected a desire for prestige: personal prestige in Chrétien's final years as prime minister, but more often Canada's international prestige, especially under Martin and the early Harper years, when the government sought to use aid to bolster Canada's place in the world, including improving its relationship with the United States. The size and nature of Canada's involvement in Afghanistan best illustrated the government's desire for the US and other Western allies to consider it a team player. The relative feebleness of Canada's renewal of aid, however, ensured that Canadians, rather than other donor countries, would be the main audience of these efforts. By 2009, notwithstanding continued involvement in Afghanistan, it appeared that the Harper government was less interested in using foreign aid to redefine Canada's place in the world and gain international prestige. It has failed to make any commitment to increasing or even maintaining aid flows after 2010, it ended Africa's privileged position as the continent that most urgently needed aid, and it embraced instead the open use of ODA for Canadian commercial self-interest, especially in Latin America and the Caribbean and in relation to the mining sector.

It should be noted, however, that self-interest and the seeking of international prestige need not be incompatible with development efforts, depending on how national interest is constructed. If Canada were to seek prominence through renewed Pearsonian internationalism, to be a leader in generous, innovative, poverty-fighting foreign aid, it could gain respect in the eyes of its donor peers and the developing world. Canada has brought new perspectives to donors' discussions in the past, including the importance of gender equality and civil society (Morrison 1998; 2000). Spearheading a similar issue in the future, such as human-rights-based approaches to development, could help provide a platform for global leadership and enhance

Canada's influence, helping it, for instance, to obtain a non-permanent seat at the UN Security Council. The question of aid policy thus encompasses not only the volume of aid and the underlying objective of Canadian assistance, but also the kind of country Canada wants to be, Canada's place in the world, and the kind of world Canada envisions.[15]

The coming years will pose additional challenges to the aid regime in general and to Canadian policies in particular. Over the medium and long term, climate change will increase the developing world's need for international assistance, particularly because of more frequent and severe natural disasters, lower crop yields, food scarcity, and higher food prices (Ayers and Huq 2009). Meanwhile, Canada's place among donors is waning, as its share of global aid flows decreases, accelerated by the rise of non-DAC donors such as China, and non-state donors, including private philanthropic organizations. The G20, where Canada's influence is limited, is supplanting the G8, where Canada sits among a select few. Canada could respond by further concentrating on narrowly defined self-interest, thereby sealing its fate as a minor player on the world stage, or it could radically rethink how and to whom it provides assistance and try to make niche contributions that would actually contribute to aid effectiveness on the ground.

Acknowledgements

For helpful comments and suggestions, I thank Chris Brown, Molly den Heyer, Brigette DePape, Tristen Naylor, Rosalind Raddatz, Arne Rückert, Jennifer Salahub, Liam Swiss, and two CIDA employees who prefer to remain anonymous. I am also grateful to the Social Sciences and Humanities Research Council of Canada and the University of Ottawa for funding that made this research possible.

Questions for Review

1. What explains the rise and fall of foreign aid budgets?
2. What are the various ways of conceptualizing aid effectiveness?
3. What are the pros and cons of focusing aid on fewer countries and sectors?
4. To what extent should foreign aid emphasize measurable short-term results?
5. Why should Canada and other wealthy countries provide foreign aid?
6. How coherent should Canada's aid policy be with other components of foreign policy?

Suggested Readings

Audet, François, Marie-Eve Desrosiers, and Stéphane Roussel, eds. 2008. *L'aide canadienne au développement: bilan, défis et perspectives*. Montréal: Presses de l'Université de Montréal.

Brown, Stephen, ed. 2012. *Struggling for Effectiveness: CIDA and Canadian Foreign Aid*. Montreal and Kingston: McGill-Queen's University Press.

Bülles, Anni-Claudine, and Shannon Kindornay. 2013. "Beyond Aid: A Plan for Canada's International Cooperation." Ottawa: North–South Institute. Available at www.nsi-ins.ca/wp-content/uploads/2013/05/BuellesKindornay.2013.CNDPolicyCoherenceEN.pdf.

Essex, Jamey. 2012. "The politics of effectiveness in Canada's international development assistance." *Canadian Journal of Development Studies* 33, 3: 338–55.

Smillie, Ian. 2009. "Foreign Aid and Canadian Purpose: Influence and Policy in Canada's International Development Assistance," pp. 183–208 in Robert Bothwell and Jean Daudelin, ed. *Canada among Nations 2008: 100 Years of Canadian Foreign Policy*. Montreal and Kingston: McGill-Queen's University Press.

References

Auditor General of Canada. 2009. "Strengthening Aid Effectiveness—Canadian International Development Agency." *Report of the Auditor General of Canada to the House of Commons.* Ottawa: Office of the Auditor General of Canada.

Ayers, Jessica M., and Saleemul Huq. 2009. "Supporting Adaptation to Climate Change: What Role for Official Development Assistance?" *Development Policy Review* 27, 6: 675–92.

Baranyi, Stephen, and Anca Paducel. 2012. "Whither development in Canada's approach toward fragile states?," pp. 108–34 in Stephen Brown, ed. *Struggling for Effectiveness: cida and Canadian Foreign Aid.* Montreal and Kingston: McGill-Queen's University Press.

Black, David R. 2005. "From Kananaskis to Gleneagles: Assessing Canadian 'leadership' on Africa." *Behind the Headlines* 62, 3: 1–17.

———. 2006. "Canadian Aid to Africa: Assessing 'Reform,'" pp. 319–38 in Andrew F. Cooper and Dane Rowlands, eds. *Canada among Nations 2006: Minorities and Priorities.* Montreal and Kingston: McGill-Queen's University Press.

———. 2013. "The Muskoka Initiative and the Politics of Fence-mending with Africa," pp. 239–51 in Rohinton Medhora and Yiagadeesen Samy, eds. *Canada among Nations 2013. Canada–African Relations: Looking Back, Looking Ahead.* Waterloo, ON: Centre for International Governance Innovation.

Booth, David. 2012. "Aid effectiveness: Bringing country ownership (and politics) back in." *Conflict, Security and Development* 12, 5: 537–58.

Brown, Chris, and Edward T. Jackson. 2009. "Could the Senate be Right? Should CIDA be Abolished?" pp. 151–74 in Allan M. Maslove, ed. *How Ottawa Spends, 2009–2010: Economic Upheaval and Political Dysfunction.* Montreal and Kingston: McGill-Queen's University Press.

Brown, Stephen. 2007. "'Creating the World's Best Development Agency'? Confusion and Contradictions in CIDA's New Policy Blueprint." *Canadian Journal of Development Studies* 28, 2: 213-28.

———. 2008a. "CIDA under the Gun," pp. 91–107 in Jean Daudelin and Daniel Schwanen, eds. *Canada Among Nations 2007: What Room for Manoeuvre?* Montreal and Kingston: McGill-Queen's University Press.

———. 2008b. "L'aide publique canadienne à l'Afrique: vers un nouvel âge d'or?," pp. 267–90 in François Audet, Marie-Eve Desrosiers, and Stéphane Roussel, eds. *L'aide canadienne au développement: Bilan, défis et perspectives.* Montreal: Presses de l'Université de Montréal.

———. 2013. "Canadian Aid to Africa," pp. 181–94 in Rohinton Medhora and Yiagadeesen Samy, eds., *Canada Among Nations 2013. Canada–African Relations: Looking Back,*

Looking Ahead. Waterloo, ON: Centre for International Governance Innovation.

———. 2014. "Undermining Foreign Aid: The Extractive Sector and the Recommercialization of Canadian Development Assistance." In Stephen Brown, Molly den Heyer, and David R. Black, eds. *Rethinking Canadian Aid.* Ottawa: University of Ottawa Press (forthcoming).

Burnside, Craig, and David Dollar. 2000. "Aid, Policies, and Growth." *American Economic Review* 90, 4: 847–68.

Cameron, John. 2007. "CIDA in the Americas: New Directions and Warning Signs for Canadian Development Policy." *Canadian Journal of Development Studies* 28, 2: 229–47.

Canada. 1987. *For Whose Benefit? Report on Canada's Official Development Assistance Policies and Programs.* Ottawa: House of Commons Standing Committee on External Affairs and International Trade.

———. 2002. *Canada Making a Difference in the World: A Policy Statement on Strengthening Aid Effectiveness.* Hull, QC: Canadian International Development Agency.

———. 2005. *Canada's International Policy Statement: A Role of Pride and Influence in the World—Development.* Gatineau, QC: Canadian International Development Agency.

———. 2007a. *Canadian Troops in Afghanistan: Taking a Hard Look at a Hard Mission.* Ottawa: Senate of Canada, Standing Senate Committee on National Security and Defence.

———. 2007b. *Overcoming 40 Years of Failure: A New Road Map for Sub-Saharan Africa.* Ottawa: Senate of Canada, Standing Senate Committee on Foreign Affairs and International Trade.

———. 2007c. *Budget Plan 2007.* Ottawa: Department of Finance.

———. 2008. *Report of the Independent Panel on Canada's Future Role in Afghanistan.* Ottawa: Manley Commission.

———. 2009. *Statistical Report on International Assistance, Fiscal Year 2006–2007.* Gatineau, QC: Canadian International Development Agency.

———. 2013a. *Global Markets Action Plan.* November. Available at http://international.gc.ca/global-markets-marches-mondiaux/assets/pdfs/plan-eng.pdf.

———. 2013b. *Jobs, Growth and Long-term Prosperity: Economic Action Plan 2013.* Ottawa: Government of Canada.

CIDA. 2008. "Canada Fully Unties its Development Aid." 5 September. Available at www.acdi-cida.gc.ca/acdi-cida/ACDI-CIDA.nsf/eng/NAT-9583229-GQC.

———. 2009. "Canada Introduces a New Effective Approach to its International Assistance." 20 May. Available at www.acdi-cida.gc.ca/acdi-cida/ACDI-CIDA.nsf/eng/NAT-5208514-G7B.

Edwards, Michael, and David Hulme. 1996. "Too Close for Comfort? The Impact of Official Aid on Nongovernmental Organizations." *World Development* 24, 6: 961–73.

Fantino, Julian. 2013. "Today, the Honourable Julian Fantino, Minister of International Cooperation issued a statement following the release of Economic Action Plan 2013." News release, 21 March. Gatineau, QC: CIDA. Available at www.acdi-cida.gc.ca/acdi-cida/ACDI-CIDA.nsf/eng/ANN-321154018-R3R.

Foreign Affairs, Trade and Development Canada. 2013. "Aid Effectiveness Agenda." 26 June. Available at www.acdi-cida.gc.ca/aideffectiveness.

Gulrajani, Nilima. 2009. "How politicization has been silently killing CIDA's effectiveness." *The Globe and Mail*, 8 June, A13.

Halifax Initiative. 2009. "Official interpretations of the 'ODA Accountability Act' one year later." Issue Brief. Ottawa: Halifax Initiative.

Hyden, Goran. 2008. "After the Paris Declaration: Taking on the Issue of Power." *Development Policy Review* 26, 3: 259–74.

Jepma, Catrinus J. 1991. *The Tying of Aid*. Paris: Organisation for Economic Co-operation and Development.

Kapoor, Ilan. 2008. *The Postcolonial Politics of Development*. London and New York: Routledge.

Kindornay, Shannon. 2011. "From Aid to Development Effectiveness: A Working Paper." Ottawa: North–South Institute.

Lalonde, Jennifer. 2009. "Harmony and Discord: International Aid Harmonization and Donor State Domestic Influence. The Case of Canada and the Canadian International Development Agency." PhD. dissertation. Baltimore: Johns Hopkins University.

Lensink, Robert, and Howard White. 2000. "Assessing Aid: A Manifesto for Aid in the 21st Century?" *Oxford Development Studies* 28, 1: 5–17.

Lumsdaine, David Halloran. 1993. *Moral Vision in International Politics: The Foreign Aid Regime, 1949–89*. Princeton, NJ: Princeton University Press.

Munro, Lauchlan T. 2005. "Focus-Pocus? Thinking Critically about Whether Aid Organizations Should Do Fewer Things in Fewer Countries." *Development and Change* 36, 3: 425–47.

Morgenthau, Hans. 1962. "A Political Theory of Foreign Aid." *American Political Science Review* 56, 2: 301–9.

Morrison, David R. 1998. *Aid and Ebb Tide: A History of CIDA and Canadian Development Assistance*. Waterloo, ON: Wilfrid Laurier University Press.

———. 2000. "Canadian Aid: A Mixed Record and an Uncertain Future," pp. 15–36 in Jim Freedman, ed. *Transforming Development: Foreign Aid for a Changing World*. Toronto: University of Toronto Press.

Nossal, Kim Richard. 1988. "Mixed Motives Revisited: Canada's Interest in Development Assistance." *Canadian Journal of Political Science* 21, 1: 35–56.

OECD. 1996. *Shaping the 21st Century: The Contribution of Development Co-operation*. Paris: Development Assistance Committee, Organisation for Economic Co-operation and Development.

———. 2002. "Development Co-operation Review: Canada." Paris: Development Assistance Committee, Organisation for Economic Co-operation and Development.

———. 2005. "Paris Declaration on Aid Effectiveness." Available at www.oecd.org/dataoecd/11/41/34428351.pdf.

———. 2007. "Canada: Development Assistance Committee (DAC) Peer Review." Paris: Organisation for Economic Co-operation and Development, Development Assistance Committee.

———. 2009. "Net Official Development Assistance in 2008." Paris: Organisation for Economic Co-operation and Development. Available at www.oecd.org/dataoecd/48/34/42459170.pdf.

———. 2011. *Aid Effectiveness 2005–10: Progress in Implementing the Paris Declaration*. Paris: Organisation for Economic Co-operation and Development.

———. 2012. "Canada: Development Assistance Committee (DAC) Peer Review." Paris: Organisation for Economic Co-operation and Development.

———. 2014. "Aid to developing countries rebounds in 2013 to reach an all-time high." Paris: Organisation for Economic Co-operation and Development. Available at www.oecd.org/newsroom/aid-to-developing-countries-rebounds-in-2013-to-reach-an-all-time-high.htm.

Pratt, Cranford. 1999. "Greater Policy Coherence, a Mixed Blessing: The Case of Canada," pp. 78–103 in Jacques Forster and Olav Stokke, eds., *Policy Coherence in Development Co-operation*. London and Portland, OR: Frank Cass.

———. 2000. "Alleviating Global Poverty or Enhancing Security: Competing Rationales for Canadian Development Assistance," pp. 37–59 in Jim Freedman, ed., *Transforming Development: Foreign Aid for a Changing World*. Toronto: University of Toronto Press.

Smillie, Ian. 2004. "ODA: Options and Challenges for Canada." Ottawa: Canadian Council for International Co-operation.

Stairs, Denis. 2005. "Confusing the Innocent with Numbers and Categories: The International Policy Statement and the Concentration of Development Assistance." Calgary: Canadian Defence and Foreign Affairs Institute.

Vollmer, Frank. In press. "Debating 'visibility' and its effects on the effective delivery of Official Development Assistance—diagnosis, justification and possibilities." *Information Development*.

Watson, Paul. 2013. "Afghan farmers worry crucial dam project will be left unfinished," *Toronto Star*, 29 May.

Woods, Allan. 2009. "Polio defeats Canada's pet project," *Toronto Star*, 16 September.

Woods, Ngaire. 2005. "The shifting politics of foreign aid." *International Affairs* 81, 2: 393–409.

World Bank. 1998. *Assessing Aid: What Works, What Doesn't, and Why*. New York: Oxford University Press.

Notes

1. It is worth underlining that this chapter focuses its analysis on changes at the policy level and does not examine the concrete impact of new initiatives on the ground, which might not yet be discernable and are only beginning to be studied in depth.

2. For instance: "CIDA will reorient its programming in the poorest countries towards new approaches that are based on the principles of effective development" (Canada 2002: 7); "In order to increase the effectiveness of the development cooperation program, we will focus our efforts in a few priority sectors and in a small group of countries and will engage in value-added, selective partnerships with Canadians and with the most effective multilateral institutions" (Canada 2005: 31); "By fully untying Canada's aid, the Government is delivering on its commitment in the 2006 Speech from the Throne to support 'a more effective use of aid dollars' and the 2007 Budget's promise not only to increase the amount of Canada's international assistance envelope, but also 'to make our existing resources work more effectively'" (CIDA 2008: 1); "With greater efficiency, focus, and accountability, our Government's new approach to Canadian aid will be even more effective" (CIDA 2009: 1); and "The Department of Foreign Affairs, Trade and Development will leverage the synergies resulting from the amalgamation to maximize the effectiveness of the resources available to deliver development and humanitarian assistance" (Canada 2013b: 241).

3. I do not mean to accept uncritically the principles of the Paris Declaration (see Booth 2012; Hyden 2008). Nonetheless, it represents the standing consensus on what constitutes aid effectiveness, to which Canada has subscribed and against which Canada's policies and practices can be assessed.

4. The first three are the main ones listed in Canada's "Aid Effectiveness Agenda" (FATDC 2013), which also includes short bromides on the importance of ownership for achieving results, transparency and accountability, and partnerships. I added the fourth item, policy coherence, in recognition of the role of non-aid policies in either reinforcing or undermining aid effectiveness.

5. In 2013, Canada was the fifteenth most generous DAC donor in terms of ODA/GNI (OECD 2014). By way of comparison, Canada was the sixth most generous country as recently as 1994 (Morrison 2000: 21). As Canada continues to cut its aid budget, its ranking is likely to slip further in coming years.

6. Namely Ghana, Ethiopia, Mali, Mozambique, Senegal, and Tanzania. The others were Honduras, Bolivia, and Bangladesh.

7. As Stairs (2005) pointed out, two-thirds of bilateral aid were already going to 25 countries—though not the same 25. This new policy would therefore not necessarily achieve any greater concentration.

8. Benin, Burkina Faso, Cameroon, Kenya, Malawi, Niger, Rwanda, and Zambia; Guyana and Nicaragua; Cambodia, Indonesia, Pakistan, Sri Lanka, and Vietnam; and Ukraine.

9. The other additions to the list in the Americas were Colombia, Haiti, Peru, and the Caribbean regional program. The other countries dropped were the two Latin American countries added in 2005 (Guyana and Nicaragua, the former now included under the Caribbean program) and two newly added Asian ones (Cambodia and Sri Lanka).

10. It added three African countries (Benin, Burkina Faso, and the Democratic Republic of the Congo), three in Asia (Mongolia, Myanmar/Burma, and the Philippines), and one in the Middle East (Jordan). Bolivia and Pakistan were removed from the list.

11. As CIDA itself has recognized, "Long-term development requires a predictable and stable source of funding to be effective" and "effective international assistance involves long-term relationships with development partners" (Canada 2005: 10).

12. OECD International Development Statistics. Available at www.oecd.org/dac/stats/idsonline.

13. Though ODA to Latin America can legitimately fight poverty and inequality (Cameron 2007), the new list notably included comparatively well-off countries (the English-speaking Caribbean) and ones where Canada was actively pursuing free-trade agreements (Colombia and Peru).

14. Prestige-seeking and compliance with norms are not incompatible. As Lumsdaine (1993: 67) argues, "doing something costly and right but doing it out of desire for approbation" is evidence of the strength of peer pressure and norms.

15. For a critique of this national(ist) framework for situating the aid relationship, see Kapoor (2008).

28 The Harper Government, Africa Policy, and the Relative Decline of Humane Internationalism

David Black

Key Terms

Counter-consensus
Global Citizenship

Humane Internationalism
Social Gospel

Much press, political, and civil society commentary has emphasized the Harper government's apparent retreat from Africa in its foreign policy. Three other trends are often linked to this one: a new emphasis on Latin America, a growing foreign policy emphasis on the pursuit of commercial opportunities for Canadian businesses, and an erosion of Canada's commitment to a poverty-focused **development assistance** program.

These trends must be kept in perspective. There has been more continuity *in practice*, both with regard to Africa and Latin America, than many accounts have suggested. Similarly, changes in foreign aid policy were very slow to be articulated, let alone implemented. As a result, much of Canada's approach in these key dimensions of its foreign policy towards the global South was guided for the first several years of the Harper era by inertia. Nevertheless, some real changes of interest, emphasis, and engagement had emerged by 2009, with potentially far-reaching ramifications. These ramifications were reinforced following the government's 2011 electoral majority and by the headline-grabbing decision announced in the March 2013 Federal Budget to integrate the 45-year-old Canadian

International Development Agency (CIDA) with the Department of Foreign Affairs and International Trade to form a new Department of Foreign Affairs, Trade and Development (DFATD). In short, there are signs of a clear shift not only from the high profile emphasis on Africa articulated in the latter years of the Chrétien government, but from 50 years of broad bipartisanship in policies toward the continent.

There are both more proximate and more foundational explanations for this apparent shift. In this chapter, I will briefly assess the former, which have received more attention and focused mainly on the role of Prime Minister Harper and the "new" Conservative party in government. However, these influences cannot be properly understood without taking account of longer-term and more foundational dynamics within Canadian political culture: the relative decline and changing character of what Cranford Pratt, two decades ago, had already characterized as "An Eroding and Limited (Humane) Internationalism" (Pratt 1989). In other words, I will focus on the longer-term trajectory of the more cosmopolitan tradition of Canadian internationalism, emphasizing the amelioration of global poverty, inequality, and injustice.

Four specific factors will be proposed as explanations for the declining influence of this tradition: the corrosive effects of attacks on the utility of foreign aid; the changing face of organized religion in Canada; the decline of radical solidarity politics; and the shift in the dominant ethical frame of Canadian foreign policy from **humane internationalism** to **global citizenship**.

In order to establish what needs to be explained, I will begin with a brief assessment of what has and what has not changed in Canada's approach to Africa and the related policy domains of Latin America and development assistance. I will then briefly review the more immediate explanations for the trends in these policy domains before exploring the longer-term decline in humane internationalist influence on Canadian policies toward the global South.

A New Foreign Policy Direction towards the Global "South"?

Characteristically, the Harper government was slow and sketchy in articulating specific policy directions concerning Africa, Latin America, and development assistance. Bold new policies were promised on both Latin America and development assistance, but for more than three years after the government was first elected, nothing was elaborated in either area. On Africa, the perceived "shift" was more a product of omission than commission: what was *not* said and done rather than what *was*.

This began to change with several documents, speeches, and announcements in 2009. The policy document *Canada and the Americas* (Government of Canada 2009), a brief policy pronouncement on aid concentration (CIDA 2009), and a May 2009 speech by then minister for international cooperation Bev Oda setting out CIDA's thematic priorities (Oda 2009) supplemented broad statements of intent (or

lack thereof) and relatively small policy openings and departures to provide observers with at least a limited basis upon which to assess government intentions.

On Latin America there was, broadly speaking, more continuity with past Liberal and Progressive Conservative policy approaches than the rhetoric of change implied. Canada's three "interconnected and mutually-reinforcing objectives" towards the region, as articulated in *Canada and the Americas*, are the promotion of democratic governance, prosperity, and security (2009: 6). Even as elaborated upon in the remainder of the document, these objectives are hard to distinguish from those of its predecessors. As Randall and Dowding (2008: 42) summarize, ". . . there is little in the Harper government's overtures to Latin America or in the concrete policies which are being pursued toward Colombia [and, one could add, other specific cases] that depart in any significant way from either the general premises of Canadian foreign and defence policy or the Canadian policies which have been pursued since the late 1980s." Moreover, because of the pattern of inconstancy in Canada's professions of intent regarding its "vocation" as a "country of the Americas," veteran policy-watchers greeted this latest round of professions with both skepticism and caution (Daudelin and Dawson 2008: 7).

Nevertheless, there have been signs of a harder edge in the Harper government's approach to the region, with more concrete and focused steps to promote free trade and establish defence linkages in hemispheric affairs as well as a discernible closeness to American perspectives and objectives. "What Prime Minister Harper has done," write Randall and Dowding, "is to wed the softer power dimensions of the former Liberal government's approach to human security to a more practical economic and defence-oriented understanding of Canada's security agenda in Latin America" (2008: 39). The most concrete manifestation of this was its precipitous decision to negotiate free trade agreements with Peru and, more controversially, Colombia, despite widespread "disbelief and anger" on the part of labour movements, human rights organizations, opposition parties, and solidarity groups in Canada, Colombia, and elsewhere. This rapid and decisive move to institutionalize a privileged economic relationship with a country "known for having the worst human rights record in the hemisphere" (Healy and Katz 2008: 35) reflected several noteworthy tendencies of the Harper government: a disdain for the critics; an ideological conviction concerning the beneficent effects of economic liberalization; and, on the analysis of Healy and Katz, a particular sensitivity to and effective coordination with the policy objectives of the previous Bush administration in the United States. Similarly, Kirk and McKenna (2009) identify a clear convergence between the Harper government's policy approach towards Cuba and that of the previous Bush administration.

On development assistance, the prime minister's September 2007 address to the Council on Foreign Relations in New York was taken to signal that major changes in foreign aid policy were imminent ("A Conversation with Stephen Harper," 2007; Freeman 2007a). Among the changes that were speculated upon was a desire to significantly concentrate bilateral aid, with the professed intent to be among the five largest donors in each of CIDA's "core countries." Despite these and other intermittent professions of intent, however, there was no clear leadership or direction on most regular aid programming for several years after the government took office. At the Heiligendamm G8 Summit in 2007, the government restated its commitment to double aid to Africa between 2003–4 and 2008–9, while at the same time stressing that it would emphasize Latin America going forward (Freeman 2007b). Through an extraordinary accounting adjustment, however, it effectively reduced the value of this commitment

from CAD\$2.8 billion to CAD\$2.1 billion. In the meantime, CIDA officials, even in "core countries" like Tanzania or Ethiopia, were left to disburse still large and growing bilateral funds with no clear marching orders.[1]

In late February of 2009, Minister for International Cooperation Bev Oda revealed a new list of 20 countries in which the government committed to concentrate 80 per cent of its bilateral funding, which potentially represented a significant degree of concentration from the previous list of 25 core development partners announced in the context of the Martin government's 2005 *International Policy Statement* (IPS), in which "at least two thirds" of bilateral assistance was to be concentrated. The 2009 announcement therefore represented one of the clearest signals to date of shifting government priorities. Several features of the new list stood out (see Tomlinson 2009). First, the government formally erased the distinction drawn in the IPS between the 25 "core development partners" and a separate funding category for "failed and fragile states." Of the 20 new core countries, five (Afghanistan, Haiti, Colombia, West Bank/Gaza, and Sudan) had previously been designated recipients through the failed-and-fragile-state window. This suggested a more strategic, security-oriented approach to aid policy. Second, Africa was the big loser in terms of the new countries of concentration, with eight of fourteen African states on the previous list dropped from the new one.[2] Similarly, several strategic priorities in the Americas—specifically Colombia, Haiti, Peru, and the Caribbean Region—as well as the West Bank/Gaza were added. Finally, the net effect of these shifts was to reduce the concentration of bilateral aid resources in countries with the highest levels of poverty. Whereas 55 per cent of designated core development partners in the 2005 list were specified as "low" Human Development Index countries in the 2008 United Nations Development Programme's Human Development Report, only 37 per cent of core recipients in the 2009 list fall in this category (Tomlinson 2009).[3]

In terms of new directions in practice, the most striking development was the rapid emergence of Afghanistan as CIDA's largest bilateral program, accompanied by the extraordinary bureaucratic reorganization of the agency's large Afghanistan Task Force to be headed by a CIDA vice-president—unprecedented for a bilateral country program. Later, as Canadian combat forces withdrew from the country, Canadian aid also declined sharply (by 46 per cent in 2012), reflecting the degree to which routine aid programming had been distorted by the unsustainable political and strategic priority placed on Afghanistan. On a far smaller scale, but of symbolic importance, was the decision in October 2006 to create a new Office for Democratic Governance as a focal point for "developing and promoting innovative and effective democratic governance programming across the Canadian International Development Agency (CIDA)" as well as to be "of service to the whole of government and to Canadians involved in democratic governance programming" (CIDA website). This office was subsequently dismantled, with a plan to inaugurate a new Democracy Promotion Agency reflecting a broader governmental foreign policy emphasis on this theme—but this agency too remained on the drawing board. Taken together, these departures reflect a certain tendency towards the instrumentalization of the aid program in support of the government's primary political objectives, as well as the ongoing trend toward the "securitization" of aid (Simpson 2007). The mooting of a new emphasis on democracy promotion reflected a certain ideological orientation on the part of the government, but the failure to act on this emphasis indicated its relative indifference toward this normative priority.[4]

After winning a majority in 2011, however, the Harper government took a firmer (if no less abrupt) approach to engineering changes in the aid program. The most striking example of this, noted above, was the sudden decision to merge CIDA and DFAIT in the March 2013 Federal Budget, with the stated aim of enhancing coherence in Canadian foreign relations. When combined with the government's November 2013 *Global Markets Action Plan*, promising that "all diplomatic assets of the Government of Canada will be marshalled on behalf of the private sector in order to achieve the stated objectives within key foreign markets" (p. 12), the merger strongly reinforced the growing perception that the poverty alleviation priorities of the aid program were increasingly subordinated to the government's trade and investment development priorities (e.g., Swiss 2013). At the very least, the precipitous manner in which the merger was undertaken indicated a cavalier disregard for its disruptive effects on aid programming.

Finally concerning Africa, and notwithstanding the streamlined February 2009 list of core aid recipients, it could be argued that Canadian policy *practice* reflected a high level of continuity. As noted above, for example, the government reiterated Canada's commitment to double aid to Africa and maintained a relatively large and (until 2009) growing aid presence there, even if its "recalculation" of this commitment meant a net loss of $700 million to projected programming for the continent. Among its security engagements, it continued to be an active participant in and the largest donor to the peace process in Northern Uganda, and a relatively major contributor to the parallel humanitarian relief effort there (Bradbury et al. 2007; Wijeyaratne 2008). It also sustained and reiterated this country's relatively large (among Western donor states) commitment to Sudan's north–south peace process, and its contribution to the international effort to ameliorate humanitarian suffering in Darfur (Black 2010a). Canadian peacekeepers continued to deploy in small numbers to these operations, as well as to the critical United Nations Organization Mission in the Democratic Republic of the Congo (MONUC) operation in the DRC, and in January 2013, the government deployed a C-17 strategic airlift aircraft along with logistical support in aid of the French-led military intervention to roll back extremist forces in northern Mali.

Nevertheless, these efforts seemed more a product of inertia than intent—simply carrying forward the commitments already made, particularly to its preferred international peers in the G8. As former Progressive Conservative prime minister and foreign minister Joe Clark wrote, "The major Africa-related decision of the Harper government was not to abandon the commitments Canada had made before. That tells us more about a prudent regard for keeping Canada's word in the G-8 than it does about an attitude towards Africa" (Clark 2007: 3). The important Ugandan engagement became almost invisible publicly. The Darfur commitment continued to serve as an exemplar for the whole-of-government approach, but again, this simply sustained a policy direction set by its predecessor in a context of extensive public and Western governmental interest.[5]

More broadly, Joe Clark usefully applied three tests to the Harper government's approach to Africa: "What does the government say? Where does it spend? Where does it travel?" (Clark 2007: 6). He demonstrated that up to the end of 2007 at least, the Harper government had had almost nothing to say about Africa; that its foreign policy spending increases have been heavily concentrated in the Department of National Defence, where Africa is of least interest and priority as compared with foreign affairs and CIDA; and that its ministers' foreign visits have been heavily concentrated in Afghanistan and Pakistan, with only three short visits to Africa for conferences and, prior to Stephen Harper's trip to the Commonwealth Heads of Government Meeting (CHOGM) at the end of November 2007, none by either the prime minister or the foreign minister. This pattern was in sharp contrast to the ministerial travel of the Martin government. While there was a small flurry of visits in the first part of 2010 by Governor General Michaëlle Jean as well as by Foreign Minister Lawrence Cannon and International Trade Minister Peter Van Loan, these can be seen as motivated primarily by a late push to promote Canada's failed bid for a non-permanent seat on the UN Security Council.

In terms of economic interests and relations, the fact that Africa has become a major focus of Canadian extractive industry investment and activity seemed initially to have negligible policy impact. This was perhaps because Canadian extractive industry activity has been even more substantial in Latin America. An apparent change of tone in this regard was signalled by International Trade Minister Peter Van Loan who, in opening the Africa Rising: Entrepreneurship and Innovation Frontiers conference in Toronto in March 2011, asserted that "our businesses are well positioned to take on a leadership role in Africa's economic development in the years ahead." Since that time, there has been a modest increase in statements regarding and travel to Africa, marked by a discursive emphasis on "Africa rising," stressing emerging market opportunities and the beneficent role of the Canadian extractive sector while saying next to nothing about the continent's continuing challenges of poverty, inequality, and insecurity. Nevertheless, of nearly 50 countries the government had initiated bilateral free trade talks with by this time, only one—Morocco—was African (Foreign Affairs and International Trade Canada, 16 March 2011). This provides a clear indication of the relative priority it has placed on economic ties with the continent.

Diplomatically, the government has closed at least four missions in Africa, further reducing what is already the smallest number of African embassies among all G8 countries save Japan (CCA 2009; see also York 2009). More specifically, whereas in the past Canadian governments have been moved by

Commonwealth and trans-societal links to play active and significant roles in the challenges facing Zimbabwe, the current government has evinced little interest in becoming engaged in efforts to mitigate that country's ongoing travails.

In short, while on each of Latin America, foreign aid, and Africa there has been considerable continuity in practice, the pattern of attention, interest, and initiative clearly reflects a de-emphasis on Africa as compared not only with previous Liberal governments but with the Progressive Conservative governments of Brian Mulroney and John Diefenbaker (see Clark 2007). This has been reinforced by the changes to (and, since the high water mark of 2010, declining) spending on aid policy in Africa and elsewhere (see Brown 2012), and a considerably more forthright and single-minded pursuit of Canadian commercial advantage in our foreign policy towards the "South." How do we explain this pattern—and how durable is it likely to be? The answer to the second question depends, of course, on how one answers the first. In the remainder of this chapter, I will argue that more proximate explanations, though clearly important, need to be situated in the context of longer term trends in the influence of humane internationalism.

Idiosyncratic and Party-Political Explanations

One compelling explanation for this shift emphasizes the influence of Prime Minister Harper. As Kim Nossal noted some years ago (1994: 91), the influence of individuals—the "idiosyncratic variable"—is typically given relatively little weight in foreign policy analysis. Nossal argues, however, that in certain situations individual influence on policy change can be decisive. Such an idiosyncratic explanation might carry more weight in relation to the current Conservative government than most,

because the government and caucus have been so thoroughly controlled and disciplined by the prime minister and his inner circle (see also Kirk and McKenna 2009: 31–33; Martin 2010).

That Harper has little personal background on, or interest in, Africa is well established. In addition, however, as an economist and economic conservative, Harper has displayed an abiding antipathy towards "big government" and socially redistributive transfers (e.g. Johnson 2009). These convictions are sharply at odds with the "logic of solidarity" that Noel and Therien (1995: 552) have shown underpins relatively generous foreign aid programs. In short, Harper's intellectual views would incline him to be deeply skeptical concerning the usefulness of aid and, more broadly, of social solidarity as a basis for policy. Lacking any real conviction concerning the potential value of stable aid relationships in fostering poverty alleviation, Harper could be expected to see the *real* value of foreign aid, beyond humanitarian and charitable impulses, as lying in the leverage it provides to the promotion of Canadian security and economic interests. This would explain both the lack of interest in the more "routine" aid programs that predominate in Africa, and the tendency towards its deployment for more instrumental purposes, in Afghanistan, Haiti, Colombia, and Peru for example.

Accompanying this intellectual understanding is a strongly pro-Western, pro-NATO, and pro-American worldview (see also Salutin, 11 July 2008). There are various examples of this, including Canada's strongly pro-Israel stance in the Middle East, and its decision to concentrate scarce security resources in the high-cost, high-risk, NATO-led Afghan operation or the 2011 operation to displace Muammar al-Qadhdhafi in Libya, at the expense of UN-led African peacekeeping operations such as MONUC. Similarly, as noted above, the decision to aggressively pursue a free trade agreement with Colombia has been linked with a particular sensitivity to, and *de facto* coordination with, the Bush administration's hemispheric policy objectives (Healy and Katz 2008). This vigorously pro-Western worldview could be understood as reflecting the "rational utility maximizing" framework of the economic conservative, insofar as Canada's core economic and security interests are seen as indissolubly linked to those of the United States in particular, and the West in general. Similarly, a tilt towards Latin America *versus* Africa could be partly motivated by the prospects of a bigger potential "up side" to investment and trade promotion activities there (Government of Canada 2009: 4–5, 11–12).

A third influence is Harper's disdain for many of the "special interest groups" and "celebrity diplomats" that have been so prevalent in the social mobilization surrounding Africa and that were regular fixtures at G8 Summits in the 2000s (see Cooper 2008). Finally, a distinguishing feature of Harper's politics has been its hyper-partisanship. In this context, his government was at pains to distance itself from prominent policies that they have seen as linked to the Liberal "brand." Moreover, "it is no secret that the current government sees Africa as a Liberal idea" (Owen and Eaves 2007)—a function of the political mileage Prime Minister Chrétien got out of his orchestration of the Africa Action Plan (AAP) at the 2002 G8 Summit in Kananaskis and, more broadly, the Africa-focused ramifications of Lloyd Axworthy's human security agenda. Hence, Harper's emphasis on Latin America, whatever its substance and merits, is at least partly as an exercise in partisan rebranding.[6]

Here prime ministerial leadership shades into party politics. How much is this intense partisanship a function of Harper's leadership, and how much of dynamics within the "new" Conservative party? The conventional academic wisdom on political parties and Canadian foreign policy is that the impact of partisanship on policy outcomes is marginal and that there has been a high level of continuity in practice (see Bow and Black 2008–9). Indeed historically, the Canadian approach to Africa and the global

South featured a high level of bipartisan continuity between Liberal and Progressive Conservative governments (Clark 2007; Owen and Eaves 2007).

The new Conservatives seemed intent on breaking this historic pattern—although as noted above, the practical repercussions of this shift are less clear. What is particularly striking about the current government's cabinet and caucus is how little evidence one finds of the "humane internationalist" tendencies and the concomitant interest in Africa that were always vitally represented in previous Tory governments—a theme to which I will return in the next section. In short, if the "new direction" in Canadian foreign policy towards the developing world reflects prime ministerial preference, there has been negligible resistance to this preference from within Harper's cabinet and caucus. In this respect among others, the "new" Conservative government is clearly distinct from its Progressive Conservative predecessors, having gained a more economically and socially conservative cast through the incorporation of the Reform/Alliance tradition and having shed most of its traditional Red Tory element.[7]

The implications of this more unadulterated Conservatism on aid policy preferences specifically, and humane internationalist tendencies generally, can be extrapolated from the work of Noel, Therien, and Dallaire (2004). They found that "[t]he rhetoric of the left about aid typically evokes social justice, solidarity, and public commitments, whereas discourses on the right refer instead to dependency, inefficiency, and waste" (38). Their survey of polling data from the late 1990s and early 2000s shows a robust correlation between party preference and level of support for foreign aid, with Reform party supporters being least favourably disposed towards ODA followed by then-Progressive Conservative supporters, and NDP supporters being most favourable. The reborn Conservative party has, of course, (re)incorporated the most conservative party-political element on the Canadian landscape from the old Reform Party, mostly in positions of leadership, and has shed its more socially progressive faction. It should come as no surprise therefore that the party has supported a tilt away from an activist policy towards the world's poorest continent and, more broadly, the politics of global poverty.

A second salient change in the policy approach of the new Conservatives is the weakening of its collective attachment to the Commonwealth specifically, among other forms of more inclusive multilateralism, such as the UN, more generally. With regard to the former, Progressive Conservative governments and their supporters in English Canada were strongly attached to the Commonwealth connection and through it the British Crown. This attachment, in turn, predisposed these governments (and, more hesitantly, their Liberal counterparts) towards active engagement with Africa, since the single largest regional grouping of Commonwealth member-states was African (see Matthews 1976; Black 2010b). The new Conservative leadership evinces little of this traditional Conservative attachment. One key marker of this is that among the eight African countries dropped as core bilateral aid recipients in February 2009, half were long-standing Commonwealth "partners." In this regard, the "new" Conservatives' variant of Conservatism has grown steadily closer to the main currents of American conservative politics, and increasingly indifferent to its British/Commonwealth roots. Similarly, the Conservatives' earlier efforts to court Quebecois voters did not lead the government to show any special sensitivity toward the member states of *la Francophonie*, since the other African countries dropped as core recipients were founding members of this organization.[8]

In short, and consistent with the predominant ideological predisposition of the Right globally (Noel and Therien 2008), the new Conservative party has demonstrated little interest in global social justice, and the support for a generous foreign aid program and for African renewal that have characteristically

been bundled with it. While this party-political shift should not be seen to have *caused* the emerging reorientations this chapter focuses on, it has certainly enabled and reinforced them. Yet the new Conservatives have not attained and now consolidated power in a socio-political vacuum. Broader trends have created an enabling environment for the transitions they are engineering.

The Declining Influence of "Humane Internationalism"

The Conservatives' apparent lack of interest in engaging with Africa's challenges, juxtaposed with the high profile initiatives on Africa that marked the final years of the Chrétien era and the Martin interregnum, could be portrayed as a sharp departure from the more ethically oriented internationalist tradition in Canadian foreign policy. To attribute this shift exclusively to the role of Stephen Harper and/or the Conservative party, however, is both to overestimate the degree of change that has taken place and to underestimate the more persistent weakness of the public culture of humane internationalism as an influence on Canadian foreign policy.

As discussed above, the degree of change in Canada's foreign policy towards the global South has been smaller in practice than the government's rhetorical framing implies. Here, however, the point I wish to emphasize is that this reframing has taken place in a highly permissive domestic political environment, in which the influence of humane internationalism has been limited and arguably weakening for several decades (see Pratt 1989).

The essence of humane internationalism in relations with the Third World, as an element of rich countries' political culture, is defined by Pratt as:

> . . . an acceptance of an obligation to alleviate global poverty and to promote development in

the LDCs; a conviction that a more equitable world would be in their (developed countries') real long-term interests; and an assumption that the meeting of these international responsibilities is compatible with the maintenance of socially responsible national economic and social welfare policies (Pratt 1989: 16).

Writing two decades ago, Pratt argued that humane internationalism constituted a vital tradition in Canadian political culture, manifested not only in the hundreds of organizations that take up these issues in communities across the country (which he characterized as the **counter-consensus**), but in the all-party support they enjoyed in Parliament. Even then, however, he argued that this tradition had little influence on Canadian policies beyond development assistance—an influence that his subsequent writing argued was steadily waning (e.g., Pratt 2003). Given the influence of the "dominant class" embedded within the state and in the capital-owning sectors of society, as well as the eroding concern with the fortunes of other Canadians reflected in the erosion of welfare state policies, Pratt argued that it is only in particular moments, or "strategic conjunctures," that humane internationalism will significantly influence policy—and then only in ways that are difficult to sustain (Pratt 2003; see also Freeman 1997: 297).

In this light, while the Conservatives' reforms to foreign aid policies and institutions, and their diminished interest in Africa, underscore the limited policy influence of humane internationalism, this broader trend is neither new nor confined to the Conservatives and their supporters. Noel, Therien, and Dallaire, writing about public support for foreign aid in the latter years of the Chrétien era, noted that despite diffuse support for foreign aid among the electorate, this support was "a mile wide and an inch deep," and that "collectively Canadians appear profoundly ambivalent, if not incoherent,

about foreign aid" (Noel et al. 2004: 37). Kim Nossal, writing in the late 1990s, noted the marked decline in "good international citizenship" and "voluntarism" in Canadian foreign policy under the Chrétien government. He argued that these more genuinely internationalist tendencies had been effectively displaced by "pinchpenny diplomacy": "seeing how low Canadian expenditures in foreign affairs can be kept without forfeiting Canada's position in international forums like the G-8" (Nossal 1998–9: 104). Mark Neufeld, writing from a neo-Gramscian perspective, highlighted both the essentially contested character of "middlepowermanship" (or Pearsonian internationalism) and the rise to the fore of a "limitationist" variant of it amongst policy elites from the Mulroney era onwards (Neufeld 1995).

It was, after all, a combination of Progressive Conservative and especially Liberal governments that undertook the most severe cuts to foreign aid in the history of Canadian development assistance during the 1990s. As reported by David Morrison (1998: 413), ODA was hardest hit of all government programs in these years of austerity, declining by 33 per cent in real terms between 1988–89 and 1997–98, as compared with a 22 per cent decline in defence spending and an average 5 per cent decline in spending on all other programs. Africa was most affected by these cuts, with a decline in bilateral aid of 7.2 per cent between 1990 and 2000, compared with 3.5 per cent for the Americas and 5.3 per cent for Asia (de Masellis 2003: 78). This sustained budgetary bloodletting occurred with impunity from the Canadian electorate. Similarly, it was the Chrétien government that, after the mid-1990s, demonstrated a clear reluctance to deploy significant troop numbers to UN-led peacekeeping operations, despite the disastrous conflicts that continued to ravage a number of African countries (see for example Smillie 2006). And it was the government of Prime Minister Paul Martin, said to be "even more committed to Africa" than Chrétien (Brown and Jackson 2009: 19) that, despite the strongest fiscal position of any G8 government, firmly resisted pressure to commit to a timetable for increasing aid to 0.7 per cent of GDP in the context of the 2005 Gleneagles Summit and parallel "Year of Africa" ("Leaders" 2005).

From this vantage the Chrétien government's late surge of interest in Africa, leading to the entrenchment of African issues on the G8 agenda (see Fowler 2003; Black 2011), can be seen not only as the very personal campaign of a legacy-minded prime minister but as an effort to deploy a humane internationalist "cover" in an expansive budgetary environment, for the far less impressive record of the government through most of its tenure. It was also consistent with an emerging transnational hegemonic consensus on a "new deal" for Africa, linking G8 member-states with a select group of Africa's "new leaders" behind the New Partnership for Africa's Development (NEPAD). This African activism can be seen, in short, as the product of a propitious "strategic conjuncture."

In this broader context, the Conservatives' "turn away from" Africa appears considerably less idiosyncratic and extraordinary. Rather, it both reflects and has been enabled by the much longer-term weakness of humane internationalism as a vital influence on public policy.

The degree to which humane internationalism has been in a state of long-term erosion or decline is less clear. For one thing, it is doubtful how much force it has ever held beyond a relatively elite minority of the "attentive public." Don Munton (2002–3), in his influential assessment of the internationalist tradition in Canadian foreign policy, argued in the early years of the new millennium that internationalist proclivities in Canadian public opinion have waxed and waned, but have remained relatively consistent and robust over time. Certainly, humane internationalist flourishes, like the Harper government's rapid and generous response to the Haitian earthquake of early 2010 or its more recent advocacy of sexual equality rights, remain conspicuously popular. However, it is widely agreed in the literature on Canadian foreign policy that public opinion has only a limited, "parameter-setting" impact on the content and conduct of Canada's international relations. More telling is the possibility that the influence of humane internationalism has weakened at the level of political and social elites. Canadians have thrice re-elected a Conservative government with no discernible humane internationalist tradition in the terms elucidated by Pratt—now with a parliamentary majority. And whereas historically, Parliamentary opinion across party lines was firmly "ahead of" government policy in championing a more generous approach on international development issues (see Pratt 2003), it could be persuasively argued that there is less depth of knowledge or interest in development and African issues in recent Parliaments than there was a generation ago. Even this assessment must be qualified, however, by the fact that in 2008 a minority Parliament unanimously adopted Bill C-293, the "Better Aid Bill," legislating that poverty reduction must be the central focus of Canadian development assistance (Freeman 2008: 1). More broadly, the vitality of a variant of humane internationalism in Canadian society is manifested in the rapid growth of international development and global studies programs in Canadian universities, as well as the continued numbers of non-governmental groups and coalitions concerned with issues of global social justice and the countries and peoples of the "developing world."[9]

Despite these ambiguities, three specific points can be made in support of an argument that the humane internationalist tradition is in a state of relative decline, in ways that have enabled the policy transitions described above. First, public and political support for development assistance as a (if not *the*) key marker of humane internationalism in Canadian foreign policy has now repeatedly shown itself to be the softest of soft targets politically. As noted above, aid was disproportionately targeted in the austerity cuts of the 1990s. More recently, in the 2010 federal budget that began to come to grips with the fiscal implications of the global financial crisis of the late 2000s, aid was once again targeted disproportionately, as the only major portfolio to be "flatlined" and therefore effectively cut in real terms. The 2012 federal budget announced a further cut of 7.5 per cent over the next three years, while an additional $300 million in aid spending was simply "lapsed" in the 2012–13 budget year, compounding the *de facto* magnitude of the cuts (see Swiss 2013). Second, the "development constituency" in Canadian civil society, which Pratt famously characterized in the mid-1980s as a part of a substantial and deeply rooted counter-consensus concerning Canadian foreign policy (Pratt 1983–84), has similarly proven itself to be a soft political target, with the church-based KAIROS coalition being summarily de-funded in late 2009 after 35 years of support by CIDA, and the umbrella Canadian Council for International Cooperation (CCIC) being similarly defunded in 2010. Third, the more idealistic and activist youth constituency that has gravitated towards international development and global studies programs in universities and to civil society groups engaged with global social justice issues has only limited concern with, and involvement in, formal political debates in Canada on these or other issues, as manifested in their low rates of electoral and party-political participation.[10]

How might we explain the evident decline in the influence of humane internationalism over the past generation? At least four elements seem to have contributed, and would benefit from further research. The first relates to the weakness of support for foreign aid. Since its "invention" in the early years of the post-World War II era, development assistance has served as a key marker of a government's commitment to global poverty alleviation

and hence humane internationalism (see Lumsdaine 1993). Yet throughout its history, aid has been subject to critiques from both the left and the right concerning the mixed motives it has served (security, commercial, and class-based as well as ethical) and the charge that it is ineffectual or even counterproductive. These critiques have waxed and waned in popularity, but over time their impact on support for this modest form of global redistribution has arguably been highly corrosive. Certainly they have been deployed to undercut the arguments of proponents of more generous foreign aid policies in Canada, especially under a Conservative government that is predisposed towards skepticism. High profile critics such as Dambisa Moyo (2009) have achieved minor celebrity status, and the broad thrust of these critiques has been echoed within this country by a Parliamentary Senate Committee (2007) that in the past might have been expected to beat the drum for more and better aid, as previous Parliamentary committees have done.

It is not possible to engage in this chapter the complex debate over whether and how aid "works." Certainly, there is much to criticize in the aid practices of Canada and other donor states and agencies. At the same time, however, much of the criticism has been ahistorical and decontextualized (see for example Moorsom 2010, on Moyo). In particular, the notion that CIDA has "wasted" vast sums of money in Africa is contradicted both by the programs that *have* worked and by the limited and highly inconstant pattern of aid spending and priorities that has undermined the potential to achieve better results. For example, the 2007 Senate report, *Overcoming 40 Years of Failure*, noted that CIDA has spent CAD$12.8 billion in Africa since its inception in 1968. Spread over 30 years and a continent that now numbers a billion people, expenditures of this modest level can hardly be expected to have had a significant impact. The point here, however, is that oft-repeated attacks on the utility of Canadian aid and aid organizations, reinforced by the still-entrenched neo-liberal common sense that markets are the answer, has undercut the political basis for one of the principal expressions of postwar humane internationalism.

Second, the foundations of humane internationalism have arguably been undermined by the changing place and face of organized religion in Canadian society. This is a strikingly understudied dynamic within postwar Canadian foreign policy. In short, many of the most prominent scholarly and organizational proponents of the humane internationalist tradition were rooted in the then dominant mainstream Christian churches—Anglican, Mennonite, Presbyterian, United, Roman Catholic, and so on—with their strong (though not uncontested) **social gospel** traditions. These included, for example, scholars like Cranford Pratt, Robert Matthews, and Douglas Anglin, and organizations like Project Ploughshares, the Taskforce on the Churches and Corporate Responsibility, and Ten Days for World Development. Similarly, a number of the leading architects of the internationalist tradition in the practice of postwar Canadian foreign policy had strong religious influences in their upbringings. To cite only two prominent examples, both Lester Pearson and Escott Reid were the sons of ministers.

These religious traditions and organizations have been in a steady, long-term decline since the 1960s (see Valpy and Friesen 2010). Insofar as there has been growth in organized religion in Canada, it has come in more conservative faith traditions—for example, evangelical Christianity (a particularly strong influence within the Conservative caucus—see McDonald 2010 and Gecelovsky 2012), Roman Catholicism, Islam, Hinduism, and Sikhism. These are obviously rich, complex, and diverse faiths. For the most part however, they lack the social gospel orientation (or its equivalent) that was so instrumental in the rising salience of a solidaristic and humane internationalist tradition in the post-World

War II era. Whether this "mission-oriented" impulse was, on balance, normatively positive or negative is beside the broader point that its decline has reshaped the social foundations of Canada's role in the world.[11]

Third, the tradition of radical solidarity politics, or "radical internationalism" in Pratt's terms (1989: 13–22), has declined markedly in the post-Cold War era. This tradition was never a significant *direct* influence on policy, nor did it seek to be. Rather, as an anti-capitalist *cum* socialist orientation, it sought to champion and support more far-reaching, transformative change and typically viewed the Canadian government as being "on the wrong side." Still, it can be argued to have had a significant *indirect* influence on policy through its research, advocacy, and coalition-building efforts. Collectives like the Toronto Committee for the Liberation of Southern Africa (TCLSAC) and Centre d'Information et de Documentation sur le Mozambique et l'Afrique Australe (CIDMAA) were substantial influences in academic centres and labour and civil society politics, within and beyond Canada. They were particularly active in support of liberation movements in southern Africa. They had substantial analogues in Latin American solidarity work. They were led by intellectually powerful and compelling scholar-activists who had a very substantial influence on a generation of students and social movements.[12]

How might we think about the influence of this sub-tradition on the trajectory of humane internationalism? Through their critical analysis and advocacy, as well as their role in graduate training and their engagement with the media, they tended to push the centre of debate in more radical directions. While it was never realistic to imagine that Canadian government policy would be brought into line with the positions they championed, their positions provided an incentive for relatively reformist and progressive political and policy elites to move official approaches some distance toward more generous and solidaristic positions vis-à-vis developing countries—notably the frontline states of Southern Africa.

With the demise of apartheid, however, as well as the end of the Cold War, this radical internationalist tradition lost much of its impetus. While radical solidarity politics have not disappeared, they have become more diffuse and unfocused as the causes for which they struggled have ended, mostly in various degrees of disillusionment. This, too, can be said to have contributed to the declining salience of the broader humane internationalist tradition.

Finally, as noted above, there remains significant evidence of something akin to humane internationalism in Canadian society. This can be seen, for example, in the popularity of international development, global studies, and environmental studies programmes in Canadian universities, with their cosmopolitan sensibility; in the many non-governmental organizations that continue to proliferate despite an inhospitable funding climate; and in the periodic upsurges of mass street-level social movement activism, seen for example in the dramatic protests that accompanied the 2010 G20 Summit in Toronto and in the 2011 Occupy movement.

Many of the protagonists of these forms of engagement and activism are relatively youthful. However, rather than framing their engagement in terms of a "humane internationalist" orientation that sees the Canadian state and Canadian foreign policy as principal targets and vehicles of their normative agenda, those who engage in these forms of activism increasingly tend to do so under a rubric of "global citizenship." This flexible and fluid frame has become increasingly popular in both public and academic discussion; Rebecca Tiessen (2011) notes, for example, that it was advanced in the Martin government's 2005 *International Policy Statement*. Tiessen defines global citizenship as "a way of understanding the world in which an individual's *attitudes and behaviours* reflect a compassion and concern for the marginalized and/or poor and for the relationship

between poverty and wealth—within and between communities, countries and regions." This is very close, in analytical and normative terms, to the definition of humane internationalism offered by Pratt a generation ago, with one key difference. Whereas humane internationalism had as the focus of its advocacy *state* obligations and policies, global citizenship reflects an ethic of global cosmopolitanism, disarticulated from national states and oriented toward transnational mobilization and direct action by engaged *individuals*. The domestic political analogue of this orientation is the tendency of young Canadians, both politicized and depoliticized, to disengage from the formal political process and public policy debates, and the tendency to see state action as comparatively ineffectual and/or irrelevant.

The point here is less that the humane internationalist tradition has declined than that it has *changed* toward a more cosmopolitan and deterritorialized orientation. The result as it relates to Canadian foreign policy would, however, be similar: a Canadian state relatively unbound from the requirement to answer to those who think its policies toward developing countries should be more generous, responsive, and self-critical.

Conclusion

The purpose of this analysis is not to discount the importance of the Harper government's efforts to reorient Canadian priorities and policies toward the developing world, and Africa in particular. Nor is it to engage in a critical analysis of humane internationalism as an orientation for foreign policy. Rather, it is to suggest that to properly understand the changes that have been unfolding under the Harper government, these changes need to be situated in relation to the persistent weaknesses and changing foundations of the humane internationalist tradition. In short, there are important reasons to believe that this vital tradition has become significantly less important politically, and that where its normative impulse persists, it has been redirected away from a focus on the policies of the Canadian state, and toward "direct" or non-governmental action. The result is a much more permissive context for changes of government policy—sometimes quite important ones—in relation to what is sometimes called the "two-thirds world." This, I think, is regrettable and worth resisting. In this regard, there is a case to be made for more firmly reconnecting the motif of global citizenship to one of responsible, indeed humane, international citizenship.

Questions for Review

1. How has Canadian foreign policy towards the "developing world" in general, and Africa in particular, changed under the Harper government?

2. What is humane internationalism, and how has it influenced the conduct of Canadian foreign policy? How should it influence the conduct of Canadian foreign policy?

3. How do you explain the apparent shift in emphasis from Africa to Latin America under the Harper government?

4. Do you agree that humane internationalism is declining as an influence in Canadian political culture? What is your assessment of the explanations offered for this trend?

Suggested Readings

Akuffo, Edward. 2012. *Canadian Foreign Policy in Africa*. Aldershot, Hampshire: Ashgate.

Black, David. 2011. "Canada, the G8, and Africa: The Rise and Decline of a Hegemonic Project?" In Duane Bratt and Chris Kukucha, eds. *Canadian Foreign Policy: Classic Debates and New Ideas*. 2nd ed. Don Mills, ON: Oxford University Press.

Brown, Stephen, ed. 2012. *Struggling for Effectiveness: CIDA and Canadian Foreign Aid*. Montreal and Kingston: McGill-Queen's University Press.

Noel, Alain, Jean-Philippe Therien, and Sebastien Dallaire. 2004. "Divided Over Internationalism: The Canadian Public and Development Assistance." *Canadian Public Policy* 30, 1: 29–46.

Senate of Canada. 2007. *Overcoming 40 Years of Failure: A New Road Map for Sub-Saharan Africa*. Standing Committee on Foreign Affairs and International Trade.

MacLean, Sandra, David Black, and Timothy Shaw, eds. *A Decade of Human Security*. Aldershot, Hampshire: Ashgate.

Medhora, Rohinton, and Yiagadeesen Samy, eds. 2013. *Canada Among Nations 2013. Canada–Africa Relations: Looking Back, Looking Ahead*. Waterloo, ON: Centre for International Governance Innovation.

References

Bellamy, Alex J. 2009. *A Responsibility to Protect*. Cambridge: Polity.

Bibby, Reginald. 2009. "Restless Gods and Restless Youth: An Update on the Religious Situation in Canada." Presented at the annual meeting of the Canadian Sociological Association, Ottawa, May.

Black, David. 2006. "Canadian Aid to Africa: Assessing 'Reform,'" pp. 319–38 in Andrew Cooper and Dane Rowlands, eds. *Canada Among Nations 2006: Minorities and Priorities*. Montreal and Kingston: McGill-Queen's University Press.

———. 2010a. "Canada." In David Black and Paul D. Williams, eds. *The International Politics of Mass Atrocities: The Case of Darfur*. London: Routledge.

———. 2010b. "Canada and the Commonwealth: The Multilateral Politics of a 'Wasting Asset.'" In *Canadian Foreign Policy*, 16, 2: 61–77.

———. 2011. "Canada, the G8, and Africa: The Rise and Decline of a Hegemonic Project?" In Duane Bratt and Chris Kukucha, eds. *Canadian Foreign Policy: Classic Debates and New Ideas*. 2nd ed. Don Mills, ON: Oxford University Press.

Bow, Brian, and David Black. 2008–9. "Does politics stop at the water's edge in Canada? Party and partisanship in Canadian foreign policy." *International Journal*, 64, 1: 7–27.

Bradbury, Adrian, Alexa McDonough, and Paul Dewar. 2007. "Quiet diplomacy or lost opportunity?" *The Chronicle-Herald (Halifax)*, 18 November.

Brown, Chris, and Ted Jackson. 2009. "Could the Senate be Right? Should CIDA be Abolished?" Paper presented to the annual meeting of the Canadian Association for the Study of International Development (CASID). Carleton University, Ottawa, 27–29 May.

Brown, Stephen. 2008. "CIDA under the Gun." In Jean Daudelin and Daniel Schwanen, eds. *Canada Among Nations 2007: What Room for Manoeuvre?* Montreal and Kingston: McGill-Queen's University Press.

Brown, Stephen, ed. 2012. *Struggling for Effectiveness: CIDA and Canadian Foreign Aid*. Montreal and Kingston: McGill-Queen's University Press.

CBC News. 2002. "Harper plans to battle 'culture of defeatism' in Atlantic Canada." 30 May. Available at www.cbc.ca/news/story/2002/05/29/harper_atlntc020529.html.

CCA (Canadian Council on Africa). 2009. "Presentation to the Standing Committee of Foreign Affairs and International Development of the Parliament of Canada by the Canadian Council on Africa." Ottawa, 3 June.

CIDA (Canadian International Development Agency). 2009. "Canada Moves on Another Element of its Aid Effectiveness Agenda." 23 February.

Clark, Joe. 2007. "Is Africa falling off Canada's map? Remarks to the National Capital Branch of the Canadian Institute of International Affairs." 6 November.

Cooper, Andrew. 2008. *Celebrity Diplomacy*. Boulder, CO: Paradigm Publishers.

Council on Foreign Relations. 2007. "A Conversation with Stephen Harper." New York, 25 September. Available at http://www.cfr.org/climate-change/conversation-stephen-harper/p14255.

Daudelin, Jean, and Laura Dawson. 2008. "A New Chapter?" *Canadian Foreign Policy* 14, 3: 5–10.

de Masellis, L. 2003. "Statistics." *Canadian Development Report 2003: From Doha to Cancun, Development and the WTO*. Ottawa: The North–South Institute.

Foreign Affairs and International Trade Canada. 2011. Press Release: "Harper Government Committed to Opening New Markets in Africa/International Trade Minister Peter Van Loan highlights new opportunities for Canadian business in Africa's emerging markets." 16 March.

Fowler, Robert. 2003. "Canadian Leadership and the Kananaskis G8 Summit: Towards a less Self-Centred Canadian Foreign Policy." In David Carment et al., eds. *Canada Among Nations 2003: Coping with the American Colossus*. Don Mills, ON: Oxford University Press.

Freeman, Aaron. 2008. "Official Development Assistance Accountability Act—Plain Language Overview." Canadian Council for International Cooperation, October.

Freeman, Alan. 2007a. "Ottawa to re-evaluate foreign aid priorities." *The Globe and Mail*, 6 October.

———. 2007b. "Harper signals shift from Africa to Americas." *The Globe and Mail*, 8 June.

Freeman, Linda. 1997. *The Ambiguous Champion*. Toronto: University of Toronto Press.

Gecelovsky, Paul. 2012. "The Prime Minister and the Parable: Stephen Harper and Personal Responsibility Internationalism." In Claire Turenne Sjolander and Heather Smith, eds. *Canada in the World: Internationalism in Canadian Foreign Policy*. Don Mills, ON: Oxford University Press.

Government of Canada. 2009. *Canada and the Americas*. Available at http://publications.gc.ca/collections/collection_2009/maeci-dfait/FR5-41-1-2009E.pdf.

Government of Canada. 2013. *Global Markets Action Plan*. November. Available at http://international.gc.ca/global-markets-marches-mondiaux/assets/pdfs/plan-eng.pdf.

Grenier, Éric. 2010. "How Parliament would look if only youth voted." *The Globe and Mail*, 7 October.

Healy, Teresa, and Sheila Katz. 2008. "Big and Little Brother Bilateralism: Security, Prosperity, and Canada's Deal with Colombia." *Studies in Political Economy* 8: 35–60.

ICISS—International Commission on Intervention and State Sovereignty. 2001. *The Responsibility to Protect*. Ottawa: International Development Research Centre.

Johnson, William. 2009. "The Outsider: How Stephen Harper brought Canada to conservatism, and the Conservatives to crisis." *The Walrus*, March.

Kirk, John, and Peter McKenna. 2009. "Stephen Harper's Cuba Policy: From Autonomy to Americanization?" *Canadian Foreign Policy* 15, 1: 21–39.

"Leaders deaf to Live 8 call." 2005. *The Globe and Mail*, 4 July.

Lumsdaine, David H. 1993. *Moral Vision in International Politics: The Foreign Aid Regime, 1949–89*. Princeton, NJ: Princeton University Press.

Martin, Lawrence. 2009. "The resurgence of the Red Tory brand." *The Globe and Mail*, 13 August.

———. 2010. *Harperland: The Politics of Control*. Toronto: Viking Canada.

Matthews, Robert. 1976. "Canada and Anglophone Africa." In Peyton V. Lyon and Tareq Y. Ismael, eds. *Canada and the Third World*. Toronto: Macmillan of Canada.

McDonald, Marci. 2010. *The Armageddon Factor: The Rise of Christian Nationalism in Canada*. Toronto: Random House.

Moorsom, Toby. 2010. "The Zombies of Development Economics: Dambisa Moyo's Dead Aid and Fictional African Entrepreneurs." Paper presented to the annual meeting of the Canadian Association of African Studies, Carleton University.

Morrison, David. 1998. *Aid and Ebb Tide: A History of CIDA and Development Assistance*. Waterloo, ON: Wilfrid Laurier University Press.

Moyo, Dambisa. 2009. *Dead Aid*. New York: Farrar, Strauss and Giroux.

Munton, Don. 2002–3. "Whither Internationalism?" *International Journal* 58: 155–80.

Neufeld, Mark. 1995. "Hegemony and Foreign Policy Analysis: The Case of Canada as a Middle Power." *Studies in Political Economy* 48: 7–29.

Noel, Alain, and Jean-Philippe Therien. 1995. "From Domestic to International Justice: The Welfare State and Foreign Aid." *International Organization* 49, 3: 523–53.

———. 2008. *Left and Right in Global Politics*. Cambridge and New York: Cambridge University Press.

Noel, Alain, Jean-Philippe Therien, and Sebastien Dallaire. 2004. "Divided Over Internationalism: The Canadian Public and Development Assistance." *Canadian Public Policy* 30, 1: 29–46.

Nossal, Kim. 1994. *Rain Dancing: Sanctions in Canadian and Australian Foreign Policy*. Toronto: University of Toronto Press.

———. 1998–9. "Pinchpenny Diplomacy." *International Journal* 54, 1: 88–105.

Oda, Beverley J. 2009. "A New Effective Approach to Canadian Aid." Speech given at Munk Centre for International Studies, Toronto, May 20. Available at http://www.acdi-cida.gc.ca/acdi-cida/acdi-cida.nsf/eng/NAT-5208469-GYW.

Owen, Taylor, and David Eaves. 2007. "Africa is not a Liberal idea." *Embassy*, 3 October.

Pratt, Cranford. 1983–84. "Dominant Class Theory and Canadian Foreign Policy: The case of the Counter-Consensus," *International Journal* 39, 1: 99–135.

———. 1989. *Internationalism under Strain: The North–South Policies of Canada, the Netherlands, Norway, and Sweden*. Toronto: University of Toronto Press.

———. 2003. "Ethical values and Canadian foreign aid policies." *Canadian Journal of African Studies* 37, 1: 84–101.

Randall, Stephen, and Jillian Dowding. 2008. "Canada, Latin America, Colombia and the Evolving Policy Agenda." *Canadian Foreign Policy*, 14, 3: 2–46.

Salutin, Rick. 2008. "Harper Sahib at the G8." *The Globe and Mail*, 11 July.

Senate of Canada. 2007. *Overcoming 40 Years of Failure: A New Road Map for Sub-Saharan Africa*. Standing Committee on Foreign Affairs and International Trade.

Simpson, Erin. 2007. "From Inter-Dependence to Conflation: Security and Development in the Post-9/11 Era." *Canadian Journal of Development Studies* 28, 2: 263–75.

Smillie, Ian. 2006. "Whose Security? Innovation and Responsibility, Perception and Reality." In Sandra MacLean, David Black, and Timothy Shaw, eds. *A Decade of Human Security*. Aldershot, Hampshire: Ashgate.

Stairs, Denis. 2005. "Confusing the Innocent with Numbers and Categories: The International Policy Statement and the Concentration of Development Assistance." Calgary, AB: Canadian Defence and Foreign Affairs Institute Research Paper Series.

Swiss, Liam. 2013. "A Remarkable year for Canadian Foreign Aid." *Ottawa Citizen* (aid and development blog site), 27 December. Available at http://blogs.ottawacitizen.com/2013/12/27/a-remarkable-year-for-canadian-foreign-aid/.

Tiessen, Rebecca. 2011. "Global Subjects or Objects of Globalisation? The Promotion of Global Citizenship in Organisations Offering Sport for Development and Peace Programmes." *Third World Quarterly* 32, 4: 571–89.

Tomlinson, Brian. 2009. "A Review of CIDA's Countries of Priority. A CCIC Briefing Note." February.

Valpy, Michael, and Joe Friesen. 2010. "A Twist of Faith." *The Globe and Mail*, 11 December.

Wijeyaratne, Surendrini. 2008. *Promoting an Inclusive Peace: A Call to Strengthen Canada's Peacemaking Capacity. Part Four: Country Study: Peace and Justice in Northern Uganda*. Discussion Paper, Canadian Council for International Cooperation, November.

York, Geoffrey. 2009. "Banned Aid." *The Globe and Mail*, 30 May.

Zorbas, Eugenia. 2010. "Canadian Policy towards the Democratic Republic of Congo." Centre for International Policy Studies Policy Brief No. 8, University of Ottawa, May.

Notes

1. On the reduced value of Canada's commitment to double aid to Africa, the Harper government recalculated this commitment from the original target, based on the *projected* value of aid spending in 2003–4, to the smaller amount derived from *actual* bilateral expenditures that year. Despite this reduced target, however, bilateral programs in core African partners continued to grow significantly.

2. Benin, Burkina Faso, Cameroon, Kenya, Malawi, Niger, Rwanda, and Zambia.

3. In fact, Denis Stairs (2005) has shown that as an exercise in concentration, the IPS process was largely illusory.

4. This brief summary draws heavily on Brown 2008.

5. Indeed much of the Harper government's emphasis in the context of the 2009 G8 Summit in L'Aquila and again at the 2010 Summit it hosted was on persuading other governments to follow its example in *fulfilling* their commitments.

6. In fairness, Kim Nossal has noted the same tendency in his analysis of the Chrétien government's "pinchpenny diplomacy": "Both the Liberal party and its leader discovered that there was considerable electoral mileage in distancing themselves from Mulroney's foreign policies" (1998–9: 94). In some respects then, the "new" Conservative approach

is merely an extension and intensification of this tendency. This larger trend could be seen to reflect the increasing substitution of partisan posturing aimed at domestic audiences for genuine engagement with the hard dilemmas of world affairs.

7. One looks in vain among the current crop of Conservative MPs for voices comparable to those of, for example, Howard Greene, Flora MacDonald, David MacDonald, William Winegard, Walter McLean, Douglas Roche, Joe Clark, or indeed Brian Mulroney in their advocacy of Canadian activism on "humane internationalist" issues.

8. Though there has been some evidence of a concerted effort to reinforce Canada's historic attachment to Great Britain itself, for example, in the new Citizenship Guide or the large portrait of the Queen mounted in the lobby of the Pearson Building housing DFATD. This is distinct from Conservative attitudes toward the broadly multilateral post-colonial Commonwealth.

9. As a rough guide, there are now 17 member-institutions of the Canadian Consortium on University Programs in IDS, and these programs are among the fastest growing at leading research-oriented universities such as Dalhousie, Guelph, McGill, Ottawa, Queen's, and York.

10. Young voters are much more likely to support parties on the political left and centre, according to opinion polling, but only 37 per cent of them voted in the 2008 federal election, compared with an overall voter turnout of 59 per cent and 68 per cent participation rates among those aged 65 and older. Early evidence suggests that this pattern has held in 2011, despite unprecedented efforts to encourage youth voting. See Grenier 2010.

11. The Roman Catholic tradition obviously contains both progressive and conservative elements. However, it is evident that the more progressive element associated in foreign affairs with liberation theology has declined in influence, in Canada as elsewhere, while the conservative orientation has been reinforced by the principal sources of growth in Canadian Roman Catholicism, associated with recent immigrants. See Bibby 2009.

12. Key examples include John S. Saul, Dan O'Meara, Linda Freeman, and Otto Roesch.

Selected Bibliography

Adams, Michael. 2003. *Fire and Ice: The United States, Canada and the Myth of Converging Values*. Toronto: Penguin.

Brecher, Irving, ed. 1989. *Human Rights, Development, and Foreign Policy: Canadian Perspectives*. Halifax: Institute for Research on Public Policy.

Carment, David, and David Bercuson, eds. 2008. *The World in Canada: Diaspora, Demography, and Domestic Politics*. Montreal and Kingston: McGill-Queen's University Press.

Carty, Robert, and Virginia Smith. 1981. *Perpetuating Poverty: The Political Economy of Canada's Foreign Aid*. Toronto: Between the Lines.

Charlton, Mark W. 1992. *The Making of Canadian Food Aid Policy*. Montreal and Kingston: McGill-Queen's University Press.

Cooper, Andrew F., and Geoffrey Hayes, eds. 2000. *Worthwhile Initiatives? Canadian Mission-Oriented Diplomacy*. Toronto: Irwin.

Donaghy, Greg. 2003. "All God's Children: Lloyd Axworthy, Human Security and Canadian Foreign Policy, 1996–2000," *Canadian Foreign Policy* 10, 2 (Winter): 39–58.

Franceschet, Antonio, and W. Andy Knight. 2001. "International(ist) Citizenship: Canada and the International Criminal Court," *Canadian Foreign Policy* 8, 2 (Winter): 51–74.

Freeman, Linda. 1997. *The Ambiguous Champion: Canada and South Africa in the Trudeau and Mulroney Years*. Toronto: University of Toronto Press.

Gecelovsky, Paul, and T.A. Keenleyside. 1995. "Canada's International Human Rights Policy in Practice: Tiananmen Square," *International Journal* 50, 3 (Summer): 564–93.

Hampson, Fen Osler, and Dean F. Oliver. 1998. "Pulpit Diplomacy: A Critical Assessment of the Axworthy Doctrine," *International Journal* 58, 3 (Summer): 379–406.

Irwin, Rosalind, ed. 2001. *Ethics and Security in Canadian Foreign Policy*. Vancouver: UBC Press.

———. Forthcoming. *Balancing Ethics and Security in Canada's International Relations*. Vancouver: UBC Press.

Kelley, Ninette, and Michael Trebilcock. 1998. *Making of the Mosaic: A History of Canadian Immigration Policy*. Toronto: University of Toronto Press.

Knox, Paul. 1995. "Trade, Investment and Human Rights," *Canadian Foreign Policy* 3, 2 (Winter): 87–95.

Lui, Andrew. 2012. *Why Canada Cares: Human Rights and Foreign Policy in Theory and Practice*. Montreal and Kingston: McGill-Queen's University Press.

Macdonald, Douglas, and Heather A. Smith. 1999–2000. "Promises Made, Promises Broken: Questioning Canada's Commitments to Climate Change," *International Journal* 55, 1 (Winter): 107–24.

Matthews, Robert O., and Cranford Pratt, eds. 1988. *Human Rights in Canadian Foreign Policy*. Toronto: University of Toronto Press.

Morrison, David. 1998. *Aid and Ebb Tide: A History of CIDA and Canadian Development Assistance*. Waterloo, ON: Wilfrid Laurier University Press.

Nossal, Kim Richard. 1988. "Mixed Motives Revisited: Canada's Interest in Development Assistance," *Canadian Journal of Political Science* 21, 1 (March): 35–56.

——. 1998. "Pinchpenny Diplomacy: The Decline of Good International Citizenship in Canadian Foreign Policy," *International Journal* 54, 1 (Winter): 88–105.

Potter, Evan. 2009. *Branding Canada: Projecting Canada's Soft Power through Public Diplomacy*. Montreal and Kingston: McGill-Queen's University Press.

Pratt, Cranford, ed. 1996. *Canadian International Development Assistance Policies: An Appraisal*. Montreal and Kingston: McGill-Queen's University Press.

——. 1999. "Competing Rationales for Canadian Development Assistance," *International Journal* 54, 2 (Spring): 306–23.

——. 2000–1. "Ethical Values and Canadian Foreign Policy," *International Journal* 56, 1 (Winter): 37–53.

Scharfe, Sharon. 1996. *Complicity: Human Rights and Canadian Foreign Policy*. Montreal: Black Rose Books.

Simpson, Jeffrey, Mark Jaccard, and Nic Rivers. 2007. *Hot Air: Meeting Canada's Climate Change Challenge*. Toronto: McClelland and Stewart.

Spicer, Keith. 1966. *A Samaritan State? External Aid in Canada's Foreign Policy*. Toronto: University of Toronto Press.

Stairs, Denis. 1982. "The Political Culture of Canadian Foreign Policy," *Canadian Journal of Political Science* 15, 4 (December): 667–90.

——. 2003. "Myths, Morals, and Reality in Canadian Foreign Policy," *International Journal* 58, 2 (Spring): 239–56.

Stoffman, Daniel. 2002. *Who Gets In: What's Wrong with Canada's Immigration Program—and How to Fix It*. Toronto: Macfarlane Walter and Ross.

Appendix A
Key Terms in Canadian Foreign Policy

Aid effectiveness: The extent to which foreign aid is able to reach its goals in relation to the amount spent.

Alliance: A mechanism by which states formally or informally partner with other like-minded states, to balance against perceived threats in the international political system. Alliances arise out of fear and are designed to enhance the probability of a state's survival in our anarchic structure.

Anarchic: The defining and dominant characteristic of the structure of the international political system. The absence of an overarching central authority.

Arctic sovereignty: The assertion by Canada of full legal control over all of the Arctic lands and waters which it claims as Canadian territory. Canada was given until the end of 2013 to submit its Arctic maritime claims to the adjudicating body under the United Nations Convention on the Law of the Sea. The United States has long contested several of Canada's sovereignty claims, notably over the Northwest Passage, which the US considers to be an international strait.

Asymmetries in Canada–US relationship: Structural differences in size, power, and national perspectives (and relative awareness) of the bilateral relationship, and its place within each country's broader national priorities.

Ballistic missile defence: A complex system put in place to act as an atmospheric shield against intercontinental ballistic missiles (carrying nuclear or other weapons of mass destruction) launched by a hostile country. The effectiveness of such a defensive system, which remains very controversial, requires that it be capable of shooting down such missiles well before they have a chance to reach their targets.

Bilateralism: The political, economic, or social/cultural relations between two sovereign states.

Board of Internal Economy: The governing body of the House of Commons comprising the Speaker, who acts as chair, two members of the Privy Council (appointed to the board by the government), the Leader of the Opposition or his or her representative, and additional members appointed in numbers so that the total results in an overall equality of government and opposition representatives (apart from the Speaker). The Clerk of the House of Commons, who reports to the Speaker, serves as Secretary to the Board of Internal Economy. Decisions of the Board of Internal Economy are made on a non-partisan basis. All recognized parties (i.e., those holding at least 12 seats in the House) are given representation on the Board.

Buy American: An aspect of the 2008 American economic stimulus program that required recipients to use government funds to purchase American goods and services.

Capacity: An organization's ability to deliver on its mandate. In the case of the public sector, this typically means a government department's ability to anticipate and prepare for events and trends, generate policy advice, and provide services.

Civil society: The sum of institutions, organizations, and individuals located between the family, the state, and the market, in which people associate voluntarily to advance common interests.

Climate change: The phenomenon in which the climate of a place or region is changed if, over an extended period (typically decades or longer), a statistically significant change occurs in measurements of either the mean state or variability of the climate for that place or region.

Committee of Supply and Consideration of Supply: Until the reforms of 1968, the Committee of Supply referred to the House of Commons sitting as the Committee of the Whole to consider the government's proposed spending plans (see *expenditure estimates*). Since 1968, when the Committee of Supply was abolished, the estimates have been automatically referred to the appropriate House standing committee for review. The granting of supply means that this proposed spending in the form of estimates votes has been approved by a majority in the House.

Supply bills, otherwise known as *appropriation acts*, are based on the estimates or interim supply as adopted by the House. They authorize the government to withdraw from the Consolidated Revenue Fund amounts up to, but not exceeding, the amounts set out in the estimates for the purposes specified in the estimates votes. Supply bills give authority only for a single year. Like other legislation, supply bills must be passed by both the House and the Senate.

Complex neo-realist perspective: Focuses on the role of hegemonic powers in ensuring, defining, and extending international order in a system in which universal values remain secondary, in which a common security calculus and interest in balance provide no substitute, and in which leadership is required to transform convergent interests into stable order.

Confidence motion: Any votable motion regarding government legislation or other matter which is deemed to constitute a test of confidence in the government by a majority of the House of Commons. Budget motions are always considered matters of confidence. In other cases, the government may deem a motion to be a matter of confidence. Opposition members may introduce a motion of non-confidence in the government. In the case of a tie vote, the Speaker, by tradition, will cast the deciding vote in favour of allowing the government to continue. If the government loses a confidence vote, it will normally go to the Governor General to request a dissolution of the House and a general election.

Continentalism: Defined by Heather Smith and Claire Turenne Sjolander, an "approach based on the assumption that the destiny of Canada (both the society and the state) is inextricably tied to that of the United States, and that it is in Canada's national interest to align itself openly with its southern neighbour to guarantee its access to the American market and keep a functional and friendly relationship with Washington."

Continuum of policy relationships: The idea that all policy relationships are fluid and need to be considered on a continuum moving from traditional concepts of the state as a unitary and rational actor to policy environments in which numerous state, sectoral, and societal actors are decentralized, often operating in a transgovernmental setting.

Counter-consensus: A term coined by Cranford Pratt in 1983–84 to refer to the "substantial number of

internationally minded public interest groups which are in serious opposition to many components of the present consensus which underlies Canadian foreign policy" on broadly humanitarian grounds. Broadly inclusive of many groups within "civil society," including faith-based groups, labour unions, solidarity groups, and many non-governmental organizations.

Crisis of overaccumulation: A moment of acute imbalance in the process of accumulation characterized by the exhaustion of profitable investment opportunities for extant capital; spectacularly manifested in speculative bubbles.

Crisis stability: A condition in which nuclear-armed adversaries are not tempted in a military crisis to escalate to nuclear warfare, primarily because most or all of the strategic weapons are secure from surprise attack.

Critical discourse analysis: A tool for examining social practices and political orders that are generally accepted as natural. The (re)telling of these practices, orders, or what are commonly perceived as truths serves to (re)construct them as so-called common sense. Embedded in all forms of language, cultural and ideological assumptions presented within these discourses often occur below the level of conscious awareness.

Democratic deficits: Aspects of government processes and institutions in democratic political systems which are considered to be undemocratic or insufficiently democratic and which require actions to promote democratization.

Democratization: The perfect democratic system does not exist; rather, democratic political development is a continuous process. In established democracies, democratization refers to efforts and measures to make government institutions and public policy processes more democratic. This may involve making them more representative and inclusive as well as more transparent and accountable to the electorate.

Denial: A policy approach that involves denying that there is a problem; used by a government when a problem is either too great to be solved or the government is unwilling or unable to solve the problem.

Diaspora: A group of people who live outside the area in which they had lived for a long time or in which their ancestors lived.

Discourse: A way of thinking that is revealed through language. Discourses affect our views on all things; they frame or define the ways we speak about issues. Discourses are seen to define the reality of the way things are.

Distribution of capabilities: Variation in quantitative and qualitative resources developed, possessed, and deployed among states and other actors.

Doha Round: WTO multilateral trade negotiations, formally known as the Doha Development Agenda, were launched in 2001 with the aim of ensuring that trade served the needs of development. As of early 2014, the negotiations remained stalled, although a substantial outcome remained within reach on agriculture and trade in goods and services.

Economic nationalism: Is a set of policies that emphasize domestic control of the economy, labour, and capital formation, even if this requires the imposition of tariffs and other restrictions on the movement of labour, goods, and capital. Economic nationalists oppose free trade and most aspects of globalization.

Emerging energy superpower: A term coined by Stephen Harper to refer to Canada's rich energy reserves (oil, natural gas, uranium, coal, hydroelectric power, etc.) and efforts to sell them to different markets.

Entrepreneurial Canadian: The contemporary Canadian identity: hyper-individualistic, and, at one and the same time, an effect and instrument of neo-liberalism.

Ethical oil: A term coined by Ezra Levant to argue that the environmental degradation of the oil sands has been greatly exaggerated by environmentalists. In addition, if Americans do not want oil sands products, the alternative is to import oil from unstable and/or undemocratic countries such as Saudi Arabia, Venezuela, Sudan, Nigeria, or Russia.

Exhortation: A policy approach wherein a government strongly encourages action by other actors (i.e., states, companies, NGOs, IGOs, etc.).

Expenditure estimates: As part of the federal budget cycle for each fiscal year (which begins on April 1), government departments and agencies are required to table in Parliament estimates documents providing details of proposed and forecast expenditures for the next fiscal year. The main estimates must be tabled by March 1. These estimates

by department and agency, grouped into a series of votes, are referred to the relevant House of Commons standing committees for study. Committees have a limited time in which to report back to the House. If they do not do so by May 31, the estimates are automatically deemed to have been adopted. (There are two exceptions involving the Leader of the Opposition: he or she may introduce a motion to allow a committee to extend the period of review for up to 10 sitting days; he or she may introduce a motion to refer the main estimates of no more than two departments or agencies to Committees of the Whole. These estimates are then deemed withdrawn from the committees to which they were referred. The Committees of the Whole must deal with the estimates by May 31 and may consider them for a period of not more than four hours each.) A committee may vote to reduce or eliminate an expenditure item in the estimates. However, it may not propose to add to any expenditure. New spending is an exclusive prerogative of the Crown (in practice, the Cabinet), requiring what is called a *royal recommendation*.

Expropriation: A mandatory legal transfer of the title (i.e., ownership) of property or the outright physical seizure of a foreign investor's assets. Normally, the expropriation benefits and is authorized by host states. *Indirect expropriation*, in contrast, refers to a process where there is no formal transfer of title or seizure but measures taken by the host state have had the equivalent effect of (or are tantamount to) interfering with the foreign investor's property rights or reducing the benefit they derive from their investment. It is these indirect measures that have been the subject of a number of disputes, especially if they involve host state regulations.

Foreign direct investment: Usually defined by economic organizations as investment that allows the investor from one country (host or capital exporting country) to have a significant influence in the managing of an enterprise operating outside the investor's own country. This is usually set at ownership of 10 per cent or more of the ordinary shares or voting power. Investors may acquire this influence by establishing a new firm (a "greenfield" investment) in a foreign (host or capital-importing) country or by acquiring an interest in an existing foreign firm (i.e., via a takeover or merger).

Foreign policy: The specific international goals of government officials and the values and mechanisms used to pursue these objectives.

Foreign policy machinery: The instruments whereby Canadian governments are able to make foreign policy decisions and conduct Canada's international relations—chiefly through the Department of Foreign Affairs, Trade and Development, and, with respect to military aspects, the Department of National Defence. Other government departments and central agencies may also be involved in the consideration of international issues—for example, the Department of the Environment on climate change; the Privy Council Office (PCO), which serves the Cabinet as a whole; or the Prime Minister's Office (PMO).

Foreign policy review: An official process by which governments evaluate their foreign policy systematically, usually using some form of public engagement.

Free trade agreement: An arrangement among two or more nations whereby they agree to remove substantially all tariff and non-tariff barriers to trade between them, while each maintains its differing schedule of tariff and other barriers applying to all other nations. GATT Article XXIV provides a framework of rules for the negotiation of free trade areas such as the Canada–US FTA.

Functionalism (*also,* **functional principle, functional middlepowermanship**)**:** A post-World War II doctrine enunciated by the King government stating that non-great powers (like Canada) could make their most significant difference in world affairs when engaged in issues in which they had pre-existing expertise and active participation.

G8: An annual meeting of the heads of government of the seven most industrialized countries in the world (Canada, France, Germany, Italy, Japan, United Kingdom, and the United States; joined by Russia in 1998).

G20: An annual meeting of the heads of government of the 20 largest economies in the world (Argentina, Australia, Brazil, Canada, China, European Union, France, Germany, India, Indonesia, Italy, Japan, Mexico, Russia, Saudi Arabia, South Africa, South Korea, Turkey, United Kingdom, and the United States).

Gender: Gender is the range of physical, biological, mental, and behavioural characteristics pertaining to and differentiating between masculinity and femininity. Depending on the context, the term may refer to biological sex (i.e., the state of being male or female), sex-based social structures (including gender roles and other social roles), or gender identity.

General Agreement on Tariffs and Trade: A multilateral treaty which delineates rules for international trade, originally subscribed to by 23 countries and now a major component of the WTO. The primary objective of GATT is to liberalize world trade and place it on a secure basis, thereby contributing to global economic growth and development.

Generation: A group of individuals, most of whom are the same approximate age, having similar ideas, problems, attitudes, and so forth.

Global citizenship: Defined by Rebecca Tiessen as "a way of understanding the world in which an individual's attitudes and behaviours reflect a compassion and concern for the marginalized and/or poor and for the relationship between poverty and wealth—within and between communities, countries, and regions."

Global governance: The process by which a range of actors, including states and international organizations, try to manage global affairs.

Golden age of Canadian foreign policy: The period generally understood to have begun shortly after the end of the Second World War and lasting until the late 1950s.

Gray Lecture: A speech by Secretary of State for External Affairs Louis St Laurent in January 1947 that outlined Canada's five international priorities: national unity, political liberty, the promotion of the rule of law in international affairs, global humanitarianism, and international activism.

Great power: Those states with significantly more combined capabilities or resources in the international political system. The number of great powers in the international political system results in different configurations: unipolar, bipolar, or multipolar.

Green paper: A formal statement of federal government thinking and proposals in a particular policy area. In contrast to a *white paper* (see below), a green paper is used to invite parliamentary and public comment prior to the government's making firm policy decisions.

Hegemony: A theoretical concept with both realist and critical meanings. As derived from the work of Italian Marxist Antonio Gramsci, and popularized by Canadian political economist Robert Cox, it is a form of dominance of one social group over another—that is, the ruling class over all other classes—featuring a high level of consent on the part of the ruled. The ideas of the ruling class come to be seen as the norm; they are seen as universal ideologies, or a common sense, perceived to benefit everyone while in reality principally benefiting the ruling class. Cox has extended this thinking to the transnational level, arguing that transnational "hegemonic orders" are pursued and sustained by transnational coalitions of elite groups.

Helpful fixer: A depiction of Canada's middle-power role in which it helps to solve some of the world's problems.

Homeland: The original country, region, or community from which a diaspora migrated.

Host state: The current place of residence for a diaspora group or immigrant community.

Human rights: Those rights to which a person is entitled simply because he or she is a human being. Human rights can also be described as being equal (the same for all human beings), inalienable (they cannot be transferred or repudiated, as one does not stop being human), and universal (applicable to everybody).

Human security: This is a concept that transcends traditional military-centred notions of security to include additional threats. The United Nations Human Development report identifies seven aspects: economic security, food security, health security, environmental security, personal security, community security, and political security.

Humane internationalism: An element of Canadian (and some other countries') political culture(s) defined by Cranford Pratt to mean "an acceptance of an obligation to alleviate global poverty and to promote development in the Less Developed Countries; a conviction that a more equitable world would be in [developed countries'] real long-term interests; and an assumption that the meeting of these international responsibilities is compatible with the maintenance of socially responsible national economic and social welfare policies."

Hyper-masculinization: As militaries require a particular ideology of manliness in order to function properly, soldiers are trained in ways that promote masculinized values: encouragement of violence and aggression, and individual conformity to military discipline, as well as an emphasis on homophobia and heterosexism.

Idiosyncratic variable: The extent or degree to which a prime minister seeks to distinguish the international behaviour of his or her government from other administrations; the way a prime minister uses the power of the office to achieve his or her goals.

Immigrant: A person who comes to live permanently in a foreign country that is not her or his country of birth.

Imperialism: Identification with the British Empire, a common feature of politics in self-governing dominions like Australia and Canada.

Independent foreign policy: An approach that seeks to differentiate Canadian foreign policy from that of the United States. The simplest—and most common—way of thinking about this is in terms of Canada's ability to pursue policies that the US opposes, without being forced to back down. But we could also think about independence in terms of autonomy more generally, in the context of a much wider variety of indirect pressures and structural constraints.

Indigenous peoples: A term that is used in reference to the natives of a region or a group of people that are considered to be the original inhabitants.

Intellectual legacy: An intellectual contribution transferred from the past, often reinforcing dominant perspectives or challenging core assumptions in a field or discipline.

Intermestic: Term coined to capture the progressive interweaving of domestic and international factors in policy-making.

International democracy assistance: Includes all forms of support given by a country, group of countries, international organization, or non-state actors (non-governmental organizations, private individuals) aiming to support the development and consolidation of democratic processes and institutions around the world. Attempts to provide outside democracy assistance can be especially controversial in countries with authoritarian governments that reject such assistance as illegitimate intervention in the country's internal affairs.

International Law of the Sea: A branch of international law, largely codified in the United Nations Convention on the Law of the Sea, which is concerned with territorial waters, sea lanes, and ocean resources.

International order: The political, economic, or social situation in the world at a particular time and the effect that this has on relationships between different countries.

International relations theory: Theories are abstractions that use simplifying assumptions to try to explain and understand international relations in different ways. Within each theoretical school there are many different spin-offs. Some of the more common theories include realism, liberalism, Marxism, constructivism, and feminism.

Intervention: Any interference in the affairs of others, especially by one in the affairs of another.

Isolationism: A desire to keep one's country out of international politics, particularly by avoiding entanglements in alliances or international agreements.

Legitimation: Although democratic election confers legitimacy on governments in a democracy, it is also important for governments to maintain democratic legitimacy for their actions in between elections. The legitimation function is to ensure that government decisions respect established democratic norms and are perceived by the voting public to do so.

Liaison committee: A permanent committee composed of the chairs of all the standing committees and the House chairs of standing joint committees. It has the authority to disperse funds to standing committees from the money allocated to it for that purpose by the Board of Internal Economy. It usually meets *in camera* to deliberate on administrative and financial matters relating to standing committees. The committee has occasionally carried out studies on the effectiveness of the committees of the House.

Liberal internationalism: An approach to foreign policy and international relations that favours the pursuit of liberal democratic goals such as human rights, democratic freedoms, mutually beneficial economic advancement, and fewer barriers between countries. This outward-looking approach tends to seek a rules-based rather than power-based international order and has been a bedrock of Canadian foreign policy.

Mandate letter: A two- or three-page note given to a minister at the outset of his or her tenure, outlining the issues and areas of importance on which the minister is to focus. The letter is written by the Privy Council Office, after consultation with the Prime Minister's Office and the deputy minister(s) affected by the change.

Message event proposal: A plan clearly outlining the speaking objective, the desired headline and sound bite, the speaking backdrop, the ideal event photograph, and the speaker's wardrobe. Prior to speaking in public, any member of the Harper government or the civil service is required to submit a message event proposal for approval.

Middle power: A country, like Canada, that is not as big as the great powers but is more important than small powers. This position allowed Canada to make a significant contribution to international affairs but without the influence or obligations of the great powers.

Militarism: Militarism is the belief in maintaining a strong military force to carry out the needs of the people. It is most prevalent in imperialist and expansionist nations.

Millennium Development Goals: Eight goals adopted in 2000 by all member states of the United Nations and two dozen international organizations. The goals set targets to be achieved by 2015 in several areas, including extreme poverty and hunger, primary education, gender equality and women's empowerment, child mortality, maternal health, and environmental sustainability.

Minimalism: A policy approach that involves taking the absolute lowest amount of action in addressing a problem.

Minority government: A situation which occurs following an election when no single political party enjoys a majority of members in the House of Commons. Since, in the Canadian parliamentary system, governments must maintain the "confidence" of the House, minority governments must obtain the support of enough opposition members to be able to pass legislation and to avoid defeat on any vote that is considered to be a matter of confidence.

Multilateralism: Working with other countries, usually in international organizations, to achieve foreign policy goals.

Multilateral trade agreements: Agreements resulting from multilateral trade negotiations conducted under the auspices of the member states of the World Trade Organization (WTO) established in 1995, and before that its predecessor, the General Agreement on Trade and Tariffs (GATT) signed in 1947. The Uruguay Round of the GATT, named after the country where negotiations began, took place from 1986 until 1994.

National identity: The depiction of a country as a whole, encompassing its culture, traditions, language, and politics. National identity is a person's identity and sense of belonging to one country or to one nation, a feeling that person shares with a group of people.

National treatment: Refers to a principle of non-discrimination central to trade and investment agreement. For investment, national treatment is the commitment by host states to treat foreign investors and foreign investments no less favourably than domestic investors and investments.

Nationalists: People who advocate an independent foreign policy for Canada in its relations with the United States. Measures should be taken to prevent economic dependence on the United States and to distance itself from American security preoccupations.

Neo-liberalism: A policy paradigm, influential since the 1970s, premised on a reduced role for the state and an enhanced one for markets. Protection of property rights and value of money are key goals. Domestically, the paradigm recommends spending cuts to ensure balanced budgets; deregulation and privatization; and, internationally, capital mobility and free trade.

Non-governmental organization: Any non-profit, voluntary citizens' group that is organized on a local, national, or international level.

Non-nuclear counterforce coercion: The ability of a nuclear weapon state to use conventionally armed weapon systems only to find and destroy an adversary's nuclear weapons, air and missile defences, strategic nuclear command and control, and political and military leadership in a campaign of steady attrition over hours or days, to a point where the adversary government feels it is on the verge of losing its ability to retaliate toward any coherent political goal as well as becoming ever more vulnerable to a completely disarming nuclear first strike.

Non-tariff barriers or measures: Government measures or policies other than tariffs that restrict or distort international trade. Examples include import quotas, discriminatory government procurement practices, and measures to protect intellectual property. Such measures became relatively more conspicuous impediments to trade as tariffs were reduced during the period since World War II. Many are now constrained by the rules of the WTO.

North American Free Trade Agreement: A trade agreement involving Canada, the United States, and Mexico, which entered into force on January 1, 1994, successor to the 1989 Canada–United States Free Trade Agreement.

Official Development Assistance (ODA): Aid provided by donor countries primarily to promote economic development and welfare in developing countries. Contributions from individuals, foundations, or private corporations do not count as ODA, nor do military assistance or export credits meant primarily to promote the sale of goods from the donor country.

Omnibus bill: A single piece of legislation introduced by the federal government that is very lengthy and that combines changes to many different laws as well as additions to Canadian law in a number of different policy areas. For example, Bill C-60 in 2013 was designed to give legal effect to the full range of policy decisions announced in the 2013 federal budget. Omnibus bills tend to be controversial and are criticized by opposition members of Parliament on the grounds that they prevent adequate scrutiny of all of their elements and force members to vote either for the entire package or against it, making it impossible to support some elements but reject others.

Order-in-Council: In Canada, a federal government order-in-council is a notice of an administrative decision issued by the Governor General, the representative of the Crown in Canada. The council referred to is the Privy Council, which advises the Crown. In reality, these orders originate with the Canadian Cabinet—the prime minister and other ministers of the Crown—and are given formal approval by the Governor General. Many orders-in-council are notices of appointments. Many others are regulations or legislative orders in relation to and authorized by existing acts of Parliament.

Pacifism: An opposition on moral, legal, emotional, and/or ideological grounds to the use of force (war in particular) to settle political differences.

Paradoxical actor: An actor who operates in a way that is logically inconsistent or self-contradictory—e.g., a governmental actor that is constitutionally very powerful but has very little actual power.

Parliamentary consent: In Canada, approval by majority vote of the members of the House of Commons and of the Senate.

Parliamentary reform: Primarily changes to the rules, procedures, and operations of the House of Commons and the Senate. Generally these involve changes to the standing orders or rules governing all aspects of how the House and Senate and their respective committees conduct their business. However wider behavioural aspects of reform, such as relaxing party discipline, improving civility in Question Period, or having more formal House debates on foreign policy, cannot be accomplished through rule changes alone.

Parliamentary supremacy: The doctrine that, as a rule of constitutional law, Parliament is the supreme law-making body both in terms of the power to enact laws and the power to amend or repeal laws, subject only to any constitutional limits on its fields of jurisdiction.

Party discipline: The degree to which members of Parliament are controlled by the party leaders and ordered to vote in accordance with the leaders' wishes. Party discipline in the Canadian House of Commons is generally considered to be the strongest of any parliament modelled on that of Westminster in Great Britain.

Peace enforcement operation: A collective use of force, under international law and Chapter VII of the United Nations Charter, to address a threat to international peace and security.

Peacekeeping: The deployment of a United Nations force involving military, police personnel, and civilians to preserve the peace.

Pearsonian internationalism: The prioritization of middle power and multilateral principles.

Performance legitimacy: Public support for a policy based on general or qualified perceptions of positive or broadly desired outcomes.

Plenipotentiary power: The authority possessed by the office of the prime minister to negotiate, sign, and withdraw from international agreements on behalf of Canada.

Policy coherence: The degree to which a donor country's different policies are complementary, rather than working at cross-purposes (for instance, when a country's trade or defence policies contradict its aid policies).

Power of the purse: In Canada, the requirement that all spending by the federal government must be approved by Parliament. The budget is always considered to be a matter of confidence in the House of Commons. The Senate must also pass all financial legislation; however, money bills can only be introduced in the House.

Principal powers: These have three characteristics: 1) they stand at the top of the international status ranking, collectively possessing decisive capability, and are differentiated from lower-ranking powers by both objective and subjective criteria; 2) they act as principals in their international activities and associations, rather than as agents for other states or groupings or as mediators between principals; and 3) they have a principal role in establishing, specifying, and enforcing international order.

Private members' bills: These are bills drawn up by backbench members of Parliament as distinct from government-sponsored legislation. More such bills are prepared during a typical parliamentary session than can reasonably be considered by the House; hence a lottery system has been devised to determine which bills will be given time to be introduced and debated in the House. Such bills may draw attention to important matters, though it is rare for them to proceed through all stages in both chambers and be passed into law.

Public diplomacy: The use of diplomatic and other foreign policy resources to promote positive communication with foreign publics such as by establishing with other countries dialogues that are designed to inform and influence public opinion in those countries. This can be done through a range of instruments and methods from personal contacts and media relations to cultural and educational exchanges, and increasingly by making use of electronic-based social media.

Quiet diplomacy: An approach in which the parties tacitly agree to negotiate in confidence, refrain from criticizing one another in public, and, more generally, avoid "politicizing" the issues by talking to the media or stirring up the general public. In the Canada–US context, it is often used more broadly to refer to a general commitment to seek influence in Washington, by going out of one's way to work closely with the US.

Realism: A school of international relations that is state-centric and prioritizes national interest and security, rather than ideals, social reconstructions, or ethics.

Realm: Connotes a sphere or domain that is both a political space and an ideational construct of political identity and community that goes beyond the state as it is usually defined in international relations.

Region: A geographic area that is marked by common characteristics.

Representation: The representation function is a crucial aspect in all electoral democracies. In Canada's electoral system, based on single-member constituencies, each member of Parliament is called upon to represent the interests and concerns of his or her electoral district in the House of Commons.

Responsibility to protect: The idea that governments have a responsibility to protect their own citizens. The concept also justifies humanitarian intervention based on political oppression or the removal of democratically elected governments.

Role or positional variable: The constitutional powers of the office, or the range of authority that any person occupying the position would possess. The four constitutional powers of the office of the prime minister, of relevance to our discussion regarding foreign policy-making, are: 1) power of appointment; 2) design of administrative structures; 3) design of decision-making processes; and 4) plenipotentiary authority.

Satellite: Canada is a peripheral-dependent/satellite country that moved seamlessly from existing as a British colonial dependency to being pulled into the orbit of the American empire.

Second reading: In Canada, all legislation in the form of bills (given a "C" number if introduced in the House and an "S" number if introduced in the Senate) must pass three readings in both the House of Commons and the Senate. First reading publishes the bill. Second reading is normally the most crucial stage since, if a bill passes second reading, it is given agreement in principle. The bill may then be referred to and studied by the relevant parliamentary committee(s) where amendments that do not substantially change the intent of the bill may be considered and voted on. Third reading is the report stage at which any final amendments may be considered. If a bill passes third reading in one chamber it will then be sent to the other chamber for similar consideration.

Security: The military ability of a state to either defend itself against the military actions of other states or to enforce its will on another state.

Social gospel: A movement and tradition originating in some North American Protestant churches in the early twentieth century that sought to apply the principles of the Gospel to society's most pressing problems and thereby promote social justice and progressivism.

Sovereign debt crisis: Occurs when a sovereign state is unable or unwilling to make regular payments on the money that it owes private banks, international financial institutions, and other bond holders. Frequently this requires the country to be bailed out by some combination of the International Monetary Fund, richer states, and regional organizations.

Sovereignty: There are three main elements of sovereignty: a defined territory, an existing governance system, and a people within the defined territory.

Special relationship: Canadian and American political leaders have long maintained that there is a special relationship between the two countries, but there is room for debate about whether that is so, and what it might mean. Usually the phrase is used to refer to the idea that the US treats Canada differently than other, similar allies or trade partners, in being more attentive to Canadian concerns and/or more forgiving of Canadian provocations.

Speech from the Throne: An address to Parliament in which the government sets out a general outline of its priorities at the start of each new session of Parliament following an election or a prorogation of the previous session. In Canada's constitutional monarchy the Speech is read in the Senate chamber by the Head of State (normally the Governor General as the representative of the Crown).

Standing committees: These are the regular ongoing committees of the House of Commons and the Senate as set out in the Standing Orders of the House of Commons and the Rules of the Senate. Special committees of each chamber, or special joint committees composed of members from both chambers, are created for a limited purpose and duration. Standing committees may be changed or eliminated through changes to the House Standing Orders or the Rules of the Senate. Memberships on standing committees are also subject to change according to the procedures set out in the House Standing Orders or the Rules of the Senate.

State-owned enterprises (SOEs): Legal entities that are created by a government in order to partake in commercial activities on the government's behalf. They can be either wholly or partially owned by a government. Concerns have been raised about whether SOEs operate as independent businesses or as instruments of the state. This has political, economic, and national security considerations.

Statutory enactment: The process of approving legislation and giving it the force of law. In Canada, this means that legislation must have passed the House of Commons and the Senate, received royal assent (a formality but required in a constitutional monarchy), and been proclaimed as having entered into force.

Strategic culture: A set of ideas (concepts, metaphors, images, symbols, etc.) shared by a given community, forming a coherent and persistent whole and helping to shape the group's attitude toward the use of force and the role of military institutions. Because a strategic culture is formed primarily by historical experience, it tends to remain stable over time.

Tariff: A duty (or tax) levied upon goods transported from one customs area to another. Tariffs raise the prices of imported goods, thus making them less competitive within the market of the importing country. After nearly eight decades of trade negotiation, tariffs are now less important measures of protection than they used to be. The tariff rate is the rate at which imported goods are taxed.

Tied aid: Development assistance that must be used to purchase goods and services from the donor country. This usually adds an estimated 15 to 30 per cent of the cost, since the same goods and services are usually available elsewhere for a lower price.

Trade policy: Focuses on the exchange of goods and services and the negotiation and implementation of international (and domestic) trade commitments that often fluctuate between protectionism and liberalization.

Transgovernmental relations: Formal and informal relations and processes between legislative, executive, regulatory, and judicial officials outside formal diplomatic channels.

Transnational historic bloc: A neo-Gramscian concept for a configuration of social forces across different states that share material interests and ideological perspectives.

Undersecretary of state: In Canada, the highest ranking executives in the bureaucracy are typically referred to as deputy ministers, but in the Department of External Affairs, the DM is still often referred to as the undersecretary of state, because his "minister" was the secretary of state for external affairs. The use of the elegant term still persists, but most government documents now refer to a deputy minister of external affairs and a deputy minister of international trade.

United Nations: An international governmental organization, created in 1945, that has 192 member states.

Value chains: Physically distributed processes of product design, production, and distribution by which "bits of value (are) added in many different locations."

Values: Values can be divided into psycho-social and politico-operational. Psycho-social values include environmental protection, democracy, social equity, human rights, and so on. Politico-operational values include the rule of law, multilateralism, security, foreign aid, and so forth.

White paper: In Canada, a formal statement of federal government policy used to set out the government's approach, decisions, commitments, and objectives in a particular area of public policy.

Whole-of-government: A deliberate design for the participation and coordinated cooperation of all relevant government departments and agencies in the development and execution of particular government policies and programs. In the case of foreign policy, a whole-of-government approach requires active collaboration among all government entities with responsibilities that involve Canada's international relations.

World Trade Organization: The successor agreement to the GATT, encompassing not only the GATT but also the General Agreement on Trade in Services (GATS), the Agreement on Trade-Related Aspects of Intellectual Property Rights (TRIPS), the Understanding on Rules and Procedures Governing the Settlement of Disputes (DSU), and a series of ancillary agreements providing more detailed rules, as well as members' schedules of specific commitments related to trade in goods, agriculture, and services. The WTO provides the governing structure for the administration, expansion, and interpretation of the constituent agreements.

Appendix B
Key Dates in Canadian Foreign Policy

BEFORE CONFEDERATION

19 June 1812   Start of the War of 1812 between the United Kingdom/Canada and the United States.

24 December 1814   Treaty of Ghent is signed, ending the War of 1812.

29 April 1817   Rush-Bagot Treaty is signed, restricting warships in the Great Lakes.

20 October 1818   Anglo-American Convention of 1818 is signed, fixing the British North America and United States border along the forty-ninth parallel from the Lake of the Woods to the Rocky Mountains.

6 June 1854   Reciprocity Treaty is signed, creating a free trade agreement between British North America and the United States.

17 March 1866   Reciprocity Treaty is abrogated by the United States in retaliation for British support of the Confederacy.

April–June 1866   Fenian raids take place from the United States into British North America.

THE IMPERIAL ERA

1 July 1867   The British North America Act unifies the British colonies in Ontario (Canada West), Québec (Canada East), New Brunswick, and Nova Scotia into the Dominion of Canada.

23 June 1870   Rupert's Land and the North-Western Territory Order is signed, transferring these lands from the Hudson's Bay Company to Canada.

15 July 1870   Manitoba enters Confederation.

8 May 1871   Treaty of Washington is signed with the United States, laying out fishing and trading rights on the Great Lakes.

20 July 1871   British Columbia enters Confederation.

1 July 1873   Prince Edward Island enters Confederation.

11 May 1880   Canada appoints its first diplomat, Sir Alexander Galt, as high commissioner to Britain.

9 October 1880   Arctic islands ceded to Canada by Britain.

12 July 1882   Canada appoints a commissioner to France.

18 March 1885   Northwest Rebellion begins, under the leadership of Louis Riel.

4 October 1899   Canadian troops depart to assist the British in the Boer War.

1 September 1905   Alberta and Saskatchewan enter Confederation.

1908   Ontario opens a commercial office in Britain.

11 January 1909   Boundary Waters Treaty signed with the United States, creating the International Joint Commission (IJC).

19 May 1909   Department of External Affairs is created.

4 May 1910   Royal Canadian Navy is created.

1911   Québec opens a commercial office in Britain.

21 September 1911   Prime Minister Wilfrid Laurier is defeated and replaced by Robert Borden in a federal election. As a result, the negotiated reciprocity (free trade) agreement with the United States does not get ratified.

FIRST WORLD WAR (1914–1918)

4 August 1914   Great War begins: Britain declares war on Germany, and all parts of the Empire (including Canada) are automatically at war.

3 October 1914   First Canadian troops leave for Europe.

2 March 1917   First meeting of the Imperial War Cabinet in London.

9 April 1917   Canadian troops fight as a distinct national corps as the Battle of Vimy Ridge begins.

29 August 1917   Conscription (military draft) becomes law.

17 December 1917   Federal election, with conscription as the major election issue, sees Borden re-elected, but without any seats in francophone Canada.

1 April 1918   Anti-conscription riot in Québec City results in four deaths.

1 October 1918   Canadian forces arrive in northern Russia to assist in civil war against the Bolsheviks.

11 November 1918   Armistice brings First World War to an end.

INTERWAR PERIOD (1919–1939)

28 June 1919   Canada signs the Versailles Peace Treaty, officially ending the First World War.

10 January 1920   The League of Nations is established, with Canada as a founding member.

2 March 1923   Canada signs its first international treaty, the Halibut Treaty with the United States.

1 July 1923   Chinese Immigration Act is proclaimed, barring Chinese from entering Canada.

14 September 1926   Mackenzie King wins a majority government in the federal election after the "King-Byng affair."

October 1926   Agreement is reached at the Imperial Conference (27 October–19 November) to grant Canada and the other dominions full autonomy in domestic and international affairs.

18 February 1927   Canada opens its first diplomatic mission, a legation in Washington.

18 September 1929   Canada opens a diplomatic mission in Japan.

29 October 1929   New York Stock Exchange crash; beginning of the Great Depression.

17 June 1930   US adopts the Smoot–Hawley tariff on imported goods; most of the rest of world also raises tariffs.

11 December 1931   Statute of Westminster gives Canada and the other dominions full sovereignty.

21 July 1932   Imperial Economic Conference creates preferential trade within the British Empire.

1935   The "Riddell Affair": Canada's representative to the League of Nations, against the wishes of the King government, pushes for economic sanctions against Italy for its invasion of Ethiopia.

29 June 1937   Mackenzie King, visiting Germany, meets Hitler.

18 August 1938   United States President Franklin D. Roosevelt visits Queen's University and issues the "Kingston Dispensation."

SECOND WORLD WAR (1939–1945)

1 September 1939   Nazi Germany attacks Poland, starting the Second World War.

10 September 1939   Canada declares war on Germany, seven days after Britain.

10 June 1940   Canada declares war on Italy.

18 August 1940   Ogdensburg Agreement on defence is signed with the United States.

7 December 1941   Japan attacks Pearl Harbor; United States declares war on Japan; Canada declares war on Japan.

25 December 1941   Allied troops in Hong Kong surrender after being overrun by Japanese forces; 2,000 Canadians are killed or captured.

1 January 1942   In Washington, 26 states (including Canada) sign the Declaration by United Nations pledging cooperation in the defeat of Germany and Japan.

27 April 1942   Referendum on conscription reveals strong support in English Canada and equally strong rejection in Québec.

19 August 1942   Dieppe Raid, Canada's first European battle of the war, leads to 3,367 Canadian casualties (killed, wounded, or taken prisoner).

9 July 1943   Mackenzie King sets forth in the House of Commons the "functional principle" for representation in international institutions.

10 July 1943   The Italian campaign begins: British, Canadian, and American troops land in Sicily.

1–16 May 1944   First Commonwealth Prime Ministers' Meeting in London.

6 June 1944   D-Day: American, British, and Canadian troops land at Normandy.

1–22 July 1944   Canada participates in the UN Monetary and Financial Conference at Bretton Woods, New Hampshire.

23 November 1944   Mackenzie King decides to implement conscription.

8 May 1945   Germany surrenders, ending the war in Europe.

26 June 1945   UN Charter is signed in San Francisco.

15 August 1945   Japan surrenders, ending the war in the Pacific.

THE COLD WAR ERA (1945–1990)

5 September 1945   Igor Gouzenko, a clerk at the Soviet embassy in Ottawa, defects with evidence of a Soviet spy ring.

13 January 1947   Louis St Laurent, Canada's Secretary of State for External Affairs, delivers the Gray Lecture, which outlines the principles of Canadian foreign policy.

12 March 1947   US President Harry Truman announces the policy of containment (Truman Doctrine) that becomes the basic principle of US policy towards the USSR.

5 June 1947   The Marshall Plan of US economic aid to Europe is announced.

9 July 1947   Brooke Claxton presents *Canada's Defence*, the first white paper on defence.

30 October 1947   The General Agreement on Tariffs and Trade (GATT) is signed at Geneva.

24 June 1948   Blockade of Berlin by Soviet Union begins (ends 12 May 1949).

31 March 1949   Newfoundland enters Confederation.

4 April 1949   North Atlantic Treaty, creating NATO, is signed in Washington.

23 May 1949   Federal Republic of Germany (West Germany) established; German Democratic Republic (East Germany) created 7 October 1949.

1 July 1949   Apartheid is instituted by the ruling Nationalist Party of South Africa.

1 October 1949   People's Republic of China, led by Mao Zedong, is proclaimed; Kuomintang (Nationalist) government under Chiang Kai-shek moves to Taiwan.

13 January 1950   Commonwealth foreign ministers meet in Colombo, Ceylon (now Sri Lanka), to establish the Colombo Plan for aid in South and Southeast Asia.

25 June 1950   Korean War begins; Canada sends destroyers and ground combat troops to serve with US-led UN force.

26 November 1950   China enters the Korean War and drives UN forces back.

31 January 1951   Canada deploys air and ground forces to Europe as part of its UN commitment.

18 April 1951   European Coal and Steel Community is formed.

18 February 1952   Greece and Turkey join NATO.

27 July 1953   Armistice agreement ends the Korean War.

30 June 1954   Canada approves the installation of the Distant Early Warning (DEW) radar line.

21 July 1954   French colonial rule in Indochina ends; Vietnam is divided into North and South at the seventeenth parallel.

6 May 1955   West Germany joins NATO; Warsaw Pact is formed in response (14 May 1955).

26 July 1956   Egypt nationalizes the Suez Canal, precipitating the Suez crisis.

29 October 1956   Egypt, French, and Israeli forces attack Egypt; Lester Pearson proposes a UN peacekeeping force to intervene.

1 November 1956   Soviet Union invades Hungary.

25 March 1957   Treaty of Rome establishes the European Economic Community (EEC).

26 August 1957   Soviet Union launches first intercontinental ballistic missile (ICBM).

4 October 1957   Soviet Union launches Sputnik, the world's first satellite.

14 October 1957   Pearson is awarded the Nobel Peace Prize.

12 May 1958   NORAD agreement between Canada and the United States is signed.

1 January 1959   Fidel Castro's revolution overthrows the Cuban government.

20 February 1959   Prime Minister John Diefenbaker announces the cancellation of the Avro Arrow, a Canadian-developed jet fighter.

26 June 1959   The St. Lawrence Seaway, a joint Canada–United States project, opens.

29 March 1960   Defence Minister George R. Pearkes announces that Canadian troops in Europe will acquire US "Honest John" rocket systems equipped with nuclear warheads.

22 June 1960   Jean Lesage and the Liberals win the Québec election; the "Quiet Revolution" begins.

17 January 1961   Columbia River Treaty on the use and control of the Columbia River basin is signed between Canada and the United States.

2 February 1961   First Sino-Canadian grain sale announced.

8–17 March 1961   South Africa leaves the Commonwealth, during a prime ministers' meeting in London, over the issue of apartheid.

12 June 1961   Canada acquires US F-101B (Voodoo) fighter aircraft, which are nuclear equipped, for North American defence.

12 August 1961   Construction of the Berlin Wall begins.

16–28 October 1962   Cuban Missile Crisis.

7 August 1964   Following a naval incident in the Gulf of Tonkin, US Congress passes Gulf of Tonkin resolution, giving President Lyndon Johnson the power to deploy US forces for the defence of allies (primarily in Vietnam).

16 January 1965   Canada–US Automotive Agreement (Auto Pact) signed by Pearson and Johnson.

27 February 1965   Québec–France entente in education.

8 March 1965   US combat troops are sent to Vietnam.

2 April 1965   Pearson gives a speech at Temple University where, in part, he criticizes US military activity in Vietnam.

12 April 1965   Paul Gérin-Lajoie, Quebec minister of education, gives a speech articulating doctrine of Quebec's competence in international affairs.

1 July 1966   France withdraws from integrated military command of NATO, but remains a signatory to the North Atlantic Treaty.

1 May 1967   The Nigerian civil war begins as the province of Biafra declares secession.

5–10 June 1967   Arab–Israeli war (Six-Day War).

30 June 1967   Kennedy Round of GATT negotiations is signed.

24 July 1967   French President Charles de Gaulle gives his "Vive le Québec libre" speech in Montréal, which appears to endorse the Québec separatist movement.

30 January 1968   The Tet offensive is launched by communist forces in Vietnam.

5 February 1968   Québec, on invitation from Gabon, participates in the Conference of Educational Ministers from francophone countries; Canada suspends diplomatic relations with Gabon on 4 March 1968.

29 May 1968   Pierre Trudeau, in his "Canada and the World" statement, announces that Canada will move to recognize the People's Republic of China and will support its membership in the United Nations.

1 July 1968   The Nuclear Non-Proliferation Treaty is signed.

20 August 1968   Soviet and Warsaw Pact forces invade Czechoslovakia.

25 August 1969 First *Manhattan* voyage through the Northwest Passage.

19 September 1969 Defence Minister Léo Cadieux announces that Canada's NATO forces in Europe will be cut in half and that Canada will disengage from its nuclear role in Europe.

20 March 1970 Agence de coopération culturelle et technique (ACCT) is created.

1 April 1970 Second *Manhattan* voyage; Arctic Waters Pollution Prevention Act introduced (8 April).

25 June 1970 Trudeau government releases its foreign policy white paper: *Foreign Policy for Canadians.*

5 October 1970 The Front de Libération du Québec (FLQ) kidnaps British trade commissioner James Cross, starting the October Crisis; Quebec Cabinet minister Pierre Laporte is later kidnapped and murdered; War Measures Act is invoked 16 October.

13 October 1970 Canada and China establish diplomatic relations.

14–22 January 1971 Commonwealth Heads of Government Meeting is held in Singapore, first CHOGM held outside Britain.

24 April 1971 Defence Minister Donald S. Macdonald tables a defence white paper, *Defence in the 70s.*

15 August 1971 "Nixon Shock": US government imposes economic measures to stem balance of payments deficit, devalues the dollar, and abandons fixed exchange rates.

12 November 1971 Gray Report recommending a foreign investment screening agency is leaked.

16 December 1971 East Pakistan declares independence as Bangladesh, following a civil war and war between India and Pakistan.

22 January 1972 EEC is expanded to include Britain, Denmark, Ireland, and Norway (Norwegians reject membership in a national referendum, September 1972).

21 February 1972 Nixon visits China.

15 April 1972 Great Lakes Water Quality Agreement between Canada and the United States is signed in Ottawa.

27 January 1973 Vietnam ceasefire agreement signed in Paris; last US troops leave Vietnam (29 March); last US prisoners of war released (1 April).

11 September 1973 Coup d'état in Chile; President Salvador Allende commits suicide and is replaced by General Augusto Pinochet.

12 September 1973 Tokyo Round of GATT negotiations begins (concludes April 1979).

6–24 October 1973 Arab–Israeli war (Yom Kippur War).

19 October 1973 Oil embargo imposed by OPEC against the United States, later extended to Japan and Europe; oil prices rise rapidly.

18 May 1974 India, using Canadian technology, explodes a nuclear device; Canada ends all nuclear cooperation.

1 August 1975 At the first Conference on Security and Co-operation in Europe (CSCE), the final agreements (the Helsinki Accords) are signed by 35 countries, including Canada.

15–17 November 1975 The leaders of France, the United States, the United Kingdom, West Germany, Italy, and Japan meet at Rambouillet, France, at an ad hoc summit called the

Group of Six; Canada attends the 1976 summit in Puerto Rico, making it the more formal Group of Seven.

16 June 1976   The Soweto uprising results in the worst racial violence in South Africa's history.

15 November 1976   The Parti Québécois, under René Lévesque, wins the Québec election.

8–15 June 1977   The Gleneagles Declaration against apartheid in sport is agreed to by Commonwealth leaders in London.

3 November 1977   French President Valéry Giscard d'Estaing publicly affirms his support for self-determination in Québec.

September 1978   Camp David Accords mark Egypt's recognition of Israel, and peace negotiations begin between the two countries.

25 December 1978   Vietnam invades Cambodia; thousands of "boat people" begin to flee Vietnam.

16 January 1979   Iranian revolution; Shah Mohammad Reza Pahlavi abdicates and leaves Iran, replaced by the Ayatollah Ruhollah Khomeini.

5 June 1979   Prime Minister Joe Clark announces that the government will proceed to move its embassy from Tel Aviv to Jerusalem; decision is reversed on 29 October, pending the settlement of the status of Jerusalem.

4 November 1979   US embassy personnel in Tehran are seized as "hostages" by Iran; Canada's Ambassador to Iran, Ken Taylor, secretly helps six members of the US embassy escape disguised as Canadians; remaining Americans released January 1981.

24 December 1979   Soviet Union invades Afghanistan.

22 April 1980   Canada joins boycott of 1980 Moscow Olympics.

20 May 1980   Québec referendum on sovereignty association is defeated.

22 September 1980   Iraq invades Iran, beginning an eight-year war.

7 June 1981   Israeli aircraft bomb a nuclear reactor in Iraq.

20–21 June 1981   Canada hosts the G7 summit at Montebello, Québec.

22–23 October 1981   International Meeting on Cooperation and Development, Cancún, Mexico, is chaired by Pierre Trudeau and Mexican President José López Portillo.

12 January 1982   Department of External Affairs is reorganized to incorporate trade and commerce.

2 April 1982   Argentina invades the Falkland Islands.

17 April 1982   Elizabeth II signs Constitution Act in Ottawa.

1 September 1983   Korean Air Lines Flight 007 shot down by Soviet fighters.

25 October 1983   United States invades Grenada.

27 October 1983   Trudeau launches his "peace initiative."

5 November 1984   External Affairs Minister Joe Clark arrives in Ethiopia and announces an emergency food aid program to address Ethiopia's famine.

17–18 March 1985   The "Shamrock Summit" between Mulroney and Reagan is held in Québec City.

14 May 1985   Government green paper on foreign policy, *Competitiveness and Security,* is published.

23 June 1985	Air India bombing is linked to Sikhs in British Columbia.
10 July 1985	French intelligence agents bomb the Greenpeace ship *Rainbow Warrior* in Auckland harbour, killing one person.
21 July 1985	South Africa government imposes a state of emergency.
1 October 1985	Canada formally requests free trade negotiations with the United States.
22 October 1985	At the Commonwealth Heads of Government Meeting in Nassau, the Mulroney government states that it is committed to keeping the issue of economic sanctions against South Africa on the agenda, despite British opposition.
17–19 February 1986	First Francophone summit, Paris.
25 September 1986	Uruguay Round of GATT negotiations launched (completed December 1993).
1 May 1987	The House of Commons Standing Committee on External Affairs and International Trade releases *For Whose Benefit?*, a report evaluating official Canadian development assistance efforts.
5 June 1987	Defence white paper, *Challenge and Commitment: A Defence Policy for Canada,* is released.
2–4 September 1987	Canada hosts the francophone summit for the first time at Québec City.
2 January 1988	The Canada–US Free Trade Agreement is signed by Brian Mulroney and Ronald Reagan.
19–21 June 1988	Canada hosts G7 summit at Toronto.
29 September 1988	UN peacekeepers win Nobel Peace Prize.
4 June 1989	Tiananmen Square massacre occurs in Beijing.
6–7 November 1989	First meeting of the Asia-Pacific Economic Cooperation (APEC) forum is held at Canberra.
9 November 1989	Berlin Wall is breached.
13 November 1989	Canada joins the Organization of American States.
20 December 1989	United States invades Panama.
11 February 1990	South African black leader Nelson Mandela is released from prison.
2 August 1990	Iraq invades Kuwait.
3 October 1990	Reunification of Germany.
19–21 November 1990	Second CSCE summit at Paris marks the formal end of the Cold War.

POST-COLD WAR ERA (1990–2001)

29 November 1990	The United Nations Security Council authorizes military action if Iraq does not withdraw from Kuwait by 15 January 1991.
16 January 1991	A US-led coalition launches air attacks on Iraq.
24 February 1991	A US-led coalition launches a ground offensive against Iraq.
27 February 1991	Iraq withdraws from Kuwait; the military offensive against Iraq ends.
13 March 1991	Mulroney and George H.W. Bush sign the first Canada–US Air Quality Accord, committing both countries to reducing the emissions causing acid rain.

25 June 1991	Croatia declares independence; civil war breaks out in Yugoslavia.
30 September 1991	Coup d'état in Haiti overthrows President Jean-Bertrand Aristide.
25 December 1991	Soviet Union formally dissolves.
21 February 1992	UN Security Council approves the deployment of a peacekeeping force for Yugoslavia (UNPROFOR).
24 April 1992	UN Security Council creates the first peacekeeping mission for Somalia (UNOSOM).
3–14 June 1992	UN Conference on Environment and Development (the Earth Summit) is held in Rio de Janeiro.
8 December 1992	US troops land in Somalia, beginning Operation Restore Hope; Canadian troops arrive 14–15 December.
17 December 1992	NAFTA is signed by Mexico, Canada, and the United States.
26 February 1993	Islamists detonate a truck bomb in the North Tower of the World Trade Center, New York.
March 1993	The Somalia affair: members of the Canadian Forces kill Somali civilians caught stealing from Canadian base in Belet Huen.
14–25 June 1993	World Conference on Human Rights is held in Vienna.
1 November 1993	Maastricht Treaty comes into force; the European Community becomes the European Union.
5 November 1993	External Affairs and International Trade Canada is renamed the Department of Foreign Affairs and International Trade (DFAIT).
11 January 1994	Canadian General Roméo Dallaire sends a fax to the United Nations regarding the need for more troops in Rwanda.
22 February 1994	Jean Chrétien's first budget includes a decrease in official development assistance spending.
6 April 1994	A plane carrying the presidents of Rwanda and Burundi is shot down; ethnic violence and genocide erupt in Rwanda, leaving 800,000 dead in 100 days.
26–28 April 1994	Nelson Mandela is elected the first black president of South Africa.
19 September 1994	After a US invasion embarks for Haiti, the military agrees to restore Aristide to power.
1 December 1994	National Defence Minister David Collenette releases *1994 Defence White Paper.*
1 January 1995	World Trade Organization is inaugurated.
7 February 1995	Foreign policy white paper, *Canada in the World,* is released.
9 March 1995	"Turbot War:" Canada arrests the Spanish fishing vessel *Estai* in international waters for overfishing.
15–17 June 1995	Canada hosts the G7 summit in Halifax.
4–15 September 1995	Fourth UN World Conference on Women is held in Beijing.
30 October 1995	Second referendum on Québec sovereignty is narrowly defeated.
21 November 1995	Dayton General Framework Agreement for Peace in Bosnia and Herzegovina is negotiated.

14 May 1997	International currency speculators assault Thai baht, marking the start of the Asian financial crisis.
20–22 June 1997	At the G7 summit in Denver, Russia joins as a full member (making the G7 the G8).
1 July 1997	Hong Kong returns to Chinese sovereignty.
5 July 1997	Canada concludes a bilateral free trade agreement with Chile.
21–25 November 1997	Canada hosts the APEC summit in Vancouver.
3 December 1997	The Convention on the Prohibition of the Use, Stockpiling, Production and Transfer of Anti-Personnel Mines and on their Destruction (Ottawa Treaty) is signed by 125 countries.
11 December 1997	The Kyoto Protocol to the UN Framework Convention on Climate Change is adopted.
May 1998	India tests five nuclear bombs, and Pakistan responds with six nuclear tests.
17 July 1998	Rome Statute of the International Criminal Court is signed.
7 August 1998	Al-Qaeda bombs US embassies in Kenya and Tanzania.
2 December 1998	La Francophonie creates the Organisation internationale de La Francophonie (OIF).
1 January 1999	Euro becomes the official currency of the EU.
16 March 1999	Czech Republic, Hungary, and Poland all join NATO.
24 March 1999	NATO commences bombing of Serbia over Kosovo; Canadian CF-18s bomb Serb targets.
20 September 1999	Security Council-authorized INTERFET forces intervene in East Timor to expel Indonesian militias; Canada's contribution (Operation Toucan) arrives by 15 October.
14 December 1999	Ahmed Ressam is arrested entering the United States with materials for a bomb he was planning to detonate at Los Angeles International Airport on New Year's Eve.
15 December 1999	First meeting of the G20 finance ministers and central bank governors is chaired by Paul Martin, in Berlin.
20–22 April 2001	Summit of the Americas, Québec City.
23 April 2001	Canada concludes a bilateral free trade agreement with Costa Rica.

POST-9/11 ERA (2001–PRESENT)

11 September 2001	Al-Qaeda hijacks four airliners and flies two into the World Trade Center towers, one into the Pentagon, and a fourth airliner into a Pennsylvania field.
12 September 2001	NATO invokes Article 5, its collective security provision, for the first time in response to the attacks of 11 September.
7 October 2001	US attacks Afghanistan, where Al-Qaeda is headquartered; Canada contributes troops.
9 November 2001	Doha Development Round of WTO trade negotiations begins.
27 November 2001	The Bonn Summit discusses the future in post-Taliban Afghanistan.

10 November 2001	China joins the WTO.
11 December 2001	The United Nations War Crimes Tribunal charges former Serbian President Slobodan Milosevic with genocide.
12 December 2001	Canada and the US issue a "smart border" declaration.
12 December 2001	Battle of Tora Bora forces the last Taliban units in Afghanistan into Pakistan.
13 December 2001	The US withdraws from the 1972 Anti-Ballistic Missile Treaty.
20 December 2001	The UN Security Council creates the International Security Assistance Force (ISAF) for Kabul.
29 January 2002	During his State of the Union speech, US President George W. Bush declares that Iraq, Iran, and North Korea represent an "axis of evil."
18–22 March 2002	The UN Conference on Financing for Development is held in Monterrey, Mexico.
18 April 2002	American fighters accidentally bomb Canadian soldiers outside Kandahar, killing four.
26–27 June 2002	Canada hosts G8 at Kananaskis.
1 July 2002	International Criminal Court at The Hague enters into force.
26 September 2002	Maher Arar, a Canadian citizen of Syrian origin, is arrested at a New York airport and is renditioned to Syria, where he is tortured; he is released to Canada on 5 October 2003.
12 October 2002	Jemaah Islamiyah terrorist attacks in Bali, Indonesia, kill 202 and injure 209.
17 December 2002	Canada ratifies the Kyoto Protocol.
12 February 2003	Canada announces that it will send 2,000 soldiers to Afghanistan as part of ISAF in Kabul.
17 March 2003	Chrétien announces that Canada will not join the US-led "coalition of the willing" in using force against Iraq.
19 March 2003	The US-led war against Iraq begins (called Operation Iraqi Freedom).
1 May 2003	George W. Bush announces that major combat operations are over in Iraq.
20 May 2003	An Alberta cow is found to have bovine spongiform encephalopathy (BSE), or mad cow disease, causing the United States and Japan to halt their imports of Canadian beef.
7 December 2003	Zimbabwe leaves the Commonwealth.
12 March 2004	Canadian forces begin deployment to Haiti.
2 April 2004	Bulgaria, Estonia, Latvia, Lithuania, Romania, Slovakia, and Slovenia all join NATO.
1–3 September 2004	Chechen militants take 1,000 children hostage at an elementary school in Beslan, Russia; 344 people are killed, more than half of whom are children.
26 December 2004	The Indian Ocean tsunami occurs; Canada deploys its Disaster Assistance Response Team (DART) to Sri Lanka.
22 February 2005	The Martin government announces it will not participate in the Ballistic Missile Defense plan with the United States.
23 March 2005	Paul Martin, George W. Bush, and Mexican President Vicente Fox sign the Security and Prosperity Partnership.

19 April 2005	The Martin government tables its *International Policy Statement* in Parliament.
7 July 2005	Islamist suicide bombers attack the London transport system ("7/7" attack).
16 August 2005	Canada assumes command of provincial reconstruction team in Kandahar City.
14–16 September 2005	The United Nations World Summit is held in New York; its outcome document endorses the Responsibility to Protect principle.
27 April 2006	Harper government announces that Canada and the United States have reached an agreement on softwood lumber.
5 May 2006	Québec is given permanent representation at UNESCO within the Canadian delegation.
6 May 2006	The Harper government announces an increase in defence spending of $5.3 billion over five years.
2 June 2006	Police arrest 17 Muslim men in Toronto, alleging a plot to detonate truck bombs against targets in Ottawa and Toronto and to decapitate Stephen Harper; the eighteenth member of the "Toronto 18" is arrested on 3 August.
12 July 2006	The war between Israel and Hezbollah in southern Lebanon begins; the Canadian government evacuates some of the 30,000 Canadian citizens in Lebanon.
9 October 2006	North Korea tests a nuclear weapon. They test again in 2009 and 2013.
13 March 2008	The House of Commons passes a motion to extend Afghanistan mission to 2011.
7–16 August 2008	South Ossetian war takes place between Russia and Georgia.
September 2008	Global financial crisis begins.
1 April 2009	Albania and Croatia join NATO.
7–18 December 2009	UN Climate Change conference is held in Copenhagen.
12 January 2010	Massive earthquake hits Haiti; Canada deploys DART.
12–13 April 2010	Nuclear Security Summit brings world leaders to Washington to discuss measures for safeguarding nuclear materials.
25–27 June 2010	Canada hosts G8 and G20 summits, Huntsville and Toronto.
12 October 2010	Canada is defeated in its efforts to secure a seat on the UN Security Council.
February 2011	Canada participates with other NATO countries in supporting a popular uprising in Libya to remove the regime of Muammar Gaddafi from power.
March 2011	A major earthquake and tsunami hit Japan; a nuclear accident follows.
9 July 2011	South Sudan becomes an independent country.
3 December 2012	Canada joins the Trans-Pacific Partnership trade talks.
March 2013	CIDA is dissolved and its foreign aid functions are transferred to a new super-ministry, the Department of Foreign Affairs, Trade and Development (DFATD).
18 October 2013	Completion of the Canada–European Union Comprehensive Economic and Trade Agreement is announced.
November 2013	A massive typhoon hits the Philippines; Canada deploys DART.

20 January 2014   Prime Minister Harper speaks to the Israeli Knesset.

March 2014   Russia invades Ukraine and annexes the Crimean Peninsula.

31 March 2014   Canada officially withdraws the last of its troops from Afghanistan.

4–5 June 2014   G7 summit is held in Brussels—the first after Russia is expelled from the group over its annexation of Crimea.

17 July 2014   After a week of competing rocket attacks, Israel launches a ground invasion of Gaza.

17 July 2014   Malaysian Airliner MH17 is shot down over a disputed part of Eastern Ukraine by Russian-backed separatists.

18 September 2014   In a state-wide referendum, Scotland votes against a motion to separate from the United Kingdom.

7 October 2014   Canadian Parliament votes to contribute CF-18 fighter jets to bomb Islamic State targets in Iraq and Syria as part of a multilateral operation.